THOMAS HARDY
THE GUARDED LIFE

'Pite's major achievement is the insight he provides into Hardy's writing itself . . . His own style is uplifted by Hardy's and his passages on the effect of Hardy's internal battles on his work are some of the best. His sensation-by-sensation creation of Hardy's mind is a beautiful thing'

Scotland on Sunday

'Ralph Pite's subtitle for his extensive and enlightening new biography, *The Guarded Life*, reminds us just how circumspect Hardy was about his private concerns, and how much conjecture has marked certain earlier biographical studies . . . Pite's assiduous modus operandi and his judicious version of events suggest that this will become the standard life of Hardy: a portrayal of an era, an examination of contemporary mores, and a tribute to the depth and complexity of Hardy's literary achievement'

Irish Times

'The portrait on the cover shows Thomas Hardy with his hooded eyes turned downward and sideways away from you. He looks waxen, shifty and evasive, like a ghost who is about to disappear. According to this biography, this is exactly what he wanted to be'

Daily Mail

'Pite achieves an admirable balance of sympathies between the rigid, reclusive writer, wrapped up in his grievances against the world, and his unfortunate, emotionally neglected wives . . . *The Guarded Life* offers many excellent insights'

Daily Telegraph

'Hardy had a keen and contradictory vision – he could be almost voyeuristic, as well as self-involved. He knew the value of small things, but despised pettiness. As biographies go, this one seems to match its subject . . . Overall, it is a brilliant book'

New Statesman

'Thomas Hardy's defensiveness was extraordinary even by the standards of the age in which he lived, and Pite is skilful, not to say ingenious, in drawing together emblems and instances of secrecy'

Guardian

RALPH PITE teaches English at Cardiff University. He has published a critical study of Hardy (*Hardy's Geography*, Palgrave, 2002), a book about Dante's influence on Romantic poetry (*The Circle of Our Vision*, Oxford University Press, 1994), and a biographical account of Samuel Taylor Coleridge (*Lives of the Great Romantics: Coleridge*, Pickering and Chatto, 1997). He is currently working on modern poetry, environmentalism and ideas of the simple life.

Ralph Pite

THOMAS HARDY:
THE GUARDED LIFE

PICADOR

First published 2006 by Picador

First published in paperback 2007 by Picador
an imprint of Pan Macmillan Ltd
Pan Macmillan, 20 New Wharf Road, London N1 9RR
Basingstoke and Oxford
Associated companies throughout the world
www.panmacmillan.com

ISBN 978-0-330-48187-8

1 3 5 7 9 8 6 4 2

A CIP catalogue record for this book is available from
the British Library.

Typeset by SetSystems Ltd, Saffron Walden, Essex
Printed and bound in Great Britain by
Mackays of Chatham plc, Chatham, Kent

Visit **www.panmacmillan.com** to read more about all our books
and to buy them. You will also find features, author interviews and
news of any author events, and you can sign up for e-newsletters
so that you're always first to hear about our new releases.

Contents

ACKNOWLEDGEMENTS

My heartfelt thanks go to Zoe Waldie, for her unfailing support of this project; to Peter Straus, for initiating it; to Charlotte Greig, Andrew Kidd and Anna South, for their perceptiveness as editors; and to Tim Hilton, for inspiration.

For their help in searching out Hardy, I'm very grateful to Susan Brandon, Sir Keith Bright, Tim Healey, Marianna Kambani, Lynda Kiss, Andrew Leah, Lilian Swindall and Dave Townsend. I've benefited throughout from research into Hardy and Hardyana by other people – the succession of editors and biographers who have served him so well and, equally important in my case, the contributors to the *Thomas Hardy Journal*. Fran Chalfont's articles there on Hardy's various homes, Celia Barclay's work on his Sparks relations, Claudius Beatty's wide-ranging knowledge of Victorian architecture, John Doheny's pursuit of Hardy's maternal ancestry, Tony Bradbury's investigation into Bockhampton's electors: these are only a few examples of the kind of expert knowledge I've relied on. Work also in the *THJ* by Simon Curtis, Peter Coxon, Trevor Johnson, Desmond Hawkins, John Pentney, Martin Ray, Patrick Roberts, Claire Seymour, Donald Winslow and many others has been just as useful in extending my grasp of Hardy's life and context. Obviously, none of these people are responsible for what I've done with their discoveries.

The book also profits, I hope, from recent critical studies that have sought to uncover an alternative Hardy – an author often more conflicted and subversive than he wanted to appear. Joanna Devereux, Roger Ebbatson, Joe Fisher, Patricia Ingham, Rosemarie Morgan, Edward Neill, Lance St John Butler, and Peter Widdowson: they may not thank me for it but I'd like to thank them. I'm also grateful to Phillip Mallett, Adam Piette, Adrian Poole, Peter Robinson, and Alan Shelston, all of whom spared time to talk things over with me.

For their companionship and encouragement, I'm indebted to Joanne Blackman, Jonathan Coe, Hester Jones, Virginia Garaux, Simon Grimble, John and Angela Lansley, Isobel O'Rourke, Mark Pedroz, Jai Penna, Peter Singer, Tom Sperlinger, and Gregory Tingay. I would like to thank Paul Symons for making sure the house did not fall down. I need to reward all my students for their patience and enthusiasm – especially (even at this distance) Joanne Chapman, Paula Cocozza, Michael Osbourne and Eric Woehrling.

Hester, Barney and Constance have had the most to put up with and they've never complained. They've given me instead 'a full-up measure of felicity', and the book is for them.

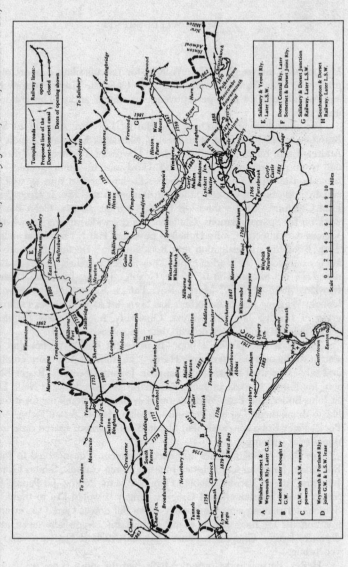

1. Railway route H was the earliest in Dorset and passed close to Hardy's birthplace. It was not extended west. The 'central route' is E. Routes F and B were crucial to Hardy's architectural career. (From Cecil Cullingford, *A History of Dorset*, 3rd ed, Phillimore & Co., 1999)

2. Detail of the Ordnance Survey, First Series map of Dorset, showing Dorchester and environs. Hardy's birthplace is named 'New Bockhampton'. Max Gate was built on the western side of Conquer Barrow.

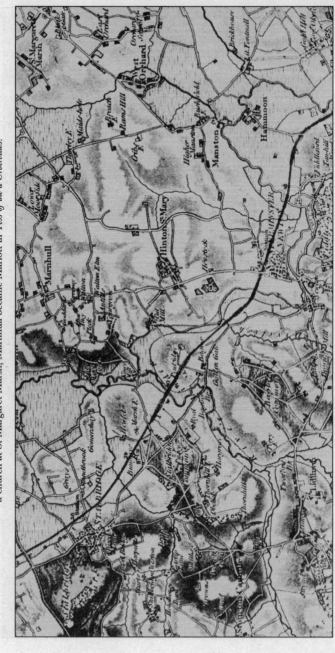

3. Detail of the Ordnance Survey, First Series map of Dorset showing Sturminster Newton, where Hardy lived 1876–78. As here, railways were etched onto the original early nineteenth-century plates. William Barnes was born in Bagber; when Hardy was working for him, John Hicks built a church at St Margaret Marsh; Marnhull became Marlott in *Tess of the d'Urbervilles*.

4. Detail of the Ordnance Survey, First Series map of Dorset showing Powerstock (named Poorstock), North Poorton and the route of the Bridport branch line. West Milton is named Milton.

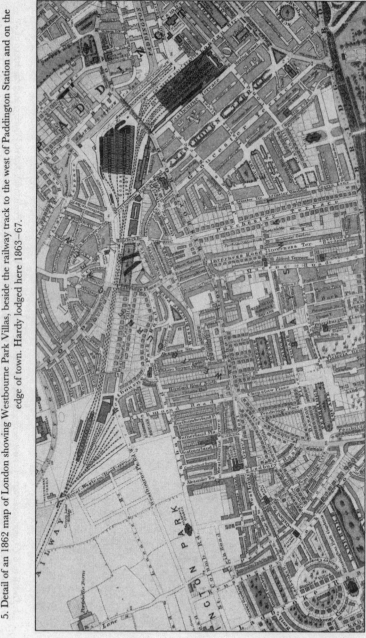

5. Detail of an 1862 map of London showing Westbourne Park Villas, beside the railway track to the west of Paddington Station and on the edge of town. Hardy lodged here 1863–67.

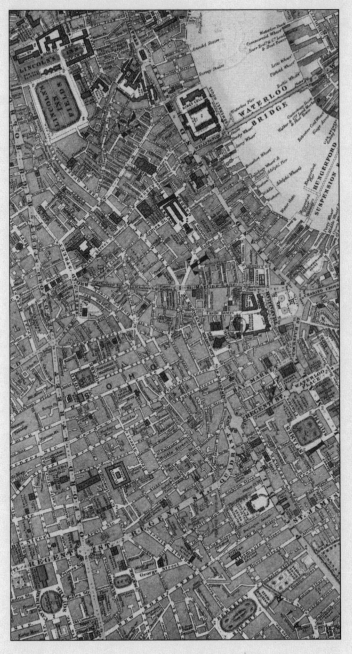

6. Detail of an 1862 map of London showing the Strand in Central London. From 1863 to 1867, Hardy worked in Arthur Blomfield's office in Adelphi Terrace, on the north bank of the Thames, about halfway between Hungerford Suspension Bridge and Waterloo Bridge.

The distressed tangle of love is Mr Hardy's subject.

Llewelyn Powys, 1901

It is a case in which we know from the art what the man was like.

F. R. Leavis on Hardy's 'After a Journey', 1975

It takes guts to be gentle and kind.

'I Know It's Over', Morrissey, 1986

Higher Bockhampton

YOU HAVE TO leave your car in the car park and walk up the lane. It's not so very far but far enough to notice – ten minutes or so, along an unadopted road that turns gradually into a track and then narrows into a path. On a wet day, it's slippery, and muddy water gathers in the potholes. The lane curves round to avoid an overhanging tree, then passes a row of small houses on the left. A field opens out on the right, sloping up to a low ridge. At this point, you first catch sight of the 'Hardy cottage'. The thatched roof and chimneys are just visible, peeping out from among some trees.

It's called a cottage and yet it turns out to be a sizeable house, with a long garden and several outbuildings. As you come nearer, the hedge encroaches on the path, squeezing groups of visitors into single file. And, from the path itself, you can see very little of the house or the garden: less and less, in fact, the closer you get. The hedge blocks your view; the two gateways, one at the end of the garden, another just beside the house, are both narrow. The notices explaining opening times are polite but coolly firm, and then, all of a sudden, you've almost gone by.

The path comes out onto the edge of a heath. Ahead of you, a track sets off across a cleared area of Puddletown Forest and at right angles to it, running north–south, lies a second track – to the right, southwards, it leads to Rushy Pond, the Roman Road, and farther on to the bluff where Rainbarrows Beacon looks out over the Frome valley; to the left, past the monument to Hardy erected by his American admirers, the path disappears into woodland. Half a mile away, it comes out on Yellowham Hill, beside the A35, the road to London. Hardy's birthplace stands at one corner of this miniature crossroads. Neighbours' paths would cross here and strangers approach. The world and sometimes his wife would come walking by. For Hardy, as he was growing up, alternatives presented themselves just outside the house. Oddly, though, neither the house end nor the rear wall has windows or doors opening onto the pathways. The house's bulky shapes look instead like defences, resisting intruders and ignoring passers-by. The house turns its back on the road and 'faces west' as Hardy said, looking out onto its own sheltered garden.

To Hardy, each of the four routes away from home possessed a set of distinctive associations and a particular meaning. Across the heath, Puddletown was filled with relatives – uncles, aunts and cousins on both his mother's and father's sides. Going that way took Hardy back into his extended family. In the opposite direction, down the lane at the front of the house, he walked off by himself to Dorchester, the county town three miles away. He went as a schoolboy first, later as a junior in an architect's office. That route took him into his future. The path behind the house, going northwards, led him into foreign parts. Hardy waited for the London stagecoach to come into sight over Yellowham Hill or to come climbing up out of Dorchester. The opposite direction, southwards, steered him towards intimate, personal places connected with his immediate family: to the Roman Road where he remembered walking hand-in-hand with his mother as a young child and to Rainbarrows Beacon where his father had pointed out the various country houses where he worked as a mason and builder. Standing at this crossroads behind the house, you can feel Hardy's life beginning around you – the great, evolving web of his endeavours and relationships spreading out over this particular piece of land. The house itself, though, stands beside you, a little unwelcoming. Visitors are received very cordially and it is beautifully kept up; nonetheless, it creates an atmosphere of resistance and inscrutability.

And Hardy himself is just the same. He is a vivid, memorable and compelling figure; at the same time, he's a stubborn mystery. In and around Dorchester, his presence is unavoidable and not simply because the tourist industry wants it that way. Hardy left his mark on the town, the district, and even the whole county; through his writing, he made all of them uniquely his own. He also imposed himself on English literature. His books are not only popular still, they are unmistakably original and distinctive. And, like the work of his near-contemporaries Dickens and George Eliot, only more so, perhaps, Hardy's stories produce a strong impression of the person who wrote them. The books conjure up a bleak, stoical figure, prompted to write by his grief and anger at the cruel treatment which the universe dishes out to the sensitive and the innocent.

To a large extent this image governs how Hardy is remembered. When people think or talk about 'Hardy', this is the side of him they usually have in mind. He is identified with his novels' unflinching sense that many people's experience was and is desperate. People do not always like that – Hardy's point of view has often been objected to; as much as he's been admired, he's been thought malicious and insincere. And even when people admire him, they do not always find it easy to be fond of him. To write a succession of such remarkable tragedies, each one worse than the last, he must have been 'like that' himself. Or so we assume. He must have been in person the dark, sorrowful genius of the novels, brooding over the universe's hostility to mankind – otherwise, how can we explain the books' existence or their extraordinary power?

Outside the novels, though, Hardy the man seems to have been quite surprisingly different. His younger sister, Kate, recalled how often he laughed and how readily he enjoyed a joke. Visitors to him in his old age recall a charming, friendly and amusing gentleman, who was a fund of information on all sorts of subjects. In these later years, Hardy also won the loyalty and affection of many younger writers, especially after the First World War – of Siegfried Sassoon, Edmund Blunden, Robert Graves and Charlotte Mew. He had been clubbable all his life. Friends as a young man with Leslie Stephen and George Meredith, later with George Gissing and Edmund Gosse, he was well known to most of the literati of the time and on good, sometimes intimate terms with aristocratic hostesses.

There are contradictions and inconsistencies in everyone, of course, and no writer corresponds exactly, if at all, to the persona presented by his or her books. There is always more to people. In Hardy's case, even so, the clash between his heartbreaking tragedies and his genial decency is so complete as to be baffling. It's mystifying and the puzzle draws you in. You think (or part of you thinks) that there must be some hidden explanation for it and some clue you have yet to find. So, Hardy's contradictions create particular problems for a biographer and particular temptations. Lois Deacon, for example, who wrote about Hardy's life during the 1960s, thought she had found the secret cause of his despair when she met the granddaughter of Tryphena Sparks, Hardy's cousin.

According to Lois Deacon, this elderly woman firmly maintained that Tryphena had been Hardy's lover, the mother of his illegitimate child and that she had deserted him for Horace Moule, Hardy's closest friend. Losing Tryphena, never seeing his son, being betrayed by Moule:

these three things together, Deacon believed, ruined Hardy's life and
she found traces of Tryphena, Hardy and Moule – of particular events
and scenes between them – encoded in his novels. The essentially tragic
pattern of his books betrayed, moreover, the imprint of Hardy's disappointed love. This was the trauma that never left him, and Tryphena
unlocked the mystery.

Not much of Lois Deacon's account is true; still, what she was
looking for is what all Hardy's biographers are prompted to look for. If
they excuse or discount Tryphena, they will usually accuse Jemima,
Hardy's mother, or Emma, his first wife, of causing Hardy the anguish
that produced the novels. And deliberately or not, Hardy encouraged
the belief that there were secrets in his life. He was instinctually shy.
There is, for instance, scarcely a single photograph or portrait of him
in which he looks towards you. He seems to have found face-to-face
encounters with other people very difficult. Likewise, he hated being
touched. Of course, as you observe him looking away all the time –
downwards, to one side, or into the distance – you cannot help but
wonder what he is so afraid of. He comes across as secretive and wary,
and you wonder why. This shyness in his character also produced,
however, a policy of self-protection. Nearly everything about Hardy
became, in fact, oblique and posed, and he went to extraordinary lengths
to control his public image.

He never published an autobiography, for instance, and neither did
he ever nominate an official biographer. Instead, he composed his own
biography, ghostwriting it in the third person and specifying that after
his death it should be published with his second wife, Florence, named
as author. Its two volumes, *The Early Life* and *The Later Years of Thomas
Hardy* (1928), remain an essential source for anyone writing about him
even though it is an extremely partial account, one that exaggerates both
Hardy's consistency and his stability. The book gives the impression of a
philosophically dispassionate character – someone who as a young man
was as resigned, melancholy and meticulous as he became when older.
The picture given by the book does fit pretty well with outsiders'
accounts of Hardy, at least in his later life, and it would not be
convincing at all were it not at least partly true. Hardy presents such
an image, though, as if it were the whole story. Reading the *Life*, it
grows easy to forget the anguish in *Jude*, the erotic intensity of *Tess* and
Far From the Madding Crowd, or the depth of misery in the 'In Tenebris'
poems.

In many ways, the *Life* allays your suspicion (and fear) that there was some dark secret in Hardy. Designed to forestall biography, it damps down speculation. The impression the book gives, whether misleading or not, is wonderfully seductive because it helps Hardy's audience to weather the storm of his tragic writings. *The Life of Thomas Hardy* assures you that his novels were never as absolutely heartfelt as you may have feared; at the same time, it confirms your belief in the artist as master – a benevolent philosopher-king of his imaginative world. It's not surprising, then, that biographers have by and large gone along with this authorized version of Hardy, accepting its attractive and reassuring view of the man and writing in accordance with its pattern of discreet, decorous biography.

Lois Deacon caused such a stir and encountered such hostility in part because she broke with the *Life*. She was her own worst enemy: reckless with her evidence and violently sentimental. All the same, the attacks on her were extreme. What they reveal is the strength of people's attachment to the serene figure Hardy presented in later life, and the reluctance of his admirers to contemplate the disturbance in him, the inconsistency, the waywardness, and the extremity – qualities that undoubtedly featured in his character. One of the most remarkable things about him in fact was his ability to keep these passions and wilful impulses under control. *The Life and Work of Thomas Hardy* typifies that ability.

'And There Was a Great Calm', Hardy wrote at the end of the First World War. 'There had been years of Passion – scorching, cold, | And much Despair, and Anger heaving high'. Now, 'Calm fell.'[1] He was working on the biography when he wrote the poem; the labour involved in the book was partly used to distract him from the horrors of the war – horrors he could barely contemplate and yet found impossible to disregard. Composing his life story calmed him in the moment and, at the same time, the book enabled him to impose calm on the whole of his life. He could pretend (not least to himself) that he had always been a steadily purposeful and emotionally self-disciplined person.

Achieving this required, however, the removal of whatever disturbed the peace – whatever external evidence there might be of trouble and strife. It necessitated radical secrecy. Hardy's extant letters run into seven volumes in the Oxford edition. An eighth volume is being compiled, consisting of letters discovered since the edition was completed in 1988. Several notebooks survive as well, plus a large proportion of Hardy's library. Apparently, then, a good deal exists outside the *Life* which one might use to contest it. Yet a mass of material has been lost, most of it destroyed on purpose. Letters from Hardy's early days are few and far between; crucial moments from his later correspondence have vanished and nearly all of what does remain, Hardy has edited. When writing the *Life*, he copied out the extracts that he wanted to keep and then burnt the notebooks they came from. Florence destroyed almost all the rest of his private papers after his death.

The bulk of what has come down proves, accordingly, to be disappointingly impersonal – the letters are for the most part concerned with business, and the notes are predominantly literary observations. Fascinating as these often are, they can be frustrating. You crave the unabashed self-declaration of Keats's letters or the reckless confessions Coleridge makes in his voluminous notebooks. And, of course, where the *Life* does reveal something more personal, your sense of precious intimacy is coloured by the knowledge that Hardy decided to preserve this piece of evidence, while much else was destroyed. What he reveals of himself is, as always, strictly on his terms. Everything is second-hand and mediated. He is present and absent too, visible and withdrawn. What persists is a feeling of tantalizing nearness – of glimpses given and instantly withdrawn. You can even begin to suspect canniness at every turn. When the mask slips, you wonder (cynically perhaps) whether Hardy has allowed it to slip – whether his momentary self-exposure is designed to mislead; that it's not in fact a 'slip' at all.

In his very last book, the collection of poems entitled *Winter Words* (1928), Hardy offered a defence of this apparently dishonest self-protectiveness. In one of the poems, 'So Various', he maintains that he was consistently inconsistent. He claims variety as his own. 'You may have met a man', the poem begins:

> – quite young –
> A brisk-eyed youth, and highly strung:
> > One whose desires
> > And inner fires
> > Moved him as wires.
>
> And you may have met one stiff and old,
> If not in years; of manner cold;
> > Who seemed as stone,
> > And never had known
> > Of mirth and moan.

The following stanzas describe other contradictions: the man seemed loyal in love, then fickle; stupid and later wise; gloomy, afterwards cheerful; adventurous, unadventurous, and so on. 'Now . . .' Hardy rousingly concludes:

> . . . All these specimens of man,
> So various in their pith and plan,
>   Curious to say
>   Were *one* man. Yea,
>   I was all they.[2]

Hardy had often been more defensive in this area. During the 1890s, he repeatedly insisted that his novels were no more than a 'series of seemings', that never would or could add up to a coherent view of the world. He resented the fact that people asked for something more authoritative from him than 'seemings' or impressions and was, at the same time, unsettled when he found he was not providing what his readers felt justified in expecting. Now, as an old man – he probably wrote this poem in his late eighties – Hardy more positively asserts that contradictoriness is nothing to be ashamed of. Making his novels into expressions of definite views distorts them, robbing them of responsiveness and empathy; likewise, the idea of him as an unchanging personality denies him humanity – it robs him of changeableness, volatility and the capacity for growth.

In terms of tone, the poem goes even further. Because it is addressed so directly to the reader, it attacks our desire to create a single, immutable image of Hardy. He refuses to be captured; he will not be summarized, nor sentimentalized, nor condescended to. He will always remain out of reach. Like Dylan Thomas in 'Do Not Go Gentle Into That Good Night', Hardy fights against the thought of being extinguished – by death in Thomas's case, in Hardy's, by other people's judgement, by their delimiting scrutiny. His forcefulness begins to sound like a victory: over his critics, over all those who tried to define him and over himself, who feared exposure so deeply. *Winter Words* as a collection is bolder and more outspoken than Hardy had risked being before. The poems in the book are at once hushed and reckless. They defy fear. Why should Hardy fear being seen, when what others see of him will always be provisional, largely accidental and probably misleading? The real Hardy cannot be found because a single, essential, true self simply does not exist. 'I was all they,' Hardy declares.

A biographer writes in a genre that imposes pattern on a life, giving it shape and meaning. The generic pattern governs the life's meaning, restricting the possibilities and inevitably producing oversimplifications. Biographies typically find it difficult to accommodate the variety people possess, either their inconsistencies of behaviour or the opposing elements within their personalities. In Hardy's case, though, variety is the key; it is exactly the thing that his biographer should try to find. There is not one big, dark secret in Hardy's life; neither though is there a consistent, constant presence, as the *Life*'s version of him leads one to believe. The anguished novelist and the sedate, philosophical artist co-exist in him; alongside both stand a multitude of other figures, other traits, other 'characters', hidden away by his habitual self-disguise, by his destruction of the evidence and by the conventions of biography itself.

Recovering Hardy's variety involves imaginative identification, of course – all biography needs that; it demands an unusual degree of scepticism too. It means going against Hardy and probing the disguises he constantly put on. It involves as well a search for hints and giveaways, a reading of his creative output that seeks to discover not so much a veiled autobiography as signs of the psychological work that his writing performed for him. All this can appear intrusive and insensitive because in finding Hardy out, you are doing exactly what he did not want: exposing to view and judgement the inner life of a person who wanted, more than anything else perhaps, to keep those aspects of himself carefully under wraps.

There are risks, then, in stepping outside the bounds of Hardy's self-image and in challenging some of the assumptions usually made by biographers and implied by the genre. Yet all these drawbacks are actually for the best. Hardy is safe now. Exposure cannot afflict him personally any longer, nor are there descendants whose feelings might be hurt. His reputation as a writer is secure. Trying to probe behind the picture Hardy constructed so carefully will not endanger that standing now, in part because the culture has changed. People are less concerned these days that the writers they admire should be flawlessly respectable people. More positively, this treatment is no less than Hardy deserves. It is needed if we are to uncover his personality, which is something that the *Life* drastically fails to do. The elder statesman figure whom Hardy presents in the book is hard to engage with. This Hardy is stifled by propriety, bathed in sepia; he obediently confines his 'experience' to what it is appropriate for a gentleman to say. The less reputable sides of his personality and the more endearing ones both disappear, not least because they depend upon contradictions and uncertainties. You lose too a sense of the complex response Hardy continually, vividly made to the world before him, moment by moment.

It's important too, I think, to release Hardy from the obligation to be a hero or an inspiration. He is frequently blamed for excluding from the *Life* everything that was remotely disreputable. To some extent all he was trying to do was avoid letting people down. He recognized how much his contemporaries had invested in the story of his life – in its narrative (its myth) of endeavour, persistence and ultimate success. He made himself appear so serene in order, partly, to ennoble ambition. That was important to him personally, of course. It also comforted the young men like Sassoon and Blunden who, after the trauma of the First World War, were seeking a motive for action that was not based on greed or self-advancement. Hardy's life as an artist provided them with an image of that ideal. The drawback was that his idiosyncrasies had to be hidden away.

Probing behind the masks to find the variety depends on inference, sometimes on speculation, and is an altogether uncertain process. Most of all, however, it relies on a form of sympathy in which honesty is paramount. For all his deceptions and silences, Hardy loved honesty. He pleaded with his first wife, Emma, near the end of their long, unhappy marriage, 'Let there be truth at last, | Even if despair.'

> nothing needs disguise
> Further in any wise,
> Or asks or justifies
> A guarded tongue.[3]

It's time to take him at his word – and to doubt his every word.

~ 1 ~

A railway bore him through

ON 2 JUNE 1840, Thomas Hardy was born in Higher Bockhampton, a tiny village lying a few miles outside Dorchester in the south-west of England. When he died in 1928, he was buried in Westminster Abbey, a figure of national importance given something like a state funeral. As an old man Hardy tried to give the impression that this extraordinary success story had taken place almost by accident – that he had never sought fame or worked to get it. This cannot possibly be the case. Growing up where he did, Hardy was on the very outer fringes of English society. It was an extremely long way from Higher Bockhampton to London, in terms of distance, time and cultural separation. If Hardy had been as passive and indifferent as he said he was, then we would never have heard of him. You might not be reading this book.

Other Victorian writers, of course, came from humble backgrounds. Upward mobility was a feature of the nineteenth century and writing was one of the best ways to rise in the world. Dickens was born in obscurity, the son of a clerk in the Navy office in Portsmouth. He died in 1870 an internationally famous man. George Eliot was as a child nothing more promising than the youngest daughter of a land agent in the Midlands. In her maturity, nonetheless, she received visits from princesses, when Queen Victoria's daughters came to her seeking words of wisdom.

Even so, Hardy's rise to fame is exceptional because his origins were uniquely obscure. Portsmouth was a key naval base with strong links to London; George Eliot's Coventry was an expanding industrial city. Dorset in 1840 was, on the other hand, one of the most remote, backward and poor counties in England. Over the next twenty years, as Hardy grew up, it became if anything more remote. While the railways drew the rest of the country closer together, making it more unified and homogeneous than ever before, Dorset was transformed into a backwater.

If you travel down to Dorset now, it still feels like an out-of-the-way place, at least by English standards. England is the most densely populated major country in Europe and its southern half is especially crowded. Settlements lie close together, running into one another in what can appear to be an endless suburb of London, and increasingly it is thought of like that: people refer to 'the south-east'; a generation ago they would have talked of Greater London and the Home Counties. City, suburb and country are blurred together in a process of development that seems now, if anything, to be accelerating. Hardy saw this coming: in 1909 he told his fellow-citizens in Dorchester that they should resign themselves to living in a suburb of London. Even so, in some ways, Dorchester and Dorset have escaped.

There are no motorways in the entire county and the railway into London does not form one of the major strands in the national network. The line runs through Basingstoke, Winchester, Southampton, Bournemouth and Poole. After the commuter belt, the industrial port and the swathes of housing behind the seaside resorts, the last little section from Poole into Dorchester has a different quality. Rural England reappears in heathland, pine forest and the winding River Frome, clear and delicate, more like an enlarged stream than a river.

That sense of escape gives the impression that Dorset is not a suburb of London at all, not yet at least, and implies perhaps that Hardy was being characteristically pessimistic. In fact, though, Dorset's idyllic rurality and almost quaint perfection were just what worried him in prospect, not least because he thought he had helped to bring them about.

*

Hardy's second published novel, *Under the Greenwood Tree* (1872), comes as near as he ever did in his fiction to portraying his family home. The Dewy family lives in a house modelled on Hardy's birthplace, and in successive editions over the years, Hardy changed the wording of the description to make the similarity more and more plain, though steadfastly denying it all the time. From the novel's first appearance, however, the likeness is present in the book because Hardy situates the house in a hamlet he called 'Lewgate' (later changed to Upper Mellstock) and the book's topography made Lewgate into an exact equivalent of Higher Bockhampton. Mellstock, Hardy wrote:

was a parish of considerable acreage, the hamlets composing it lying at a much greater distance from each other than is ordinarily the case. [. . .] There was East Mellstock, the main village; half a mile from this were the church and the vicarage, called West Mellstock, and originally the most thickly-populated portion. A mile north-east lay the hamlet of Lewgate [. . .] and at other points knots of cottages besides solitary farmsteads and dairies.[1]

'East Mellstock', later renamed Lower Mellstock, corresponds to Lower Bockhampton, on the edge of the water meadows, where the village schoolhouse stood in both novel and reality. West Mellstock, the name later reduced to simply Mellstock, maps onto the actual Stinsford; its tiny church is described in accurate detail a few chapters later. Lewgate, a 'mile north-east' must be Higher Bockhampton. Hardy may even have chosen the name because it would provide a hidden clue. Within the family, 'Lewgate' was remembered as a name they had thought of using for the house where Hardy was born.

The likenesses continue beyond this central layout. When the novel moves towards Yellowham, for instance, renamed Yalbury (where Geoffrey Day's cottage lies hidden in the woods) it continues to depict Dorset realities. Details of the scenery recall Hardy's surroundings – the patchwork of woodland and heath, intersected by compact, lush river valleys, and the sunken lanes, sometimes made into tunnels by a roof of intersecting tree branches. Figures in this landscape also recall real people whom Hardy knew. Reuben Dewy is a musician, as Hardy's father was; Reuben's father, William Dewy, is leader of the band: a venerable, authoritative figure, similar to Hardy's paternal grandfather (though Hardy had never known him). Dick Dewy, the son and grandson in this family of players, sang the treble part and played the violin – again, as Hardy had done himself. Some of the events are historical too: the novel opens with the Mellstock Quire singing carols around the parish at Christmas time – something that Hardy remembered, having probably taken part himself when a boy. His family had maintained the tradition of 'going the rounds' for generations. Although by the time he wrote the novel the practice had died out, in the 1840s of his childhood, where he set the novel, it still continued.

Under the Greenwood Tree presented this rural world with great affection as well as literal accuracy. Fondness and honesty come into conflict in the book, nonetheless, and there's no doubt that it smoothes away the rougher edges of rural life. Heavy manual labour, poverty and hunger are all kept out of sight although in reality the first two were accepted as inevitable while the third was a constant threat. Instead, Hardy's rustics are buffoonish and endearing. Michael Mail, for instance, an old member of the choir, recalls sitting one day eating a meal in an inn and hearing a brass band playing outside in the street. He found himself compelled to chew in time to the music. 'Truly, now [. . .] there's a friendly tie of some sort,' he declares, 'between music and eating.'[2]

When he came to revise the book as a middle-aged man and again in old age, Hardy worried that its comedy was not as harmless as it had first appeared. The book had slotted Hardy's personal history into a conventional point of view, converting old friends and neighbours into stereotypical rural characters. Perhaps there was something vulgar and appeasing about doing that. The 'realities out of which [the narrative] was spun were material for another kind of study', Hardy commented, with his characteristic, rueful understatement – a novel very different from 'the chapters here penned so lightly, even so farcically and flippantly at times'. But, Hardy continues, 'circumstances would have rendered any aim at a deeper, more essential, more transcendent handling unadvisable at the date of writing'.[3] As a young writer, just starting out, Hardy was forced to compromise; at least, this is what he claims, and he had good reason to. Hardy's readership was made up predominantly of people living in cities, most of them middle- or lower middle-class. A direct challenge to their assumptions about rustic folk would not have been published. Reviews of the book – even a supportive one, written by his friend Horace Moule – show the tightness of the constraints Hardy was compelled to work within.

In the novel Reuben and the rest of the choir are under threat from barrel organs and harmoniums. These recently invented instruments were being introduced into churches in the mid nineteenth century and, inevitably, their presence made other musicians redundant. Hardy records the historical change and also makes the clash between choir and organ into the novel's symbolic keystone. Early on, he presents the rustics inveighing against their rivals, these newfangled instruments. William Dewy takes the lead, calling them, 'Miserable machines for such a divine thing as music!' In his review, Moule picked up on this apparently innocuous turn of phrase. Such formality showed, he said, how the country people were made to speak 'in the language of the author's manner of thought, rather than their own'.[4] Rustics must not be too articulate or clever because then they would not be proper rustics.

Hardy dutifully changed the wording of Dewy's speech in later editions. Still, the first version was probably the more accurate one. It's perfectly possible that Hardy's grandfather and others like him – church-going, musical people whom Hardy knew – could and would have used exactly the same words as William Dewy does. They would have heard every Sunday the words of the Prayer Book and the Bible, memorizing much of what they heard and absorbing biblical language into their vocabulary. Hardy's urban audience, though, had set ideas about 'rustics' in which this sort of sophistication found no place, and Hardy's writing was pressured to conform to those expectations. If it didn't, then his representation was not believed. He was faced by a conundrum. If he produced a true record of what he heard around him in the countryside, it would be perceived as a distortion of the reality. He would be accused of interfering. He had to make his country characters speak in the language expected by the audience if he was not to be criticized for imposing on them the audience's language.

Hardy did manage to find ways around this problem even as early as *Under the Greenwood Tree* and addressed it again many times in his later novels. It became habitual with him to provide the standard image and to undermine it at the same time. Nonetheless, as the later preface to *Under the Greenwood Tree* reveals, Hardy was liable to feel uneasy about his role. He was in his novel-writing always an intermediary, who was attempting to translate one way of life into the terms of another, hoping to make it understood, a little at least, by people whose lives were very different. In that undertaking he continually ran up against the preju-dices of those he spoke to – the terms on which they were prepared to accept the 'other' world that Hardy came from. At times, unfortunately, it appeared to him that his compromises with prejudice had helped reinforce it. Perhaps he had not done enough to challenge his audience's assumptions. Perhaps he had participated in the process of turning Dorset into an olde worlde sort of place.

His career as a novelist continually placed him, therefore, in between two societies. To the city-dweller, he was a rural novelist and a Dorset man; an exotic creature, who was condemned to remain something of an outsider however much he assimilated. To the rural communities that Hardy described, he was an outsider as well. Even if his subject matter lay close to home, and even if he stoutly defended country life against the routine disdain of city folk, his writing about the countryside at all set him apart from it. Hardy's livelihood depended on literate, leisured people, on publishers and novel-readers, nearly all of whom lived miles away; his line of business separated him from the economy that drew the rest of community together. And perhaps, as Hardy himself sometimes feared, his work also made him a traitor to his background.

Certainly, he won few friends among the locals. A string of anecdotes records the hostility to Hardy felt by ordinary Dorsetshire people, who repeatedly said when asked about Hardy that they could not see much point in writing books at all, but especially not ones as miserable as Hardy's. Within this forthright philistinism there was, I suspect, an undercurrent of suspicion – either that Hardy was making capital out of rustic mannerisms (laughing at country folk with his city friends) or that he was presenting country people as worse than other folk – irreligious, licentious, coarse, morbid and generally unrespectable. In other words, while his metropolitan readers demanded a condescending version of rurality, his and his family's neighbours felt they were being shown up if Hardy was more candid. It looked as if he would be accused of betraying them whatever he did.

Because he became a writer, Hardy was particularly exposed to this problem. His profession divided his loyalties. That division, though, only reflected a more fundamental rupture in him. He was born in the heart of the English countryside and was surrounded from boyhood by a feudal society and a peasant culture that was essentially medieval. He grew up, however, just as it was undergoing drastic change. His was the first generation in Dorset separated by the Industrial Revolution from the continuum of the past. Surrounded by and intimate with something from which he was also divided, simply by the date of his birth, Hardy could never feel himself to be either a part of the rural world (as his father was) or safely distanced from it (as the next generation would be).

*

This turning point in history arrived with the railways. When Hardy was born, there were none in Dorset, though they were starting to be built in other parts of the country. The first Dorsetshire railway was constructed in 1847, linking Dorchester to Southampton, with connections from there to London. The route ran along the Frome valley and passed within two miles of Hardy's childhood home. Standing in the garden, you can still hear the whistle of the trains, and from Rainbarrows Beacon you can see them, on the far side of the water meadows. Steam trains would have been still more eye-catching than modern diesels.

Before the railways came, Dorchester was an important regional centre. Families in the county had town houses there; every year, there was a 'season' when the landed gentry moved in from their country seats to enjoy parties and 'routs'. Like other provincial towns and cities, Dorchester was a world unto itself to an extent that is now difficult to imagine; even so, it was not cut off. Coaches ran regularly to and from London; in the mid century more than forty coaches a week changed horses at the King's Arms on High West Street. They travelled on westwards, beyond Dorchester, to Exeter and the strategic ports of Falmouth and Plymouth. Dorchester lay, in other words, on the main route south-west out of London. It was one of the stopping-points on the Western Circuit too. Several of 1688's Bloody Assizes were held in Dorchester and, even in Hardy's day, hangings still took place at the county gaol. Hardy was seven by the time the railway was built, so he could remember Dorchester as it was before – as a place that enjoyed daily contact with London via the coaches and preserved its independence too, with its own social world, its own dialect and traditions. With the arrival of the trains, Hardy wrote, the ancient folk ballads were 'slain at a stroke by the London comic songs that were introduced'.[5]

With improved communications, the capital was bound to exert greater control over the regions, both economically and culturally. This happened throughout nineteenth-century England. Unlike many other places, though, Dorchester (and Dorset as a whole) did not receive very much in return. There was little investment or development and the economy remained almost exclusively agricultural. The county had too few of the natural resources – coal, iron ore, tin or china clay – that brought industry to other rural areas and so, as industry became more important nationally, Dorset was left behind. Similarly, when agriculture entered a long period of depression towards the end of the nineteenth century (a depression produced in part by improved international trade), Dorset suffered disproportionately. Employment declined as farms enlarged. Unemployment and emigration became widespread.

The population grew nonetheless, partly because so many incomers arrived. The majority of these were middle class city-dwellers, 'townies', retiring to the country. They moved there in the hope of finding a stereotypical rural world, full of peace and tranquillity, and their expectations influenced the 'old Dorset families' who started to value their county in similar terms. Newcomers and the established county set both had little interest in helping the area move forward into the modern world; in fact, quite the opposite. Dorset was to remain a little piece of paradise. Anything that did not fit in with this image was disapproved of, actively discouraged or ignored.

Throughout Hardy's life improvements were made in and around Dorchester: drains were built, cleaner water was provided, disease banished, and old, insanitary housing was replaced by neat rows of labourers' cottages. Other Victorian novelists, such as Anthony Trollope and Margaret Oliphant, described the same process as it took place in other parts of the English countryside and, like Hardy, they noticed that the changes pursued a narrowly defined set of goals. Improvements were designed to conserve the past and, simultaneously, to redefine it – to ensure that only a gentrified version of the old order survived. Dorset was one of the counties in which that agenda was most damaging. Its distinctive ways of life (curious but intelligible as these were) gradually turned into heritage.

The railways brought Dorset a deadening version of modernity; progress, you might say, slowly sent the county backwards, reducing it to a stylized image of its past. For Hardy, invasion by the industrialized world created opportunity and produced disinheritance simultaneously because he was old enough to remember what was disappearing. He was too young to be anything except a child of the new, more urban world and yet he was personally linked to – imaginatively formed by – the vanishing rural ways of life. They formed an environment he could revisit as an adult, both in his mind and to an extent physically as well; he could become through his work old Dorset's historian and advocate but he could never be 'of' it. Very quickly, it was not there any more to re-enter. Traces remained – in the few elderly people who somehow kept themselves apart from the changes going on all around, in the memories that were preserved via family traditions, and in the time-honoured country songs. These, Hardy came to believe, should at all costs be preserved – through local histories, through photographs and through the art of fiction.

The (sometimes brutal) candour in his writings about rural life was in part, therefore, a response to the prevalence of sentimental nostalgia. He was trying to disrupt a twee perspective on the countryside that dominated it increasingly in the course of his lifetime. Even so, Hardy was not and could never be part of the untouched rural world he was trying to depict. And neither were his readers, however much they might have liked to pretend that they were or, perhaps, that he was. Neither, though, was Hardy comfortably separate from the fading country life. It was not something he could recreate as a historical novelist might recreate the distant past because this particular piece of history lay closer to him than that. His childhood and earliest memories had been fashioned by it and although that lent authenticity and conviction to his evocations of rural life, it meant too that his writings always carried somewhere within them the burden of his loss and regret.

At the time, however, when the railway first arrived in 1847, the sense of opportunity eclipsed all anxieties about the future. Within a year or so of the railway's opening, Hardy travelled up to London for the first time – going with his mother and taking the train. It was a thrill he never forgot and it was shared, one way or another, by everyone in the county. The railway promised to bring them into the modern world at last – the world that had been leaving them behind. In addition, by connecting Dorchester to the new transport system, it promised to make the town as prominent under the new dispensation as it had been under the old. Everyone took for granted that the railway would soon be extended further westwards – to Bridport, Honiton, Exeter and beyond – along the line of the old coach route.

There were perfectly good grounds for assuming this would happen, but it never did. A branch line was constructed as far as Bridport in 1857 and other lines were built during the 1860s, which crossed Dorset from north to south – one linked Dorchester to Yeovil, another connected Wimborne to Wincanton, via Blandford Forum and Sturminster Newton. Even so, the long-awaited route, westwards from Dorchester, never materialized.

The first trains into the south-west of England had run along Brunel's broad-gauge Great Western line, from London to Bristol and then on to Exeter. This route was completed during the 1830s, early in the railway boom. Following in its wake, Brunel's rivals, the narrow-gauge companies, could not decide where to build a line to challenge it. Dorchester lay on one of the options, the 'coastal route' that followed the old coach road. The other was the 'central route', going from London to Exeter via Salisbury and Yeovil. After years of wrangling, the central route was chosen, received Parliamentary approval and was built finally in 1860; the moment it opened, Dorchester became a dead end. The great world left it behind and left behind the county too, which was crossed by major railway routes only at its northern edge, near Gillingham and Sherborne.

Hardy went to school in Dorchester from 1849 to 1856, and for the next six years he worked there in an architect's office. He grew up, therefore, while the battle for the 'coastal route' was fought and lost. It was early in 1862, that he left Dorchester for London. Whatever his personal reasons were for leaving, he took the decision just when the town's prospects were in decline. People were already starting to suspect that it was doomed to turn into a merely residential town – a place to retire to; somewhere that young people would move away from. It would become sleepier and old-fashioned, more conservative and hidebound than before. It would be politer, altogether more genteel, cleaner and healthier too with considerably improved drains. At the same time, it would lose its vitality and self-confidence.

The present look and feel of Dorset can be traced back to this decision about the railways, taken a hundred and fifty years ago. The choice of route preserved a rural county; it helped ensure that 'the Hardy country' became a much-loved backwater, filled with refinement and a gentle pathos.[6] As these changes gradually took place, they established for Hardy a feeling of congruence between his own life and the history of the district – a congruence that increased his sense of identification with his home county. Like him, Dorset was neither being incorporated into the modern world nor could it remain independent of it. It was perceived in a particular, stereotypical way – as tranquil and marginal – and it was developed in such a way that it conformed to expectation.

This state of affairs contributed to Hardy's reticence before the public. He resisted being identified or pigeonholed (by journalists or critics or biographers) because he felt he had always had to withstand people's tendency to stereotype the places he came from. In a similar way, his development as a novelist shows him working to find ways of adapting to (rather than succumbing to) the pressures placed on a 'rural writer'. *Under the Greenwood Tree* combined perfect conformity to expectation with hints of subversion – hints so remote as almost to need a code-breaker to bring them to light. *The Mayor of Casterbridge* (1886), written when Hardy was in his mid forties and had recently come back to Dorchester to live, can be seen as an exploration of the divided person he felt himself to be – a person divided by the railways and what they brought with them, who was now living in a county where the past was being smothered by nostalgia for the past.

*

Most of the action of *The Mayor of Casterbridge* takes place during the 1840s – the period of Hardy's childhood, when traditional rural life stood on the verge of the enormous changes that the railways plus the Corn Laws would bring. The story contrasts Michael Henchard with his younger rival, Farfrae, who gradually replaces Henchard in business and, in the end, as mayor too. Henchard's decline through the course of the novel is made to parallel the disappearance of old, rural life: Henchard has made his money and risen to power by employing old-fashioned farming and trading methods; Farfrae brings new techniques and a new style. He is a cultured man of the world, whereas Henchard is cruder, more forceful and more direct, earthy where Farfrae is bland. This means also that Henchard is more independent. He is more 'himself' than modern people seem able to be. Consequently, there is something dreadful about his slow removal and eventual death although there is nothing really to object to in his successor.

As these events unfold, Casterbridge loses its independence too. When first described, the town stands alone in the landscape and still resembles the provincial capital founded by the Romans. By the end it has been linked more closely to Budmouth – the equivalent Hardy provides for Weymouth – and, although the railways are scarcely mentioned in the book, the novel's contrasts are structured along the lines of the future railways. Farfrae comes up from Budmouth when he first arrives, supposedly on his way to Bristol. Often later on, he is seen travelling to and fro along the Budmouth Road. His movements run along the route of the railway linking Weymouth to Bath. By contrast, all the places Henchard goes to during the novel lie on the old coach road from London to Falmouth: the route that the layout of the railway system had effectively destroyed. This remains Henchard's habitual trajectory – one he cannot alter or shift away from, and that inability leaves him ruined and abandoned in the end, just like the coach roads themselves. Meanwhile, Farfrae prospers and Casterbridge modernizes.

Clearly, *The Mayor of Casterbridge* depicts a universal human situation – the clash between old and new, the Oedipal struggle between father and son. The locations Hardy chooses, in place and time, allow that conflict to reflect Dorchester's situation as it confronted Victorian

England – as a previously independent and in some ways 'primitive' community came up against the bourgeois values of modern society and its subtly coercive conformism; and furthermore as the rural world was invaded by metropolitan values and its local economy disrupted by external pressures. Farfrae and Henchard evidently represent the two sides in that struggle – a struggle that was taking place inside Hardy as well.

By the time he came back to live in Dorchester, Hardy was a middle class professional, with an RP accent and London connections. Henchard's rustic style, his downright manner, his doggedness and his cunning, though they were part of Hardy, were part of his past. They were what he needed to suppress in order to do well in his career, which depended upon providing a London audience with entertainment they would enjoy. Farfrae resembles that more polished side of Hardy: the clubbable, literary man and the efficient producer of novels, who took pride in always delivering his work on time. By coming back to Dorchester, Hardy was bringing these two sides of his life into renewed contact: within him, the professional, well-read, *au courant* novelist confronted the 'Dorset man', still wedded to his old-fashioned and unfashionable roots.

What is most striking about the book, perhaps, is the impossibility of compromise. The two sides are set against one another almost against their will: Henchard treats Farfrae at first as he might a long-lost son and Farfrae seems perfectly well disposed towards his new friend and employer. Yet, over time, they cannot live in peace together. They adapt to one another and distort one another. Farfrae's presence casts Henchard as the boorish rustic; he makes the older man look and feel out of date as he creates – he forces on Henchard – a different and uncomfortable self-image. That is unavoidable; it also works in the other direction because equally Henchard's proximity establishes Farfrae's belief that he is the coming man. As soon as old meets new, positions become entrenched. The new makes the old older and the old makes the new newer. Stereotyping begins.

Throughout his writing life Hardy saw himself as caught up in just such a web of projection and denial. Being between two worlds did not give him privileged insights into both (as you might imagine it should). Rather, it made him acutely sensitive to the impact expectations could have. People were fashioned by the way they were seen; they were assigned roles and functions, put in their place, and prevented from being different. Nowhere was exempt from the tussle for dominance. Rural places might be thought to lie 'outside the gates of the world', as Hardy put it, and for someone from the busy cultural centre, being outside the world would imply peace and quiet – a retreat or an idyll.[7] To the inhabitant, though, being 'outside the gates of the world' meant exclusion and imprisonment. You were given a particular status and the behaviours it was assumed to imply.

One of the purposes of Hardy's novel was to count the psychological cost of progress and development. In a sense, the railways had ruined Dorchester, eroding the distinctive life of its community. Similarly, the modernity that the railways brought with them could not tolerate Henchard. His character was no longer deemed suitable and so he has to leave. His ejection and death rehearse a process that Hardy was compelled to undergo, along with many of his contemporaries. He and they had to suppress their Henchard-like qualities, refuse that inheritance and adapt instead to the world as they found it. The novel's ending mourns Henchard's passing, sensing that his character traits were valuable and will be missed in the future; it also shows him resisting absorption and sentimental affection right until the end, hinting that Henchard will always persist, like an inner child, raw and unreconciled despite the adult's sensibly businesslike attitude to life.

Despite the professional difficulties and the personal heartache it caused, Hardy's suspension between different eras and different communities was his greatest piece of good fortune as a writer. The place where he was born and the time when he was born gave him the opportunity to feel immediately the self-division, the deracination and lack of certainty that afflicted so many other people at that time. Hardy's plight and Dorset's chimed with the wider culture's anxieties – anxieties that have not yet gone away. An entire generation of Victorians felt ousted from their true, rural home and their sense of exile was heightened by (while it also came to represent) the loss of other certainties – a secure religious system and a stable social hierarchy. Hardy's circumstances enabled him to speak with special conviction to that audience.

He recognized as well that everybody else was actually just like him, in standing at a point of conflict between different points of view. That was troubling, perhaps, but at the same time it was revealing: it showed that society did not really possess essential unity or harmony. There was no authoritative, unifying myth, and no narrative could reconcile social differences. It was this perception that helped set Hardy apart from his predecessors, the High Victorian novelists, and gave his work its modern edge. Given that everywhere was contested and everyone conflicted, the only way forward for a writer was to show the coexistence and the clash – to show Farfrae and Henchard fighting it out.

– 2 –

One who lived and died where he was born

DORCHESTER'S fate seemed an object lesson in the need to keep abreast of things. Whatever the drawbacks might be of taking an active part in modern life, the alternative was decline. You would be ignored at first, patronized and then invaded – economically and culturally. Taking part was not a straightforward business but it could not be evaded; neither, in fact, should it be. Hardy was brought up (despite everything he said to the contrary) in an aspirational, upwardly mobile family; he grew up too at a time when Victorian self-confidence was at its height. By background and by culture, he was taught to embrace change and, like everyone born in 1840, he was led to believe in progress.

During Hardy's childhood, industrialization and urbanization developed rapidly in Britain, altering fundamentally the social structure, the economic system and the landscape. There were new ways forward in life and new dangers. A widespread fear developed, for instance, of the growing cities' overcrowded slums. The urban masses appeared anarchic and revolutionary because, living in poverty and disease, they seemed likely both to infect and overthrow their masters. At the same time, industrial power was breathtaking. It could make unprecedented fortunes for individuals and it energized the collective effort that built the great Victorian cities of Liverpool, Manchester, Birmingham, and Glasgow. London, meanwhile, became the first world city, vastly expanded, redesigned and rebuilt, and the hub of an expanding empire. The mid-century period seemed to offer the nation an opportunity to take over the world, as was demonstrated by the Great Exhibition of 1851. This celebration of British industrial might also revealed its extent for the first time, and for many Britons, it was the moment when they saw what they were achieving and what they might soon achieve.

Such evidence of success inevitably had an impact on Victorian culture so that nineteenth-century intellectual life became dominated by ideas of progress. Its historians thought habitually in terms of improvement over time. Civilization had emerged from barbarism and, despite setbacks, it had gradually moved forward. The present was history's highest point, which would be surpassed only by the future. The theory of evolution by natural selection (first put forward by Charles Darwin in 1859) contributed to this world view and was itself influenced by it. Nature, it now appeared, moved forward from the simple to the more complex, from the amoeba to the human mind. The development of complexity seemed in fact one of the principles of life itself. The overwhelmingly positive implications of the theory were mingled with a more forbidding idea. Darwinian theory suggested that older forms of life – those that were, for whatever reason, less well adapted to present circumstances – were bound to die out and be replaced. Progress was both inspiring and ruthless.

Hardy could not escape this atmosphere, not even in the depths of Dorset. The signs of change were all around – in the railways, in agricultural innovations, and in the constant drift of the population towards the cities. The advocates of self-help were present too. The first book he ever bought was *The Boy's Own Book: A Complete Encyclopaedia of all the Diversions, Athletic, Scientific and Creative of Boyhood and Youth.* He was fourteen at the time and what he got for his money (earned by playing music at weddings and dances) was a manual of social advancement. Hardy's mother, Jemima, disapproved of the volume, refusing 'to see any merit in a book which was chiefly about games', yet *The Boy's Own Book*, like all such mid-century texts, used games to encourage what she constantly encouraged herself: busyness and self-improvement. There were articles teaching the refined pursuits of cricket and fencing, swimming and angling. Hardy could and did teach himself chess by consulting it; he made notes on the 'Deaf and Dumb Alphabet'. Though there was fun in the volume, it was restricted to the good, hearty fun cultivated by the public school ethos.

Hardy said much later in life that he 'used to stare at this work in a bookseller's window at Dorchester and crave to have it as his own'. It was, according to the *Life*, a 'coveted volume'. He remembered himself as a boy desperate to know the latest thing – keen to imitate how other, more privileged boys behaved. At the beginning of *Jude the Obscure*, the young Jude has similar feelings when he watches the schoolmaster, Phillotson, setting off for Christminster. In the big city, Jude is convinced,

Phillotson will start a fascinating life. Out there beyond the village is the world of fencing and swimming, cricket and angling and chess.[1]

Though his *craving* the book comes from a remark he made as an old man, it feels quite convincing. Hardy comes across as a very recognizable fourteen-year-old when you imagine him poring over this small, private encyclopaedia. The *Life* always emphasized his physical and emotional frailty: at birth, he was given up for dead, it says, until the nurse noticed signs of life; in childhood, he was 'fragile' and 'his parents hardly supposed he would survive to grow up'; and as a boy, supposedly, he cared little for life in the great world beyond Bockhampton.[2] Hardy's enthusiasm for *The Boy's Own Book* suggests someone much more vital than this – someone more outward looking, ambitious, and simply more boyish too. Furthermore, despite Jemima Hardy's apparent dislike for *The Boy's Own Book*, this energy and desire for life were qualities Hardy inherited from his parents.

*

Hardy's birthplace in Higher Bockhampton was first built at the beginning of the century by his great-grandfather, John Hardy, who lived in Puddletown, a large village lying three or four miles away to the northeast. The building plot was cut out of heathland and the house established a new settlement – what was then called 'New Bockhampton'. Even when Hardy was a boy, the wilderness could still creep back in. One of the few family stories that Hardy retells about his infancy involves a snake.

> [O]n his mother returning from out-of-doors one hot afternoon, to him asleep in his cradle, she found a large snake curled up upon his breast, comfortably asleep like himself.

The *Life* tells few outright lies so probably the incident did take place. Hardy's place of birth meant he grew up with nature at his door and snakes in his bed.

John Hardy built the house for Thomas, his eldest son and his new daughter-in-law, Mary, née Head. They moved in during 1801, with the first of their children still a baby, and they lived there for the rest of their lives, raising a family of three daughters and three sons; a seventh child, a daughter, died in infancy. Thomas Hardy the first was a 'livier': that's to say, although the house and its plot of land belonged to the local manor of Kingston Maurward, he held them on a lease that would not expire until his death. Before that took place, the lease would be extended, making Thomas's sons liviers in turn and ensuring that the landlord could not reclaim the house before the death of Hardy's father. He was not yet thirty when Hardy was born and the family's tenure had already lasted forty years; it would continue for another half-century until Hardy's father died in 1892.

Hardy wrote about people in this social bracket several times in his novels and was concerned to point out there and elsewhere how minutely stratified his background was. Being a 'livier' set you apart from the peasantry. Labourers were hired for set periods (increasingly short periods as time went on) and were frequently compelled to move from place to place; by contrast, liviers were well-nigh permanent residents. In the Hardys' case, they ran a business too – a 'building and master-masoning business' set up by Hardy's grandfather and taken on by Hardy's father. A middle class person visiting a rural community like Stinsford might not have observed the differences in status but everyone around recognized them instinctively. As a 'livier' family the Hardys enjoyed greater independence than workers attached to an estate and more security than workmen for hire. Like other local tradesmen, they formed part of 'an interesting and better-informed class', as Hardy put it, 'ranking distinctly above' farm labourers. The two groups, peasants and tradespeople, continually met and depended on each other, yet they did not mix. Intermarriage was surprisingly rare. Furthermore, Hardy, though he is easy to label as a rustic or peasant writer, was never quite that. Unlike Robert Burns, for instance, or John Clare, he was by birth one step above (and away from) the labouring class.[3]

Another sign of the family's local prestige is the fact that the first Thomas Hardy was an elector of the parish – one of the few people in it entitled to the vote in parliamentary elections. This was a considerable privilege. In addition, he and his sons were excellent musicians, and Hardy inherited much of their talent. He played the violin very well from an early age and remembered folk tunes perfectly. They were still vivid to him when he was more than eighty years old.[4] His grandfather, however, and his father too, at least as a young man, had played for the services in the local church at Stinsford week by week. Before church organs became the norm, music in English churches was led by a group of musicians occupying a gallery at the back of the church (the west end, often beside the tower). There would be a group of singers in the gallery too, leading the worship and occasionally dominating it.

Modern Anglican church music carries on in the shadow of innovations introduced by the Victorians. As organs were installed during the 1830s and 1840s, chancel choirs developed too and plainsong chanting of the psalms was revived, particularly in Tractarian and High Church parishes. During the seventeenth and eighteenth centuries the psalms had been sung in metrical versions that were the equivalent of modern hymns. In fact, a few of these versions are still used as hymns: 'Through all the changing scenes of life', for example, or 'As pants the hart for cooling streams, | When heated in the chase'. By reviving the chanting of the psalms, the Victorian reformers aimed to create a feeling of timelessness and dignity in church services. This was the church's ancient music and its introduction would displace the boisterous tunes and the sometimes raucous delivery of the metrical psalms.

As this took place, local traditions were replaced by something more standardized and national. The new forms of worship brought into parish churches music that, up until then, had been restricted to cathedral services and a few wealthy city parishes. A process of centralization was at work in musical life, as it was in so many other aspects of Victorian culture. The music that Hardy's family performed originated before these changes occurred and has disappeared almost completely since. It is difficult to bring back to life, though some of it has begun to be performed again recently (by groups such as the Mellstock Band and Vital Spark).[5] Perhaps because of this, historians have tended to pass over eighteenth-century English church music, focusing instead on the great achievements of the seventeenth and nineteenth centuries, on Purcell and Stainer. Neglect creates ignorance, which in turn creates dismissiveness. It is easy to assume that the style practised by Hardy's family – 'country psalmody' as it was called – possessed little worth or musical sophistication.

With the choir at one end and the priest at the other, beside the altar, musicians and clergy were always liable to be at odds over who really ran the service – the priest and reader saying it or the musicians leading the musical sections. Most surviving accounts of the music were written by clergymen and so, inevitably, they tend to be biased against the musicians. The minstrels in the galley are seen as overvaluing both their contribution to the services and their musical gifts. The music itself is described as rough in performance and rudimentary in composition.

Some clergy, though, did recognize the importance of musicians in creating links between church and parishioners. Music gave one sizeable group in the community a stake in the services. If that made them overbearing or pompous at times, it was a small price to pay. And there's clear evidence that the music itself was often more complex as well as more proficiently performed than many records imply. The tradition of country psalmody produced notable composers: William Knapp, from Poole, was just one example. It was also an eclectic style: folk melodies certainly provided the major source for the tunes of the metrical psalms but art music was incorporated as well. Tunes by Haydn come up in the music books of Dorset parishes.

Such range and skilfulness are not really surprising. People with a musical ear are born into every class and every age, and they usually have a very retentive memory for tunes. Moreover, tunes were passed around. Each local group or family of musicians, like the Hardys, kept a collection of manuscript music, in which secular and sacred music was combined. Musicians could copy tunes performed by other groups and melodies could even be obtained from the shops where music was sold. The poet John Clare, who was a gifted fiddle-player, visited music shops in order to copy out the music that he found there. This was an accepted practice and it made it easy for opera melodies and fashionable London waltzes to mix with folk music traditions, creating a form that was nothing like as crude as it's been taken to be.

In Stinsford, the music seems to have been particularly good. There were only four instrumentalists in the gallery – Hardy's grandfather on the cello (or bass-viol) and three other strings, among them Hardy's father and uncle. The four-part choir was positioned so that each voice stood beside the instrument playing their part. Other churches in the district boasted larger numbers and woodwind as well as strings; none, however, according to Hardy at least, had such a talented group. The Hardys 'maintained an easy superiority' over their rivals in neighbouring parishes, so much so that members of the family, Hardy's grandfather in particular, were asked to help out elsewhere.

One reason for their excellence was the support of the vicar. Edward Murray came into the parish in 1822 and remained until 1837; he was an upper-class man with family connections to the Earls of Ilchester and he could afford to live in the rather grand Stinsford House, in preference to the vicarage. Murray organized regular rehearsals in the house for the church musicians and encouraged them to be ambitious. They performed 'Elaborate Canticle services' as Hardy called them, such as 'Jackson in F' and 'Jackson in E flat'. William Jackson (1730–1803) came from Exeter and his music was quite well known in the West Country, but performances of it were usually confined to churches larger than Stinsford.[6] Jackson's musical idiom, similarly, lay much nearer to cathedral music than to country psalmody. The Hardys' willingness to take on his works implies (despite Hardy's urbane modesty about their accomplishments) that they were a group of skilful and cultivated musicians.

An elector of the parish, who was accustomed to visiting the vicar's house, led the music in church every Sunday and lived in a dwelling that was in effect his own, could hardly be called a peasant. Hardy's grandfather was, in fact, a leading figure in his community, long established commercially, comparatively well off and widely respected. While his music linked him back into an almost ageless tradition of folk tunes and popular culture, it linked him up and out as well: he was on good terms with the well-born incumbent and was performing music designed for elite city congregations. Working in the building trade, though it seems at first glance to tie the family into the working class, had a similar consequence for his class position, allowing both rootedness and mobility.

Hardy's grandfather was a businessman, employing labourers and owning a brickworks across the Frome valley near Broadmayne. Most of his work was supplied by the local gentry – by the lord of the manor at Kingston Maurward and, to a lesser extent, by other landowners in the surrounding area. He and his son, Hardy's father, needed to deal with people above and below them on the social scale and Hardy's father was particularly good at charming the clientele. 'To the courtesy of his manners,' Hardy wrote, 'there was much testimony among the local county-ladies with whom he came in contact as a builder.'[7] He was a good-looking man by all accounts and Hardy enjoys the thought that he was attractive to upper-class women. It is especially pleasing to him that his father's popularity derived less from some kind of rugged earthiness (which is what the situation might lead you to expect) and more from 'courtesy'. Thomas Hardy, senior, proved that a commoner could behave like a gentleman and he did so without pretending to be a gentleman born. There was no servile imitation of genteel manners – in fact there was nothing pretentious about his behaviour; there was only courtesy. Self-reliance was combined with politeness and self-respect led to a proper respect for the customer. The absence of servility was, in fact, the way to get on.

*

Hardy inherited comparable attitudes and similar ambition from the other side of his family, though in this case they were coloured by a more troubled history. His maternal grandmother, Elizabeth Swetman, known as Betty or Betsy, was an educated woman; at least, that was what Hardy claimed.

> She knew the writings of Addison, Steele, and others of the *Spectator* group, almost by heart, was familiar with Richardson and Fielding and, of course, with such standard works as *Paradise Lost* and *The Pilgrim's Progress*.

She was reputed to be the owner of an exceptionally large collection of books and thirty gowns as well, although these details are almost certainly exaggerations.[8] Betty's family had, it is true, been established for several generations in Melbury Osmond, a village in north-west Dorset, halfway between Maiden Newton and Yeovil, and, like the Hardys, the Swetmans held their property, a farm of fifty acres, on a long lease that passed down from one generation to the next; their lifehold of the farm had continued, in fact, all through the eighteenth century. Consequently, Betty grew up in a family that saw itself as occupying a very different social plane from peasants or labourers. That did not guarantee, even so, that they were well off or even comfortable and there's no evidence they had the means to purchase fine clothes and books – books were rare luxury items in eighteenth-century rural communities. Betty's mother, Maria (1738–1802), was born into the Childs family, however, and they were involved in publishing, so Betty may have inherited by that route a library something like the one Hardy describes.

In the normal course of events, Betty's brother, John, would have inherited the lease to the farm. For some reason he never did so and eventually he moved away to live in Southampton. That may have been his choice: farm incomes were falling at the beginning of the nineteenth century and city life offered (or seemed to offer) better opportunities. Equally, his departure may have been the result of a new landlord, the Earl of Ilchester, refusing to extend the lifehold. The Earl would very probably have wanted to farm the land himself, incorporating its acres into a larger, more cost-effective operation. If this was the reason why

John did not receive what he would have seen as his inheritance, it would have felt to the family like an eviction – an unjust though legal appropriation of customary rights. Betty's father remained on the farm until his death in 1822; then control over the land reverted to the lord of the manor. The outcome for Betty and her sisters was not only a perceptible loss in status; it brought poverty nearer too.

When Betty's mother, Maria, died in 1802, Betty was twenty-four. Soon afterwards, she fell in love with a local man, George Hand, became pregnant by him and the couple married in December 1804. George Hand was nothing more than a servant. Although in some of the records his status is raised a little to that of gardener, this is attempted only in places where he was not known. He was nothing like good enough for the Swetmans and Betty's father, John Swetman, strongly disapproved of the match. His family's recent misfortune contributed to that disapproval, making him more insistent about his daughter's social superiority and more determined that she should marry well. Worse still, though the evidence is meagre and some of the sources unreliable, it does look as if George turned out to be a bad husband. Stories of his drunkenness, adultery, violence and spendthrift habits were frequently related in the family and Betty insisted that he be buried beside his mistress.

George died in 1822 and Betty's father died in the same year, leaving her an unprotected widow with seven children to support. Maria, the eldest, was seventeen and would soon be off her hands, but the two youngest, Mary and Martha, were still little children and Jemima, Hardy's mother, was only nine. The long-foreseen loss of the farm occurred at the same time and was compounded by Betty's double bereavement. She was left without either financial resources or family support; the result was first hardship and later destitution. In 1829, she was compelled to 'go on the parish' – that is, to live on the equivalent of social security benefits – and this humiliation was never forgotten. 'I should not have been poor if right had took its place,' she wrote in 1842, aged sixty-three.[9]

Betty had of course been powerless to oppose the will of the lord of the manor, when he took back from her family the land they had farmed for a century. Still, the conviction that she had suffered such an injustice did preserve her self-respect. Hardy remembered Betty from his early childhood – she died in 1847 – and absorbed directly the embattled self-reliance that her life story had instilled in her. Similar convictions were present in his mother too, of course, handed down to her from Betty during an impoverished childhood. Jemima shared her mother's instinc-tual self-reliance, her pride in family and her dislike for the arbitrary power of local aristocrats. She followed her mother also by being 'omnivorous' in her reading (as Hardy described it, perhaps a little patronizingly). Eager to educate herself, she was fiercely anxious that her children should do the same; her mother's influence was powerful too in the way that Jemima kept house.

Betty had 'doctored half the village' by consulting 'medical books in her possession'.[10] We have only Hardy's word for this but supporting evidence comes from the mere fact that her children survived. Despite poverty and the many deprivations it caused, not one of them died – something which at that period was highly unusual. Likewise, infant mortality among Betty's grandchildren was comparatively low, particu-larly among the children born to her daughters. The four girls produced twenty-five children in all between them; of these, twenty-two are known to have lived into adulthood. This is a high degree of success for the time and could not have been achieved without a combination of expertise and self-discipline. In those days, a mother could hope to keep her child alive by knowing herbal medicine (there was no other kind you could afford), by keeping herself and her house as clean as possible and by avoiding anything or anyone who was diseased. Survival depended upon running your own house strictly and being very careful whom you mixed with. These habits followed from the belief in self-reliance that the family's history had engendered. It meant too that Hardy and his cousins grew up in an environment where both discipline and wariness were taken for granted.

Jemima Hand was reputedly the most intelligent and talented of Betty's children. She was brought up to go into service, as a cook, and was employed first of all at Maiden Newton, quite close to home. In 1837, she joined the staff of Stinsford vicarage, where at first she worked for Edward Murray, though soon afterwards he left the parish. Hardy claimed that his mother had been employed in London and in Wey-mouth before going to Stinsford. Although there's no evidence either to support or contradict this, Jemima thought of herself as someone who knew the world beyond the backwoods parish where she had come to live.

The Stinsford area was full of family connections – her father, George, had originally come from Puddletown nearby and her eldest sister, Maria, married since 1828 to James Sparks, was raising a family there. Recently, her brothers Christopher and Henry had moved into the district as well. Now, Jemima was doing the same and sticking close to the tribe, as she would do all her life. Nonetheless, a desire to remain slightly set apart persisted. She was not one to forget the cultured way of life she had observed elsewhere – whether that was in London or in the well-to-do household at Maiden Newton where it is known that she worked. Swetman family pride had been handed on to Jemima and if anything had been heightened by her childhood experience of severe poverty. She was resolved to be true even in adversity to her background and so she tended to separate herself from her peers. This was all she deserved, it was healthier and it kept in view the prospect of rising once again in the world. After her marriage, apparently she would not allow the Dorset dialect to be spoken inside the house.

His parents' ideas about their social position and their concern to maintain it inevitably had an impact on Hardy, and probably on him more powerfully than on his younger brother and sisters because, as the first child, he was especially subjected to the burden of their expectations. His father had joined the family firm; Hardy was groomed to do the same. That was why, as a teenager, he was directed towards architecture. Skills he acquired in that profession would prove useful to the business because, later on, assuming that Hardy got established locally, he would send work the family's way. For similar reasons, Hardy's parents encouraged him to mix with the Moule children whose father, the Revd Henry Moule, was Vicar of Fordington, a suburb of Dorchester. Jemima positively admired Henry Moule, for his sincere religion and personal courage. She also saw his family of seven Cambridge-educated sons as offering Hardy a route to superior culture that did not involve his leaving the district.

This forms one pattern visible throughout Hardy's upbringing. None of his three siblings – Mary, Henry or Kate – ever married and all of them stayed close to home nearly all their lives. Mary and Kate did travel initially, going away to college in Salisbury to train as teachers, and for the first few years of their careers working in schools some distance away. As soon as they could, though, they returned to Dorset, teaching at a girls' school in Dorchester, where Mary became headmistress, and living in a house that Hardy had bought for them. In retirement, they gravitated back to Higher Bockhampton and until 1913, well into old age, they lived in their childhood home. When at last they did leave, it was only to move in with their brother, Henry, who had taken over the family firm and never left the district at all. The three of them shared Talbothays Lodge, a considerable dwelling that Hardy had designed and Henry built. It stood only two or three miles away from the house where they were born.

Hardy's cousins did marry and have children; many of them left the area too, moving to London, Bristol or Plymouth. This was the more usual course of events in Victorian society, in which people were moving around more and more. Hardy and his siblings seem to have been unusually wedded to their parents' home territory but that attachment does not at all imply inertia. All four children grew up with the expectation that they would make their way in the world, succeed professionally and advance socially. They were pressured to rise from the higher ranks of skilled labour and small business to enter the lower ranks of the professions and they were taught to pursue the high culture that their family had always aspired to, through reading, music and painting. Mary became an accomplished portrait painter, and Hardy was a skilled draughtsman, with notebooks full of 'artistic' sketches. These advances were to be achieved, however, without the family unit breaking up. Entering the professions must not challenge the primacy of loyalty to the family; neither its business interests nor its balance of relationships should be threatened and no one was to move away, not permanently at any rate. Hardy was expected to avoid becoming assimilated to his rustic surroundings and yet never to abandon them.

Such a degree of submission to their parents does not come about in children by accident. A parent would need to possess not only authority to bring it about but some cunning as well. Hardy's account of his parents does not present them in this light at all; he makes them neither manipulative nor pushy; furthermore, the *Life*'s devotion to the memory of his mother encourages the idea that she was the power in the marriage. From that narrative and from the family myth more generally, Jemima emerges as the one keeping the household together. Nonetheless, one or two signs do remain not only of the parents pressurizing their children but also of Hardy's father's being a determined character – someone as concerned as his wife was that their first-born son should do their bidding.

*

Jemima Hardy and Thomas Hardy, senior, were married on 22 December 1839, less than six months before Hardy was born. Marrying because of pregnancy was fairly common in that community and not disgraceful. Both Hardy's grandmothers, Mary Hardy and Betty Hand, had been married in the same circumstances so, in isolation, Jemima's pregnancy does not imply a shotgun wedding or a marriage that was unloving. Betty, it is true, had been miserable with George Hand but Mary had lived happily with Thomas Hardy the first, Hardy's grandfather, for well-nigh forty years. For Hardy's parents, marriage was neither as contented as that nor as grim as Betty's had been.

Hardy depicted their life together as a clash between his father's unworldliness and his mother's drive. She was 'a "progressive" woman, ambitious on [Hardy's] account though not on her own.' His father, on the other hand, 'was in nature the furthest removed from a tradesman that could be conceived'.

> Instead of waylaying possible needers of brick and stone [. . .] he liked going into the woods or on the heath, where, with a telescope inherited from some collateral ancestor [. . .] he would stay peering into the distance by the half-hour; or, in the hot weather, lying on a bank of thyme or camomile with the grasshoppers leaping over him.

Hermann Lea, one of Hardy's closest friends in later life, had heard about this telescope too. According to him, Hardy's parents would take the boy for a walk on the heath every Sunday afternoon. From its highest point, Rainbarrows:

> with the aid of a telescope, his father would point out places of interest, houses and other buildings on which he was then working.

This version creates a slightly different impression, particularly of Hardy's father who seems much more positive and less dreamy. The telescope brings knowledge of the wide world into the family's isolated home. It reveals how the man of the house is extending his reach into the neighbourhood and it shows the little boy that his father has influence and power, that he is a kind of hero.[11]

Hardy evidently did have feelings of admiration for his father, bordering on hero-worship. The last entry in his first literary notebook is a quotation from one of the Norse sagas, as translated by William Morris: 'He was nowise of such wondrous growth & strength || as his father had been.' The first entry in the book was from Shakespeare's *Timon of Athens*: 'It is I | That all the abhorred things o' the earth do mend | By being worse than they.' The last entry mirrors the first, enclosing the book in self-deprecation. That is typical of Hardy. He tended from the beginning to suffer from low self-esteem and his parents' relation to him may have contributed to that. From the note-book, it appears as if he felt unable to live up to their expectations of him, not least (and this is the surprising thing by comparison with the *Life*), not least his father's expectations and example.[12]

If Hardy's father was in fact more driving – more driven – than one would guess from the *Life*, that does not mean his mother was less so. Despite appearances, they probably held rather similar views about the need to get on and certainly, by the time Hardy was old enough to remember walks of this kind, the couple had made themselves a powerful presence in the extended family. How they did so sheds light on the side of Hardy's father that Hardy himself tended to obscure.

When Jemima married her husband, her mother-in-law, Mary Hardy, still owned the family business. Mary had been widowed in 1837 and since their father's death, Thomas and his elder brother, James, had carried on the work. (The eldest of the three sons, John, had already moved into Dorchester.) Within a few years of the marriage, however, the business had been divided. James continued to live close by with his growing family but relations between the brothers and their families were chilly and remained so. Theresa, James Hardy's daughter and Hardy's cousin, lived in the same house down the lane from Hardy's birthplace into her old age; though living as a neighbour, she stubbornly refused to have any dealings with her relatives. She would not even enter the house. Similarly, when Hardy was growing old, it was sug-gested that he should make Basil Augustus Hardy his heir. Basil was James Hardy's great-grandson and so Hardy's great-nephew. Since Hardy had no children of his own, there was no one more directly in the line of succession and, by all accounts, Basil was an eminently suitable character – respectable, pleasant and the son of a clergyman. Despite all this, Hardy refused point-blank to consider the idea.

This degree of lingering animosity implies a bitter dispute. The *Life*, though it mentions the division of the family firm, gives no convincing reason for that change and glosses over any family rift. It encourages you to ignore the fact that the two couples and their children continued to live only yards apart, that James's two younger children, Augustus and Theresa, were of an age with Hardy and his sister Mary, and that James continued to work in the same line as his brother – in the 1851 census James is referred to as a 'mason employing two labourers'.[13] The relatives living nearest to Hardy disappear from the story of his childhood, in which otherwise the extended family figures prominently. There must, though, have been many opportunities to reconcile the two families. The *Life* elides this aspect of things and creates too a hint of contradiction. If Hardy's father been as easy-going and unambitious as Hardy suggests, surely he would have found a way to patch things up.

The received idea of the relationship between Hardy's parents, which follows the image created by his own account, assumes that in the early years of their marriage Jemima pushed her new husband into making the break with his brother – a break that, left to his own devices, he would never have made. Her ambition, in other words, disrupted the harmony of the family. Although this is part of the story, it is not all of it. For one thing, when he first married, things seem not to have been going especially well for Hardy, senior. His father's electorship was not handed on when he died; neither Hardy, senior, nor any of his brothers were deemed suitable, though nobody knows why; perhaps these youngish men were thought not to possess the same gravitas as their father. In the same year, 1837, the new incumbent, Arthur Shirley, arrived, replacing Edward Murray. Under the new regime, the west gallery musicians were not encouraged and by 1843 the band had disappeared, a barrel organ taking its place. The loss of church favour reduced the status that the family had enjoyed in the parish before and may have had financial implications as well.

Traditionally, the parish had given some money to its musicians, though the sums did little more than cover their costs. 'Going the rounds' at Christmastime brought some financial reward, and fiddle-players could always make extra money by playing at dances and weddings. Some musicians at the time were able to become at least semi-professional. For his part, Hardy claimed that he and his family were never paid – it was, he said, 'a firm principle with them' to charge nothing for their services – but it is doubtful whether this is entirely true. After all, Hardy bought *The Boy's Own Book* out of money he had earned playing the fiddle. That fact was suppressed by Hardy (it survives thanks to J. M. Barrie) who wished in all areas to make his family appear more genteel than it actually was. In fact Hardy's father's violin-playing would have supplemented the family income, at least to a small extent, especially when times were hard. When the church band was dispersed, opportunities were reduced, even though the Christmas tradition lived on, and the openings that did remain were the less respectable ones. Overall, disbanding the gallery musicians meant for Hardy's father that music came into conflict with his work as a builder. Playing the violin and rehearsing the band at Christmastime became a costly hobby, and a drain on his time and money, whereas previously it had helped establish his credentials in the eyes of the county families for whom he worked.

Another sign that Hardy's parents married in straitened circumstances can be found in the house at Higher Bockhampton. After her husband's death, Mary Hardy continued to live there; when her son planned to marry, he built an extension for her, adding it on to the right end of the house (looked at from the front). The workmanship of the new section is noticeably worse than the rest of the building. It seems to have been built cheaply and in a hurry. Thomas Hardy, senior, was not an incompetent builder and the poor quality of the extension is unusual. It increases the impression that he did not find it easy to step into his father's shoes. The new vicar's treatment of the musicians did not help and neither did the decision over the electorship, where the vicar's opinion may have counted against him once again. At least, opposition from the new incumbent may easily have been suspected. Hardy's father felt himself suddenly snubbed and dispensed with by the gentry-folk, in ways that indirectly harmed his business. It no longer looked quite so well established without Hardy's grandfather at the helm and that raised doubts as to whether it could support both brothers and both their families.

Hardy's father had reasons of his own, then, for splitting from his brother. Probably, he did not actively pursue a breach; rather, as he saw it, things had simply changed since their father's death and the business needed to respond to the harsher conditions it now faced. Continuing in the same old, generous way would lead both brothers to ruin in the end. And where he had made a decision, Hardy's father could be doggedly obstinate. The *Life* emphasizes, for instance, how persistently during Hardy's childhood Jemima wanted to leave Higher Bockhampton and move into Dorchester instead. This issue comes up regularly in the opening chapters. The only obstacle to what would have been a sensible, advantageous change was the opposition of Hardy's father. He absolutely would not go, and so the family stayed put. Reading the *Life* you are seduced by the image of Hardy's father as a kindly countryman into ignoring the character traits implied by this refusal.

While Hardy makes it easy to forget his father's strength of will, he also soft-pedals the vulnerability of Jemima's situation when she first married. She was a forceful but also a traumatized woman whose childhood had undoubtedly left its mark on her. There were, Hardy said, some experiences from her past that she could never speak of and she never lost her fear of poverty. She loathed idleness because idleness had ruined George Hand, her father, and impoverished his children. Habitually, she saw life as a fight to gain and keep hold of the means to live. Thomas Hardy, senior, had had by comparison a much easier time of it. His father's business had been sound and he had been brought up to continue it, either in partnership or alone. Financial means had given his family the leisure to pursue their music, inside the church and out, whereas Jemima could not even play the piano. Hardy remembered her gazing at the keys, wishing she could play and reminded by the instrument of what she had been denied. This personal history meant she would criticize her husband for not being active enough in business. His assurance seemed like slackness to her, although in fact pretending to be a little off-hand was to your advantage when running an established business, because it gave the impression that work was in strong supply. This manner was habitual to Thomas Hardy, senior, and an aspect of his family pride, but to Jemima it was distressing. Compulsively, she would push him and thus make herself appear the pushy one.

Her husband's oblique, casual-seeming manner was the more troubling to Jemima because of how tightly knit the Hardy family was and how much power her mother-in-law wielded in it. When Mary Hardy died in 1857, she left everything to Thomas Hardy, senior, even though he was the youngest of the three sons and his elder brothers were still living. John and James both had the prior claim in law and an equal claim according to natural justice. Mary's will had been drawn up as early as 1841 and she stated in it that she chose Hardy's father as her heir, 'for his kindness and affection towards me'. She never swerved from this point of view and her decision about her money, even though, by 1857, both of Hardy's uncles were, unlike his father, already grandfathers – they stood at the heads of strong family lines, which promised a safe long-term future for the family firm. Even so, neither brother ever received a penny from their mother.

Thomas Hardy, senior, had been Mary's favourite child from the beginning. It was one reason why he never left home – why he lived and died where he was born. Though Mary moved into the granny flat next door when Jemima arrived, her presence was still pervasive in the

Higher Bockhampton house and Jemima remained an outsider, whom Hardy's father had married probably more out of a sense of duty than anything else. She would want to have a greater say in the affairs of the firm less out of relentless ambition than out of a need to establish herself within the family. Jemima's fears about money and the threat of indolence would have led her to take an active part in her husband's business anyway. To those innate characteristics was added her feeling of not being part of the family group. Rather than Jemima and Thomas simply taking over the business, therefore, something subtly different took place when the firm split; the triumvirate of Thomas, James and their mother, Mary, was replaced by a second, consisting of Thomas, Mary and Jemima.

It's wrong to see Jemima's demonic energy shattering the calm of the Hardy family; what occurred was both more complicated and tauter than that. Rivalry between the brothers existed already, thanks to their mother's favouritism, and anxiety about the firm's prospects was already increasing, after the death of Thomas Hardy the first when the family's local standing suffered. Under these circumstances, a split was not unlikely, quite apart from what Jemima may have wanted. In addition, Hardy's father was not someone who could easily be pushed, except in a direction where he was predisposed to go. He may have been more relaxed and easy-going in manner than Jemima was, but he was never the dreamy rustic idler depicted in the *Life*. He died in 1892 and the elegy Hardy wrote for him, 'On One Who Lived and Died Where He Was Born', gives the more rounded picture. Hardy wrote there of his father's 'vigour | And fine, forceful frame'. The *Life* allows 'fine' – it emphasizes his attractiveness so much in fact as to leave the suspicion he was unfaithful; it does not allow 'vigour' or 'forceful'.

Mary, Hardy's sister, produced accomplished oil portraits of both their parents. In her picture of her mother, Jemima is reading, with glasses on the end of her sharp nose and with her mouth firmly set. She looks the domineering character of family tradition. The painting of Thomas, senior, is copied from a photograph; in it his mouth looks shy and there's diffidence about his eyes. The photograph itself reveals a livelier person, more energetically uncomfortable, as if formal clothes and posing for photographs were things he actively disliked. He looks slyer and impatient to get away. The difference between photo and picture shows Mary doing something similar to what her brother did in the *Life*. She shifts the image of her father away from that of a suppressed rebel and presents him as more like the stereotypical, softly-spoken working man.

The available evidence of what Hardy's father actually did gives the impression of someone rather different. He may not have been particularly in a rush to expand his business, he may have preferred fiddle-playing to making money; still, the business flourished and his son, Henry, took it over in a good state. Moreover, he took active steps to ensure that both his sons could, at the very least, take his place. He hoped his eldest, Hardy, would better himself by moving into architecture. Paying for Hardy's training was, as far as his father was concerned, an investment to secure the firm's interests into the future. And it was Hardy's father, Hardy says, who 'insisted' that Hardy 'make an income in some way by architecture' when his training was completed. He was not willing to see good money go to waste. Similarly, a few years earlier, it had been Thomas – and not Jemima – who vigorously disapproved of Hardy's going around the district, playing the violin at weddings and parties. Like his wife, he wanted nothing to interfere with his son's advancement. And, when Hardy moved to London in 1862, it was his father who came up to visit him and see the sights, while Jemima remained at home. That stage in his son's progress was also one he wanted to encourage, even if his wife had her doubts.

The concern that his son should do well may have originated in feelings of inadequacy. Hardy's father had lived for a long time in the shadow of his own father whose name he shared and who had established the business originally, pioneering the wilderness of 'New Bockhampton'. He had worked for his father and played for him too, accepting his lead in the gallery of Stinsford church as much as in the building yard. This dutiful and submissive side to his personality appears again in his waiting until his father died before getting married, and the same family loyalty was displayed in his choice of Hardy's Christian name: Thomas yet again, after his father and grandfather, placing his son in a line of succession. And, clearly, he played the part of the dutiful son by looking after his mother into her old age.

Hardy himself often feared that he had let down his predecessors and, particularly, that his lack of children proved his unworthiness to follow in the family line. It seems an odd feeling given Hardy's international fame – his extraordinary pre-eminence by comparison with all his relatives. It would be a more natural one in Hardy's father, who had achieved comparatively little on his own account and who died without living grandchildren or any in prospect. Probably Hardy inherited the feeling from him. In both men, there was a tendency to accept other people's dominance and to resent it at the same time, to submit to others and, rather than opposing, to evade them. Within that disposition, a sense of failure lingered – the fear of not quite being a man.

Hardy's father must have been someone who masked self-certainty, even obstinacy, behind diffidence and charm. He was a good-looking, relaxed character who knew how to enjoy life. You would only find out if you knew him very well, how decided he could be about the things that mattered to him. And what mattered was often what lay near at hand – his mother, the house where he was born, the family business and family tradition. Another side of the same characteristic was the way he stood back and let Jemima do the talking. Socially, sometimes professionally and even within the family, he would use his wife's more outspoken and forceful personality to achieve what he wanted himself. She seemed, therefore, more dominant than she actually was. She controlled the family more than she did her husband because on crucial matters he would not give way. He would not discuss them and retreated instead – onto the heath with his telescope or across the fields to dances, carrying his violin. Jemima remembered most vividly the figure he cut, his striking appearance as he, his father and brother walked along the lane to church. She remembered someone, in other words, who would not be mastered, whose accommodating ways and unflappable steadiness were a kind of power.

Hardy wrote about his parents' courtship when both of them were dead. In his poem, 'A Church Romance', Jemima turns to look at Hardy's father, playing in the gallery:

> in her pride's despite
> One strenuous viol's inspirer seemed to throw
> A message from his string to her below,
> Which said: 'I claim thee as my own forthright!'

For the man to 'claim' the woman is, of course, only the traditional arrangement. To say anything else would be remarkable, even for Hardy who was famous for showing how variously power was shared between the sexes. Yet Hardy says the traditional thing very forcefully here. His father does not only claim Jemima, he does so 'forthright'. 'Forthwith' is part of the meaning and you can think for a minute that that is what the line primarily means. The more unusual word, 'forthright' makes Thomas Hardy, senior, sound bold as well as quick, decisive and unabashed as well as unhesitating. He may be 'strenuous' in his playing – more energetic than polished and almost comically vigorous – so that it is slightly humiliating for Jemima to find herself falling for someone so unsophisticated. All the same, she does fall for him. He will not allow her to escape.

~ 3 ~

She who upheld me and I

HARDY portrayed his father as the principal source of his love of music and love of the countryside. Although Jemima told him a great deal, Hardy said, about country ways and superstitions, his father was closer to nature itself and even able to blend in with it, 'with the grasshoppers leaping over him'. Nonetheless, it was from his father that Hardy learnt more worldly skills as well, observing and imitating his strategic charm and hidden obstinacy. In later life, Hardy was willing to appear henpecked if that helped to preserve his actual independence within the marriage. This too, probably, he had seen his father do. And both men viewed their families with love and fear in equal measure, loyally devoted to a tradition they believed they had let down. Most obviously perhaps, Hardy repeated his father's devotion to his mother. Jemima became in Hardy's later life a revered figure: 'I have always found that what my old mother said was right,' Hardy told Robert Graves when Graves was visiting in 1920.[1]

The children of alcoholics, particularly the daughters of alcoholic fathers, are often characterized by extreme self-control and reticence, especially about their feelings. Jemima's refusal ever to speak about some things in her past suggests she was self-controlled in this way and to this extreme extent. She had been nine years old when her father died – old enough, therefore, to have experienced his drunkenness, unreliability and neglect at first hand, to have felt and understood it. She may also have witnessed his violence towards her mother. When he died, Maria, Jemima's eldest sister, went to live with her grandparents in Puddletown and her mother, Betty, was compelled to find work. Jemima, the middle daughter, had to take responsibility for her two younger sisters, Martha and Mary, who were six and seven years old at the time. Her own childhood abruptly ended.

Jemima grew up to see her brothers, Henry, Christopher and

William, all display some of the weakness for drink and the violent tendencies that had marked their father. Her family had been and remained strongly matriarchal – Betty, Maria and herself were its dominant forces. It also huddled together. Most of the family followed Maria to Puddletown though William did not, Betty moved only in her extreme old age and Martha moved away when she married. All the others – Maria, Jemima, Mary, Henry and Christopher – lived and died in and around the village, raising their children there. They were a close-knit and inward-looking group. The poverty in their early lives had taught them to rely on their own – no one apart from family could be relied on to help and no one outside the family should know how bad things were. In Jemima's case, ties with her younger sisters, to whom she had been a second mother, reinforced those habits and assumptions.

When Jemima first married, Martha and Mary were both living nearby. Their presence supplied in some ways an emotional counterweight to Jemima's mother-in-law. Having them around enabled her to keep up in her new life the essential relationships from her old, rather as her husband did through his mother's presence. After 1841, when Martha married and left the area, Mary's companionship became all the more important. In 1847, Mary too was married and, although she continued to live in the district – in Puddletown with her shoemaker husband, John Antell – her marriage contributed to a crisis in Jemima's.

Betty Hand, their mother, had died the same year. She was buried on 1 June, the day before Hardy's birthday, and Mary was married in November. As the last unmarried girl, it had fallen to her to look after Betty in her final years and, as was often the case, the mother's death released the daughter. Then, six months later, in May 1848, Martha, now living near Hatfield in Hertfordshire, lost one of her children, Martha Caroline, born in 1846. At some unknown point in the previous few years, Jemima had suffered a miscarriage and had been seriously ill afterwards. She was still recovering when her mother died, followed by her niece, and her youngest sister married. Family tradition has it that the miscarriage and subsequent illness changed Jemima, making her into a harder woman, who was more obstinate and inflexible than before. Really it was the combination of illness, bereavement and separation that affected her.

In the aftermath of Martha Caroline's death, Jemima went to visit her sister and took Hardy with her. They travelled up by train to London and stayed there overnight before going on to Hatfield, where they they remained for almost a month, living with Martha's family – her husband John Brereton Sharpe, Hardy's 'favourite uncle', and their two surviving children, Frederick and Louisa. It was a long enough stay for Hardy to be placed in the local school. He vividly remembered the excitement of the journey, the sights of London and his sense most of all of being his mother's companion. Jemima said that she needed little Tommy with her in order to ward off the unwanted attentions a single woman might receive while travelling. This, though, sounds distinctly like a pretext. By taking Hardy with her, she was taking him into her side of the family. Now that her sisters were leaving and her mother dead, Hardy was to be her support when the marriage was difficult or her spirits low.[2]

How close Jemima came to leaving the marriage altogether is hard to say. It's certainly possible that she thought of staying on permanently in Hatfield. Jemima's niece, Rebecca (Maria Sparks's eldest daughter), did something similar a few years later. After a brief, unhappy marriage, she separated from her husband and went to live in Plymouth with her younger sister, Tryphena, becoming a second mother to Tryphena's children. Unlike Rebecca, Jemima had her own children to take into consideration, though at this time only two. Hardy himself was with her; Mary, a year younger, could have stayed with her father and grand-mother had Jemima decided to leave, or she would not have been an impossible burden for one of Jemima's married sisters in Puddletown, Maria or Mary, to take on.

Whatever Jemima's hesitations about her marriage, she and Hardy did come back to Bockhampton and quite soon afterwards, she became pregnant once more. Hardy's brother, Henry, was born in 1851, ten years after Mary; after a gap of a further five years, Kate, the youngest child, was born, by which time Jemima was nearing forty. Her miscarriage had certainly contributed to the long gap between Mary and Henry, but poverty may have played a part as well. The 1840s were a time of widespread economic depression, giving rise to social unrest and the Chartist movement. Jemima's sister, Maria Sparks, who had had four children between 1829 and 1836, delayed her fifth child, Nathaniel, until 1843; her sixth, Tryphena, did not enter the world until 1851, the same year as Henry. Jemima may have been following her example albeit unconsciously.

In those days, the only reliable mode of contraception was absti-nence. This would have been easier for Jemima if she felt disaffected towards her husband already, though it was likely to alienate the couple still more. The further gap between Henry's birth and Kate's certainly increases the suspicion that the marriage was uneasy and sexually unfulfilled. After that, the dynamic of the relationship was altered by the couple's advance towards old age and, more specifically, by the death of Mary, Hardy's grandmother, in 1857. Crucially, it is clear that, amidst the ups and downs of her married life, Hardy became the focus for Jemima's most intense feelings. The journey to Hatfield established a link between them that was never lost. She became jealous about him, possessive and astringently demanding. Hardy became, in response to this, devotedly loyal towards her. His first encounter with the world outside the village coincided with his being made his mother's intimate, her ally and her man-at-arms. They had gone on jaunts together before – on 'various expeditions', according to the *Life*, including one 'in fantastic guise' to play a trick on relatives in Puddletown. 'They were excellent companions, having each a keen sense of humour and a love of adventure.'[3] The stay in Hatfield changed this playful companionship into something more serious. It established in Hardy a sense of responsibility towards his mother and a lasting nostalgia for their time together. He saw the two of them united against the world.

Jemima in Hardy's poetry is the one 'Guiding my infant steps, as when | We walked that ancient thoroughfare, | The Roman Road.' This road crossed the heath near Hardy's birthplace and Hardy confessed to being frightened of walking there when a child. Her presence helped him confront such fears. In 1896, during his most serious period of depression, Hardy recalled a similar scene. He would have been happy, he wrote, had his life ended years before – on, for instance:

> that loneliest of eves when afar and benighted we stood,
> She who upheld me and I, in the midst of Egdon together,
> Confident I in her watching and ward through the blackening
>   heather,
> Deeming her matchless in might and with measureless scope
>   endued.[4]

The poem wishes for something impossible. Life would have been so much better had he never lost the childlike, total confidence in his mother, which was bound to diminish as he grew up. He could not always think of her as 'matchless in might', not as she grew old (and by 1896 she was in her mid eighties). All the same, he would have been far happier had they never changed from what they were then – surrounded by a sinister world and confronting it together. Jemima's protection 'upheld' him then and he wished it could do so still.

Similarly, of course, the *Life*'s account of things is profoundly committed to Jemima. It gives her side of the story in several family disputes; it celebrates both her wisdom and her drive. When he was writing it, however, Hardy told his second wife: 'I do not ask for much – I only want a *little* affection.' Many things could have prompted him to say such a thing; what is arresting about it is the sense of neglect – the child's protest that he has not been loved enough. Despite the *Life*'s rather cosy account of Hardy's upbringing, hints exist within it and evidence comes from elsewhere which suggest that he did not receive very much affection as a child. One reason for this may have been that soon after returning from Hertfordshire he was caught in the crossfire of his parents' troubled relationship.

*

At the age of eight Hardy began attending the village school, situated in Lower Bockhampton a mile or so away from his home. The school had been set up only quite recently and a new schoolhouse built, thanks to the efforts of Lady Julia Martin, whose husband had bought the Kingston Maurward estate in 1844. Lady Julia was an energetic lady of the manor and saw it as her role to help improve life in her husband's villages. Founding and funding a 'national school' – that is, a Church of England one – was a first step in that direction. She 'made it her hobby', Hardy remembered, 'till it was far superior to an ordinary village school'.[5]

Hardy was known as 'Tommy' when a little boy and, according to the *Life*, because Lady Julia had 'no children of her own':

> she had grown passionately fond of Tommy almost from his infancy
> – said to have been an attractive little fellow at this time – whom
> she had been accustomed to take into her lap until he was quite a
> big child. He quite reciprocated her fondness.

When Hardy was nine, however, Jemima decided that he should be sent to a different school – one run by the renowned schoolmaster, Isaac Last, in Dorchester. Last was a Nonconformist but, Jemima learnt, 'an exceptionally able man' and the schooling he offered was reputed to be the best in the district, better even than that of Dorchester Grammar School.[6] Whatever Last's merits may have been, another factor prompting Jemima to act was Lady Julia's evident fondness for her son. The one thing Jemima would not tolerate was another woman poaching her Tommy from her.

Lady Julia, in turn, was offended by Jemima's decision to withdraw her child. It was a piece of insubordination that did not sit well with her paternalistic attitudes. By way of punishment, she persuaded her husband to withdraw all the estate's building work from Hardy's father. This was a serious blow to the business, potentially a considerable financial loss, and it cannot have made life any easier between Hardy's parents. Jemima's jealous high-handedness threatened the firm and it compelled Hardy's father to begin looking further afield for work. It was in his nature to express anger indirectly, through coldness and withdrawal; in this instance, he had every opportunity to do so and every excuse since, after all, it was Jemima's fault that he was away so much.

The *Life* exonerates Jemima in this dispute, claiming that she did what she did solely out of concern for Hardy's progress in life. His father's loss of income is downplayed as well; the narrative emphasizes how quickly he gained new customers, thus revealing his 'easy superiority' as a builder as well as a musician. The reality at the time was more fraught for all the family and not least for Hardy, because parting from Lady Julia caused him considerable pain. Even in the *Life* he confesses that he 'secretly mourned the loss of his friend the landowner's wife', that he felt for her almost as a lover would and that he had 'grown more attached than he cared to own'. When the chance presented itself of seeing Julia again he 'jumped at the offer', going with a young girl from the village to a local harvest supper which Lady Julia would attend. When they met, Lady Julia reproached him: 'O Tommy, how is this! I thought you had deserted me!'

> Tommy assured her through his tears that he had not deserted her, and never would desert her: and then the dance went on.

When Hardy got home that night, after three in the morning, 'A reproof from both his parents [. . .] ended the day's adventure.' It also ended the connection. Hardy did not meet Lady Julia again until 1862, when he had moved to London. She was one of the first people he looked up when he arrived in the capital, going to see her the moment he went beyond his mother's reach. Though he was disappointed to find how old she had grown and did not repeat the visit, the instinct to look her up as soon as he could indicates the strength of his childhood feelings.[7]

The depth of Hardy's attachment to Lady Julia and its lastingness formed a pattern that was repeated later in life with other aristocratic women; it contributed no doubt to his fascination with glamour. The feelings Lady Julia aroused also lead one to suspect something lacking in his mother's affection. Jemima was evidently possessive of her boy, and ferociously hostile to Lady Julia's probably overbearing intrusiveness. She was not herself comfortable expressing affection. Though she took effective and determined steps to break off Hardy's relations with this surrogate mother, she did not (perhaps she could not) supply what Hardy quite naturally needed. Instead she sent him off every day to school in Dorchester. Meanwhile, his father travelled around the district in connection with his work and often spent time away, his wife's behaviour creating physical and probably emotional distance between him and the children.

Hardy's father, nonetheless, would have been no more pleased about his son's feelings for Lady Julia than Jemima was. If he resented the way his wife had crossed the lady of the manor and offended his principal customer, he would have been impatient with his son too – for being so childish and soft. His own devotion to his mother meant that in his eyes, your natural mother was, of course, the person you should be most attached to. His experience after his father's death, over the church music and the electorship, had already formed in him the conviction that it was idle to suppose the upper classes genuinely cared about their social inferiors. Hardy's going off to school in Dorchester would, both his parents hoped, toughen him up physically and help him forget the silly nonsense of his infatuation with Lady Julia.

Hardy, as an elderly man, remarked that 'he did not like going to school as a boy – & he remembers being sent when he was really ill'. The *Life* mentions that he was so physically frail when young that his parents believed he probably would not live to be an adult. Yet, over his schooling, they were apparently willing to take risks. Sending him to Last's school meant a six-mile walk – three miles there, three miles back – and although such distances were not unusual – some of Hardy's classmates walked in from Charminster, a village a few miles outside Dorchester to the north – and although Hardy was stronger by the age of ten, when he started the routine, nonetheless it's worrying to learn that he was sent when he was 'really ill'. It implies a draconian regime, even a punitive one.

Hardy's writings often declare his lack of ambition and his lazy satisfaction with what he had in his obscure rural childhood. Hardy was proud of never having wanted to better himself because that proved he had succeeded without really trying and so confirmed how innately gifted he was. It suggested too that he had always been genuinely more interested in Dorset than in London. His books repeatedly asserted that the quiet world of the countryside was preferable to the frantic pace of city life; a lack of ambition proved that this was something he genuinely felt and so made his art sincere. Nevertheless, there are many moments in the novels and several poems which sound guilty about idleness.

His first published novel, *Desperate Remedies* (1871), can be read over-all as an exploration of the need to be motivated. In *The Hand of Ethelberta* (1876), the narrator says of the hero, Christopher Julian, that though 'a thinker by instinct, he was only a worker by effort. [. . .] It is a provoking correlation, and has conduced to the obscurity of many a genius.' In 'Four in the Morning', a poem from *Human Shows* (1925), Hardy describes himself waking up and delighting in the morning, partly because he thinks he is alone. Then outside, he hears somebody sharpening a scythe and the noise sounds like a rebuke.

> – Though pleasure spurred, I rose with irk:
> Here is one at compulsion's whip
> Taking his life's stern stewardship
> With blithe uncare, and hard at work
> At four o'clock!

This is the only poem Hardy published where he gave 'Bockhampton' as the place of composition.[8] He seemingly connects his birthplace with a salutary and enlivening work ethic. This is something he is reminded of – something he can recapture – when he goes home.

The hard-working and stern aspect to his home life naturally created in Hardy a hunger for pleasure. 'A Young Man's Exhortation', written in 1867, exhorts us to:

> Exalt and crown the hour
> That girdles us, and fill it full of glee,
> Blind glee, excelling aught could ever be
> Were heedfulness in power.
>
> Send up such touching strains
> That limitless recruits from Fancy's pack
> Shall rush upon your tongue, and tender back
> All that your soul contains.

And other poems written much later – 'Great Things', for instance, or
'Lines to a Movement in Mozart's E-flat Symphony' – similarly relish
'blind glee'.[9] The later poems are more confident, however, that life's
pleasures have been fully enjoyed, at one moment at least in the past.
The earlier ones are filled with the fear that pleasure is passing the
speaker by and that he will always be deprived.

The dominance of the work ethic in Higher Bockhampton is
confirmed by another anecdote Hardy recounts in the *Life*. On one
occasion, he made the mistake of confessing his lack of worldly ambition
to his mother. He came, with childish self-importance, to the decision
that he 'did not want at all to be a man, or to possess things, but to
remain as he was, in the same spot'.

> Afterwards he told his mother of his conclusions on existence,
> thinking she would enter into his views. But to his great surprise
> she was very much hurt, which was natural enough considering she
> had been near death's door in bringing him forth. And she never
> forgot what he had said, a source of much regret to him in after
> years.[10]

A child moaning that they 'never asked to be born' does of course sound
ungrateful. Hardy, though, was not quite saying that and really, it *is*
surprising that Jemima was not pleased by what he told her. All her life,
she pressured the children to stay nearby; Hardy was fully entitled to
expect her to be gratified to hear that this lonely place, with only his
family for company, was quite enough for her favourite son. Her
opposite reaction bears out the feeling – elsewhere rarely acknowledged
– that Jemima pushed Hardy. Staying at home did not imply in her
mind any loss of ambition. Of course her children should do well and
make her proud. They should carry on their parents' good work, extend
the business, and struggle to regain as far as possible the family's lost
status and wealth.

Jemima's refusal ever to forget Hardy's childish remarks sounds
manipulative as well, as if she were always throwing them back in his
face and using against him this example of his supposed ingratitude.
Whenever he was slow or disobedient, she could remind him that he
had never appreciated the sacrifices she had made on his behalf. And,
clearly, she was setting up a double bind: if Hardy enthused about a life
of future success, then he was abandoning her; if he did not, then he
was disappointing her hopes. Reluctance meant he was slipping back

into the ruinous idleness of his grandfather, George Hand; ambition meant he had no respect for his family and no real attachment to his lonely mother in her unhappy marriage. Jemima's solution to the conflict she established was a strictly defined idea of what Hardy should aim for: his mission was to help the family colonize nearby Dorset in the same way that a previous generation had colonized the lonely heath. Anything else was a kind of betrayal. Hardy, for his part, did not just absorb this project: he absorbed the threat of betrayal too. He had a pained sense of obligation and he suffered guilt about even wanting to go his own way. At the same time, he had a baffled suspicion that he was expected to go his own way; he must do so, however, on his parents' behalf and with their interests in view, as much as and perhaps more than his own.

Hardy's father, lingering in the background, shared some of his wife's anxieties and most of her ambition for their children. The local aristocracy had done him no favours. His eldest brother, John, had been driven from the district by the landlord, who was lord of the manor. He himself had suffered at the hands of an officious new vicar; more recently, his business had been seriously compromised by the whimsical jealousy of a childless woman, who just happened to be wife of the squire. Insidiously, behind the scenes, Lady Julia had compelled him to make his own way in the world. That was a sign of the times. Hardy's father felt, with some justification, that he had been treated more harshly than his father or even his grandfather had been. There was no longer a stable feudal order in which the poor were cared for by the rich and estates managed for the benefit of all. If that world had ever existed, it certainly did not do so now. You might yearn for it; music might transport you back into a dream of it; traces of it might be detected in the innocent country folk you mixed with. Everyday modern life, however, was a more sober, unforgiving affair.

Hardy's father went 'further afield to replace' the estate work he had lost, 'soon obtaining a mansion to enlarge'. He expected his son to do the same, to go as far afield as necessary. Likewise, Hardy's father 'remained' in the house where he had been born. Because 'the rambling dwelling, field, and sandpits attached were his for life he remained'.[11] Hardy himself would not be so lucky, as everyone in the family foresaw. Their ownership of the Bockhampton house lapsed on the death of Hardy's father and would not be renewed. Later in life when family history became very important to him, Hardy dwelt particularly on the Swetman family's decline and fall. The Swetmans had been important members of the community for more than a century; at that time their present landlords – the landlords depriving them of their patrimony – were no better than peasants. Now, exactly the same thing was happening to Hardy and his immediate family because their lifehold would soon be taken away.

Hardy's and his siblings' childhood was, therefore, a preparation for departure. They faced the same task as their mother had – that of finding their way and their place in life; at the same time, like their father, they took on responsibility for a family business – a business that would have eventually to be carried on in new premises. Hardy's genuine and powerful desire never to grow up and leave home, his wish to be still and invisible within the landscape, on a bank of camomile, hopped over by the grasshoppers like his father or hidden away amongst the ferns as he had been himself when a child – these feelings arose from his knowledge that he could not stay. They found a focus in his two grandmothers – particularly, his father's mother, a woman who had been able to reside in a single dwelling all her adult life and who came to represent for him the stability he was denied. The importance of these grandmother figures in his writing also bears out the suspicion that it was from them, rather than from his parents, that Hardy received some of the affection he craved.

*

Both of his grandmothers were already widows by the time Hardy was born; their husbands had been local men, born in Puddletown, whereas both wives were outsiders. Betty Hand came from the north of Dorset; Mary Head, from even further away – from the village of Fawley, near Wantage in Berkshire. (Hardy set his last novel there, encoding the family connections: Jude the Obscure's surname is Fawley and he grows up in the village of Marygreen; this is modelled on the actual Fawley and is named, partly anyway, after his grandmother.) The two women also shared a history of early trauma. Betty had lived with an abusive husband and had been ostracized by a vindictive father; Mary was an orphan. Her father had died the year she was born, her mother when she only six. She grew up in extreme poverty and, before she married, she may have given birth to an illegitimate child. Like Jemima, Mary was unwilling to talk about the desperate times from her past and, partly as a result, little is known for sure about what exactly happened to her.

Instead, both Hardy's grandmothers became treasuries of local knowledge and family history. Betty, Hardy says, could be relied upon to know what had taken place in the parish: 'if ever there was any doubt as to the position of particular graves in the churchyard, the parson, sexton, and relatives applied to her as an unerring authority'. Mary is highlighted in several places in his writing; in his earliest surviving poem 'Domicilium', for instance, and in 'One We Knew', written in 1902. In 'Domicilium', she tells Hardy how the Bockhampton house looked 'when first she settled there', fifty years before. In 'One We Knew', Hardy remembers that 'She showed us the spot where the maypole was yearly planted', 'She told of that far-back day when they learnt astounded | Of the death of the King of France', 'She said she had often heard the gibbet creaking' and so on. Each stanza begins with one of her memories, one of the pieces of history she passed on.[12]

It is hard to disentangle what the grandmothers were really like and how Hardy related to them as a boy from the role they performed in his later view of things. As he grew older and the past receded further, his grandmothers came to represent a lost haven. By talking of them, he could convey his distance as a grown man from the life of his childhood. He did something similar in the way he portrayed his father because by making Thomas Hardy, senior, so straightforwardly rustic, Hardy could suggest his separation from the previous generation's culture and way of life.

There were reasons for his doing this in his portrayals of both generations, his father's and his grandmothers', and there were different reasons at different times; even so, beneath these changing motives runs the continual feeling that as a boy, Hardy was as close to his grandmother, Mary Hardy, as he was to anyone. 'Domicilium', written soon after her death, pays devoted homage to her, 'my father's mother, who is now | Blest with the blest'. *Two on a Tower* (1882) depicts her once again, this time as the sole carer for the novel's young, orphaned hero, Swithin St Clare, a 'woman of eighty [who] retained faculties but little blunted'.

> She was gazing into the flames, with her hands upon her knees, quietly re-enacting in her brain certain of the long chain of episodes, pathetic, tragical and humorous, which had constituted the parish history for the last sixty years.[13]

There is noticeable affection in the portrait – reverence for her steadiness, 'quietly re-enacting' the past, and still a sense of the twinkle in her eye as she recalls 'humorous' episodes along with the tragical ones. This fondness for her and the warmth of her relationship with Swithin suggests by contrast the ambivalence of Hardy's feelings for his parents – an ambivalence that dated back to his boyhood, even though it worsened at points during his adult life. He was unfailingly loyal to both Jemima and Thomas Hardy, senior, yet he never gives the impression of ever being quite confident with them. He found comfort and affection instead elsewhere in the family: in his sister, Mary, and in his grandmothers.

One of their great attractions for him was their supply of memories. In 'One We Knew', Hardy's grandmother, Mary:

> told how they used to form for the country dances –
> 'The Triumph', 'The New-rigged Ship' –
> To the light of the guttering wax in the panelled manses,
> And in cots to the blink of a dip.

Jemima, by contrast, had rather mixed feelings about the old country dances and she would rebuke her husband for 'performing them with all the old movements of leg-crossing and hop, to the delight of the children'. Doing things in the old way risked causing positive harm, she believed, because 'this fast perishing style might tend to teach [the children] what it was not quite necessary they should be familiar with'. Hardy's grandmother worries less about what might or might not be necessary. Like her son, she aims to give delight and her recollections seem to offer an escape from tension.

All the same, she chooses her memories very carefully and, like all of Hardy's significant relatives from childhood, she is resolutely silent about personal things. She would not speak of her childhood any more than Betty or Jemima would, and her son, Hardy's father, was habitually elliptical and evasive about his feelings. The one thing all of them would talk about was 'parish history'. Knowing the district better than anyone proved that you belonged. It gave you a better right to claim true ownership than anyone else, more even than your 'betters' who were the legal owners, and more than the vicar or lady of the manor who had done you down. By acquiring local knowledge you could also gain some degree of compensation for injustice. Psychologically too you could establish yourself because meticulously recording events stabilized experience; it gave order to the past and alleviated trauma. By keeping the history, you could hold together a life that had been disrupted – by familial violence in Betty's case, by sudden poverty in Jemima's, and in Mary's case by the early death of her parents.

Hardy became a meticulous man who remembered things, who

sought to preserve the past in all its detail. His novels often make use of stories told him by his mother and grandmothers or stories drawn from back-numbers of the local paper; furthermore, books' concern more generally is with 'parish history', with 'episodes pathetic, tragical and humorous' that took place in a particular district. In his personal and domestic life too, Hardy maintained order, particularly in times of emotional crisis or pain. He had grown up in a house where nothing was said about what really mattered – where history filled the silence and annals of the parish supplanted personal lives. He grew used to secrets; he absorbed habitual strategies of self-control. While the past could sometimes offer a sanctuary, a comforting memory of secure affection, it could also be used as a defence.

Taking in and remembering, becoming an accurate, impersonal chronicler of events, was one way in which he achieved this. The habit enabled him to maintain belief in his own distance from events and from suffering. That had been part of the point for Jemima and the others too. Being able to record things precisely implied that you were detached from them, unaffected and unharmed. It also made fact into a place of safety. If you were troubled, you could turn to matters of fact, to musical or building techniques and, if you were a writer, to dictionary definitions, for security and consolation. Thirdly, within these anecdotes of local history and country life you could find, without admitting it to yourself, equivalents to the pain or trouble you were trying to control. You could release your feelings without confessing them, sometimes without even realizing that you had these feelings and wanted to release them.

Hardy has often been criticized for being an unconscious writer. In fact, it is his unconsciousness that makes him so good. Rather like Alice in the looking-glass world, he went away from things in order to approach them. Traumatic feelings and transgressive impulses that would otherwise have been censored out, half-unconsciously, are allowed to burst through in his books because, like his mother and grandparents, he was rigidly, determinedly sticking to the facts. Stories from country life often challenged people's conventional expectations of decency or moral uprightness. Hardy was keen on that unsettling power which they possessed so clearly. In addition, being no more than a historian liberated him from his own moral judgements, which were often rather prim and allowed profound unacknowledged feelings to come into play.

What was good for him as a novelist had much less beneficial consequences in his private life. He wrote so well because otherwise he was so buttoned up, so like his mother in his reluctance to confide or confess. He could adopt all too easily the late Victorian and Edwardian ideas of gentlemanly conduct and, in fact, he put on the mask more completely than many of his contemporaries. He turned into someone who could very rarely unbend, not even to his closest intimates. There were, it is true, understandings within the family. Mary, his sister, as well as being the person who knew most about his childhood, could intuit something of his real feelings and Emma, his first wife, shared his inner life, with its hopes and fears, for something like ten years. It was because they had been so unusually intimate that Hardy's coldness to her in middle age and beyond was decided, absolute and cruel. Similarly, in his sixties, he did confide a little in his friends Hermann Lea and Edward Clodd. Still, with these few exceptions, Hardy's upbringing guaranteed that he died, for all his fame, hardly known as a person at all.

‒ 4 ‒

‘The playground of TH’s childhood’

WHEN he started at Isaac Last’s Dorchester school in 1849, Hardy began living in one place and working in another, with an hour spent on the journey each way. This remained his way of life for nearly ten years, because it was not until he was well established in his apprenticeship as an architect, during his late teens, that he began to sleep in Dorchester during the week and visit home only at weekends. Travelling to and fro every weekday, he saw ‘rustic and borough doings in a juxtaposition peculiarly close’. The ‘railways and telegraphs and daily London papers’ of Dorchester made, as he said in the *Life*, a vivid contrast with life in a hamlet ‘three miles off, where modern improvements were still regarded as wonders’.[1] Hardy found himself living in two worlds at the same time and two very different historical periods.

In the *Life*, Hardy uses his schooldays as an example of what he felt about himself more generally: that he was uprooted from a timeless rural world by accidents of history and personal circumstance. And, to a certain extent, that is what happened. At the time, as a teenager growing up, Hardy’s feelings about going to school cannot have been quite so nostalgic for what he left behind, though evidently he did start there unhappily. He missed Lady Julia and felt that he was being unfairly driven away from her. Distress at losing his surrogate mother would have made him resent all the more the strictness of the regime imposed by his natural parents. On the other hand, he excelled academically at Last’s school and seems to have enjoyed his success. Plainly, he was an unusually clever boy. He had started to read when very young, perhaps as early as three years old, and on his recent visit to Hatfield, he had proved himself more than the local children’s equal in mathematics and geography. In Dorchester, similarly, there are several accounts of his helping his schoolmates with their homework and, unsurprisingly, he won prizes as well.

Isaac Last, Hardy reports, 'finding that he had an apt pupil who galloped unconcernedly over the ordinary school lessons' allowed him to begin studying Latin from the age of twelve. At the Academy, a more advanced school Last opened when Hardy was thirteen or so, Hardy went on to win 'Beza's Latin Testament for his progress in the tongue' and another prize for diligence and good behaviour. Generally, he was 'extraordinarily quick in acquisition'. He learnt some French and German, and 'In applied mathematics he worked completely through Tate's *Mechanics* and Nesbitt's *Mensuration*.' He 'found a certain poetry in the rule for the extraction of the cube-root, owing to its rhythm'.[2] Hardy was not only intellectually talented, then, he had a broad range of aptitudes: his retentive memory would have helped him in all subjects. Geography, for instance, consisted at that time in little more than memorizing the names of capital cities and longest rivers. His excellence in mathematics, however, shows a capacity for abstract thought as well as a good memory, and languages, music and drawing each require different sorts of skills.

Hardy's novels later reflected his intellectual range, showing his receptiveness to and delight in all branches of knowledge, however dry or academic they might initially appear. Geology, the Napoleonic Wars, the laws of perspective, Druids, cider making, history, social science, astronomy – ideas and subjects of every kind found their way into his books. Many novelists (such as Dickens and Joyce, for example) have attempted to portray the whole world within the confines of one work. In Hardy's case, the breadth of subject-matter also gives the feeling that he has other strings to his bow. He does not sound like a novelist who has dutifully done his research and now knows about farming or astronomy or whatever; he sounds instead like someone who could have turned his hand to anything, if he had not happened to choose writing as his profession.

The eclectic style also characterized the way that Hardy related to the literary world during his career as a novelist. Employing it enabled him to give the impression that he was not simply a writer and not solely preoccupied with literary success. By presenting himself as genuinely interested in these other areas, he could claim as well that he had a more authentic and disinterested sensibility than other novelists. The feeling that he could do (and be) several things at once, that he was not committed to any particular project or role, enabled Hardy both to stand up to competition and, at the same time, to stand aside from it.

Signs of this tactic appear, however, much earlier in his life, before he began to write. Hardy had innately not only the gifts of a polymath but also the instincts of one, and he sought out variety, partly because it offered him disguise.

This was a side of his temperament encouraged by the way he lived as an adolescent, fitting into contrasting places. He seems to have defined himself as an outsider, malleable and amenable certainly to what different circumstances required but secretive as well, with a private territory of his own. He could, for instance, have taken more than one route from Bockhampton into school. Down the lane at the front of the house, tracks and field paths led into Dorchester via the main road from London, which Hardy could join at several different points. Or he could cut down beside Stinsford church, then follow a path beside the river and across the water meadows into town. A third alternative was to set off around the back of the house, along the path towards Rushy Pond, which led down the hill through Bhompston Farm and Lower Bockhampton; from there, he could follow the river into Dorchester.

These different routes meant he could define and explore a whole little district, in the shape of a sharply pointed triangle. Dorchester stood at its apex, Higher Bockhampton at one corner and the London road and the River Frome formed its two long sides. Within that area, all sorts of different landscapes could be found: the remote heathland, the tree-lined road to Grey's Bridge with the spires of Fordington and Dorchester rising beyond, water meadows, the Frome's pretty river-banks, an elegant country house and landscaped gardens at Kingston Maurward, and Stinsford's ancient churchyard. Hardy did travel to places outside this area, both physically and imaginatively. His father's work expanded his horizons, music took him around the nearby country-side and he visited relations at Upwey, near Weymouth, as well as in Puddletown. Going to school in Dorchester created, all the same, an irreplaceable intimacy with this one small area, which was to be, for the rest of his life, a personal domain.

He became possessive about it. As a schoolboy, the *Life* declares, Hardy 'loved being alone':

> but often, to his concealed discomfort, some of the other boys would volunteer to accompany him on his homeward journey to Bockhampton. How much this irked him he recalled long years after.[3]

It seems to have been especially irritating for Hardy to be bothered by other people on this 'homeward journey', as if he viewed that part of his day and that part of the world as his alone. It is remarkable too how rarely Hardy writes about the inside of his childhood home. *Under the Greenwood Tree* is the only case when he does so in his fiction and in the *Life* nearly all of his boyhood memories relate to places away from the house – to the dances where he played violin, to incidents at school and, most of all, to meetings on the country roads and the footpaths which took him to and fro. Perhaps these outdoor scenes were his truer home.

In Hardy's day, it was quite natural to think of the inside of the house as a female space. All through his childhood, Jemima, with Mary, her mother-in-law, and Mary, her daughter, did the household chores. Taught by her mother, Hardy's sister became in fact an excellent cook. His father's work, on the other hand, was conducted outside, either nearby or at a distance. He had no room of his own in the house, not even a separate office for the business (not at least until the late 1850s, when the house was rearranged after the death of his mother). For a boy, the house was somewhere you left behind in the quest to become a man.

It is not in the least surprising then that, when Hardy wanted to remember *his* childhood, he focused on places outside in the countryside nearby, and this inclination can be found earlier than the *Life*. In 1871, he painted three small watercolours, more carefully finished than the many sketches he drew as a young man. One was of the back of the Higher Bockhampton house, one was of Rainbarrows Beacon and the third showed Dorchester, seen from the top of Stinsford Hill. Beneath this one is a title in Hardy's neat handwriting: 'The Playground of TH's Childhood'. A golden rainbow arches over the houses of the town, rather like a halo.[4]

It is an odd place for him to find a playground, one might think, especially given his complaints about being sent off to school. Yet the title confirms both his attachment to the area between home and school and his sense of possessing it personally. It suggests, too, excitement, a boy's thrill at setting out on the adventure of his life and leaving his family behind. By going off along the lane to school, Hardy could enter a playground, escaping the watchful, critical atmosphere at home and able to forget the tensions between his parents, tensions that were often channelled through their ambitions for him. Out there, too, he was moving beyond their sphere of influence because, while Puddletown was full of relatives, Dorchester was the place to which his father would not move. Hardy was, as far as the family was concerned, breaking new ground and, although that was part of the point as far as they were concerned, it brought for him, nonetheless, a feeling of release.

With freedom came solitude and his mode of life as a schoolboy inevitably confirmed Hardy's love of being alone. Mary, hitherto his frequent companion in walking or climbing trees, did not join him at Last's school and two hours a day walking by himself (not in the school bus or on a train or sitting in his mother's car) – doing this was bound to increase Hardy's already pronounced self-sufficiency, just as it was certain to develop his imaginative life. Gifted children tend to be loners anyway. Their talent sets them apart and many of them become very skilful at hiding their powers or deploying them only when it's advantageous to do so. Hardy tended to do the same. 'He used to sit away by himself,' one of his schoolmates recalled after his death. 'He was always in a stud' (sic).[5]

The isolation was not simply his free choice, however, because he was kept apart from the other boys by external factors. He had his lunch every day with his great-aunts, who lived in Dorchester close to the school and, like the other pupils who travelled in from outlying villages, he was on the fringes of the playground groupings. Being top of the class made him still more of an outsider and there are hints that he was picked on as a result. A shop in South Street, Dorchester, was kept by a formidable woman, Sally Warren.

> To enter the shop one descended a step. The boys sometimes threw Hardy's cap down into the shop, and when he entered to retrieve it the old woman belaboured him with a broom.[6]

Horse-play perhaps; or perhaps a sign of something worse. Hardy was physically slight and so a likely target. Moreover, if he was bullied, it would help explain why there's no record of any schoolboy friendships and why he made no attempt to stay in touch with any of his schoolmates after he left. It would explain why he seems to have wanted to put the experience behind him.

While his schooldays lasted, Hardy did not assimilate to the place so much as make himself invisible within it. If other boys wanted to walk home with him, he did not object but he did not encourage them either. If they wanted help with their work, he would provide it, though he never offered or used his cleverness to curry favour. He stuck instead to what interested him personally. It's notable, for instance, how enthusiastically he kept up his music while at school. As well as travelling every day from Bockhampton into Dorchester and back again, he frequently went out in the evenings for 'adventures with the fiddle', playing 'in farmers' parlours', at an 'agriculturist's wedding, christening or Christmas party [. . .] not returning sometimes till nearly dawn'.[7]

Hardy was rapturous about music, which partly explains his persisting with it, despite being so stretched by his daily routine. Particular tunes would unfailingly bring him to tears, and playing at dances put him into a kind of frantic trance. But there were other attractions too. Jemima did not oppose his going out to these dances, 'possibly', Hardy says, 'from a feeling that they would help to teach him what life was'. He would see grown-ups drinking, carousing and flirting, and there was a chance he might join in. As is still often the case, music could make it easier for a shy adolescent to meet the opposite sex. Hardy's account of his father's attitude is more contradictory. Thomas Hardy, senior, is said to have objected to his son roaming the neighbourhood in this way; yet several of the anecdotes Hardy provides feature his father, as if the two of them went out playing together. There's a suggestion here that Hardy was being trained up as part almost of a family band. Whatever the truth of this, the inconsistency about his father's feelings reveals Hardy's double loyalty to music: he loved it both for its connections with the past, including his family past, and just as much for the way it offered him excitement and experience of his own, independent of anyone else. The other, musical life he led outside school and outside the family gave him, in other words, a sense of himself. He clung on instinctively to the feeling of being different from other people that music gave him – different and, at the same time, in touch with his roots and his family.

Staying in touch with those local, family roots became increasingly important to him as his years of schooling slowly drew him further away. Hardy's academic gifts were exceptional by comparison with those of the rest of the family. Mary, the family member he was closest to in feeling and temperament, had nothing like his talents and neither did Henry or Kate. His cousins, the Sparks children – Rebecca, Martha, Nathaniel, James and Tryphena – were bright, but they provided little intellectual companionship. So, as Hardy achieved what the family expected of him, those achievements set him apart.

Music was one route back and it allowed him to feel that he was keeping a foot in both camps. It did not heal the rift (except momentarily perhaps, while he was actually playing), but it did maintain the balance between his competing loyalties. More pervasively, his effort to balance the two (and balance himself between the two) encouraged the non-committal manner that became so characteristic – the impression Hardy sought to give (not least to himself) that he could get on anywhere and do almost anything. He could be a clever schoolboy, a helpful companion, a dutiful son and brother, a devout churchgoer (his family thought that he might make a priest in the end) and an accomplished fiddle-player. He could perform equally well in all academic subjects, and he knew town life as well as country life. By adopting this stance of the all-rounder, he avoided exposure. He pleased everybody and was committed nowhere. He could keep out of sight the question of what he might really want for himself.

*

Meanwhile, his parents' plans for him continued to be put into effect. In 1856, Hardy was asked by his father to make a survey of Woodsford Castle. These remains of a medieval keep, being used as a farmhouse at the time, stood a few miles east of Dorchester, just beyond West Stafford. They were being restored by John Hicks, a Dorchester architect, and Hardy, senior, had been taken on as one of the building contractors. Performing the survey was an opportunity for Hardy to demonstrate to Hicks his skills as a draughtsman and his potential as an architect; when it was proficiently completed, Hicks duly agreed to take him on as a pupil in his office. Hardy's father paid Hicks a substantial amount of money for training up his son and Hardy, just turned sixteen, was taken out of school.

He cannot have been entirely surprised and the routine of his life scarcely altered. Hicks's office was in the centre of Dorchester, like Last's academy, and Hardy went on living at home, walking into work every day. Moreover, according to the *Life*, Hicks was a kindly, liberal employer and 'exceptionally well educated, for an ordinary country architect'. For the first few years, he ensured that Hardy's duties did not become too onerous. Hardy's fellow-pupils were also, Hardy says, 'well educated' and one in particular, Henry Bastow, had 'a liking for the classical tongues' and 'regretted his recent necessity of breaking off his studies to take up architecture'. The two young men began to read together, Hardy took up Greek (which he had not learnt at school) and Hicks apparently smiled upon their efforts, even though 'during the ensuing two or three years [Hardy and Bastow] often gave more time to books than to drawing'.[8] It would be surprising if Hardy had not, like Bastow, felt some regret about the sudden end of his academic pursuits because they had given him status and fulfilment for a number of years. It eased the change from scholar to clerk to find that he was able to carry on studying. And, after being an outsider at school, he seemed to have found as soon as he left a like-minded companion. Bastow became over the next few years Hardy's first friend.

He was a year or two older than Hardy and further on in his schooling, having attended a school 'in or near London'. Similarly, Herbert Fippard, Hicks's senior pupil when Hardy arrived, made 'one or two trips to London' during the brief period when the two of them overlapped. Fippard was only the son of a Fordington grocer but he could fascinate Hardy by 'whistling quadrilles and other popular music' heard in London or by giving racy 'accounts of his dancing experiences at the Argyle Rooms and Cremorne'. His stories were almost certainly fabriacted, but the tunes were genuine and Hardy insists that he never forgot them. At school, then, Hardy had been odd and, intellectually at least, he had stood supreme; in Hicks's office, he was more at home and a little bit more threatened. Here were people who had the same hopes and ambitions as he did. Here were others who had been forced to take up architecture because they could not afford the classical education they desperately wanted. Hardy wanted to emulate them and compete. He wanted to share their knowledge of a wider world.

Bastow was a Baptist and serious about his faith, so much so that he decided while Hardy knew him to undergo adult baptism. It is a sign of their intimacy that Hardy began to wonder whether he ought to do the same, even though for an Anglican like him, it would be highly unusual. Lengthy discussions of the relative merits of infant and adult baptism took place between Hardy, Bastow and two other friends, who were also Baptists. Hardy, being outnumbered, felt under pressure to improve his knowledge of the Greek New Testament and the Church Fathers so he began to combine his work drawing in the office with hours spent, early in the morning, mugging up Latin and Greek.

Studiousness was a genuine feature of Hardy's character and a lasting one. But by taking up the debate, he was also doing something else very characteristic of him – trying both to adapt to a new environment and to remain in touch with his background, in this case the 'High Church principles' of his upbringing. Unlike the school, Hicks's office challenged him to hold his own and it was in that environment –

stimulating and rivalrous, stimulating because rivalrous – that he began to write. 'Domicilium', his first extant poem, dates from his early years in Hicks's office. He may too have had a comic article printed in the local paper around this time – written in the form of a letter composed by one of the town-clocks, which had recently been removed. Later in his career, Hardy found it increasingly difficult to combine literature and architecture, and eventually he was forced to choose between the two, several times. These decisions were made all the more painful by the hopes that were raised during his time with Hicks. There it seemed to be taken for granted that following the profession of architecture could be both rewarding in itself and a path to higher things – to a classical education and literary achievement.

*

It was not the office alone that encouraged this idea. An important additional source of Hardy's hopes and excitement was a school next door, because its schoolmaster was William Barnes. Barnes (1801–86) was a remarkable person – a wide-ranging scholar, who could read sixty languages, a talented draughtsman and a nationally known poet, as well as a gifted teacher, who was both dedicated and progressive. Unlike nearly all his contemporaries (Isaac Last included) Barnes hardly ever employed corporal punishment and his curriculum was unusually imaginative. Instead of dinning the classics into his pupils, Barnes taught them science as well, demonstrating the power of electricity, the working of steam engines, and the principles of bridge building – all to little boys whose peers in other schools were facing a legion of Gradgrinds. Frederick Treves, for instance, the surgeon at the London Hospital famous for his care of the Elephant Man, Joseph Merrick, grew up in Dorset and was taught by Barnes. He never forgot 'the good old man' who 'knew boys better than most'.[9]

Hardy came across Barnes as an avuncular presence, who could be relied upon to resolve disputes in the architect's office. He recalled running into the school to ask Barnes's expert opinion on the questions of Latin and Greek grammar that periodically exercised the scholarly architectural clerks. Of course, Hardy also claimed that Barnes always decided in his favour and, although this is hard to believe, it shows how much he invested in Barnes and Barnes's learning. His enthusiasm for the classics contained, that's to say, a strong desire to align himself with educated people. The parallels with Jude and Phillotson in *Jude the*

Obscure are marked (and Hardy drops hints in the novel that he is thinking of Barnes in connection with Phillotson). When Barnes kindly welcomed Hardy and endorsed Hardy's self-taught expertise, he seemed to be opening a door for him socially. At the same time, Barnes's life story seemed to prove that Hardy's hopes were well founded and this encouraged Hardy to take him as a role model.

Certainly, Hardy's fondness and admiration for the older writer was lifelong. In 1879, he wrote a celebratory review of Barnes's recently published *Collected Poems*. It was extraordinary for Hardy to write a review at all because reviewing was one of the routes into the literary world that he had refused to follow. Three years earlier, he and his first wife, Emma, had moved to Sturminster Newton and lived there, very happily, for two years. Sturminster was an out-of-the-way place with apparently little to recommend it apart from seclusion and tranquillity. There was no obvious reason for Hardy to choose it in 1876 except, perhaps, that Barnes had grown up there. Interestingly, too, while Hardy was living in Sturminster he wrote dialect poems similar to Barnes's.[10]

These decisions suggest some impulse towards discipleship on Hardy's part, though discipleship was something he never liked to confess, either in relation to Barnes or anyone else. It continued, nonetheless, to crop up in Hardy's relationship with the older man. After Barnes's death in 1886, Hardy wrote an obituary full of admiration and love for him. He wrote almost as few obituaries as reviews and those he did write are often somehow barbed; with Barnes again he made an exception. And, in the novel that he was finishing at the time, *The Woodlanders*, Hardy began to write a further elegy for Barnes through the death of the book's hero, Giles Winterbourne. Giles, in his integrity and kindliness, became in many respects an image of Barnes as Hardy saw him.

Hardy paid such close attention to Barnes and followed his example so often because he saw in him an exact precursor. Barnes had grown up on a tiny farm near Bagber, a village close to Sturminster Newton. Aged fourteen or so, he had become a clerk in a solicitor's office in Sturminster, walking in and out of the town. In his early twenties he changed course and branched out on his own, setting up as a schoolmaster, first at a school in Mere, near Gillingham in Wiltshire, before moving twelve years later to Dorchester. While he was teaching, Barnes pursued his research into comparative philology, in which he gained an international reputation, and wrote numerous other books – on the laws of perspective, on the Ancient Britons and on geography. He composed original poetry too, in dialect and standard English, publishing *Poems of Rural Life in the Dorset Dialect* (1844) and *Hwomely Rhymes* (1859) before the collected edition that Hardy reviewed. Amidst all this work, Barnes registered for a university degree, becoming what was known as a 'ten years' man', and graduated from Cambridge in 1850, by which time he had also been ordained.

From peasant to priest was an enormous distance to travel in nineteenth-century English society. Barnes achieved it without sacrificing his principles (he was a sincere Christian all his life) and without souring his family life. His marriage was evidently a profoundly happy one and, although his wife died young, Barnes was comforted in old age by the devoted love of his children. Neither did Barnes lose touch with his roots – he remained a Dorset man through and through, popular locally for his recitations of dialect poetry and widely respected as a knowledgeable Dorset antiquarian.

Although, Hardy could not follow exactly this path – he never gained a degree or entered the Church – still the similarities are very close and Hardy was at pains to draw attention to them in his obituary. He made great play of the fact that Barnes, like him, was picked out as a boy and trained up in one of the professions; also that, as an apprentice, Barnes alternated between life at home in the fields and office work in the country town. Nor were the likenesses superficial. One of Hardy's fundamental concerns as a writer was to depict his home territory both honestly and affectionately. Barnes had done that a generation earlier and Hardy was aiming for most of his career simply to carry forward Barnes's achievement, continuing it amidst what Hardy regarded as much less favourable circumstances. Barnes also showed him the merits of variety. He was extraordinary in the breadth of his interests and abilities, many of them self-taught, and that encouraged Hardy to explore many different areas of interest, as and when they cropped up.

Barnes showed Hardy too not only what you might accomplish as an autodidact but what you could combine as well: a modest schoolmaster, supporting his family, could become a world authority in linguistics, a graduate of Cambridge and an original writer. Moreover, this could be done in Dorchester. His presence in the town perfectly exemplified what Hardy increasingly believed as he grew older that intellectual and professional freedom was something only a countryman could enjoy. In town, workers and professionals were compelled to specialize and were restricted to their specialism, whereas a countryman could range wide. Barnes had fully realized that freedom, even like Hardy taking pride in his skills as a draughtsman. Most importantly of all, perhaps, Barnes instantiated a Victorian ideal. 'A more notable example of self-help,' Hardy wrote in his obituary of him, 'has seldom been recorded'.[11] For the rest of Hardy's life, Barnes was a source of inspiration, a model for his own ambitions and an example of uncompromised success. The irony is that while they were working so close to one another, Barnes's triumphant self-help was what kept them apart.

In his schoolroom beside Hicks's office, Barnes lay apparently within Hardy's reach – close enough to be asked questions and always willing to provide an answer; at the same time, it was plain that Hardy himself was never going to attend Barnes's school. His station in life denied him access to Barnes's teaching, his learning and his paternal affection. Hardy remained outside the charmed circle of the boys whom the 'good old man' understood so well. For Hardy, therefore, discipleship was bound to be a solitary affair. Emotionally distant from his parents and increasingly separate from them culturally, he sought out surrogate fathers. Barnes was the first of these: his intellectual powers, his kindness, and his artistic sensibility all attracted Hardy. But Barnes's very success meant that only the rich could afford his teaching; poorer people, people closer to Barnes himself, had to make their own way as best they could without his direct help. Self-help, therefore, was always *self*-help because those who bettered themselves were divided from those like themselves, who needed their assistance most.

By comparison with cosmopolitan Dorchester, Bockhampton had come to seem to Hardy a restrictive, feudal place. The free exchange of ideas in Hicks's office and the Nonconformist self-reliance of his friends there, suggested that the hierarchies and paternalism of village life had been rendered anachronistic by the modern world. When he found Barnes so near to him and yet so tantalizingly far, that hope was disappointed. Class proved as powerful a force in Dorchester as in Bockhampton and the two adjoining houses in Dorchester's South Street, Hicks's office and Barnes's school, remained set apart. Though he could emulate Barnes – in his reluctance to become restricted to any single specialism; in his ambition as a writer; in his aim to combine writing with a breadwinning occupation; and even in his unfailingly polite and kindly demeanour towards the strangers who sought him out, children in particular – Hardy could never sit at his feet. And as much as he had learnt as a schoolboy to keep his true talent and his real interests hidden from view, so now he must not protest against what his betters had decreed. If, in fact, Barnes taught Hardy anything, it was that he would be wisest never to complain.

– 5 –

His kindred they, his sweetheart I

MEANWHILE, Hardy and Bastow continued their self-education. Hardy would get up at five in the morning (even earlier during the summer months), read until eight, and then walk into work. That way he got through, as he modestly put it, 'a moderately good number of the usual classical pages' – Virgil, Horace and Ovid among others. Somehow, though, he still found the time and energy to go out and about in the evenings playing his fiddle at dances. This well-established routine was broken only in 1860 when Bastow left Dorchester, first for London and soon afterwards for Tasmania, where he lived and worked for the rest of his life. In his absence, Hardy was asked to take on wider responsibilities. For the previous four years, he had been employed mostly on the routine work of copying drawings; now he was asked to travel around Dorset, surveying the buildings that were to be restored, and gradually he became involved in the designs themselves. It was because of these extra demands on him that Hardy began to sleep in lodgings in Dorchester during the working week. Despite Hardy's pleasure in the greater interest of his work, it did not compensate for the loss of Bastow's companionship.

Bastow's letters to Hardy during the 1860s, written from the other side of the world, are full of affection. They address him as 'dear Brother' and 'dear old Tom'; they offer advice freely and confidently; in particular, they exhort him not to lapse from his religious commitment: 'and oh do let Jesus have the very best of all your time & thoughts', Bastow told his friend. Given the fervour of Bastow's Christianity, it is not surprising he made these pleas. Even so, the tone can be startling. Later they lost touch and when Bastow died in 1920, Hardy was not told. As late as 1927, however, he still remembered his old friend. When Hardy spoke about him, Florence Dugdale, Hardy's second wife, gained the impression that 'he would like to meet this man again more than anyone in the world'.[1] Perhaps that is an exaggeration, as Florence tended to overstate Hardy's feelings and Hardy was himself liable in old age to feel plangent nostalgia for the innocence of his early life. Nonetheless, he was remembering a relationship of genuine intimacy. After Bastow's departure in 1860, the correspondence between them lasted for several years (which is not often the case with Hardy's friendships) and it petered out only reluctantly. Their friendship lasted so long principally because the religious fervour Bastow displayed was at the time fully shared by Hardy.

He recalls in the *Life* attending a prayer meeting held by Bastow and his two friends, Frederick and Alfred Perkins, who were sons of the local Baptist minister. It is presented as an amusing, callow business. Hardy arrived on time, anxious not to be late, and found himself the only one there. When his friends finally tumbled in, it emerged that they had gone to the fair instead and forgotten all about the meeting. The anecdote implies that, beneath the religiosity, Hardy and his friends were really quite normal chaps – easily distracted by the fun of the fair and keener anyway on boyish, gladiatorial disputes over arcane points of doctrine than on the solemn, possibly embarrassing business of praying together. It is furthermore the only such meeting Hardy admits to, although Bastow's letters suggest that there must have been others. In 1861, he urged Hardy not to 'forget our little meetings together at our place of assignation'.[2]

Intensity of feeling was not unusual in Hardy's male friendships and Victorian men generally were often by our standards almost alarmingly uninhibited about expressing affection for one another. There would have been, for Hardy and Bastow, no undertone of sexual innuendo about saying a 'place of assignation'. The phrase suited the romance of their friendship, as it developed between two otherwise rather isolated young men: one an outsider, schooled in London; the other solitary, sensitive and growing apart from his family. As much as Barnes was becoming a kind of surrogate father, Bastow became during Hardy's teens a surrogate elder brother, and such devotion to the people around him, especially to those who could offer him an example to follow, remained the pattern of his male friendships for many years, certainly into his thirties.

Partly thanks to Bastow's influence, Hardy became a devout Christian, with Evangelical leanings (despite his family's being more High Church). His faith had a profound impact, moreover, on his understanding of the profession he was entering – that's to say, on what Hardy believed architecture could and should accomplish. Nearly all of his work was connected with church restoration – the rebuilding of the medieval parish churches of England according to the principles and habits of Victorian Gothic. In middle age and afterwards, Hardy looked back in horror at the destructiveness of the Victorian fashion for 'restoration', seeing only the harm it caused – the loss of 'memories, history, fellowships, fraternities' and 'the rupture of continuity' brought about when old buildings were rebuilt insensitively and according to a standard model.[3] This entirely understandable change of heart has obscured his feelings and views while a young man, in the same way that his later loss of religious faith has hidden his youthful Christian faith. At the time, Hardy could see his architectural work in an idealistic light, thanks to the ideas that lay behind Victorian Gothic and thanks too to the character of John Hicks.

Hicks himself was the son of a clergyman, James Champion Hicks, from Rangeworthy in Gloucestershire. His elder brother followed his father into holy orders, becoming Vicar of Piddletrenthide, north of Dorchester. When soon afterwards Hicks moved his practice to Dorchester from Bristol, he travelled in the hope that his brother's position would improve his connections with the church hierarchy and so bring work his way. This hope was slowly beginning to be realized when Hardy joined the firm six years later. Progress was slow because Hicks was competing with London architects: Benjamin Ferrey (1810–80), who had grown up in Wimborne, built Dorchester's All Saints' Church on High East Street in 1845, as well as the town hall and the new hospital.[4] A. W. Pugin restored the chancel of the village church at Rampisham, north-west Dorset, in 1845–7. George Gilbert Scott also worked in Dorset, building a church at Cattistock in 1857, and G. E. Street, designer of the Law Courts in London, contributed to the rebuilding of Bere Regis church as late as 1874–5.

Hicks did secure the restoration of his brother's church in 1852, and three years later, he took over work on Powerstock church, when the architect originally assigned the project suddenly died. This was a significant building – its chancel arch and the south doorway are exceptionally fine – and Hicks's successful completion of the commission helped to make his name in the district. More substantial undertakings started to come his way: he completed Pugin's church at Rampisham, rebuilt Woodsford Castle, where Hardy was introduced to him, and began restoring St Peter's, Dorchester, a church standing right in the centre of the town. Hardy's father may have sensed Hicks's rising reputation and Hicks may have been more willing to take Hardy on because his business was expanding. One of Hardy's first tasks, at any rate, was to help on the drawings of St Peter's.

Hicks was an unusual architect in his day because his restorations exhibited such restraint and sensitivity. Though, like all his contemporaries, Hicks did destroy many features of the original buildings that people would now want to preserve, he was nothing like the worst in this regard, rather the opposite. He was not a dogmatic architect, so he did not insist upon the purity of a single style (as Pugin did), nor did he impose one style inflexibly, indifferent to local conditions. Wherever he worked, Hicks would not use anything except materials locally available, and he preserved as many as he could of the existing elements.

The Victorian Gothic insistence on building showy new churches in obscure villages was certainly questionable as it could easily become a piece of vulgar display by the vicar or the squire. More insidiously, while such building purported to be for the benefit of the local populace, it might very well be harmful – removing the odd, local features of buildings in favour of a uniform, 'pure' Gothic style, stripping out historical associations, and thereby robbing people of their sense of belonging. Hardy had seen enough while still a boy to feel some wariness about aristocratic attempts to better the conditions of those around them. Lady Julia's new school had been admirable and attractive but as soon as her authority was challenged over it, she took her revenge by having Hardy's father sacked. Paternalist generosity disguised, in other words, a self-centred will to power. Furthermore, as Hardy knew from his family's experience, old-fashioned music was tolerated no more than old-fashioned architecture. Improvement eradicated idiosyncrasy; it uprooted indigenous forms, with their long-standing customs and privileges.

What Hardy saw Hicks doing ran counter to these more cynical anxieties. With him, improvements seemed genuinely to be improvements as his buildings helped bring education and spiritual comfort to those most in need of it. The majority of Hicks's churches were built in the most obscure parts of the county. North Poorton, near Powerstock, where he worked in 1862, was a tiny hamlet lost in a tangle of steep little hills and valleys. It registered sixty-one inhabitants in the census of 1881. Bettiscombe, further west, where Hicks built a new church at the same period, was equally remote and so was Stour Row, south of Shaftesbury, where he designed a single-cell church later in the 1860s.

These churches often served communities whose earlier centres of worship had fallen into disrepair. North Poorton was one instance of this; so was West Milton nearby, where Hicks's successor, G. R. Crickmay, inherited from him the commission to build a new church. Both churches lay within the Powerstock parish boundaries and their construction was possible thanks to the efforts of Thomas Sanctuary, vicar of Powerstock. Sanctuary saw it as his religious duty to rebuild the Established Church's decaying fabric and to erect new village schools alongside them. He was an especially energetic and sincere man, whose faith led him to seek the welfare of his flock in all areas of their life: material, cultural and spiritual. Other clerics may have had more doubtful motives when raising money for a new church. Even so, Sanctuary was not an eccentric. Hicks, himself the son of one cleric and related to another, would have respected those ideals and in all likelihood he shared them. His background encouraged him to view architecture as a form of philanthropy – as an activity that could improve the spiritual lives of ordinary people.

This would have been in the high-minded spirit of Victorian Gothic. New churches, in the old style of architecture, were built with an almost missionary fervour because Gothic architecture was seen as embodying a better form of life. The Victorians imagined the medieval world to have been more harmonious, more stable and more socially cohesive than their own society, disrupted as that was by industrialization. Building in medieval forms would help cure the ills of the modern world; it would renew a sense of community; it would reveal and develop people's sense of interdependence and, at a time of religious uncertainty, it would secure them in the time-honoured truths of the faith. Hicks's modest work, in poor parishes where help was genuinely needed, epitomized those hopes. Poor people in lonely places were given a focus for their communal life, the chance of a decent burial, and the uplifting music of the services week by week. Church schools built beside the churches brought literacy and the chance of empowerment.

The naively fervent quality of Hardy's friendship with Bastow would have chimed with these aims and even exaggerated them. Victorian Gothic in the hands of a decent and conscientious man such as Hicks allowed a sense of mission to flourish in young men like Hardy and Bastow, even though the movement's idealism – and still more his own idealism at the time – were later erased from the record Hardy left of himself. Undoubtedly, though, Hardy was an earnest young man;

someone whom 'Everybody said [. . .] would have to be a parson.'[5] Failing that – if his father could not afford to send him to a university – Hardy could, like Hicks, become an architect working for the Church. It was a profession that could be seen as a calling and a way of spreading the gospel.

Terms like these feel out of place when you are talking about Hardy, whose writings are so unsympathetic to dogmatic religion, still less to preaching religion, even if they remain nostalgic for religious forms of life. Nonetheless, these are the terms Hardy would naturally have used during his adolescence. He was, after all, going to prayer meetings with his work colleagues, and meanwhile a religious revival was taking place in his hometown. Moreover, this 'awakening' of 1859 was led by the father of Horace Moule – the most important friend Hardy ever had.

*

It is not known when Hardy and Moule first met. He may have become acquainted with the family through Moule's younger brother, Handley, who was close to Hardy in age and went to Isaac Last's school. Handley had a telescope, mounted on the vicarage roof, and was a keen amateur astronomer; several of Hardy's novels, from as early as *Far From the Madding Crowd*, show unusually detailed knowledge of the stars, and it's quite possible that Handley fired this interest. The eldest brother in the family, Henry Joseph Moule, may also have linked the families. Their father, Henry Moule, Vicar of Fordington since 1829, was an inventor as well as a cleric and took an interest in improving farming methods. He proposed renting some land from Hardy's father to carry out experiments and Henry Joseph acted on his behalf, visiting Higher Bockhampton to negotiate terms. Henry Joseph was also an accomplished painter, especially in watercolours, as was Hardy's sister, Mary. Hardy at this time was either teaching himself to paint already or was inspired to do so through meeting Henry Joseph.

Amidst these various shared interests, religion played a part as well, because Hardy's getting to know the family closely coincided with Fordington's religious revival. Henry Moule had not been popular when he first arrived thirty years earlier. He was a committed Evangelical, hostile to drink and gambling, and more concerned with personal salvation than with maintaining the status quo. The parish he entered was, moreover, extremely poor. The cottages were, as Moule wrote, 'of the most wretched description' and their inhabitants 'utterly destitute of the ordinary conveniences of life'. 'Vice, in its worst forms, abounds among them.'[6] To the poor, the Anglican church was seen as part of the Establishment, with the vicar assumed to be the ally of the squire and the landlord; and, where Nonconformism was strong, as it was in Dorchester, Anglicanism, the official state religion, was tolerated, not embraced. Meanwhile, the local gentry did not care to have their customs and their status challenged by someone they regarded as a servant. An Evangelical cleric interfered with the few pleasures that poor and rich held in common, notably gambling.

Henry Moule achieved standing in the community only when cholera broke out in Fordington in the summer of 1854. At great risk to his own life, he visited the sick and comforted the dying; he organized the burning of all contaminated clothes and mobilized the community to defend itself. This saved many lives. As he acted, Moule also lobbied, sending a series of letters to the Prince of Wales, officially Fordington's landlord. These letters, with their detailed account of Fordington's grisly squalor, were published in newspapers and later collected in a volume. Gradually, they led to changes in Fordington and to real 'improvements' in the conditions of its poor. Dorchester's civic dignitaries honoured Moule for his efforts while the poor of Fordington loved him for the risks he had taken, and the solidarity he had shown at a time when it would have been quite open to him to decamp. From then on, his congregations rapidly grew.[7]

It may be that Dorchester's religious revival was carried forward by the aftermath of the cholera outbreak – on the wave of affection felt for Henry Moule and out of the sense of visitation and impurity that the epidemic instilled. Whatever the cause or causes, in 1859:

> many hundreds of people [. . .] were awakened, awed, made con-
> scious of eternal realities. And a goodly number shewed in all their
> after life that they were indeed new creatures.

This is from the account given much later by Handley Moule who, like his father and his missionary brothers George and Arthur, remained all his life a devout Anglican Evangelical. Handley's writing catches the tone of the period he is remembering.

> A great social uplifting, wholesome and permanent, followed the
> Revival. In particular, a vigorous movement for temperance and

thrift arose spontaneously among the work-people, and was wisely fostered and organized by my Father and his friends.[8]

At this time Hardy was busily debating infant baptism with Bastow and the Perkins brothers. Even though he disagreed with them over doctrine, he learnt to respect their 'finer qualities'. The Perkins family:

> formed an austere and frugal household, and won [Hardy's] admiration by their thoroughness and strenuousness. [. . .] It was through these Scotch people that Thomas Hardy first became impressed with the necessity for 'plain living and high thinking', which stood him in such good stead in later years.[9]

'Temperance and thrift', austerity and frugality, plain living and high thinking: Jemima had instilled these virtues before; now the revival and Hardy's office friendships meant that he was surrounded by a comparable bracing atmosphere.

It was in this context that Horace Moule entered Hardy's life. Horace was by then in his late twenties, the fourth of the sons, his mother's favourite and a charismatic figure. Handley remembered his 'hundred charming ways of interesting and teaching me, alike in scholarship and classical history'.

> He would walk with me through the springing corn, translating Hesiod to me. He would draw a plan of ancient Rome with lines of pebbles on the lawn.

Handley describes his brother through Christlike imagery, drawing on the Gospel stories that all the family was steeped in. Jesus walks with his disciples through fields of corn, and when he stops the adulteress from being stoned, he writes in the dust on the ground. Handley presents his brother as a hero and clothes him in glory as his writing slips into poetry: 'corn' rhymes exactly with 'lawn' and the rhythms, especially in the second sentence, are iambic. 'With línes of pébbles ón the láwn'. It sounds for a moment like Tennyson, with Horace being mourned in the same way that Tennyson mourned his lost friend, Arthur Hallam, another heroic figure.

Although an aura of tragedy surrounded Horace's memory by the time Handley wrote his memoir, this image of him is not simply fanciful. Horace was the cleverest in a family of clever children, a fine musician and a gifted scholar as well as an accomplished teacher and public speaker. He was also in worldly terms the least successful of the sons, the least able to fulfil his family's expectations or cope with the world's pressures. Their father had graduated from St John's College, Cambridge. Handley became a fellow of Trinity and later Bishop of Durham. Henry Joseph became a private tutor and travelled Europe with well-born English families. George Moule was ordained Bishop of China in 1880. Charles Moule, two years younger than Horace, ended his career as President of Corpus Christi College, Cambridge.

Horace, by contrast, could not complete even his first degree, though he went up to Oxford and later transferred to Cambridge, distinguishing himself at both places. By the time his friendship with Hardy blossomed, he had been awarded the Hulsean prize at Cambridge for his study of the oratory of the early church. Even so, without a degree and with a worsening reputation for unreliability and alcoholic episodes, he was condemned to an inglorious future as a private tutor and occasional reviewer. In the end, he earned his keep as a Poor Law Inspector until finally he committed suicide in 1873. Around 1860, though, when he was tutoring Handley at home, teaching other pupils from the town and arranging a literary society, Horace was still in his prime. 'Wonderful was his faculty', Handley wrote, 'for imparting [. . .] a living interest in the subject-matter, and for shedding an indefinable glamour of the ideal over all we read.'[10] He addressed public meetings and met with acclaim. He charmed Hardy into hero-worship.

In many ways, Horace brought into Hardy's world the 'glamour of the ideal'. He was born into the educated upper-middle classes; he was cultured, 'a fine Greek scholar'; he was everything Hardy wanted to be. Furthermore, he seemed available to Hardy in ways that Barnes could never be. He tutored him but it scarcely felt like instruction. There was no money involved, no curriculum, only the free exchange of ideas and thoughts, as the two of them went walking in the fields. Horace gave the impression of an intellectual fellowship that could overcome every social barrier. Moreover, that impression was not dishonest; he and Hardy did become close, personal friends.

All the same, class continued to divide them. Moule, like his father, sincerely wanted to better the lives of the poor and the less advantaged. He lectured to the local branch of the Working Men's Mutual Improvement Society on 'Oxford and the Middle Class Examinations', explaining how access to the University was being extended. His lecture enthused about the widening of opportunity: one of its great advantages,

Moule said, would be to make classical literature accessible to a far wider cross-section of the public. Moule had grown up in exactly the atmosphere of idealism and practical benevolence that would encourage such enthusiasm. His father had spent his energies attending to his parishioners' needs, physical as well as spiritual, and Horace carried on that mission.[11] He could not offer religious succour as readily because of his doubts about the Christian faith, and he was less practical than his father, so instead he pursued the same goal through education – education that extended to and depended upon friendship.

*

While on Hardy's side, the relationship with Moule was the deepest friendship he ever knew, on Moule's, there may have been elements of sexual love involved. His alcoholism and melancholia could certainly be symptomatic of repressed or guilt-ridden homosexual feelings. In the *Life*, Hardy does stress Moule's love of Greek and that may carry the encoded implication of Greek love. There is little in Hardy's temperament to suggest that such feelings would have been reciprocated. Hardy is insightful about male friendship, while instinctively distinguishing it from erotic love, which in his novels seems to exist only between men and women. Relations between men sometimes seem more profound and in some respect more stable precisely because they are free of sexuality's compulsiveness. And often in Hardy such relations are at their most intense when they are unequal: Jude is strongly attached to Phillotson, his teacher; Stephen Smith in *A Pair of Blue Eyes* (1873) is devoted to Henry Knight, his mentor and hero; Henchard and Farfrae are like father and son, rivalrous and yet bound up with one another. His relationship with Moule both generated that pattern and followed it. Moule answered his need for a mentor and their changing relationship during the 1860s enabled him to reflect upon, and grow wise about, the pitfalls of admiration.

The *Life*'s version of their friendship restricts it to a literary companionship and that element was undoubtedly important: at New Year 1862, Moule gave Hardy a copy of Palgrave's *Golden Treasury*, the famous Victorian anthology of English poetry, first published in 1861. Hardy cherished the volume all his life and stated once that his sole ambition as a poet was to write a poem good enough to be included in Palgrave's collection.[12] Moreover, the two friends discussed literature endlessly and when Hardy began to try and write professionally, he consulted Moule on questions of style, taking on many (though not all) of his critical opinions. When their friendship first developed, however, Hardy was not in any sense a man of letters; both he and Moule were troubled by other questions than those of literary composition. They saw writing, literature and culture in general always in relation to social questions (Who should be educated and how should opportunity be widened?) and in relation to religious ones.

Evangelicals believed that faith was the one thing needful for salvation; grace, rather than culture, would bring you to God. If that was true, literature was ephemeral – ornamental rather than essential, a luxury and not a necessity. Liberal Anglicans in the Victorian period, most eminently Matthew Arnold, saw culture differently. It offered an alternative to orthodox religion because it provided a means of acquiring personal serenity and securing social order, during a period when religious dogma was under threat and society in chaos. Moule was stressfully caught between these two positions. He was drawn intellectually towards the more liberal point of view and was also half-unwillingly loyal to his father's more dogmatic position, centred on grace.

In 1859 Horace published *Christian Oratory: An Inquiry into its History During the First Five Centuries*. The book was 'Affectionately Inscribed' to 'My Father'. The study demonstrated how the early Christian orators were crude in comparison with their classical contemporaries. This lack of art was unimportant, however, because in preaching, 'an artless but faithful and earnest man' would perform 'a great and solid work', whereas a mere rhetorician would achieve nothing. Preaching, Moule said, 'proves itself to be a strange leveller in the matter of intellectual distinction.'[13] His father would have readily accepted these judgements and by dedicating the book to him, Moule was highlighting their agreement. More worryingly, Moule was himself a gifted orator and an accomplished classical scholar (as *Christian Oratory* revealed). The book dismisses both these accomplishments. The tension between what Moule was good at and what he valued – what he was brought up to value – is acute in the book and its conclusions feel like self-reproach.

Hardy records how he and Moule discussed the most advanced thought. Moule, he says, gave him his copy of G. A. Mantell's *The Wonders of Geology*, a book that his father had banned from the house because of its heresy. Similarly, in 1860 they eagerly discussed *Essays and Reviews*, the volume of liberal theology that was causing a furore. In the same year, however, Moule underwent a crisis. He was employed as a tutor in Salisbury but went AWOL during a visit with his pupil to Paris. Soon enough he turned up safely back at home, though not before Charles and Henry had been sent in search of him. After this episode, pressured both by his family and by his own conscience, Moule made an effort to reform – he lectured on temperance and began to help his father evangelize. It looks as if he experienced a conversion, along the Evangelical pattern.

There is little direct evidence about Hardy's religious position at this time, but what there is suggests that he too drew nearer to Evangelical Christianity just when his friend did. Hardy's Bible has survived and the marginal notes, though few in number, are revealing. In 1860, Hardy marked in his Bible verse 9 of Psalm 119: 'Wherewithal shall a young man cleanse his way: even by ruling himself after thy word.' The text echoes the strenuous self-discipline of the Perkins family. The following year, the number of notes increases and Hardy shows particular interest in St Paul's First Letter to the Corinthians, chapters 14–16. Beside chapter 15, he wrote 'Fordington, 1861', as if he linked it (possibly after the event) with this time in his life. The chapter is full of references to conversion, atonement and new life: 'For I delivered unto you first of all that which I also received, how that Christ died for our sins according to the scriptures' (verse 3), and 'For since by man came death, by man came also the resurrection of the dead. For as in Adam all die, even so in Christ shall all be made alive' (verses 21–2). The chapter provides an essential set of texts for the Evangelical understanding of Christianity.

Hardy's commitment lasted until he moved to London in 1862, where it altered and then gradually fell away. His first surviving letter, addressed to Mary and dated 17 August 1862, mentions attending church ('I just come [*sic*] from the evening service at St Mary's Kilburn', St Mary's being 'rather to my taste') and repeats his favourite quotation from the Bible: 'After the fire a still small voice'.[14] Elijah in the wilderness hears the 'still small voice' of God in the hush that comes after earthquake, wind and fire. Hardy's feelings about religious experience, about God and about true speech, were all profoundly influenced by this story: God spoke after turbulence and disruption; He spoke with a persuasive understatement and an authoritative quietness. God could accept and endure all the worst that life could inflict, and then speak afterwards, unperturbed and unaltered. Acquiescence, resilience, calm: these are Hardyan virtues. There should be nothing strident and nothing cowardly either.

This story from the Bible and this particular verse became so important to Hardy partly because they recalled the intense faith of his Evangelical phase and, at the same time, his instinctive reservations about Evangelical Christianity's forthright tone – reservations which, as time went on, seemed more and more well-founded. Moule's trajectory – his erratic behaviour followed by a compulsive return to traditional, dogmatic faith – suggested that modern progressive liberal thought produced impossible doubts and was bound in the end to lead to personal breakdown. That collapse provoked, in turn, a violent recommitment to a primitive form of Christianity – emotional in its appeal and intellectually repressive.

Years after Moule's death, Hardy amidst his doubts and unbelief went on yearning for the 'still small voice' of God – a form of faith, in other words, that avoided controversy, dogmatism, emotionalism and stridency. Moule's experience also helped establish Hardy's conviction that his generation had become obsessively preoccupied with religious questions. Earlier generations had enjoyed a simpler and more kindly way of being Christian; as things stood now, belief and unbelief were both equally unsatisfactory, and equally self-destructive. Doctrinal controversies had eroded trust in ordinary, human affection.

In his poem 'Afternoon Service at Mellstock', one of the first in *Moments of Vision* (1917), Hardy recalls his churchgoing youth, the 'afternoons of drowsy calm' when he sang the old metrical psalms.

> So mindless were those outpourings! –
> Though I am not aware
> That I have gained by subtle thought on things
> Since we stood psalming there.[15]

It is a characteristically understated poem, almost legalistic in its caution. Hardy is not aware that he has gained; how much he feels has been lost remains for the reader to decide. And present caution makes a disappointing contrast with Hardy's carefree youth of mindless outpourings. You might expect this value judgement to be reversed – empty-headed babble would normally be ranked below careful consideration of serious matters. Hardy disagrees and so does his character Mrs Edlin in *Jude the Obscure*, who strongly disapproves of young people taking marriage vows so seriously and regrets how they torture themselves with unreal scruples.

Hardy even makes a similar point about Moule's own family. *Tess of the d'Urbervilles* includes an affectionate portrait of Moule's parents in the form of Angel Clare's parents. His mother and father are neither self-righteously orthodox (as his brothers are) nor racked by doubt (as Angel is himself). They treat Angel well, love him dearly and would have extended their charity without hesitation to Tess when she was in need, only she feared to ask. The pathos surrounding her reluctance to ask them, in a crucial scene in the novel, is partly generated by the connection in Hardy's mind between Tess and his old friend, Moule. If only, in his hour of need, Moule had dared to ask their help, he might have been saved. Part of Hardy's feeling was that the zeitgeist had conspired against Moule (and against Hardy too, to a lesser degree) turning his strengths into disadvantages, and his virtues into dangers. His delicacy of mind, his flawless integrity, his acute intelligence, and his sense of duty were all admirable, yet they helped to destroy him. His culture did not provide enough of the commonplace warmth and accepting toleration that Moule needed for his talents to flourish. In that respect, sadly, he represented his generation.

Hardy himself was luckier because their backgrounds were crucially different: Hardy's family was conventionally religious (as was required in their time and society) but they were not especially devout. For Moule and his brothers, religion lay at the heart of everything. Not only careers and beliefs but the family's sense of identity as well was bound up with faith. Their different ages during the Dorchester revival also altered the degree of pressure – Hardy was in his late teens, Moule approaching thirty. Hardy could more easily afford to experiment a little with his beliefs; in the midst of his enthusiasm, part of him could also step back. He was attuned in any case to a relaxed scepticism about Christianity, whereas Moule's situation was more claustrophobic and the issues more absolute.

In Dorchester in the early 1860s, Hardy did not perceive all of this but he could intuit some of the uncertainty that lay beneath his friend's confident manner. Perhaps he alone recognized how far Moule's idealism was driven by an urgent need to find some purpose in life. And because he accompanied his friend, following Moule along the path from dormant faith to renewed commitment, he could understand (as it were, from the inside) the lingering doubts and self-doubts from which Moule suffered. This closeness over religion also implies, naturally enough, that Hardy was caught up in Moule's life at the time, intimate with him and, more than that, devoted to him.

The closest portrayal Hardy gave of his relationship with Moule, though it is far from biographically exact, occurs in his early novel *A Pair of Blue Eyes* (1873). Stephen Smith, the book's hero, is a young man from the country fiercely loyal to his friend, Henry Knight, a metropolitan, educated man. Smith is a budding architect, Knight a established critic and reviewer. Though much else in the novel derives from Hardy's first meetings with Emma Gifford, his future wife, this relationship dates back earlier and one of the most striking things about it is Smith's spontaneous hero-worship of the older man, which blinds him to Knight's faults. Moreover, Hardy always showed great respect for devotion.

It is present in Tess, for instance, when she cannot abandon Angel however badly he treats her. Devotion like this is not a dignified emotion and it may even become degrading. Hardy presents it to some extent in a good light, even so, and from that evaluation arise some of his most original moral perceptions. The simplicity and innocence of devotion, its spontaneous wholeheartedness, struck him as valuable – perhaps supremely valuable – and it is possible that this understanding springs from his friendship with Moule. Looking back, Hardy recognized in his younger self a commitment to Moule that he could not easily explain – one that looked a little embarrassing, yet struck him nonetheless as the beginning of wisdom.

*

In *A Pair of Blue Eyes*, however, Henry Knight is an ambiguous character who behaves in absurd and sometimes cruel ways, so that Smith's devotion to him looks at times pitifully naive. Devotion might be a good thing but in this case it seems to have chosen an entirely unsuitable object. If this aspect of the book suggests that Hardy was disillusioned with Moule when he wrote it, during 1871–2, the process of disillusion-ment had started years before. Despite his increased workload after Bastow left Hicks's office, Hardy continued to study intensively. He wrote pieces for the local paper, including reports on church architec-ture, and worked his way through Greek tragedies in the original. It became, though, increasingly difficult to do everything at once and he asked Moule's advice.

> on his inquiring of Moule [. . .] if he ought not to go on reading some Greek plays, Moule's reluctant opinion was that if Hardy really had (as his father had insisted, and as indeed was reasonable [. . .]) to make an income in some way by architecture in 1862, it

would be hardly worth while for him to read Aeschylus or Sopho-
cles in 1859–61.

Moule's views were plainly disappointing. Hardy 'had secretly wished
that Moule would advise him to go on with Greek plays' and yet 'felt
bound to listen to reason and prudence'. If the decision had gone the
other way, who knows what would have happened? Hardy speculates
that he might very well have gone to university and become a don in
the end. 'But this was not to be, and it was possibly better so.'[16]

'Possibly' here sounds an unwilling concession – so unwilling as to
be almost a denial, although requisite modesty is playing a part too.
Hardy could not go much further than this without sounding disparaging
about the universities. However these nuances function precisely, the
passage vividly evokes the moment when Hardy discovered that, actually, he was still trapped in the course of life assigned him by his class
and background. Moule might appear a liberating force who introduced
him without hesitation to the culture usually reserved for the rich, doing
so because he believed in widening access to the universities. When it
came to the crunch, however, Moule still insisted on reason and
prudence, and consigned Hardy to his place.

This judgement not only threw into question the reality of Moule's
friendship, it also led Hardy to doubt the ideas of equality and social
mobility which supposedly animated both Moule and his family. His
closest friend and ally seemed now, like Lady Julia earlier, all too willing
to invoke the proper order of things, reason and prudence, as a way of
keeping Hardy down. Hardy's unforceful temperament discouraged him
from kicking against the pricks or flying in the face of his friend's advice.
He would have revered Moule too much to disagree and he was too
attached to him to find fault.

Moule's decision caused a practical difficulty, nevertheless, as well as
personal unease. If Hardy were to continue as an architect and go
forward in the profession, Dorchester was not the place to stay. Bastow
had gone to London to better himself and he had advised Hardy by
letter to do the same. It was the natural move in a profession where
power was concentrated in the capital. In many ways, all the same, the
prospect of leaving home was deeply unappealing to Hardy; it implied a
narrow commitment to architecture and architecture alone. Hardy's
literary interests, his tentative steps towards writing, his music – all these
would have to be placed on the back burner. In addition, of course, he

would have to leave behind the scenes and countryside that were so important to him.

Moule's disappointing advice helped him to make the break. Bastow's example was one he could follow – and follow all the more easily if he began to feel that his connections with people outside his class were illusory and frail. Moreover, it seemed an opportune time to leave because others were doing the same. William Barnes learnt in January 1862 that the living of Winterborne Came would become vacant within six months and that he would be invited to take it up. He could give up schoolmastering at long last. Meanwhile, Barnes's pupil, Hooper Tolbort, who was a friend of Hardy's and Moule's too, was preparing for the Indian Civil Service examinations. He would sit them in the summer and then, presumably, depart for the subcontinent. Three years before, in 1859, Tolbort had come first in languages and second in English out of all the candidates for the Oxford Middle Class Examinations. There was no doubt he would do well again. Another of Hardy's Dorchester friendships would thereby be brought to an end and another of his contemporaries would act on the assumption that their future lay elsewhere.

He had family reasons to fear staying behind. His uncle, John Antell, was an impressive autodidact, accomplished in Greek and Latin, but he was also unfortunately an embittered and impoverished alcoholic, who made a poor living as a shoemaker. His was not a good example to follow. As far as his immediate family was concerned, time in London made excellent sense, so long as the move did not become permanent. Hardy's father, like Hicks, saw the benefit of his son acquiring up-to-the-minute professional expertise. Hicks gave him letters of introduction, one to the famous architect Benjamin Ferrey, another to John Norton, one of Ferrey's pupils who was an old friend. His parents gave him, as his leaving present, a copy of the Book of Common Prayer.

For Hardy, while leaving was inevitably a wrench, it was more importantly a comedown. He was accepting his family's expectations for him and jeopardizing his dreams of a higher, literary life. Characteristically, his only way of rebelling was by falling in love. Throughout his time working for Hicks, Hardy had inhabited a very male environment. He had lived among men and his emotions had been concentrated on them. The schoolboy crushes that he recalls (on Rettie, for instance, on 'Louisa in the Lane' and several others) all occurred earlier in his teens and were eclipsed by his subsequent male friendships – with Bastow, the Perkins brothers and lastly Moule. The one exception to this is a story that in 1862 Hardy proposed, rather suddenly, to a local girl, Mary Waight. In Hardy's circumstances at the time, marriage was completely out of the question. The idea did not remotely accord with either reason or prudence. Anyway Mary did not love him and she turned him down. So Hardy went away and not long afterwards Mary married someone else. Her grandchildren remembered visiting Hardy in Max Gate years later and being made welcome there.[17]

Foolish, impulsive, largely groundless, Hardy's proposal was really a doomed attempt to stay in Dorchester and make a life there. It suggests both his reluctance to leave and his instinctual retreat from external pressure into the arms of an older woman. Mary was nearly thirty, Moule's age; Hardy was only twenty-one. She would have been rather like a mother to him, securing him in his familiar world. At the same time, marrying her would have given him the feeling of doing as he chose. In that respect, though the proposal looks like a bid to hold on to the past, it was a sign of things to come. Freedom and security were the conflicting desires Hardy always wanted to balance and the hope of combining them underlay his actual marriage ten years later.

One who walks west, a city-clerk

WHEN HARDY stepped off the train in April 1862 and walked out into the streets of London, he was still a very young twenty-one. It was his first visit to the capital since he travelled through the city as a boy. This time, he was on his own and was planning to stay.

Hardy had letters of introduction to well-established London architects and through family connections he had suggestions about possible places to live. Though Hardy tended in retrospect to disguise the fact that he linked up with Dorsetshire people when he arrived in London, he relied on such contacts, both professionally and domestically, and quickly enough they helped him settle into London life. Nonetheless, he stood out a mile: although he had been taught standard English at school and at his mother's insistence had spoken it at home, he must have had, even so, a noticeable West Country accent. Everything else about him gave away the country boy as well. His clothes were too neat and too clean. His hopes were too orderly. His cast of mind was too idealistic for the driving world of the capital. That, at least, was what he came to feel.

And to Hardy's eyes the place was huge – London's three million inhabitants completely dwarfed Dorchester's few thousand (fewer than three thousand in 1821; fewer than ten thousand in 1901). While Dorchester's streets might be bustling on market days, they could be almost eerily quiet at other times, day as well as night. In London, the streets were constantly choked – with carriages and hansom cabs, with wagons transporting goods between the main railway stations, with animals being herded to market and, more than anything else, with people. By modern standards London covered a very small area: it was continuously built-up only between Paddington in the west and Poplar in the east, from Islington in the north only as far south as Walworth. Camberwell and Peckham were leafy suburbs; Fulham was a separate settlement. Similarly, on the northern side, Willesden, Highgate and Stoke Newington remained outlying villages; Clapham lay on the edge of town to the south, and Herne Hill (where Ruskin had grown up) was still a place of fields, orchards and market gardens. London Docks, that lay just beyond the Tower, were still in existence and in use, though new docks were being built to rival them further east, on the Isle of Dogs.

It is hard to imagine what it was like for three million people to live in such a confined area. The overcrowding was terrible, especially in the East End. Hardy had seen poverty and squalor before, notably in Fordington, which had all the features of a London slum: poor housing, insanitary conditions and the danger of cholera. The poverty he encountered in London was, however, on a scale quite new to him and cholera, now eradicated in Dorchester, still persisted. There were outbreaks in the East End as late as 1866. Moreover, the poor were all around you – visible, audible, tangible. You rubbed against them on the pavements. Costermongers and beggars accosted you. Prostitutes walked the streets quite openly day and night, especially around the Haymarket and Leicester Square, places that Hardy walked through every day on his way to work.

Londoners were avoiding these problems by moving out into the quickly expanding suburbs. Ribbon development along the major routes – usually in the form of substantial villas – was replaced in the 1860s and 1870s by enormous swathes of speculative building, usually of smaller houses. Clapton, Hackney and Dalston; St John's Wood and Gospel Oak; Lambeth and Norwood were all developed at this time. As fast as the city spread out, however, its population increased. By the census of 1881 it had reached nearly five million. Newly built tramlines and railways enabled middle-class and lower middle-class people to live outside the crowded centre, in places that, at the time, offered easy access to the countryside. The centre itself remained intractably over-crowded and its poorer regions, despite improvements in public health, were disease-ridden and dangerous.

Hardy did not go so far afield but he did find ways of distancing himself from the city. As an architect he fell on his feet. Ferrey was of no help but Norton was, giving him a nominal task in his office so that he had a base from which to begin, and almost at once Hardy was taken on permanently by Arthur Blomfield's practice. Blomfield (1826–99) was in his early thirties, energetic, efficient and increasingly successful. He became very eminent in his day, was knighted and, although his work now compares unfavourably with the great achievements of Victorian Gothic (made by Pugin, Scott, Street, Pearson or Butterfield), Blomfield was never less than competent. He was also a forward-looking architect, willing to experiment with the new building materials (such as steel and concrete) which Victorian technology made available. Hardy was, naturally, grateful to him for taking him on and remained so; indeed, the two men became lifelong friends. Within a few months of Hardy's beginning to work for him, Blomfield moved the firm into new, enlarged offices on the first floor of Adelphi Terrace, on the Strand overlooking the Thames. Demolished now, Adelphi Terrace was a fine building, designed and built by the Adam brothers in 1768, and the move declared that Blomfield was the coming man. Hardy remembered himself and the other junior colleagues decorating their new office's antique white marble mantelpieces with pencilled caricatures.

Hardy could have found lodgings nearby but chose to live instead on the other side of town: he spent the first year in Kilburn, in Clarence Place, now forming part of the east side of Kilburn High Road, north of the railway station. In April 1863, he moved to 16 Westbourne Park Villas, a mile and a half away in Westbourne Grove, west of Paddington. This was at the time on the edge of the built-up area. Hardy recalled the bus conductors at Kilburn calling out 'Any more passengers for London!' and open fields lay to the left of the Edgware Road as you drove north. There, the only sign of London's approach were cemeteries laid out amidst parkland. South of Westbourne Grove lay Bayswater, Ladbroke Grove, Notting Hill and Holland Park, designed and built as a grand westerly urban development twenty years earlier. Hardy's house lay on the northern fringes of this, right beside the Great Western Railway. Beyond it, there was very little housing – Portobello Lane ran out to Portobello Farm. From his bedroom at the back of the house, Hardy could see the spires of the new churches built for the well-off congregations of West London. At the front, the railway line ran out towards Acton, Ealing, Reading and beyond.

So, day by day, like Dickens's character Wemmick in *Great Expectations*, Hardy walked across London to work – through Paddington, Marble Arch, Soho and Covent Garden down to the river near Charing Cross. He may sometimes have taken the omnibus that ran along the Marylebone and Euston Road; and certainly once in 1863 he tried the newly opened underground railway running from Paddington in the same direction. Usually, though, he would walk. It was cheaper (Hardy was always careful with money) and it provided healthy exercise. Living in Westbourne Grove as a pedestrian commuter meant that Hardy's life in London started to repeat the rhythm of his Dorset days. The walk from Bockhampton into Dorchester had been a mile or two shorter and far less busy. Now, though, as before, he could immerse himself in a big city and then purposefully and methodically he could step away from it.

Living where he did gave him a breath of country air as well every evening on his return, a glimpse of the sunset and the sound of the trains setting off for the West Country and home. In particular the trains linked him to his sister Mary. Soon after Hardy moved to London, Mary took a job as a schoolmistress in Denchworth, a village near Wantage in Berkshire, where their younger sister Kate lived with her for a while and attended her school. Hardy visited his sisters in this village (and drew sketches of the churchyard) so he knew that it lay very close to the Great Western line and that the trains running beside his lodgings would pass near his sister's schoolhouse within an hour or two.

*

Hardy's decision to live in Westbourne Grove may have been another instance of local connections influencing him: next door at number 18 lived a father and son, both architects, who had done work for the brother of the new owner of Kingston Maurward House. Going there also accorded with his desire to keep the darker, more threatening aspects of London at arm's length. The same is true of his focused self-cultivation. Hardy visited the exhibition at South Kensington almost as soon as he arrived; he spent his lunchtimes in the National Gallery; he became a keen theatregoer and opera-lover. In 1864, he started to learn French at evening classes in King's College, London. There is an almost relentless quality to this self-education, a driven determination not to let a single chance of improvement pass him by.

Hardy, though, was more reluctant to explore London itself. He restricted himself to the culturally elevated aspects of the urban experience and led a quiet life. He pursued architecture seriously, becoming a member of the Architectural Association in 1862 and entering its competitions – his design for a country mansion took first prize in 1863; he won a silver medal from the Royal Institute of British Architects later the same year for his essay 'On the Application of Colored [*sic*] Bricks and Terra Cotta to Modern Architecture'. He went to church regularly and read his Bible and he played his violin, sometimes joined by another of the lodgers in the house. It was an austere, dutiful and lonely existence that continued much of what he had grown used to in Dorchester. That familiarity helped him to manage and he was happy to find that he could manage. Meanwhile, in his professional life, he was doing as well as anyone could ask.

For his part, Hardy's father was excited to have a son in the capital. His visit in 1862 took place very quickly and was a lively affair. The two of them went together to the opera but, as Hardy wrote to Mary, 'nothing would satisfy Father unless he went to see the Thames Tunnel', that ran from Wapping to Rotherhithe. Hardy was typically reluctant to go to 'one of the lowest and most crowded parts' of the city, but his father went anyway. He agreed a rendezvous at the Monument, with 'Miss A.', an unidentified family friend and, arriving 'a little too soon, he went to the top of the Monument (200 feet). "Just to pass away the time".[1] Thomas Hardy, senior, comes across as a bustling, energized presence, quite different from Hardy himself, who was circumspect as a rule. And this letter gives a very different impression of Hardy's father from the image Hardy produced in later years. The peacefully contented rustic workman and church musician, who lived and died where he was born, does not match up with this vigorous personality, eager to see the sights.

Hardy's wary concern about safety stands out against his father's unabashed pursuit of his own enthusiasms. The Thames Tunnel was not a fashionable place to visit. Nathaniel Hawthorne had come back distinctly unimpressed: 'an arched corridor, of apparently interminable length, gloomily lighted with jets of gas at regular intervals'.[2] This was the customary judgement but Hardy's father took no notice. To him, the engineering involved was interesting in itself and, indifferent to received opinion, he was equally blasé about filth and pickpockets. Hardy noticed more than anything his father's belief that really there was nothing to be afraid of. It struck him as both naive and enviable.

Nonetheless, there's an edge of prim disapproval in Hardy's response to his father – a cagey recoil from his uninhibited enthusiasm which is similar to Hardy's recoil from London generally. Part of that was to do with his mother, who never visited him in London and who always urged him to be careful. London, in Jemima's eyes, was a corrupting place, from which her son must keep himself pure. Hardy's 1918 poem, 'The Woman I Met', written when he was visiting London for the first time in several years, recalls his mother's concerns and his response to them – the purity he cultivated in himself as a young man and the lack of self-awareness that it produced (or so at least he came to believe).[3] His impulse to back away from ordinary experience had, however, little ultimately to do with his mother, being intrinsic to his temperament.

Hardy's novels are full of male characters who are morally scrupulous and isolated – isolated because morally scrupulous. It was a type he understood thoroughly. In *A Pair of Blue Eyes*, when Smith first visits Knight in his elegant London lodgings, the two men look out into the crowd of ordinary people rushing through the street below. Their privileged, outsider's point of view creates what Knight calls his 'humanity show'. It is an uneasy moment in the book and in the characters' relationship, mixing fascination about what is seen outside the window with a sense of exclusion from the human race. Knight's name for the spectacle appears dangerously detached too. Should humanity be reduced to a mere show, even if that does 'show' you something? Is Knight not part of humanity himself?

The passage shows Hardy's beginning to wonder whether he and Moule and others like them protected themselves too much from the normal jostling of everyday life. One consequence was unconscious ignorance; another was isolation; and a third was thoughtless self-righteousness. Hardy grew utterly convinced in his maturity that belief in your own moral superiority was destructive. The first signs of that conviction appear in Henry Knight, a character who epitomizes judgementalism. Knight is out of touch with his own emotions and insensitive to those of others; at the same time, he is forever laying down the moral law to people. He is an unconscious hypocrite, motivated by emotions and drives he does not acknowledge in himself – which he has consistently claimed both to understand and to be unaffected by.

Knight is based partly on Moule and Hardy portrayed him in this way while Moule was still alive. Before Moule's unexpected death, therefore, he was thinking that an extreme version of his friend's attitudes would lead to snobbishness and self-ignorance. This, though, does not mean that Hardy was ever simply hostile to the idea of looking on at life with philosophical detachment. Evidently, it was something he found instinctual in himself and yet was troubled by.

At New Year 1864, Moule gave him a copy of the *Thoughts of the Emperor Marcus Aurelius*. The book became one of Hardy's treasured possessions; he marked and wrote comments in it, quoting it several times in his own writings. Marcus Aurelius's classical Stoicism embraced passivity; it sought release from physical temptations, from both fear and desire, and recommended a fatalistic acceptance of whatever took place. One should enjoy the spectacle of the world while remaining undistracted by its charms or possible rewards. Truth to oneself implied a withdrawal into oneself, and concern for others demanded a degree of detachment from them. Without that, you would be so strongly swayed by other people and by your own emotions that you would be unable to do any good in the world.

Keeping your distance from things, avoiding entanglements and the seductions of the world, all chimed with Hardy's character. Meanwhile, his mother's anxieties, his own Christianity, his friendship with Moule and his reading of Marcus Aurelius, helped to bring these traits to the fore. They accentuated his high-minded idealism, his personal reticence, his passivity, his hunger for calm, and even his fair-mindedness, which could sometimes prove relentless. The difference was that in London he gradually saw this highly moral, sometimes aloof approach to life as a choice, possibly a mistaken choice, whereas in Dorchester it had seemed inevitable and natural.

Losing faith in his and Moule's idealism was a change that did not by any means take place overnight. Hardy's disillusionment was strangely gradual in fact, though that may be an impression created by his habitual secrecy. Moments of crisis were one of the things he was most determined retrospectively to smooth away. The more likely pattern in the moment (judging from what happened later on in his marriage to Emma) was one of hectic fluctuation, to and fro between opposing feelings and opinions, in which very slowly one point of view won out. And it was not only a matter of disillusionment. As Hardy's horizons were broadened by London, he saw the possibility of making choices and, with that, the opportunity for a greater degree of self-definition.

His initial decision to go there had already implied this, to an extent. However much he had been pressured into going, Hardy had nonetheless given up one set of options and chosen another: the serious pursuit of architecture as a profession. He was still following the course laid out for him by his parents (and behaved in London initially just as they would have expected him to), but inevitably the city with its crowds, its prostitutes, its rule of every man for himself, and its giant size, showed him other paths. Though nearly all were to be avoided and no more than one or possibly two could be followed with the necessary blinkered careerist obstinacy, Hardy confronted alternatives at every turn.

Hardy perceived London's effect on him gradually and to a large extent after the event. Even his first, wary approach to London life, however, was conducted with a new degree of self-consciousness. Part of him treated life in the capital as a matter of seeing through a required period of time before going home again. He ought to try and gain the most from the experience, professionally and culturally, while it lasted – the most, that is, according to how his family would define the word. The habit of keeping himself at one remove from London, plus his laughable accent and out-of-place tidiness, made Hardy feel set apart as well as alone. He grew aware of never being quite present in London and certainly never properly an inhabitant. He was always passing through and always therefore something of an observer. As time went on, he doubted the wisdom of keeping his distance in this manner. It seemed, among other things, a decision about his lifestyle that his background had imposed upon him. Those doubts were beginning already in 1862 in Hardy's competitive hostility towards his father, who had immersed himself in the city's strangeness apparently without a second thought.

If London gradually threw everything into question for Hardy, in two areas the impact was especially serious. Starting there as an obedient son, preparing himself to enter the family business, he ended five years later having deliberately disappointed his parents' hopes and become painfully alienated from them. The breach that took place during these years was not repaired before Hardy entered his forties and it was never properly healed. It occurred principally because Hardy's belief in his profession evaporated. 'Belief' is the right word because Hardy had seen architecture as part of a wider task, underpinned by religion and energized by a social conscience. He came to the unhappy realization that architects in London were in this respect quite different from those he had known in Dorchester.

*

Hardy's work in Blomfield's office was almost exclusively concerned with the drearier aspects of getting buildings built – as in his early years at Hicks, he spent his time copying out senior partners' designs. He soon found that 'architectural drawing in which the actual designing had no great part was monotonous and mechanical'.[4] His work also trapped him in the office; during the previous couple of years, he had been out and about in Dorset and beyond. He had been given responsibility and independence whereas his new post with Blomfield was both more prestigious and more menial. Discovering this presented Hardy with an unforgettable irony: getting ahead meant losing your personal freedom; success restricted the development and expression of your abilities.

Meanwhile Hardy's ambition was growing. He had been in architecture for six years already and he had been sent up to London not least because he was evidently quite good. His success in winning architectural competitions during 1863 strengthened his feeling that he deserved better. What emerged, however, was a second awkward truth about life in the capital. By moving from Dorchester to London, Hardy had moved from meritocracy to privilege, from an earnest sense of mission to a more complacent atmosphere of dominance.

Arthur Blomfield was a good architect as well as a successful one; still, he owed his success in large part to his father, who was Bishop of London from 1828 to 1856. Bishop Blomfield was energetically committed to building churches for the new districts of the expanding metropolis: districts and populations that would otherwise slip out of the church's grasp. Ninety-four new churches were built in the metropolitan area between 1824 and 1856: three on average every year. Most of this enormous programme was concentrated in places like Paddington, Islington, or Lambeth where the population was growing fast. Driving it forward was Bishop Blomfield, with his son poised to benefit. By specializing in church architecture, Arthur Blomfield could help to realize his father's vision and, in the process, he would establish himself professionally as a leading ecclesiastical architect. Church-building involved fund-raising; in this case, a large part of what the father helped raise went straight into his son's business.

Hardy could not have helped noticing that Blomfield stood in the same relation to his father, the Bishop, as Hardy was expected to take up in relation to his own father. That was reassuring in some ways. It confirmed that there was nothing shameful or vulgar about following the profession that your parents wanted for you. But it was also proof of exclusion because Hardy's father was by no means the Bishop of London. Hardy did not have the connections required to advance himself far and the only ones he did have were back in Dorset. Blomfield confirmed the truth that everyone apart from Hardy took for granted:

before very long he would return home, become Hicks's assistant, and probably in the end his successor. He would spend a few years acquiring London polish, and subsequently make a living by bringing the latest fashionable designs to his provincial clients, making use of his Dorset contacts (as Hicks himself had done, when he moved there from Bristol). That was his assigned role, professionally and socially. It would take either extraordinary energy or extraordinary talent – talent like Ferrey's – in order for him to escape.

Hardy's first published novel, *Desperate Remedies* (1871), reveals a remarkable, sardonic awareness of how important it is to be well connected. In its opening chapters, several people place advertisements in the newspapers, either offering or asking for work. In each case, nothing whatever happens until personal recommendation comes into play. The heroine becomes a lady's companion because her lover suggests her; and the villain becomes a land steward because he is the lady of the manor's illegitimate son, whom she wishes to help. Several other more suitable candidates are cast aside, including the heroine's lover, who is modelled on Hardy. It all proves that the arbitrary preferences of those in high places determine success or failure. For those seeking to make their way in life, happiness or misery comes down to the whim of an aristocrat. This is one of the inescapable conditions of existence. All you can hope to do is find the situation dryly amusing by learning to observe it.

Hardy wrote the book in 1869–70, a few years after leaving London. It radiates a powerful feeling of rejection although this manifests itself only in a pointed contempt. There is no violent denunciation (as there had been a little earlier, in writings that were never published); instead, Hardy takes pride in showing up the system's unfairness. The novel is self-consciously accomplished, so much so that its skilfulness becomes another example of how merit goes unrecognized. The book possesses in these respects a more self-assured point of view than Hardy could possibly have reached when he first arrived in London and first came up against its rigid hierarchies. At that stage, Moule's advice was still ringing in his ears.

Moule had crushed Hardy's literary and academic hopes a few years before, yet he was undoubtedly sincere in his desire to see opportunity widened. Moule wanted a meritocratic world and thought it was a scandal that connections counted for so much. He hoped and believed that this national disgrace would slowly be removed by fair competition.

Hardy had learnt to share Moule's ideals and then made the painful discovery that even Moule was unable to see them through entirely. Now, in London, he found the same disheartening lesson being repeated again. Connections mattered more than anything, even in the one arena where Hardy thought he might possibly escape their influence: the profession of architecture, known in its day as a means of rising in the world.

Along with the placemen culture went self-satisfaction. In London, architecture's moral point seemed to have disappeared. Easy-going though Hicks was as a person and an employer, his churches often had unusually prominent pulpits: the tiny St Mary Magdalene, North Poorton, and St Martin's, Shipton Gorge, both built in 1861–2, have two of the best examples, still well preserved. 'Preach the Word' is carved into the pulpit of Shipton Gorge. Working very often for sincerely benevolent clergymen, such as Thomas Sanctuary, Hicks saw his work as rather like preaching so that building modest but serviceable churches in out-of-the-way Dorset parishes was a kind of crusade. Hardy, influenced by Bastow and by the Dorchester revival, saw the process in similar terms.

Hardy wrote in the *Life* that he was brought up in 'High Church principles', and Blomfield's practice was filled with 'Tory and Churchy young men' – it was somewhere Hardy might have been expected to feel comfortable. Elaborate disputes over adult versus infant baptism, even Evangelical fervour itself, were things he might now consign to his unsophisticated youth. Moreover, Blomfield was like Hicks an avuncular, kindly man, never too strict with his employees and keen on music. He welcomed his new recruit into 'the office choir' that sang 'glees and catches at intervals during office hours'.[5] On the other hand, the 'Churchy' young men were defacing Adams's eighteenth-century interiors and, without Blomfield's knowledge, they mercilessly made fun of the members of the Reform League – a progressive, left-wing political group, occupying the floor beneath. These high jinks were, no doubt, exciting at first. They increased Hardy's sense of being let off the leash. They were what he would never dare do himself.

Later, though, such antics seemed to him juvenile, complacent and philistine. More than anything, Hardy discovered that following his father's profession had led him into one of the centres of the Establishment – into one of its engine rooms. The churches he was now helping to build served the interests of that Establishment. They were designed, funded, and erected in order to stabilize the status quo. The anarchy of the slums was to be held back not by increasing wages, improving housing or by giving people reason to hope for a better life for themselves or their children. Instead, the Church asserted itself, teaching submission, the hierarchical structure of its buildings reflecting the social hierarchy it helped sustain. Ridiculing the Reform League epitomized all too exactly what church architecture suddenly seemed all about.

These dawning perceptions coexisted with a loyal attachment on Hardy's part both to Blomfield himself and – at the time – to the Church as well. Hardy's fondness for Blomfield never disappeared; nonetheless, his office was something of a shock to Hardy's high-mindedness. The shock challenged his hitherto unquestioned belief that the building of these churches was valuable because they improved the life and morals of local congregations. Hardy had seen his work as progress, as his way of participating in 'the march of mind' – the Victorian world's advance from darkness to light.

So, as he came to doubt the value of what he was doing, not only did his sense of a career path falter but other things faltered too: his religious faith was thrown into question; his acceptance of his family's allotted role for him became more uncertain and he began to have doubts about established Victorian orthodoxies: belief in an ordered society, and belief in progress. He was made to think twice about his culture's self-confidence. The new churches did not prove that things were getting better, only that the ruling class was stamping its authority on those beneath. The Establishment was colonizing working-class London in just the same way as it colonized the world. 'Progress' looked like a euphemism – a way of justifying conquest. Hardy experienced these dissenting, sceptical opinions as an unspecific, simmering unease, growing as he stayed in London, which reached clear expression only after he had reached breaking point. That happened during 1866.

*

Hardy's first impulse was to reach a compromise, an accommodation with architecture and with his parents. Earlier, when listening to Moule's advice, 'he felt bound to listen to reason and prudence'; similarly now, he 'was forced', he said, 'to consider ways and means'.[6] He could not afford simply and romantically to abandon his job. He was too prone to self-doubt to take the risk and still too concerned with what his parents would think. Instead, from around the beginning of 1864, he decided to keep up his architecture, at least as the day job, while devoting all his free time to interests he could believe in. Rather than put in for architectural competitions, Hardy returned to literature, reading hard in his lodgings evening by evening. The difference from his Dorchester days was that the two spheres, architecture and books, did not overlap any longer or form parts of a whole. Rather, Hardy began to lead a double life; like Dickens's Wemmick again, he strictly divided office from home.

Moule evidently encouraged this shift of focus. Enthusing about the liveliness and comedy of Hardy's letters to him, Moule wondered breezily whether Hardy might become the London correspondent for a country newspaper. He might earn surprising amounts by 'a column of condensed London news & talk'. 'You know the sort of berth I mean.'[7] Though Hardy did learn shorthand, he did not follow up Moule's suggestion any further. It was an oddly ill-judged idea, because Hardy was certain to find the work trivial and demeaning. Furthermore, a London correspondent was bound to take an interest in London society – in gossip, scandal and the latest news. The job was founded on the assumption that all these ephemeral things were somehow interesting.

Hardy had, he said, 'neither the inclination nor the keenness for getting into social affairs and influential sets which would help him to start [an architectural] practice of his own'.[8] Unlike Moule, who was perfectly at home in middle-class, professional circles, Hardy was bound to feel the difference between entering 'influential sets' as an equal and entering them from below, as a social climber. Moule could be the former while Hardy was condemned to be the latter. Becoming a London correspondent would involve Hardy still more in flattering people and ingratiating himself with them. Worse still, as a gossip columnist, he would be trying to persuade innocent, provincial people that the capital city was a fascinating, glamorous place. He would be made to feel inferior and would be making his audience feel inferior in turn.

His preferred instead to try to become an art critic, specializing in architectural art. That would unite his interests and talents better and it would feel far more worthwhile. But breaking into the world of arts journalism was no easier than getting on in architecture. If anything, it was more difficult because in arts circles Hardy had no professional status and would be more than ever an outsider pleading for acceptance. Moule also suggested that Hardy might advertise his services as a London correspondent. If he ever did so, nothing came of it, except perhaps his use of advertisements in the plot of *Desperate Remedies*, plus a sense that things were not quite as straightforward as Moule assumed, not for somebody like Hardy anyway. These half-hearted moves towards journalism provided more than anything else further evidence of unjust exclusion. 'The world does not despise us; it only neglects us,' he wrote in his journal in 1865.[9]

As his hopes of a career as an art critic proved illusory, Hardy tried in a more head-on way to reform architecture. According to the *Life*:

> he used to deliver short addresses or talks on poets and poetry to Blomfield's pupils and assistants on afternoons when there was not much to be done, or at all events when not much was done.[10]

'There is no tradition', Hardy adds, rather dryly, 'of what Blomfield thought of this method of passing office hours.' What his fellow-workers thought is also unrecorded but there is no mention of their taking much notice. In Dorchester, earnest, intellectual and artistic conversation had been the norm. Here in London, surrounded by art and culture, Hardy was confronted by indifference to both. Everyone else in the office was much more concerned with celebrity gossip and upper-class scandal.

Countering all this by giving lectures was not quite as eccentric in those days as it would be now, even though Hardy's memoir does tend to play the scene for laughs. Lecturing was a well-established element in Victorian cultural life, occupying some of the space now taken up by broadcasting. And Hardy had again an example to follow in Moule, who had educated the working men of Dorchester via evening lectures. Hardy was doing really only what might be expected of him as a cultured and Christian young man and he would have been surprised as well as disappointed to find that he was thought odd and tiresome, or worthy and provincial. At the same time, his giving these lectures at all suggests that Hardy was still, fundamentally, unafraid. His seriousness lent him self-possession as the idealistic principles he lived by continued to sustain an identity.

The lack of response from his colleagues – they showed a thorough lack of interest in poetry, for instance – confirmed the awkward fact that architecture had little to do with art and less with morals. As far as its practitioners in London were concerned, it was a business like any other. Despite the high ideals that lay behind the Gothic revival, on the ground, in Hardy's immediate experience, buildings were not thought about in terms of moral improvement or political reform. And what social impact all these churches did have, seemed to be conservative, even repressive. Pugin's or Ruskin's hope for a religious reawakening and William Morris's socialism – none of these seemed to be on their way to being realized by London architects.

*

Moule's suggestion of 'chatty' journalism as a way forward for Hardy may have been tactless and probably looks peculiar in the light of his later tragic novels. Hardy, though, always had a comic gift. His reviewers constantly praised the humour of his rustic characters and *The Trumpet-Major* (1880), a book that is little read now, was a notable success in its day, largely on the strength of its comedy. Moule was perhaps right to observe that insistent, almost punitive high-seriousness coexisted in Hardy with a practised sense of humour, and to encourage him to make the most of it. For his part, comedy was a skill Hardy was barely interested in. People had liked his light-hearted, observant writing ever since he contributed squibs to the local paper in Dorchester. He could produce such work quite easily and was glad if it won him some praise. As a young man, 'cast upon the billows of London with no protection but his brains',[11] Hardy wrote comedy to amuse himself and his few friends.

'How I Built Myself a House', published in *Chambers's Journal* in 1865, was Hardy's first successful attempt of this kind. He had been writing poetry for several years without seeing any of it in print. Now, he dashed off a droll account of the pitfalls confronting those who set about building their own house – the smart, pushy architect, the builder with his unbudgeted extras, the surveyor in league with the builder – and suddenly he found himself a writer. Years later he suggested it might 'have been acceptance of this *jeu d'esprit* that turned his mind in the direction of prose'.[12]

What is more remarkable at the time is the absence of any follow-up or continuation. In this adeptly comic piece, Hardy had found a way of writing successfully while remaining an architect. Instead of lecturing his colleagues, he had started to tease them a little. This was enjoyable and it might even prod them in the direction of greater respect for the client and for the work itself. It also showed that he could follow Moule's advice and write in a chatty style without compromising his self-respect. Yet nothing further came of it.

In its light-heartedness, the piece was adapting to the tone of life in Blomfield's office. The writing is as knowing and urbane as Hardy's colleagues were or sought to be. As he wrote it, however, Hardy was starting to face up to more deep-seated reasons for disillusionment even than those that faced him in Adelphi Terrace. By 1865, his cherished religious faith was starting to fail him. With it disappeared any desire to build churches, any interest in whether architecture was being pursued in the correct spirit, and any genuine motivation either to join the profession or to reform it.

~ 7 ~

If but some vengeful god would call to me

LIKE HIS disillusionment with architecture, Hardy's loss of faith occurred gradually. In a sense, religious belief never left him completely – in old age, he was still loyal to the Church and never the enraged atheist of legend. Furthermore, because he was so deeply attached to religion, what happened during his twenties was traumatic.

Hardy portrayed his parents as pragmatically religious – not hypocritical, exactly, but sceptical amidst required piety. Their children were baptized but only, according to Jemima, because it would do no harm. Similarly, although Hardy's father, like his grandfather, was devoted to church music, his first love was the music. Everywhere in his writings, country people of his parents' generation are shown as being more or less attached to the church without taking its claims too seriously. They rub along with the institution and its local representative, the vicar, in the same way that they rub along with each other. People like Hardy's parents did not imagine anything much would come of their Christianity. But there it was.

Hardy's nostalgia for an instinctual, uncomplicated religion – a religion that was just a part of life – was something he shared with many of his contemporaries. As religious doubts arose in the period, they engendered the myth of a peacefully devout past, when such difficulties did not. Present worries led to an idealization of the past, particularly of the Middle Ages, which were seen as a time of faith and certainty, unity and concord. Contributing to this was the idea that religious doubt was a peculiarly modern phenomenon, caused by recent advances in science and philosophy. These had robbed the Victorians of their inheritance and divided them from the past, even the very recent past, which now seemed like an age before the flood.

Darwin's theory of evolution, first put forward publicly in 1859, is the best known of these disruptive innovations. Darwin confirmed what geology had been suggesting for the previous half-century or more: that the Bible's creation story could not be given a literal interpretation. God had not created the world in seven days; the process of evolution had done so over many millions of years. More seriously, Darwin's theory implied that if nature were an image or reflection of God then God was horrible – either blindly indifferent to what He created, or a Being that used predation and brutality in order to achieve its ends. In addition, evolution suggested that man's superiority was neither moral nor even objective; it was amoral and contingent. Humanity was not superior to other species, only better adapted to present circumstances. If the world changed (if the climate changed), that superiority would pass to other species, probably new ones.

Similarly, research into antiquities – languages, texts and archaeological finds from the ancient world – revealed that the books of the Bible were mutually contradictory and that they shared material with the scriptures of other contemporary cultures. The Bible did not look any longer like a divinely inspired text, dictated by God Himself; instead, it was a collection of biased histories, filled with superstition and propaganda. And as similarities to other ancient religions became clearer, so did the suspicion that the doctrine of Atonement, central to Christianity, was primitive and morally dubious. Should God really demand a blood-sacrifice in order to cleanse mankind from sin? The religion began to appear distasteful.

These new discoveries in science and archaeology, plus new developments in ethical thought, destroyed many people's religious faith. There were Christians who committed suicide when they read Darwin's *Origin of Species* (1859). Just as significantly for Hardy, however, where faith did survive this onslaught, it changed. Believers had more opponents to contend with and conflict altered the quality of their belief. Christians were required to be more self-conscious, more determined and argumentative so that the faith's earlier naturalness and innocence were lost. Many of Hardy's writings about religion, particularly poems written in later life, emphasize evolutionary theory as the nemesis of Christianity. It has become almost a cliché to say that his work expresses the despair felt by a Victorian sensibility as it faced up to a Darwinian universe. Hardy's feelings about evolution were in fact more ambiguous than this received idea of him implies and his spiritual history was more complicated too.

Much closer to the heart of his religious feelings is his famous poem

'The Oxen' (1915), in which Hardy yearns after the fanciful, almost fairytale belief his 'childhood used to know'. 'So fair a fancy few would weave | In these years!' he admits. Yet he would love such a belief to be true. He would go 'in the gloom, | Hoping it might be so'.[1] Hardy's affection for his parents' faith − for their near-indifference to something they never questioned − dovetailed with memories of his childhood world before the railways came to Dorset, a world where folklore blended with orthodoxy, whimsy with sincerity, and humour with emotional depth. Losing religious faith created a powerful nostalgia for those securities, in Hardy as in many other people at the time. Their faith's disappearance seemed to be accompanied by the loss of unconditional acceptance. When God the Father vanished or turned cruel, it felt as if their parents had abandoned them. It was an end of innocence, and a Fall into the modern world's individualism and conflict. Victorian images of the medieval past linked up, therefore, with Hardy's recollections of his Dorset childhood and that congruence helps explain why his poetry moved its first readers so deeply, despite the strangeness of its language and form.

The poems are so peculiarly impressive, though, because of their roots in some of Hardy's deepest formative experiences: his time of allegiance to the Evangelical faith of Dorchester's religious revival, and his early, intimate friendships with devout young men. Both his religious and anti-religious poems employ dry, cerebral terms and appear to analyse a general cultural malaise; this quality disguises their links with Hardy's personal history. The poems offer, in fact, one of the very few sidelights on this part of Hardy's life and personality − areas which otherwise he kept severely under wraps.

*

When Hardy went to London, he went as a committed Christian, who attempted, following Horace Moule's strained example, to find continuity between his religion and his culture − between his and his mother's enjoyment of books and the severe morality of Evangelical Anglicanism. In some ways, Hardy envied the Perkins brothers because they found it so unproblematic to put their religion first and their learning second. In other ways, though, he felt he was better than that. Moule and Moule's family implied that your religion should have an influence over all aspects of your life. The same was true, in a gentler spirit, of William Barnes's religion. Both contributed to the serious tone in which Hardy practised church architecture and hence derived too, initially at least, his earnest approach to writing poetry.

Although Hardy and Moule remained in touch when Hardy moved to London – they met when Horace came to town and between visits they corresponded – it was inevitable that their relationship would alter. Hardy's poem 'A Confession to a Friend in Trouble', dated 1866, reflects some of this change. 'Your troubles shrink not, though I feel them less | Here, far away, than when I tarried near'.[2] The speaker seems to know, with mournful clarity, both that the troubles remain and that he does not feel them as once he did. Involvement in the friend's life has turned into a more dispassionate and observant awareness of it. All the same, increasing separateness was still combined with Hardy's habitual deference.

None of Hardy's letters to Moule survive but a few of Moule's to Hardy do. It's clear from these that Hardy continued consulting his friend. He asked his advice about possible directions he might follow in his career; he wanted Moule's opinion on literary matters, and they went on discussing religion. In 1865, Hardy was reading John Henry Newman's recently published autobiography, *Apologia Pro Vita Sua*. The *Life* copies out an extract about Newman from one of Hardy's notebooks written at the time.

> Worked at J. H. Newman's *Apologia*, which we have all been talking about lately. A great desire to be convinced by him, because H.M.M. likes him so much. Style charming, and his logic really human, being based not on syllogisms but on converging probabilities. Only – and here comes the fatal catastrophe – there is no first link to his excellent chain of reasoning, and down you come headlong. Poor Newman! His gentle childish faith in revelation and tradition must have made him a very charming character.[3]

Newman had been the leading figure in the Oxford Movement, which had endeavoured to make the Anglican Church more Catholic and more sacramental. In 1845, he had converted to Roman Catholicism – the logical end point as he saw it to his journey of faith. Other Anglo-Catholics felt deeply betrayed nonetheless by Newman's shift of loyalty. In the *Apologia*, Newman presented his self-defence, showing the sincerity of his position at every turn and the overall coherence between what he had once believed and what he now believed. In doing so, he argued forcefully for the rightness of the Roman Catholic position. His personal fame and the religious controversy ensured that the book caused a great stir, among agnostics as well as Catholics and Anglicans. George Eliot said when she read it first that the book had 'breathed much life' into her.

Hardy's reaction illuminates several things – first of all, his religious views at this stage; secondly, his continuing keenness to argue about religion and, thirdly, the state of his relationship with Moule.[4] Moule and Hardy had repeatedly disagreed over style and its importance in writing. Their letters from 1863 show them debating the point already. Moule always maintained that style itself did not matter; so long as the thinking was good, the writing would take care of itself and this position fitted with his earlier book, *Christian Oratory*. Hardy, on the other hand, gave meticulous attention to stylistic rules. Concentrating on these externals was, according to Moule, something of a distraction.

That longstanding, often amicable disagreement sheds light on this notebook entry because in it Hardy essentially says that Newman has a charming style but his thinking is all wrong. This implies that style does indeed have a power of its own – a power, moreover, that Moule, 'who likes [Newman] so much', has unwittingly succumbed to. Newman's style has made Moule lose sight of the logical inconsistencies in Newman's arguments. So, if style has such an impact in this case, then Hardy is right to study it carefully and Moule is wrong to be so dismissive.

Hardy sounds supercilious about 'gentle childish' Newman. The entry has the competitive arrogance of a smart undergraduate and it is trying at the same time to catch out Hardy's mentor, Moule. Hardy talks about the superiority of a 'really human' logic, but he practises here something more inhuman and insistently logical, in order to show himself the intellectual equal, even the superior, to these two authority figures. And if Newman is 'childish' in his faith, Hardy is being boyish when he takes such pleasure in the discovery that faith is founded on contradictions. His own logic-chopping and point-scoring seems inhumane.

During 1864, the markings in Hardy's Bible and in his Prayer Book petered out and his attendance at church gradually declined as well. On 11 September 1864, he wrote 'Doubt' in the margin beside chapters 44 and 45 of Isaiah. Later the word was heavily erased. These chapters of Isaiah speak of divine justice being present on earth: God's people will prosper; whereas the heathen and evildoers will suffer and perish. They also foreshadow St Paul's teaching about salvation: 'I have blotted out, as a thick cloud, thy transgressions, and, as a cloud, thy sins: return unto me; for I have redeemed thee.' (Isaiah 44:22.) They would have reminded Hardy of the passages in 1 Corinthians that were one of the foundations of his Evangelical belief.

London seemed to be proof that justice did not operate in human affairs, and that the vision of an orderly, organic human society was illusory. It was not realizable simply because the world was not like that. There was no justice in nature or evolution; there was no continuity between the moral order and the natural order. Instead, there was a fight for supremacy, a *'struggle for life'* – a phrase that coloured the 1860s in the aftermath of Darwin's work; even Henry Bastow, Hardy's fervently Baptist friend, used it in a letter of 1863.[5] In this amoral environment, 'red in tooth and claw | With ravine' (as Tennyson wrote in *In Memoriam*), the Christian doctrine of the blotting out of sins did not seem false so much as meaningless.

When Hardy rubbed out the word 'Doubt' from the margin is not known. It is usually assumed that he did things like this much later in order to cover his tracks. From 1864 onwards, however, Hardy's mood was highly volatile. As he said about reading Newman, he still had 'great desire to be convinced', and not least for personal reasons: 'because H.M.M. likes him so much'. Moule did not want to lose his family over religion; Hardy did not want to lose his friends. Yet he did not want to be a hypocrite and the Church appeared, in many respects, the embodiment of hypocrisy – complacent, self-regarding, and oppressive while preaching the gospel of love and human brotherhood. Writing 'Doubt' and then, almost at once, erasing it again would not have been surprising, given his state of mind.

Hardy said of his mother Jemima that she saw in early life 'some very stressful experiences of which she could never speak in her maturer years without pain'. Her refuge from these afflictions was reading: 'she appears to have mollified her troubles', he said, 'by reading every book she could lay hands on'.[6] This may not have been actually true; nevertheless, it was a strategy she taught her son. The best way forward was to suppress your feelings and find useful occupations for your mind. Hardy's habitual cure for misery was busyness and during his writing career the focused efficiency he needed to practise frequently achieved that end. As a young man in London, he cured loneliness through self-improvement. The gallery-visiting, theatregoing and lessons in French were all parts of that effort.

Books were a more dangerous source of distraction because they were more a matter of personal choice. Hardy was drawn to those that expressed similar anguish to his own which meant he did not read indiscriminately so much as avidly. What captured his interest were books that expressed and so reawakened the feelings of betrayal, beleaguered insecurity and disillusionment he was struggling to keep under control. Unconsciously, it led him to convert reading into study. From early on, Hardy's studiousness had been marked. It was habitual with him to take up areas of knowledge and make himself master of them. In London, the schools of Renaissance painting, the styles of Gothic architecture, the great works of English and French literature, were all thoroughly researched at one stage or another. Like his parents and grandparents, who became experts in parish history in order to keep trauma at bay, Hardy used the pursuit of knowledge as a way of suppressing feeling.

Later, in his novels, he worried about the consequences of stifling your emotions and replacing them with the acquisition of factual information. He saw it as one of his own mistakes and one that his society encouraged. It might occasionally have comic consequences but it could also have disastrous ones. As 1864 turned into 1865, however, and Hardy felt himself to be increasingly adrift in London, his need for some kind of control over and structuring purpose for his life was overwhelming. In response, he began to compile a self-consciously literary notebook, entitled 'Studies, Specimens &c'.

*

By 'Studies' and 'Specimens' Hardy meant turns of phrase, unusual epithets, striking usages and so on, which he collected from his reading. He made lists of examples, quoted from Shakespeare, Spenser, Walter Scott, Palgrave's *Golden Treasury* – from any poet he was reading at a particular time. Byron, especially *Childe Harold's Pilgrimage*, comes up frequently; so do Shelley and Keats; and there is a single, long section from Tennyson's *In Memoriam*. The notebook is one of the very few documents to survive from this period in Hardy's life and he saved it from destruction probably because of its literariness. Its existence supported the image he wanted to present of himself as a natural-born writer, whose other occupations had always been diversions from his true path. The notebook showed Hardy already practising, despite his architectural labours, the craft that would become his career – the craft that was always his first love.

There is some truth in this image and self-image, but not the whole truth. Neither is the notebook quite as formal or purely technical as it might appear. This transcript of his literary apprenticeship naturally reveals something of what was happening to Hardy emotionally. In that respect, it is uniquely valuable: there are scarcely any letters, no anecdotes, perhaps a single photograph, which date from these years. There are poems (especially from 1866 on); these, however, have been carefully selected. The notebook alone, Hardy let slip through the net.

Initially, though, it looks pretty arid and, consequently, it suggests a stereotypically academic mode of reading – a detached, technical, professional state of mind in which you comb texts for their verbal oddities. So, for instance, when he was reading Wordsworth's sonnets, Hardy noted down:

> fulgent / trim array / what boots it /
> stress / bedimming / sepulchral / sky
> muffled in clouds

The underlinings show his concern with unusual words or combinations of words – a sky 'muffled' in clouds, for example; 'dimming' made transitive as 'bedimming', and so on. These lists continue for page after page, the phrases nearly always remaining out of context. It is scarcely an arresting read, yet hidden inside these word lists lies something personal too.

The last four of the phrases quoted above ('stress / bedimming / sepulchral / sky muffled in clouds') are taken from an obscure Wordsworth poem, entitled 'Even as a dragon's eye that feels the stress'. It describes a taper placed in a cottage window in a 'black recess | Of mountains'. Nothing exists to 'mitigate and cheer its loneliness' there; it is a 'joyless Thing | Which sends so far its melancholy light'. Even so, Wordsworth adds, around this light:

> Perhaps are seated in domestic ring
> A gay society with faces bright,
> Conversing, reading, laughing;—or they sing,
> While hearts and voices in the song unite.

Evidently, this sonnet talks about things that mattered to Hardy. It juxtaposes a solitary existence with all the joys of home: friendship, reading, conversation, and above all music; Hardy's London bedsit with the fireside circle at Higher Bockhampton. In other words, Hardy was recording the poetic technicalities of a poem that touched him deeply.

The poem expressed as well an idea that became important to his books. Although to an outsider the rural world might look miserable and poverty-stricken (its cottages like melancholy tapers set in the midst of darkness), to its inhabitants it was a world of love and joy. Wordsworth's poem implies this. When reading it, Hardy's personal nostalgia would have been combined with the sense that Wordsworth had recognized the kinds of prejudice Hardy himself encountered. The poem instructs the educated reader to reconsider the rural world; in that respect, it – and Wordsworth more generally – is a significant influence on Hardy's point of view and his sense of what his own books might set out to achieve. The sonnet was therefore a significant poem for Hardy and one that he was likely to find especially poignant at this point in his life. The notebook both records that incident and instantly controls the feelings provoked. It is as if Hardy channelled his feeling into a technical study of particular phrases, so keeping the feeling itself at arm's length.[7]

Longer quotations (that is, complete sentences or stanzas) are pretty rare in the notebook and all the more interesting for that. The first entry of all comes from Shakespeare's comparatively little-known play, *Timon of Athens*:

> It is I
> That all the abhorred things o' the earth <u>do mend</u>
> <u>By being worse than they</u>.

In a jumble of words and phrases from Shakespeare's sonnets, Hardy copies out a few pages later, 'Ah, yet doth beauty like a dial hand, steal from his figure & no pace perceived' (from sonnet 104). Similarly, when he's reading Palgrave's *Golden Treasury* he comes across the Renaissance poet Thomas Lodge's 'Rosalynde's Description'. Suddenly, lines appear amidst the string of words:

> with orient pearl, with
> sapphire blue with marble white, with
> ruby red her body every way is fed
> yet soft in touch & sweet in view

All of these sudden introductions of line-length quotations have a personal edge to them. Miserably low self-esteem afflicted Hardy in London and remained a danger all his life. He was also acutely sensitive to the effects of ageing: 'I look into my glass | And view my wasting skin', he wrote in *Wessex Poems*. Thirdly, he wrote some of the most erotic prose and poetry in the language.[8]

The notebook focuses, then, on things essential to Hardy – as a writer and as a person. It reveals his character; it writes his history. And what stands out particularly is the frequency and intensity of the erotic feeling, both the strength of his sexual drive and the powerful efforts he made to restrain it. Hardy had been learning shorthand in 1864. In the notebook, he uses it occasionally, and almost always when sex is involved. Quoting a line from Shakespeare's *Pericles*, 'That he went to bed to her very description', Hardy wrote 'went to bed to her' in shorthand. He noted a phrase from *Richard II*, 'frowning brow to brow' and added, again in shorthand, 'therefore loving lip to lip'. Possibly Hardy was frightened that someone might come across the notebook – perhaps his sister Kate who was still a child. It is more likely, though, that the encoding was for his own benefit.

We associate the Victorians with prudishness and sexual repression, often unfairly. Because it was designed to be read by an audience that included children, Victorian literature was routinely censored and often the writers did this themselves, having internalized the expectations of their publishers. The result conveys a false impression of Victorian behaviour and, to a lesser degree, Victorian attitudes. It implies an obsession with chastity that is at odds with the amount of recorded prostitution at the time and the numerous forms of pornography (written, drawn and photographed) that were in existence too. Hardy seems, nonetheless, to be fully committed to official Victorian values in his reluctance about putting sexuality into words. The shorthand fits with the impression he later gave of having been a withdrawn, self-consciously pure young man. Even the subject of sex had somehow to be translated into a different language as if, without this barrier, Hardy would be brought too near to its disturbing influence.

On the other hand, Hardy seemed unable to avoid the subject. As he went on reading and noting down words, sex figured more and more. Soon after reading *Richard II*, Hardy read Spenser's celebration of married love, *Epithalamion*; on the following page are phrases noted from Robert Burns ('knacks o' love, wiles o' love', 'her brow, her blush, her eyes'). Then, as happens increasingly as the notebook goes on, Hardy started to develop ideas of his own based on what he's reading. Using shorthand for the word 'breasts' he wrote: 'her breasts two heaving young mushrooms with lady birds set on their crowns that never have seen the sun'. 'Snowy' is inserted above 'heaving', 'new' above 'young' as Hardy sought the exact nuance he wanted. However he chose to phrase it, the image is eerie. Oddly, perhaps, mushrooms represented purity to Hardy: 'as mushrooms bore thro' the earth, & keep their cleanness', he wrote in the same section. Likewise, the woman's breasts are white because they have never been shown – they 'never have seen the sun'.

This is the first time in the notebook that Hardy allowed his mind to dwell for a moment on a woman's body. As he did so, he tried to keep it virginal and that helped again to place its sexuality at a distance from him. The bizarreness of the comparisons helps to assert the man's mastery – over the woman, over himself and the situation generally. All these endeavours cannot help but reveal, even so, Hardy's intense fascination with the woman he imagines, the body he desires. Hardy's novels later became extraordinarily insightful about this contradictory impulse within male sexual desire. Angel Clare's unthinking mistreatment of Tess (by idealizing her) or Clym Yeobright's unforgiving cruelty to the woman he is obsessed with, Eustacia Vye: these imaginary actions draw upon tensions Hardy had registered in himself much earlier.

While the novels made possible meditated reflections on male fantasy, at the same time Hardy used his writing less consciously as a way to re-enact his desires, in all their discomforting complexity. The novels were valuable to him partly because they helped him achieve some sort of perspective on his own, conflicted sexual feelings. In his mid twenties, he seems to have lost that distancing control – not to any extraordinary degree by most people's standards but enough to terrify someone like him, for whom self-control, order and privacy were so important. In the course of the notebook, in other words, a kind of sexual awakening seems to be taking place. What could not be said at first except in shorthand gradually became the only subject worth talking about and even the Bible was mined for material to use in love poetry.

Whether this awakening had any equivalent in Hardy's personal life is more difficult to say, due to the lack of evidence. It would not have been unusual for someone of Hardy's age and class to visit prostitutes; still less, for lovers to become sexual partners. It was not quite respectable – it could 'ruin' a girl – yet it was known to go on all the time. Hardy does seem to have had girlfriends while he was in London and it is possible that he slept with them – possible, but in his case unlikely. Hardy drops heavy hints in his novels that the country dances where he played the violin as a teenager involved drunkenness and sex and that may have been the context in which he lost his virginity. But who can say? Certainly, he had been exposed to a promiscuous environment, even if he had not participated in it. Later, though, his circle of friends narrowed to a group of young men for whom chastity was the measure of manhood, and not sexual prowess. Masculinity was defined in the period as the ability to hold in check the animal passions so that purity was made into a sign of strength. This had a gendered aspect because women were defined as lacking the strength to control their sexual instincts and for that reason they needed the dominance of men. The entire social order depended in fact upon male sexual self-control.

Hardy had imbibed – partly from his Baptist friends, partly from Moule's ideal of the scholar-gentleman, and partly from his own sense of vocation – this adherence to sexual purity. Hard as it may be to believe now, he would have remained true to that ideal while living in London. The notebook's preoccupation with sexuality was, therefore, more of a response to sexual frustration (initially spontaneous, later more self-aware) and less an exploration through language of some new, sexual experience. Sexuality became a focus of guilt and anxiety, in part because it threatened to shatter Hardy's carefully maintained serene exterior and partly because once welcomed, or acknowledged even, sex would challenge his already fragile religious faith.

*

About halfway through the notebook Hardy began to make notes from the Bible, particularly the Old Testament prophetic books of Isaiah, Jeremiah and Ezekiel. But instead of simply jotting down interesting phrases (as he had with his earlier reading of poetry), Hardy constantly adapts them and adapts them in the same direction. So, for instance, he notes down:

> nourishing eyes, glance
> abundant hours of love, glances of love, beauty:
> the abundant blushes: loving-place : briars:[9]

The source of these is Isaiah 7:

> And it shall come to pass in that day that a man shall nourish a
>   young cow, and two sheep;
> And it shall come to pass, for the abundance of milk that they shall

give he shall eat butter: for butter and honey shall every one
eat that is left in the land.
And it shall come to pass in that day, that every place shall be,
where there were a thousand vines at a thousand silverlings, it
shall even be for briers and thorns.

There's no connection between the source and Hardy's versions, except
the single words he has taken over: nourishing, abundant, place (turned
into loving-place) and briars. It is almost comically incongruous. Hardy
seems to be ignoring the Biblical passage, mining it solely for ways in
which its language might enrich possible erotic writing of his own.

Experimenting with language and developing his techniques as a
writer: these remain Hardy's primary concerns. Focusing his attention
on those things disguises the sexual imperative that is at work too. And
that disguise helps liberate his sexual urge. Over the page, Hardy again
uses a passage from Isaiah as his jumping-off point: 'needy heart, her
needy eyes, glance, my needy lips, her needy beauty: my hope died
childless: I left my hope on .. : bowed down by love : if I fall under : love
is a moaning thing'.[10] Isaiah in the Bible is denouncing the ill-treatment
of the poor; he's not talking about 'love' at all. Hardy plays around with
the original, working on the possibilities created here and there by the
original's wording. Hardy saw himself, probably, as doing nothing more
than this. In the process, he hits upon expressions that matter to him –
phrases of bitterness and resentment, of dislike at being encroached
upon.

A few pages further on in the notebook, Hardy began an alphabetical
list of phrases and usages. These do not have any particular source any
longer, which marks another stage in the notebook's development, as for
the first time, Hardy begins to compose on his own account. First he
had just transcribed lines and phrases from the literature he had been
reading; then he began to expand on the quotations, as in the passages
from the Bible, which he developed in such extraordinary ways. Now he
was writing independently of any source. As you read through the
notebook, following the chronological sequence it records, Hardy seems
to be slowly emboldened, willing to risk his own ideas once he has
dutifully absorbed the best of previous writers.

This self-realization comes about in conjunction with two other
things at the same time: Hardy's near-obsessive focus on sexuality and
his transformations of the Bible. Selfhood, sex and rejection of religion

go together. In fact, when Hardy first begins to write for himself in the notebook, all the phrases are to do with sexual love:

> soft accent of thy heart : sweet
> ache of n—k, l-p, s—l : soft acts : swift
> acts of thy eyes: warm action of pulse, blush :
> acute sweet, blood, blush [. . .]
> the hot ado of blushes : the sharp ado of
> sweet & bitter : the dear adulteries of lid
> with lid, pleasure & regret.

And so on, as far as the letter 'd': 'dim love, dim kiss: dip of thy lip into mine : deep dips : dip into thy neck : soft dip of thy throat : as thy bosom dipped and filled'.[11] The repetition in these passages lends them enormous rapidity and fluidity. Words and phrases seem to be pouring out of Hardy. You can sense the breathless rush of desire and his eagerness to break free of authority. If only for a moment, the genie has got out of the bottle.

*

Whether as symptoms of this rebellion or as additional causes for it – perhaps both – Hardy faced other disappointments around this time. Following his unsuccessful attempts to become a journalist, an art critic, or a poet, and with his continuing sense of disillusionment with architecture, Hardy had considered joining the Church. In the *Life*, he referred to this as 'a scheme of a highly visionary character', and in a surviving letter to Mary, written in 1866, he called this 'notion [. . .] far fetched'. It would take too long – seven years or more – and it would cost too much to be worth attempting. So, as he wrote to Mary, it seemed 'absurd to live on now with such a remote object in view'. The letter sounds defeated and dejected, more so than the *Life*, which tried to give the impression that Hardy never took the idea too seriously, not least because he had never really believed what the Church taught.[12]

This is evidently disingenuous. Even though, by 1866, Hardy was no longer a confidently committed, believing Christian, he had been so very recently. While his faith lasted, entering the Church would have made sense to him on idealistic grounds as well as practical ones. It was also genuinely possible in the Church to pursue artistic interests, so perhaps it would prove a better place than architecture for the exercise of Hardy's talents. Since 1862, Barnes had been vicar of Winterborne Came, just a few miles from Dorchester. In 1866, he was still publishing both poetry and scholarship while simultaneously fulfilling his duties to his parishioners and winning their devotion. His life showed what a clergyman could achieve in a quiet country parish when he was equally devoted to his flock and his art. Hardy still respected Barnes and admired his poetry more and more. (There are several entries from Barnes in the 'Studies, Specimens &c' notebook.) The older man's happiness and usefulness in both spheres would have been powerful incentives to Hardy to go the same way.

Because Hardy took the idea of becoming a clergyman seriously, he was dejected when it proved impossible. His letter to Mary registers that despondency but also disguises Hardy's other feelings – his rancour towards the unfairness of the system and his sense of resentment, directed once more against Horace Moule. Moule was in Cambridge at the time and had sent Hardy the ' "Students Guide" to the U. of C.' This was the document that showed exactly how long Hardy would take to gain the necessary qualifications, how much it would cost him, and how absolutely the goal lay out of his reach. Moule, with his own privileged background and his ordained brothers, seemed implicated again in the forces that kept Hardy back. It was an unfortunate reminder of what had happened in Dorchester a few years before.

Mary was fond of Horace Moule and probably attracted to him; for his part Hardy never relinquished his affection for his friend, despite their differences. Instead, he disguised his anger from himself by embracing a fatalistic melancholy. This was what Marcus Aurelius would recommend and was how his own family tended to approach disappointment. Hardy took that tone in the letter partly for Mary's benefit as well. Mary was more pious than Hardy had now become, and she remained so. While unquestioning piety was expected of Victorian women, Mary's faith had been increased by the Dorchester revival. It comes as no surprise then to find Hardy unwilling to tell his sister the other reason for his decision – that he had abandoned the life of faith because his faith had abandoned him. This nonetheless was part of what he felt. Hardy's faith had become a listening for the 'still, small voice', which the prophet Elijah heard, in the passage from the Bible that Hardy loved more than any other. When he found he could hear it no longer, he was left not only personally bereft and socially isolated, he was denied choices of a career.

Perhaps his doubts led him to give up the idea; perhaps the unworkability of the idea contributed to his doubts. If the Church was so hidebound by class that it had no room for him, perhaps it was not so very different from 'the world' after all. In which case, it looked as if belief made actually rather little difference to behaviour and there was, therefore, no reality to the new life in Christ. In any event, doubt and disappointment were a bleak combination and as they descended upon Hardy his personal life disintegrated.

– 8 –

Red roses and smug nuns

HARDY'S first book of poetry, *Wessex Poems* (1898), contains a sequence of sonnets, entitled 'She, to Him' and dated 1866. Probably they really were written then and little altered afterwards. In style, they resemble Shakespeare's sonnets, which Hardy was reading closely at the time, as quotations in the 'Studies, Specimens &c' notebook reveal. Like other poems in *Wessex Poems*, the 'She, to Him' sonnets help to make the book feel obscurely autobiographical, offering clues and hints about Hardy's personal history. The 'She' of the poems has been passionately in love with the 'Him' and been abandoned by him. Like 'Neutral Tones' and 'Revulsion', other poems from 1866 included in the volume, the sonnets reveal a depth of feeling hitherto not found in Hardy's writing. They are direct and convincing, where his previous work had tended to be rhetorical, overblown, even histrionic. From the poems, it is hard not to suppose that in this year Hardy went through a serious love affair, probably his first.

It has been suggested that the girl involved was Eliza Nicholls, a year younger than Hardy, and working in service in a house near Hardy's lodgings. Eliza came from Kimmeridge, on the Dorset coast near Lulworth, and she may have met Hardy before he came to London. Soon after Hardy moved to Westbourne Park, however, Eliza left the city and went to work in a house in Godstone, Surrey; in 1866 she shifted again and went to live with her parents, who had moved from Dorset to Findon in Sussex. It is known that Hardy visited her that year at Whitsun – he kept the sketch he made of the parish church. Hardy never referred to Eliza and the *Life* made no mention of her so the only evidence for the relationship comes from Eliza's descendants (who cannot necessarily be relied on), and the sketch of Findon church.

Hardy's autobiography contrives to make all his early relationships with women sound trivial. They are comic episodes of puppy love and principally show the depth of his later feelings for Emma Gifford. This contrast was partly a show of proper, conventional respect for his dead wife – no one had rivalled her, the *Life* declared. And it is true that no one really had. On the other hand, the 'She, to Him' sonnets evoke a relationship that was not trivial. As soon as he confesses its existence in *Wessex Poems*, Hardy covers it up once again, leaving no other biographical clue and saying only that these sonnets came from a larger collection, the rest of which he destroyed.

Eliza Nicholls (if she was the girl in question) was and remained a devoutly religious person, respectable and chaste. Her relationship with Hardy may have begun as early as 1863, when Hardy too would not have approved of sex before marriage. By 1866 (the more likely date for the beginning of a relationship between them), Hardy's views on the subject and his feelings about it had changed. He no longer accepted religious dogma without question and his understanding of love had become much more sexualized.

In the course of the sonnet sequence, for example, the speaker makes the alarming discovery that love 'puts all humanity from me'. 'Believe me,' she says in the fourth poem:

> Lost One, Love is lovelier
> The more it shapes its moan in selfish-wise.

This is a particularly frightening discovery if you start where Hardy (and Eliza) would have started from – that is, with the Christian idea of love. St Paul's charity, which 'Beareth all things, believeth all things, hopeth all things, endureth all things', seems almost the exact opposite of the love that 'shapes its moan in selfish-wise'. Sexual love turns out to be more insistent than the woman speaking (and Hardy writing) had thought before – amoral, grasping and, even more strangely, the lovelier for being like that. At the same time, this sort of love was more threatening than its Christian counterpart. Desire was a need – a need felt by both men and women: 'her needy eyes, glance, my needy lips, her needy beauty', as Hardy wrote in the notebook. Sex endangered your freedom. 'But this I know,' the woman says in the same poem, 'my being is but thine own – | Fused from its separateness by ecstasy.' 'Separateness' was profoundly important to Hardy, both as an ideal and as a burden. 'Ecstasy' relieved the burden and destroyed the ideal.[1]

We do not know for certain what happened to Hardy, whether he had an affair with Eliza Nicholls, with someone else or with no one.

What does come through in these poems and what fits with the notebook is the unstable mixture in him of attraction and recoil when it comes to sexual feelings. The poems suggest that he would have recoiled from the sexual ecstasy he imagined or foresaw with a woman (or was offered by one) in rather the same way that he recoiled from the crowds and delights of the London streets. His desires created the abreaction. And as much as he feared the consequences of sexual success, he feared the impact of failure too. Hardy as a young man was more than usually unwilling to be hurt. As he wrote in 'Revulsion': 'For winning love we win the risk of losing, | And losing love is as one's life were riven'.[2]

Hardy's surviving poems suggest a more steadily melancholic state of mind than emerges from the notebook. In this respect they resemble his letters. Sorrowful resignation was the stance he usually adopted in public, which was an understandable thing to do and also part of the truth of his feelings. He could reach that point of fatalistic acceptance, and writing sometimes helped him to do so. It was, in fact, one of the reasons why he wanted to write. Behind the scenes, even so, he was more troubled.

Sexuality, like religion only more so, was a taboo subject. Hardy's fellows in the office were as ignorant as he was. They 'really knew nothing at all' about the 'romantic and *risqué*' women they were fascinated by.[3] Moule too was, if anything, more repressed than Hardy himself, despite being ten years older.[4] Meanwhile, Hardy's other frustrations did not diminish: his by-now continual weary rage with God, with the professions, with London, and with the entire order of things. Training himself in poetry was designed to keep these reasons for desperation at bay and, typically, to complement his study of poetry, Hardy bought a rhyming dictionary in 1865. The emotional turbulence brought out by his reading would, of course, prove beneficial in the end, both to his imaginative sympathy and his writing. At the time, it only added to his sense of instability. And in the following year, 1866, when some sort of love affair began, Hardy also came across for the first time Algernon Charles Swinburne's recently published *Poems and Ballads*.

*

Swinburne (1837–1909) was a scandalous figure. A friend of the Pre-Raphaelites, he had lived for a time with Dante Gabriel Rossetti at Rossetti's house in Cheyne Walk and the *Poems and Ballads* volume was dedicated to the painter, Edward Burne-Jones. Like his friends, Swinburne enjoyed a reputation for Bohemian excess and dubious morality. Before *Poems and Ballads*, his plays, *Atalanta in Calydon* and *Chastelard*, both published in 1865, had attracted widespread praise. Hardy took notes from *Chastelard*, either in 1865 or 1866. *Poems and Ballads*, however, was more controversial. The poetry's eroticism and outspoken atheism created a furore. Swinburne was condemned and adored in equal measure and with equal ferocity. Hardy remembered how the attacks on him in the press at this time 'made the blood of some of us young men boil'.[5]

Such men were not, by and large, architects working for Blomfield, the son of the Bishop of London, with commissions from Oxford Tractarians like Thomas Combe (1797–1872). Swinburne was asked to stand as an MP, unlikely as that may sound now and the people who asked him were members of the Reform Club, the much-mocked institution occupying the floor beneath Blomfield's offices. For Hardy, commitment to Swinburne meant dissent from his workplace and his colleagues. Perhaps that was part of the attraction.

Swinburne's work can often feel now like a calculated assault on Victorian pieties – provocative, attention grabbing, and 'sensational'. For Hardy, though, Swinburne was revelatory. He brought into the open ideas and feelings that Hardy was struggling towards. There were, for instance, Swinburne's notorious anti-Christian pronouncements. 'Thou hast conquered, O pale Galilean; the world has grown grey from thy breath'. There was a pervasive nostalgia too for the classical world, 'the fair days when God | By man as godlike trod, | And each alike was Greek'. And there were also more disturbed moments:

> As one who hidden in deep sedge and reeds
> Smells the rare scent made where a panther feeds,
>   And tracking ever slotwise the warm smell
> Is snapped upon by the sweet mouth and bleeds,
>
> His head far down the hot sweet throat of her –
> So one tracks love, whose breath is deadlier,
>   And lo, one springe and you are fast in hell,
> Fast as the gin's grip of a wayfarer.

Capture and torture become in Swinburne things to be desired.

> By the ravenous teeth that have smitten
>   Through the kisses that blossom and bud,
> By the lips intertwisted and bitten

> Till the foam has a savour of blood,
> By the pulse as it rises and falters,
> By the hands as they slacken and strain,
> I adjure thee, respond from thine altars,
> Our Lady of Pain.[6]

This sado-masochism emerges several times in the poems and was known to correspond to Swinburne's personal taste for flagellation.

There's no sign of Hardy's responding specifically to that side to Swinburne. His enthusiasm came, first and foremost, I think, from Swinburne's explicit rejections of Christianity which he found liberating and euphoric. Although, for example, there are many quotations from *Poems and Ballads* in the 'Studies, Specimens &c' notebook (several longer than anything Hardy quoted from anyone else), the longest quotation of all comes from *Atalanta in Calydon*. Copied out over three pages, the extract includes that poem's infamous chorus:

> Who makes desire, and slays desire with shame;
> Who shakes the heaven as ashes in his hand;
> Who seeing the light & shadow for the same,
> Bids day waste night as fire devours a brand
> Smites without sword, & scourges without rod;
> The supreme evil, God.[7]

For Hardy, this violent reversal of received opinion felt long overdue. In Swinburne, he found someone who was finally willing to say things of this kind – out loud and for all to hear. Swinburne made it seem suddenly possible to declare your unbelief in public and, more than that, your hatred of what was commonly believed and its moral offensiveness. You did not have to pretend any longer that you respected the established Church with all its oppressiveness and hypocrisy – hypocrisy that, furthermore, particularly damaged sexuality and love.

Hardy came back repeatedly to the first line of this stanza, 'Who makes desire, and slays desire with shame'. He copied it out at the back of the notebook in what appears to be a list of literary touchstones. Swinburne was, once again, saying what few would dare to say though many thought it: God had created sexual desire and then condemned it. Religion, in other words, and its moral codes repressed entirely natural impulses, making them appear shameful and making people ashamed of what was utterly instinctive. His fondness for this particular line, plus the evidence of the notebook as a whole, strongly suggest that Hardy felt this at a personal level – that Swinburne's writing precipitated a recognition that he had been made to feel morbidly guilty about natural feelings. Swinburne showed him his repression and showed him too who he could blame for it.

Religion's pharisaic, repressive power was not the only thing Hardy gleaned from Swinburne's work. Swinburne's writing also tapped into a vein of feeling about the female body that Hardy shared. On several occasions, Hardy refers to the impact made on him by the sight of a woman being hanged – something he witnessed at close quarters when young. In describing this event years later, Hardy mentioned (almost as a matter of course) the way the woman's body became attractive in death. Its desirability increased as it hung before him. A voyeuristic element, related to his feelings about the hangings, can be found all through Hardy's life and career; it's connected less to Swinburne's poetry about sado-masochism than to his representation of love as a source of torture. Hardy's reading seems to have focused less on Swinburne's desire for pain than on his sense of love consisting of agony amidst delight.

> A great elder-tree
> Held back its heaps of flowers to let me see
> The ripe tall grass, and one that walked therein,
> Naked, with hair shed over to the knee.
>
> She walked between the blossom and the grass;
> I knew the beauty of her, what she was,
> The beauty of her body and her sin,
> And in my flesh the sin of hers, alas!
>
> Alas! for sorrow is all the end of this.
> O sad kissed mouth, how sorrowful it is!
> O breast whereat some suckling sorrow clings,
> Red with the bitter blossom of a kiss![18]

Swinburne's poetry accentuated, in other words, Hardy's pre-existing tendency to fear sexual love – to fear its violation of self and its power to destroy peace of mind. At the same time the erotic force of the poetry was compelling.

Hardy was so taken by Swinburne in 1866 and so influenced by him over the next few years because Swinburne expressed just what Hardy was starting to feel himself. Swinburne's boldness in doing so struck him as heroic and inspiring. Here was someone at last whom Hardy felt he wanted to imitate and defend. London had offered him precious few others. He was leading an obscure, mundane existence; his circle of uplifting, idealistic friends was broken up and scattered across the globe, while Blomfield's office constantly implied the overwhelming power of the status quo and his closest friend, Moule, similarly conveyed the necessity of compromising with the system. This was something Moule found difficult himself and insisted upon the more stringently as a result. Swinburne, on the other hand, resisted all these disillusioning imperatives, denying their validity, defending personal preference and recklessly making honesty his god. But there was something else too: Swinburne made these revolutionary assertions in highly formal verse.

Later in life, Hardy met Swinburne and became a close acquaintance, if never quite a friend. After Swinburne's death in 1909, Hardy wrote for him one of his finest elegies, 'A Singer Asleep'. He recalled there:

> that far morning of a summer day
> When, down a terraced street whose pavements lay
> Glassing the sunshine into my bent eyes,
> I walked and read with a quick glad surprise
> New words, in classic guise, –
>
> The passionate pages of his earlier years,
> Fraught with hot sighs, sad laughters, kisses, tears;
> Fresh-fluted notes, yet from a minstrel who
> Blew them not naïvely, but as one who knew
> Full well why thus he blew.

The poem celebrates the way in which Swinburne's explicit sensuality disrupted the mid-Victorian world: 'It was as though a garland of red roses | Had fallen about the hood of some smug nun'.[9] He evokes too, of course, the excitement he felt, as he walked to and from the office, reading as he walked. Thirdly, though, he says that Swinburne was always completely in control of his work. There was far more passion in his poems than in those of any other writer of the day; even so, they were the opposite of naïve. The poems sounded 'fresh-fluted notes', but these were produced deliberately, with complete self-awareness about both intentions and consequences.

In other words, Swinburne managed somehow to remain serene amidst all the violent feelings he portrayed. The 'Studies, Specimens &c'

notebook reveals as nothing else does Hardy's increasing volatility as his years in London frustrated him, sexually, professionally, and personally. At the same time, the notebook shows that literature (and literary technique in particular) seemed to provide a way out of his difficulties – a way of regaining equanimity, focus, purpose and calm. Swinburne's elaborate, supremely technical writing offered him a triumphant example of that artful serenity. Swinburne, moreover, achieved this success without becoming merely accomplished because his poems were charged with the most extraordinarily intense emotions. The complexity of Swinburne's poems – their metrical sophistication, their verbal inventiveness, their classicism ('New words, in classic guise') – became so powerful an example to Hardy because this skilfulness suggested how you might maintain control over the passions you no longer denied.

Consequently, Swinburne's work justified the strictly technical attention to poetry that Hardy practised in his notebook – justified it against the criticisms Moule, for one, might make. Swinburne's poems also implied that within metrical forms it was possible to address all subjects, all areas of experience, however extreme or even abnormal. In the craft of words, the poet possessed a means of distancing himself from all he touched upon. That gave him the freedom to write about anything. It also meant he stayed at one remove from things. The classical Stoicism of Marcus Aurelius had found a poetic equivalent.

Swinburne created for Hardy a feeling of sudden, absolute release on several levels. He need not any longer submit to Christian doctrine or conventional morality. His sexual feelings were nothing to be ashamed of and neither should he be frightened any longer of putting his love into words. The poet's vocation allowed him to address any subject and exploit any material. He would be fully justified in reworking texts from the Bible, for example; he was justified as well in developing as far as he could a vocabulary of physical, sexual experience, whatever 'abnormal' impulse that undertaking might lead him to discover or express.

As a result, in the notebook, when Hardy is reading Swinburne he keeps up his usual stance of professional, technical interest. He copied out, for instance, the following lines from Swinburne's 'Satia te Sanguine':

> As the lost white feverish limbs
> Of the Lesbian Sappho, adrift
> In foam where the seaweed swims
> Swam loose for the streams to lift

These highly erotic lines are included, Hardy says, because they provide an example of the present tense introduced by 'where', an unusual and intriguing grammatical device. Similarly, the alphabetical list of words and phrases – 'soft accent of thy heart', 'dear adulteries of lid with lid', 'as thy bosom dipped and filled' and so on through the letters of the alphabet – often resembles pieces of Swinburne's poetry. Sections of the list seem to have been put together actually while reading Swinburne. Hardy was mining these poems, just as he made use of the rest of his reading. Doing this proved that he was as much of a technical connoisseur as Swinburne was himself, with his dazzling range of forms and startling epithets.

Swinburne's poetry called up all Hardy's repressed sexuality and, at the same time, offered him a way of distancing himself from those sexual feelings. In this way, the poems resembled the family's habit of using factual accuracy as a means of both evading and addressing traumatic events in the past. Hardy wanted to learn from Swinburne how to achieve an assured combination of honesty and self-awareness, passion and collectedness. Yet, actually, Swinburne's example contributed to Hardy's distress. He was in a sense simply too young for the poems, though they appealed especially to young men. The themes, in tandem with the style of Swinburne's poetry, wound up to a higher pitch the clash that already existed between Hardy's desire to fight against repression (whether political, social, religious or sexual) and, on the other side, his wish to keep control, his love of neatness, detail, meticulous workmanship, his insistence on decorous relations with other people and on his own personal privacy.

Swinburne had such an impact on Hardy because his structured, highly formal poetry challenged the foundation of Hardy's morality at the time, with its emphasis on restraint and self-denial. Swinburne asserted that repression was an evil, and Hardy could readily welcome that. The reason he gave, however, was more shocking: repression did not hold back natural desires that were naturally good. It was an evil because it thwarted our experience of pain and torture – the agonies that, according to Swinburne, were inseparable from ecstasy and the shame that was bound up with love. As he made these disturbing claims, all of Swinburne's artistry declared that he had survived the agony and kept his humanity. He made violent agony and mental torture appear to be compatible with the most civilized forms of experience.

Although Hardy tried to emulate Swinburne's poems, they ran way ahead of his experience. He could not match their elegant, knowing poise, though they enforced the illusion that he might – that through dedication to art he could acquire an artist's calm. In reality, calm was the last thing Swinburne would produce in someone like Hardy, situated as Hardy was.

*

In one of the last sections of the 'Studies, Specimens &c' notebook, Hardy began to rework passages from the minor Old Testament prophet, Habakkuk, doing with this book what he had done a short while earlier with Isaiah. On this occasion, he referred to the result as a 'concoction', sounding more self-aware about what he was doing. The verses he used as his starting-point were an anguished cry against God:

> O Lord, how long shall I cry, and thou wilt not hear! even cry out
>   unto thee of violence, and thou wilt not save!
> Why dost thou shew me iniquity, and cause me to behold
>   grievance? for spoiling and violence are before me: and there
>   are that raise up strife and contention.
> Therefore the law is slacked and judgment doth never go forth: for
>   the wicked doth compass about the righteous; therefore wrong
>   judgement proceedeth.

Hardy makes of these:

> violent kisses : delight
> too violent for me : violent days : she showed
> me smiles : I thought what the turned years
> had showed me : her red spoilt eyes : her
> lips slack with sorrow : if time would slack
> a little : his love is slacked : the fall of mouth
> upon mouth : the fall of time : there never go
> forth from you pleasant speeches : whatever the
> years may tell : the end of her pulses : the end of
> her eyes : your heart will rock, sway, wave on in
> its low sweet pace is mine wild heavy or still
> Is it I to chide you that these things show? Is it
> I to chide you that you took me so ill, wear me down?[10]

At first, there is a remote connection between the two passages. Words from the Bible passage, such as 'violent', 'showed me' and 'slacked', are turned over and over in Hardy's mind as he tries to find new, arresting contexts for them. Then, in the last few lines, the writing alters and leaves the Bible behind. It begins instead to sound like a soliloquy of unrequited love, remembering (as Swinburne's work so often does) the ecstasy of sexual contact, of mouth falling upon mouth. These prompt in turn confused feelings of anger and resentment.

Clearly, Hardy had not left behind completely his religious doubts. Choosing these verses from Habakkuk suggests that he was still preoccupied by moments in the Bible where people complain to God. Just earlier in the notebook, for example, Hardy had written, 'I have put by faith', a phrase noted from Psalm 4. He began developing it at once: 'I have put by faith: like dreams that die in handling : like tunes in the mind that die being tried'.[11] '[D]ie in handling', he rewrote several times, trying 'crumble', 'waste being thought of', 'fade'. Evidently, this was a feeling of loss he wanted to catch exactly. The last phrase too ('like tunes in the mind that die being tried') suggests, very movingly, that Hardy feared he was beginning to lose touch with the old folk tunes that had been his emotional lifeblood while at home, and kept him in touch with home until now. He thought he could remember them but when he tried, he found he had forgotten them. Likewise with faith: it seemed present still, or very nearly present, but when he tried to practise it – in prayer or Bible reading – all his past conviction evaporated. These were the desolate feelings that made Swinburne's serenity so enviable to Hardy. Their persistence shows, meanwhile, how far out of his reach that state of mind still was.

And when he began to explore Swinburnian physicality – 'her red spoilt eyes : her lips slack with sorrow' (phrases that evoke Pre-Raphaelite paintings, especially those by Dante Gabriel Rossetti) – when he does this, Hardy begins almost at once to start writing more confessionally, more 'naively' than Swinburne ever did. Within the neatly handwritten words of the notebook, an aesthete's tender consideration for the finer points of language, for its possibilities and refinements, comes up sharply against a young man's quite normal struggle to control unfamiliar feelings, intensities and uncertainties he had never expected. Is his heart 'wild heavy or still'? He does not honestly know.

*

Hardy's efforts to write were demanding and unrewarded: no one would publish the poems he composed and composing them drained him emotionally and psychologically. Meanwhile, his religious faith broke down, blocking one of his imagined escape routes from a profession that was disappointing him. And, not surprisingly in these circumstances, he found it impossible to sustain relationships with women. All of these factors combined led to Hardy becoming exhausted and probably depressed. He found it hard to concentrate at work – he 'scarcely had physical power left him to hold the pencil and square' – and finally in July 1867, Blomfield advised him to return home.

Later in life and in his autobiography, Hardy blamed his ill-health on the stench of the Thames, which ran outside the office windows at Adelphi Terrace. No doubt that didn't help. Up until 1858, the year of the 'Great Stink', human waste had flowed directly into the Thames. As the city's population grew, the river became an open sewer and in summer particularly, when water levels dropped and the river flowed more slowly, the smell was almost unbearable. A new drainage system was instituted in 1858, designed by Joseph Bazalgette; it opened in 1865. The smell was significantly reduced, however, only after 1875 when Bazalgette's system was completed. Even then, the improvements were gradual. Throughout Hardy's London years, his working environment was unhealthy and over time that would have taken its toll on him.

Hardy also mentions his habit of 'reading incessantly' after work, from 'six to twelve' at night. This sounds hyperbolic but probably was not. Hardy always had remarkable powers of application and could drive himself very hard, especially at times of emotional crisis. Inevitably, though, this sort of regime would make him ill in the end. Hardy claims that 'When he visited his friends in Dorset they were shocked at the pallor which sheeted a countenance formerly ruddy with health', and says that his leaving London was made easier when John Hicks wrote to him.[12] Hicks needed to find an assistant and wrote asking Hardy to look out for one on his behalf. Hardy took up the offer himself, agreed with Blomfield a leave of absence until October and hastily made his escape – most of his books and papers were left behind in Westbourne Park Villas. Outwardly, at least, he left on the understanding that he would soon return. In the event, he never came back; over the next five years, he made only rare, brief visits and it was nearly ten years before he lived in the city again.

− 9 −

Believed-in things

HARDY'S return was scarcely triumphant. Unwell and overwrought, unsure of his future, he was nonetheless intent upon making some sort of break with the past, and that would involve confronting somehow his parents' ambitions for him. It was not, by any means, an easy moment. Remarkably quickly, though, Hardy bounced back. He picked up where he left off in his architectural work, with the advantage now of going freelance and so choosing what and how much to do. In the spare time that gave him, he was able to write a full-length novel, completing the first draft in around five months. It felt like a miraculous recovery. 'A few weeks in the country [. . .] completely restored him, ' Hardy later wrote.

Leaving behind the 'fitful yet mechanical and monotonous existence' of his London days, 'suddenly he became more practical'. He:

> queried of himself definitely how to achieve some tangible result
> from his desultory yet strenuous labours at literature during the
> previous four years.[1]

His parents were probably asking him the same question and asking each other what their son thought he was up to. Certainly, Jemima never saw much point in acquiring unnecessary skills: she had told her husband off when he taught the children dance steps that had gone out of fashion and she never lost her sense that life was filled with obstacles and opponents – that you could ill afford to idle.

Hardy had often hated (and would grow again to hate) the pressure he was put under to achieve. At this moment, though, his parents' dynamism felt welcome. Being forced to be practical seemed healthier than the feverishness and directionless languor of his London days – there seemed more purpose in such a life and more hope. Bustle might also prove his parents wrong. If he could write and publish a novel, it would show that all his bookishness had been worthwhile. Architecture would be revealed as only one among many ways forward in life. And Hardy would also be able to declare that, thanks to five years spent in London, he now knew as much as his parents did about 'ways and means'.

His parents probably treated this new enthusiasm for novel writing as little more than a phase. It reassured them that Hardy was still working part-time for Hicks, and had not thrown away his chances there; moreover, he had been quite seriously unwell. If trying his luck as a novelist cheered him up, then little was going to be gained by opposing the idea. Their marriage survived on the basis of tolerance and distance so that family life was reticent, indirect and watchful. They were not inclined to challenge Hardy and knew, in any case, that he was very strong-willed. A handful, his grandmother had called him early on, and these judgements often stick, whether they are true or not. So, for the moment, they let him get on with it.

*

The book Hardy wrote was entitled *The Poor Man and the Lady* and he finished it, during the autumn of 1867, when he was only twenty-seven years old. In the first months of the following year, he copied out the manuscript, making revisions as he went. He started sending it to publishers in July 1868. The book was never published and, unfortunately, the manuscript was later destroyed. It does survive in part, however, though only in shadowy ways. 'An Indiscretion in the Life of an Heiress', a short story Hardy published in 1878, reproduces with alterations probably about a third of *The Poor Man and the Lady*; other sections were cannibalized earlier in the decade and included in published novels. This is especially the case with his second novel, *Under the Greenwood Tree* (1872); and even a novel written as late as 1875, *The Hand of Ethelberta*, owed something to this first extended piece of writing.

Judging from the surviving extracts and fragments and from Hardy's few remarks about the book, it was a fiery piece of work – 'a striking socialistic novel', he later called it. There was, not unusually for a first novel, a lot of autobiography too. The hero, Will Strong:

> was the son of peasants working on the estate of the great local squire. [. . .] The hero showed remarkable talent at the village school, and was [. . .] educated as a draughtsman. [. . .] the lad was

sent up to London, where he was taken into the office of an eminent architect, and made striking progress.[2]

So far, so directly modelled on Hardy's career to date.

In London, Will Strong 'took up radical politics'. This was out of 'pique', Hardy said, because the 'great local squire' had opposed Strong's love affair with his daughter and used his influence to separate them. Strong had moved to London as a last resort after the squire helped evict him from his family home. The parallels with Hardy's life are less exact here and heightened for effect since, as far as is known, he never did fall in love with a squire's daughter. It has been suggested that he was introduced to the aristocratic mistress of one of his senior colleagues at Blomfield's but there's no evidence for this and it does sound fairly implausible.

The emotional centre of this episode in the book was Hardy's passion as a boy for Lady Julia Martin, and hers for him. Like Will Strong, Hardy had been separated from this love and his family had been punished. Coming back home would have helped reawaken his past and his feelings for Lady Julia in particular. In Stinsford church were buried 'William O'Brien with his wife Lady Susan, daughter of the first Earl of Ilchester' – a 'handsome Irish comedian' and an aristocratic lady, whose 'secret marriage in 1764' had caused a scandal.[3] Hardy was fascinated by this romantic story and, to some extent, he rewrote it in this earliest piece of fiction, projecting himself as the poor man and drawing on his relationship with Lady Julia. It reveals the persistence of his attachment to Lady Julia and the dependence of his imaginative energies on childhood experience. The novel (as far as it can be reconstructed) had a kind of reckless bravado – an adolescent fury it is perhaps surprising to find in someone already in their late twenties. Alongside this was a turn inward, bringing back remote personal experiences, dwelling on these, and probing their true meaning.

One sign of Hardy's imaginative return to his relationship with Lady Julia comes from the relative absence of eroticism in the writing (at least what survives of it in 'An Indiscretion in the Life of an Heiress'). That text is charged instead with feelings of devotion and longing so that there's chivalric nobility in the love, particularly the man's for the revered lady. The love is so courtly and ideal in part because Hardy uses the love story to address other issues – social and political questions, surrounding the hero's process of disillusionment and persecution; the love affair remains secondary to that. The thematic significance of the 'Lady', as a symbol of a glamorous, monied future, outweighs her sexual presence.

For Hardy, though, the class system and sexual mores were entangled in one another. A man needed money before he could marry and prior to marriage, sexual contact was especially risky for aspiring people who traded on their respectability. And Hardy, whether as an author wooing his public or an architect competing for clients, found himself obliged to be respectable. Accordingly, in a sense, class position unmanned him; it enforced chastity. Being relegated sexually, socially and professionally all seemed part of the same process. Around this time, Hardy referred in one of his notebooks to the '"grand scheme of subordination" [class to class]'. He was a politically radicalized young man by 1867–8 and sensed at least that one of this pernicious scheme's effects on him was a kind of emasculation.[4]

In London, these conflicts had been heightened for him by reading Swinburne. In Dorset, he felt rather differently: reminders of Lady Julia called up lost simplicities, a youthful tenderness of feeling that was threatened by Swinburne's strange and wild sexual impulses. In other words, Hardy made *The Poor Man and the Lady* such a fervent and romantic book, as well as one so lacking in sensuality, because he was reacting against Swinburne's eroticism. That was part of the book's practical impulse. Hardy wanted to rid himself of Swinburne's fever and keep hold of his hero's radicalism. Equally, though, and more intimately, Hardy was trying to recover a purity of sexual feeling that he felt he was in danger of losing. The prospect of that was terrifying to him; it seemed part of an illness he had recently gone through, part of an infected world he had been fortunate to escape in time. So, in place of fevered desire and keeping a lid on such desire, Hardy embraced an ideal of ardent, self-sacrificial romantic love, in tune with his state of mind ten years earlier – the headily idealistic days of his friendships with Bastow and Moule.

*

The other parts of this first novel, particularly those that survive into *Under the Greenwood Tree*, tell a second story about Hardy's feelings when he went home. The 'Studies, Specimens &c' notebook shows that when he returned to Dorset, Hardy's reading habits altered. In place of Swinburne, he studied Shakespeare and that change corresponds to his novel's retreat from the erotic to the romantic; it also began to restore his sense of humour. Hardy made notes from *Antony and Cleopatra*, *As You Like It*, *The Merchant of Venice*, *Much Ado About Nothing* and *Love's Labours Lost*. Though entries from these plays coincide at first with quotations from Swinburne, Swinburne soon vanishes and examples of Dorset idioms and dialect take his place. Moreover, the 'concoctions' disappear, with all their anguish and muddled rage; instead Hardy quotes instances of Shakespeare's wit. 'Portia concerning her suitors – There is not one among them but I dote on his very absence.' He seems delighted suddenly by the playwright's foolish characters, especially the group in *Love's Labours Lost* made up of Costard, Moth, Pompey and Holofernes. At the same time, in other notebooks, he began to record details of rural life. The first entry in the 'Memoranda' notebook (compiled later from early materials) was dated 1867. It concerned 'My father's description of the funeral of a singer or violinist at Stinsford formerly'.[5]

These are the beginnings of Hardy's rustic comedy – convincingly detailed, endearing and often owing its inspiration to Shakespeare. The Dewy family in *Under the Greenwood Tree* resemble Shakespearean rustics; so does William Worm in *A Pair of Blue Eyes*, and so too – most successfully of all, perhaps – do the chorus of farm labourers in *Far From the Madding Crowd*. Though Hardy always disliked admitting to his literary influences, the notebook gives away the nearness between the Elizabethan original and Hardy's imitation. It shows too that this interest began during the summer when Hardy came home. In *Far From the Madding Crowd*, one of the rustics, Joseph Poorgrass, is given the novel's final words: 'But since 'tis as 'tis, why it might have been worse, and I feel my thanks accordingly.' These are almost a paraphrase of a passage from *Love's Labours Lost*, spoken by Holofernes. Hardy had noted it down in 1867: 'This is a gift that I have, simple, simple; a foolish extravagant spirit [. . . .] But the gift is good in those in whom it is acute, & I am thankful for it.'[6]

Holofernes could be Hardy himself at the time he made the note – full of relief and delight at escaping from London. In the world's eyes, he might look simple; he might be thought foolish for allowing the pressure of the capital to get to him; and his love of home might be regarded as extravagant – it might even be extravagant; nonetheless Hardy felt extremely thankful for it. Shakespeare allowed ordinariness to be valuable. He laughed at simplicity and respected it too. Although Hardy's relationship to Dorset remained vexed and complicated in several ways, when he returned home his first reaction was to reassert his rustic identity. He set aside the intervening London years, recalling his dearest memory from childhood and writing about it in a novel; simultaneously, he began to follow his family's example and made minute observations of his surroundings, the customs, the landscape, and the local history. This was, after all, a place that nobody else much cared for and nobody knew better than he did. He was unrivalled and in possession, and he could find his emotional balance once again. In his notebook, he started to invent phrases describing nature: 'clanging thunder, humble bee, pealing waves, whooping storm' and so on. As he honed his skills, technique in itself became less central. There's greater simplicity and more exuberance in his writing, more clanging and whooping.

Inevitably, though, return brought tensions as well as a sense of relief, particularly when Hardy began to write about being at home. He wrote in the *Life* that, when he came back to Dorset in 1867, 'He easily fell into the old routes that he had followed before, though', as he adds, 'with very different ideas of things.'[7] Dorset offered him sanctuary, clearly, from a bad time in London. His health improved and his mood was transformed. He felt secure within familiar scenes, familiar characters – within an apparently timeless, unchanging environment where people accepted both him and one another. Bockhampton impressed him now as a humorous, tolerant, unambitious place; muddle was acceptable; a patient interest in things (instead of a hurried manipulation of them) was part of daily life.

At the same time, there was a sense of separation. Hardy stood apart from the previous existence, which was summoned up wherever he went. He did not feel quite right there. His 'different ideas of things' gave him new perspectives on what he had previously taken for granted and having 'different ideas' at all was as much the problem as what those different ideas might be. He felt special and conspicuous, as he had never done before. This produced in Hardy, almost as soon as he re-entered his parents' house, a feeling that things could not be quite the same as they had been before. The five years in London had irrevocably divided him from the old country life. He did not yet feel nostalgic for Bockhampton and Dorchester; rather, there were the beginnings of disquiet, registered in his notebooks at the time as in the *Life* later. It was a disquiet that Hardy sought to allay by writing his novel.

On his return, Hardy could not help but feel something of an outsider in Bockhampton; that distance, though, encouraged him to speak all the more forcefully on behalf of 'the peasantry about him – his mother's ancestry [. . .] his old acquaintances, neighbours and [. . .] familiar friends, with their rough but honest ways'.[8] As an onlooker now, he could be a spokesman for his people and that was in a sense all he could be, because his years in London had made it impossible for him fully to reincorporate himself into their world. Aligning himself with Dorset, refusing to let its rural life be patronized, speaking on behalf of those without a voice: these are the linked imperatives behind his first novel, and its moral fervour answered the psychological necessity of finding a way to fit back into his home. At the same time and in the same state of mind, Hardy fell in love with one of his 'familiar friends', his cousin Tryphena Sparks.

*

Exactly when this happened, how long the affair lasted and how deeply Hardy felt for Tryphena: all of these have been disputed. Lois Deacon maintained that Hardy fathered a child by Tryphena and that she jilted him for Horace Moule. She also believed that Hardy's marriage to Emma Gifford was poisoned from the beginning by his lingering, unrequited love for Tryphena.[9] All of these claims are equally doubtful; unfortunately, because the relationship has been sensationalized in these ways, it has also been dismissed too easily. Michael Millgate is remarkably off-hand about it and effectively replaces Tryphena in Hardy's emotional life with Eliza Nicholls and her sister Jane, even though their relationships with Hardy are if anything more difficult to feel confident about. Martin Seymour-Smith is franker about the obscurity that surrounds this phase of Hardy's life and in response to it, he refuses to elevate Tryphena above the various other women Hardy may or may not have had love affairs with during his twenties.[10] Both biographies are, in my view, playing down Tryphena's importance to Hardy. The truth is that, like many other things in his life, the affair with Tryphena was both outwardly unremarkable and profoundly significant.

Hardy, characteristically, left a tantalizing uncertainty surrounding Tryphena. One poem in *Wessex Poems* refers to her: 'Thoughts of Phena. At News of Her Death', written in 1890 but scarcely a single other clear-cut reference to her exists in his extant writings, though ambiguous hints are dropped here and there. 'Thoughts of Phena' (like 'Neutral Tones' and the 'She, to Him' poems) arouses interest in Hardy's past and then refuses to satisfy that interest. Furthermore, the time when he was close to her remains one of the most hidden periods in his life. The *Life* devotes only ten pages to the years between summer 1867 (when Hardy came home) and April 1870 (when he met Emma Gifford); these pages are given over almost entirely to his working life – as a part-time architect and aspiring novelist. Similarly, there are only six surviving letters from these years and all of them are written to publishers. The 'Studies, Specimens &c' notebook, hitherto the principal source of direct, contemporary evidence about Hardy's emotional life, peters out around 1867. The 'Memoranda' notebook (compiled later) only really gets going after April 1870 and the same is true of the 'Literary Notes'. A big gap in the record like this arouses suspicion, even in Hardy's case when much of the record is thin – suspicions increased by 'Thoughts of Phena' and several other poems, dated by Hardy to 1869 and published later. Hardy was hiding something, clearly. He wanted people to know that there was something to hide.

Tryphena was the youngest daughter of Maria Sparks, née Hand, Jemima Hardy's eldest sister. The family lived in Puddletown, two miles or so across the heath behind Hardy's house and the two sets of children had been friends from childhood. Maria's third daughter, Martha Mary, was six years older than Hardy; the two sons, James and Nathaniel, were respectively three years older and three years younger than he was. The cousins played together indoors and out. They stayed in touch into old age. Martha is reputed to have been the most beautiful of the sisters and there are family stories of Hardy's being in love with her. According to these, Hardy's aunt, Maria, opposed the match, on the grounds that her daughter and Hardy were first cousins. If so, this was not a very good reason since first cousins were allowed to marry, then as now.

Tryphena was by far the youngest of the family. Born in 1851, she was eight years junior to Nathaniel, the next youngest, and seventeen years younger than Martha Mary. More than twenty years separated her from the eldest daughter in the family, Rebecca. She was the same age as Hardy's brother, Henry, and so ten years or more younger than Hardy himself. Surviving photographs show that the sisters all looked rather alike, with dark eyes, strong eyebrows and lustrous black hair. The similarities between them, plus further family stories, have led to the idea that Hardy was successively in love with all three – Rebecca, Martha Mary and finally Tryphena. (There was a fourth sister, Emma, who married in 1860.) In Hardy's last novel, *The Well-Beloved*, the hero falls in love with a woman, then her daughter and lastly her granddaughter, and this has been used to support the idea of his being in love with all three of his Sparks cousins.[11] The similarity is probably coincidental because the plot of *The Well-Beloved* has closer biographical links with Hardy's unhappy love life during the 1890s. If Hardy did have feelings for Rebecca or Martha Mary, they do not seem ever to have been of the same order as his feelings for Tryphena. Lois Deacon also suggested that Tryphena was illegitimate and that Rebecca was her mother, as clearly Rebecca was old enough to be so. She argues that Rebecca's decision in 1873 to go and live with Tryphena in Devon, after her own brief marriage failed, indicates a special degree of intimacy between the two women – closeness more likely between mother and daughter than between sisters. Rebecca may easily have taken over her mother's role towards the youngest child in the family but that was not at all unusual and their mother was ailing as Tryphena grew up. It does not remotely imply that Rebecca was Tryphena's birth mother.

When Hardy arrived home in 1867, Tryphena was sixteen and working as a pupil–teacher in Puddletown school. Her mother, Maria's, worsening health was evident to all her family and relations and at some point, Tryphena moved in with her aunt, Mary Antell, who also lived in the town. Mary had four children close to Tryphena in age so it would have been natural for Aunt Mary to take Tryphena off Maria's and Rebecca's hands at this difficult time. That would help Rebecca, the eldest daughter, run the household in place of her mother, and protect Tryphena from some at least of the stress of her mother's illness. It was typical of the families to help each other out and it would not have been at all surprising if Jemima had asked Hardy to help out too. He had learnt some French in London; Tryphena was bright and already aiming to become a schoolteacher so French would be a useful extra to her. Obviously, he could and should give her a helping hand. It may also have crossed Jemima's mind that Tryphena's vitality and sense of humour would do her mournful son some good.

Biographers have usually assumed that Jemima opposed the relationship between the cousins, rather than encouraging it. Michael Millgate states that to Jemima's 'jealous eyes' Tryphena was not 'an especially good match for an up-and-coming young professional man'. But no direct source is given for her supposed jealousy.[12] Guided by the story of Maria's disapproval of Hardy's attachment to Martha Mary and influenced too, perhaps, by the plot of *The Poor Man and the Lady*, Millgate and others have presented Hardy and Tryphena as lovers cruelly separated by self-interested parents. Jemima's interests lay, in fact, mostly in the other direction. Meanwhile, her real, if often suppressed, affection for Hardy may have played its part as well. What could be more natural than for a mother to find her unhappy son a nice young girl to take an interest in?

Hardy's sister, Mary, described the Sparks's home in Puddletown as a 'cheerful house with the sparkling river in front, and in the near distance the old Church tower with the clock & rambling chimes'. Everyone in Hardy's immediate family, including Jemima, knew that they by contrast sometimes led a gloomy life, away from everyone on the heath. They were by temperament the kind of people who needed to make sure they had things around that would cheer them up or keep them occupied. Music and painting, reading and storytelling were not so much luxuries as necessary therapies. Jemima's low self-esteem could make her neglect her children too and try to palm them off on others. It was an impulse that could be cruel, admittedly; in this case, it would have been sensible.

Jemima would also have been reasonably content at the prospect of something possibly developing between Hardy and Tryphena. She was not especially keen on any of her children marrying, preferring to imagine the four siblings living as two couples: the elder pair, Thomas and Mary, and the younger pair, Henry and Kate. Although this never happened, Hardy's sisters did live together for most of their lives, and later they shared a house with Henry. Still, if Jemima had to contemplate the prospect of her children's getting married, she wanted them to stay within reach. That would be more likely if they married 'in' and her tribal instincts would be satisfied as well. Tryphena was obviously a capable girl, perhaps the brightest of her sisters, and, through school-teaching, she had the chance to go up in the world without leaving her native place. Jemima foresaw that possibility for her daughters and planned for it. She would have seen Tryphena in a similar light.

And as well as being bright, Tryphena was brisk – as brisk as her mother, the eldest of her family, and Jemima, her aunt, a capable, even formidable woman. Tryphena looked as if she would keep any future husband on his toes so that Hardy's tendency to lassitude would find an opponent in Tryphena, just as his father's had in Jemima. Moreover, the big difference in age meant that the couple might enjoy a loving relationship that would never become entirely intimate (or would not do so for many years). Hardy's marrying Tryphena would not take him away entirely from his mother, either physically or emotionally. And, as the couple started 'walking out' together, Tryphena's dying mother would be glad to know that her youngest daughter was going to be looked after. Now, all this does not imply that Jemima actively schemed. Hardy did not need much encouragement, anyway, to find Tryphena charming and attractive but nonetheless his mother, looking on, would have seen her niece as perfectly acceptable – useful, even – as a match for her son.

Some evidence in support of this can be gleaned from Hardy's novels. *The Poor Man and the Lady* was not directly or deeply concerned with events in Hardy's love life at the time he wrote it. He narrated this period more closely ten years later in *The Return of the Native*. There, Clym Yeobright, much of whose experience is modelled on Hardy's own, remembers his mother's feelings about his cousin, Thomasin.

> Years ago there had been in his mother's mind a great fancy about Thomasin and himself. It had not positively amounted to a desire, but it had always been a favourite dream. That they should be man and wife in good time, if the happiness of neither were endangered thereby, was the fancy in question.[13]

If Jemima did have such a 'fancy', it would be an additional motive for her opposing Hardy's relationship with Emma a few years later. And Tryphena would have provided the focus for Hardy's sense that he was going against his family when he married.

How though did the relationship develop? How deep was it and how serious? Lois Deacon in particular saw the affair in terms of a grand, all-consuming passion, doomed to tragedy from the beginning. Even though things were probably serious between them, at least for a time, that account does not quite ring true. In 'Thoughts of Phena', Hardy writes of her more fondly:

> Did her gifts and compassions enray and enarch her sweet ways
> With an aureate nimb?

The poem celebrates her sweetness, in other words, and thinks of her as a delightful person, not as a *femme fatale*. Hardy makes her seem more like Thomasin than Eustacia Vye, the seductress of *The Return of the Native*. In pictures, similarly, she looks like an attractive, vivacious girl, rather than a classic beauty. Whereas Martha Mary was thought to be the best-looking girl in the family, Tryphena had the liveliest mind.

Likewise, 'Thoughts of Phena' remembers her 'when her dreams were upbrimming with light, | And with laughter her eyes'. Her 'sweet ways' were the feminine equivalent of the 'rough and honest ways' of Hardy's countrymen (as he described them in *The Poor Man and the Lady*). She attracted him in large part because she embodied for him the values and pleasures of an ideal, rural life – on his social plane, with similar aspirations, shared memories, and the same local knowledge. Added to that, Tryphena possessed charm, kindness, and hopefulness too. She reassured him that the world was not as cruel or miserable as he had begun to believe. She was balanced, funny and flirtatious. Her sexuality was not fiercely repressed, and on the other hand neither was it (as Swinburne had led Hardy to imagine) an irresistible, insatiable power, ready to devour him. Without trying and without even being aware of it, she declared that there was an alternative to London's extremes of ecstasy and despair, success and failure.

Hardy often connected Tryphena with his sister Mary. 'Thoughts of Phena' was first published alongside 'Middle-Age Enthusiasms', dedicated to 'M. H.', that is, to Mary, his nearest companion when growing up.[14] His novels frequently contain women who resemble Mary: Thomasin in *The Return of the Native*, and Fancy Day in *Under the Greenwood Tree* both recall her.[15] Fancy Day also resembles Tryphena very clearly. She has the same dark hair and she lives at roughly the same distance from Dick Dewy as Tryphena did from Hardy, though not in precisely the same direction. Mary and Tryphena seem to have mingled in his imagination very early and the link is perpetuated by *Wessex Poems*, thirty years later.

When Hardy returned to Bockhampton in 1867, Mary was running a school in Minterne Magna, ten miles due north of Dorchester. The two of them took day-trips together whenever Mary had a holiday. Minterne Magna was not Bockhampton, even so. The single major difference between Bockhampton in 1867 and Hardy's childhood memories of home was Mary's absence. Hardy came back to a family home that did not contain his dearest childhood friend and Tryphena filled that gap. She became a kind of replica of Mary. She came to represent the innocent, vibrant country world – the not-London – that he associated with Mary, remembered so vividly and feared that he might have lost.

Hardy, who was frail still and unnerved by his loss of Christian faith and his sense of waging a losing battle against the Establishment, became

powerfully attached to Tryphena, not least because of what she represented to him. Through 1868 and 1869, they were involved in a deeply
felt love affair, with even some thought of marrying. Tryphena became
the 'one believed-in thing' that Hardy could pin his hopes on as he
wrote his first novel. When the relationship later went wrong, it was not
because Tryphena disappointed Hardy – by running off with other men,
or by flirting, or by refusing to marry him. All these suggestions, plausibly
put forward by other biographers, assume that Tryphena was responsible
but, probably, the end of the affair had very little to do with her. Instead,
she had become too closely identified with Hardy's ideas, aspirations
and convictions at a particular stage. That had been on his side the
major source of the attraction from the beginning. As soon as his
opinions and sense of himself altered, there was little Tryphena could do
that would stop him from letting her go. She, as an individual and as a
person, had played too little part in his feelings about her.

This process of cruel disenchantment occurred in parallel with (and
was partly provoked by) Hardy's first encounter with London's publishing world.

10

Rising and falling with the tide

HARDY finished the manuscript of *The Poor Man and the Lady* in June 1868 and sent it off a few weeks later to Macmillan, a leading London publisher with a reputation for publishing serious fiction – what would now be called 'literary fiction'. He enclosed a letter of introduction by Horace Moule, who was quite well known in London literary circles for his reviewing work. Enclosed too was a letter Hardy had written, explaining his intentions to the publisher.

> Sir,
>
> In writing the novel I wish to lay before you – "The Poor Man and the Lady" (sent by today's post) the following considerations had place.
>
> That the upper classes of society have been induced to read, before any, books in which *they themselves* are painted by a comparative outsider.
>
> That in works of such a kind [. . . .][1]

And so on. Hardy gives five reasons in all why the book is the way it is, presenting the rationale all too rationally, as if personal feelings (of indignation, say, or resentment) had not played any part. He makes himself appear implausibly distant from his work.

That impression would have been increased when his readers opened the book itself. Alexander Macmillan, then head of the firm, sent it out to be read by John Morley, a man of letters and biographer who later went into politics. Morley's report was not so much mixed as divided; the book, he said, was:

> a very curious and original performance: the opening pictures of the Christmas Eve in the Tranter's house are really of good quality: much of the writing is strong and fresh. But there crops up in parts

a certain rawness of absurdity that is very displeasing: the thing
hangs too loosely together.

Morley suggested that Hardy 'study form and composition, in such
writers as Balzac and Thackeray'.[2] He gained in fact the clear impression
of an angry young man, intemperate and a little naive, despite Hardy's
best efforts in the covering letter to appear the opposite.

Probably hoping to decide one way or the other about the book,
Macmillan read it himself. On 10 August he wrote a long letter to
Hardy, praising the novel rather warmly and, all the same, finding
himself in agreement with Morley's criticisms. It is a kindly letter,
encouraging and fair-minded: 'Much of the writing seems to me admirable,' Macmillan said, 'full of real power and insight. And the characters,
on the whole, seem to me finely conceived and presented.' And rather
than be offended by Hardy's treatment of the upper classes, Macmillan
found the portrayal of them unbelievable. For much of the letter, he
pleads with Hardy to reconsider; surely, Macmillan exclaims, they
cannot really be as bad as this. 'Even the worst of them [the upper
classes] would hardly, I think, do the things that you describe them as
doing.'[3] Hardy came up against this response again and again during his
career; the more accurate he was, apparently, the less likely he was to
be believed. This applied whether he praised the rustics for their
sophistication or condemned the aristocracy for its selfish narrow-
mindedness. It was what he faced whenever he reversed customary
judgements and challenged ideology.

Tactfully softening the blow of this disappointing response, Macmillan promised in his letter to show the book to 'another man [. . .] who
knows more of the upper class'. Then, nothing happened. No doubt, the
pressure of other business pushed Hardy's manuscript to the back of
Macmillan's mind. The uncertainty (increased by the continuing possibility of a third opinion) left Hardy fretting. He wrote back to Macmillan
after a month: 'I have become anxious to hear from you again.'

As the days go on, & you do not write, & my production begins
to assume that small & unimportant shape everything one does
assumes as the time & mood in which one did it recedes from the
present I almost feel that I don't care what happens to the book, so
long as something happens. The earlier fancy, that *Hamlet* without
Hamlet would never do turns to a belief that it would be better
than closing the house.

His tone has shifted completely. Brittle authority has given way to a confiding dependency. 'I have been hunting up matter for another tale,' Hardy says, 'which would consist entirely of rural scenes & humble life'; one, that is, that will play to his perceived strengths; but, Hardy goes on, 'I have not courage enough to go on with it till something comes of the first.' And more poignantly still, he adds in a postscript: 'Would you mind suggesting the sort of story you think I could do best, or any literary work I should do well to go on upon?'[4]

Behind the apparent superiority and indifference of Hardy's first letter lay a quite natural dream of instant success. He would not admit he was hoping for anything so unlikely; still, until the final answer came, he could not help believing that, just possibly, the book would be accepted. Now disappointment, and the apparently indefinite postpone-ment of any further feedback, forced him to reconsider. Publishing the novel, however faulty it might be, would be better, he says, than giving up altogether, better than stopping the show and, as in a theatre, 'closing the house'. With Hardy, being practical often went with being downcast, but it revived as well the habits of a businessman. He began to flatter Macmillan, to ask his advice and accept his judgement. He knew from working in architecture how important it was to keep people sweet.

'How I Built Myself a House' and Hardy's 1867 poem, 'Heiress and Architect', dedicated to Blomfield,[5] both cleverly depict the power games involved in the relationship between buyer and artist. In each stanza of the poem, the architect gets what he wants while seemingly devoted throughout to the client's convenience. Meanwhile, as the poem goes on, the (female) client's fanciful notions gradually surrender to the architect's more prosaic priorities. Now, a year later, in the literary world, Hardy found himself involved in similar negotiations. He sounded much more personable in the second letter and much more subservient too. That was the only means he had of exerting any pressure, of nudging the publisher along and trying to make things happen. It was not, in fact, a new tone for him to adopt; it was an all-too-familiar one.

This reawakening in September to life's tawdry realities was already familiar in another way too. It repeated the disillusionment that had descended on Hardy the moment he completed the manuscript. He recorded 'a time of mental depression over his work and prospects' in June/July when the book was finished. And 'Cures for despair', he wrote in his notebook for 1 July 1868:

To read Wordsworth's 'Resolution and Independence'.
   "   " Stuart Mill's 'Individuality' (in *Liberty*)
   "   " Carlyle's 'Jean Paul Richter'.

Similarly, at this period, Hardy 'lent some more help to Mr Hicks in his drawings for church restorations, reading the seventh book of the *Aeneid* between whiles'.[6]

These are telling selections. 'Resolution and Independence' (subtitled 'The Leech-Gatherer') describes the poet waking up after a stormy night and feeling weighed down by fears and anxieties. He walks out into the fresh morning and meets a resilient, unconquerable old man, stoically going on with his unglamorous life. The poet finds in him indomitable determination, simplicity and a personal strength that defies external judgment. John Stuart Mill, similarly, argues in 'Individuality' that personal freedom must never submit to social pressure. Book Seven of Virgil's *Aeneid* also follows a crisis. Aeneas has travelled through the underworld in Book Six and in Book Seven, he re-enters the everyday world – he attempts to deal with politics, history, war and betrayal.

For Hardy in summer 1868, dealing with publishers was a bit like becoming a politician. After the heroic independence of writing his radical novel, he had to resume the sordid business of persuading other people to do what he wanted. He had to make compromises; he had to be, where necessary, mealy-mouthed, and sometimes an actual liar. Instead of the artist's freedom, Hardy had to confront once more the usual, inevitable 'struggle for life'. And, in particular, he was woken up to the necessity of dealing with London. While living in London and writing poetry, Hardy had remained a purist and baulked at the thought of deliberately setting about a literary career in the normal way. Now, it was from Dorset, strangely enough, with the manuscript of a novel on his hands, that he was obliged to become more involved. A novel celebrating the country over the city needed the city's favour if it was ever to see the light.

Quite what transpired during the autumn is unclear. There were probably further letters from both Hardy and Macmillan that have been lost. Possibly too, Hardy made some revisions to the manuscript before returning it to Macmillan and then travelling up to London in early December to hear the publisher's verdict on the revised version. Then, Macmillan broke it to him that he could not publish the novel himself, sugaring the pill by suggesting that another publisher, Chapman & Hall, might take it on. 'Edward Chapman was a man of the most scrupulous morality', however, so scrupulous that he had refused to publish Mrs Henry Wood's *East Lynne* in 1861.[7] He was unlikely to view Hardy's incendiary manuscript any more favourably than Macmillan had done but whether or not he suspected this, Hardy was not in a position to turn down possible openings. He called on Chapman & Hall almost at once and left the manuscript with them.

'I fear the interview was an unfortunate one,' Hardy noted in a diary.[8] Perhaps he got the sense instantly that his sort of novel would not go down well and perhaps he was starting to recognize that he might be pushing too hard – that he could be amenable one minute and overbearing the next; that, perhaps, he was being presumptuous, naively arrogant. It was nearly six months since he sent off the book and he was yet to gain a clear response from the first publisher he had tried. That was in some ways promising – and more encouraging than the string of rejections his poems had received two or three years earlier. It was frustrating too, of course. When he finally went to the effort and expense of travelling up to London, he did so full of suppressed anxiety and irritation – emotions he felt so strongly that he feared they would alienate the very people he needed to please. Yet he persisted too. This is the most striking difference, perhaps, from the Hardy of the London years. In 1868–9, he was no longer the sort of person who would meekly accept disappointment or let his novel fade out of sight as his poems had done.

Hardy had gone back to assisting Hicks during the late summer and into the autumn of 1868 as his possible publishers held fire. The firm had a good deal of work on, much of it in the north of Dorset: during 1867, Hicks had completed small churches at Stour Row and Compton Abbas, both villages in the Blackmore Vale, south-west of Shaftesbury. Now, he was working on plans for a church at Turnworth, south of Blandford. Hardy's main expertise from his time in London lay in ecclesiastical architecture: his drawings for All Saints' Church, Windsor, consecrated in 1864, were rediscovered in the mid 1970s and Hardy may have had a hand too in the chapel at the Radcliffe Infirmary, Oxford (1864), which Blomfield was commissioned to build.[9] Hicks was likely to use Hardy on churches (rather than, for instance, on the town hall in Wareham that Hicks was also designing at this time) and Turnworth Church has been identified as largely Hardy's own.

Hardy's renewed involvement in architecture in 1868, once his novel

was finished, seemed to augur that he would return to his original profession full-time before too long. His parents were waiting for that to
happen – for his novel-writing ambitions to die a death and for common
sense to reassert itself. When he came back from London in December
1868 with nothing more than a definite rejection from Macmillan and a
vague promise from Chapman & Hall, they may have thought the end
was in sight. Unknown to them, probably, church building was increasingly distasteful to their son and that dislike, as much as anything,
prompted him to make further attempts to escape architecture as a career.

The longer that Chapman & Hall kept Hardy waiting, the bleaker
he began to feel about the likely outcome. By January 1869, he felt 'a
vague sense of ominousness at getting no reply' and decided to travel
back up to London once more. The previous visit had succeeded in
moving the situation forward a little and perhaps the same thing would
happen again. The repeated delays proved, if nothing else, that Hardy
needed to be proactive if his ambitions were to progress. Back in
London, he saw Macmillan and Morley once more and they made the
sensible, predictable suggestion that Hardy should help launch himself
into literary London by writing reviews. Morley offered to introduce him
to the editor of the *Saturday Review*. This was a valuable offer and Hardy
may have been tempted. Ultimately, though, he turned down the idea.
He seems, in fact, to have been remarkably nonplussed.

The *Saturday Review* was an advanced magazine, with a reputation
for a rather supercilious tone. Moule wrote for it and perhaps for that
very reason Hardy wanted to keep his distance. He was rejecting more
than simply this one magazine, however, and his decision to do so
suggests that Hardy's sense of his own position and project was already
starting to crystallize. He was putting himself at a disadvantage, clearly,
by refusing a good opportunity when it came up. But, as earlier when
Moule suggested, even more implausibly, that Hardy should write a
gossip column, Hardy seemed to back away instinctively, as if he sensed
that writing reviews was bound to shift his loyalties away from the rural
world. How could he produce novels satirizing the emptiness of London
culture, while also writing ingratiating reviews of its products and their
producers? Perhaps there was something self-protective at work too. If
staying on the margins of the literary scene looked to an outsider like
headstrong folly, it probably felt to him like a necessity, since he could
not face struggling to the top of the greasy pole of a second profession,
with the self-promoting mentality that would demand. It seemed com-

mon sense instead to keep himself to himself and for the time being to stick to architecture as a source of money.

Meanwhile, as Chapman & Hall continued to deliberate about *The Poor Man and the Lady*, Hardy hung around in London. He studied the pictures in the National Gallery and read a little. Then, suddenly in February 1869, as if to justify Hardy's self-belief, the firm accepted the book. They asked him only to put up £20 as a guarantee against loss, which was not an unusual arrangement for a publisher to make with an unknown author. Hardy agreed to their terms without hesitation and soon afterwards he left London for Dorset, 'expecting proof-sheets soon to be forwarded'. His personal sense of elation must have been tremendous. And, as likely as not, his parents were pleased as well. Getting his book published proved he had not been entirely wasting his time; it proved he had some talent and that his application had paid off. So, as long as success did not turn his head or lead him to forget his duties to the family, they could enjoy it with him.

Then there was a hitch. Chapman & Hall wrote to Hardy in March asking if he could come back to London urgently and talk to their reader. When he arrived, he was 'ushered into a small office with glass partitions, on the ground floor at 193 Piccadilly' and introduced to yet another person employed to pronounce judgement on his work. The man in question began, without any preliminaries, to analyse Hardy's novel. Never, Hardy later said, 'had he heard so much good criticism packed into so little space.'[10] The reader was, as it turned out, George Meredith (1828–1909), then just forty and with a growing reputation as a novelist and poet. Meredith was also notoriously fastidious and extremely cautious. He had advised Chapman & Hall against publishing the runaway bestseller *East Lynne*; he later persuaded them to reject both Samuel Butler's *Erewhon* (1872) and Sarah Grand's *The Heavenly Twins* (1893), both notable successes in their day.

Self-consciously high artistic standards were coupled in Meredith with an ingrained fear of causing offence. His sequence of poems, *Modern Love*, had appeared in 1862; and his best-known novel, *The Ordeal of Richard Feverel*, in 1859. Both of these had created a scandal, particularly *Richard Feverel*. Usually in the mid nineteenth century, English novels were published first of all as a serial and in a three-volume edition, scheduled to appear as the serial came to end. The 'three-decker novel' as it came to be known, was too expensive for most of its audience and was aimed in fact at libraries, in particular Mudie's Circulating Library, which effectively controlled the market until the 1890s. Mudie could make or break an author by deciding whether or not to purchase copies of the first three-volume edition. Subsequent cheaper editions would be unlikely to appear if the novel had not gained at least some momentum from the first, and such momentum depended on Mudie's approval. Mudie, a Scotsman of strict religious views, could be brutally censorious. He disliked *The Ordeal of Richard Feverel* and cancelled the library's original order of 300 copies, claiming that the book was unsuitable for a family audience. But for Mudie's decision, Meredith would probably not have been forced to stoop to earning his bread as a publisher's reader. His own harsh experiences returned, therefore, whenever he undertook this task for Chapman & Hall, colouring his judgement.

As Hardy listened to Meredith's characteristically thorough discussion of his work, it dawned on him that he was being asked to reconsider. Despite Chapman & Hall's prior acceptance of the book, Meredith now wanted to dissuade Hardy from going ahead with it. *The Poor Man and the Lady* was, he said, too explicit in its attack on powerful institutions. It would draw down on its author's head violent condemnation from the reviewers and such an assault would have serious consequences for Hardy's chances of future success. There was a real risk that the book, instead of starting his career, would effectively end it, just as *Richard Feverel* still threatened to hang over Meredith's future. It was not until 1871, with the publication of his successful novel, *The Adventures of Harry Richmond*, that Meredith felt he had lived to fight another day and he sincerely wanted Hardy to avoid enduring the same sort of difficulties.

Meredith was careful not to criticize the book itself; that, he guessed, would have been counterproductive. And there were things to praise in it: both achievements in its writing and views Meredith himself was broadly in sympathy with. He had himself published a regional novel, *Rhoda Fleming*, in 1865 and, albeit obliquely, his writing like Hardy's consistently satirized the complacencies of English life. So, he warned Hardy only about the novel's probable reception and advised him to withdraw, at least for the moment. It might be worth rewriting and toning down, or (and this was Meredith's preferred option) Hardy should set about writing something else – something more palatable and commercial. The direct expression of Hardy's true feelings would be best postponed, perhaps indefinitely.

Years later, when he and Meredith had become friends as well as allies, Hardy recalled this meeting fondly, expressing his gratitude for

Meredith's sound advice. At the time, it was a bitter pill to swallow. Hardy agreed at least to think the matter over; and then, forlornly, he took his manuscript away. Probably he went home, though for the next few months his movements are unknown. Certainly, he did not give up on the book at once. Three months or so later, on 15 April 1869, he wrote from Bockhampton to another London publisher – Smith, Elder & Co. – offering the book to them, but by 30 April, they had evidently rejected it. Hardy wrote a letter that day asking for the manuscript to be returned.

This latest rejection seems to have been the turning point. According to the *Life*, it was 'at the end of April' when George Crickmay wrote to Hardy, asking him to take on further responsibilities as an architect. John Hicks had died during the winter and Crickmay (who had taken over the business) needed someone to help with the outstanding church building. Hardy accepted Crickmay's offer and during May he worked in Hicks's old offices in Dorchester. After that, he was taken on for the whole summer and moved down to Weymouth, where Crickmay was based. Hardy found lodgings there in June 1869 and did not leave until the following February. The decision and the move were both significant steps. Hardy had resumed architecture almost full-time (after a gap of nearly two years) and he had left home once more.

Perhaps Crickmay did just happen to write at the same time as *The Poor Man and the Lady* was rejected yet again, just as in summer 1867 Hicks had happened to write to Hardy, in search of a young assistant for his Dorchester practice. It's more likely, though, that Hardy in 1869 had been holding out for a few months against offers of architectural work, hoping against hope that his novel would find a publisher and set him going on a literary career. It may very well be that in April, when he was let down again, he decided to accept a long-standing proposal.

As far as architecture went, the new job was a promotion and an opportunity. Hardy went to Crickmay as a more senior member of the team, with special duties and a recognized specialism and he could not convincingly pretend this new assignment was simply a stopgap; the day-job was beginning to encroach. As it did so, clearly, Hardy was putting aside what he saw as his mission in life. Even at the time he would have recognized the danger that by going to Crickmay he was shifting his priorities, at the very least. There would have been family pressure on him to go in this direction plus some degree of personal loyalty to Hicks's unfinished projects, several of which Hardy had been involved with before. Perhaps, though, the most powerful influence on him was his desire to escape from the turmoil of hope and rejection, which had been the currency of his experience with publishers. He could find relief from it in the purely mechanical tasks architecture often demanded.

Actually, of course, Hardy had done rather well with the book and there was a great deal to feel encouraged about. Eminent publishers and men of letters had taken his work seriously, read it carefully and seen both accomplishment and promise in it. Only a few novelists get as far as this at their first attempt; even fewer see their first manuscript published. All the same, from Hardy's point of view, he had ended up with a book that nobody was willing to publish and, if their praise was at all sincere, then their refusal to do so must be based principally on fear – fear of unfavourable reviews, fear of offending the sanctimonious Mudie, fear that one scandalous book would taint the reputation of the whole firm. Publishers seemed, in consequence, fearful of anything and everything that threatened to rock the boat. Perhaps, in that case, what he wanted to write was doomed never to see the light of day and he should give up a game that he could never win.

Perhaps cruellest of all, however, the block on the book was not absolute. Chapman & Hall would not renege on their promise to publish the book should Hardy still ask them to go ahead. In the light of Meredith's recommendation, the firm would strongly advise him against publishing; only Hardy, though, could make a final decision. This was honourable of Chapman & Hall, but it was also unfair. How could an unknown like Hardy take the risk involved, particularly without his publishers' full support? He was not the sort of well-heeled Bohemian (like Rossetti or Swinburne, say) who could afford to offend the world, and who even enjoyed causing outrage to bourgeois sensibilities. Notoriety would hurt Hardy as an aspiring mainstream novelist (that part of Meredith's argument could not be denied), whereas for Rossetti or Swinburne, scandal secured a coterie reputation.

There was therefore no actual alternative for Hardy but to follow Meredith's advice. Chapman & Hall may have had legal reasons for leaving the ball in Hardy's court as well as a sense of scruple; whatever their motives, the effect was to compel him to give up the book himself. Their action – or rather their inaction – forced the young novelist to perform an act of submission. He must give way to the realities of the marketplace; he must recognize his own comparative insignificance.

That was bad enough: what accompanied it was an insight into the workings of the Establishment, which proved how naive he had been. People in high places were not going to listen humbly to criticism and they had well-established means of silencing rebellious voices like Hardy's, of humiliating and ousting them. Everyone else took that for granted. The publishers, in their desire to protect Hardy from the consequences of his youthful hot-headedness, conveyed to him, inevitably, their sense that he had really no idea who or what he was pitting himself against.

Hardy did succumb to the pressure and withdrew *The Poor Man and the Lady*; moreover in June 1869 he began to write a book along the lines that Meredith had suggested – a story with more plot, more excitement and less of the earnest agitprop. The result was *Desperate Remedies*, a sensation novel. Hardy completed his first draft within nine months – by March 1870 – and a year after that, the book was published, not, admittedly, by either Macmillan or Chapman & Hall, but published nevertheless. Within two years, therefore, Meredith appeared to have been vindicated. Even so, as he wrote *Desperate Remedies*, Hardy continued to send out the earlier manuscript to publishers and he found ways subsequently of smuggling many parts of it into print, hidden in other novels or turned into a short story. He never accepted to his dying day that *The Poor Man and the Lady* had not been good enough to publish.

*

It took Hardy three months to decide that he could and should follow Meredith's advice. After the long palaver over *The Poor Man and the Lady*, he might be better off settling down as an architect. Crickmay was offering him that possibility and Hardy accepted it, at least for the present. Doing so proved to be liberating, however. His ambition and resolve were both renewed when he moved away from home, almost as if he had been released from a prison of self-doubt. One reason for this was the place he moved to: Weymouth.

King George III had visited the town regularly during the late eighteenth century, on the recommendation of his doctors, who prescribed sea bathing as a cure for his bouts of madness. Farmer George was much loved and his patronage made the town into a fashionable watering place, despite its distance from London. During the Napoleonic Wars, it became a key military base as well, its elegant, Georgian esplanade filled with officers and fine ladies. Even in 1869, when Hardy moved there, signs of this elegant past remained, particularly in the buildings; meanwhile, the town was reinventing itself as a more popular seaside resort. The railway had been completed ten years before, connecting Weymouth to London and, northwards, to Bath, Bristol and, most lucratively, Swindon, a rapidly expanding railway town. These links brought new holidaymakers in and ensured that Weymouth did not go into quaint decline – that it was not completely supplanted by nearby Bournemouth or by the English Riviera of Devon and Cornwall, also now made more accessible by the railways. The town was the exception to the Dorset rule and was keeping pace with modern life.

For Hardy, recently twenty-nine, there were echoes here of his London years, in the Georgian architecture of the town and in the glamour of the well-dressed, fashionable ladies who went walking beside the sea. Perhaps to his own surprise, these ephemeral charms came as a great relief. Semi-permanent work had fallen into his lap and he had lodgings of his own, only a hundred yards from the beach. This was something he particularly enjoyed.

> Being – like Swinburne – a swimmer, he would lie a long time on
> his back on the surface of the waves, rising and falling with the tide
> in the warmth of the morning sun.

This 'tonic existence by the sea seemed ideal', Hardy claimed, 'physically he went back ten years in his age almost as by the touch of an enchanter's wand.'[11] He was caught up, it seems, in a magic indolence, swooning as much as swimming – drowsing and dreaming, and regaining his lost youth. The sudden improvement in health, both mental and physical, which he experienced when he returned to Dorset two years earlier now happened again, as powerfully as before. When summer turned to autumn, Hardy joined a dancing-class 'where a good deal of flirtation went on'.[12] Weymouth felt like a holiday and *Desperate Remedies*, begun during the summer, reflects the freedom, ease and playfulness that came over Hardy as he began this new phase of life. Writing the novel also contributed to that mood because in writing it Hardy was embarking on unknown territory.

A sensation novel was a new genre in 1869, with new rules. To produce one that would succeed, Hardy had to learn how to construct an intricate, yet suspenseful narrative and how to entertain. Novels of this kind were understood to be playful; they consciously tried to offer an alternative to Victorian high seriousness – the social commentary and spiritual travails of Elizabeth Gaskell or George Eliot, for instance. Their unwillingness to be serious about anything caused as much consternation as their sensuality did. Sensation novels were artful as well as cynical; their authors not only produced 'sensations', they conveyed too a sense of control, of achieving and deploying effects. The reader could share in that feeling of superiority, so that the style's hedonism brought with it a kind of cool.

Meredith had not suggested a 'sensation novel' specifically; he had recommended Hardy write 'a novel with a purely artistic purpose'. *Desperate Remedies*, because it demanded so much technical skill, created that sense of a purely artistic purpose. Hardy could bring to novel writing the love of technique that he had learnt through studying poetry two or three years earlier and aesthetic distance promised to restrain the fury of *The Poor Man and the Lady*. The genre's delight in poise would have reminded him of Swinburne – the famous swimmer – and reawakened his allegiance to Swinburne's style, its classicism balancing its erotic force.

And as with Swinburne, focusing attention on artistry alone made for a different kind of rebellion. Through their style, sensation novels gave the impression of having gone beyond indignation and protest. Likewise, the world's usually moralizing judgement of the end product could be made irrelevant because the writer would remain unperturbed. Writing *Desperate Remedies* allowed Hardy to float, 'rising and falling with the tide'; he could be observant of the world's ways, alerted to their corruption and yet untouched – an aesthete, neither angered nor deterred.

It was a seductive prospect. And it helped to calm some of his social fears. In *Desperate Remedies* the upper classes are neither homogeneous nor respectable. Members of the elite show ordinary weaknesses and consequently the social order is less of a bugbear than it had been in *The Poor Man and the Lady*. Macmillan's feeling that Hardy had treated the aristocracy unfairly before may have contributed to this. Secondly, social mobility is now possible, where in the first novel it was resolutely obstructed. In *Desperate Remedies*, if you are lucky, you can always get ahead. Often all you need do to be accepted as an aristocrat is to dress up like one. Most people, whatever their origins, can perform the role of a wealthy lady or gentleman. And, at the end, this is what the hero and heroine do. Though by no means to the manner born, they become lord and lady of the manor. They gain that identity. This reward – this happy ending – hints that identity itself may be something you acquire or put on. In this novel, people do not have integrity; they reveal themselves to be flexible personalities who adapt to circumstance.

Hardy was doing just the same, as he fell in with Weymouth people and left Bockhampton behind. The shift was exciting and the ease with which he made it may have troubled him. Life now appeared full of possibilities, if one were open enough – passive enough – to accept them. Yet if he could so readily change, there must be doubts over the person he essentially was – even questions as to whether he was essentially any one person. The stance of *Desperate Remedies* was helpful here once again because becoming a self-conscious artist provided Hardy with a role and an identity. It created for him a form of self that could accommodate variety, unpredictability, and an ironic relation to accepted certainties, including belief in a self.

It is no surprise then that *Desperate Remedies* was a highly artful book, sensational and full of quotations. Critics have tended to dislike this latter quality, accusing the book of being over-literary and heavy-handed. All the echoes of other writers have been taken to prove that Hardy had a chip on his shoulder about his lack of a university education and compensated by displaying too showily what learning he had acquired. This critical judgement arises out of (and tends to disregard) the critics' own desire to display superior learning – a superior knowledge of when and where it's appropriate to reveal your literary education. The judgement keeps Hardy in his place, as a provincial, autodidact novelist who would have benefited from going to Oxbridge. The book and its allusions strike me as more controlled than that.

Hardy calls his leading man Aeneas, for example, and makes him a devious, manipulative murderer, the opposite of Virgil's morally scrupulous and conflicted figure. Similarly, his heroine and his villainess are both named Cytherea, one of the names of the goddess Venus. The ageing, vindictive woman at the centre of the plot looks like a ghastly parody of Venus and Hardy's Aeneas seems to parody Virgil's. Hardy's names (and his quotations too) are a means of looking askance at and even toying with the classics – the writings he had been prevented from studying properly. Because of his ignorance of them, he had been denied access to the Church, the higher professions, and the educated classes. A year before, this unjust treatment had still enraged him; now it seemed he could view it almost with disdain. Even so, for all of this self-assurance, relaxation and sense of purpose, Hardy did pay a price.

*

The plot of *Desperate Remedies* articulates his sense of reawakened possibilities as Weymouth reminded him of everything about London that had been exciting and desirable. It inspired him to believe once again that there was more to life than a provincial architecture practice and that writing was the means for him to attain it. Writing could offer him a way to establish himself and through writing he could make himself eligible to women from a higher social class. Furthermore, the new, urbane style he was adopting in his new novel implied a change of heart. At Bockhampton, he had been fiercely loyal to home, indignant and idealistic, romantic and devoted. More isolated in Weymouth, he became more self-sufficient too; writing became less an opportunity to release pent-up emotions and more a process that helped create a self. You could not write a sensation novel on behalf of anyone or in defence of a downtrodden community. The style was more self-referential than that and less idealistic.

Because of this self-involvement, Hardy's excitement about living in Weymouth began to be tainted by a muddled sense that he and Tryphena were drawing apart. Undoubtedly, when Hardy moved there, the couple would have found it more difficult to meet up, even though the distances involved were tiny by modern standards. Tryphena remained in Puddletown – a village without a railway – and had been a pupil–teacher there since 1866. Such a post normally lasted for three years, to be followed by teacher training at a college far away – in Salisbury, perhaps, where Hardy's sisters trained, or even in London. Tryphena was, therefore, expecting to leave Dorset early in 1870 and, meanwhile, her duties took up nearly all her time – she was not even at her mother's bedside when she died in November 1868. With the pair living apart and both working, meetings cannot have been frequent and Tryphena's departure put pressure on the relationship at just the wrong moment.

As far as Hardy was concerned, Weymouth's glamour confirmed Tryphena's simplicity while mixing with people closer to him in age meant that Hardy noticed her youthfulness more. Certainly, glamour remained a double-edged quality for Hardy. Weymouth was always on the brink of appearing corrupt to him, given his prim reflexes along with the scholarly, dutiful and moralistic sides to his character so that Tryphena, quietly living and working in the countryside, could represent its opposite. She could perpetuate, like his sister Mary, an image of the pure and the 'believed-in'. As Hardy's home receded from him, however, the virginal seemed more and more like the unsophisticated and at the same time, Tryphena became linked in his mind with feelings of claustrophobia. *Desperate Remedies* tended to emphasize the pressurizing qualities of village life, the atmosphere they produced of inquisitiveness and entrapment. Weymouth's freedom brought that out by contrast and Tryphena suffered by association.

Essentially, Hardy started to judge her more. He looked at her with London eyes and she seemed far less special than before. Now she appeared 'but one | Of the common crowd'.

> She seemed but a sample
> Of earth's poor average kind,
> Lit up by no ample
> Enrichments of mien or mind.

These lines are from 'At Waking', a poem written in Weymouth in 1869. It is an anguished piece, as powerful as anything Hardy had written before, in which he confronts the bleak experience of waking up from a dream to find everything prosaic and plain. He was to have the same experience again, many times. On this occasion, it is love that becomes illusory and Tryphena does seem to be secretly referred to.

In his much later poem, 'Thoughts of Phena', Hardy referred to her as his 'lost prize'. 'At Waking' ends, defiantly loyal to the woman:

> Off: it is not true;
> For it cannot be
> That the prize I drew
> Is a blank to me![13]

'Prize' again. These are not, of course, the only two occasions when Hardy uses that word but, nonetheless, it seems a telling conjunction. And, miserably, in autumn 1869, it *was* true, try as Hardy might to deny it and hold on to his relationship with Tryphena. She was becoming 'a blank' to him – not just valueless and not wicked or deceitful (there's no sense of Hardy's being jilted here); instead Tryphena has somehow become meaningless to him, empty and ungraspable. Try as he might, resist it as he might, nothing could halt the dream's decline.

Other poems from this period – such as 'The Dawn after the Dance' and 'In the Vaulted Way' – are variants on the same essential situation, confirming that Hardy went through some change of heart, which he could scarcely account for himself, still less explain satisfactorily to anyone else. 'At Waking' is closest in feeling, however, to the desolation expressed in his earlier poem 'Neutral Tones', and out of these experiences Hardy later wrote with extraordinary insight about the way that love could mysteriously disappear – how lovers could be abandoned by love itself. As a novelist, he became painfully alert to the suffering of women, such as Fanny Robin, for instance, who had been abandoned and to that extent, it *is* true to say (as Lois Deacon claimed, for different reasons) that Hardy's whole life and work were marked by his affair with Tryphena. Likewise, the end of this romance – his almost involuntary ending of it – enabled Hardy to see something of himself in capricious, fickle men like Sergeant Troy or in somebody like Angel Clare – a man who first idealizes an ordinary, local girl and then dismisses her. Angel misjudges Tess's simplicity in the same way that Hardy had misjudged Tryphena, making her into an image of perfection and then, inevitably, being disappointed by her. Tryphena had not been either ideal or commonplace; she had been an individual in her own right and Hardy had ignored that simple truth. It was what he came most to regret about his treatment of her.

11

With magic in my eyes

IN JANUARY 1870, Tryphena left Puddletown for London, where she began to attend Stockwell College (on the southern outskirts of the city) to train as a teacher. Soon afterwards, in February, Hardy left Weymouth and returned to Bockhampton. He worked hard at home on his first draft of *Desperate Remedies* and on 5 March he sent off a nearly complete version (lacking only the final few chapters) to Alexander Macmillan. Perhaps at this point, as they went their separate ways, Tryphena's and Hardy's love affair came to an end but it's more likely I think that, although the relationship was under strain, there was no decisive break.

It could be that Hardy felt able to go home in February precisely because Tryphena had left the district. Or his desire to finish the new novel as quickly as possible could imply persisting feelings for her because if they were still, in some way, involved with each other, they could meet much more easily when the book was done. She was in London and Hardy's visits to publishers would give them the chance to see one another. Meeting there, away from family scrutiny, might also be more comfortable for both. And if he could remain close to Tryphena as she began to adapt to town life – and began to make the same changes Hardy had made at the same age – he might discover whether she was more than simply a delightful country girl. He might be able to decide whether or not there was any future for them.

In the midst of these struggles and uncertainties, something quite extraordinary happened.

A few weeks before the novel was finished, Crickmay wrote to Hardy asking him to travel to St Juliot in Cornwall to survey a church and plan its restoration. St Juliot stood in the Valency valley, a few miles inland from Boscastle, on the remote north Cornish coast, roughly halfway between Padstow and Bude. The incumbent of the parish, the Revd Caddell Holder, had known Hicks years before, when both were based near Bristol and, as often in these matters, personal connections were decisive. Crickmay found himself inheriting from his predecessor another church commission in an out-of-the-way place. This one was more attractive than some, however, because it extended the practice's range into hitherto uncharted territory. On the other hand, the journey to Cornwall was arduous and time-consuming. In these circumstances, Hardy was the natural person for Crickmay to ask because of his expertise in church building and because, as an unmarried man without dependants, he could travel without difficulty.

Initially, according to the *Life* anyway, Hardy was reluctant and changed his mind only after he had sent off *Desperate Remedies* (all bar the very last chapters). This version of events is dubious, not least because it exaggerates Hardy's freedom to pick and choose. Hardy would have been short of money by Eastertime, having given up his job at Christmas, and he still had no long-term source of income apart from architecture. Probably, he asked Crickmay for a stay of execution, finished the new book as best he could, and then hurried away to Cornwall. After his experience with *The Poor Man and the Lady*, he would welcome the distraction. Some drawing and surveying – some 'mechanical' work – would help him forget about Macmillan, publishers' readers and what reception they might be giving to his new book.

It is unlikely he was fully aware of how drained he was by the effort of completing the novel. One of Hardy's lifelong friends, Sir George Douglas, remarked after his death on:

> the reaction which, however temperately a man may live [. . .] must infallibly follow intense and prolonged application to imaginative work. In Hardy's case this reaction was apt to be of extreme severity.[1]

In 1870, as he took a series of trains and lastly a carriage in order to reach St Juliot, Hardy was at just this point of extreme reaction: he was exhausted, as much emotionally as intellectually, and liable to violent mood-swings between euphoria and melancholy. This state of mind had afflicted him in summer 1868, when he sent *The Poor Man and the Lady* to publishers for the first time, and produced both his imperious letters to Macmillan and his dejected ones. Even so, Hardy is unlikely to have realized when he travelled down to Cornwall how vulnerable his tiredness made him and how liable to extremes of both despair and excitement.

In this state – no longer burdened by the novel but no longer secured by it either and feeling peculiarly exposed to life – Hardy met Emma Gifford. He arrived at St Juliot vicarage late at night, after a journey that had begun at four in the morning; his knock at the door was answered not by a servant or by the lady of the house (as would be normal) but by a woman his own age. The vicar was confined to bed, suffering from an attack of gout, and he required 'the constant attention of his wife', Emma's sister, Helen; so it fell to Emma to make Hardy welcome. She had, she said, 'to receive [Hardy] alone' and felt:

> a curious uneasy embarrassment at receiving anyone, especially so
> necessary a person as the Architect.[2]

She cannot have expected someone so young or so interesting – a handsome, unmarried man with a manuscript poem peeping out of his jacket pocket. A starchy middle-aged professional would have been far more likely. And Hardy can scarcely have set out for darkest Cornwall in the expectation of meeting on the vicarage doorstep an educated, refined, rather beautiful woman, with literary interests like his own. For both of them, romance came suddenly to life before their eyes.

*

Emma came from Plymouth originally and had been living in St Juliot for a little over two years, as a companion for Helen. Caddell Holder was many years older than his wife and had grown-up children from a previous marriage. There was little prospect therefore of Helen ever raising a family of her own and the sisters, though they quarrelled frequently, remained unusually close. Helen had been seriously ill before her marriage, as a result of a carriage accident, and Emma had nursed her back to health. She had become, in fact, indispensable. Emma's age – she was, like Hardy, already nearing thirty – intensified the attachment, because by now her chances of marrying were growing slim. The geographical and social isolation of the parish seemed likely to guarantee this sad outcome, so that the love of her sister was perhaps the most Emma could hope for. She had no money of her own with which to attract suitors and was too grand for the locals. It would have been degrading for her to marry any of them.

Emma was musical and especially good at singing. Hardy's memorial to her, placed on the wall of the restored St Juliot church, recorded that she led the church music, just as Hardy's family had done. The rest of her time was spent with her sister or riding (Emma was an excellent horsewoman) or in parish-visiting. It was a monotonous, sometimes lonely life though not an unusual fate: Victorian society contained many middle-class spinsters, pious and dutiful, sometimes sentimental, who lived as companions and poor relations. Emma was not yet condemend to that role, although it beckoned, and she sustained herself with romantic hopes. Devoted to the landscapes of the Cornish coast near her present home – the towering cliffs and secluded coves, the narrow fishing villages and steep, wooded valleys, the wild seas breaking on the rocks of Pentargan Bay and the cliffs nearby – she believed also that she had inspired passionate, devoted love in several young men who lived nearby. Despite appearances, she still trusted that she would one day find her perfect partner in life. Hardy fulfilled these hopes exactly; he fitted perfectly into her romantic narrative and not least by falling in love with Emma as swiftly as she fell in love with him.

Hardy's first visit to Cornwall lasted a matter of days. He needed only to survey the church and complete some preliminary drawings. Back in Weymouth with Crickmay, he could decide what should be done – how much of the old fabric could be saved and what should be built in its place. He began his surveying the first morning after his arrival and rapidly fell into a familiar routine – he had been surveying churches off and on for ten years or more – a routine that left time for several excursions: to Boscastle, the nearest town; to Tintagel and its ruined Arthurian castle, standing a few miles along the coast; and to Beeny Cliff nearby, which rose higher than Beachy Head.

Though Hardy destroyed so many of his diaries, he chose to keep the records of this visit – honouring Emma's memory once she was dead – and this means that their movements can be followed precisely. On 9 March, he 'Drove with Mrs Holder and Miss Gifford to Boscastle', the next morning he 'Went with E. L. G. to Beeny Cliff. She on horseback'. That afternoon he walked to Boscastle, 'E. provokingly reading as she walked'. Within a day and a half, Emma changed from 'Miss Gifford' to 'E. L. G.' and then to 'E.'. On only their second outing, Helen was left at home and by the third Hardy was annoyed that Emma would not give him her exclusive attention.

The trip to Beeny Cliff was their first time together unchaperoned and, of course, Hardy never forgot it. After Emma's death, he went back. His poem 'Beeny Cliff: March 1870–March 1913' remembers where they 'laughed light-heartedly aloft on that clear-sunned March day' and Hardy hopes against hope to hear again 'the sweet things said'. The drive to Boscastle was imprinted indelibly on his mind too. When the two of them got out of the carriage, 'in dry March weather' and walked up the hill to ease the horse's burden, their climb:

> filled but a minute. But was there ever
> A time of such quality, since or before,
> In that hill's story?[3]

As he remembered it, anyway, the feeling between them developed instantaneously.

Hardy visited again in August and stayed much longer. He and Emma again travelled 'to the various picturesque points on the wild and rugged coast near the rectory'. They read together, sketched and 'Walked under a sky | Of blue with a leaf-wove awning of green, | In the burn of August to paint the scene'. Some of the sketches survive: of Emma by Hardy and Hardy by Emma, little portraits that could serve in place of photographs. They went on a picnic together too: 'placed our basket of fruit and wine | By the runlet's rim, where we sat to dine'. During that summer, the first powerful attraction between them deepened into love. There was by then 'a vague understanding between the pair', Hardy later stated – one that was firm enough for Hardy to tell Horace Moule about, even if no one else.[4]

From the beginning, they wrote frequently, though none of the correspondence survives (beyond two fragments Hardy copied into notebooks). In 1871 and 1872, Hardy visited Cornwall whenever he could: in May 1871, in October, in August 1872, and around Christmas and New Year 1872–3. The couple met up for a holiday in Bath in June 1873 and that year Hardy again spent Christmas in Cornwall. There may have been other meetings. Hardy was still living in Dorset for much of this time and could travel up to London fairly easily. Emma had relatives in London and in her memoirs she mentions visiting them. The couple could even have arranged a rendezvous in the capital and told nobody. Hardy is probably remembering some such event in his poem 'The Change', written much later. Its opening stanzas describe the couple's first week together in March 1870 and then move to a railway station in London. There at some unspecified time Hardy awaits Emma 'In a tedious trampling crowd' where 'the twanging of iron wheels gave out the signal that she was come'. Emma was 'Half scared by scene so strange' but speaks ardently to him: 'O Love, I am here; I am with you!'[5] Meetings such as these could have taken place very rarely, nevertheless. Cornwall was so far away and Emma enjoyed only limited freedom of movement.

Periods of enforced separation between courting couples were not uncommon at the time, when travel was difficult and conventions strict; nonetheless, it was painful for them, and troubling. Hardy's financial circumstances and the differences of class between his and her families meant that there was no certainty of their ever marrying; doubt was hanging over them all the time, accompanied for Hardy by a sense of having to make himself worthy of her and intensified for Emma by her knowledge that the biological clock was ticking. Meanwhile, during their times apart, Emma was exiled in Cornwall, with only her married sister and elderly brother-in-law for company, while Hardy was either marooned in Dorset (with relatives who did not like the sound of this new girlfriend) or struggling to make a living in London. He wrote in a poem from 1871 of 'the grey gaunt days dividing us in twain', the 'slow blank months'. During these expanses of time, he complained, 'So harshly has expectance been imposed | On my long need'.

In another poem, 'Love the Monopolist', begun the same year, Hardy reveals some of the anxiety that went with their separation. The poem's young lover tells his beloved to 'eye | All neighbour scenes as so much blankness | Till I again am by'. He tells her to ignore autumn's beauties – 'Ripe corn, and apples red, | Read as things barren and distasteful | While we are separated!' – and his jealousy disappears only at the close.

> When I come back uncloak your gloom,
>   And let in lovely day;
> Then the long dark as of the tomb
>   Can well be thrust away

This is, from its subtitle, a 'Young Lover's Reverie', and its closing lines sound too neat, almost as if Hardy is retrospectively making fun of youthful ardour; it's nearly a parody of that young man's, long since vanished, confidence. This does not make it any the less autobiographical even so. The woman is described in the poem as 'An airy slim blue form', just like Emma elsewhere in Hardy's poetry – the woman dressed in 'the original air-blue gown' of his famous elegy 'The Voice'. The passionate speaker of 'Love the Monopolist' does represent Hardy himself, as he was around 1871 – possessive of Emma and, at the same time, possessed by her, possessed by his feelings for her.[6]

Later in life, Hardy wanted always to present himself as detached and philosophical, and as generally 'impassive' in his approach to experience. Emma is the one usually accused of being jealous and highly strung. His poems, however, written at the time they first met, make him appear quite as obsessive and as almost violently committed to her. This strength of feeling did not diminish over the following months and years, even though the two of them met little more than twice a year. Certainly, if Hardy's feelings had changed, he could have left Emma behind and she would have had no means of redress. Moreover, judging from his earlier love affairs, Hardy was liable to grow disillusioned with women. The odd thing is, really, that this relationship did not peter out as all the others had done. Hardy's feelings did not change and, in 1874, the couple were finally married.

*

It is tempting to think that the relationship lasted precisely because of the distance between them and biographers have often viewed it as fundamentally an imaginary love affair: Emma found in Hardy someone who could rescue her from spinsterhood and isolation, while Hardy found in Emma an image of refinement and purity conjoined; she was to him another Lady Julia, lying this time possibly within his reach. These fictional images of each other survived, so it is assumed, because the couple lived apart so long; when marriage brought them into contact with the real, difficult person beneath the imaginary ideal, their fantasized love evaporated.

Hardy's family began this view of the marriage. Latterly, Kate and Mary would tell visitors that Hardy had fallen in love with an image in his own mind, with someone who bore no relation to the actual Emma. They had their own reasons for stating this – for believing it, even – and certainly Emma did alter drastically in later life. Still, it does not quite ring true. Nor do the stories that Emma (with Helen's and Caddell Holder's connivance) set out to entrap Hardy, whether by making him feel he had committed himself and so must do the honourable thing or, more graphically, by pretending that Emma was pregnant. For one thing, Hardy would have been very difficult to capture from such a distance.

He would have felt remorse, no doubt, if he had ended the relationship, but he could and would have done so if his feelings had changed or someone else had entered his life. And there's no evidence of Emma's either becoming pregnant or pretending that she was. The story is entirely speculative, drawn illegitimately from Hardy's fiction, and it runs up against the problem of Hardy's sexual repression. At this stage, he still felt a considerable investment in chastity and his later novels' advocacy of sexual freedom arises in part out of his reaction against this earlier point of view. In the early 1870s, even had Emma been willing (like Arabella in *Jude*) to ensnare Hardy sexually, he would have been wary. She would have risked disappointing his ideal view of her and so of driving him away.

What held them together was companionship – a feeling of having shared pursuits and shared goals. Emma recalled their times together early on as collaborative.

> The rarity of the visits made them highly delightful to both; we talked much of plots, possible scenes, tales, and poetry and of his own work.

She mentions too that she 'copied a good deal of man[u]script which went to-and-fro by post' and 'was very proud and happy doing this'. Hardy confirms this in the *Life*:

> during the autumn of this year 1870 there were passing between him and Miss Gifford chapters of the story [*Desperate Remedies*] for her to make a fair copy of, the original MS having been interlined and altered, so that it may have suffered, he thought, in the eyes of a publisher's reader by being difficult to read.

He says too that he 'kept up a regular correspondence' with her and 'sent her books'. It later became a terrible bone of contention with them how far Emma had helped with the composition of Hardy's novels. She claimed at times that she had virtually written them while he tried to cut her contribution (small as it often was) out of the record entirely. It's all the more noticeable that he mentions her involvement at this stage.[7]

None of his previous girlfriends had been able to offer him anything comparable in the way of help and encouragement. Even Tryphena, who was the best educated, had not been particularly interested in literature. She could not be the confidante that Emma became. Neither could she support his ambitions by bolstering his confidence and, in

March 1870, Hardy needed precisely this kind of support. He was fretful after working hard to complete a second novel in the space of nine months soon after his first had been rejected. He had published nothing else beyond a couple of light-hearted pieces and he was risking his future as an architect by spending so much time trying to get ahead as a writer. Last of all, he was getting older. Three months after meeting Emma, Hardy was thirty. Of his literary heroes, Keats had died aged twenty-five and Shelley aged twenty-nine. Swinburne had been nationally famous by the time he was Hardy's present age – undergraduates had marched through the streets of Cambridge declaiming his poems at the tops of their voices. Hardy was beginning to wonder whether it was already too late for him, and whether he should perhaps resign his youthful hopes of artistic glory.

Three days in Cornwall – he had arrived late on 7 March and left again at dawn on 11 March – did not establish their relationship on this footing, of course, and it was only after Hardy's much longer, second visit in August that Emma began actively to help him. In the interim, Hardy was rudderless much of the time, uniquely for him and bafflingly.

Desperate Remedies, though he claimed to have completed it before going to Cornwall, was not properly finished until the autumn but while he revised it, Hardy did not fill his time with architecture as you might expect. Blomfield and others offered him work when he returned to the capital late in the spring, but he showed little interest in taking it up. He seems instead to have felt strangely at a loss. The poem, self-deprecatingly entitled 'Ditty', which he wrote at the time and inscribed with Emma's initials, registers the curious mixture of excitement and disorientation Hardy was feeling, as he recognized his commitment to Emma and the fact that the merest accident had brought them together. 'Devotion droops her glance | To recall | What bond-servants of Chance | We are all.'[8]

One further reason for hesitancy was, oddly enough, his making a breakthrough with his writing. When he first came back from Cornwall, he resumed full-time work at Crickmay's office and moved once again into lodgings in Weymouth. These were the obvious things to do. Within a few weeks (on 5 April), Macmillan wrote rejecting *Desperate Remedies* but, undeterred, Hardy sent the book off again at once, though not to Chapman & Hall, his previous second choice. Instead, he sent it to Tinsley's, a more downmarket publishing house, known for its sensation fiction. He would still have resented perhaps the way that Chapman &

1. Hardy's birthplace at Higher Bockhampton, Dorset, photographed c.1900.

2. Hardy's mother, Jemima Hardy (1813–1904), photographed in 1876 by W. Pouncy, a Dorchester photographer.

3. Hardy's father, Thomas Hardy (1811–1892), photographed in 1877, also by Pouncy.

4. Hardy aged eighteen or nineteen, while he was working for the architect John Hicks in Dorchester.

5. Horace Moule (1832–1873), Hardy's closest friend as a young man.

6. Tryphena Sparks (1850–91), one of Hardy's first cousins on his mother's side, with whom he was probably in love before his marriage.

7. Hardy's designs for a townhouse made in 1861 though never built. Notice the enormous scale of the rooms.

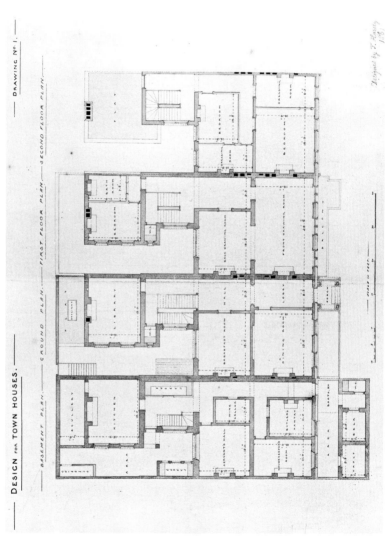

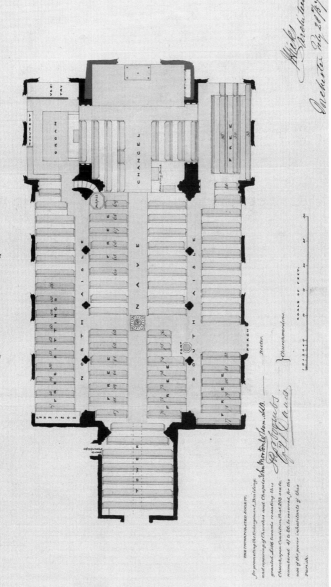

8. Groundplan of St Peter's, Dorchester, drawn by Hardy in 1856.

9. Hardy's sketch from the window of his lodgings at 16 Westbourne Park Villas, drawn in 1866.

View from my window
16. W. P. V.
June 22-66.
¼ past 8 in evening.

10. Hardy's watercolour, *The Playground of TH's childhood*, painted around 1871.

11. Emma Lavinia
Gifford (1840–1912),
the woman Hardy fell
in love with, from an oil
painting of c.1870.

12. Hardy in around 1870, as he would
have looked when he first met Emma.

13. Hardy's map, drawn for the 1912 'Wessex Edition'. A slightly simpler version of the same essential design had appeared in his first collected edition in 1895–6.

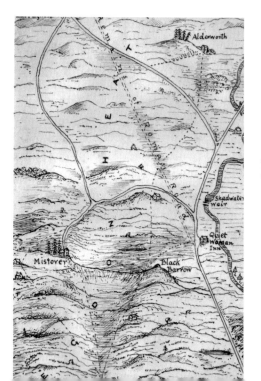

14. Hardy's sketch-map for *The Return of the Native*; an engraved version was printed in the first and second editions (1878 and 1880) but then discarded.

Hall had dealt with him over the first novel and he did not want to risk either Meredith's interference again or the firm's dithering. Anyway, he always wanted to succeed on his own terms, if possible, and had no desire to become a Meredith product.

The strategy worked. At the beginning of May, Tinsley wrote back accepting the novel and offering the same terms that Chapman & Hall had suggested for *The Poor Man and the Lady*, with Hardy once again having to pay a guarantee against loss. Despite this, the minute he heard the news, Hardy gave up his job at Crickmay's, left Weymouth and moved to London. He wrote later that he went reluctantly, 'for he had left his heart in Cornwall'9 but, all the same, as early as the middle of May, he was set up in lodgings in 23 Montpelier Street, off the Brompton Road in Knightsbridge. Montpelier Street lay within easy reach of the South Kensington museums, which Hardy had always enjoyed visiting when in London. The wide expanses of Hyde Park were nearby too and, as at Westbourne Park Villas, he was living close to both the centre and the outskirts of London. It was a cultured and relatively quiet part of town – an ideal place perhaps to finish a book.

That may have been a more arduous process than he was later willing to admit. Hardy was, instinctively, a detailed reviser of his work and remained so throughout his writing career, though he tended to say little about it.10 He consistently downplayed the care he took with his novels, out of a desire to present them as potboilers mostly and nothing like as important to him as his poetry. Naturally, at the time, the knowledge that *Desperate Remedies* was really going to be published would have made him more determined than ever to get everything *exactly* right. We've seen, at any rate, that his revisions were so extensive that they made the original manuscript illegible and Emma had to transcribe a fair copy later in the year. That much rewriting could have taken him the summer and then been disguised afterwards, leading to this appearance of a hiatus. There is, though, more to it than that.

It's hard to imagine that meeting Emma did not leave him unsettled. He had promised both Emma and Crickmay that he would revisit Cornwall in August; until then he was in a kind of limbo – not suspicious or sceptical about his own depth of feeling, perhaps but uncertain nonetheless about where it could possibly lead. Could he seriously intend to marry this genteel woman, living hundreds of miles away? It was presumably a vain hope, given what he had learnt about the class system over the last fifteen years and so it must be foolish to go on with the affair – destructive to do so and self-destructive too. Meanwhile, living in Knightsbridge, he had easy access to Tryphena in Stockwell, if ever he wanted to visit her. Her teacher training college lay only three or four miles away, the other side of the river, and his choosing that part of London hints that their relationship had not yet come entirely to an end. Hardy looked round the Stockwell college years later after Tryphena's death and was evidently moved by it. Nothing is known, however, about any possible meetings during 1870. If he did not meet her, though, while living so close by, he would be decisively rejecting her and, inwardly at least, making a commitment to Emma. After a three days' acquaintance, that decision seemed almost impossible to comprehend, let alone justify.

This was the central uncertainty that left a gap in Hardy's life and he filled it by reviving old male friendships and starting new ones. Moule was around in London, his company making 'the time [. . .] pleasant enough', as Hardy later recorded. When he was not meeting him, Hardy did a little work for quite a famous architect, Raphael Brandon (1817–77), and became fond of him. These two friends – one nearly sixty, the other approaching forty – became connected forever in Hardy's mind and were linked to this desultory period in his life, this time hovering on the brink. Both men were worthy and yet, in the end, unsuccessful. It seemed that both, for some accidental or unidentifiable reason, some intrinsic quality of character, could not make the compromises necessary for success in a mediocre world. Moule was still at the point where he had been a decade before; his prospects and mental health were, if anything, getting worse. Brandon was a comparable type, at a later stage.

He and his brother, Joshua, had published an *Analysis of Gothic Architecture* in 1847, the year of his brother's death and it became an important work at the time (Hardy consulted it and copied some drawings from it into his architectural notebook). Raphael followed up its success with two further works based on research he had undertaken with his brother: *Parish Churches* (1848) and *Open Timber Roofs of the Middle Ages* (1849). All three presented English styles of medieval architecture with remarkable accuracy and detail, in authoritative studies that were also groundbreaking, because they revealed to the Victorian public the fine qualities of buildings that were either little known or taken for granted.[11] They were less concerned to declare dogmatically what the best version of Gothic was than to reveal the variety of its English forms.

Raphael gained considerable respect and even fame through these books at mid century; ever since, however, he had struggled to make his way. His preference for English Gothic, rather than French, remained unfashionable; he came to seem too scholarly and even his literary talents were held against him because, despite endless learned disputes in the pages of Gothic-revival journals, such as *The Ecclesiologist*, most working architects were impatient with too artistic an approach to the business of building. Partly because of his diminishing success, partly because of personal tragedy – his wife and only child both predeceased him – and partly as a result of his temperament, Brandon became a depressive, who ended, in 1877, by killing himself.

Initially, in summer 1870, Brandon's unworldly style – his indolence and expert knowledge – attracted Hardy, as if he were coming across a kindred spirit amidst the philistinism of London architecture. Brandon's offices in St Clement's Inn, in 'an old-world out-of-the-way corner', became a retreat from the turmoil of the city and perhaps from the uncertainties of Hardy's situation too. A serious love affair brought with it the onerous responsibility of making yourself rich enough to marry the girl. Emma in Cornwall – in the 'vague romantic land of "Lyonnesse"' – meant Hardy's involving himself thoroughly in the hard-headed, altogether unromantic world of London. He saw the need for that and was pursuing it too as he rewrote *Desperate Remedies*, trying his best to ensure the book would do well.

Hardy could afford to be a little bit more confident too because he had his book now. Tinsley's was not as prestigious as Macmillan, but it was a start. Hardy had made the transition from writer to author, amateur to professional, and could now go forward along that path. Doors were still open to him in the architectural world too. Even the increasingly well-respected Blomfield was welcoming him and so he could envisage a more settled future, either writing full-time or able to combine his two professions. Despite all this, part of Hardy flinched from the prospect and retreated into Brandon's obstinately *un*professional backwater. Part of him wanted to be back in Weymouth, swimming in the bay and idly floating with the tide. He looked back on that previous summer as an idyll, as the last phase of youth, and he tried, for the first few months in London, to live that sort of life once more.

As the summer went on, however, events challenged his affectionate, perhaps rose-tinted view of Brandon and of Moule too. The Franco-Prussian War broke out and became at once 'a cause of much excitement to Brandon', who bought all the papers and read them avidly, including the 'leading articles on the war', many of which were written by Moule. To some extent, Hardy went with the flow of the moment too, growing 'as excited' as Brandon and visiting the Waterloo veterans in the Royal Hospital, Chelsea. All the same, what he found there disappointed him: 'tattered banners mended with netting and [. . .] the old asthmatic and crippled men'. Although later, Hardy grew fascinated by the Napoleonic Wars, at this point he felt like a bemused onlooker. It made him despondent to see his older, supposedly wiser friends getting caught up in things that could not really touch them. It seemed proof that beneath Moule's intellectual self-assurance and Brandon's soft-spoken, gentlemanly modesty lay a consuming desire for heroism. Unfulfilled ambitions and thwarted hopes must be producing this impassioned involvement in a foreign war.

Hardy's friend Edmund Gosse observed something similar happening to his father during the Crimean War of the mid 1850s. Philip Gosse was a fundamentalist Christian convinced of the nearness of Christ's Second Coming and of the emptiness of all worldly things. Nonetheless, during the war, he became a fervent, even jingoistic patriot.[12] Perhaps (as happened again later in life), the 1870 war spurred Hardy into action too, because his friends' behaviour began to look like a warning. In Brandon's quaint backwater, in Moule's delicacy and high-mindedness there was no true contentment or peace. That was to be found, if anywhere, in action and decision, in taking the plunge.[13]

It was with these feelings in his mind that Hardy 'severed his temporary connection with Brandon' on 8 August and returned to Cornwall, where this time he stayed for a matter of weeks: 'the visit was a most happy one', Hardy later wrote, not least because his hopes were fulfilled and not his fears. He went half-expecting to be disappointed – to find that the beauty he had glimpsed in Emma was illusory, a fantasy of his own projected onto her. Instead, he found her more beautiful than ever, 'metamorphosed into a young lady in summer blue, which suited her complexion far better'. And as that doubt was resolved, so his energies returned. From Cornwall, he went back to Dorset not London and continued *Desperate Remedies* there. Emma helped him; she galvanized her future husband, encouraged him, and provided the companionship he had hardly ever found before. She did so, moreover, in the knowledge that authorship was not the quickest way for Hardy to make the money they could marry on. It offered a far more uncertain future for them than architecture did. Despite this, she had no hesitation proving, if proof were needed, that she was not aiming to entrap him. Nevertheless, how, and how quickly, they could hope to marry were questions all the more on Hardy's mind after his second visit. They had reached some sort of understanding by now so Hardy needed to consider very carefully what path to take for the future. Architecture and literature were thrown into conflict once again.

*

Desperate Remedies was published in three volumes in March 1871. Hardy had had to supply Tinsley with £75 (out of his total savings of £123). So £75 was a lot of money to Hardy, and roughly what he could expect to earn in six months from his architectural work. Initially, the book received good reviews, from the *Athenaeum* and the *Morning Post*; then on 22 April, the *Spectator* attacked it, calling it 'a desperate remedy for an emaciated purse'. Hardy read the piece near his home, sitting 'on a stile leading to the ewe-leaze he had to cross on his way home to Bockhampton'. It left him utterly desolate: 'The bitterness of that moment was never forgotten; at the time he wished that he were dead'. Moule made kindly efforts to reassure him, first in a letter telling Hardy to take no notice, later in a favourable review of his own, but the damage was done. Hardy was by nature too sensitive to brush aside such criticism and, from this moment, was doubly fearful of what reviewers might decide to say; meanwhile, sales of the book suffered. In May, Hardy visited Cornwall again, escaping the literary fray; as soon as he left, however, signs of the book's failure assaulted him again. On his way home, he saw remaindered copies on a railway station bookstall; whatever his friends said, whatever encouragement and comfort Emma offered, Hardy was convinced that the *Spectator* had ruined his chances.

The rest of the year became a struggle. Hardy spent it back in Dorset, working for Crickmay once again, and writing another novel: *Under the Greenwood Tree*. John Morley, when he read *The Poor Man and the Lady* in 1868, had admired the rustic scenes in the book, and reviewers of *Desperate Remedies*, whatever else they might dislike, praised its rural elements, what the *Spectator* called the 'unusual and very happy facility in catching & fixing phases of peasant life'. Hardy now used these as his starting point for a short, pastoral book, quite unlike *Desperate Remedies* in terms of plot and quite unlike *The Poor Man and the Lady* in terms of tone: that novel's inflammatory radicalism disappeared completely; so did the arch artfulness of *Desperate Remedies*. Hardy presented instead a country world that was as charming and sweet as any city-dweller could wish, hoping that this portrayal would appeal to a conservative publisher, such as Macmillan.

Hardy sent the manuscript to them on 7 August, calling it 'entirely a story of rural life'. He abandoned *Desperate Remedies*' focus on plot and suspense – 'I thought it just as well not to dabble in plot again at present', he told Malcolm Macmillan (Alexander's eldest son) on 17 August. Instead, he made his home territory marketable and unthreatening, concluding from the reviews that 'a pastoral story would be the *safest* venture' (Hardy's italics). Even if this approach involved the suppression of some of his true feelings about country life, that restriction was no worse than the unhelpful plot constraints that *Desperate Remedies* had placed upon him. So, at least, he now believed.

Malcolm Macmillan wrote back to Hardy encouragingly on 11 September, enclosing a copy of John Morley's report: 'so favourable a judgment', Macmillan wrote, 'makes us feel strongly inclined to avail ourselves of your offer'. There then followed a by-now familiar pause. Hardy wrote again a month later, mentioning a recent good review of *Desperate Remedies* (written by Moule, though Hardy didn't point that out). A few days later, Alexander Macmillan, the head of the firm, wrote back, not decisively rejecting the book but dashing Hardy's hopes all the same:

> I think the public will find the tale very slight and rather unexciting.
> The first 50 or 60 pages too are really rather tedious [. . . .]
> It is difficult to know in what form it would best attract the public [. . . .] We could not venture on it now.

His only concession was to express an interest in considering the book again after Christmas, 'if you should not arrange otherwise before the spring'.[14] And back came the manuscript.

This rejection, following a hopeful first response, followed exactly the pattern of Hardy's experience with *The Poor Man and the Lady*. It was especially disappointing because Moule's review had at the same time revived his hopes for *Desperate Remedies*. He had written to Tinsley on 3 October from Cornwall, asking whether the good reviews could be advertised and even whether Hardy himself might fund extra publicity. Tinsley's answer (sent on the 23 October, three days after Hardy heard from Alexander Macmillan) brought him further bad news. Sales of

Desperate Remedies remained poor and that further narrowed Hardy's options. He would have been hoping that the first novel might at least break even, allowing him to recoup his initial outlay and giving him the funds to finance a further novel, if the publishers again required a guarantee against loss. Tinsley's answer seemed to scotch that plan; if he lost his £75, or even a fair proportion of it only, he would not have the means to take the same path again.

A few days after Tinsley's reply arrived, Hardy left St Juliot and went back home to Bockhampton. Away from Emma, he lost heart: he had tried three sorts of novel, one had been rejected, another seemed doomed to failure, the third, though it had appeared, had been slated and remaindered. There seemed little point and little financial sense in sending out *Under the Greenwood Tree* anywhere else, and still less good in going on with any future writing projects. Quite apart from the anguish the experience was causing him, it damaged Emma's chances of happiness and, Hardy felt, it took advantage of her generosity of spirit. He announced to Emma (in a letter that does not survive) his intention of giving up writing altogether and, as he says in the *Life*, he threw aside the manuscript of *Under the Greenwood Tree*:

> into a box with his old poems, being quite sick of all such, and began to think about other ways and means.[15]

The only realistic alternative open to him – his only other way or means – was to knuckle down to architecture and make a decent living at it.
Emma, to her credit, tried to make him change his mind.

> [W]ith that rapid instinct which serves women in such good stead, and may almost be called preternatural vision, [she] wrote back instantly her desire that he should adhere to authorship, which she felt sure would be his true vocation.

Hardy, however, would not be persuaded.

> From the very fact that she wished thus, and set herself aside altogether – architecture being obviously the quick way to an income for marrying on – he was impelled to consider her interests more than his own.

All this is written much later – a fact that Hardy highlights at this point in the *Life*, drawing attention to the absence of contemporary letters 'between the couple [. . .] to show the fluctuation of their minds on this vital matter'. He coyly implies once again a significant silence, a secret never to be told, and then goes on, rather brutally:

> But what happened was that Hardy applied himself to architectural work during the winter of 1871–72 more steadily than he had ever done in his life before.[16]

This account, as far as it goes, does ring true: Emma ardently supported Hardy's ambitions as a writer throughout their courtship and early married life; his vocation was an essential part of the romance he had brought into her life; and it defined both her role and their relationship. Hardy, on the other hand, had a powerful sense of his responsibility to her as an avowed lover – a sense that he ought to be making himself eligible, regardless of her willingness to sacrifice her hopes. Naturally, though, he gave up his ambitions as a writer resentfully; he was angry about Macmillan's contradictoriness over *Under the Greenwood Tree* and about Tinsley's unwillingness to support *Desperate Remedies*. He moved back to Weymouth once more, so as to be available to Crickmay full-time, and sent curt business letters to Tinsley, asking for details of the account between them. Steady application to architecture was his overriding priority now and over the next year or so – his last year as an architect – Hardy achieved a good deal.

*

Crickmay's practice was expanding partly because, with Hardy's help, he had consolidated Hicks's legacy. Hicks, for example, had built a single-cell chapel at Stour Row in 1867. In 1870, Crickmay restored Buckhorn Weston church, just a few miles away, on the other side of Blackmore Vale, and in 1872–3, he erected the large, new church of St Margaret, Margaret Marsh, within two miles of Stour Row. Likewise, between 1869 and 1874, he was building the sizeable new church of St Mary Magdalene, West Milton, in the parish of Powerstock. Hicks had first begun to establish himself in Dorset through his work in the parish and Crickmay was evidently thought to be a competent successor. Similarly, the firm's work on Turnworth parish church led to their restoring the nearby church of All Saints in Stoke Wake (completed 1872), a village on the slopes of Bulbarrow, just a few miles from Turnworth.

Crickmay was more used himself to domestic and commercial architecture: he had done work for Weymouth College in the mid 1860s, for instance, and for Weymouth Royal Infirmary in 1870. In 1871, he was designing an eye infirmary in Weymouth, private houses at Green-hill, Weymouth, and extending several local schools. For the first time, in the winter of 1871–2, Hardy began to contribute to this sort of work, integrating himself much more fully into the practice than before. More emphatically, during spring 1872, Hardy followed through on this change of direction. He returned to London, rented lodgings at Cellbridge Place, back near Westbourne Park Villas, and began working for the architect T. Roger Smith. Following the 1870 Education Act, new board schools were being built in and around London (as elsewhere in the country), creating a lot of work for architects. Hardy took this opportunity to extend his repertoire beyond church restoration and he began to cultivate contacts too: he spent 'some occasional evenings in preparing drawings for Blomfield, with whom Hardy was in frequent and friendly touch'. He seemed to have consigned the dreamy, artistic young man of 1870 resolutely to the past and was turning himself instead into a rounded, professional architect. That spring, he could not even spare the time to travel down to Cornwall and attend the opening of the restored church in St Juliot. His architectural notebook, similarly, exchanged Gothic details (reminiscent of Brandon's published works) for drawings of hinges, window designs, and the outlines of drainage systems.

After Hardy became such a great novelist, his architectural work was often either forgotten or seen as simply hack work. That was all the easier because the buildings he was involved in were modest, for the most part rather plain and Hardy later belittled his own accomplishments. As a young man, clearly, Hardy was much more invested in his buildings than he liked to pretend when looking back. He was also more characterful and inventive in his architecture than has usually been allowed. Within the churches he helped to build, there are curious signs of a distinctive emphasis, almost a style. As you would expect, this was developed most in the work he did for Hicks and then Crickmay between 1868 and 1872, after his return from London.

In St Juliot, rebuilt to Hardy's designs between August 1870 and April 1872, as everywhere else, Hardy and Crickmay stuck to Hicks's habit of preserving the original fabric as far as possible. Rather than replace medieval windows, for instance, they would repair and some-times relocate them. Appropriate local building materials were used: flint and rubble at St John's, Hinton Martell, near Wimborne (restored 1869), and stone at West Lulworth (restored the same year). Hicks had also paid careful attention to internal carving and Hardy/Crickmay took that concern forward. The carved capitals of the pillars in Turnworth are only the best-known example; West Lulworth has carved capitals too and so does Hinton Martell, where the nave arch meets the chancel. Hinton Martell, like Turnworth, also has decorated corbels, supporting the roofbeams. These show the Evangelists, just as in Hicks's church, St Martin's, Shipton Gorge (1861–2), where St Matthew and the other Gospel writers look down soberly on the congregation. In St Mary Magdalene, North Poorton (1861–2) – one of the tiniest churches Hicks built – carved corbels again appear, this time showing angels and foliage springing out of the low walls.

Within the plainness and restraint of these buildings, then, there is unusually good workmanship and detailing. Moreover, where Hardy is involved, there are hints of dynamic energy, sometimes willing to overload a building. At Turnworth, for example, where the capitals are most elaborate, and undoubtedly Hardy's, the pillars are strangely short. The roof is low and the arches deep, so that the top of the pillar, where it meets the arch, is at little more than head-height from the ground. The carving is made both very present to the congregation and disproportionate to the space. Similarly, the most highly decorated of Hicks's interiors date from 1861–2, the period when Hardy was most actively engaged in the designs. By contrast, Stour Row, designed in the mid 1860s when Hardy was in London, though it does have carvings on the pillars supporting the chancel arch, keeps these modest and generic; they do not disturb the simple and conventional lines of the whole.

Hardy tended towards larger gestures elsewhere: St John's, Athelhampton (built by Hicks in 1861–2) has, for example, an exaggeratedly large porch. The building is little more than a chapel, without tower or aisles, but it has, comparatively speaking, a huge porch attached to the south wall, the effect increased by the small size of the door set within it. It's an impressive feature – impressive but startling. Similarly, the porch of West Lulworth church is outsized and emphatic. It forms the ground floor of the church tower and the tower is broad for its height, its breadth stressed by angled buttresses. Consequently, the door seems to be taking you into a bigger building than the one it is attached to.

There's disproportion here but a dramatic impulse is at work too, a wish to be glorious and impressive amidst restricting circumstances. The grandiose little gestures seem to defy the rule, which dictates that only the large can be grand, and only the wealthy can be elaborate. It is a baroque impulse, too, perhaps; one that uses imbalance to create tension and interest, even if that is at the expense of order and proportion with the comforts that these bring. If this is Hardy's signature as an architect, his buildings resemble his novels, with their conscious exaggerations and their desire to magnify tiny things in order to declare the grandeur of obscure places. Hardy claimed repeatedly that fiction required a disproportioning of realities if it was to succeed and his often-neglected work building and restoring churches hints at exactly the same conviction. His churches suggest how much he was giving up by becoming a writer and how fundamentally similar instincts governed his work in both careers.

~ 12 ~

That there should have come a change

DESPITE HIS determination to be practical, Hardy remained inwardly volatile. According to the *Life*, he was diverted from his chosen career path simply by two accidental meetings: one with Moule, and a second with Tinsley, his publisher. Both asked Hardy what he had been writing, and both expressed regret when he told them he 'had thrown up authorship for good and all'. Moule was especially worried that architectural drawing would damage Hardy's eyesight (as it had for a time in 1867); without writing, he would then have nothing to fall back on. Tinsley, apparently an avuncular, humorous man, had no such feelings of bleak foreboding; he was straightforwardly concerned with Hardy as an author with potential and insisted that he send him the manuscript of *Under the Greenwood Tree*, even though Hardy claimed not to know where it was and to have no interest in it.

These passages from the *Life* do sound embroidered, though the meetings themselves probably did take place. Even the smallest encouragement would have weakened Hardy's resolve, since his giving up authorship was something neither he nor Emma actually wanted. The most important source of encouragement, however, is not mentioned in the *Life* and was more mundane – money. In early March, Hardy heard in detail how things stood with regard to *Desperate Remedies* and on 19 March he received a cheque for £60. The book had cost him only £15 in the end and so was not a complete flop; if he liked, he could repeat the experiment. From this moment on, things moved rather fast: on 8 April, Hardy wrote to Tinsley, sending him *Under the Greenwood Tree* and saying that he had 'decided to proceed [. . .] as rapidly as possible' with a new, three-volume novel.

Tinsley accepted *Under the Greenwood Tree* immediately and proofs started to arrive in early May; the novel appeared before the end of the month. Reviews were favourable – as kind and gentle as the story itself

– and on the back of its modest success, Tinsley asked for a further novel, this one to be serialized in his magazine as well as published as a book. Magazine publication was an important element in the marketing of mid and late nineteenth-century fiction. Though censorship was tighter in magazines because they were aimed at a family audience, the financial rewards were considerable. By the end of July, Hardy and Tinsley had reached an agreement (after a bit of bargaining, in which Hardy showed a new degree of cunning). Hardy was to receive £200 for the combined rights – that is, for the serial and the first edition, which would appear as the serial concluded – and the serial itself would begin as early as September.

So rather suddenly in Hardy's early thirties, he was making real money as a writer and could now reasonably hope to make more as his career progressed. Authorship could certainly become lucrative: George Eliot's historical novel *Romola* (1863) had earned an extraordinary amount, £7000 for its serialization rights alone. Though this was exceptional, the £600 Elizabeth Gaskell received for *North and South* (1855) was not. Even if Hardy never achieved George Eliot's stature, he could begin to expect to make a good living from books. Literature, which had hovered near for so long, tantalizing Hardy with its unattainable possibilities, now seemed to be promising an income, and one substantial enough to enable him to support a wife.

Just as importantly, he began to see his writing career in this light. As late as April, he had been willing to sell Tinsley the copyright of *Under the Greenwood Tree*, and accepted a mere £30 for it, far from the 'liberal terms' he said he was aiming for. Now, he was reading books on the laws of copyright, negotiating his fee with a publisher and signing a contract only when his future possession of copyright was guaranteed.[1] This was far better practice commercially – George Eliot never sold her copyrights – not least because it looked forward to possible reprints and new editions. It also reveals a rapid transformation in Hardy's approach, as if he grabbed the chance of a literary career as soon as it became even remotely possible.

The *Life* stresses Tinsley's jovial encouragement and Moule's solicitude. Moule's support was certainly constant. His reviews of *Desperate Remedies* and *Under the Greenwood Tree* were both prominent and favourable. However cruelly he had discouraged Hardy about university, he believed in him as a writer. Tinsley, too, thought Hardy was worth investing in and, crucially, so Emma did as well. Hardy turned to her each time he was rebuffed by publishers. She discussed his work with him, more sympathetically than anyone else could, and offered practical assistance. In the *Life*, partly because of its rigid gender roles and partly for other reasons, Emma's active help tends to be played down. She is cast in the role of muse and inspiration but this image isn't fair either to her intelligence or her usefulness. Nonetheless, it praises her as a partner in Hardy's ambitions. He even compares their relationship to that between Robert Browning and his wife Elizabeth Barrett Browning – a famously romantic and harmonious union between two successful writers.

At the time, Hardy responded to his sudden success by proposing marriage. He signed an agreement with Tinsley at the end of July and immediately afterwards travelled down to Cornwall, leaving his employer, Roger Smith, somewhat in the lurch. He stayed in St Juliot for the whole of August and, towards the end of the visit, approached John Gifford, asking him for his daughter's hand in marriage. Gifford turned him down, rather indignantly by all accounts and Hardy and Emma would not marry for another two years. It's surprising in some ways that they ever did.

Perhaps John Gifford's refusal proved Emma right. Writing was not only Hardy's true vocation, it was his way up the social ladder. Steady application to architecture, supplemented by a minor degree of success as a writer, would not be enough to overcome John Gifford's class prejudice. And it was through writing and the great triumph of *Far From the Madding Crowd* that Hardy finally made himself good enough for his wife's family. The first episode of that novel appeared in the well-known *Cornhill Magazine* in January 1874; its reception showed that Emma's 'desire of a literary course for Hardy was in a fair way of being justified' and nine months later they were married.[2]

This is apparently a happy conclusion for Emma, a vindication of her faith in Hardy, a victory over her family and testimony to her devotion. She could take some credit for helping him succeed. Her contribution also appeared to ensure her at least a supportive role in Hardy's working life from then on. Sadly, although some kinds of collaboration remained a source of pleasure and stability in their life together, this two years' delay caused lasting problems and can be blamed for a great deal of what later went wrong.

*

The relationship had not been entirely easy from the beginning. Emma had written in October 1870 that: 'I take him (the reserved man) as I do the Bible; find out what I can, compare one text with another, & believe the rest in a lump of simple faith.' Hardy copied out the remark, struck by its generosity and lack of fear. He had seen even earlier, almost as soon as they met, that with lovers, 'in spite of her orders to him to fetch & carry, of his devotion & her rule, he is in essence master'. And, in December 1870, he commented:

> An experience, hard-won, by an inferior mind, often prompts a remark of profundity & originality not to be surpassed by one of her superior calibre.

'One of her superior calibre', 'he is in essence master': both sentences have the same absolute conclusion. They suggest a tone in Hardy's disposition that would prove formidable to someone like Emma.

A few months later, in February 1871, Hardy observed more tartly, 'Nothing so interesting to a woman as herself'.[3] He was himself by nature highly self-contained and his writing was bound to increase that tendency. He was also liable to be impatient with other people – with their interest in themselves, which was not interesting to others, and certainly not to him. So he was amazed – alarmed even, sometimes awestruck – when he came up against Emma's willingness to accept him totally and without question. She seemed to be devoted to him, in a literal, quasi-religious sense. That made him cherish her all the more – she offered him the unconditional love he had never properly received from his parents. It also made him sense a thrill of power. He had had mentors before but never disciples; his friends had always tended to be older than he was, role models and surrogate parents. Emma was his own age, his social superior and yet she bowed down before him – out of love.

This was astonishing to him (though in some respects it was only the conventional stance for a woman in love); moreover, as Hardy himself began to realize, it was dangerous too. Emma's submission invited Hardy to adopt the domineering, masterful role of the Victorian husband. Hardy didn't know whether it was a role he might benefit by accepting (through gaining greater confidence and poise) or whether it might bring out his authoritarian streak – the forcefulness and self-will he had inherited from his mother and tried to keep in check. Hardy had little choice, however, during 1873 and 1874, because unless he pushed himself forward, he would never make it as a writer and never be able to marry the woman he loved. It was as simple as that and the forcefulness required probably began to appear morally right.

John Gifford's refusal, in other words, put Hardy on his mettle. Gifford demanded a better showing from the young man and that was exactly what Hardy provided. All well and good. The father could feel that he had only been acting responsibly by insisting that this obscure young fellow prove himself. He had taught the naive lovers a valuable lesson in how the world worked. The downside, though, was Hardy's private feelings because naturally enough, Gifford's rejection made him feel resentful and aggressive. He was insulted by the request that he show himself worthy – it confirmed all his suspicions about so-called 'superior' people – and he was put out as well, because the Giffords' snobbish opposition would not make it any easier for him to persuade his own family that Emma was a suitable wife. Since, however, the demand had been made, he would set about fulfilling it. His pride in himself and his origins demanded no less. As always when confronted, Hardy responded with far greater determination than people expected. They looked at him and saw an intense, unworldly, callow youth – lovesick and malleable. They found after a while that they were dealing with an unyielding personality, who would not be gainsaid – someone who was, on his territory, dictatorial.

There's no reason to think that Hardy blamed Emma for what her father had done or that the relationship itself was soured. Indeed, they seem to have pulled together. John Gifford might care about social differences but, for Hardy and Emma, at least at this stage, they cannot have mattered. Later in her life, Emma became fixated on her genteel background and berated both Hardy and his relatives for their commonness. In the 1870s, though, she happily threw in her lot with a comparatively poor man, whose prospects were a gamble. She must have been a more liberal-minded person in her thirties than she became later and, probably, overcoming family opposition gave them common cause. Furthermore, it was now settled between them that Hardy would take the riskier path, the one that Emma had always encouraged. During the autumn of 1872, T. Roger Smith wrote to Hardy asking him to return to London and carry on the board school work they had begun over the summer. They had been successful in six of the competitions and Smith was now willing to offer Hardy an improved salary. Hardy decisively refused the offer and did not prevaricate any longer: he announced to Smith that he was now a novelist. He would never work as an architect again.

*

John Gifford's rejection of him as a future son-in-law was also liberating, however, because it gave Hardy a reason outside himself for pursuing his ambitions. Emma's need for a financially secure husband had encouraged him to work hard as an never architect the previous winter. Now, it seemed that he would never escape from the prison of his class until he had achieved some greater degree of worldly success. This challenge meant he could write single-mindedly, unworried about the ultimate value of his efforts. He was able, as he put it, 'to stifle his constitutional tendency to care for life only as an emotion and not as a scientific game'.[4]

Hardy's letters to his publisher Tinsley had often been notably practical earlier. He requested statements of account; he negotiated over copyright; he suggested reviewers; during the summer of 1872, he even supplied the names of people who might be interested in subscribing to Tinsley's magazine on the strength of its serializing *A Pair of Blue Eyes*. All this was no more than common sense; even so, Hardy's business acumen is unexpected, especially given the image of himself that he created later. Life as an architect helped him to treat authorship as just another trade. Nonetheless, during 1873, a further change takes place – a change in tone, manner and self-presentation.

Late in 1872, when Hardy was back in Dorset writing, Leslie Stephen (1832–1904), editor of the famous *Cornhill Magazine*, wrote to him asking for a novel. This became *Far From the Madding Crowd* and it made Hardy's name. Hardy accepted the offer (an offer he could scarcely refuse) though with the rider that he was already committed to *A Pair of Blue Eyes* and must ask Stephen to wait. Even by accepting the offer on these terms, though, he was certain to offend Tinsley, who would quite reasonably have expected first refusal on a new book.

Hardy wrote the final chapters of *A Pair of Blue Eyes* in March 1873; when the novel appeared in volume form in May, it was altered in several places from the serial version – alterations that Hardy must have made in the interim. So it can only have been after this point that he began work on *Far From the Madding Crowd*; in September, he sent what he had written so far to Stephen and they agreed terms late in October. The first number of the story was planned for as early as the third week in December; and subsequent instalments would be monthly from then on so Hardy had committed himself to another tough schedule.

Tinsley knew nothing about these arrangements until they had been finalized, and he protested. Hardy was forced to write some sort of explanation to him on 30 November 1873.

> Dear Sir
>
> I am truly sorry that you consider there was a breach of courtesy in my not mentioning about the Cornhill to you sooner. I write to assure you that it was quite unintentional, & to express a hope that you may see there was nothing unusual in it, under the circumstances. Should this event, or any other, tend to put an end to the good feeling which has hitherto existed between us, I for my part shall sincerely regret it –
>
> > Very truly yours
> > Thomas Hardy[5]

The tone is exaggeratedly polite. This may be the product of embarrassment – something that would also account for the letter's amnesia about the recent past because Hardy had, in fact, been relying on Tinsley completely for several years. Nobody else had taken on his books, despite Hardy's repeated attempts to interest other publishers. It was Tinsley who had brought out the three novels that gave Hardy a foothold as a writer and led to this better offer from Stephen.

Tinsley's own version of events, published many years later, emphasizes Hardy's dependence on him, as you might expect. Tinsley points out that he made no money from his various attempts to launch the unknown author. He tried three editions of *Under the Greenwood Tree* (in two volumes, one volume and in paperback), but none of them would sell; he even 'tried Mr Hardy's third novel [. . .] but it was by far the weakest of the three'. And there is a note of pique in his references to what happened over *Far From the Madding Crowd*:

> Of course, Mr Hardy was quite within his rights in not offering me [the] book, although I had paid him rather a large sum of money for *A Pair of Blue Eyes*.

Even at the time, Tinsley became frosty. When a year or so later, in the winter of 1874–5, Hardy asked to buy back the copyright of *Under the Greenwood Tree*, Tinsley demanded £300 for it, ten times what he had paid in 1872. The sum was so large as to amount to a refusal, 'an intimation', as Hardy wrote, 'that you do not wish to part with it'.[6]

Hardy's overformal and rather lofty manner with Tinsley continued as *Far From the Madding Crowd* succeeded. By the time he asked to buy back the copyright, the novel had appeared in volume form (on 23 November 1874) and glowing reviews were just coming out. Hardy had been asked 'for another story' by George Smith (1824–1901), founder of the publishing firm Smith, Elder, which published the *Cornhill*. Smith wanted it to 'begin as soon as possible in 1875'. Hardy had gained an American publisher as well. *Under the Greenwood Tree* and *A Pair of Blue Eyes* were published in the US in 1873, *Desperate Remedies* and *Far From the Madding Crowd* the following year. These were heady days and perhaps Hardy was swept off his feet.

Certainly it was premature of him to tell Tinsley that he wanted *Under the Greenwood Tree* back in his own hands because 'A collected edition of my other stories will probably be published, & I should like to add this one to it, if possible.'

Tinsley's refusal pushed Hardy onto the defensive and he offered a practical explanation of his grandiose plans.

My idea was that [the novel] might be made more of if issued as one of a set than standing alone, people being in the habit of buying books that form a series.

At this time – January 1875 – Hardy had published four novels, and only the most recent of them had been even remotely successful in commercial terms so 'A collected edition' was scarcely likely yet. It was unrealistic (vainglorious really) to speak of the prospect blandly as a probability.[7]

Collected editions were not usually attempted until late in a writer's career; that was true of Dickens and Thackeray, for instance, and Hardy had the same experience. His 'Wessex Edition' appeared in 1895–6, when he was in his mid fifties and had spent almost a quarter century publishing novels. Earlier in a writer's career, novels, if issued by the same publisher, would often be presented in the same format, so as gradually to form a series. This was the case, for instance, with Elizabeth Gaskell whose works came out in Germany in a 'Collected Edition' between 1849 and 1857 – in other words as they were published – and something comparable happened to Hardy with Smith, Elder during the 1870s and 1880s. Even so, the impression he gave to Tinsley was a bit presumptuous, as Tinsley knew better than anyone.

Hardy seems to have absorbed this and, second time around, he spoke of his ambition with a more deflated, practical air, sounding almost apologetic. It was not arrogance, he suggests, only good business practice to think of his books a 'form[ing] a series'. Although the letters do show how early in his career, Hardy had in mind a sequence of novels, they also reveal the qualities of character that became established from now on. The all-conquering self-belief of the first letter slips out at an unwary moment; immediately afterwards, in the second letter, Hardy reasserts his modesty and good sense. He presents himself as altogether prosaic and down-to-earth. The second attitude comes in the wake of the first, covering its tracks, pretending that the earlier, wilder outbursts were nothing of the sort, only common sense – and that he meant no harm. Nonetheless, he had given a glimpse of his ambition and his cool, almost regal self-assurance.[8]

Leslie Stephen's offer had already bolstered Hardy's self-confidence during 1873, as he completed *A Pair of Blue Eyes* and before he had the external proof of success that came when *Far From the Madding Crowd* appeared. Throughout that year, passing remarks in Hardy's letters reveal the new self-assertiveness that came with greater self-belief. In April 1873, he wrote to Tinsley:

> I will call when I come to London, though it will not be so early in
> the season as usual. I have an idea of going abroad for a short time.

This is his first reference to 'the season', though he was often in London at that time of year. Its first appearance accompanies his first mention of foreign travel. He has 'an idea of going abroad', he says, with mannered unconcern, as if it were the most natural thing in the world. He presents himself as someone who shares the same aspirations and language as his target audience and it is as if he has only been waiting to be justified in doing so.[9] Other letters show how rapidly (and again somewhat prematurely) Hardy took on the voice of the established writer. He repeatedly sounds lofty and, when he deals with money, he becomes rigorously lucid. It is not that he was putting on airs exactly, rather he was adapting himself to the part he had to play. This was fair enough perhaps, but it did him little good in his private life.

*

You can track a similar change in the novels Hardy wrote just before and just after his marriage in September 1874 – that is to say, in *A Pair of Blue Eyes* (1872–3) and *Far From the Madding Crowd* (1874). In both of these, Hardy raises questions about the relation between love and power, and he repeatedly connects these to concerns about writing. In *A Pair of Blue Eyes*, the whole tangle is addressed with almost frightening rawness. There seems to be a real worry in the book that becoming an author can take you over – that it can destroy your sympathy for others, and for women especially.

Elfride, the novel's heroine, and her lover, the young architect Stephen Smith, are undoubtedly modelled on Hardy and Emma, even though Hardy denied the similarity all his life. The fictional romance takes place in the same scenes as the real-life love affair and, as was painfully the case with Hardy too, Stephen's humble origins enrage his lover's father. Stephen is compelled to travel abroad and make his fortune, in the hope of marrying Elfride in the end. While he's away, his friend and role model from London, Henry Knight, meets Elfride and falls in love with her too. Partly because the novel has such a clear autobiographical foundation, Knight has been equated with Horace Moule. That connection may have been somewhere in Hardy's mind when he wrote but there's no evidence at all that Moule was ever in love with Emma.

Henry Knight, like Moule, is a reviewer and magazine journalist. When they meet, he has already reviewed Elfride's anonymously published novel and treated it harshly. Although older and apparently wiser than the innocent, ineffectual young Stephen, Knight lacks first-hand emotional experience. He knows about love in theory, but

> In truth, the essayist's experience of the nature of young women was far less extensive than his abstract knowledge of them led himself and others to believe. He could pack them into sentences like a workman, but empirically was nowhere.[10]

He is cruelly demanding of Elfride whereas Stephen is seen as being too accommodating of her. Knight bullies her and then sets her quite unrealistic standards of behaviour, dragging from her the confession that she has been loved – and kissed! – by other men before him. This is a contrast that Hardy returns to. The men in his novels are very often either firm to the point of harshness or gentle to the point of weakness. They treat women either too indulgently or too severely. How, Hardy asks, can a man fulfil a woman's (supposedly) natural desire to be led, without imposing on her and crushing her?

In this respect above all, Knight is not simply Horace Moule and represents instead something that Hardy was afraid of in himself. *A Pair of Blue Eyes* places Hardy's younger, passive, gentle self (Stephen Smith) against the strict authority of the grown-up literary man (Henry Knight). The contrast is energized by Hardy's concern with the effect on himself and on Emma of his years spent, like Knight, in solitary, ambitious reading and writing. As Knight bullies Elfride (into misery and illness), he begins to sound like the speaker of Hardy's poem 'Love the Monopolist'. The successful man of letters in Hardy, the London Hardy, is risking his happiness by demanding so much control over and so much obedience from the woman he loves.

Far From the Madding Crowd stands at a greater distance from Hardy's own experience than the earlier book so that its heroine, Bathsheba Everdene, is much less like Emma Hardy than Elfride is and the hero, Gabriel Oak, cannot be seen as a self-portrait. Even so, in one respect at least, the book does come near Hardy's experience because from Gabriel's point of view, the story is concerned with being made to wait.

At the beginning, Gabriel is trying to go up in the world. He is a shepherd who aspires to running his own business. When all his sheep are accidentally killed, this hope evaporates. At the same time, Bathsheba inherits money and rises socially out of his reach, destroying hopes of ever marrying her. By the closing chapters, however, Gabriel has regained Bathsheba, they marry and seem on the threshold of a happy future. Gabriel wins her back, despite the social divide, not by climbing up the social scale himself but instead through his heroic ordinariness, by sticking to what he knows. In several episodes of their turbulent courtship, Bathsheba is forced to recognize Gabriel's innate worth and he proves to her how much she needs him. When the sheep on Bathsheba's farm fall ill, for instance, and only Gabriel can save them, he refuses to help until she asks him respectfully.

> He says he shall not come unless you request him to come civilly in
> a proper manner, as becomes any person begging a favour.[11]

Gabriel insists that the woman from a superior class who has previously been his employer must learn to treat him as an equal. Though he still loves her, love will not make him submit to her. In fact, the opposite happens: love demands civility.

Similarly at the end, when Gabriel and Bathsheba are finally united, the couple are seen as 'tried friends' for whom 'pretty phrases and warm attentions' are no longer necessary. They feel 'substantial affection' for each other because they have common interests.

> This good-fellowship – *camaraderie*, usually occurring through simi-
> larity of pursuits, is unfortunately seldom superadded to love
> between the sexes, because they associate not in their labours but
> in their pleasures merely. Where however happy circumstance
> permits it development the compounded feeling proves itself to be
> the only love which is strong as death – that love which many
> waters cannot quench, nor the floods drown, beside which the
> passion usually called by the name is evanescent as steam.[12]

Gabriel has become Bathsheba's social equal again (as he was at the novel's opening) and their marriage is based on a partnership of equals. As Hardy and Emma had done and would do again, the two 'associate [. . .] in their labours' and not 'in their pleasures merely'.

When Emma read this happy ending she was a recently married woman and in many ways it would have been reassuring to her. Hardy seemed to be declaring how much he still appreciated both her and her collaborative help. His words sounded like a hymn of praise to the life of mutual cooperation she thought they were embarking on. On the other hand, the paragraph points a severe moral for a couple just beginning married life. Passion has been outgrown and replaced by friendship; romance has been put aside in favour of 'hard prosaic reality'.

Likewise, although the story affirms Gabriel's constancy, it punishes Bathsheba. She has been taught harsh lessons – in maturity and in respect for others – and she has been obliged to accept the equality that Gabriel demands. There is more forcefulness in the novel than is usually recognized. The ending is hopeful, certainly, more so than many of Hardy's later novels, but its muted optimism is shadowed by the memory of Gabriel's strength of will; his determination not only to win Bathsheba's love but to command her respect. Hardy's resentment at John Gifford's refusal of him lingers in Gabriel's sense of grievance and Bathsheba must compensate. Likewise, Emma must take Hardy as he is and never look down on him as her father had done.

Gabriel is no monster though and no fool, whereas, in many ways, Henry Knight was both. *A Pair of Blue Eyes* worries constantly about Henry Knight's desire for power over Elfride. That desire ends by destroying her and from the beginning it ruins her peace of mind. The older, more literary man is much less attractive, finally, than the younger, gentler more innocent one. By 1874, some of these worries have disappeared. Gabriel can assert control without becoming cruelly obsessive like Henry Knight (or Boldwood, the more sympathetic and pitiful of his rivals in the later novel). He can be strong and determined without losing the reader's sympathy.

The novel seems to have resolved the problem posed by the one before. It is convinced that masculine firmness can be reconciled with kindness, and control joined with love. Although Hardy's confidence about Gabriel reflected his confidence about himself and the progress of his life at this time, the more tentative world of *A Pair of Blue Eyes* would have been a kinder one. You might prefer to think of Emma as Elfride, devotedly adored by Stephen Smith, instead of seeing an image of her in Bathsheba, dominated by Gabriel, with her caprice and wilfulness enchained. Emma might have preferred it too.

Bathsheba's destiny seems to show what Emma and Hardy must give up in order to go forward together – the impossible, romantic self-sufficiency of their Cornish days. They never went back to St Juliot and its environs during all the many years of their marriage, which seems inexplicable, given the magic of their shared times there, and cruel too, if it was Hardy's stubborn refusal to travel that stopped Emma from returning. Naturally, though, as the marriage soured, neither of them would have been keen to revisit the places where so many hopes were raised, and so many painful consequences unwittingly begun.

As far as Hardy was concerned, however, St Juliot now simply lay outside the real world. It epitomized a form of love that would not endure the business of living. If he based his marriage on the pattern of *A Pair of Blue Eyes*, he would make himself either ridiculous (Smith) or cruel (Knight). In either case, he would be dodging maturity. He began to move instead towards a relationship in which passion came second to friendship and romance gave way to practical considerations; passionate, self-sacrificial love was turned into something more mundane and in some ways more difficult – 'the mutual help and comfort that the one ought to have of the other both in prosperity and adversity', as the Anglican marriage service puts it.

*

This change between the novels is more a change of tone than a change of heart. Emma had always helped Hardy and she had been attractive to him partly for that reason. There was nothing new in that respect in the conclusion Hardy wrote for *Far From the Madding Crowd*. Emma was willing too that Hardy should leave his Stephen Smith persona behind; she had always thought him far older than he actually was, Hardy later said. She had had the quite natural expectation, given her time and background, that the man in a love affair should be an authority figure, and a kind of father. Similarly, as a child of her time, she could easily separate marriage from romance: the one was frequently a matter of convenience and even expediency, the other could be confined to a realm of fantasy and dreamy consolation. There was nothing, in other words, intrinsically odd about what Hardy was saying in the novels, nothing that in itself Emma could or would object to. Nevertheless, something was hardening in him and she began to sense the change.

In July 1874, only three months before they married, she wrote to him, rather plaintively:

> My work, unlike your work of writing, does not occupy my true mind much ... Your novel seems sometimes like a child all your own & none of me.

What else she may have written, we do not know because these are the only extracts Hardy kept from their correspondence at this time. Perhaps he chose them for what it turned out they foreshadowed, the childlessness that afflicted their marriage, and for what they conceded: that Emma's engagement in her work was less profound than Hardy's was in his. This was a point she disputed, often acrimoniously, in their later life. Whatever Hardy's later reasons for keeping these sentences, they undoubtedly betray Emma's perplexity that summer, while Hardy was in London, 'having to write against time' and finishing the last few chapters of his novel 'at a gallop'.[13] She sounds as if she already feared he was outgrowing her.

Naturally enough, during 1873 and 1874, as he grew so busy, Hardy had less opportunity to visit Cornwall. He was either in London or Dorset and Emma could not leave St Juliot for any length of time. There was no question of her living with him in Bockhampton or sharing his lodgings in London and staying somewhere else was tricky – hotels were expensive and Emma's relatives could be prevailed upon only so much. They enjoyed one holiday together in Bath in June 1873, chaperoned by Emma's friend, Miss d'Arville, and Hardy spent Christmas that year in Cornwall. Meanwhile, however, Hardy was becoming less of a recluse. From January 1874 onwards, as *Far From the Madding Crowd* was serialized and caused something of a stir, he began to be taken up. Other writers, journalists, London hostesses and literary societies all wanted to meet him, and he started to correspond with well-born ladies who had an interest in fine writing. It's clear that he appreciated the attention.

Early in 1874, when Hardy was living at home, he was invited to dine by Emily Geneviève Smith, wife of the rector of West Stafford, Reginald Southwell Smith, the son of a baronet. West Stafford was only two miles away from Bockhampton, across the Frome valley. Hardy's father had carried out repairs to the manor house there, Stafford House, during the 1850s, and to Woodsford Castle nearby as well. Hardy had met the family before: he had been a guest in the West Stafford house in 1866, though the visit had not, apparently, been a success. The squire's butler, Mr Pole, had refused to wait upon Hardy because of his supposed ill-treatment of Pole's daughter, Cassie. This time the occasion was much more harmonious.

Geneviève Smith (Hardy used her second name though she was also called by her first) was in her late fifties, an accomplished and educated woman, and known as the 'Dorset Nightingale' because of her talent for singing Her husband had been given the living of West Stafford by his old schoolfriend, John Floyer, who was the squire. Floyer was an MP too and married to the daughter of another MP, George Bankes (1788–1856), judge-advocate-general in 1852. The Smiths were, there-fore, well-connected people, better established socially than the Moules were, though in many respects the two families were rather similar. Theirs was also a more feminine household than Fordington vicarage could ever be, crowded as that was with seven sons and overseen by a powerful father. The Smiths had a family of twelve children, girls and boys, though many of them like their father suffered from tuberculosis and several died young.[14]

This welcome from the Smiths was, within the strictly demarcated hierarchy of country society, a key moment of recognition for Hardy. On the strength of his books alone, he was being invited into upper middle-class society. Though his father and grandfather had mixed with such people, they had always done so as privileged servants and employees. Similarly, with the Moules, Hardy had been welcomed as Horace's protégé. Now, his status was subtly different. Certainly, he remained inferior socially – that was accepted by all; nonetheless, as a literary success he was his own man. Over the years, he established himself as a friend of the family, becoming particularly close to Reginald

Bosworth Smith (1839–1908), known as Bosworth. They were close in age and in interests; Hardy had read Bosworth's book, *Mohammed and Mohammedism* in London in 1870 and later when Bosworth was a schoolmaster at Harrow, Hardy and Emma visited him there. The Smiths' younger daughters, Evangeline, Eva for short, and Blanche, both wrote stories and Evangeline became one of the first aspiring writers to ask Hardy for criticism and advice.

Hardy accepted Geneviève's invitation in 1874 (as was pretty much required of him) and then genuinely enjoyed the evening at the West Stafford rectory. In his letter of thanks, he wrote:

> I cannot help thinking of your varied knowledge & experiences, which are of that precise kind that has a peculiar charm for all engaged in such pursuits as mine – & for myself doubly, from having been denied by circumstances until very lately the society of educated womankind, which teaches men what cannot be acquired from books, and is indeed the only antidote to that bearishness which one gets into who lives much alone.[15]

These sentences are handled with conscious elegance – with an over-elaborateness that seems effortful. Though Hardy wants to sound socially and intellectually self-assured, he reveals the desire more than the reality, and that desire encourages him to discount Emma: he had known her for nearly four years, so it was not really true to say that 'until very lately' he had been denied 'the society of educated womankind', not at least in letters. Had Emma ever read this sentence she would have thought it at least ungenerous if not disloyal.

Those things would not make it dishonest, of course. It is all too likely that living alone did produce 'bearishness' in Hardy – discontent and a persistent sense of unspecific grievance. In its effects on Emma, the result was a vicious circle: Hardy's busyness excluded her, and as they saw and heard less of each other, Hardy grew self-absorbed and drove her away more. The work which used to draw them together was now 'none of me', 'a child all *your* own', intruding where one of their own should be. Meanwhile, and perhaps more worryingly, Emma was now a latecomer to Hardy's expanding social life.

It is notable, too, how firmly Hardy asserts his identity as a writer; writing to Geneviève, he speaks of himself as someone 'engaged in such pursuits as [his]'. To some degree, this boldness is required by the social situation – when Hardy is being acknowledged as a writer, he has to describe himself in the terms in which he is being perceived. He had, however, thoroughly internalized that idea of himself. The pattern of his life, too, was beginning to be set, even down to the annual London visit and the occasional trips abroad. By mid 1874, he could feel that over the previous two years he had established himself in a career and done so almost in isolation from his future wife. Tinsley and Leslie Stephen had given him a chance; Moule had advised; Emma had inspired. Hardy could and did feel, nevertheless, that it had been his achievement alone.

Maybe Emma's ability to assist Hardy would always have been short-lived. She was a less talented writer than he was; her mind and sensibility were much more straightforwardly conservative and she remained all her life a devout Christian so differences would have been certain to emerge. Hardy, though, had been forced to make his way as a writer while living apart from her and barely seeing her. Writing had ceased to be a shared arena. Now, it was an occupation (neither a hobby nor a romantic dream) and it was his occupation, not hers or theirs. Though he might sometimes, generously, open up his literary world to her, he also reserved the right to withdraw into it. Increasingly, too, writing became his social life as well as his private business. If he was going to require Emma's assistance, it was more likely to be as a hostess than as a writing partner. If she herself were to succeed as a writer, she would have to emerge from out of his shadow. Had they married in 1872 and lived together while Hardy made his first breakthrough as a writer – had she been alongside him, encouraging, reassuring, and helping him, relieving his bearish moods – their future together might possibly have been rather different.

*

Almost inevitably, as Hardy's horizons broadened and his self-confidence improved, he met a woman who rivalled Emma. Geneviève Smith, in her late fifties, may have been an attractive mother figure, as Lady Julia had been before, and Hardy's feelings about such women were always eroticized. Her musical gifts would have appealed to him too; however, she was no threat to Emma. The danger came from Helen Paterson (1848–1926), who was illustrating *Far From the Madding Crowd* as it came out month by month in the *Cornhill*. Hardy had been helping by providing the publishers with sketches of 'smockfrocks, gaiters, sheep-crooks [. . .] and some other out-of-the-way things that might have to be shown', and in May he wrote directly to Helen, giving details of the story that he thought might be relevant.

Helen Paterson was a gifted painter and Hardy admired her illustrations greatly. When he moved back to London during summer 1874, they met on several occasions and years later Hardy said he regretted that they had not married. He told Edmund Gosse in 1906 that 'but for a stupid blunder of God Almighty' they would indeed have done so. It is hard to know how seriously to take this remark. In the same letter, Hardy willingly confessed that he had 'never thought of [Helen] for the last 20 years'. On the other hand, he included 'The Opportunity: (For H.P.)' in his collection, *Late Lyrics and Earlier* (1922):

> Had we mused a little space
>   At that critical date in the Maytime,
> One life had been ours, one place,
>   Perhaps, till our long cold claytime.[16]

Given these later sentiments, it seems, certainly, 'an odd coincidence', as Hardy put it in the *Life*, that Helen 'had also thought fit to marry' during that summer. Her wedding to William Allingham, the diarist and friend of Tennyson, took place in August 1874, a few weeks before Hardy married Emma. It is therefore just possible that Hardy went ahead with his own long-delayed marriage to Emma only when Helen Paterson was no longer available.

When Hardy had lived through the long years of his ruinous marriage, this missed 'opportunity' would of course have struck him much more forcefully. At the time, as he admits, they did not even think of it. 'We parted with smallest regret', Hardy wrote in the poem, 'Strange, strange that we lived so lightly!' The summer of 1874 was a very busy and carefree period in Hardy's life, hectic, thrilling and suddenly filled with many different calls on his time. While writing hard, Hardy was also, for example, dealing with his American publisher, Henry Holt – he sent him his portrait-photograph in July – and having to clear up with Smith, Elder a misunderstanding over how his books would be handled for the American market. As tended always to be the case, professional success gave a great boost to Hardy's self-confidence; that made him flirtatious, and it was at these times of elation and excitement that he tended to fall in love. Probably, for a while anyway, he felt like that about Helen Paterson, who was beautiful and talented, and an artist like Hardy's sister. He was, nonetheless, so caught up in what he was doing, so thrilled by his first success, that he hardly noticed his feelings. Both of them were already spoken for anyway and could enjoy a harmless, permitted flirtation.

*

Beneath these changes in Hardy's sense of himself and in his relation to Emma lay something more serious still. 'Lightness' is, in fact, an odd word for Hardy to use to describe these months. *Far From the Madding Crowd* was and is an impressive achievement, with comic elements certainly. It is also, however, a much weightier novel than anything Hardy had written before. The style is ornate, and the narrator sententious. It's highly intellectual at points and even though that's not new for Hardy – *A Pair of Blue Eyes* contained all sorts of up-to-the-minute references to evolution and religious doubt – it's a more thoroughgoing piece of work than any he had produced before. In it, a whole world view is being articulated. There had been an anarchic quality to *Desperate Remedies* so that the novel feels at times like a reckless parody of itself. *Under the Greenwood Tree*, likewise, was too perfect: the idyll gave away its quaintness. *A Pair of Blue Eyes* played with genre too – it was identifiably a 'romantic novel' and simultaneously a pastiche of the form. Everything Hardy had written up to *Far From the Madding Crowd*, in other words, possesses an ironic self-awareness. That was perhaps the lasting consequence of Meredith's advising him to write in an artificial style.

Far From the Madding Crowd did not relinquish this artistic self-consciousness but the novel is no longer content simply with showing up to canny readers the limitations of conventional novels and the dangers of writing them. That was not, after all, an effect you could pursue forever; nor was it one that would sit well with the *Cornhill*, a magazine which, under Leslie Stephen's editorship, was consciously serious, and even earnest. Leslie Stephen's impact on Hardy's book was profound and his influence over Hardy lasted for the remainder of the 1870s. Although Stephen was an unusually gifted and charismatic man, who attracted disciples, nonetheless he played such an important role in Hardy's life only because Hardy's existing confidant and mentor, Horace Moule, suddenly vanished from it.

A Pair of Blue Eyes was properly finished by the end of May 1873 and, before embarking on his next book, Hardy needed to relax. Moule was passing through London at the time; they went to the theatre and, on 15 June, before Moule travelled on to Ipswich, they had dinner together. A few days later, after spending some time in London with his brother, Henry, Hardy took the train up to Cambridge, timing his visit to coincide with Moule's. Moule was now a workhouse inspector, employed by the Local Government Board, and, since the job took him around East Anglia, he used Cambridge as his base. On 20 June Hardy dined in Moule's college, Queens', walked with him along the Backs and stayed in college overnight. Next day, Moule showed him round. As Hardy wrote in his diary at the time, it was a 'never-to-be-forgotten morning'. They climbed up onto the roof of King's College Chapel, 'where we could see Ely Cathedral gleaming in the distant sunlight'.[17] Then, in the afternoon, Moule went with him to the station and Hardy returned to London by train. He was never to see his friend again.

Moule's job was a desperate comedown for someone who had grown up with such high expectations. It must also have been dispiriting work, assessing the destitute. Meanwhile, his less talented brothers were doing far better than he was. Charles was already a Fellow of Corpus Christi College. Frederick had a living near Peterborough. At least they were both nearby and able to keep an eye on him, because Horace's instability was worsening: he was more than ever prone to depression and alcohol abuse, with the erratic behaviour that inevitably followed. His family believed that his failure to fulfil his potential at Oxford 'preyed upon his mind ever afterwards'. There is also a quite credible story that Moule got a girl into trouble in Fordington sometime in the 1860s.[18] He would have been unable to marry her and the family would have needed somehow to help her out. One lurid version has it that she emigrated to Australia where their son ended up hanged as a criminal. If any or all of this actually took place, Moule's betrayal of the girl would have tormented him. He may also have been engaged during the early 1870s and been jilted sometime in 1873. By the summer of 1873, at any rate, he was subject to profound depression.

Probably Hardy noticed nothing unusual when he visited at midsummer. He was used to Moule's moods and knew of his drinking. Moule would anyway have been cheered up by seeing Hardy and could be relied upon to make a good show for his admiring friend. Three months later to the day, however, on 21 September 1873, Moule committed suicide. He was once more living in his college rooms in Queens' and once more suffering from depression. Charles was on hand to look after him and came over from Corpus Christi to keep him company. By the end of the evening they spent together, and after a long talk, Charles felt confident enough about his brother to leave him alone for the night. Soon after he left, though, Moule went into his adjoining bedroom and cut his throat. Though Charles was called at once, he arrived too late. He never forgave himself for not preventing his brother's death.

Hardy heard the news three days later. The following evening, 25 September, he visited the newly dug grave in Fordington churchyard and on 30 September he sent off to Leslie Stephen what he had so far written of the new novel. Then, for a month or more, he could do nothing. Sending off the manuscript bought him time, since there was no point in writing anything further until he heard back from his potential editor but Stephen replied quickly, and encouragingly, accepting the book on the basis of what Hardy had sent. Hardy remained immobilized, even so. He did not agree terms with Stephen for more than another month and it was only when, at the end of October, Stephen suddenly asked if the serialization could begin earlier, in January instead of March or April, that Hardy could respond more positively. By the end of November he had negotiated £400 for the serial rights and, from then on, he was committed to working extremely hard on the book.

All through October, in other words, he had written very little, and probably because he simply could not bring himself to. He was deeply shaken and traumatized by Moule's death, and his first response was to regress – to retreat back into his childhood among the ferns. He helped at his father's cider-making, for instance.

> It was the last time he ever took part in a work whose sweet smells and oozings in the crisp autumn air can never be forgotten by those who have had a hand in it.

Immersing himself in this work, he was trying to recapture the security of his father's life, its unchanging rhythms and seasonal rituals.

Hardy later planted a small orchard in the rear garden of Max Gate, just outside the back door, and the trees for it came from his home in Higher Bockhampton. Giles Winterbourne, too, the hero of *The Woodlanders*, is constantly linked to cider-making and apple trees. It was for Hardy an activity deeply imbued with his love of home and powerfully expressive of the world in which he had grown up and whose history he wanted to record. One of the long-term effects of Moule's suicide was to reinforce in Hardy the impulse to be a chronicler – to keep in memory hidden lives and neglected values. I suspect too that as he went into the orchard he remembered his dead friend.

Moreover, during October 1874, Hardy tried to make even his writing physically part of his home environment. He says that he was writing 'sometimes indoors, sometimes out'; if he had no paper with him 'he would use large dead leaves, white chips left by the wood-cutters, or pieces of stone or slate that came to hand'.[19] These are bizarre claims, and not literally true, I expect. The point of them is to make his work natural somehow, rather than willed or ambitious. This may have been especially important to Hardy at this time if, as is likely, because he feared that his success had contributed to Moule's misery. It was one thing for Moule, as a teacher and guide, to support Hardy in his efforts to write, give him good reviews and console him about the bad ones; it was quite another for Moule to see himself outstripped by his most faithful disciple. In Cambridge at midsummer, Hardy had been at a good point, on the up with his career and perhaps even unthinkingly a little brash. For Hardy to pursue his personal ambitions was almost unbearable if he thought their fulfilment had killed his closest friend. Yet it was urgent that he keep on writing. He was on the brink of success at last – after six or more years of struggle – and he could not afford to let Leslie Stephen down.

Fate seemed to have intervened and blocked his path. Emma's uncomplicated enthusiasm, her love of life, her wish for achievement, had been helpful to him over the past three years. She had rescued him in many ways from his mother's melancholy – her obdurate determination and its opposite, her depressed passivity. After Moule's death, he lost sight of that optimism; back for nearly a whole, uninterrupted year in his mother's house, and now stricken by grief, he slipped back towards Jemima's point of view – he began to share her feeling, confirmed as it was by Moule's sudden, ill-timed death, that 'a figure stands in our van with arm uplifted, to knock us back from any pleasant prospect we indulge in as probable'.[20]

That darker sense of what life can indiscriminately or malevolently inflict on people produced the more sombre tone of *Far From the Madding Crowd*. Moule's death, which had at first immobilized him, gradually changed into the single event that drove him most doggedly on. The suicide seemed the almost inevitable end-result of despondency and lassitude. Lose your hope of advancement and success (however empty those things might be) and your vitality would start to ebb away. Hardy had seen before that without ambition you could end up adrift like Raphael Brandon; now it appeared the results could be worse still.

The death altered and deepened his sympathies as well, particularly for high achievers. Henry Knight, in *A Pair of Blue Eyes*, was a fundamentally comic depiction of academic isolation and self-involvement, with the blindness to human feeling these engendered. His nearest equivalent in *Far From the Madding Crowd* is Farmer Boldwood, who enters the story only in the sections written after Moule had died. Eligible but solitary, Boldwood looks like a confirmed bachelor but when Bathsheba half-jokingly sends him a valentine, he becomes obsessed with her. Love utterly destroys his cherished self-possession, his dignity and his moral sense. He ends up shooting his rival and escapes the gallows only by pleading insanity.

Similarly, in the single poem Hardy published about Moule's death, Hardy writes about his friend's unrecognized need for love. The poem sounds very like one of Robert Browning's dramatic monologues and, as Browning sometimes does, Hardy leaves it unclear who is being spoken to. The poem is called 'Standing by the Mantelpiece' and subtitled '(H. M. M., 1873)': Moule's initials, often used by Hardy in referring to him, followed by the year of his death. Moule, speaking the poem, tells an unidentified listener that they should not be surprised about his suicidal feelings nor 'embittered' about what has happened between them.

> Since you agreed, unurged and full-advised,
> And let warmth grow without discouragement,
> Why do you bear you now as if surprised,
> When what has come was clearly consequent?[21]

Agreed about what or to what? And what is it that has come, so predictably? The poem never gives an answer to these questions. Is it a pregnancy and is the person addressed a woman, who is trying to act surprised when the consequences of 'warmth' were obvious? Or is a man being spoken to? Is it Hardy, who is being rebuked by Moule for not noticing that Moule was falling in love with him? – or for backing away when he knew or should have known how much pain it would cause?

There have been different interpretations, by both critics and biographers, and evidently Hardy wanted to leave questions hanging in the air. He had published a touching short poem, 'She at His Funeral' in *Wessex Poems*, dating it '187–', and it seems to refer to Moule's funeral. The poem is spoken in a woman's voice – perhaps the voice of Moule's lover, sent away to Australia, or perhaps Hardy's feelings masked by a female persona; perhaps both. In his copy of Tennyson's *In Memoriam*

Hardy wrote several marginal notes linking Tennyson's feelings for Arthur Hallam to Hardy's for Moule, and Tennyson's poem repeatedly expresses love for the dead Hallam.

Sexual orientation was differently understood and therefore differently experienced in the nineteenth century from the way it is now. 'Straight' and 'gay' are categories that do not apply very exactly to the range of feelings involved and the kinds of relationship that were possible. Male friendships could be profound, intense attachments, sometimes combined with erotic feelings about the male body. This sort of involvement with another man was not seen as homosexual love, however; the distinction was carefully and firmly made between the two. Homosexuality remained taboo and at the end of the century was forbidden by law. Nonetheless, in the mid century at least, 'love' for another man was accepted as something an ordinary heterosexual man might experience.

Hardy and Moule had such feelings for one another and, after his death, Hardy cherished the memory of Moule almost as if he had lost a lover. He sketched in the situation of 'Standing by the Mantelpiece' so vaguely perhaps because he sensed the new cultural situation of the early 1920s, in which homosexuality was more likely to be imputed to descriptions of male friendship. Really, though, he makes things vague because the situation itself is not what matters. The poem is more concerned to say that, whether it arises between two men or between a man and a woman, love is inevitable. Intimacy leads to attachment, as night follows day. You cannot just be friends with people; either physically or platonically, you become lovers. Whether or not Moule made a pass at Hardy when they met for the last time, Hardy came to feel that no one, himself included, had recognized Moule's perfectly natural, and entirely human need for love. In the same way, Bathsheba, like everyone else in *Far From the Madding Crowd*, had ignored the fact that Boldwood was as vulnerable to these feelings as anyone else would be. As Hardy sensed this truth, it lent his writing a new quality of compassion for the privileged and the supposedly powerful – for those, in other words, whom he had frequently condemned before.

– 13 –

Wasted were two souls in their prime

THROUGH the winter of 1873–4, writing his novel distracted Hardy from his grief and hopelessness. His family had always preferred to shut down their feelings in times of crisis – to say nothing and try to feel nothing – and Hardy's surviving notebook entries from this period reveal the same desire. They either concern natural phenomena – the noises made by a thunderstorm or the precise look of a sunset – or they record local history. Five pages of the book are devoted to 'Kenfield, the mail-coach guard from London to Dorchester' – to his life, habits, uniform and so on. Hardy was always interested in such things, but particularly when they offered him a source of stability amidst emotional pain.[1] It was an isolated existence, however, and one made lonelier by Moule's death. There was nobody else in Dorset that Hardy could confide in. And in Moule's absence, there was nobody whose advice or critical judgement he could call upon as he tried to write what was by far the most important novel in his career to date. The one person he could turn to was his editor, Leslie Stephen, and, as Hardy sent off sections of the book during the winter, Stephen began to occupy the gap that Moule had left.

When he commissioned *Far From the Madding Crowd*, Leslie Stephen had been editor of the *Cornhill* for two years; though only in his early forties, he was a dominant figure already in the London literary world. Stephen's wife was Thackeray's daughter; his friends included notable men of letters, like John Morley and George Meredith, Frederic Maitland, who later wrote Stephen's biography, and James Russell Lowell, the American poet. Stephen's eminence impressed Hardy and assisted him: when the serial of *Far From the Madding Crowd* began to prove a success, Stephen was ideally placed to help Hardy make the most of it. The London elite now opened its doors to him and he began to mix with the editors who had rejected his early poetry.

In another respect, Stephen hampered Hardy. He was peculiarly anxious about the suitability of his magazine for a family audience and elaborately cautious over anything that might possibly cause offence. In Hardy's novel, for example, Fanny Robin is pregnant with an illegitimate child when she dies. Hardy originally mentioned the fact that the two bodies were buried together, the child in its mother's arms. Stephen thought this too graphic and asked Hardy to gloss over the details. This was by no means exceptional treatment. Stephen implored another contributor to cut out a reference to the German philosopher, Schopenhauer, because 'the ordinary person, who is the general object of my dread, has never heard of Schopenhauer, but he may scent infidelity in a German name'.[2]

Stephen also suggested cuts to Hardy's manuscript, reducing its pictorial elements – the descriptions of rural life especially – and asking Hardy 'to catch the attention of the readers' by providing more action though Stephen assured Hardy, rather defensively, that he did 'not want a murder in every number'. Perhaps the *Cornhill* would have done better if he had; during the eleven years of Stephen's editorship (1871–82), its circulation halved, from 25,000 to 12,000. Still, Stephen recognized correctly that serialization demanded event. 'When the novel appears as a whole,' he reassured Hardy, the cut pages could easily be replaced.[3] Whether all this interference improved the novel can be debated but Hardy felt, looking back, that Stephen had been meddling, particularly in his more prudish objections to the book. At the time, he encountered an unprecedented degree of engagement with what he wrote. Tinsley had been by comparison slapdash; Stephen appeared personally committed to both the book and its author.

His editorial concern developed into friendship and, over the next few years, as Hardy continued to write for him, Stephen exerted a significant influence over his young author. Like Moule, Stephen had been brought up as an Evangelical Christian who doubted his faith as he grew up. In 1871, he had resigned his Fellowship in Trinity Hall, Cambridge because of his scruples about accepting the Thirty-Nine Articles of the Church of England (all dons were required to declare their orthodoxy at this period). Stephen remained uncertain, however, about what he could and did believe. He told Hardy in 1875 that 'he had "wasted" much time on systems of religion and metaphysics' and that the newest theory 'had "a staggering fascination" for him'.

Agnosticism did not produce in Stephen the moral revolt that atheism set free in Swinburne, nor the disdain for virtue felt by the aesthetes. Quite the opposite. Stephen was a severe moralist, a painfully scrupulous editor and a famous mountaineer. He was also outspoken; his *Essays on Free Thinking and Plain Speaking* (1873) practised both: they defended rational, unprejudiced inquiry and presented that defence forcefully, even aggressively. On paper at least, Stephen had some of Hazlitt's pugnacity. These qualities – physical strength, moral as well as physical courage, openness to new ideas coupled with intellectual rigour – proved that virtue could be separated from religion and Stephen always insisted that you could renounce the one without losing the other.[4]

Hardy's intellectual development was changed for good by this friendship. Stephen was especially impatient with liberal attempts to disguise the clash between Christianity and the modern world. For him, with his Evangelical background still in his blood, either you were a Christian or you were not. It did no good to try and fudge the issue, as the Broad Church tried to do. One of its most eminent theologians, F. D. Maurice, had argued against the Christian doctrine of eternal punishment in Hell, but could not bring himself to reject it outright. Stephen thought his position untenable. Maurice, he said, had proved everlasting damnation 'to be a most edifying and consolatory doctrine – only that everlasting did not mean everlasting, nor damnation, damnation'. This pungent manner was typical of Stephen's polemical style; within it lay the fear that intellectual evasiveness would lead to catastrophe.

> It is melancholy to see so much genuine fervour running to waste, not in preaching the truths which are most urgently needed, but in trying to make fiction do the work of truth.[5]

Hardy's anti-Christian statements, written much later in his life, still carry the echo of Stephen's characteristic tone: his ferocity and earnestness. He inherited too Stephen's conviction that candour was not only admirable, it was essential.

Stephen's own standpoint was increasingly influenced by positivism – a philosophy developed by the French writer Auguste Comte and put forward most influentially in English culture by George Eliot. Positivists could no longer accept the supernatural aspects of Christian doctrine – the belief that Jesus Christ was the Son of God and that he had worked miracles; they nonetheless believed that people could act as Christ acted. Positivists looked for a human Christ. People could become Christ to one another in the moments when they behaved with selfless love. That, and not any metaphysical system or theological doctrine, was the essence of Christianity.[6]

These opinions were not restricted to Stephen and George Eliot; John Stuart Mill, another of Hardy's intellectual heroes, professed and expounded them too; so did Harriet Martineau and, among people Hardy knew personally, John Morley, Frederick Harrison and, most importantly, Horace Moule, who had given Hardy a copy of Comte's *A General View of Positivism* (1865). Positivist ideas were in fact highly fashionable during the 1860s and 1870s and it would have been difficult for Hardy to avoid coming across them. In Stephen, he encountered an impressive embodiment of these ideas – a person who combined religious doubt and moral resolve. Moule's doubts had produced a long trauma and played a part in his suicide. In Swinburne, religious unbelief produced wild amorality and self-involved withdrawal. Stephen's feats of masculine strength, both on mountains and in arguments, declared that the agnostic could be a hero, that Swinburne's 'pale Galilean' could be replaced by a figure of power and influence – not a 'muscular Christian', perhaps, but a muscular positivist.

One result of this was Gabriel Oak – the hero of *Far From the Madding Crowd*. He is a figure with symbolic connections to Christ who yet remains fully human. Oak and the novel are, in that respect, a positivist creation and readers at the time saw similarities between Hardy's novel and those of George Eliot. It is one of the few resemblances Hardy accepted when he came to write the *Life*, though he stressed the differences too (all of which turned out, unsurprisingly, to be in Hardy's favour). More recently, critical analysis of the book has brought forward its underlying tensions, finding signs in it of Hardy's impatience with bourgeois values and the censorship – the dishonesty – which those values produced. While he went along with Stephen's demands, Hardy found ways of insinuating what he was not permitted to state clearly, suggesting the unpleasant truths that were habitually denied.

These signs of dissatisfaction are genuinely part of the book; nonetheless, the remarkable thing about *Far From the Madding Crowd* is its firmness – the lack of ambiguity with which it puts forward a positivist view of the world. It would be wrong to take this as expediency on Hardy's part. No doubt he had to woo Stephen and his public but he was, at that moment, convinced of the truth of what he was saying. He had, like Stephen, been wrestling with religious doubts for a number of

years and he found in positivism a belief system that offered him the
consolations of religion while removing the conflict between faith and
reason. Positivism held on to religion's power to inspire, hearten and
motivate – it held up an ideal just as orthodoxy did – but, unlike
traditional faith, it did not demand the sacrifice or the distortion of your
intelligence.

One of Hardy's contemporaries whom positivism touched was
Emma. She was receptive to advanced religious ideas when they first
met and remained so for the early years of their marriage. She believed
in God without having fixed or absolute views about most of Christian
doctrine. Secondly, because she accepted conventional gender roles and
wanted, even expected, her husband to be a kind of hero, what Leslie
Stephen articulated about moral strength in men she would have
instinctively agreed with. Just as Moule's death had begun to intensify
Hardy's seriousness of purpose as a writer, Stephen's influence during
1874 taught him to see his work in terms of a mission – to preach 'the
truths which are most urgently needed'. Emma, though she feared
rejection and felt rejected by Hardy's self-involvement, could also
respond to his self-image as a heroic writer, engaged in a noble
undertaking. This was exactly the kind of person with whom she believed
she had fallen in love four years earlier and now, thanks to her loyalty
and devotion, they were able to marry.

*

Pictures survive, of Emma and of Hardy, from the time of their courtship
and marriage. A portrait in oil of Emma shows off her mass of ringlets,
her full bosom and her pretty clothes. She is looking to one side. Her
face is steady and sensitive, yet she gives the impression of having to
conquer shyness and a lack of self-belief. Hardy appears with a full
beard, which he was to keep for another twenty years, and his hair cut
short at the back. On top, it was beginning to thin and recede. He
looked much older in the early 1870s, more sombre and also more self-
possessed, than he had done only a few years before. When he first
arrived in London, he wore sideburns and a moustache, and his hair
had been longer and glossier, probably oiled. Where he had once
appeared cagey and watchful, he seemed by his early thirties composed
and philosophically calm. He had been modelling himself on Swinburne
but when Emma met him, he looked more like Tennyson. Emma would
always see him in that light and until the bitter end she believed that

Hardy was 'the one intended for me'.[7] Fate had miraculously brought them together, so they must have been meant for each other. It was Emma's destiny to accept this gifted and authoritative man, whose intense scrupulousness and commitment to his life's work made him so similar to the moral arbiters both of them admired – to the bearded sages, like Carlyle, Ruskin and Tennyson himself, on whom the Victorians relied for spiritual guidance.

The marriage took place on Thursday, 17 September 1874, in St Peter's Church in Paddington. Emma's uncle, Edwin Hamilton Gifford, a Canon of Worcester Cathedral, married the couple, and her younger brother Walter, who lived in London, attended the ceremony. Although her father, John Gifford, remained unreconciled to Hardy as a son-in-law, others in her family supported her. On the other hand, not a single member of Hardy's family appeared, though some or all certainly could have come, had they wanted to (or had Hardy wanted them to). Henry had stayed with Hardy for nearly a week in London only the previous summer. In their absence, Hardy wrote to Henry (not his parents) on the following day, 'to tell you all at home that the wedding took place yesterday'. He placed an announcement in the *Dorset County Chronicle*, which appeared on 24 September.[8]

By then, he and Emma were on honeymoon for a fortnight in Paris (or as Hardy put it more prosaically in the same letter to his brother, 'I am going to Paris for materials for my next story'.) When they returned in early October, they moved into a villa in Surbiton, then a village on the southern fringes of London, sharing a four-bedroom, detached house with another couple and their young daughter. Surbiton was seemingly an odd place to choose but it had its attractions. There was a station there on the railway line running from London Waterloo into the southwest – towards Basingstoke, Winchester and Dorchester. Hardy was choosing a halfway house between London, where his profession was centred, and the country, where both he and Emma would have preferred to live. On this side of London, Hardy was within easier reach of home than in the Paddington area and in the suburbs, Emma could adapt to city life without being swamped by it.

Surbiton also contained one of Hardy's Dorset connections – Frank Honeywell (1839–1903), a violinist and organist, whom he may have got to know in Weymouth. (Honeywell had been organist of St Mary Woolnoth, Weymouth.) Honeywell ran a successful music shop in Surbiton, gave music lessons and in 1877 he became organist of All

Saints, Kingston-upon-Thames, a few miles away. The two men were, according to Beatrice, one of Honeywell's seven children, 'great friends', close enough for Beatrice to refer to Hardy as 'Tom'. It may be the case in fact that Honeywell helped Hardy find the house, because its availability was never advertised in the press.[9]

The street where they lived had a tollbooth on it, charging people other than locals a penny before allowing them through. They had for company the rural, non-literary friends whom Hardy was most at ease with and Emma would find unthreatening. So, it was a secluded, peaceful situation, in many ways ideal for both of them. Unfortunately (and as would happen again and again), Hardy's profession soon drew him back into town. They lived in Surbiton for only six months in the end, before moving back to lodgings in Westbourne Grove in March 1875 – returning to Hardy's bachelor haunts.

By then, Hardy had completed the book version of *Far From the Madding Crowd*, which came out in November 1874 with Hardy's name given on the title page and used in advertisements; he had also started work on his next book, *The Hand of Ethelberta*. On the back of his success with *Far From the Madding Crowd*, Smith, Elder offered him £700 for the serial rights and first edition rights of the new novel. This was agreed in March when arrangements were made for the new story to begin appearing in the *Cornhill* in July. Several scenes were set in the capital and Hardy claimed that his reason for moving was the need to research them. He was also getting involved in the Copyright Association, lobbying Parliament to set up an inquiry into the copyright laws, and that interest was typical of his anxiety to become a fully-fledged professional writer. As much as he loved Surbiton's seclusion, the quiet made him restive; it felt like a luxury he could not afford.

The pull of London was, nonetheless, very much the pull of male friendship. Hardy and Emma moved on 22 March, and the very next day, Hardy left Emma behind in their unfamiliar flat and spent the evening with Leslie Stephen. It was probably the first time they had met for several months and while Hardy was there, Stephen asked him to act as a witness to his final renunciation of holy orders. When Hardy recalled this incident in later life, he made a good story out of it, playing up the quaintness of Stephen's High Victorian seriousness – his furrowed brow that was set off to perfection by the dark, Gothic surroundings of his study. At the time, he found it more alarming than that and from then on, as it turned out, the two men had less to do with each other – less, perhaps, than either of them was expecting.

This was partly as a result of events in Stephen's personal life. Later in 1875, his wife Harriet Thackeray, known as 'Minny', died aged thirty-seven, after the premature birth of their second child. Stephen was heartbroken and never entirely recovered. He was married again a few years later – to Julia Duckworth, née Prinsep, herself recently widowed – and so became stepfather to Julia's three children. He had one daughter of his own already, Laura, aged five when her mother died, and he and Julia subsequently had four children of their own, including Virginia Stephen, who later married Leonard Woolf. Stephen clung to his family life amidst recurrent depression following his bereavement and Julia too continued to mourn her first husband as she brought up a second family. They became a notoriously formidable couple.

Hardy knew Minny's sister, Anne Ritchie, née Thackeray (Virginia Woolf's Aunt Anny), and records her commenting that 'when she calls on L. S. and his wife she feels like a ghost, who arouses sad feelings in the person visited'. Hardy had a similar effect, perhaps, though to a lesser degree, because his friendship with Stephen dated back to the time of Stephen's first marriage. Certainly in subsequent years, Hardy found him difficult: 'Called on Leslie Stephen. He is just the same or worse; as if dying to express sympathy, but suffering under some terrible curse which prevents his saying any but caustic things.' Henry James, similarly, wrote of Stephen's 'ineffable and impossible taciturnity and dreariness'.[10]

Hardy had seen this kind of behaviour before in his friend Moule and, as much as Stephen withdrew into his family, Hardy backed away from his friend's darker states of mind. During the mid 1870s, Hardy had an especially strong, though largely unacknowledged, fear of depressives, which resulted from Moule's suicide and his continuing suppression of his feelings about it. From 1875 onwards, he and Stephen remained in touch and Hardy continued to respect Stephen's critical powers, though he noticed more often as time went on the contradiction between Stephen's avowal of candour and 'plainness', and his primness when editing novels. At crucial moments in his career until the mid 1880s, Hardy would still turn to Stephen for advice. Nonetheless, their friendship had somehow failed to blossom.

Intimations of this and his usual discomfort in London once he got there prompted Hardy to think of moving further away. In July, he began to explore possible places; he travelled to Dorset and made inquiries in Shaftesbury, Blandford Forum and Wimborne – all of them small towns in the north-east of the county with railways links to London, offering something like Surbiton's balance between remoteness and access to the capital. On 12 July he and Emma went down together to Bournemouth, probably with the same idea in mind, and on 15 July they travelled on by steamer to the then-remote fishing-port of Swanage, on the Isle of Purbeck, the far side of Poole Bay. Bournemouth was a rapidly developing holiday resort, with good connections to London. Swanage, which did not have a railway of its own for another five years, was more romantic yet not hopelessly inaccessible. You could take the boat to Bournemouth and catch a train up to London from there. Maybe this would be perfect. In any event, they decided to stay. Hardy, 'suspending his househunting, settled down there for the autumn and winter' and finished *The Hand of Ethelberta*.[11]

Deciding where to live remained, nonetheless, a persistent problem during the first ten years of his marriage to Emma. They moved to Yeovil in March 1876, to Sturminster Newton in July, back to London two years later, and then to Wimborne in July 1881. Only from the summer of 1883 onwards were they settled finally in one place – Dorchester, Hardy's old hometown. Each move had its own particular circumstances but the essence of their restlessness was the tension already visible: the pull in Hardy between the peace he needed in order to write and the busy, literary world where he needed to make his name. Emma's discomfort in the capital played its part, too, as did the conflict between her love of romantic solitude and her desire (like Hardy's) for middle-class friends. Nonetheless, moving so many times was disturbing to them both, particularly Emma, who had a deep-seated cultural expectation of having a home of her own now that she was married. She noted down their various changes of address during the summer of 1875, starkly listing them one after another in her diary. The following year at the end of a holiday, she wrote: 'Going back to England, where we have no home & no chosen county.'[12]

Their choosiness and changeableness suggest too that, as a couple, they found it awkward to negotiate. Hardy vividly remembered the day in Bournemouth in summer 1875 when they were together looking for a place to live. It was 14 July, St Swithun's day, and it rained very heavily – traditionally a bad omen, presaging forty days of rain. 'We were irked by the scene,' Hardy wrote, and 'by our own selves'. (Or, as he wrote in the manuscript, 'by each other'.)

> For I did not know, nor did she infer
> How much there was to read and guess
> By her in me, and to see and crown
> By me in her.
> Wasted were two souls in their prime,
> And great was the waste, that July time
> When the rain came down.[13]

He did not recognize Emma's remarkable qualities while she, for her part, grew impatient with his unresponsiveness – she did not see anything interesting behind the gloomy exterior. Probably, they would forget about all this soon enough when Swanage turned out to be such a delightful place. The poem wonders though whether their failures of sympathy at this moment were the source of their future unhappiness, and the 'waste' of their lives.

Meanwhile, Hardy was trying to coming to terms with his parents' disapproval of his marriage. They had grown accustomed to thinking of him as a professional architect who pursued an amateur interest in literature. Meanwhile, his protracted stays at home (in winter 1872–3 and as recently as the first six months of 1874) had led them to assume that Dorchester would remain a base for him. His marriage challenged both assumptions. Hardy showed no sign of planning to bring his wife home to live near the family and he seemed intent upon abandoning architecture completely. They saw too that Emma was a genteel woman with literary pretensions, more a writer's wife than an architect's.

His parents' hostility made Hardy stubborn in return and Jemima responded to what she saw as his rejection of her by in turn rejecting him. The support Hardy's family and home had given him, almost without his noticing it, was absolutely removed. That made him rely on Emma as much as he had done when they first met. And, just as John Gifford's opposition had driven Hardy to make himself into a successful writer, so his family's rejection meant that he felt he was taking a stand. In spite of the obstacles that fate and his family threw in their way, he had gone ahead with the marriage and, consequently, if ever it started to go wrong, his determination would look like blindness and folly. So as well as having a wife to support and a career to maintain, Hardy was now under pressure to ensure that marriage never gave even the slightest sign of faltering.

*

The progress of the couple's early married life together can be followed much more closely than their courtship because, very fortunately, two of Emma's early diaries survive. The first begins on her wedding day in September 1874 and covers the following year: their honeymoon, plus some details of where they lived afterwards. The second covers Emma's holiday with Hardy in May 1876 'to Holland; the Rhine, Black Forest, &c'. Hardy had by then finished *The Hand of Ethelberta*; they had left Swanage for Yeovil and were soon to move on from there to a large house in Sturminster Newton. The holiday filled the intervening time. Other much later diaries, from 1887 and 1897, also exist, recounting foreign travel: specifically journeys to Italy and Switzerland.

Each time the narrative breaks off soon after their return to England, sometimes on a gloomy note. At the end of the honeymoon, Emma wrote:

> Thursday Oct – 1–1874
> Arrived at London –
> Dirty London. Very
> wet –
> > Friday morning
> > Drive to
> > Waterloo station for
> > Wimbledon
> Met Mrs Rousehill
> > Sunday 4th
> "Freeman's Arms" – Wimbledon
> – very wet – raining perseveringly

The same thing happened a year and a half later, when they returned from Germany. Once the holiday was over, Emma added only a few more, desultory entries: a note of the places where their luggage was searched, their new address in Sturminster Newton and some dates of visits later in the year. After that, nothing.[14]

Writing journals of one's holidays was common practice, especially for women in the Victorian period, and so was the idea that your everyday existence was not worth recording. Similarly, the contents of these diaries are, in many respects, conventional. Emma filled them with information and detail – about cookery and travel arrangements, adding her own sharp-eyed observations about foreign ways. Sometimes her comments overlap with Hardy's observations. In 1876, for instance, he noted that Rotterdam looked 'over-clean and new, with not enough shadow, and with houses nearly all out of the perpendicular'. Emma wrote of their visit:

> We had hot water at Rotterdam brought up in the morning in pint cups – two – Shrubs & trees in gardens like ours – laburnums in flower. All the people talk English.
>
> Houses are peculiar in these respects – a great deal of glass but the windows rather plentiful than extending across the fronts as shop windows in England – yet large & long [,] frameworks always white & everything painted white that can be in the house & outside[15]

She is busily receptive and particular. It is an almost exaggerated femininity that concentrates so much on small things, leaving the grander statements to her husband.

This feeling of conscious womanliness excludes most personal testimony. Emma's emotions do peep through in the diaries now and then; when they do, though, they are usually framed by an apology. She noticed in Paris that 'Wherever I go, whoever I pass [. . .] the people gaze at me as much or more than I at them & their beautiful city.' She was curious about this: 'Query – Am I a strange-looking person – or merely picturesque in this hat.' At once, however, she corrected herself: 'As it is remarkable I note it.' The passage makes her appear highly sensitive and alert to people's attention, yet not simply vain. An almost aristocratic air of finding oneself amusing coexists with naive vulnerability and a lack of cunning. Alongside these is a well-drilled habit of modesty – a reluctance to draw attention to oneself, even one's own attention to oneself.[16]

Particularly in 1874, the diaries also give the impression of an anxiously dutiful person. There are many sketches, some of significant objects, such as Napoleon's tomb or the fine tables in the hotel courtyard, and some like holiday snaps, showing the cliffs on the Isle of Wight or the landscape of Holland seen from the sea. Sketching was another ladylike accomplishment and Emma's are perfectly good, though unremarkable. (She and Hardy had sketched each other in Cornwall.) Her diary pictures are most characterful when she chooses unexpected details – door-handles, flower boxes, baguettes or bonnets. One of her impulses here is to gather interesting facts to talk about to friends, at dinner parties or over tea; another is to obediently make the most of the experience; while a third, certainly, is to delight in curiosities for their own sake.

She also uses such activities to stave off the boredom she readily felt. On honeymoon, she notes:

> Sunday night
> a thunderstorm.
> Morning T gone out
> Cat at the Hotel magnifique
> Sitting in the courtyard

These words run to the bottom of the page; the next begins, 'Description of Courtyard'. This description covers the rest of the page and includes one or two sketches.[17] Cats became an important source of comfort to Emma later in life, so it is interesting that when Hardy has 'gone out' Emma focuses on a cat and then finds herself something useful to do. The pet and the exercise of writing a detailed account of her surroundings, almost an inventory of the scene, seem to help her avoid feeling too sorry for herself.

Emma was always an active person, a fine horsewoman and later a keen cyclist. She became increasingly brusque about Hardy's melancholy, thinking it morbid and unhealthy. These diaries, however, amidst their slightly feverish energy and their feeling of a strangely youthful unself-consciousness – she was nearly thirty, after all – also reveal a woman eager to please her husband. She evidently believes in a clear division between a woman's part and a man's: hers are the 'home duties', his the more public ones. Even when, in her sixties, she became a keen supporter of women's suffrage (which Hardy opposed), Emma still thought that men and women had different gifts and naturally took different roles. It was her part to acquiesce and she obeyed that principle all her life – to a surprising extent, given her reputation as a domineering woman.

On their 1876 tour, it is Hardy who seems to have been demanding. They came home via Brussels, partly because of Hardy's work. As he put it with his customary dryness in the *Life*:

> Here Hardy – maybe with his mind on *The Dynasts* – explored the
> field of Waterloo, and a day or two later spent some time investi-

gating the problem of the actual scene of the Duchess of Richmond's Ball[.]

Emma does not mention the Duchess of Richmond's Ball (which was
held in Brussels the night before the Battle of Waterloo) but their visit to
the battlefield takes up several pages of her diary. It was a strenuous
business: 'great fatigue, so ended Waterloo day', Emma notes the next
morning and confesses,

> Today I am still greatly fatigued, & Tom is cross about it – Just
> been to see lace made in one of the manufactories[.]

The day after, the Wednesday, she is still tired.

> Tom is gone to see the picture gallery which was closed yesterday
> so I have missed it altogether[.] Quite worn out with the day at
> Waterloo[.][18]

They had arrived in Brussels on Sunday 11 June and visited Waterloo
the day after. Just two days earlier, in Strasbourg, Emma had been rather
unwell: 'Very weak & ill. Ulcerated throat – feel as if I was either
recovering from or going to have a fever.' She was still recuperating
when they explored the battlefield. She also suffered 'occasional lameness
[. . .] from early childhood' so that walking long distances troubled her;
hence her preferring to ride or take a carriage and in later life to go by
bicycle. Because her exhaustion was so understandable, Hardy's crossness
looks ungenerous, whereas Emma seems kindly and helpful, even if she
did moan a bit. And she missed the pictures. When they visited Antwerp,
a few days after Brussels, she made detailed notes of the paintings they
saw. In Brussels, though, as was all too usual, Hardy's wishes came first.
They followed a tight, inflexible schedule and she lost out.[19]

The diaries bring out Emma's kindliness, her wish to be a helpful
and accommodating wife, and the goodness of heart that had won
Hardy's love originally. Sadly, too, they show the area where the
marriage confronted its greatest difficulties, both early on and later,
because Hardy's tendency to get irritated with Emma always arose from
his sense of being intruded upon. One of the most poignant entries
comes when Emma and Hardy are staying in a hotel in Rouen, their
very first destination on the Continent.

> Chambermaid enters our room in the evening not knowing we
> were there. Sees us writing at our table. She bows curtseys waves

her hand at us smiles chatters her apologies places a <u>pail</u> beneath our wash stand. Then <u>spins</u> still smiling & chattering out of the room.

'Sees us writing at our table.' The chambermaid's charming confusion, eagerly described, is really Emma's own excitement. As late as 1910, she wrote to Lady Hoare that, while Hardy was away:

> I am ensconcing myself in the Study in *his* big chair foraging – he keeps me *out* usually – as *never* formerly – ah well! I have my private opinion of men in general & of him in particular[.]

This comes from an angry though not a hate-filled letter and its anger originates in Emma's feeling excluded from '*his* big chair', the place where he wrote. Thirty-five years earlier, Emma began her marriage hoping and rather expecting an intimate, literary partnership.[20]

Some Recollections emphasizes how Emma actively pursued literary interests before she ever met Hardy:

> Sometimes I visited a favourite in the scattered parish – an amusing woman, pleasant-mannered and lively – who told me fine old tales and strange bye-gone experiences of her own young life and hardships endured in service, which I took down afterwards in my pocket book for matter with which to begin writing country stories, having come to the conclusion that I was hearing from one [and] other of these country-folk a good deal that was fresh, peculiar, and not yet written about.[21]

No such 'country stories' have ever come to light, and it has usually been assumed that Emma was exaggerating her gifts as a writer along with her commitment to the life of writing. But she certainly was writing during the early years of the marriage. In Swanage, she composed a long short story or short novel, *The Maid on the Shore*, which has never been published, although a typescript survives. It may not have been completed until as late as 1889, but it was begun within a year of their marriage. Drafts of it appear near the back of the 1874 diary.

High-pitched, idealized and romantic, *The Maid on the Shore* is nothing like as striking or complex as one of Hardy's novels and that has made it easy to despise. Its settings, furthermore, are the same as those of *A Pair of Blue Eyes*, so it has been thought merely derivative. Direct comparison misses the point, though, because Emma's work is not trying exactly to rival Hardy's. *The Maid on the Shore* is less an imitation than a feminization of his novels and corresponds to Emma's consistent desire to complement her husband. In literature as in their domestic life, she hoped she could be both the assistant and the equal. She had been of practical help ever since they met and her moral support had helped him when discouraged. She was also convinced that Hardy's masculine powers would benefit from her feminine logic of the heart. His dark and melancholy realism should be balanced by the inspiring idealism that was natural to her, as a person and as a woman. Accordingly, *The Maid on the Shore* is described on its first page as 'a story of fair passions, and bountiful pities, and loves without stain'. Partly for the same reason, it is effusive, even rather amateurish in style, whereas Hardy's early novels tended to be analytical and, if anything, overwritten.

Emma, in other words, wanted to influence Hardy for the better (as she saw it) and to insinuate herself back into this part of his life, which had recently become closed to her. Her efforts were not kindly received this time, although when they first met, Hardy had welcomed her advice and discussed his work very freely with her. In their first years of marriage, she found herself in rather the same situation as Elfride in *A Pair of Blue Eyes*, almost as if Hardy knew before he married her what was likely to happen. Emma too, if she did not predict this outcome, saw it happening. She could have been writing of herself when she describes her heroine in *The Maid on the Shore* as:

> One of those people who lost their proper assertiveness on being snubbed, and could be altogether extinguished by a continued course of it [. . . .] Such self-effacement as she was capable of would prove an effective bar to happiness if she should become united to a man of caprices (or moods), for he would grow exacting upon it.[22]

This passage sounds too self-aware for Emma in 1875 and seems to betray too much experience of married life. Perhaps it was written later but, if so, the passage points to vulnerabilities that had been in her character from the beginning: a desire to please, which could be exploited, and a fragile self-confidence, which could be corroded.

As a writer (and to some extent as a person), this is indeed what happened to Emma during her marriage. She wrote hardly anything after *The Maid on the Shore* and, before the last year of her life, she published hardly anything either. She decisively lost her place at the writing-table. Yet the character analysis from *The Maid on the Shore* is a remarkable piece of self-understanding. The Christian principles of her upbringing plus her original, devoted love for Hardy kept her loyal to the marriage. Yet what she saw as his mistreatment of her changed the ardent, trusting, girlish young woman into a more critical person, able to make this clear-eyed self-analysis. Hardy's repressive treatment compelled her, as she saw it, to insist on her rights and to do so with unnatural, unwomanly firmness. That was one of the reasons why she hated his behaviour so much and why her forcefulness alternated with depressed subservience. Underlying all their later quarrels was Emma's belief that her good faith had been made use of, that 'such self-effacement as she was capable of' had been insisted upon.

The paradox was that in her approach to the marriage she had invited Hardy's 'assertiveness', only she wanted his dominance to be gracious and courtly. She also assumed that in several areas she would still dominate; she expected her judgement to be respected on the topics where she was, in her view, naturally expert – in domestic matters and in delicate questions of behaviour or feeling. Hardy resisted this: he built the house they lived in and in his books he flaunted his contempt for customary good feeling and taste. By doing so, he not only offended Emma's sense of what was respectable, he overruled as well her feminine judgement.

These actions left her both hurt and indignant. And, because she was by nature easily snubbed, easily put down, she turned into a caricature of the severe, married lady stiffly insisting on her due. Hardy responded to this by adopting an equally conventional manner; he deferred to his wife and made his conduct impeccably appropriate – in public at least and so long as all the things that really mattered remained strictly under his control. This shared code of behaviour was observed by their friend, George Douglas.

All who knew them, Douglas said:

> must have been struck by [Hardy's] desire, as far as possible, to 'take her with him' in his pursuits – whether it was a question of reading books together, cycling, or sight-seeing or of associating her with his literary labours.
>
> [. . . .] But no less striking certainly were his unremitted deference and chivalrous consideration where his wife was concerned[.]

Emma's critical judgement of his books received from Hardy, Douglas goes on, 'a deference which, to speak frankly, it scarcely deserved', for Emma 'was always very much on the side, if not of the angels, at least of the proprieties'. Douglas writes warm-heartedly about both Emma and Hardy ('It would have been impossible, I fancy, to find pleasanter visitors than the Hardys proved themselves to be'), and he wants to counter the widespread view that the marriage was an unmitigated failure.[23] This agenda colours what he says, but other contemporary accounts agree with Douglas that Hardy was remarkably polite to Emma, considerate and gallant. All the same, his deference was superficial. His career as a novelist became a sustained and sometimes reckless attack on the proprieties that Emma stood by.

Superficial it may have been; uncaring and cruel it was not. Hardy was evidently a moody person, who was completely caught up in his work for much of the time. He could recognize this and was aware of Emma's sensitivity, the vulnerability to attack of this woman who possessed 'spirit and the power of deciding for herself' (as Douglas put it). He knew about these weaker sides of her in part because, in his bad moments, he knew so well how to take advantage of them. To compensate, he would try at other times to bolster and protect her self-esteem.

Douglas assumes that Hardy's work naturally did and should take precedence and Hardy shared that point of view. That made his accommodation of his wife into a generous action whereas her accommodation of him was no more than her duty. Emma would not necessarily have disputed that account of her marriage, believing like any good Victorian Anglican that her role as wife meant she should 'honour and obey' her husband. It was not humiliating for her to be meek because that was her duty, and likewise it was the duty of a good husband to be benevolent, paternal and courteous. For many years, Emma and Hardy played out these parts together, performing the marriage with an elaborateness and precision that tried to make up for the widening differences between them.

− 14 −

Lifelong to be I thought it

THE HAND of Ethelberta, written in the first year of the marriage, is marked already by some of these tensions. Its hero, Christopher Julian, eventually gives up hope of ever marrying the grand Ethelberta and settles for Picotee, Ethelberta's younger, more homespun sister instead. Picotee had always been devoted to him and in the end he does not regret his choice. Ethelberta resembles Emma at points and Christopher is, likewise, in many ways a portrait of Hardy so Christopher's choice of Picotee over Ethelberta might be taken as an indication of Hardy's beginning to regret marrying Emma and not, say, Tryphena. The feeling in the novel is not as simple as that, however; opting for Picotee reflects just as much Hardy's and Emma's shared preference for the country over the city, and for Swanage over London. What might appear more worrying in retrospect is Picotee's lack of definition as a character. There is no spirit in her to be crushed, as there was in Elfride, or wilfulness to be tamed, as there was in Bathsheba. Those traits are exclusively Ethelberta's and she is consigned to a loveless marriage with a seedy aristocrat. The novel punishes proper assertiveness in women, and that was a worrying sign.

Fortunately in some ways, the book was a failure and that made the marriage easier. The novel appeared in two volumes in April 1876, at the close of its serialization run. After *Far From the Madding Crowd*, expectations had been high but, from the outset, reviews were lukewarm. In March 1876, Hardy already feared what might be coming.

> You may possibly by this time have formed an idea of what sort of reception *Ethelberta* will meet with − but please read to the end before judging.

He curtailed the project, completing the novel in eleven numbers instead of the planned twelve, and, as he did so, he called a more general halt, saying in the same letter:

> I do not wish to attempt any more original writing of any length
> for a few months, until I can learn the best line to take for the
> future[.]

He had begun to move in this direction a few months earlier. In
November 1875, he was offered the chance of serializing his next novel
in the *Examiner*, a prestigious magazine with a large circulation but he
turned the offer down.

> I am afraid that I cannot at present enter into any engagement. My
> intention is to suspend my writing – for domestic reasons chiefly –
> for a longer time than usual after finishing *Ethelberta*[.]

True to this resolve, Hardy waited before beginning another book. He
and Emma left Swanage, took a continental holiday, and in the summer
moved to Sturminster Newton, a little town in the Stour valley. Here,
after their two-year nomadic existence, they stayed at last.[1]

They seem to have been genuinely happy in Sturminster. As often
in their married life, Hardy turned to Emma for comfort and support
when his career ran into trouble whereas, often without meaning to, he
ignored her when things were going well. He had more room for her
too because, after working so feverishly hard – between 1871 and 1876,
he had been producing almost a book a year – Hardy now paused. *The
Return of the Native* was a far more considered book and one that Hardy
prepared for very carefully. He was anxious, for one thing, to avoid a
second false move, after the failure of *The Hand of Ethelberta*.

In the aftermath of that disappointment, in May 1876, Leslie
Stephen had written Hardy a kindly letter, offering encouragement and
some advice.

> I think as a critic that the less authors read of criticism the better.
> You e.g. have a perfectly fresh and original vein, and I think the
> less you bother yourself about critical canons the less chance there
> is of your becoming self-conscious and cramped[.]

This was tactful, both in its oblique reference to Hardy's bad reviews
and in its affirmation of his talent. Stephen went on to recommend that
if Hardy read anything it should be the works of George Sand (1804–76),
the French, woman writer whose novels depicted working-class life in an
idealized countryside. Stephen was managing to agree with the critics

that *The Hand of Ethelberta* was bad, while encouraging Hardy to ignore them and get on with what he was good at, regardless of critical fashion.

Hardy later became protective about *The Hand of Ethelberta* and its spiky comedy, claiming that the book did not succeed simply because it was ahead of its time. In 1876, he was willing to believe he had made a mistake. Even so, Stephen's recommendation of George Sand struck the wrong note. Hardy always disliked comparisons and he was determined now to follow his own 'perfectly fresh and original vein', as Stephen was himself saying.[2] Moreover, stories of charming rural life were precisely what he wanted to get away from now that he was living in the actual country once again. He began instead to write ballad poetry, something he had done only once before, in 'The Fire at Tranter Sweatley's', written in 1866.[3] Hardy published the poem in November 1875, calling it in the subtitle 'A Wessex Ballad' (his first use of the term Wessex in reference to his works), and other ballads soon followed, even though they remained unpublished for twenty years.

Hardy's desire to align himself with country life appears too in his admiration for R. D. Blackmore, whose novel *Lorna Doone* (1869) he read in 1875. He told Blackmore in a letter of a 'kindred sentiment between us in so many things'. 'Little phases of nature,' Hardy said, 'which I thought nobody had noticed but myself were continually turning up in your book.' Pursuing the acquaintance, Hardy sent Blackmore a copy of the Tranter Sweatley ballad in November and was keen then to point out that he had moved to Swanage: 'I am a countryman again, as you see.'[4] He chose Blackmore over Sand because Blackmore's landscapes were both wilder and harsher, and his novel allowed into portrayals of country life a more dangerous primitiveness.

Moving to Sturminster was another aspect of the same concern with the real, unvarnished form of rural life. Hardy was fond of the whole district: the Stour Valley that ran down south-eastwards to Wimborne, Shaftesbury lying to the north and the Blackmoor Vale to the west (which he later made Tess's birthplace). This part of Dorset was linked in his mind with William Barnes, who had grown up there, and with his own explorations of the county as a young architect. Margaret Marsh, Stour Row, Buckhorn Weston and Turnworth all lay nearby. It was also peculiarly unspoilt. The old Dorset dialect was still spoken in its pure form. Personal associations and language meant that, in and around Sturminster, Hardy could return to the way of life he had grown up with, little changed by the intervening years.

He had changed, of course, and looked with the eyes of a novelist who had a growing reputation. Professional success confirmed Hardy as an outsider, so that coming home to Dorset was again awkward as well as comforting. The distance was much greater than it had been in 1867 when he first retreated from London to Bockhampton because he was now established in metropolitan, literary circles and had married into genteel society. Both he and Emma were respectable middle-class people revisiting the country and that distance from their surroundings gave them common ground. It also meant that Hardy's writing became more dispassionate about the rural world he looked in on, more inquisitive about it and less devotedly loyal towards it. He became instead something of a student of remote communities. To do so he drew on books, oral history and, curiously enough, on his wife's experiences as well.

Soon after they arrived, Hardy set out on an extensive programme of reading. Where earlier he had generally read poets and novelists for the most part, he now broadened his interests, studying philosophers, sociologists, historians and what would now be called anthropologists, though anthropology was in its infancy and scarcely named. (The first use of the word in its modern sense was in 1861.) He became especially interested in books that described and compared primitive ways of life from around the globe. *The Return of the Native* reflects this reading – generally, in its deliberately heavyweight, intellectual manner; specifically, in its presentation of Egdon Heath as a 'primitive' environment – antique and elemental.

Emma joined in the work, by copying into Hardy's notebooks numerous quotations from the books he had been reading. Perhaps this sounds a dreary, even a humiliating task, but Emma, I think, definitely enjoyed it. She felt useful and appreciated and she also found the books interesting in themselves, because like her husband she had been denied the education her intelligence deserved. Emma also proved particularly helpful to Hardy's thinking when it came to local knowledge, so that in effect *The Return of the Native* brought together his Dorset and her Cornwall, making out of these two the bleak environment of Egdon Heath. The imaginative mingling of both their home territories reflects the happiness of their married life together and also, naturally, it helped to bring such happiness about. In Sturminster, Emma could feel for the first and probably the only time that the writing-table was theirs.

Ever since 1867, Hardy had noted down Dorset stories, traditions and superstitions, mostly related to him by members of his family.

Several of these are used in *The Return of the Native* to help convey the strangeness of Egdon Heath.[5] Emma became another source – two peculiar little anecdotes about Cornwall survive into his memorandum book. Furthermore, in *Some Recollections*, Emma describes St Juliot as a place where:

> the belief in wit[ch]craft was carried out in actual practice amo[n]gst the primitive inhabitants. Traditions and strange gossipings [were] common talk, and, I must add, evil-speaking [was] indulged in by these isolated natives [of a parish] where newspapers rarely penetrated[.][6]

The Return of the Native depicts a very similar, archaic environment where witchcraft and evil-speaking are practised, unusually by Hardy's 'isolated natives'.

The authentic material Hardy gathered from both Emma and his family helped him to reveal a pagan community at the heart of the charming world of rural Dorset, thus enabling him to unsettle his audience's assumptions about the countryside. Emma was an especially valuable source because in Cornwall, as an off-comer from genteel Plymouth, she had come up against a 'dull, aggressive' society. She remembered meeting with suspicion and witnessing extreme cruelty, right in the midst of nature's inspiring beauty.[7] Her mixture of delight in and distaste for rural life reflected the feelings of many in Hardy's audience, for whom the country was lovely to look at and impossible to live in. Hardy no longer patronized that point of view; he was becoming particularly interested in it because he was beginning to shared it.

*

As Emma assisted Hardy with *The Return of the Native*, both practically and more intimately, the marriage found a stable footing for the first time. They bought furniture – something they had not done before – and entered Sturminster society, which was dominated by clergy families, a class of people Emma always felt at ease with. They also began to make tentative contacts with Hardy's relations. This process was an especially important one for Victorian wives because a woman was still regarded as joining her husband's family when she married, taking his name, moving to his home, and placing all her property legally in his hands. For someone of Emma's background, remaining estranged from Hardy's family stopped her from being properly his wife.

Her 1874–5 diary shows how keenly she sought acceptance. On a memorable outing from Swanage to Corfe Castle in September 1875, which Hardy used as a basis for scenes in *The Hand of Ethelberta*, he and Emma were joined by his sisters, Mary and Kate. It was probably the first time she had met her sisters-in-law since the marriage and Emma's diary entry for the day begins:

Sep. 13th 1875. 10.30. A.M.
Corfe Castle
    Breakfast Picknic.
    Tom. Katie. Mary. Emma.
        Hardy.
    Drove in Sommer's Van, leaving
    Swanage at 7. with 15 people [. . .][8]

'Hardy': her new married name and shared by all four; and that name centred on the page, like a declaration, like breathing a sigh of relief. The name draws the group together with Emma and Tom framing Katie and Mary, guarding and securing them. During this 'splendid day', a year after the wedding, Emma thought of herself as assuming finally her rightful place in the family. Thrilled by that, she at once became affectionate. When Mary and Katie left, Emma and Hardy 'scrambled down the slope on that side of the castle' and 'watched them out of sight'.

Around the same time, Emma made overtures to her mother-in-law as well, though without success. Jemima briskly rebuffed her, using Kate as her mouthpiece.

My dear Emma
    Mother is much obliged to you for your kind invitation but she
is so very busy just now that she cannot possibly come. She would
like to have come as she says she wants to see you again.

There are two further sentences in the letter; the first relaying Jemima's advice that they should not bathe in the sea, for fear of coming 'to some untimely end', and the second more barbed: 'You would be much safer she says on Rainbarrows or Crowstairs.'[9] That's to say, back near the parental home in Bockhampton. A year later, Emma and Hardy did spend Christmas at Bockhampton with the family and, by all accounts, this attempt to thaw relations proved another failure. With Kate, nonetheless, Emma did strike up a friendship.

Kate was nearly twenty at the time and soon to start training as a teacher in Salisbury. There, she attended the same college as her sister Mary had done, fifteen years before. During her training, Kate and Emma corresponded, though none of the letters survive; a few years later, in 1881, when Kate was teaching at a school near Sherborne, she referred back to their earlier letters.

> You write soon and then I'll answer you again like you used when I was at Salisbury. I remember the autumn there so well.

She had been miserable as a student, as she recalled again in 1882, in another letter to Emma.

> I met a college girl in Sherborne last Sat. Talking over the Salisbury times to her made me feel quite antiquated. I think they are having rather better times than we used to have but I dont mind if Tom publishes how badly we were used. Give him my love and the same to you[.]

Both letters are written thanking Emma for gifts: 'I have paraded about the room with my cape on and I am delighted with it,' Kate wrote in one. In the other, she enthused, 'I cant think how you could know just what I wanted in the shape of gloves. They are exactly the colour of my dress.'

Both these letters to Emma are warm-hearted, trusting and spontaneous – quite different from Kate's style when writing from home, either in Bockhampton or later from the house she shared in Dorchester with Mary. Another letter, from the same period, begins, 'My dearest dears'; one announcing her imminent arrival warns them:

> I shall eat such a lot and talk a great deal so I shall be rather troublesome. Come to meet me mind and make a fuss about my coming. I hope you've got some cake.
>
>   Yrs affectly
>   Katie[10]

Kate was by nature more outgoing than the rest of her family and her relationship with Emma encouraged her in that. Emma gave Kate something of the same supportive warmth that she gave Hardy while Kate in return gave her the chance to behave in a more feminine way than Hardy encouraged. They talked about clothes and fashion; Kate rather excitedly mentioned 'gentlemen' who visited the school and relayed a compliment paid her by Mrs Esdaile, with whom she lodged.

Likewise, Emma sought to help out the extended family as and when she could. When they were living in Tooting in the early 1880s, for instance, they employed Hardy's cousin, Mary Hand, as a domestic servant. She had recently been bereaved. 'I feel I owe you a great deal,' Mary wrote to Emma, 'for your kind consideration when my poor Father died.'[11] Extending kindness and sometimes charity to relations was perceived as very much the woman's role so Emma was acting only as was expected of her, and it is more than likely she was acting sometimes at Hardy's prompting. If he could, he was anxious to do well by the family, and be seen to be supportive of them. Emma was eager to please him and eager too to adopt the wifely role, even though taking it up was bound to place her at odds with Jemima.

Residing at least semi-permanently in Sturminster Newton gave Emma the context and security in which she could start to play the part of wife at last. She and Hardy were within reach of the family but not at its mercy; and to some extent, at least, they could dictate terms. Moreover, should they stay in the town, Sturminster might eventually become a new centre for the family – a new hub for it to revolve around as Hardy's parents aged; in the meantime, they could enjoy their secluded freedom. The shift of primacy from Jemima's household to their own would not come about of course unless Emma and Hardy provided what, as it turned out, they never could provide: children.

*

Hardy's 'How I Built Myself a House', his earliest surviving publication, begins:

> My wife Sophia, myself, and the beginning of a happy line, formerly lived in the suburbs of London, in the sort of house called a Highly-Desirable Semi-detached Villa.[12]

The successful, bourgeois male has one child already and expects to have more. This is a matter of course. To start a family and move house is to follow the proper pattern of life. Hardy's piece makes fun of his narrator but it accepts these assumptions and throughout his life, he remained someone who wanted children – someone who saw parent-hood as so natural and intrinsic that it became almost a necessity.

In June 1877, during their second summer at Sturminster, Hardy and Emma experienced trouble with their servant Jane. Her boyfriend had, they discovered, been staying overnight in the house. Immediately she was found out, Jane ran away. Hardy remarked in the *Life*: 'The further career of this young woman is not recorded, except as to one trifling detail.' Only over the page, in the extracts included from his 1877 diary, did Hardy explain what that 'trifling detail' was – as if, even in his seventies, he found the experience hard to revisit.

> Aug. 13. We hear that Jane, our late servant is soon to have a
> baby. Yet never a sign of one is there for us.[13]

They had been married for very nearly three years and Emma would be thirty-seven in November. Time was getting on.

Many couples find it hard to conceive. In Hardy's day, modern fertility treatments were unavailable and women often went through the menopause at an earlier age than they do now. (The average age is now fifty-one; in the nineteenth century, it would have been around forty-five.) Childbearing was riskier too then than now, especially as women got older. Still, it was quite possible to start a family late. Robert Browning's wife, Elizabeth, although an invalid when single, recovered after her marriage and bore her first child in her early forties. Much closer to home, Martha Mary Sparks, Hardy's cousin, got married in 1869 when she was in her mid thirties; she had three children soon afterwards; Nathaniel, her brother, married a woman of thirty-seven, Ann Lanham, and they had two boys. Emma, marrying at thirty-three, going on thirty-four, certainly had reason to hope.

All the evidence indicates that Emma was a maternal person. She doted on babies when she was older; earlier, she and Hardy looked after her nephew and niece, Gordon and Lilian Gifford. Sent out of London by their father, Walter, for the good of their health (sometimes as far as Cornwall, where they stayed with Helen and her husband), the two children lived at Max Gate for long periods from the mid 1880s on. They became something like adopted children.

Hardy too was actively involved in caring for Gordon and Lilian. Around 1885–6, he drew several pages of little pen-and-ink sketches, illustrating scenes from Greek history; these were made 'To please L. G. (a child)' – Lilian, that's to say, who would have been around six years old at the time. Hardy's stick-figure pictures show: 'Plato teaching in the avenues of the Academy' or 'Olympic games. The reward: a laurel crown'. Hardy drew them, I imagine, as he was telling Lilian the stories (a bit like Rolf Harris). And, characteristically, while he wanted to please her with the charming, engaging little illustrations he was also providing a thorough grounding in Greek history. There are pictures of Philoctetes, the Oracle of Trophonius, Eteocles and Polynices, and much else – each character and incident concisely explained. The classical world was traditionally male territory but Hardy gave Lilian access to it and did not flinch from telling her about its barbaric cruelties; one picture shows the 'Spartans exposing their children'.

Hardy and Emma arranged the education of both children and Hardy later pulled strings so that Gordon, as a budding architect, could join Blomfield's firm. Lilian, as an impoverished, highly neurotic lady of leisure, continued to be made welcome in the Hardy household even after Emma's death. Both she and Gordon remained deeply attached to Emma and Hardy, more deeply than to their natural father. So, although Hardy may have found them an increasing burden as they grew up and even put up with them largely for his wife's sake and later her memory's sake, his initial response, during the 1880s, to the chance of raising two surrogate children was plainly enthusiastic.[14]

There's no doubt at all, then, that not having children was a tragedy for Hardy and Emma, and a source of lifelong regret. Why it happened cannot be said for sure. Infertility on one side or the other is the simplest, least sensational answer and probably it is the true one. None of Hardy's siblings married so there's no evidence about possible fertility problems running in his family. Cousins on both his mother's and father's side did have children, though. Similarly, in Emma's family, Walter, her younger brother, raised a family (George and Lilian), while her sister, Helen, did not. But Helen was married late to a very old man, so her childlessness does not tell us very much.

Whatever the medical situation, both Hardy and Emma when they married were inexperienced sexually; Emma was almost certainly a virgin and, though Hardy may not have been, his previous experience had more often been of love than of sex. His sex drive, judging from his writings, was strong and straightforwardly heterosexual. The novels, poems and notebooks all reveal someone who was neither sexually ignorant nor agonized by transgressive desire (as Moule may have been). Neither is there any indication of impotence, though that has been given as the reason why the couple never had children. On the other hand, as a young man, Hardy had strict sexual morals. His religiosity and later his agnostic high-mindedness both encouraged the repression of eros.

Furthermore, sexuality, because of the emotional turbulence it created, was always likely to trouble someone with Hardy's very controlling temperament. He could recoil from it in panic. There are signs too of something voyeuristic in his make-up.

Many of the sources for Hardy's voyeurism are merely rumour – stories of him as an old man, walking near Max Gate, discovering couples *in flagrante* and watching them with interest; or stories of his brother Henry using a telescope for the same purpose. There's also a letter from 1926 where Hardy recalls the sight of a murderess, Martha Browne, being hanged seventy years before – an event he had witnessed aged sixteen.

> I remember what a fine figure she showed against the sky as she hung in the misty rain, & how the tight black silk gown set off her shape as she wheeled half-round & back.[15]

This is written too late in life to offer much reliable evidence of how he behaved or felt when younger; even so, it ties in with the persistent impression in the *Life* and his notebooks that looking was for Hardy a highly erotic activity. Women are gazed at, with an eye that is almost voracious. The female body is regarded, anatomized, and appreciated – it is visually consumed. Likewise, Hardy's beautiful heroines, women such as Eustacia Vye and Tess, are imagined very visually. He writes unusually detailed descriptions of their physical form, giving the impression of something like connoisseurship.[16]

Voyeurs do not necessarily make good lovers and, in addition, Hardy had been a bachelor throughout his twenties. By the time he married, his sex life had been dominated by fantasy – by looking and imagining – for nearly twenty years. The psychological impact of that was apparent in the 'Studies, Specimens' notebook: in its moments of sexual obsession and its emotional volatility. He connected Emma with escape from those dangers and so with poetry celebrating virginity and chastity, in particular Edmund Spenser's *Epithalamion*. She was so compellingly attractive to him because she presented an image of purity, both sexual and moral. That impression was encouraged by her class – she could seem to stand above the sordid struggle for life Hardy himself had to undergo – and by the place where he found her: an unknown spot, which the modern world had never violated. These associations do not mean he was not sexually attracted to her; clearly he was and she to him. Instead, it allowed his sexual feelings to appear purified. This was true love, he felt, because it made desire pure.

Consequently, in some respects, a long, unconsummated courtship suited Hardy. It postponed the sexual intimacies of married life, which were likely to have been as frightening for him as they are for many men. His sexual inexperience (whether it was absolute or only relative), plus his conflicted feelings, are likely to have made his and Emma's love life awkward at the beginning and in those circumstances, Hardy was the kind of person to back away. He was emotionally cautious, ferociously self-protective and always liable to introversion. His excessive, miserly, selfish emotional caution was the quality in his conduct towards Emma about which he felt most remorseful after her death; and it had, I suspect, an unstated sexual aspect.

As has often been pointed out, Hardy's writings show an unprecedented awareness of female sexuality: both what arouses women and how they behave when aroused. Leslie Stephen had censored out Hardy's descriptions of Bathsheba's erotic feelings but Grace Melbury in *The Woodlanders* (1887) is an extraordinarily insightful study of sexual awakening, of how vulnerability and fear are combined with thrilled excitement. It is this quality in his sensibility that prevented Hardy's writing from being simply voyeuristic or pornographic. For all his repression and prickly resistance to physical intimacy – he loathed being touched and would avoid even handshakes if he could – Hardy had a lover's intuitive responsiveness not only to women's beauty but to their sexual need. When he was cold to Emma, he knew what suffering he was causing her (better sometimes than she did herself) and recognized the strength of the instincts he was denying.

Emma, though of a very different temperament, was in some respects similar to Hardy in her feeling about sex. She saw her marriage in a stylized light, thinking of it as a romance. As a respectable woman, she was to be wooed; as an imaginative young woman, raised on Tennyson and Sir Walter Scott, she expected chivalry and gallantry. Her background led her to assume that she was the object of sexual desire, rather than a participant in it. Moreover, women were frequently described in the Victorian period as creatures possessing no sexual impulse and deriving no pleasure from the act. Many Victorian women knew this was not true, of course, just as Hardy did himself. Emma comes across, however, as someone who had internalized this point of view.

Before his marriage, Emma's father, John Attersoll Gifford, had been in love with her mother's sister and had been engaged to her until, tragically, she died of scarlet fever at the age of eighteen. He married

Emma's mother in place of the woman he had lost and his old love
haunted the household where Emma grew up. Emma's father was an
argumentative man, educated and freethinking whereas her mother was
devoted to reading the Bible and raising her children. These character
types foreshadow Emma and Hardy in their later years – so too does
the presence of a dominant mother-in-law. Emma's paternal grandmother lived with the family throughout Emma's childhood, and her
father's relationship with his mother seems to have been quite as intense
as his feelings for his wife, probably more so. After his mother's death,
he drifted into worsening alcoholism.

It cannot have been a warmly affectionate home; there was little
love between the parents, who were increasingly preoccupied with
keeping up appearances as their income declined. Passion, if it had ever
existed in her parents' marriage, was consigned firmly to the past. The
woman's role, as exemplified by Emma's mother, was to carry on
running the house regardless. Daily life and personal interactions were
self-consciously formal. Music was very important and became a major
channel for the expression of feelings, hopes and yearnings that were
otherwise kept hidden.

Emma's father, however, chose to see in Emma the image of her
dead aunt, his lost love. She had been 'a lovely golden haired girl' and
Emma was her father's:

> only *fair* child with bright hair, which he would stroke with sighings
> occasionally.[17]

This resemblance (whether actual or imaginary) drew Emma more
closely into the family legend, obliging her to play the part of the
devoted daughter beside the forlorn father. The situation also confirmed
the view that love affairs took place above and beyond the sphere of
everyday life, in some ethereal, often tragic realm. Meanwhile, her
siblings did little to disturb that picture.

Emma was the fourth child, with one elder sister, Helen, and three
brothers, two older and Walter who was younger. Helen and Walter did
get married in the end, though not until Emma was in her late twenties;
the two other brothers, Richard and Willie, never married. Emma was
not brought up in a household busy with intrigue or thronged with
possible suitors so she did not have an opportunity to watch true love
running its uneven course with an elder brother or sister. The internal
structure of the family and its social position encouraged both ignorance

about sexuality and romanticized ideas of love. And, as with the Brontës in Haworth, it led to powerful feelings developing between brothers and sisters.

Emma was devoted to her mother, admiring and emulating her; in a more volatile way, she was devoted to her sister too. After Emma's death, Florence Hardy claimed that 'the sisters had violent quarrels'. Quite possibly; yet despite the distance from Dorset to Cornwall and despite Hardy's discouragement, Emma remained in touch with Helen, wrote to her regularly, visited her when her husband died in 1882 and looked after her in old age. Helen died in Lee-on-Solent in 1900 and Emma spent two months nursing her through her last illness.[18]

Similarly, she wrote of an aunt who entertained them when children:

> She chatted, and laughed, and 'badinaged' and feasted us like a very fairy god-mother, and wore light-coloured ringlets I thought lovely by the side of her good-looking countenance, and the first moment I saw her I loved her, though I was not demonstrative about my affection.

This is the only time in the memoir that Emma speaks of loving someone. She never uses the word of Hardy. The strength of her feelings suggests a neglected child, just as her well-mannered secrecy about it implies that she was used to having her feelings ignored. Because *Some Recollections* was written when Emma was nearing seventy, the difference between her love for her aunt and her 'affection' for Hardy might be dismissed as simply the product of her embittered old age. That contributed, no doubt, and Emma's feelings for Hardy when they met were clearly passionate as well as sincere. What the passage really shows is Emma's separation of the feelings she has for men from those she had for women. Both may be based on 'affection', but relations with men begin in romance; they are public and stylized. Relations with women are more personal to her and more intimate.[19]

This is by no means unusual for a Victorian woman. It's the emotional aspect of the 'doctrine of separate spheres', in which the sexes were seen as complementary but very different. A woman must love her husband and serve him but she confides only in her beloved female friends. Similarly, a man cherishes his wife and spends his evenings at his club, following masculine pursuits. This set of assumptions made it easier for Emma and Hardy to grow apart in later life. At the beginning, crucially, they helped to divide love from sex. Emma would have found it particularly hard to make the transition from rapturous admiration to physical passion because her family background dovetailed so exactly with Victorian mores.

She was also, from her upbringing, more at ease with women's physicality than with men's. In autumn 1874, when returning from honeymoon and crossing the Channel in bad weather, Emma observed a woman on board:

> The lady on the highest berth in the Steam-boat on our return journey – opposite me – had firm flesh & complexion which can only belong to high-fed & comfortably-living people. The combination grand. In her chemise she was a perfect Juno. Flesh, tinted – neither dark nor yellow white – perfect flesh & form –

This entry finishes one page of Emma's diary and on the next, Emma wrote down a number of what look like titles – 'Merry Maidens', 'Village maidens', 'Maids in moods', 'Moods in men', 'Juno on Earth', 'Venus embodied', and so on.[20] The passionate quality of the description is marked and part of it derives from Emma's feelings about class: the woman proves that only the wealthy and genteel can be truly beautiful. Part of it though is straightforwardly sensual. Emma dwells on the woman herself, on her 'perfect flesh & form'. Emma was not a lesbian, but there is an undercurrent of lesbian feeling here, though, as with male homosexuality, Victorian culture allowed for intimate, eroticized relations between the sexes without naming them as such.

All these things contributed to making sexual relations between Emma and Hardy uncertain when they began. If they continued to encounter problems, both would have been inclined to withdraw – into imaginary loves, into memories, into various versions of 'romance'. That, combined with a woman's naturally declining fertility in her thirties, would have been enough to make children unlikely. If there was some other specific medical explanation, neither Emma nor Hardy ever offered it. Hardy's comment in 1877 is all he says; and none of Emma's letters survive from the time when children were still a matter for hope or discussion. Later, childlessness became for her a matter of poignant regret – no one was to blame, God in his wisdom had decreed.

The consequences, anyway, are more significant than the possible causes. Childlessness is the unexplored hinterland of their estrangement, creating resentment and making resentment feel unjustified. However much they wished to blame the other, neither of them could be sure they were not to blame themselves. For Emma, the result was a significant loss of status, particularly in relation to Hardy's family, who could always use it against her. Having children was less an option than a duty in the nineteenth century, especially for women, and infertility was stigmatized. The childless woman had failed in her social as well as her marital obligations. The childless man, meanwhile, was a failure in Darwinian terms. He had proved that he was not among the fittest and that he would not survive.

For Hardy, not having children proved what he was always likely to fear, that he was inadequate and weak – the last, degenerate example of a race that had once been strong. He had let down his family and he had no future. It was a profound and absolute humiliation that drove him on as a writer because his works offered a chance of immortality and success was a proof of worth. Emma had felt as early as 1874 that Hardy's writing was like a child to him and there's little doubt that Hardy came to share that belief. Childlessness also made it easy, of course, for Hardy to wish he had married somebody else or married no one.

Suppressed recriminations and anxieties about the future cooperated to make Hardy hanker after London – its companionable alliances and rivalries between men, its promise of achievement and recognition. There, when they moved in March 1878, he and his wife began remorselessly to drift apart.

~ 15

Some hid dread afoot

TYPICALLY, Hardy emphasized afterwards the professional logic of
the move.

> Despite the pleasure of this life at Sturminster Newton Hardy had
> decided that the practical side of his vocation of novelist demanded
> that he should have his head-quarters in or near London.[1]

He believed this principally because *The Return of the Native* was so difficult
to get published. In February 1877, he sent what he had written so far –
no more than the opening few chapters – to Leslie Stephen, who was
still editor of the *Cornhill*, but Stephen proved unenthusiastic. He found
the plot unsuitable for a family audience and his judgement probably
led Hardy to alter the book's focus, shifting attention away from
Thomasin and on to Eustacia Vye. He revived his original storyline
more than ten years later when he wrote *Tess*.[2]

Despite the change of direction, Hardy approached other publishers
soon afterwards, trying John Blackwood first. *Blackwood's Magazine* was
famous for its gothic fiction and seemed likely to welcome *The Return of
the Native*'s sinister settings and melodrama. He would have had high
hopes when he sent the first third of the book to Blackwood in April
1877. It was rejected, however, and then rejected a third time by George
Bentley, for his magazine *Temple Bar*. Hardy did not find a publisher
until August when the new firm of Chatto & Windus agreed at least
to serialize the novel. The firm had recently taken over the *Belgravia*
magazine, until 1876 edited by Mary Elizabeth Braddon, the sensation
novelist. Hardy's story would fit in nicely there. The *Belgravia*, though,
was nothing like as famous as *Blackwood's* or as prestigious as the *Cornhill*.
Naturally too, it paid much less well.

Hardy received £240 for the serial rights to *The Return of the Native*; a
year later, the volume rights brought him another £200. By comparison,

The Hand of Ethelberta, two years earlier, had made him getting on for twice as much – £700 for serial and volume rights combined. And he would have been hoping to improve on that. Blackwood had paid Margaret Oliphant £1500 for her novel *The Perpetual Curate* (1864), published when she was still making her name, and a reasonably well-established journalist and novelist, like James Payn, expected to generate as much as that annually. From two years' work, Hardy was making only one-third of the amount.[3]

Stephen's rejection of the book was not really surprising. As well as being too frank about sexual matters (though this was not very frank at all by modern standards), the new novel attacked Stephen's progressive beliefs. According to *The Return of the Native*, history revealed superficial change rather than advancement and 'improving' old-fashioned ways of life did no good, either to the improver or the supposedly improved. Nonetheless, Hardy had expected to keep his friend on side. He had, after all, only been accepting Stephen's advice when he decided to follow his natural bent without regard for critical opinion. More serious than his disappointment, however, was Hardy's sense of having to do without his most eminent advocate in the London literary world. His vulnerability was driven home when, subsequently, other doors refused to open. Although there were some reassuring signs – a celebratory essay in the *Examiner* by Charles Kegan Paul and a commission for a Christmas short story – Hardy began to worry that he was losing ground.

A further sign of this anxiety was his watchful concern for *The Return of the Native*. As it started its magazine run in January 1878, he worried insistently about the illustrations. On 8 February, when he was visiting London, he wrote to Arthur Hopkins, the illustrator, and complained about what he had seen so far, suggesting various changes, particularly in the depiction of Eustacia. He went on to declare that:

> My opinion, & I believe that of most novelists, is that the writer & illustrator of a story can hardly ever be in thorough accord unless they live in constant communication during its progress, & in these days that is almost impossible. However I trust some day to make your acquaintance, & obtain your pardon for my remarks[.]

On 20 February, Hardy wrote to Hopkins again, including this time sketches of rustic costumes and of a mummer's pole; by August, he was congratulating Hopkins on his success with Eustacia: 'she is certainly just what I imagined her to be'.[4] Hardy had fussed about the illustrations to

Far From the Madding Crowd; still, during 1878, there was more of an edge to his involvement and greater assertiveness too. Perhaps with a man instead of a woman (*Far From the Madding Crowd* was illustrated by Helen Paterson) Hardy found it easier to be outspoken. All the same, there is something authoritarian in his manner.

His determination to get everything right may have been heightened by the death in November 1877 of his old employer, the architect Raphael Brandon. Hardy had linked Brandon and Moule together in his mind since summer 1870 and Brandon's suicide confirmed his two friends' sad kinship. It reinforced his belief that, even if no human achievement had any final value, misery – perhaps suicide – was bound to follow if you did not pursue attainable goals of some kind. His conviction that idleness was dangerous drove Hardy forward and accentuated the tension in him between acceptance and ambition.

In *The Return of the Native* Hardy had embraced passivity. On Egdon Heath, though there is a lot to be improved, no improvement is possible. Trying to make matters better, as Clym the hero does, either has no effect or it makes things worse. People on the heath are living fossils, exotic because they have not moved with the times. In their essentials, however – in their drives and emotions, and in their confrontation with inexorable natural forces – there is no difference between them and modern, advanced people. Humanity is, here as everywhere, unchanging: 'slighted but enduring'.

Far From the Madding Crowd had been far more affirming: Bathsheba does remove the unjust steward and Gabriel does rise in the world. It had been fair to see similarities to George Eliot's works because Hardy's plot left the heroine chastened, as Eliot's heroines were chastened, and his hero's final vindication argued that through modest hard work a better future could be gained. *The Return of the Native* turned its back on those sources both of optimism and of moral authority. There was nothing to be done and therefore no sense in exhorting people to improve themselves. This change of view meant that, from now on, Hardy was to become a writer who had, in a sense, nothing to say. His 'fresh and original vein' was to affirm nothing and to become instead a mere looker-on at life – at its seasonal rhythms and impersonal powers. Accordingly, he would not take up the role of Victorian sage and so denied his audience the pleasure of being instructed.

On the other hand, the difficulties Hardy found in getting *The Return of the Native* into print created an imperative to act. He could not afford to be as passive as his novel suggested one ought to be. If he did not exert himself, then as a writer he was going to disappear. Two years of reading, thinking, and artistic self-fashioning in Sturminster had consolidated Hardy's belief in his originality and power. Even so he had now to prove it was true.

It was in this combative mood that he moved to London, and the undercurrents of anxiety about the change were quelled for the moment by the excitement of resuming the struggle. He was 'primed for new scenes with designs smart and tall'.[5] He and Emma rented the whole of a sizeable end-of-terrace house in Tooting, a suburb on the southwestern outskirts of London. The house was on four floors including the basement and, front and back, there were views over fields dotted with villas, with the wooded parkland of Wandsworth Common only a few hundred yards away. It was nearly in the country and yet the nearby railway station took you into Victoria, via Clapham Junction. Hardy wrote to his brother Henry in September, 'Tell mother she must make up her mind to come while the fine weather lasts. I will [m]eet her at Clapham Junction.' Tooting seemed to offer the compromise that Hardy and Emma so often tried to find between country and city, home and profession, family and marriage.

In addition, it was rather a fashionable suburb. Alexander Macmillan lived in a spacious house, Knapdale, half a mile away on the Tooting Bec Road. Hardy dined there and at Macmillan's garden parties he and Emma could mix with London literati: with Thomas Huxley, for instance; John Morley (who had read *The Poor Man and the Lady*) and Henry Holt, who published Hardy's novels in America. Whether he chose Tooting in order to cultivate the Macmillans cannot be said for sure; it was certainly an advantage to be close to this eminent publisher, especially as Leslie Stephen became ever more withdrawn.

Anyway, literary connections did become the all-consuming focus for Hardy's social life as he made a concerted effort to further his career. He worked enormously hard in Tooting. Apart from *The Return of the Native,* whose monthly instalments came out over the course of 1878, Hardy's short story, 'The Impulsive Lady of Croome Castle' appeared in April. (It was later used in *A Group of Noble Dames*). 'An Indiscretion in the Life of an Heiress', based on parts of *The Poor Man and the Lady*, appeared in July. At the same time, Hardy was working on a dramatization of *Far From the Madding Crowd* and, from May onwards, he began research for *The Trumpet-Major*, his historical novel set in Dorset during the Napoleonic Wars. Two poems connected with the novel – 'Valenciennes' and 'The Sergeant's Song' – were written during the year, and the novel itself was composed during 1879. Beforehand, Hardy spent many hours in the British Museum working on archive material. Two long short stories were written at this period as well: 'The Distracted Young Preacher' (April 1879) and 'Fellow-Townsmen' (April 1880). Both of them run to more than 20,000 words and *The Trumpet-Major* is nearly 130,000 words.

Smith, Elder, who had published *Far From the Madding Crowd* and *The Hand of Ethelberta*, accepted *The Return of the Native* for volume publication in autumn 1878. This was a cheering achievement, placing the new novel in a series with his old, and boding well for the future. Leslie Stephen still refused to consider Hardy's novels for the *Cornhill*, however, even though Smith, Elder published the magazine. Eventually, *Good Words* accepted *The Trumpet-Major* and began to serialize it in January 1880, by which point Hardy was already beginning work on his next book, *A Laodicean*. Harper & Brothers had asked him for a magazine story during 1879; by March 1880, Hardy had agreed terms for a serial to begin in January 1881. The commission was another good sign in itself and *Harper's New Monthly Magazine* paid well (£100 per instalment); Hardy would also become better known in the United States. Unhappily, though, he was putting himself under severe time-pressure.

Meanwhile, the editor of *Good Words*, the clergyman Donald Macleod, kept demanding that Hardy censor *The Trumpet-Major*. His requests were so finicky that Hardy began during 1880 consciously to write two versions of the book: one for the magazine and a second, closer to his original intentions, for volume publication. It was a strategy he returned to with *Tess* and *Jude*. On this occasion, it heightened his workload all the more, particularly when Smith, Elder agreed in July 1880 to publish *The Trumpet-Major* in volumes. These needed to appear promptly because it was normal practice for the parts to be bound together as a book as soon as a serial ended. If the first volume edition was to have any sales, it needed to forestall this semi-pirated version. During summer 1880, therefore, Hardy was completing *The Trumpet-Major* and, at the same time, revising it; when he was not doing either of these, he was first preparing and later writing the opening sections of *A Laodicean*.

It was a formidable burden and came at the end of two arduous years because amidst it all, Hardy had invested heavily in his profile: while in Tooting he began dining out regularly, joining the Savile Club and later the Rabelais Club, which was restricted to literary men. He met Matthew Arnold, Tennyson (who praised *A Pair of Blue Eyes*), Henry James, Richard Jefferies, Mary Braddon, Walter Besant, Sir Percy Shelley (son of the poet Shelley), Monckton Milnes and Charles Kegan Paul. He got to know Anne Procter better, the widow of the Romantic poet 'Barry Cornwall', and through her he met Robert Browning many times. All Hardy's labour, writing and networking, did certainly appear to pay off. Smith, Elder became his established publishers; respectful accounts of his work started to appear in heavyweight periodicals, and he was paid more and more for his work. Nonetheless, his writing remained a struggle, both effortful and against the grain.

The Return of the Native never received enthusiastic praise and would not sell; it was thought too gloomy and too intellectual. When he approached John Blackwood about his next book, Hardy was quick to reassure him that the *The Trumpet-Major* was 'above all things a cheerful story, without views or opinions, & is intended to wind up happily'. He said much the same thing to another publisher, J. P. Lippincott, a few weeks later: 'I may add that [*The Trumpet-Major*] is to be a cheerful, lively story, & is to end happily.'[6] He clearly wanted to dispel the unfortunate impression left by *The Return of the Native*. *The Trumpet-Major* is, undoubtedly, lighter in tone and it did achieve something of the desired effect. Reviews were kind, sales good and Hardy regained his reputation for pastoral comedy. It was a relatively minor hit nonetheless. Macleod's continual, niggling objections undermined Hardy's confidence that he could provide the pictures of rural life that his editors, if not his audience, wanted from him. There seemed to be something rebellious in his writing, try as he might to make it conventionally respectable.

His unease was clear when, immediately after *The Trumpet-Major*, he veered off in another direction again. *The Trumpet-Major* had been an historical novel; with *A Laodicean* Hardy now began a mixture of sensation novel, rural tale and romance, which he subtitled, '*A Story of To-Day*'. In it, he abandoned real locations too. *The Trumpet-Major* had been very precise, and originally gave the actual place names. *A Laodicean* used instead a vaguely West-of-England setting. And the new book was consciously intellectual once more, filled with the 'views and opinions' (many on currently controversial subjects) that *The Trumpet-Major* had avoided.

Artistic uncertainty reflected self-doubt and made it worse. As the summer continued, Hardy's correspondence began to reveal an almost manic relentlessness about his work. He needed an illustrator for *A Laodicean* and personally approached Helen Allingham, Frank Dicksee and William Small, before George du Maurier accepted.[7] Similarly, he wrote to R. B. Bowker, editor of *Harper's*, asking first for proofs, then enclosing corrections, then requesting that proofs be sent to du Maurier, and finally asking for 'yet another copy of proofs' for himself. His normally unflappable efficiency was coming under visible strain.[8]

The same was true when he and Emma went on holiday. They spent two weeks in Normandy during late July and August, between the end of *The Trumpet-Major* and the beginning of his writing *A Laodicean* – a time, that is, when his usual exhaustion at the completion of a novel was overshadowed by his gearing himself up already to begin a second. In the *Life*, which supplies the only record of the trip, Hardy mentions two supposedly comic incidents. At Le Havre, the couple took a room in a hotel and found they did not like it at all.

> Mrs Hardy fancied that the landlord's look was sinister; also the landlady's; and the waiter's manner seemed queer. Their room was hung with heavy dark velvet, and when the chambermaid came and they talked to her, she sighed continually and spoke in a foreboding voice; as if she knew what was going to happen to them, and was on their side, but could do nothing. The floor of the bedroom was painted a bloody red, and the wall beside the bed was a little battered, as if struggles had taken place there.

It emerges that on the coach to the town Hardy had told a fellow-traveller that he was carrying 'money with him in Bank notes'. This was, of course, 'a thing one never should do; yet he had done it'. Remembering his mistake in this eerie room threw Hardy and Emma into a panic which was made far worse when they discovered in the room a cupboard that 'had at its innermost recess another door, leading they did not know whither'.

Gothic menace generated farce.

> With their luggage they barricaded the closet door, so jamming their trunks and portmanteau between the door and the nearest bedstead that it was impossible to open the closet. They lay down and waited, keeping the light burning a long time.

It is a funny anecdote, in some ways, and a familiar tourist's alarm. Yet you worry for them too, dragging their suitcases around, barricading the door, and then lying awake. You worry because it is so unlike them. Both could be fussy abroad and Emma especially could imagine hostility but they were experienced travellers, resourceful and bold. Normandy, furthermore, was almost home from home. They had been there on honeymoon and Hardy in particular loved its beaches and cathedrals. It makes you wonder what it was, really, that prompted such antics.

A few days later in Honfleur, Hardy was frightened again.

> On a gloomy gusty afternoon, going up the steep incline through the trees behind the town they came upon a Calvary tottering to its fall; and as it rocked in the wind like a ship's mast Hardy thought that the crudely painted figure of Christ upon it seemed to writhe and cry in the twilight: "Yes, Yes! I agree that this travesty of me and my doctrines should totter and overturn in this modern world!" They hastened on from the strange and ghastly scene.[9]

A Laodicean was in many ways an autobiographical novel and it drew especially on Hardy's time as an architect in the late 1850s and 1860s; then he had been a committed Christian. The book also raised religious questions directly, by quoting from 'Familiar Conversations on Modern England' by Karl Hillebrand, a recently published article concerned with the anxiety created when traditional faith disappeared.[10]

For nearly fifteen years, Hardy would not have called himself a Christian and for most of that time, especially latterly, his loss of faith had not troubled him, partly because it had been replaced by positivism. Suddenly, this summer, religious anguish welled up in him. As he looked at the scene of Christ's death (frequently displayed by the roadside in Catholic countries), he felt the need for Christ to reassure him – for Christ to agree that it was right to reject Christianity. That impulse revealed how much he still wanted Christ's forgiveness – forgiveness in his case for abandoning faith in Christ. He seemed desperate that Christ should go quietly – that Christianity should fade out of history. At the same time, he wanted the opposite. If only Christ himself would tell Hardy that he was still faithful despite his unbelief and that his rejection of modern Christianity proved his loyalty to Christ.

*

The strain Hardy was undergoing during the summer of 1880 had been building up ever since he arrived in London two years before. Anxiety about his religious feelings had been provoked in particular by a bereavement earlier in the year, and from that flowed a confrontation with his past that proved, in the autumn, nearly fatal to his well-being.

In February 1880 Horace Moule's father, Henry, died. As Vicar of Fordington, he had been a leading light in the 1859 revival that touched Horace and, through him, Hardy too. His death reminded Hardy of the faith he had lost and prompted memories of familial happiness – the brothers' affection for one another and their tender care for their parents, especially in their distress after Horace Moule's suicide in 1873. He sincerely wanted to travel down to Dorset for the funeral and yet felt he could not spare the time. The impossibility of it made him realize how horribly London was imprisoning him.

Handley Moule, the youngest son and Hardy's near contemporary, posted a copy of the funeral sermon to him. 'I cannot refrain from sending you a line,' Hardy wrote in thanks, 'to tell you how deeply it has affected me.'[11] Touched and grateful, Hardy started to renew his acquaintance with the family, concerned to keep in contact with a past that threatened to fade away; also, from this point on, he began to imagine returning home for good. In a letter to Henry written in April 1880, Hardy mentions 'the plot of ground we want to get in Dorchester'. This is the first sign that he wanted to build a house in his hometown; though the plan did not come to fruition until five years later, it originated here.

When his father died, Handley Moule was a Fellow of Trinity College, Cambridge, and his brother Charles was in Corpus Christi. They responded to Hardy's friendliness during spring 1880 by inviting him to visit them and, in mid October, with *The Trumpet-Major* out of the way and *A Laodicean* making progress, Hardy felt able to take up their offer. He and Emma travelled up on 16 October and were shown round 'the usual buildings and other things worth seeing', as Hardy put it in the *Life*, 'though Cambridge was not new to Hardy'. He had seen it all before, in the summer of 1873, with Horace Moule. Their last meeting, Moule's 'last smile' were inevitably brought back to him as he walked the Cambridge streets once more. 'After the first day or two,' Hardy's account continues, 'he felt an indescribable physical weariness [. . .] but he kept going.' When their week-long stay was over, the couple returned to Tooting, arriving back 'the very day *The Trumpet-Major* was published', and at that point, Hardy finally could 'keep going' no longer. He collapsed, seriously ill, and did not step outside his house again until 10 April the following year, nearly seven months afterwards.

What precisely the matter was, nobody knew or knows for sure. The medical diagnosis, according to the *Life*, was internal bleeding but that sounds suspiciously like a catch-all or a euphemism. Geraldine, the heroine of 'An Indiscretion in the Life of an Heiress', died when she 'ruptured a blood-vessel internally'. Hardy may have employed an indefinite, rather romantic affliction to disguise more sordid details. He suffered from recurrent bladder infections in later life and may have had a stone in his urinary tract at this time or possibly a kidney stone. But neither of these would have caused such a lengthy illness; normally the patient would either have died or got rapidly better. His doctors offered Hardy the alternatives of a serious operation or several months bedridden; when he chose the latter, he was prescribed a restricted diet and the regime may have slowed down his recovery.[12] Whatever the physical illness involved, however, the root of the problem was psychological. Essentially, Hardy had a breakdown, brought on by two years' overwork and the impact of his visit to Cambridge.

During their stay, he and Emma had gone to Evensong in King's College Chapel. Hardy observed how the wax gathered on the candles and dripped to the floor.

> They were stalactites, plumes, laces; or rather they were surplices,
> – frayed shreds from those of bygone 'white-robed scholars', or
> from their shrouds – dropping bit by bit in a ghostly decay.
> Wordsworth's ghost, too, seemed to haunt the place, lingering and
> wandering on somewhere alone in the fan-traceried vaulting.

Sensing Wordsworth's ghost, Hardy was also remembering Horace Moule, who made a point of showing him the Chapel during the brief time they were together in Cambridge in 1873. 'M.', Hardy noted, 'opened the great West doors to show the interior vista' and took him up onto the roof.[13] For seven years, he had managed to suppress his feelings about Moule's death, often by burying them beneath the workload demanded by his career ambitions. Now, when he was at a low ebb professionally, this unfinished business came back to haunt him.

Partly, as with everyone, Hardy's grief was for himself. Wordsworth reminded him of his youthful ambitions to be a poet; Cambridge itself brought back his thwarted hope of entering the University. It seemed an institution that belonged to the fortunate people, like Charles and Handley Moule, who fitted in naturally with middle-class expectations. Wordsworth, as *The Prelude* showed, had been unhappy as a student; the

University had never rewarded Moule despite his exceptional talent; and Hardy had been shut out by the class system. All three of them seemed outcasts, permitted to visit but never accepted.

Because of the pressure he was under and the bereavements he had suffered, recently and more distantly, Cambridge in October 1880 made Hardy feel that the last seven years had been in vain. He had found no one to replace his old friend and similarly, there was nothing in his present life that compensated for the loss of childhood certainties, youthful hopes and religious faith. He felt himself to be 'lingering and wandering on somewhere alone', friendless and compromised, doing well enough but accomplishing nothing of real worth. These feelings would have been less powerful had he still felt himself comforted by a loving marriage, but signs that the relationship was under strain had been building up for a while. In Moule's absence, Emma had given Hardy the emotional security and encouragement that he needed during the first few years of their married life and that Moule's friendship had offered before. Now, sadly, amidst his trials and in part because of them, Emma could be of little help.

*

Hardy wrote on 21 February 1880 to George du Maurier, his future illustrator for *A Laodicean*, who drew cartoons for *Punch*. His letter contains a suggestion for a cartoon 'as promised':

> [Scene – After dinner in a fashionable London Drawing-room, before the men have come up.]
>
> *Mrs Tregushing* (young married lady from Cornwall, in town for a fortnight) "O yes – there are huge grand cliffs in Cornwall, & seals, & sea-gulls, & the most magnificent wild waves you ever saw!"
>
> *Mrs Fitzsneerly* (allowing her eye to travel slowly over Mrs T.'s person) – "Are there any dressmakers in Cornwall?" (Extinction of young Mrs T.)[14]

Fortunately, du Maurier did not take up the suggestion, which is not especially funny and filled to overflowing with animus against Emma; she was a married lady from Cornwall, who was liable to wear extravagant and unfashionable clothes and liable too to gush about the magnificent scenery of her homeland. 'Extinction of young Mrs T.' is a threatening phrase as well; the young woman's discomfiture kills her off.

In 'Fellow-Townsmen', published two months later, Hardy introduced for the first time a figure who later recurred in his fiction: the dissatisfied husband of a unloving wife who wishes he had married someone else. So far in Hardy's work, it was the women who made the wrong choice. Most recently in *The Trumpet-Major*, Anne Garland was caught between several men, between her impulses, her duties and her society's expectations. She was another version of Elfride, Bathsheba and Ethelberta. Mr Barnet in 'Fellow-Townsmen' is by contrast a new departure and foreshadows Henchard and Jude.

In the story, furthermore, Mr Barnet is given the opportunity to murder his wife with impunity: she has been involved in a boating accident and is thought to be dead from drowning. The doctor has declared as much. When Barnet is left alone with her, however, he notices traces of life.

> Barnet had a wife whose presence distracted his home; she now lay as in death; by merely doing nothing – by letting the intelligence which had gone forth to the world lie undisturbed – he would effect such a deliverance for himself as he had never hoped for, and open up an opportunity of which till now he had never dreamed.

An opportunity, that is to say, to marry the woman he really loves. She still lives nearby and from the bedroom window he can see the chimney of her house. His eye falls on it as he stands beside his 'dead' wife.

> There he saw that red chimney still smoking cheerily, and that roof, and through the roof that somebody. His mechanical movements stopped, his hand remained on the blind-cord, and he seemed to become breathless, as if he had suddenly found himself treading a high rope.

It is wonderful moment – vertiginous, like Henry Knight hanging from the cliff, and yet grounded too because, as Barnet is tempted to let his wife die, Hardy remarks that some 'honest men' will 'deliberate' indefensible actions while other 'honest men' will not.[15] A person's honesty does not depend on what they imagine, it depends on what they do, and many entirely decent, moral people in Barnet's situation would, like him, find themselves contemplating murder. It is impossible to tell who will and who will not be tempted in this way, but you can be sure that proper conduct does not imply serenity. The virtuous man does not escape his yearnings, his frustrations or his moments of malevolence.

The story prefigures *The Mayor of Casterbridge* in many ways and most important of these is its acceptance that people always struggle with the unacceptable desires they have. They cannot be improved, still less perfected; the most you can hope for in human beings is self-restraint. Strangely enough, Hardy had never quite reached the point of saying or believing this before. A more optimistic, earnest strain had lingered in his work even when it attacked earnestness and derided optimism. And it was the unhappiness in his marriage that produced his deeper disillusionment.

The moment in 'Fellow-Townsmen' provides another hint that Hardy felt estranged from Emma in early 1880. His imagination was producing ways of humiliating her and opportunities to get rid of her – opportunities that he knew he could not take. He was being forced to contemplate the prospect of a permanent doubleness at the heart of his life, shows of patience and affection keeping in check his feelings of hostility towards his wife. And he sensed that, in London at least, she would never cease from getting on his nerves. She did not fit in, either with London society or with Hardy's literary life. She had not lived in the capital before, not for any length of time, and she had no friends there. Nobody was around to advise her or smooth her way. Consequently, her social life depended more than ever on Hardy, who was himself edgy and tending to retreat in any case into contexts that excluded her. In 1878–80, as Hardy 'by degrees fell into line as a London man again', Emma could not join him. She was sidelined and as at the beginning of their marriage, Hardy began to ignore her, almost at times as if he simply forgot she was there.

It was in their house in Tooting, Hardy says, that his and Emma's 'troubles began'. What these 'troubles' were exactly, the *Life* will not say, only that 'they seemed to begin to feel that "there had past away a glory from the earth".' His phrasing – 'they seemed to begin to feel' – is exaggeratedly cautious and heavy-handed and he follows it with a quotation that had already become proverbial. It seems as if he is extremely reluctant to say anything more specific and this reluctance has created the embarrassment revealed in his style here. Two poems, however, written in the Tooting years suggest instead that he was genuinely baffled by what had happened.

'A January Night (1879)', published in 1918, and 'Snow in the Suburbs', not published until 1925, are both wintry poems. Cold and rain invade the house. With them come ghosts and uncertain fears.

The tip of each ivy-shoot
Writhes on its neighbour's face;
There is some hid dread afoot
    That we cannot trace.

Is it the spirit astray
Of the man at the house below
Whose coffin they took in to-day?
    We do not know.

The couple seem united only in their sense of hidden dread, some anguish they cannot trace back to its source.[16] As their marital problems began, Hardy did feel simply and bleakly unable to explain why they had occurred. He saw only that love was dying.

In some ways, he needed it to be like because he needed to ignore the extent to which his choices and actions were placing his marriage second and putting it at risk. From Hardy's point of view, he was working so painfully hard because it felt as if work was all he had – faith had gone, family was remote, home empty and the hope of children fading. He had come to London fearing that even novel writing would be taken away. However much he wanted to, he could not have stayed in Sturminster writing novels that wouldn't sell. Having a wife compelled him, he felt, to make this crushing effort – to write to order and write a lot. The personal cost had to be borne, even if that included the decline of their marriage.

As he felt the chill of love's decay, of course he turned even more towards the work that felt like his one support. Inevitably, too, that turn away from Emma made matters worse. It was a vicious circle that contributed to his illness but it was the illness (even though he later called it 'A Wasted Illness') that helped to rescue him.

— 16 —

No such bower will be known

WHEN HARDY fell ill late in October 1880, the serial of *A Laodicean* was about to start. The first instalment, dated January 1881, would actually appear a month beforehand, so as to catch the Christmas market. He was too sick to write the book but it was extremely late in the day for him to withdraw. He feared the impact on his professional reputation and declaring his sickness to the world was, in any case, the last thing he wanted to do. Fortunately, he did have some breathing space. The first three instalments had been sent to the publishers already by the end of September and part four was sent off in early November, just after he collapsed. He had been writing it during October and may have made some headway with part five too. 'Part V is nearly ready,' he assured his publishers from his sickbed, 'but I will not forward it unless desired.' It's not clear when he did send it, possibly not until the end of the year. Parts six, seven and eight, however, were sent off in rapid succession during January and February 1881 and the writing was completed by early summer.[1]

There seems, then, to have been a complete interruption in his work during November and December, and this shows for one thing how serious the illness was. The 'troublesome local irritation', as he called it, actually left him prostrate. Until Christmas, the situation was manageable. All Hardy needed to do to stay on schedule was correct proofs and Emma could do most of that for him. In the New Year, though, the publishing schedule was bound to start catching up with him and still he did not regain his strength. He remained confined to his bed and, if the book were to continue at all, he would have to dictate it, with Emma as his amanuensis.

The likelihood is that Emma became quite actively involved. From part six onwards the novel changed markedly; the style became more sentimental and the plot more episodic. In its settings, it drew on the couple's 1876 holiday in Holland and Germany and their more recent trip to Normandy. If these parts weren't Emma's suggestion (Hardy had used his holidays before, in *The Hand of Ethelberta* for example), nonetheless, they made it easier for her to offer ideas and participate imaginatively. And the ending in particular strikes a highly romantic note, unusual for Hardy, in which the heroine retrieves the situation, acting more energetically than is strictly ladylike and being rewarded with marriage to a humble architect.

The parallels are suggestive between these events and the Hardys' situation as the book was finished. *A Laodicean* retells the *Poor Man and the Lady* narrative and it reuses characters from *A Pair of Blue Eyes* – the aspiring architect and the well-born lady. From the outset, Hardy had been revisiting his early adulthood as he wrote the novel. Now, in the happy ending, the book shows a partnership of equals; unlike Elfride, this heroine is not crushed by men or oppressed in marriage. She is named Paula Power and she exerts her power; meanwhile, true love makes class differences irrelevant. It reads rather like a wish-fulfilment for Emma, who always wanted to play a part in Hardy's writing life and with this book had had the chance to do so, at long last. The way the book was written epitomized Emma's hopes for their life together and the story it told celebrated her ideal form of marriage. It was perhaps, from Hardy's point of view, a tribute to her and to her devoted support, which had rescued his novel, saved his reputation and seen him through a dangerous illness.

Nonetheless, when the book was done, Hardy knew he had to take stock. He could not think of it as anything much better than hack work, done to order, against the clock, in unfavourable circumstances and being so ill proved that he could not go on like this. His illness seemed to prove that Hardy simply could not cope in London. For some unclear temperamental reason, he could not flourish as a person, still less as a writer, unless he went away. During the winter, he reached that conclusion once and for all. Hardy had reached forty in June 1880, a few months before he broke down, and his illness was a form of midlife crisis, provoked by a whole range of uncertainties – about his career path, his marriage, his relation to his family and, underlying all of these, doubts about the ultimate worth of what he did.

As Hardy lay sick in bed through the winter of 1880–81, two literary giants passed away: Thomas Carlyle, the historian, essayist and sage, and George Eliot. During the same period, the entries in Hardy's notebook change in tone. Matthew Arnold, for instance, one of the leading critics and thinkers of the day, is starkly condemned: 'Arnold is wrong about provincialism', Hardy wrote. And in May, when he was just beginning to walk outside by himself again, he reached, 'after infinite trying', some 'General Principles'. These included judgements he would not alter for the rest of his life.

> The emotions have no place in a world of defect, and it is a cruel injustice that they should have developed in it.[2]

He was also reading Leslie Stephen again, in particular a long article, 'The Moral Element in Literature', published in January 1881. Stephen sees the writer as, potentially, a moral influence for good who must, in consequence, prove himself worthy of the reader's 'love or reverence'. He or she must also be utterly sincere. The poet:

> like the man, is lower in rank so far as he is wanting in sincerity, & therefore puts us off with sham conventional phrases[.]

Hardy was growing convinced that this was exactly how he had fallen short in his most recent novels.[3]

Stephen remained influential on Hardy, especially on a question such as what makes a writer genuine. He had followed Stephen's advice in 1876, by trying to pursue his 'perfectly fresh and original vein'. In 1879, he had noted down Stephen's dictum: 'The ultimate aim of a poet should be to touch our hearts by showing his own.' This demand only came home to him fully, however, as he lay on his sickbed. From 1881 onwards, he set himself the task of risking honesty, ignoring critical opinion and striking out on his own. Perhaps George Eliot's death helped free him to do this, allowing him to feel he was no longer in her shadow and could declare himself more fully. Even so, he found it an extremely difficult task to fulfil. It was to be more than five years before he felt he was even beginning to achieve artistic independence.

*

The first step was to leave London and he set about this as soon as he could. On 20 April he informed his landlord of his intention to leave and a few days later he drove down to Dorset with Emma in search of somewhere to live. Hardy had had it in mind for more than a year to buy a plot of land in Dorchester but either none had come available thus far or he was still wary of taking that final, probably irrevocable step. Instead, in June 1881, he rented a house in Wimborne Minster, a small town in the east of Dorset near the New Forest.

Wimborne now is rather enveloped by Bournemouth. In 1880, it was more a place unto itself and more of a local hub, because the London railway connected here with the Stour Valley line. Hardy's house, Lanherne (later renamed Llanherne) stood in a newly developed part of town between the old centre and the outlying station. In one direction, towards the railway, were workers' cottages; in the other, nearer town, were more middle-class dwellings – a veterinary surgeon, a Wesleyan minister, and some retired professional people. Wimborne offered the Hardys some of Sturminster's seclusion and more in the way of society. They mixed with educated people and joined in readings of Shakespeare; within six months they were being invited to the lord of the manor's shooting-party. Frank Douglas, a young man studying land agency, lived nearby and sought them out. His brother George Douglas, a Scottish landowner, was an admirer of Hardy's work and soon became a trusted friend. There were good bookshops too and a fine Minster church – a building that Hardy especially loved.[4] He and Emma travelled around the district, with Kate joining the party once again, and Hardy took a renewed interest in local history – in the gossip about Miss Drax, for instance, who owned Charborough House nearby, in the life histories of coachmen and generally in 'The slow meditative lives of people who live in habitual solitude'.[5]

He told his cousin John Antell in July that they had moved to Wimborne 'for the air, which is considered necessary for my complete restoration' and through the autumn, he wrote very little, only two minor short stories, 'What the Shepherd Saw' and 'Benighted Travellers', which appeared for Christmas 1881. In the New Year, he accepted a commission for another novel, with the first instalment due to appear in May, but, unusually for him, he had done hardly any work on the project before setting up the deadline. For the preceding six months, he had spent his time enjoying the quiet of a country garden with:

> all sorts of old-fashioned flowers, in full bloom: Canterbury bells, blue and white, and Sweet Williams of every variety, strawberries and cherries that are ripe.

When he did work, proof reading *A Laodicean* mostly and revising it for volume publication, it was seated 'under the vine on their stable-wall' where the sun shone 'through the great leaves, making a green light on the paper'. His convalescence had otherwise been interrupted only by a holiday, spent in Scotland during August 1881.[6]

The rest did him good. Wimborne proved congenial and the year ended, as he remarks in the *Life*, 'with a much brighter atmosphere for the author and his wife than the opening had shown'.[7] So long as he kept his distance from London, Hardy's state of mind and body improved; soon enough, unfortunately, he was drawn back into trying literary 'squabbles'.

On 29 December 1881, a play, *The Squire* by A. W. Pinero, was given its first night at St James's Theatre. Similarities to *Far From the Madding Crowd* were seen at once and made more suspicious by the fact that the same theatre had been offered Hardy's dramatization of the novel during the previous year. Hardy was plainly upset because his letters refer several times in early 1882 to this piece of shady dealing. He was then accused of plagiarism himself – in sections of *A Laodicean* and *The Trumpet-Major*. The accusations were quite groundless and, as Hardy remarked to his American publisher, 'it is hardly matter for surprise that, in view of recent events connected with the stage, such a counter-charge should have been made'. Later in the year, rather bad poems started to appear in London magazines under the name 'Thomas Hardy'. They were nothing to do with him and Hardy was provoked so much that he wondered whether he could copyright his name.[8]

Even so, Wimborne made it easier for Hardy to brush off these irritations. He was enjoying his work on the new novel, *Two on a Tower*, and when it was finished in mid September, he and Emma went on holiday, first touring the West Country and then, in October, travelling to Paris.

> [T]hey stayed for some weeks, away from English and American tourists, roving about the city and [. . .] practising housekeeping in the Parisian bourgeois manner, buying their own groceries and vegetables, dining at restaurants, and catching bad colds owing to the uncertain weather.

It is like a repeat of their early married life, with its Bohemian shapelessness, its sense of spontaneity and improvisation. Exactly two years earlier, Hardy had fallen ill and a relapse of some sort always threatened when he finished working on a book. The cure this time was to suspend for a moment his regular, disciplined life and to regress. The two of them were 'playing truant', as Hardy called it.[9] They may also have been trying once more to conceive a child. Emma was nearly forty-two and Hardy's mother had been forty-three when she gave birth to Kate. There was reason to think they still had just a little more time. And, as Martin Seymour-Smith points out, solitariness, seclusion and domesticity would all have been conducive.[10]

Whatever their hopes, when they came back to Wimborne they found themselves thrown back into the gloomy realities of adulthood. Caddell Holder, Emma's brother-in-law and still rector of St Juliot, had died while they were away and Emma quickly went down to Cornwall to comfort her sister. Hardy felt the loss personally because he was fond of Holder, an old-fashioned and broadminded cleric, who was not too fussy about doctrine, not too exacting about morals and known instead for his funny, sometimes risqué stories. Hardy celebrated these qualities when he recalled Holder in the *Life* but he began his eulogy on a bleaker note. At Holder's death, Hardy and Emma:

> realized that the scene of the fairest romance of their lives, in the picturesque land of Lyonnesse, would have no more kinship with them.

Cornwall had suddenly become another place where they would never go again. The world of Emma's youth and the most important of her imaginary retreats had disappeared, just as for Hardy his life as 'a London man' had recently vanished – he knew he could never live and work there again. By closing the door on Cornwall, Caddell's death was a painful, private loss for Emma but it was a severe loss to the marriage as well.

Soon afterwards, Hardy wrote to his friend Edmund Gosse telling him that 'We propose to leave Wimborne for good about March: the house we are in lies rather too near the Stour level for health.' Perhaps this was one of their reasons; more significant was the fact that some suitable land had finally become available near Dorchester and, at the end of November, Hardy had begun the slow process of acquiring it. After more than two years' wait, he was impatient to get on.

In January 1883, he wrote again to Gosse.

> We were discussing just now the curiously tonic effect (morally) of having to get up by candlelight on a dark morning early for some bustling mean utilitarian purpose. If you have not tried the plan do so the next time you feel in a nervous overdone state. I

trust however, & believe, that you never reach any such unhappy
condition.

Building a house for her and resolving to settle outside London in a
genteel country town was in some respects what Emma had always
wanted Hardy to do. And he did present it in that light by referring to
Max Gate frequently as a house he designed for her. Even so, the
impulse behind the move was more self-centred and less romantic.
During the first few months of 1883, Hardy was determined to wake up
from dreams and shed illusions – resolved to embrace once again the
bustle of the mean and utilitarian because that was all there was. He did
so reluctantly in some ways and reluctance made him all the more
uncompromising.

Wimborne may always have been a stopgap, a place of convalescence
that Hardy planned to move on from quite swiftly. It had offered, even
so, a meeting place between London and Dorset. 'I seem to see more of
London now than when we lived in the suburbs,' he told Alexandra Orr.
'I very frequently run up, & enjoy those very commonplaces of town life
which used to be a weariness.'[11] This was in December 1881; a year
later, returning home from Paris, his mood had changed. In Wimborne,
as elsewhere, his and Emma's lives seemed to be ebbing away.

And so they moved. The purchase of land outside Dorchester on the
Wareham road went through during the spring and Hardy signed the
lease on 14 June 1883. By the end of June he and Emma had moved
into a rented house, Shire-Hall Place, near the centre of Dorchester.
And by the year's end the ground was being prepared for the building
of Max Gate. Legal matters, the move itself, starting to design the house
and then overseeing its construction – all these took up Hardy's energies
and distracted him from the despondency which seemed always about
to descend during the early 1880s. For Emma too, though Hardy's
family were unwelcoming, Dorchester offered more than Wimborne and
the thought of entering a house of her own, built by her husband, would
have lifted her spirits.

*

Hardy's principal feeling in moving back home was not nostalgic, though
that is what one might expect and what has usually been assumed, by
both critics and biographers. Instead, he was looking forward, and
putting the past behind him in order to address the realities of his

situation – his time of life, his gifts and his limitations as a writer, and the prospect of never having children. There were to be no more indolent holidays in Paris and no more running away to live in romantic seclusion deep in the countryside. Dissatisfaction with what he had achieved so far convinced him that he must focus his powers more narrowly – he had to put into practice Leslie Stephen's maxims: embrace the sincerity essential to great art and avoid becoming distracted by changing literary fashions, by critical orthodoxies or by prudish editors.

Hardy told the critic, Kegan Paul, just before he left London in 1881 that 'the worst work I have ever done has been written under the influence of stupidly adverse criticism'.[12] He knew that he was someone it was comparatively easy to blow off course; the more difficult thing was to find a context where he could keep going at his own endeavour without sinking into lassitude or despair. In Dorchester he did manage that. Sticking to his own inspiration led to the sober intensity of the four great novels he wrote over the next twelve years: *The Mayor of Casterbridge*, *The Woodlanders*, *Tess* and *Jude*. Yet he did not accomplish these things swiftly or easily. There were long periods of inertia and despondency during the mid 1880s, not least because, as he made the decision to return home, he knew he was taking an enormous risk.

Dorchester had its compensations. His family was nearby. Indeed, within a few months, Hardy's father and brother were at work building Max Gate. And, unlike Wimborne or Sturminster, Dorchester offered Hardy numerous contexts outside the marriage where he could busy himself, be entertained and find companionship. He was a son of the town, so relatives and acquaintances, if not close friends, were all around. The new setting, though apparently at the opposite extreme from Tooting, resembled it to the extent that it provided Hardy with a social context from which Emma was excluded.

Some affection for her remained, as did Hardy's underlying emotional dependence, revived as that had been by his illness. Nonetheless, from now on, Hardy would have little time for Emma's fancifulness and naivety (whether affected or natural); he would disapprove of her absurd, flamboyant clothes – like 'a vague recollection', as Gosse put it, 'of some nymph in a picture by Botticelli' – and feel contemptuous of her airy unworldliness.[13] For all Emma's attachment to the proprieties, it was Hardy who now masked his rebellious spirit beneath rigid respectability – beneath the conventional social manner he needed to adopt if he were to turn himself into Thomas Hardy, the famous author.

One poem gives us a glimpse of Hardy's deepest feelings at this time.
During his career as a novelist (between 1872 or so and 1895), he wrote
very few poems and they are nearly all marked by particular personal
resonance. At some stage during 1883, he composed 'He Abjures Love'.
'At last I put off love,' it begins, 'For twice ten years | The daysman of
my thought, | And hope, and doing'. He refuses its charms and its
anxieties. He will not any longer:

> by wilful ways
> And baseless ires,
> Return the anxious smiles
> Of friendly faces.

He prefers instead to live without illusions.

> No more will now rate I
> The common rare [. . .]
> Things dreamt, of comelier hue
> Than things beholden!

He will be steady, clear-eyed and kind. He will understand how outward-
going friendliness often masks insecurity and no longer reacts to it with
'baseless ires'. Yet, all the while, he will be in despair. Whatever
tranquillity he gains from such clear-headedness and moderation, it will
be no true recompense for love itself.

The final stanza goes back on all that been said before.

> – I speak as one who plumbs
> Life's dim profound
> One who at length can sound
> Clear views and certain.
> But – after love what comes?
> A scene that lours,
> A few sad vacant hours,
> And then, the Curtain.[14]

This poem has the feelings characteristic of Hardy's work over the next
ten years: the wistfulness, the stoical realism and the desire to bring
loving kindness into a loveless, empty world. Biographically, it reflects
how he wanted to live his marriage. He would leave behind the illusions
of love – that were both precious and destructive to him – and amidst
this disappointment, he would do his best to go on being affectionate

and kind. Abandoning passion was, he believed, the only way for him to carry on – to avoid illness, take steps against professional failure and prevent marital conflict. The troubles between him and Emma could never be resolved and he must somehow resign himself to them.

In 1880, Hardy had been tempted to humiliate his wife via cartoons and he had even imagined her death; in Wimborne, he had realized that their old idyllic life together could never be resumed. If he were going to preserve his peace of mind and his respectability, he would have to learn to leave passionate feelings behind. He must try not to count too carefully the cost of that renunciation.

*

Hardy's retreat from the marriage was made easier by his involvement in building Max Gate. Hardy had always taken an interest in house building and rarely had the opportunity to pursue it. Before leaving for London in 1862, he had drawn up designs of a grand town house, presumably in order to show off his abilities to prospective employers in the capital. Blomfield had built churches almost exclusively and by the time Hardy was working for Crickmay he had been turned into something of a church building specialist. With Max Gate, he could at last build a house of his own without having to take into account the views of either clients or senior partners so his obsession with the project was perhaps understandable. He designed the entire structure, down to the details of drainage and fittings, and was an exacting supervisor – builders came to dread working for him. He had no intention of giving his brother and father a free hand, even if they were family, and, according to Nathaniel Sparks, Hardy's cousin, the result was a quarrel. Thomas Hardy senior vowed, when the work was finished, that he would never build such a house again for the £1,000 Hardy had paid him.

Hardy's fascination extended to the plot of land, especially when Roman remains were found there. Digging the foundations uncovered three skeletons buried in separate, oval graves – 'the tight-fitting situation strongly suggestive of the chicken in the egg shell', as Hardy observed, rather eerily. Urns were buried with the bodies and in one the builders found a 'fibula or clasp of bronze or iron, the front having apparently been gilt'. In May 1884, Hardy read a paper about these finds to the Dorset Natural History and Antiquarian Field Club and the following year, he wrote an archaeological story, 'Ancient Earthworks and What Two Enthusiastic Scientists Found Therein', which is set on Maiden

Castle, an Iron Age fort visible from Max Gate. The scientists of the title unearth Roman objects there, including a statue of Mercury. Similarly his first magazine interview, published in 1886, finds him at home in Max Gate. Nearby Maiden Castle, Conquer Barrow, and the Hardy monument on Black Down Hill are all pointed out with affection and pride. The interview was extensively ghostwritten by Hardy and both tone and content reveal his investment in this particular spot. Of course, the site of Max Gate was not absolutely of Hardy's choosing (he had had to take what was on offer, as and when it came on the market), but he was now intent upon establishing his claim to it.[15]

In the *Life* Hardy gave the impression that he was more offhand about Dorchester and Max Gate. When they first arrived, he and Emma 'did not foresee' staying in the town for 'the remainder of their lives', though 'in the long run it proved not ill-advised' to do so.[16] This is a lawyer's answer, not inaccurate but designed to give a misleading impression. In truth, everything about their move to Dorchester implied a coming to rest. There was a far greater chance that they would feel imprisoned than that they would ever leave. For Emma, this was particularly the case, partly because the house Hardy could afford to build was actually rather cramped.

When it was first built in 1885, Max Gate was L-shaped, with two rooms on the ground floor, plus a kitchen and scullery at the back. Above, at the front, were the master bedroom and across the landing Hardy's study, with a dressing room in between. A second bedroom lay at the back, over the kitchen, and the servants slept in the attics above Hardy's study. The couple's homes in Wimborne and Tooting had both been larger than this and in Wimborne they had enjoyed a spacious garden as well. All that surrounded Max Gate was an open field. 'The only drawback to the site seemed to be its newness', as Hardy later wrote – a rawness that was not offset by discovering antiquities, however fascinating these might be.

Hardy did set about planting a garden straight away, asking his cousin John Antell for advice about which trees to choose. Gardens take time to mature and inevitably Max Gate remained in an exposed position for a number of years. Outdoors you could readily be seen from the road and even indoors your privacy was compromised. Hardy designed and built peculiar window shutters that could be raised from below, parallel with the sash. Light could still enter through the upper half of the window while the people inside were hidden behind the shutter covering the lower half. This arrangement gives an indication of how much he and Emma valued their privacy and how much Max Gate endangered it.[17] It was also a rather enclosing design; when the shutters are raised, they give the sense that the room is half underground, like a basement flat.

Similarly, although their most recent home, Shire-Hall Place in Dorchester, had not been large, with little by way of a garden and no view other than that of Dorchester jail, the town had been all around. Now for the first time since she married, Emma was living out-of-town, isolated from neighbours. In addition, Max Gate was Hardy's through and through. Apart from running the household (which she never much enjoyed), Emma had little opportunity to make her mark. She loved gardening and Hardy laid out a garden for her, but somehow it was John Antell who chose the trees. Perhaps without even intending it, Hardy had built his wife a gilded cage, shut her up in it and left her to herself.

Taking the universe seriously

IT HAS BEEN almost taken for granted that when Hardy came back to live in Dorchester he was returning to the bosom of his family, that the more than decade-long rift Emma had caused was now healed and his bond with his mother restored. In line with this, Hardy's recovery of an intimate connection with home, roots and family has been presented as the crucial reason why his writing improved in the following years. It's a version of events that allows biographers to treat Hardy's marriage as an aberration and it also simplifies his relationship with Dorset, both the way he portrayed it in his novels and how he felt when he returned home. Clearly, Hardy did see more of his family when he was living in Dorchester and his relationship with Emma became increasingly distant as he grew older. Nonetheless, he did not simply shift his affections from one to the other, from wife to mother, when he moved to his home territory. It's truer to say that he kept himself insulated from both.

There is unusually little evidence about Hardy's state of mind during his first few years back in Dorchester. The *Life* gives only a dozen pages to the years 1883–85; there are very few entries in the surviving 'Personal Notebooks' – only one for the whole of 1884 – and Hardy's extant letters are concerned, as usual, mostly with business matters. It seems a significant and mysterious gap in the record, comparable to the one surrounding 1869–70, for example, or later times when his personal life was potentially scandalous. In this case, though, you are somehow left with the impression of silence at the time rather than of Hardy's destroying the evidence afterwards. Hardy seems for a while to have been too preoccupied and withdrawn to leave much trace behind. He cuts a forlorn figure, wary and self-involved as often, but more despondent too.

There were several factors contributing to this loss of heart. He had reached the conclusion that his marriage was a failure and would, from now on, be a burden he must learn to bear. He was, as before in

Sturminster and Wimborne, at home in Dorset and yet not at home – uncomfortable and unsure of himself. In *The Return of the Native*, he had asked himself whether the native could ever return. Now, in 1883, the same question disturbed him more than ever because he felt he would never thrive anywhere else. He was convinced that he had 'lived too much in the country to bear transplanting to town'.[1] His recent illness inevitably left its mark as well. As he looked back on it, the winter of 1880–81 looked like the end of his youth. He must take greater care of his health from now on and concentrate his resources, resisting the encroachments of 'never-napping Time'. Even so, perhaps the most important reason for Hardy's gloom was his nagging uncertainty about his career, as he struggled to find a direction that would release him from the mediocrity he seemed to have been sinking into.

His loss of confidence had been made considerably worse just before he moved to Dorchester by the reception of *Two on a Tower*. Most of the reviewers in autumn 1882 treated the book as minor – acceptable and pleasant enough even though not up to the standard of Hardy's earlier achievements. Several of the critics, however, decided it was 'repellent', 'unpleasant' and 'objectionable', although the public was more encouraging. As Hardy commented to his old friend Anne Procter, 'by their buying, & enthusiastic letter-writing to me on the subject, [they] show that their interest in it is greater than in anything I have done latterly'. The critics, meanwhile, 'have been quite acid'. 'Which,' Hardy asks, 'am I to believe?'[2]

The scandal in *Two on a Tower* was mild enough – so mild in fact that the critical hostility does seem contrived. Hardy's heroine is a married woman, Viviette, whose husband is abroad and may be dead; in his absence, she falls in love with a far younger man, Swithin St Clare. Viviette is too susceptible to Swithin's charms to be quite admirable and Hardy reminds the audience of the moral conundrum she faces – almost certainly she is a widow and free to marry Swithin; only an accidental lack of information makes her natural instinct an adulterous one. Hardy turns this mild satire on respectability's contradictions into something more serious when Viviette and Swithin conceive a child. Soon afterwards, Swithin leaves for South Africa to pursue his research as an astronomer, still not knowing that Viviette is pregnant. At this point Viviette learns that her first husband actually has died but instead of releasing her, as it would have done just a little earlier, the news threatens to be ruinous. The only way she can see to escape from disgrace is to marry someone else as quickly as possible and, conveniently, a bishop is already pursuing her. By adding deceit to her fornication, she leads the bishop to stand father to a child he soon realizes is not his own.

There is evidently comedy here and Hardy responded to the reviewers' outrage by accusing them of having no sense of humour: 'I conclude that we are never never again to be allowed to laugh & say with Launce – "it is a wise father that knows his own child." '[3] It is a fair enough riposte to critical primness but a disingenuous one too. Nothing compelled Hardy to choose a bishop and the book gave that character no credit for his actions. We are told that he does not broadcast the scandal (or divorce Viviette) only because doing so would harm his own reputation. Similarly, the novel forgives Viviette for having sex with Swithin outside marriage. She is seen as loving and altruistic and Swithin is praised for his enduring loyalty to her. Set against them is a self-important cleric who receives the comeuppance he hardly seems to deserve. By implication, 'loving kindness' between fornicators is more valuable and more virtuous than upholding moral decency. Redemptive love inhabits the sexual, romantic world and not the religious one.

These are provocative things to imply and Hardy must have known, at some level, that he was giving cause for offence. All the same, in his letters around Christmas 1882, he sounds genuinely surprised that the book has produced an outcry. The immediate result was that he found it difficult to go forward. While completing the novel, he wrote a brief short story, 'A Tradition of 1804', and before the reviews came out he wrote 'The Three Strangers', one of his most vivid tales. Both of these are distinctively local – 'A Tradition of 1804' recalls *The Trumpet-Major* and 'The Three Strangers', like 'The Distracted Preacher', previously entitled 'The Distracted Young Preacher', celebrates the lawlessness of rural people. They harbour convicted criminals, saving them from the gallows, but their actions reveal only that they live by a higher standard of morals than their masters, the official upholders of morality. It is the same point he was making in *Two on a Tower*.

Hardy seemed, in other words, to be doing rather well in Wimborne during 1882 as he recuperated and there was a lot that was good in *Two on a Tower*, even though he had written it very fast. It had charm as well as originality; there was more depth of feeling in it than in either *A Laodicean* or *The Trumpet-Major* and likewise, 'A Tradition of 1804' was entertaining and almost effortless to write. As for 'The Three Strangers', it was a triumph: sardonic, kindly, closely observed, and elegantly constructed; it was also a success in the terms Hardy was now setting himself – both a 'precise transcript of ordinary life' and narrating something 'uncommon in human experience'. Though all this boded well, 1883 turned out to be an almost uniquely unproductive year and 1884 was little better. Hardy would not publish another novel until 1886.

There had never been such a gap in his output before and it can be accounted for only in part by his being so busy designing Max Gate and overseeing the building work. When he left London in 1881, Hardy had been assuming that his health and creativity would soon revive in the country (as they had done before, so dramatically, in 1867); in Wimborne, at first, exactly that appeared to take place because *Two on a Tower* and the short stories proved so easy and enjoyable to write. The novel's reception then threw this optimism into question. Even if he felt reinvigorated by Dorset, perhaps his London audience would prove obstinately hostile to what being in the country inspired him to write. That had been his experience in Sturminster five years earlier when *The Return of the Native* proved so stubbornly unsuccessful, and that had been the problem he attempted to solve by moving to London in 1878. The reviews of *Two on a Tower* showed that he was still caught between compromise and sincerity. Coming home, however good for him personally, left him in no-man's-land nevertheless.

There's no doubt that he faltered and what little he produced in 1883–4 became generic – conventional and proficient but lacking in distinctiveness and imaginative energy. He wrote first a long short story, 'The Romantic Adventures of a Milkmaid', published in the summer of 1883. It came out in seven parts in America, in *Harper's New Monthly Magazine*; in Britain it appeared entire in the special summer number of the *Graphic*, a weekly magazine, whose large format allowed for unusually large and high-quality illustrations.[4] The *Graphic* later became an important outlet for Hardy's work – *The Mayor of Casterbridge*, *Tess* and *A Group of Noble Dames* all appeared there and Hardy came to rely on Arthur Locker, editor of the magazine. The rhythm of the *Graphic*'s weekly parts and the prominence it gave to pictures both had an impact on Hardy's style, contributing to its eventfulness and visuality. It may be one reason why his books have been so successful as films.[5]

In 1883, all this lay in the future. The story he sent to Locker at the end of February was overfamiliar and oddly unconvincing. A striking loss of self-confidence is evident in the story, as if the reviews of *Two on a Tower* had reawoken Hardy's fear of rejection and his belief that he could not afford to speak his mind. Perhaps he was only marking time but if so, the next story he wrote was worryingly similar. *Youth's Companion*, an American magazine, asked Hardy to write for them in April 1883. Accepting the offer, he assured the editor that:

> You may depend upon my using my best efforts to please your numerous readers; & that the story shall have a healthy tone, suitable to intelligent youth of both sexes.

This sounds like Hardy four years earlier, reassuring editors that *The Trumpet-Major* would be 'a cheerful, lively story' by contrast with *The Return of the Native*.[6] He also sounds very willing to adapt himself to editorial requirements – he will write as the servant of his paymaster, as someone who could be depended upon to provide the appropriate kind of work. Like 'The Romantic Adventures', the story he wrote, 'Our Exploits at West Poley', has some interestingly doubtful implications, especially if read in a Freudian light. It remains, even so, a completely acceptable example of the genre Hardy was being asked to write – a boyhood adventure, comparable to (although less good than) Richard Jefferies's *Bevis: The Story of a Boy*, published in 1882.

Meanwhile, Hardy was turning down requests from more major editors and agents. Alfred Austin, later Poet Laureate, wrote to him in December 1882, hoping for something to help launch the *National Review*. The first issue was planned for March 1883 and Austin was co-editor. Hardy said he might be able to help, though not for a while. There was another approach in January, perhaps from the literary agent, A. P. Watt, and once again Hardy refused, pleading pressure of work, although actually he had very little on the stocks. He seems at this time to have selected out-of-the-way commissions deliberately, in the more downmarket, throwaway *Graphic* or in obscure American journals, rather than take on a major project. He would rather for the moment write to order – impersonally and, as it were, semi-detached from what he did.[7]

*

Hardy's fortunes as a writer were revived and his whole career turned round by his breaking away altogether from fiction for the first time and beginning to write 'a sketch, or series of sketches' of rural, working-class life in Dorset. Margaret Oliphant (1828–97), the novelist and journalist, had requested this piece from him in July 1882 but Hardy declined at the time, claiming to be 'so hopelessly behindhand' with other 'less substantial productions' that he could not take on anything else. He did promise, however, to 'communicate with Mr Longman as soon as I am in a position to write a paper of the sort' because, he said, he had often thought 'of taking the labouring poor of this my native county seriously'.[8] Margaret Oliphant probably did not set too much store by these assurances and would have been surprised when a year later Hardy came up with 'The Dorsetshire Labourer'.

When it was published in June 1883, Hardy called it modestly a 'merely descriptive' piece; similarly, he told John Morley, his old acquaintance, who was now involved in politics, that 'Though a Liberal, I have endeavoured to describe the state of things without political bias.'[9] He claimed to be putting before the public nothing more than a faithful account of how the people around him lived and worked so that his discussion of a controversial topic – the condition of the labouring poor – would be quite neutral. So far during 1883, he had been writing stories that fitted with generic expectations, largely as a result of a self-protective reaction when *Two on a Tower* caused offence. He was holding his creativity in check and making himself obedient and dispassionate instead. In 'The Dorsetshire Labourer' the same absence of innovation or daring – the same lack of imagination, one might say – was just what was required because in order to be accurately descriptive it was necessary to remain passive before the facts. Fiction's cheeky, occasionally provocative distortions (like those most recently in *Two on a Tower*) must be given up in place of patience, clear-headedness and objectivity. Moreover, this artistic self-denial was an exact equivalent to Hardy's abjuring love.

The political situation at the time encouraged this change in approach. On 15 March 1883, a bomb exploded in Westminster, planted by the Fenians. The threat to Prime Minister Gladstone and other members of his government created panic in the authorities, so that all forms of dissent looked threatening, whether they arose out of the Irish situation, industrial relations or the depression in agriculture. Farm labourers were known to be enduring hardship and their plight had been in the news several times that year already. Hardy did not wish his piece to be attacked as an untimely encouragement of rebellion. Indeed, despite his socialistic youth and his consistently left-wing sympathies, he did not believe in rebellion any longer, if he ever had, and that too led him to embrace a passively realistic mode of writing, committed to and absorbed in the facts themselves.

In April 1883, he took lengthy notes from a magazine article, 'The

European Terror' written by Émile de Laveleye, and then referred to it in 'The Dorsetshire Labourer'.[10] Laveleye differentiated in his essay between several kinds of socialism: the nihilist and anarchist thread, the collectivists and the 'Possibilists' – i.e. those who believed in social evolution instead of revolution. Hardy connects this last, more moderate, gradualist group with the trade union leader Joseph Arch (1826–1922), one of the heroes of his own essay. Arch had been first president of the National Agricultural Labourers' Union, founded in 1872, and had toured the country recruiting members. Hardy had heard him speak and what he recalled was the 'remarkable moderation in [Arch's] tone'. Arch refused to exaggerate the miseries of the poor and he even sang the praises of cottage life. It was this evident accuracy about the advantages of the poor man's existence as well as its afflictions that made Arch persuasive. According to Hardy, it was this truthfulness that had made him successful in his campaign for improved wages. Arch's 'remarkable moderation', as Hardy called it, was made possible, he goes on to say, because Arch was both a 'humorist' and 'a man by no means carried away by an idea beyond the bounds of common sense'.[11]

In all these respects, Hardy began taking Arch as his example. Keeping your sense of humour was essential, and so was a sense of perspective, if you were not to overstate your case and so destroy it. Hardy began, in other words, reaching towards a way of writing that was cautious, even quietist at points, and yet would never become time-serving or dishonest. The essay has been criticized, certainly, for placating the powers-that-be – for painting too rosy a picture of rural life and disguising its poverty, the near-starvation many suffered and the actual starvation that afflicted a few. That criticism is unfair because, although it is deliberately understated and unsensational, Hardy's article is also detailed in unexpected ways and at unexpected moments. In it, for example, he draws a poignant sketch of an old shepherd no longer of sufficient use to be hired by a farmer.

> 'There's work in en,' says one farmer to another, as they look dubiously across; 'there's work left in en still; but not so much as I want for my acreage'. 'You'd get en cheap,' says the other.

Hardy makes no comment on this, observing and letting it be observed that the man is being treated just like an animal.

Meanwhile, Hardy displays scrupulous fair-mindedness. He does not exclude the fact, for example, that where wages were low, there could be compensations – a cottage and garden rent free, and 'Fuel, too, is frequently furnished, in the form of wood faggots.' Similarly, he includes a lengthy paragraph arguing that 'The question of enough or not enough often depends less upon [. . .] the earnings of the head of the household than upon the nature of his household.' A family with lots of daughters would be bound to be less well off than one with several 'strong boys', old enough to work alongside their father.

The telling anecdote and the curious detail are both integral to Hardy's 'merely descriptive' writing. He does not inveigh against the sentimental image of the countryside held by his urban readership; rather, he indirectly challenges it simply by presenting agriculture's forms of casual harshness and, secondly, by drawing his readers in, intriguing them with peculiarities and oddities they would never have foreseen. These nuggets of information do not disrupt the received idea so much as make it irrelevant. Meanwhile, the absence from the essay of personal intervention, polemic or editorializing was a way of taking people as seriously as they deserved. Just observing, without preconceptions, was a way of viewing country people with respect.[12]

Farm labourers were known generically at the time as 'Hodge'. 'Hodge', Hardy says, was assumed to be 'a degraded being of uncouth manner and aspect, stolid understanding, and snail-like movement'. Such people were easy for visitors to find, especially in Dorset, 'where Hodge in his most unmitigated form is supposed to reside'. Yet, actually, the stereotype does not exist. Suppose a visitor from London were taken by 'Hodge' to live with him at home; he would soon become 'conscious', Hardy says, 'of a new aspect in the life around him'.

> [W]ithout any objective change whatever, variety had taken the place of monotony; that the man who had brought him home – the typical Hodge, as he conjectured – was somehow not typical of anyone but himself[.]

After six months, the visitor would find that Hodge 'has become disintegrated into a number of dissimilar fellow-creatures, men of many minds, infinite in difference'. You can discover this, Hardy asserts, only from the inside. You can know the individual labourer only if you 'take pot-luck with him and his, as one of the family'.[13]

For a writer, like Hardy, who is trying to present Dorset to Londoners – to an educated, urban readership – the problem is how to remove the lens of caricature. Your writing must somehow repeat the sequence of events described at the beginning of the essay – the process, that is to say, of gradually bringing your readers up close and personal with the ordinary and yet unexpected world of Dorset people, in all its oddity and particularity. You would learn nothing by anatomizing a problem, like the 'philosophers who look down [. . .] from the Olympian heights', as Hardy put it in the essay; instead, the local historian, just like the visitor from London, needed to take 'pot-luck'; that is, accept hospitality at a meal without special preparation – taking whatever happens to be in the pot at the time. So, in an extended sense, you must take what's on offer at any given moment, suspend your judgement and preferences. Taking pot-luck involves a receptive, absorbed attentiveness.

By temperament, Hardy craved order and invulnerability, but now he found that his novel writing required him to be tentative and open. For a writer, taking pot-luck meant adopting a merely descriptive attitude, one in which you refused to impose your prejudices, your ideas or your preconceived opinions. You had to receive Hodge and receive from him. Elizabeth-Jane, the young heroine of his next novel, *The Mayor of Casterbridge*, is constantly placed where she can watch. She, 'being out of the game, and out of the group, could observe all' and this might be Hardy speaking of himself, out of things in Dorchester because no longer truly 'native', yet able to see all. And, writing again about Elizabeth-Jane, Hardy claims that 'To learn to take the universe seriously there is no quicker way than to watch.'[14]

Away from the hurry of city life and, particularly for Hardy, away from literary gossip and literary fashion, you may gain the opportunity to perceive, recognize and portray things that others have missed – histories and truths that have been passed over by people preoccupied with their own rightness. No longer hoping for anything from the system and being satisfied with 'tentativeness from day to day' leads Hardy to develop his sense of the story-teller simply watching what goes on around: passive, unprejudiced, non-judgemental, and inquiring. This watchfulness is a kind of indolence and so it began to justify the passivity Hardy always wanted to find in himself when he looked back on his career as an old man. But it also risks everything on nothing. Hardy's whole future depended on whether he could make anything out of staying in Dorchester and merely watching.

*

For the rest of the summer of 1883, after 'The Dorsetshire Labourer' was completed, Hardy was largely taken up with Max Gate. Percy Bunting, who had recently started to edit the *Contemporary Review*, asked him to write something similar to 'The Dorsetshire Labourer', on, as Hardy put it, 'the question of the labourer & his vote'. Either because something too explicitly political was being asked of him or for other reasons, Hardy turned Bunting down, though not before compiling some preliminary information.[15] Instead, once he had sent off 'Our Exploits West Poley' (obediently produced on time but not to be published for years), Hardy began to search for an equivalent in fiction to the stance and approach of the essay.[16]

He had recently bought a new notebook, roughly the size of a school exercise book, and entitled it 'Facts | from Newspapers, Histories, Biographies, & other chronicles – (mainly Local)'. During the autumn of 1883, Emma copied into the book various anecdotes about rural ways of life, culled from recent newspapers and from the autobiography of a local poet, J. F. Pennie (1782–1848), *The Tale of a Modern Genius*. Hardy took over the work from Emma in November, copying out further extracts, most of them selected at first from the *Daily News*. Later he added material from Hutchins's *History and Antiquities of the County of Dorset*, from *The Times* and elsewhere.

In March the next year, Hardy began a more systematic trawl through the back numbers of the *Dorset County Chronicle*, starting with the file for 1826. By May, he had reached the end of 1829. The *Chronicle* was a weekly paper, consisting of four broadsheet pages, closely printed in five columns. Hardy read through all of these, borrowing them from the County Record Office, almost next door to his house in Shire-Hall Place. Again with some help from Emma, he recorded in the notebook stories that were remarkable – murders and suicides, successful and unsuccessful forgeries, the tricks used by burglars – and noted down details that illuminated the daily life of early nineteenth-century Dorset. People's clothing especially interested him; so did the extremely long distances people walked, the fairs and wrestling matches that entertained them, and the poverty they suffered.[17]

By early summer 1884, Hardy was beginning to conceive his next novel, *The Mayor of Casterbridge*, and one reason for researching the *Dorset County Chronicle* was simply to provide background for the book. He was doing what he had done when preparing *The Trumpet-Major* five years before, and some incidents from the *Chronicle* reappear little changed in the novel; Henchard's selling of his wife matches an account from the newspaper, and so does the way he humiliates Abel Whittle. The notebook is more wide-ranging in its interests, even so, and contains far more than could be used in *The Mayor of Casterbridge* or even in the rest of Hardy's fiction, though he continued to draw from it. The sheer amount of material suggests a larger intention.

Like his decision to live in Dorchester, the 'Facts' notebook has been taken as a sign of Hardy's re-immersing himself in his background and, to an extent, he was certainly doing that. Several of the pieces he copied out offer accounts of events he had heard about already. On Christmas Eve 1827, Hardy's uncle, John Hardy, had been set upon by members of the Fordington Mummers, because he was a member of the rival, Bockhampton band. The case came to court in January 1828 and the *Chronicle* duly reported proceedings. Reading its account, Hardy could check the facts behind this family story and similarly at other points he compared reports in the newspaper with 'M's description to me' – his mother's account, that is.[18]

Though it often corroborated family stories, the *Chronicle* also supplied Hardy with an independent witness to the same events and an alternative body of knowledge. He could begin to look at these incidents more dispassionately than before because events that might be highly charged for him found their place in the *Chronicle* cheek by jowl with mundane news items or other similar stories; no doubt these had been just as painful or appalling to the participants as the clashes and dramas that affected Hardy's own family. So the newspaper assisted him in developing a merely descriptive style for his fiction but it was liberating too, because after studying it he would no longer have to defer to parental authority when recounting Dorset life; instead, he had acquired his own route into that shared past. Hardy came from a long line of local historians and now, by reading the *County Chronicle*, he was becoming one himself. He can be seen as taking possession of the county's past and of the family traditions in the same way that he was beginning to find his own particular territory in the area of Max Gate.

Making his own home in the district and grasping its history on his own terms were assertions of himself that Hardy needed to make if returning to Dorchester were not to become either regressive or suffocating. They were an essential part of making sure that by coming home he continued to take forward his writing career. Yet they were bound to isolate him, too, and despite its gradually becoming clearer to him, from writing 'The Dorsetshire Labourer' and working on the notebook, how he should begin to write from now on, he continued to find it very hard to make progress. He could to some extent explain and excuse the slowness of *The Mayor of Casterbridge* by saying he had been so taken up at the time with building Max Gate. He could manage to work only 'off and on' during the summer of 1884, he said, and in April 1885, when the book was finally complete, he complained again about being 'frequently interrupted' while writing it. His next novel, however, *The Woodlanders*, proved just as awkward and that was more difficult either to account for or accept.

He began work on the book as soon as *The Mayor* was finished, feeling under pressure because the previous book had taken so long, but by November 1885, even so, he was still struggling miserably with the outline of the plot. 'In a fit of depression', he felt as if he were 'enveloped in a leaden cloud'. 'Sick headache' followed two days later and his mood did not lift for the rest of the winter. On New Year's Eve, he wrote:

> This evening, the end of the old year 1885 finds me sadder than many previous New Year's eves have done. Whether building this house at Max Gate was a wise expenditure of energy is one doubt which, if resolved in the negative, is depressing enough. And there are others.

One source of his misery and the lasting difficulty he found with his work was simply loneliness. Hardy had access to few distractions and fewer friends. Hardly anyone he knew from London would visit him, especially not during the winter, and few, if any, of his Dorchester intimates still lived there. Horace Moule was dead; the other Moule brothers were far away, in Cambridge or the Far East, the only exception being Henry J. Moule, the eldest son. He, with his antiquarian interests and his gifts as a painter, did become a trusted friend but nonetheless Hardy cuts a forlorn figure at this period. He became fascinated by circuses and especially by their doleful clowns.

Particular bereavements made matters worse: by an odd coincidence, his old schoolfriend Hooper Tolbort had returned to Dorchester at the same time as Hardy did. After his outstanding performances in national examinations, Tolbort had had a distinguished career in the Indian Civil Service. He did not come home in triumph, however, to retire and build a mansion. He arrived, instead, as a widower and a consumptive.

To Dorchester he again returned [. . .] shattered in health, but still full of plans for the future. A sudden accession of his dreadful cough broke down his fragile frame completely, and in five days after his arrival he was dead.[19]

Hardy never completely shrugged off his mixed feelings about Tolbort. They had been rivals as schoolboys and, even in this generous obituary, there are still hints of resentment. 'Tolbort lived and studied as if everything in the world were so very much worth while,' Hardy noted, rather tartly, soon after his friend's death. 'But,' he immediately continued, 'what a bright mind has gone out at one-and-forty!'[20] He disparaged Tolbort impatiently for his innocence and yet felt acutely bereft of his 'bright mind'. The two feelings coexisted because, although Tolbort's presence had been an entirely unexpected bonus for Hardy, he could ill afford to lose him when he died. It robbed him of one of the town's few kindred spirits.

Loneliness lay at the heart, too, of the first significant piece of fiction Hardy produced in Dorchester, 'Interlopers at the Knap', a short story he began around Christmas 1883 and published in May 1884. It is intrinsically one of his best stories (and unlike his other most recent short fiction he included it in *Wessex Tales* a few years later); it seems also to be addressing Hardy's deepest concerns at this time: his isolation, his relationship to his family and to Dorset, and his search for a way of writing fiction that satisfied both his artistic instincts and his commercial ambitions. The story recounts the romantic history of Sally Hall, a woman who decides in the end to live unmarried and give up the hope of children. Hardy tells us in his final sentence that she 'strictly adhered to her purpose of leading a single life' and seems to invite our admiration for that choice, unconventional as it may have been. His account ends on a note of praise for her refusal to sacrifice her own preferences in order to lead a more normal life.

Isolation seems acceptable and even admirable, yet Sally's unmarried state possesses darker implications too, because she is closely modelled on Hardy's own mother. The village where she lives corresponds to Melbury Osmond, where Jemima lived before her marriage, and her suitor, Farmer Darton, travels up from near Dorchester, making the same journey that Hardy's father made the night before the wedding. Even minor details in the tale – an incident with a blank signpost, for example – derive from family tradition, and Hardy's characterization confirms the autobiographical resonances.[21] Sally is, like Jemima, a brisk businesswoman while Darton is described as someone who possessed 'an unambitious, unstrategic nature' and 'allowed his mind to be a quiet meeting-place for memories and hopes'. These descriptions match the portraits Hardy habitually drew of his parents and once recognized they turn the story into a sequence of events in which people resembling Hardy's mother and father never marry or have children.[22]

This sort of biographical connection in Hardy's work is frequent and is usually taken to be ornamental but on this occasion it goes deeper. Consciously or accidentally, the story touches on areas where Hardy felt profoundly conflicted. Sally is, in some ways, doing what he was trying now to do himself – disengaging from the world, following her own, in some ways eccentric, course and coming to terms with childlessness. She seems a defence of the decision to hide out in the wilds of Dorset and do what is most truly right for your personality – a defence, that is, of Hardy's retreat from London. On the other hand, she is secretly connected by the text with Hardy's mother and suggests a Jemima who is happier without him. Hardy's non-existence allows Sally/Jemima to go on living an undisturbed life in a rural idyll.[23]

This would not be the only time that Hardy's fiction contemplated his own non-existence. Jude, so autobiographical a figure for Hardy, murmurs on his deathbed Job's desire that: 'Let the day perish wherein I was born.'[24] Henchard, too, in *The Mayor of Casterbridge*, admits to being depressive and says that during his 'gloomy fits' he could, like Job, 'curse the day that gave me birth'. 'Interlopers at the Knap' views the same possibility and does so almost indifferently, as if soothed somehow by the idea of non-being. Coming home could easily have induced feelings of failure in Hardy and the suspicion that his own, independent life had achieved nothing. His intrusion on the world was concluded now, by his being absorbed back into the anonymity of Dorset, so he might as well never have been born.

'Interlopers at the Knap' shows the presence of such world-weariness in Hardy when he found himself back in Dorchester and suggests too that one way he had of coping with the thought of ultimate failure and insignificance was to imagine that he had never existed at all. In his beginning to make accurate observations of Dorsetshire life, in his withdrawal from human contact and now in his imaginative work, he seems to have been attempting to make himself invisible and transparent. In his fiction as much as in his copying out of newspaper articles, he would become a chronicler of histories, an anonymous transcriber of events (rather like the reporters on the *Dorset County Chronicle*); he would make himself into someone whose mind had become a quiet meeting place for facts and nothing more.

Clearly, reading the story like this also unsettles the received view that Hardy regained in Dorchester the love of his family. And there is in fact little evidence of warmth. Hardy's parents remained people it was easier to admire or emulate than to love. And, although he felt he must look after his relatives – a sense of obligation that increased as he became wealthier – he did not receive much emotional support in return. He set aside money to support his unmarried sisters in their old age, sent work the way of his brother and visited his parents without fail every Sunday afternoon. All this was his duty as firstborn son and a duty he felt with the excessive force characteristic of eldest children. His family, meanwhile, accepted such help and recognition as no more than its due. Pride would not allow them to admit anything else. As a result, Hardy's emotional attachment to 'family' consisted during the 1880s in attachment to the name and its history. He looked to discover continuity with his prestigious ancestors, even when the connections were remote – with Captain Thomas Hardy, who fought at Trafalgar, and with Thomas Hardye who founded Dorchester Grammar School. Knowing the link to be extremely tenuous, Hardy nonetheless pointed out to every visitor Captain Hardy's monument on Black Down, visible through the Max Gate windows. As well as a source of pride, it was an attachment he clung to.

*

In resolving now to do no more than watch, Hardy seemed to accept that nothing could be done to make things better. There was in other words a deep vein of fatalism in the 'merely descriptive' style he now embraced. He had been at different times a Christian, a socialist and a positivist, and these ideals had successively informed his sense of himself as a writer. He was now following out to its logical extreme the bleakness of *The Return of the Native* and accepted, more personally and entirely than before, the powerlessness which the earlier novel had presented as mankind's inevitable condition. Prospero in Shakespeare's *Tempest* had used the word 'abjure'. 'But this rough Magicke | I here abjure' he vows at the end of the play: 'deeper than did ever Plummet sound | Ile drowne my booke.' Hardy needed to abjure love in order to survive his marriage and likewise he renounced imaginative freedom in order to accept his homecoming and find his way forward as a writer. That meant giving up any lingering belief he may have had that an artist could change the world, yet gradually Hardy was led to think that watchfulness, passivity and resignation could be forces for good.

In *The Mayor of Casterbridge*, Henchard survives, as Hardy was surviving in Dorchester, by the suppression of his feelings. He cauterizes his emotions, warding off the violence that he knows he is capable of and, inevitably, restraining his native warm-heartedness as well. He is forcing himself against the grain to do what Farfrae, the more successful and more superficial man, does without effort, because it comes naturally to him. Despite Henchard's tragic fall and Farfrae's equally inevitable rise, the novel does show Henchard being rewarded for this arduous, sometimes painful self-restraint. He is a self-centred man, by and large, but he is taught by events to feel love for a woman, Elizabeth-Jane, in whom he can have no investment. By the time he realizes how utterly he cares for her, she is married to Farfrae (from whom Henchard is estranged) and he knows that she has never been his daughter. In exile from Casterbridge, Henchard knows too that he is not even her neighbour and never can be; he has no kind of claim on her nor she on him yet, despite this, he cannot cease to care for her. He is held by the pull of a love that is now disinterested.

What Henchard learns corresponds to the book's emphasis on watching because watching can be, it seems, a kind of care. The objective, self-denying form of writing that Hardy began to practise in Dorchester originated in despair. Nothing can be done; indeed, all efforts to act are harmful. Whatever we may like to believe, we are passive in the face of the natural forces that control us, and we should as far as possible be unmoved and resigned when considering our lives and hopes – lives that will lead nowhere and hopes that will be disappointed. Observation, accurate description, mechanical functioning – these are the corollaries of that passivity and loss of hope. Yet they may bring something about as well. Watching can bring us to the kind of selfless devotion to others that Henchard learns to feel.

Elizabeth-Jane, who has the last word in the book, embodies the selfless and skilled care for others that Hardy is advocating. Her keeping still is partly self-protective (because, like Hardy, she has been hurt by passion) but it is seen as a way of cherishing others too. Reserve is a form of kindness; watchfulness is even a form of love, perhaps the only form it was safe to hope for. Hardy, like Henchard, was drawn towards a half-automatic, cauterized existence. By setting aside personal desire, he sought to avoid further pain. Slowly, however, he came to believe that this self-denial could create a way of looking on at life that was also tender towards life. He started to hope that by viewing the world with detachment, he might come to feel for it again.

– 18 –

Life-loyalties

IF THIS WAS a coherent and self-consistent mode of life and work, it was not without strain. Hardy was compelling himself to resist some of his most powerful impulses: his quizzical, teasing, satirical style, that made fun of the powers-that-be; and his sense of the ecstatic in life, found through music and dancing, as well as through love. All the 'Great Things' he would later celebrate – love, cider, and dancing – were studiedly renounced.[1] When asked early in 1883 whether drink assisted him to write, he replied that in his experience it was more a hindrance than a help and that, with one or two 'rare exceptions I have taken no alcoholic liquor for the last two years'. That is, since his illness, perhaps.[2] Avoiding alcohol implies as well however that, during his early years in Dorchester, Hardy was returning to the principles of 'plain living and high thinking' that he had learnt from the Perkins brothers, the Baptists he had been friends with when first working for Hicks. As much as ever, though, he hankered after what he denied himself. The dance melodies and songs brought back from London by his workmates had entranced him in the 1850s. Now, nearly thirty years later, he was intoxicated by the capital again, this time by its upper-class society.

From the beginning of their time in Dorchester, Hardy and Emma made a habit of visiting London for several months every year. There were sound professional reasons for keeping up contacts in the capital, especially when you were deciding to settle permanently in the country. These were not just business visits, though; especially during the early years in Dorchester, before Max Gate was built and while it remained an uncomfortable, 'raw new' house, Hardy was delighted by escaping to London. It let him off his self-imposed leash. He could exchange the magistrates' bench for the salon and the soirée.

Usually it has been accepted that Emma initiated this interest in society London and compelled Hardy to accompany her. This was the impression given by Hardy's family, for their own reasons. The evidence suggests, however, that of the two Hardy was the one keener to mix with London's elite and that, at best, Emma was sharing in his excitement. Hardy always tended to assume that Emma was enjoying the things he expected her to enjoy – this had happened even on their honeymoon. He also found it easier to do what he wanted if he could think of it as done partly for her benefit. He had thought in this way of his labours designing and building Max Gate; in his fascination with London high life, he tended blithely to make the same assumptions.

Hardy and Emma visited London for several weeks in the early summer of 1883, during the 'season', and did the same the following year. From this date, too, Hardy became noticeably more interested in society – in people with titles, country houses and daughters who were debutantes – and he began to compile lists of his aristocratic friends, many of which were later cut from the *Life*.[3] In 1884, for instance, he and Emma met 'an artistic crowd which included Burne-Jones'; the next year, 'they found themselves on a particular evening amid a simmer of political excitement', surrounded by Conservative lords and ladies, all discussing the fate of General Gordon. Wimborne had been a retreat from London (though Hardy did travel up for occasional visits); his years in Tooting had been an immersion in the literary world. Now, living in Dorchester, Hardy sought to enter more elevated circles. And from the spring of 1885, he began to do so by himself, even though the people he met were frequently connections of his wife.

Mary Jeune, for example, was an important London hostess and one of 'Mrs Hardy's relations'. Her husband, Francis, was related by his first marriage to Emma's family. Nonetheless, it was Hardy who gradually took her and her family over; he started to travel up to London before Emma did, staying on longer after she had gone back to Dorset and making short trips at other times of year. Early in 1885, when they were invited together down to Devon (Emma's native county) to stay with the Earl and Countess of Portsmouth, Hardy once more went by himself. It was sickness that forced Emma to stay behind – 'in benighted Dorset', as Lady Portsmouth called it – and eighteen months later when Hardy visited the Earl and Countess again, Emma did come too. Still, from her point of view, the first visit was unfortunate. Hardy thoroughly enjoyed his time and did none of the work he was expecting to do, being distracted instead by 'an extraordinarily sympathetic group of women' –

Lady Portsmouth and her brood of girls. Hardy said the mother was 'one of the few, very few, women of her own rank for whom I would make a sacrifice', and her pretty daughters attracted him.[4]

Emma could not help noticing that Hardy's supposedly cynical cultivation of these aristocratic connections made him highly excited. He could scarcely claim he was just carrying out a wearisome professional duty when he was so much enjoying being flattered by beautiful women, made much of and entertained. Developing a social life in London and elsewhere was designed to relieve the depression that Dorchester brought on in him and to some extent in Emma too. Clearly, it did improve his mood and Emma benefited from that improvement. Life in Dorchester was cheerier when her husband was, as she saw it, less morbid. More worryingly perhaps, though he had abjured love, he seemed not to have renounced flirtation.

*

Before *The Mayor of Casterbridge* began to be serialized in January 1886 and again when it was about to be published complete in May, Hardy was nervous about its reception. He felt uneasy about the amount of incident he had introduced in order to create excitement in each one of the *Graphic*'s weekly, rather than monthly, parts. Smith, Elder, who published the volume edition, unnerved him too by worrying initially about the absence of any genteel characters. It was natural for him to be nervous anyway, because the book had taken such an enormous effort to write and had then been held up, in part by delays over the illustrations. Fortunately, the pictures, by Robert Barnes (1840–95), an artist who specialized in rustic subjects, turned out very well in the end, and the novel was well received.

The Hardys were in London when it appeared as a book. In May, Hardy told Jane Panton, a novelist friend, that 'I have had no high hopes of it, & am therefore the more surprised to find that it seems to be thought so well of.' By June, he was beginning to grow used to what he had initially found (or modestly pretended to find) surprising. He told Christina Reeve that 'The book is doing very well (as the publishers express it).' Oddly enough, only the *Saturday Review*, which Moule had written for, disliked the book.[5]

As *The Mayor* came out, so did *The Woodlanders*. The serial began in May, in monthly parts in the prestigious *Macmillan's Magazine*. Until recently, Hardy had found the novel heavy going. In November 1885, he told Frederick Macmillan that the new story 'has hardly passed out of the chaotic stage as yet' and asked whether the start of publication could be put back to June 1886.

> I may have put you to some inconvenience already by delay. To set against this however there had been the advantage of a longer time for incubation – a great gain, for I am very anxious that the story may be in every way worthy of the high character of the magazine.

Possibly, being commissioned at last by Macmillan, whom he had approached repeatedly at the start of his career, now intimidated Hardy. What held him back far more, though, was worry that *The Mayor* would ultimately fail – rather as *The Return of the Native* had done in 1878. When it went well, the relief was enormous and his self-confidence blossomed. Through the summer of 1886 *The Woodlanders* progressed without a hitch.

Renewed confidence showed itself in lots of other areas too. In London that year, Hardy revived several old friendships, notably with George Meredith, whom he had scarcely met for fifteen years, ever since Meredith advised him against publishing *The Poor Man and the Lady*. Now, he need no longer be embarrassed about that early novel's rejection. He made new literary friends as well and observed fellow-authors with unabashed perceptiveness. The American writer, Oliver Wendell Holmes, was 'a very bright, pleasant, juvenile old man'; Henry James 'has a ponderously warm manner of saying nothing in infinite sentences' and Walter Pater gave the impression of someone 'carrying weighty ideas without spilling them'.

Similarly, though he had always taken an interest in politics, he now became particularly taken up by the argument over Irish Home rule and attended Parliamentary debates. He was willing to meet politicians and assess them: 'Plenty of form in their handling of politics, but no matter or originality,' he observed, authoritatively.[6] And he was not swept away by success. Amidst his active social life, Hardy spent a lot of time in the British Museum library, reading philosophy, including the works of Hegel.

Praise seemed almost literally to rejuvenate him. He told Robert Louis Stevenson (1850–94) in June 1886 that he felt 'several inches taller at the idea of your thinking of dramatizing the *Mayor*'. Stevenson's appreciation of the book was shared by another rising star, George

Gissing (1857–1903), who wrote to Hardy during this year, seeking advice and guidance. '[I]n your books,' Gissing wrote, 'I have constantly found refreshment and onward help.' Hardy's own letters became more forthcoming as a result. He gave robust advice to Edmund Gosse when Gosse's latest book was attacked in the *Quarterly Review*. 'Do not, my dear Gosse, let it interfere with your digestion or your sleep for a single day.' 'I repeat *don't* take it to heart.' It was unusual for him to be so bold and, although there is great sympathy in the letter and an undertone of alarm – a fear of the consequences of taking these things to heart – Hardy insists that such silly criticisms can be laughed off just as they deserve to be.

In addition, and again this is a change, Hardy was willing to talk of his own work – its aims and its failings. 'Somehow I come so short of my intention,' he confessed to Gissing. Thanking Coventry Patmore for his kind words, Hardy was similarly self-deprecating.

It is what I might have deserved if my novels had been exact transcripts of their original irradiated conception, before my attempt at working out that glorious dream had been made – & the impossibility of getting it on paper had been brought home to me.[7]

Ruefulness of this kind implies a new degree of self-belief. Two or three years earlier Hardy had been bleakly silent about his work. Now, he could afford to be dissatisfied.

*

Hardy returned to Dorchester later in the summer, in better spirits than he had enjoyed for many years. Nearby, however, his old friend William Barnes was growing frail and, in October 1886, he died peacefully in the vicarage at Winterbourne Came, a mile or so from Max Gate.[8] Hardy had always kept in touch with Barnes. He had made a point of calling on him whenever he came to live in Dorset – in 1878, 1882 and again in 1883 – as if by seeing Barnes, he could touch base. Similarly, for as long as he lived at Max Gate, Hardy's preferred route home from Dorchester was not the most direct one. Instead of taking the main road, he would follow the path across the fields towards the rectory at Winterbourne Came, and then turn aside near his own house. His reverence for Barnes entered *The Woodlanders*, which became in places an elegy for Barnes's rural world and a celebration of the selfless kindness he practised in his life. Elegy, though, was coupled in this case with renewed hope because, thanks to his own improved state of mind, Hardy was able tentatively to believe that Barnes's virtues could live on still.

In July 1883, he had taken his trusted literary friend, Edmund Gosse, to meet Barnes and had been struck by Barnes's refusal to impress his visitors. Barnes was taking a church service and his two admirers joined the congregation.

> Barnes, knowing we should be on the watch for a prepared sermon, addressed it entirely to his own flock, almost pointedly excluding us. Afterwards walked to the rectory and looked at his pictures.[9]

There was no question in Barnes's mind of putting the wishes of these 'important' outsiders before the needs of his own parishioners. Without seeking to cause offence, Barnes refused to be distracted from his concern with those he was commissioned to help.

This incident typified Barnes's untroubled self-sacrifice, the instinctual way in which he put his own interests second, either to those of his pupils, when a teacher, or his flock, when a priest. Barnes was the finest example Hardy ever found of genuine altruism and that was why he revered him so much. On the other hand, the way that Barnes ignored Gosse and Hardy was comically rude. Hardy rather enjoyed being given the choice by Barnes of either being amused or taking offence. He also saw the serious point. Though he and Gosse had made a special effort to come, that made not the slightest difference to Barnes. There were more important things at stake than other people's self-regard. Barnes was defying people's self-centred expectations and their expectation that he would be selfish or self-aggrandizing in return. He was being something of a 'humorist', as Hardy described Joseph Arch.

The characterfulness of the man does not come through in Hardy's Giles Winterbourne, the hero of *The Woodlanders*, who in other respects embodies all the qualities Hardy admired in Barnes: his devotion to the world he knew, his intimacy with it and care for it, and his thorough superiority to the smart folks who looked down on rustic simplicity. Yet Barnes's defiant, unafraid self-belief, present within his infinite kindliness (and not conflicting with it) was what impressed Hardy most. Selflessness could live with eccentricity. It could be comic and characterful.

As Hardy's own confidence recovered during 1886, he became more concerned with the value of a personal perspective and how you might combine that with the purely descriptive, impersonal approach he had developed since coming back to Dorchester in 1883. A major influence on him as this change took place was Impressionist painting. In 1886–7, he rushed to see the first London exhibitions and wrote animatedly about the new style. The 'principle' of Impressionism, he said, is:

> that what you carry away with you from a scene is the true feature to grasp; or in other words, *what appeals to your own individual eye and heart in particular* amid much that does not so appeal, and which you therefore omit to record.

Hardy did not want any longer to see 'scenic paintings' of landscapes but instead 'the deeper reality underlying the scenic'.[10] For this to emerge, you have to pick and choose so your own peculiarities of taste and temperament need to be engaged. You cannot pretend to be objective and you must take a chance instead on your own perceptions.

At the beginning of 1887, when Hardy thinks through what he wants to do as a writer, he once again employs the terms of painting.

> The 'simply natural' is interesting no longer. The much-decried, mad, late-Turner rendering is now necessary to create my interest. The exact truth as to material fact ceases to be of importance in art – it is a student's style – the style of a period when the mind is serene and unawakened to the tragical mysteries of life; when it does not bring anything to the object that coalesces with and translates the qualities that are already there, – half hidden, it may be – and the two united are depicted as the All.[11]

Four years earlier, Hardy had argued that you needed to be at home with the Dorsetshire labourer in order to understand him. Now, in 1887, he took that idea one stage further: close observation is seen as personal observation. In fact, it must be thoroughly personal because otherwise it will slip away from its material and become lofty once again. Personal preferences (even foibles and peculiarities) are justifiable in an artist; you might even start to believe they were necessary to art.

Impressionist paintings do possess the qualities Hardy finds in them. Though committed to the accurate transcription of external things, the paintings of Monet, Pissarro and Manet and the other Impressionists are all highly personal works as well. The choice of subject is often unusual, even idiosyncratic; the compositions break the received rules of art whenever that is required for the transcription of what is important –

for the pattern, that is to say, which a particular artist is moved to observe. The works insist on reflecting the painter's focus of attention even as they try to give an accurate impression of what is immediately there, so they are designed to give priority to a subjective viewpoint and make the painter's personality visible in the picture.

Accordingly, an impersonal style began to seem naive to Hardy. If you were to see the underlying truth of things, there must be some meeting – some coalescence, as he put it – between your personal vision and the objects you attend to. And this is not artistic arrogance or Romantic egotism. Your watching had to be yours if it was to avoid turning into some kind of false objectivity – a way of looking at things that was both presumptuous and reductive.

Watching and mere description had been the modes Hardy clung to in his first unhappy years back in Dorchester. By 1887, with one successful book published and another being serialized, with Max Gate built and he and Emma settled there, Hardy began to feel that he both could and should trust his idiosyncrasies more. Barnes, who had never minded very much about conforming either to intellectual dogmas or to society etiquette, left Hardy this legacy: the duty to be unashamed about your own convictions and to put your trust in them.

As his approach to writing changed, his notebooks and letters naturally changed as well. In 1880 and again in 1883, for example, he had trenchantly upheld the benefits of provincialism, attacking Matthew Arnold in particular for his belief in the superiority of the cultural centre. During the 1880s, though, he became gradually less shrill: in 1884, he 'liked Arnold better now than he did at their first meeting'. By 1889, writing to the poet and critic John Addington Symonds (who was living in Switzerland), Hardy wrote more dispassionately about the whole question.

> I, too, am in a sense exiled. I was obliged to leave Town after a severe illness some years ago – & the spot on which I live is very lonely. However I think that, though one does get a little rusty by living in remote places, one gains, on the other hand, freedom from those temporary currents of opinion by which town people are caught up & distracted out of their true courses.

It is a measured, even-handed discussion. One loses, but, 'on the other hand', one gains. And 'true courses' may be found. There is such a thing as what's best for you – for you personally – and what's best will be what is true to you. This personal truth, for Hardy, is something you discover through your surroundings – through observing them in your own, 'idiosyncratic' way.

Peculiar and personal description of nature is one of the most impressive features of *The Woodlanders*: Hardy had always been an acute observer of the natural world, its minutiae and its grandeur but he had never written about it so precisely, so movingly or, at times, so strangely as he did in the novel he completed while Barnes was dying. Casterbridge in *The Mayor of Casterbridge* had been depicted with extraordinary topographical accuracy and with a new degree of alertness to social history. *The Woodlanders* remains an accurate picture, filled with knowledge of rural life, but what is added so strikingly is a subjective point of view, with its own distinctive emphases and interests. Hardy chose to locate the novel in the area of Dorset where his mother grew up; he noticed its peculiarities and highlighted them. His descriptions are, literally, impressionistic and many elements in the picture that one would normally expect to find are left out entirely or sketched in only vaguely.

*

When *The Woodlanders* was about to be published in volume form and, therefore, about to be reviewed, Hardy went on holiday. Instead of choosing Normandy or Paris or Scotland, he and Emma set off this time for Italy, carrying 'into effect an idea that he had long entertained'. The choice of destination is another sign of Hardy's growing self-confidence. Finally, he was going to make the Grand Tour; finally, he would be 'among the poets', as Keats, one of his poetic heroes, put it. Hardy and Emma journeyed in Shelley's footsteps and Hardy sent Edmund Gosse violets picked from Keats's grave in Rome. On several occasions, he visited sites connected with Napoleon and the Napoleonic wars, as he had done last in 1875. He felt bold enough to begin contemplating once again his epic history of the Napoleonic Wars.

Emma wrote a diary of their Italian holiday, which survives and reveals, surprisingly perhaps, how well they were getting on. By this time, they had learnt to give themselves a break from each other, now and then. In Milan, towards the end of the trip, Hardy went off to Lodi (where an important Napoleonic battle took place) while Emma 'went about Milan – took trains'. She looked after herself more readily than before, even though she could still sometimes feel rather abandoned. When 'T. H. went out again' without her, Emma:

found the same black cat prowling about & whilst calling, the
Japanese child came with the chambermaid, & we all went to look
at the picaninis, & they were in a little loft-like chamber, but on the
same floor, on straw, 4 little tabbies, the child and I made friends
over them[.]

Children and cats consoled her in Hardy's absence, just as they had
done in Paris on honeymoon.

By now, though, Emma bore her disappointments with very little
complaint. In Venice, they were given introductions to eminent English
expatriates but Emma could not take them up.

Afternoon resting – my knee being jointless. T. H. has taken
letters of Int: [Introduction] to the ladies – Very disappointing for
me – (For the best always)

In the diary, Emma sometimes uses 'T. H.', sometimes 'Tom'; 'T. H.'
is always less friendly and 'Very disappointing for me' sounds stiffly
cross. The last four words here, however, are fitted into the end of a
line and look as if they were added later. The next paragraph begins
'Evening'; perhaps as soon as that, as she read over what she had
written earlier in the day, Emma could decide to put her annoyance
behind her.[12]

Her generosity on this occasion makes some of her other remarks
read more sympathetically. She records early on that they were charged
six francs each for their lunch at Dijon. It made 'Tom very vexed.
Dyspeptic before and worse now.' Taken in isolation, this could seem a
gleeful observation, even a vindictive one – as if Hardy's miserliness
deserved to be punished by indigestion. In the run of the diary, though,
it conveys a more simple concern for him. In Rome, similarly, Emma
sounds just pleased that there were 'two nice letters for Tom from
Kegan Paul & Gosse about Woodlanders'. And it was in Rome that she
impressed her husband most.

In the diary, all Emma says is that they bought a picture and:

Tom walked with it along a narrow street St. Marco. The attack by
confederate thieves dreadful fright to me – got into omnibus & back
to hotel[.]

Hardy mentions the same incident. The three men who attacked him:

could see that both his hands were occupied in holding the picture, but what they seemed not to be perceiving was that he was not alone, Mrs Hardy being on the opposite side of the narrow way. She cried out to her husband to be aware, and with her usual courage rushed across at the back of the men, who disappeared as if by magic.

Emma could certainly be fierce. Just earlier in the diary, she mentions a 'Little shoe-black persistent at Forum Sunday morning', adding '[I] broke my umbrella beating him off.' She sounds for a moment like the Red Queen in *Alice in Wonderland*.[13] For Hardy, Emma's boldness was one of her most compelling qualities, partly because he so often lacked it himself. Also he recognized that Emma's forthrightness did not derive from innate stridency; rather, she was a naturally shy person who was able courageously to overcome her shyness on behalf of others. He would have known without needing to be told that the encounter was a 'dreadful fright' to her.

It was a tiny incident yet Hardy was the kind of person for whom such things mattered enormously. He records in the *Life* a notebook entry from January 1886, entitled 'Misapprehension':

The shrinking soul thinks its weak place is going to be laid bare, and shows its thought by a suddenly clipped manner. The other shrinking soul thinks the clipped manner of the first to be the result of its own weakness in some way, not of its strength, and shows its fear also by its constrained air! So they withdraw from each other and misunderstand.[14]

This was often what he and Emma did. They were frequently unhappy together simply because each of them withdrew from the other in fear. Both adopted a clipped manner because they could not bear to have affection rebuffed. An incident like this one at Rome released them from their habitual anxieties not least because it proved beyond question that Emma still cared for her husband. It cleared up and made a mockery of their joint misapprehension.

Later in 1887, Hardy began a poem, related to *The Woodlanders* and entitled 'In a Wood'. It was not completed until 1896, though exactly what was written when, nobody knows. The poem contrasts the natural and the human because in the wood is found the Darwinian world, where living things prey on each other and compete for limited resources. In this environment, giving way to the other means death; the trees are:

> Combatants all!
> Sycamore shoulders oak,
> Bines the slim sapling yoke,
> Ivy-spun halters choke
> Elms stout and tall.

Nature in *The Woodlanders* is the same as this; the forest trees can be heard 'rubbing each other into wounds'. Among human beings alone is it possible to find sympathy and mutual affection. According to the novel, what Marty South and Giles Winterbourne do for one another and for those they love, the natural world can never do.[15]

The poem ends by making the same transition back from the natural to the human.

> Since, then, no grace I find
>   Taught me of trees,
> Turn I back to my kind,
>   Worthy as these.
> There at least smiles abound,
> There discourse trills around,
> There, now and then, are found
>   Life-loyalties.

Emma's courage in Rome reawakened Hardy to the loyalty she had given him through a period of years when he had given her little in return. They remained prickly with each other, subliminally rivalrous and often distant; nonetheless as Hardy's inner confidence grew during 1887, so did his confidence in Emma. He became more open to the idea that people could be committed to each other and, in his own case, that they might even be loyal to him – more committed and concerned than he found it easy to believe.

This was a revelation to him and a surprise because he had got used to thinking that human sensitivity was an evolutionary accident with usually catastrophic consequences. Being responsive to other people's feelings no longer appeared a piece of hypersensitive derangement, as he had often feared it might be. William Barnes had shown compassion to others throughout his long, fulfilled life and Emma, despite Hardy's neglect and thinly disguised contempt, still cared for him, genuinely and instinctively. Both people seemed proof to Hardy that loving kindness was not only humanity's unique gift and burden, it was also the foundation of the affection he had himself actually received.

This renewed conviction brought Hardy back nearer to the positivism he had been influenced by a decade earlier. As early as the summer of 1885 he was attending lectures in London held by the Positivist Society and Emma had gone with him. When Church disestablishment became an election issue later in the year, Hardy wrote to one of his campaigning positivist friends, John Morley:

> I have sometimes had a dream that the church, instead of being disendowed, could be made to modulate by degrees [. . .] into an undogmatic, non-theological establishment for the promotion of that virtuous living on which all honest men are agreed.[16]

This sounds very like positivism's 'religion of Humanity', which tried to avoid metaphysics and to nurture instead humankind's unique capacity for altruism.

The Woodlanders reflects this change of emphasis in Hardy's views. Giles, like Gabriel Oak, has Christ-like attributes and his merely human goodness reveals the divine. Barnes had always been a Christian and so too was Emma. Although Hardy could not regain his faith, this novel, imbued with Barnes's example, made his peace with Christianity, probably for the first time since the summer of 1880. The book found evidence in the world that Christ's teaching could be followed, despite the distortions inflicted on that teaching by the Church.

*

On their return from Italy at the end of April 1887, Hardy settled back at once into productive work. He wrote a short story, 'Alicia's Diary', over the summer, which drew on the Italian trip and in June, he accepted £1000 as an advance on a new novel. This was a larger sum than Hardy was used to and it came from Tillotson and Son, a publishing agency and distributor, whose arrangements allowed them to publish work through a number of outlets, at home and abroad. Through them, Hardy would be distributed more widely than before. He could feel, as he told Gosse in August, that he had got through the worst of things.

> As to despondency I have known the very depths of it – you would be quite shocked if I were to tell you how many weeks & months in

byegone [*sic*] years I have gone to bed wishing never to see daylight again. This blackest state of mind was however several years ago – & seldom recurs now.[17]

He believed he had reached a point where he could look forward to the years ahead, assured that he would find at least some degree of fulfilment in them.

In this mood during September, he wrote two of his best short stories, 'The Waiting Supper' and 'The Withered Arm'. He sent the second to the editor of *Blackwood's* thinking that its 'weird nature' might suit the magazine, which often published gothic tales. *Blackwood's* accepted the piece, much to Hardy's excitement (they had rejected *The Return of the Native* ten years earlier) and published it in January 1888. Almost at once, Hardy suggested to Macmillan that they might produce a volume of his stories. Again, this idea was swiftly taken up and *Wessex Tales* came out in May 1888 – one year after *The Woodlanders* and only two since *The Mayor of Casterbridge* was published as a book. Hardy sent complimentary copies to Robert Browning and to the eminent positivist, Frederic Harrison.

Wessex Tales, as it first appeared, contained 'The Withered Arm' and four other stories: 'The Three Strangers' (1883), 'Fellow-Townsmen' (1880), 'Interlopers at the Knap' (1884) and 'The Distracted Preacher' (1879). There were a number of others Hardy might have included, several of them rather good. It's odd, for instance, that he did not include 'The Waiting Supper'. Selecting these five focused the collection on concerns shared by the two novels he had written most recently – on a rural way of life that was in retreat before modernity; and on what happens to people when they come up against the harshness of that modern world. There are 'moments of vision' in nearly all the stories – moments of aghast recognition – and in their aftermath a few, redeeming instances of kindness.

It was the first time Hardy had used 'Wessex' as a title (since his 1875 'Wessex' ballad, 'The Bride-Night Fire', at any rate). Eight of his novels were published in a uniform, one-volume format by Sampson, Low, Marston between 1881 and 1893 and at some point in this period, probably again during 1888, Hardy asked Edward Marston, 'Could you, whenever advertising my books, use the words "Wessex Novels" at the head of the list?'[18] As in 1875, when he tried to buy back the copyright of *Under the Greenwood Tree* from Tinsley, his publisher at the time, Hardy was thinking ahead to a collected edition. It was his instinctive idea as soon as he began to make headway and this time, he imagined it in relation to Wessex.

In *Wessex Tales*, each of the stories is located in a particular area of Dorset and each connects with one of his novels: 'Fellow-Townsmen' with *The Mayor of Casterbridge*, 'Interlopers at the Knap' with *The Woodlanders* and so on. The book presents an epitome of the district, rather as *Tess*, the novel he was already thinking about, takes its heroine all around the county. Hardy had established a base in Max Gate and, in his mind, it occupied the centre of the landscape; Maiden Castle, Conquer Barrow, Black Down were all configured by him in relation to the house, as satellites or outposts. In this way, he occupied his setting, making it his own. Now he was starting to extend that imaginative conquest, such that Dorset and the surrounding counties would eventually be made into the Hardy country.

Finding outlets for his work had suddenly become unusually easy for him and as a result, he began to write more quickly. He went on with further short stories as soon as *Wessex Tales* was complete. 'The Melancholy Hussar of the German Legion' (later added to *Wessex Tales*), 'A Tragedy of Two Ambitions', and 'The First Countess of Wessex' were all written during 1888. As he worked on them, he was planning *Tess of the d'Urbervilles* (his novel for Tillotson's) plus a sequence of short stories, *A Group of Noble Dames*, published in 1890–1. Because there is a gap of three years between *Wessex Tales* (1888) and Hardy's next novel, *Tess of the d'Urbervilles* (1891), there seems to be an interruption in his output, comparable to the earlier ones around 1876–8 and 1882–6. Certainly, you might predict some slowing down after the high productivity of 1886–8. But in fact, Hardy in 1889 was buoyed up by his recent success and inspired by the Impressionists to believe that self-expression was justified, even essential.

He did grumble all the same about having 'to cover so many pages a year', as he remarked to George Douglas at the end of 1888. A few months later, he told Arthur Locker, editor of the *Graphic*, that he had 'in contemplation some other work than serial fiction, besides the novel I mentioned'. The novel was *Tess*, his current project; the 'other work' is probably a glancing reference to what became *The Dynasts* in the end, Hardy's long-cherished Napoleonic poem. Part of Hardy, in other words, impulsively sought a change from writing fiction almost as soon as he had become established in it. The desire not to be confined had

contributed to the restless variety of his earlier novels and now surfaced
once again in a slightly different form.

Yet to the same publisher, only a month later in March 1889, Hardy
wrote:

> Can you give me any idea how much you would be disposed to
> pay for [. . .] a Christmas story – same length as the "Romantic
> Adventures of a Milkmaid"? [. . .] I think I could write such a story
> some time next year.

Locker jumped at the chance and the two men rapidly reached an
agreement. The previous year Hardy had turned down a request from
Locker and sweetened the pill by adding, 'I shall be sure to write to you
as soon as I feel courage enough to commit myself anew.' Now,
apparently, he had the courage to take on not only *Tess*, which he was
actively working on, but the long short story that would become *A Group
of Noble Dames*.[19]

A year earlier, Hardy had told Lady Margaret Wallop, one of Lady
Portsmouth's daughters, that after 'The Withered Arm' he had 'some
more creepy [stories] in my mind: yes – creepier ones still!'[20] *A Group of
Noble Dames* contains several of Hardy's creepiest and the collection
evidently took shape in his mind amidst the euphoria of his finding 'The
Withered Arm' so eagerly accepted by *Blackwood's*. More generally, in
Hardy's letters at this time, there is an unnerving feeling of his getting
overexcited. He was taking on far too much, recklessly and almost
arrogantly. It was not as if he needed money so desperately any longer,
or that he needed to prove himself. He had a series of genuine successes
under his belt. Yet he seemed unable to rest on his laurels.

Success had been achieved on his own terms. At one remove from
London and ignoring literary fashion, Hardy had realized his potential
without compromising his independence. He had been vindicated. His
parents might still have preferred an architect for a son but, even if they
did, they could no longer claim he had failed in his chosen profession.
And his wife, despite their differences, had shown that she cared for him
still; perhaps the marriage was not the outright failure he had feared it
was. Achieving his ambitions would have made Hardy a less difficult
person to live with, to start with in any case, and it helped bring about
the generally more hopeful atmosphere of his life in the later 1880s. It
also, however, encouraged him to think he could afford to be 'creepier',
both more daring and more candid in his writing.

After his triumph with *Far From the Madding Crowd*, *The Hand of Ethelberta* had been an extravagantly bold move and Hardy's career repeated that pattern several times; rather than consolidate success, he would leap ahead, defy expectation and assert his freedom. In 1888–9, he saw this as an obligation as well as a right because otherwise, his art would never live up to the example of the Impressionists. He felt as well that by now he could afford to take the risk: where his critics were not won over, they would either forgive him or be fearful of attacking him. Thanks to a large extent to Barnes and Emma, Hardy was willing to believe that people could indeed behave with loving kindness; if so, they should be able to acknowledge and tolerate difference. They would welcome Hardy's idiosyncrasies, even if they disagreed with him.

These hopes were too sanguine; without Hardy's realizing it, self-belief had turned into overconfidence and he was overlooking his audience's prejudice and hypocrisy. As he rushed ahead, believing his time had come and that he must seize the moment, believing too that the public were sympathetic and fair-minded, Hardy was pulled up short by an absolute resistance. He found that candour was not something his editors, his publishers or even his readers were prepared to tolerate – not in 1889 any more than in 1882.

– 19 –

If the true artist ever weeps

HARDY SPENT the spring and summer of 1889 planning *Tess of the d'Urbervilles* and, according to the *Life*, he settled down to the actual composition of it only in August, when, at the end of the London season, he moved back to Dorchester. By 9 September, however, he already had half of the book in draft, which suggests that he must have started earlier. In London, despite the impression he gave of visiting endless plays, art galleries and acquaintances, Hardy usually spent a good deal of time working and this summer was no exception. Unfortunately, when Tillotson's read what Hardy sent them they were horrified and rejected the book almost at once, cancelling the contract. Soon afterwards, Hardy tried *Murray's Magazine* with the book and after their equally rapid rejection of it, he turned to Macmillan. By the middle of November, they had turned it down as well.

By 1889, Hardy was no longer accustomed to his books' being refused by publishers; indeed, during the last few years, they had been queuing up to take his work, despite the fact that it was sometimes unusually explicit about sexuality. R. H. Hutton thundered in the *Spectator* that *The Woodlanders* was 'a picture of shameless falsehood, levity and infidelity'; even so, the novel had been taken by Macmillan, the publisher whose respectability Hardy had always seemed to endanger, and it sold better than almost anything else Hardy had written before.[1] Its popularity seemed to indicate that Hardy could now approach dangerous subjects – his personal standing and a more tolerant public seemed to have given him liberty to speak his mind.

After this string of rejections, *Tess* did not appear in print for almost two years: the serialization began finally in July 1891 in the *Graphic* and the first edition came out in time for Christmas that year. Then it became Hardy's greatest success to date, a best-selling and critically acclaimed book, which shot him to fame. At that point, when his problems with the book had ended so happily, Hardy saw his whole career during the 1880s as an attempt to overcome the primness and cowardice of the publishing world and to make novels more honest.

> Ever since I began to write – certainly ever since I wrote "Two on a Tower" in 1881 – I have felt that the doll of English fiction must be demolished, if England is to have a school of fiction at all [. . .] the development of a more virile type of novel is not incompatible with sound morality[.][2]

Though this has the false clarity of hindsight, at some less conscious level Hardy had been moving towards greater explicitness. *The Woodlanders* took greater risks than *The Mayor of Casterbridge* had done and was more willing to risk controversy for the sake of expressing Hardy's point of view. When in autumn 1889 *Tess* was so summarily dismissed, this endeavour – the life-shaping project to reform the English novel – was thrown suddenly into doubt because it seemed as if the doll simply could not be demolished. At the same time an upheaval took place in Hardy's personal life. The winter of 1889–90, as Hardy began to approach the landmark of his fiftieth birthday, became an emotional turning point.

*

Hardy found a solution to the problem of *Tess* by offering the manuscript to Arthur Locker, editor of the *Graphic* (where *The Mayor of Casterbridge* had first appeared). He claimed later that, for a time, he considered not publishing the story in a magazine version at all. That would have been an entirely new departure for him, after writing nine novels in sixteen years, all of which appeared first in serial form; probably, too, he could not easily afford the financial sacrifice. Looking back, when he was far better off, Hardy tended to forget (or disguise the fact) that, even in his late forties, he earned his living from the money magazine editors gave him for his work. In no position, therefore, to ignore conventional mores, Hardy agreed to bow to them, at least as far as appearances went, and the version of the novel that he sent to Locker was already expurgated when it arrived. To avoid his publishers' prudish hostility, he censored himself. In the *Life*, written a quarter of a century afterwards, this policy is hailed as ingenuity outwitting primness. The new 'treatment was a complete success', Hardy says, 'and the mutilated novel was accepted'.[3] At the time, nevertheless, it was both an extremely arduous process ('sheer drudgery', Hardy says) and an emotionally demanding one.

Hardy changed the text for the serial while also preserving and revising the original version. This process required meticulous care; several different-coloured inks had to be used to distinguish between the various sorts of alteration and to ensure that the original was not accidentally lost. It must have been a confusing and tiresome business. Emma's handwriting appears in the manuscript and proves that, as so often before, she was supporting Hardy at a stressful moment in his career. None of this activity began, however, until the late summer of 1890 – almost a year after Hardy had sent off the first version of the book and more than six months after its rejection by three prestigious magazines. By that stage, Hardy was writing in many respects a different novel – two different versions of the original novel, one might say – and he could approach the task with some degree of equanimity. During the previous winter, he had been absolutely furious about the rejections and unable to return to the novel at all, unable to regain anything like his usual philosophical composure in the face of disappointment.

His anger reveals how much he depended throughout his career on his audience's sympathy. Hardy was not by nature a confrontational person, rather the opposite. He wrote no manifestos; he usually refused to write reviews; and he did not, as Oscar Wilde had done, set out to offend people in order to attract attention. Instead, his approach had been to try to effect a gradual shift in opinion and taste, bringing it about without his audience's noticing. When *Two on a Tower* caused offence, he regrouped and slowly (over several years and several books) worked towards a position where he could repeat that earlier novel's attack on accepted morality. Similarly, in all of Hardy's indignant responses to (what he saw as) unfair criticism, he betrays his hunger for acceptance. 'A man must be a fool to deliberately stand up to be shot at,' he declared when harshly reviewed and to Hardy, it did feel like being shot at. He could not dismiss bad notices as an occupational hazard and still less could he see them in a positive light, treating any publicity as good publicity.

Hardy was so vulnerable because he wanted mutually contradictory things: to be admired and, at the same time, to be unflattering about the people whose admiration he sought; to be accepted and to behave unacceptably. He felt a far stronger need for appreciation than was wise in someone who was challenging his readers on essential issues: on sexuality, religion, and the social order. George Gissing, seventeen years younger than Hardy, was quite different in this regard. He admired

Hardy and Hardy him; they shared a commitment to 'high artistic aims' rather than 'circulating-library popularity', and to 'literature as distinct from the profession of letters'. Gissing, though, was more uncompromising. His novels are dark, sometimes forbiddingly so. His best books – *The Nether World* (1889), *New Grub Street* (1891), *Born in Exile* (1892) and *The Odd Women* (1893) – though moving and occasionally funny never set out to be entertaining; they are austere in tone and sometimes relentless. Not surprisingly, perhaps, he remained comparatively unsuccessful despite his talent and his brother's novels, forgotten now, achieved far better sales. Yet still Gissing refused to compromise. Everything remained, as he put it to Hardy, 'subservient to my ideal of artistic creation. The end of it all may prove ineffectual, but as well spend one's strength thus as in another way.'[4]

Hardy never felt quite so self-reliant because popular success mattered to him far more and partly for class reasons. Gissing did not come from a wealthy background but he had been on course for university when his life took a different turn; consequently, he had a firmer sense of having chosen his path and could even find something to be proud of in remaining unrecognized as a novelist. Hardy, on the other hand, had not torn up his ticket to social advancement and become a writer instead. He had had no ticket except writing – architecture would have consigned him back to his provincial roots soon enough – and succeeding as a writer was therefore fundamental to his self-worth. In addition, *Far From the Madding Crowd* had given him a thrill he could never forget. For fifteen years, he had been trying to recapture that moment of acceptance and elation and, for the last three or four years, he had felt he was at last beginning to reap his reward. Consequently, when *Tess* was turned down, he was incensed and also terrified.

In February 1890, he wrote one of his very few literary critical essays, 'Candour in English fiction'. He had published 'The Profitable Reading of Fiction' in 1888 and would write 'The Science of Fiction' in 1891. Though his notebooks and letters reveal how self-conscious he was as a writer, these are his only critical essays as such,[5] and his willingness to publish critical work is a further indication of his increased self-confidence at the end of the 1880s. 'Candour in English Fiction', though, is more a denunciation than a discussion. In it, Hardy makes a sustained and impassioned attack on the magazine publishing system that had rejected *Tess*.

Magazine publishing is responsible, Hardy says, for the 'lack of sincerity' evident in contemporary novels. It produces their failures in honesty ('candour') and in conscientiousness; it gives rise to their 'charlatanry' and 'quackery'. Secondly, though, the restrictions imposed by magazine morals deny the writer proper access to his readership. Because magazines will print a story only when it is entirely respectable, they compel its author to censor his or her best impulses. He or she is forced:

> to belie his literary conscience, do despite to his best imaginative instincts by arranging a *dénouement* which he knows to be indescribably unreal and meretricious, but dear to the Grundyist and subscriber. If the true artist ever weeps it probably is then, when he first discovers the fearful price that he has to pay for the privilege of writing in the English language – no less a price than the complete extinction, in the mind of every mature and penetrating reader, of sympathetic belief in his personages.[6]

The anger here is hard to miss, along with Hardy's contempt for the system that demands such 'indescribably unreal' products. The price the artist pays is, nonetheless, more intimate: he or she loses the readers' 'sympathetic belief' in what has been written. The artist weeps because an essential tie has been broken.

Two years earlier, Hardy wrote in 'The Profitable Reading of Fiction' about the ideal version of this relationship. The best readers of a novel, he asserts, 'exercise [. . .]a generous imaginativeness' that adds to the story, filling in the gaps.

> Sometimes these additions which are woven around a work of fiction by the intensitive power of the reader's own imagination are the finest parts of the scenery.[7]

This may sound like no more than a gallant compliment. To Hardy, though, the readers' actions were understood to lie at the heart of his writing. The audience's imaginative participation in and elaboration of what Hardy wrote was, in his view, absolutely essential to a novel's effect. An impressionist writer had to bring something to the object 'that coalesces with and translates the qualities that are already there'. So too, Hardy realized, did impressionist readers. They had to make something of what they were given, just as the writer did and, accordingly, there needed to be a relationship of mutual trust. Where that broke down – where it was either absent in the audience or prevented by censorship – the writer was left in a hopeless situation, speaking into a void.

Reviewers were increasingly describing Hardy as an 'artist': of the two greatest living novelists, Coventry Patmore said in 1887, 'Hardy, though less perfect, is much the greater artist.' In 1891, William Minto wrote that Hardy was 'emphatically an artist, a creator of beautiful and noble things'.[8] The freedom of the 'artist', his or her suffering and nobility, were more and more frequently assumed during the 1890s as the Aesthetic Movement became more influential, and Minto's claim could easily be mistaken for something written by Wilde or Aubrey Beardsley.

'Candour in English Fiction' shows that Hardy largely accepted this understanding of the novelist in general and of his own work, so that some of his indignation in the essay arises out of a passionate commitment to art above everything else. Yet the essay reveals just as clearly Hardy's lack of the Aesthete's imperturbable self-assurance. The result of adapting to respectability is, Hardy says, 'the complete extinction, in the mind of every mature and penetrating reader, of sympathetic belief in his personages'. There is no question of his shrugging this off or laughing at the situation. He cannot find comfort in the idea that a censorious public made writing foolish and its end product a joke. Nor can he, in reality, treat the issue with 'cynical amusement' and look down disdainfully at the demands of the market, even though this was a stance he did resort to, especially in retrospect, and one he could adopt even in 1890. His immediate reaction is more candid and self-revealing. He admits that Grundyism ruins his books because it destroys the foundations of a writer's life: the sympathetic belief of his readership. There's nothing unusual in this. In fact, it is rare for an author not to invest in his relationship with his audience, despite the many protestations to the contrary. During the winter of 1889–90, however, Hardy was especially vulnerable to this sense of desertion because his professional life so dismally repeated events closer to home.

*

In London, during the summer of 1889, Hardy had got to know Rosamund Tomson, an up-and-coming poetess. In June, he invited her to the dinner of the Incorporated Society of Authors in the company of two other women writers, Mona Caird and Mabel Robinson. Mabel Robinson he had known for several years and she visited Max Gate;[9] Mona Caird was a novelist and campaigner for women's rights. A few months later, Hardy assisted her in trying to publish 'an article on

Evolution in Marriage'. It was Rosamund Tomson, nevertheless, who made the deepest impression on Hardy, not least because she began to pursue him. She sent him a copy of her latest book, *The Bird-Bride*, inscribed to 'Thomas Hardy, with the sincere admiration of G. R. T.' ('Graham R. Tomson' was her pseudonym) and followed this up later in the year first with a copy of *Selections from the Greek Anthology* and then in December with two portrait photographs for Hardy to choose between.[10]

Hardy was captivated enough to hope that Rosamund would come down to visit Dorset. 'When are you going to haunt these scenes?' he asked in September. Her husband was a painter, Arthur Tomson, famous for his Dorset and Sussex landscapes, as Hardy knew. 'You should have come in August,' he wrote, '& all the painter-friends at your heels.' When the visit was deferred again and again, Hardy complained.

> We are greatly disappointed to learn that you are not able to include Dorset in your programme. [. . .] No: I cannot come to Sussex either: but then my conscience does not prick me in saying my negative as yours ought to prick you in saying yours; for, you see – I had never raised anybody's hopes. But I should much have liked to come[.][11]

There is some playfulness here: as Hardy tells Rosamund off and wags his finger at her, he manages to sound archly flirtatious and avuncular.

Hardy had behaved like this before with other attractive younger women – like Mabel Robinson, or his friend Mary Jeune's daughters by her first marriage, Madeleine and Dorothy Stanley. Fashionable women's attentiveness brought out in him something equally charming, humorous and considerate, and he became in middle age and beyond a popular guest with cultured families. To women young enough to be his daughters, he could be the perfect uncle. There is, nevertheless, something more to his feelings for Rosamund Tomson and he deploys a more plangent tone – 'But I should much have liked to come,' he says. For all his wish to make Rosamund feel guilty, he still comes across as personally hurt.

Rosamund was twenty-six in 1889 and an enviably successful writer. She was an acknowledged beauty and, while energetically cultivating Hardy, she made herself appear sexually available. Hardy wrote later that he thought he had found in her 'an enfranchised woman' – that's to say, a sexually liberated one. In 1896, Rosamund, who had divorced before marrying Tomson, divorced a second time in order to marry her lover, the novelist Henry Marriott Watson. Her actions caused a scandal and damaged her career but they proved to Hardy that he had been right in some ways. Rosamund had indeed been flirting with him.

Her effect was so profound and ultimately drastic, because she reawakened and then disappointed feelings that Hardy thought he had outgrown. Within six months or so of their first meeting, as Hardy lingered in Max Gate and Rosamund failed to visit him there, he came to the conclusion that her supposed interest in him had been in fact utterly self-serving.

> Her desire [. . .] was to use your correspondent as a means of gratifying her vanity by exhibiting him as her admirer, the discovery of which promptly ended the friendship, with considerable disgust on his side.[12]

Hardy reacted to her neglect of him by assuming he had been deliberately humiliated – that Rosamund had not admired him, only sought to pass him off as her admirer and thus exploit his reputation to her own advantage. To win his admiration gratified her vanity and was likely to improve her reputation since, as Hardy was well aware, his endorsement could help other writers. Though he was generous about helping in this way, especially when the request came from younger women, his assistance was always based on the presumption that both parties were disinterested. As Hardy saw it, Rosamund had broken this fundamental rule by attempting to flaunt his admiration of her and expose him as in thrall to her beauty and talent.

In doing this, though, she had behaved only as society's prudish moral guardians did when they censored novels: she had destroyed trust. She did not want Hardy's admiration for itself; she did not wish to relate to him at all, in fact, not with any sincerity, and instead of defying conventions, instead of proving herself liberated ('enfranchised'), she only proved herself to be thoroughly conventional. Like so many others, all Rosamund wanted was success, professional and social advancement, and she was prepared to use the normal, insincere methods to attain the normal, worthless goals. This was how the world worked and, just as disturbing truths could not be tolerated in the world's fictions, so sincere feelings did not fit with a careerist agenda. Sincerity might need, at times, to be faked but real emotions were too wayward to be reliable, too demanding and complex to be of use. They upset the best laid career plans as much as they disobeyed the rules of propriety.

The 'considerable disgust' Hardy felt at Rosamund Tomson's treatment of him dovetailed with his feelings about *Tess*'s rejection to produce a hatred of institutionalized dishonesty and a violent abreaction against educated, London society – the world that produced and required such an order of things. It was this impulse that first produced the 'Candour' essay and then coloured everything Hardy wrote during the rest of the spring. He had satirized genteel pretensions and well-heeled, empty-headed London types before – in *The Hand of Ethelberta* most fully; he had never been so bitter about them before, or so unremitting as he became over the next few years.

The rejections of *Tess* had disrupted Hardy's timetable because he was already contracted to write a short novel for Locker in time for Christmas 1890 and had expected to start on it as soon as *Tess* was complete. Now, though, Locker was taking on *Tess* as well and it transpired that there would be no room for it in his magazine until July 1891, so the second contract would have to be fulfilled first. The rejections meant, in other words, that Hardy had to stop work on his novel and begin instead the sequence of short stories that was to become *A Group of Noble Dames*. In these, he drew attention repeatedly to the cruelty of aristocratic men and the perversity of their aristocratic wives. The only way of escape from a life of pampered imprisonment, deceit and selfishness was to embrace rural simplicity. Similarly, during the autumn, when he began rewriting *Tess*, Hardy introduced the question of her aristocratic family history. Tess's rape by Alec with all its terrible consequences is made only at this stage into an act of retribution. Tess is being punished for the treatment her 'mailed ancestors' dealt out 'even more ruthlessly upon peasant girls of their time'.[13]

Such hostility persisted. It can be found undimmed, for example, in the short stories Hardy began to write when *Tess* was finished late in 1890: 'For Conscience' Sake' and, particularly, 'The Son's Veto', both published in 1891, reveal an extreme hatred of class ambition and the self-righteousness it engenders. Similarly, *The Pursuit of the Well-Beloved* (as *The Well-Beloved* was entitled in its serial version), written in 1892, makes rather tired fun of London society's artificialities and pretensions, its tediousness and self-involvement. Hardy even makes Rosamund Tomson into his model for one of the characters, the London hostess 'Mrs Pine-Avon'. The male protagonist, by contrast, although he is absurd at times, does possess some capacity for depth of feeling and, as in *A Group of Noble Dames*, emotional honesty is to be found outside London in rural seclusion, in this case in the Isle of Portland, near Weymouth. Hardy recognized soon enough the unattractive aggression in the 1890 short stories and attempted, in public anyway, to disavow them. *A Group of Noble Dames* was published first in the *Graphic* at Christmas 1890 and again six months later, in an extended version as a book. It was, he said, 'a frivolous little volume' published 'by way of relaxation'; or, as he put it in a second letter from 1891:

> rather a frivolous piece of work, which I took in hand in a sort of desperation during a fit of low spirits[.][14]

It was another 'desperate remedy', he claimed – employed on this occasion to relieve misery – so its brittle heartlessness should not be taken too seriously; rather it should be excused as the product of a bad moment.

*

What he was remembering a year afterwards was not only *Tess*'s failure to find a publisher and Rosamund Tomson's teasing exploitativeness, but bereavement too. On 5 March 1890, Hardy sketched out the first few lines of a poem: 'Thoughts of Phena', as it was later entitled, 'At News of Her Death'. He claimed that he began the poem before he had any inkling that Tryphena was dying or even ill; instead, 'It was', according to the *Life*'s drily oblique account, 'a curious instance of sympathetic telepathy.' As had happened several times before, bereavement produced in Hardy a grim resolve to do his work – to endure pain by losing himself in the routines of professional existence. Nonetheless, though he had lost touch with Tryphena, hearing of her life in Devon, her marriage to Charles Gale and their children only at one remove via the family network, her death reawakened his feelings for her and his loyalty to what she represented. The distaste for sophistication that marks his writing over the next few years had, that's to say, a positive aspect because it marked a return to the convictions that underlay *The Poor Man and the Lady*, from more than twenty years before. Tryphena had to some extent inspired Hardy's belief in the virtues of country life and now Tess, the heroine of his next novel, was made to epitomize them.

For Emma, however, the consequences were altogether unhappy. Hardy's infatuation with another woman, albeit brief, followed by the revival of his affection for Tryphena, brought about a crisis in the marriage, from which in many respects it never recovered. The evidence for this change is typically indirect and emerges mostly from arrangements inside Max Gate. When he first designed the house, Hardy made it face north-east – that is, towards Higher Bockhampton. By the time it was built, he had turned it round. Facing south, the house would certainly be warmer and more comfortable, but in addition it would have its back to Hardy's family home. And, curiously, no windows look in that direction anywhere in the house. Perhaps Hardy was recalling *The Return of the Native*, thinking first of a house, like Blooms-End, which looks backwards into the heath and the past, and then changing his mind so that Max Gate when it was actually built looked forward instead. Over three generations, Hardy's family had moved westwards – from Puddletown to Bockhampton and now to Dorchester – and Hardy placed Max Gate in the line of that progress, as if not looking back once he had set his hand to the plough.

He and Emma shared the bedroom on the first floor and Hardy had a study across the landing – an airy, spacious room with windows looking out to the front and the side. From his desk Hardy looked westwards, as the Higher Bockhampton house had done. Captain Hardy's memorial was visible in the distance before him, to inspire and give a sense of belonging, and so was William Barnes's vicarage at Winterbourne Came. Indeed, it was in this room that Hardy wrote *The Woodlanders*, aware as he sat at his desk that his old friend Barnes lay dying close by. Soon after finishing the book, though exactly when is not known, Hardy moved his study into the back bedroom of the house and turned the original study into his private bedroom. Possibly Hardy found it too distressing to look out towards Winterbourne Came and be reminded that Barnes was dead. Perhaps, too, his next book required a new space as Hardy had hardly ever written two books in the same house before. Since 1875 he had lived in Swanage, Sturminster Newton, Tooting, Wimborne, Dorchester and Max Gate: with the exception of Tooting (and that had ended badly), each of these locations was connected with only a single novel. Moving studies in Max Gate was perhaps as close as he could come to a new beginning.

Of course, though, shifting his bedroom was not essential when he moved his study. Guest bedroom and study could simply have been swapped around. Whenever the change was made – at some date between February 1887, when *The Woodlanders* was finished and 1890–1 when the bulk of *Tess* was written – and whatever the writerly motives may have been, it expressed a decision to occupy separate bedrooms. Such an arrangement was not very unusual for middle-class Victorian couples and it does not in itself necessarily imply marital estrangement. For Hardy and Emma, even so, it does seem to have been the beginning of the end. And although the date when the change took place is not known for certain, the most likely time (to my mind) is the first half of 1890, during what Hardy remembered as a fit of low spirits.

Hints of marital breakdown had been accumulating already, most notably the fact that from the mid 1880s on, Hardy's sexual life was becoming imaginary. His books had always been intensely erotic, though none more so than his most recent, *The Woodlanders*. Edred Fitzpiers, the outsider in the novel, is eagerly promiscuous and one of the local girls, Suke Damson, shamelessly leads him on; Mrs Charmond, the more 'enfranchised' lady of the manor, also has an affair with Fitzpiers and talks of desire building up in her like the charge in a battery, demanding release. Juxtaposed with these characters are those for whom sexual feelings struggle against extreme repression. Giles Winterbourne refuses to sleep with Grace Melbury, even though he loves her and even though she evidently wishes him to do so, and while his dogged self-destructive refusal may have morality on its side, it feels compulsive.

Hardy's siblings may have been somewhere in his mind as he wrote the book, since none of them ever married. Though the novel, in other words, frequently seems to celebrate the values of rural life, it also sees suffocation there – stifled aspirations, stifled hopes and, in particular, stifled sexuality. Partly this is a sensitive piece of social observation because chastity was enforced with particular rigour on Hardy's class, which needed to marry respectably and could not afford scandal. Nonetheless, the pressure in either direction in the novel – the felt power of Eros and the imprisoning force of repression – are new to Hardy, and furthermore all the characters with whom he could identify most easily desire a sexual freedom that circumstances forbid.

In a similar way, Hardy's diaries became peopled at this time more and more by beautiful women.

> That girl in the omnibus had one of those faces of marvellous beauty
> which are seen casually in the streets, but never among one's friends.
> It was perfect in its softened classicality [. . . .] Where do these
> women come from? Who marries them? Who knows them?

'[A]mong his friends', even so, Hardy did find Lady Coleridge, who had 'really fine eyes' and Lady Rothschild who was 'amply-membered'. At Mrs Jeune's, a 'Miss Amélie Rives was the pretty woman of the party':

a fair, pink, golden-haired creature, but not quite ethereal enough,
suggesting a flesh-surface too palpably. A girlish, almost childish
laugh, showing beautiful young teeth.[15]

Hardy repeatedly mixed this sort of unfeeling assessment with outbursts
of desperate sexual longing. He notices perfections like a connoisseur,
judging women's faces like pictures, but then 'Who marries them?' he
asks, bewildered and disconsolate. Why are such 'faces of marvellous
beauty' never 'among one's friends' though they are visible all around?
– even among the 'harlots' of Piccadilly where 'A girl held a long-
stemmed narcissus to my nose as we went by each other.'[16]

Hardy's poem, 'At Middle-Field Gate in February', written in 1889,
finds the same clash between the acceptable and the desired. He
remembers in it the 'far-back day':

> When amid the sheaves in amorous play
> In curtained bonnets and light array
> Bloomed a bevy now underground!

The present of the poem is desolate, by contrast, as mist condenses on
the bars of the gate 'Like silver buttons ranged in a row, | And as evenly
spaced as if measured'.[17] The 'measured' (the mechanical and rigidly
constrained) has replaced 'play', which was licentious and unashamed.
You can hear the change in the neat, clickety-click rhythm of the final
line. Meanwhile, the speaker seems to have missed his chance and is
living on, envious of what others had.

Tess gives the clearest picture of Hardy's longing for sexual intimacy
at this time in his life. 'I, too, lost my heart to her,' he admitted later
and, at points, the novel feels as if he is writing out a sexual fantasy.
Angel Clare's declaration to Tess, for instance, comes when he is
watching her milking.

> Eyes almost as deep and speaking he had seen before, and cheeks
> perhaps as fair; brows as arched, a chin and throat almost as
> shapely; her mouth he had seen nothing equal to on the face of the
> earth. To a young man with the least fire in him that little upward
> lift in the middle of her red top lip was distracting, infatuating,
> maddening.

Angel sounds like Hardy himself when he observes Tess so carefully:
'that little upward lift in the middle of her top lip' reminds Angel of 'the

old Elizabethan simile of roses filled with snow', which was a simile Hardy was fond of too. 'Of all the people I have met this summer,' he wrote in his diary during 1889, one lady's 'mouth recalls more fully than any other beauty's the Elizabethan metaphor "Her lips are roses full of snow."' It is a coolly literary and self-respecting comparison, yet what Angel and Hardy observe so dispassionately is distracting too, 'infatuating, maddening'.[18]

The writing in the novel is energized, clearly, by erotic desire. Beneath the language of aesthetic appreciation, there's a powerful sexual impulse and Hardy as he writes is drifting towards voyeurism. This is the pattern of his 1860s 'Studies, Specimens &c' notebook, where (as it happens) Hardy first notes down the 'roses full of snow' simile. Looking at women with a supposedly objective eye, to assess their beauty, disguises your desire for them and so releases it. The difference in *Tess*, however, lies in the fact that desire is now prompted most of all by the promise of sympathy. When, for example, Tess and the other milkmaids are walking to church and find their way blocked by a flood, they cling 'to the roadside bank like pigeons on a roof-slope'.

> Their gauzy skirts had brushed up from the grass innumerable flies and butterflies which, unable to escape, remained caged in the transparent tissue as in an aviary. Angel's eye at last fell upon Tess, the hindmost of the four; she, being full of suppressed laughter at their dilemma, could not help meeting his glance radiantly.

As she glances back, Tess is not leading Angel on so much as instinctively sharing the joke with him. The word 'radiantly' hints that this could be taken as an opportunity – the comedy of the moment allows eye contact and so it reveals some of the feelings Tess has for Angel. What it hints more strongly, though, is the absence of any design. The incident remains a childlike moment, free from innuendo and innocent of the usual power struggle between the sexes. Angel and Tess are laughing together and out of that begins arousal and consummated love, so that sexuality seems to be innate in companionship.

Hardy was imagining in Tess a woman who had no side to her and no thought of exploiting her beauty to her advantage, someone like Tryphena 'whose dreams were upbrimming with light | And with laughter her eyes'.[19] He started to imagine too a relationship that was naturally intimate – one where sex was not set apart from friendship and simply expressed instead, in physical terms, the ties of affection that naturally grow up between people when they are living and working together. Emma could no longer offer that, not least because almost from the time they first married and more decisively during the 1880s, their relationship had survived by choosing friendship over passion. Love as loyalty, as affection, as companionship was what they had and sex was almost its opposite. Because sexual desire was so mobile and so easily transferred, it threatened their life together; for that reason it had had to be blocked out, and the initially powerful sexual attraction between them repressed. Desire's sudden, wayward imperatives would destroy the long-standing moderately happy way of life they had devised together.

Though he saw the danger, Hardy could not respond to it. He had been willing to settle for a steady, rather melancholy personal life but now, the intimacy Tryphena had once given him and Rosamund recently denied him became his most pressing need. He had been searching already, albeit unconsciously, for love, erotic contact and, most of all, for sympathy even before the winter and spring of 1889–90, as his diaries and notebooks reveal. Now, Hardy's greater awareness of his own feelings was fatal because his high sense of personal integrity would dictate that he move into a bedroom of his own, unable to perpetuate what now appeared a travesty of love.

The physical estrangement was especially painful for Emma because the previous two years or so of their marriage had been encouragingly harmonious, as Hardy's mood improved with his growing recognition as a writer. It was also inevitable that as Hardy began to despise high-class London society, some of that animus was displaced onto Emma, who could conveniently embody for him gentility and pretentiousness. In their Tooting years, Hardy had found Emma an embarrassment to his social and professional ambitions, but it was only during the 1890s that her class itself became a target for him. From that period, too, clear evidence starts to emerge of his relatives' contempt for her, and perhaps Hardy was starting to licence that treatment of her, possibly without even realizing he was doing so. And as much as he attacked Emma's social position and aspiration, he shrank away from her, reliving his feelings for Tryphena as he imagined his new heroine.

These were changes that gradually took place over the following few years. Immediately, in spring 1890, Emma was confronted by undoubted evidence of Hardy's sexual interest in other women – an interest that in secret had been intensifying for several years. What she discovered frightened and angered her and probably seemed repellent as well, although fortunately, as far as she was concerned, nothing had come of her husband's foolishness. If anything, the young lady in question seemed to have humiliated him and he might even be expected to learn his lesson. Emma was always one to brush aside despondency by trying to make the best of things, and, by the autumn, equilibrium seemed to have been largely restored. Her helping to transcribe *Tess*, which was such an arduous task, may have been a reconciliatory gesture on both sides.

Hardy had gone into retreat, all the same. His new study at the back of the house had a much less promising view and, by moving into it, he was turning away from the prospects offered by his old study at the front. And *Tess*, as its second version gradually formed in that room, became elegiac and inward. All his most recent novels were set in the past and had considered historical change, a process that *The Mayor of Casterbridge* had tried to accept as inevitable and *The Woodlanders* suggested had a kind of merit to it, because the old order was seen as unfit to survive, whatever its virtues might be. *Tess* is a more anguished and unambiguous book, in which history is an assault – the rape and destruction of a distinct, unique culture by indifferent, outside forces. What Alec does to Tess, in other words, London is doing to Dorset.

Hardy's harshest words in the novel are reserved for Angel Clare, however, and in that respect the book carries on the angry protest he made in 'Candour in English Fiction'. Though Alec seduces (perhaps rapes) Tess, he tries later on in the book to take her back and make her at least passably respectable. Tess is, in fact, the only person Alec ever begins to love. Angel, on the other hand, seems to love her and wins her love in return, only to reject her when he finds out the guilty secret of her illegitimate child. His rejection is far crueller to her than Alec's sexual assault and more destructive as well. Angel, despite seeming 'enfranchised' – that is, liberated and progressive in his views – turns out to be as narrow-minded and moralistic as the worst of his contemporaries. Tess tells him her story – the story we have just been reading – and Angel's inability to sympathize makes him into an epitome of the bad, censorious reader. He refuses to fill in the gaps in the picture. Rather than Alec's new money, it is Angel's new, heartless and self-righteous morality that is ruining Tess.

If then Tess represents an ideal woman – Tryphena by contrast with Rosamund Tomson – she also represents a ideal relationship, the ideal form of generous, unselfish, instinctual love that modern 'morality' obstructs. And Hardy, just as he had put so much of himself into Ethelberta fifteen years before, put a lot of himself into Tess. The sympathy she was denied, he was being denied as well. In Rosamund Tomson's behaviour he had been exposed to the values of the ordinary world, the duplicity it found acceptable and the sincerity it deplored. This perception (unfounded or not, naive or profound) set him in the future at odds with his audience and he grew from this point on far more willing to offend his readership. Not only candidly accurate about uncomfortable realities and not only willing to express his natural bent, Hardy became positively challenging as well. *Tess* and *Jude* were both more heightened novels than those he had written before and deliberately *un*realistic at points. It is as if Hardy were using his books to test out whether his readers were really on his side or only pretending to be. He was still seeking sympathy from them, but insisting now that it be absolutely genuine.

The intensity of that effort was, in part, another attempt to compensate for his soured marriage because with Emma there was now none of the intuitive understanding which Hardy sought from his ideal reader. There was little or nothing left of what he found a few years later in a real person: Florence Henniker.

– 20 –

That we had all resigned for love's dear ends

TESS, when it finally appeared in time for Christmas 1891, became an instant bestseller: 'its exceptional popularity' transformed Hardy from a well-respected writer into a famous man. The best London hostesses wanted him to grace their parties and the book's rapid sales began to make him wealthy. A new Copyright Act had recently been passed in America, which meant that Hardy could profit from the US market in a way that had been impossible before. All the ghastly delays surrounding the novel (which he had started more than three years before) now seemed fortunate; without them, his most popular book would have earned him nothing abroad.[1]

Though Hardy remained cautious with money, signs of his growing wealth became apparent over the next few years. In 1893, on their annual visit to London, for example, he and Emma 'took a whole house' for the first time. They 'brought up their own servants, and found themselves much more comfortable [. .] than they had been before'. They stayed longer than usual too – from early April until early July.[2] Hardy also began to consider his and his family's financial future. Sometime in the late 1880s, he had bought a terraced house for his sisters in Woolaston Road, Dorchester, just around the corner from the girls' school where they taught. In 1892 he invested in further property – a house in central Dorchester, which he rented out – and in shares as well, some of which were placed in Kate's name.

These decisions may have been influenced by the death, during the summer of 1892, of Hardy's father, creating in Hardy a feeling of personal responsibility for his unmarried sisters and his widowed mother. Henry took over the family business, as had been foreseen for years, and he promptly set about the construction of a new house, Talbothays Lodge, built on land Hardy's father had bought a little while before. The site lay just outside West Stafford, halfway between Higher

Bockhampton, on the north side of the Frome valley, and Broadmayne to the south. It was two miles to the east of Max Gate. Hardy designed the house for Henry, on a grander scale than Max Gate, and designed as well the two rows of workers' cottages that were put up nearby. These are of a high quality and have long gardens, big enough for apple trees. One row is beside the road and the other, next to it, is set twenty or thirty yards back. Instead of one long row, huddled together and cramped against the road, Hardy's arrangement creates a sense of space and freedom, and was also likely to be healthier. Henry was planning to marry, it appeared, and of course he could afford to at last. The Lodge reflected his new status as head of the family firm, while the cottages declared that he was a dynamic businessman and considerate employer.

The pair of houses, Talbothays and Max Gate, showed the brothers both progressing in their own lines; to judge from their houses both were prosperous and considerable men, who had done well – as well as the family could have hoped and better than many of their cousins. Both possessed their land freehold – Hardy had bought the plot from the Duchy of Cornwall in 1885, a few months after moving into Max Gate; Henry had inherited his from the family – so they were independent of the landlords who had controlled their father's life. Henry's new house, built on such a scale and so soon after his father's death, conveys a feeling of release and self-assertion. Now forty years old, he had at last a chance to make his mark – on the firm and on the landscape – and to make his escape from the family into a marriage. Though he never married, as it turned out, he moved into Talbothays all the same and, in old age, his sisters joined him there.

Though the death of his father had a similar psychologically liberating impact on Hardy, as far as buildings were concerned, he was forced to wait. He had become the head of the family; only when his sisters' needs were catered for and Talbothays complete did he begin to extend Max Gate, though he had wanted to do so for some time. Late in 1894, work began on new servants' quarters at the back of the house: a new kitchen, an extended scullery, plus a larder and storerooms. The old kitchen was used to house Hardy's and Emma's bicycles and later on, it became a second living room. Above the new rooms, Hardy built a third study for himself, as large as his first one at the front of the house. His second study, where he had written most of *Tess*, reverted to being a spare bedroom. At this time or soon afterwards, a second turret was added as well, on the eastern end of the front. Externally, it balanced the turret on the other end; internally, it aggrandized Hardy's bedroom, giving him views east-wards and south-eastwards, in the same direction as his new study's window. All the changes to the house benefited Hardy, in fact, much more than they did Emma. The only real advantage to her was that, in a larger house, there was greater scope for the couple to avoid one another; Hardy's study now lay some distance away at the end of a gloomy corridor instead of being right next to her bedroom. Even so, Hardy may have appreciated this greater separation more than Emma did.

The new arrangements gave Hardy a grander room to work in, better lit and with an east-facing window that looked out over the garden. Hardy designed the window to have one large, square pane at the centre and smaller ones around it, so that glazing bars did not interrupt his view. Hardy was a small man and the clear centre of the window was set at just the right height for him to look through. This tailor-made room contrasted powerfully with the hole-and-corner aspect of his office in the spare bedroom, where he had been working for three years or more. It also placed him near the servants, whose conversation he could overhear through the floor.

Maybe, Hardy's construction of a room all to himself, close to the servants, was another example of his shifting his allegiances away from Emma and towards his roots. Emma, at least, could well have felt it as such, despite the benefits to her of living in a larger, implicitly partitioned house. Certainly, their estrangement was now worsening. Emma may have hoped and half-expected that with the novel's triumphant success the opposite would happen. She was accustomed to Hardy's self-involvement while he was working hard on a book and she knew too all about his dark response to adverse criticism and the consequences of that for their relationship. Only five years before, on the other hand, when *The Woodlanders* started to do well, their relationship had improved. In 1892, however, the result was different because, as in 1874, she now had to cope with Hardy's feverish delight in acclaim.

In some respects, success did mellow him. As he received popular recognition and critical approval – the first full-length study of his work, Lionel Johnson's *The Art of Thomas Hardy*, was under way – his highly-strung sensitivity to criticism eased and his writing proceeded with less of a struggle as well: during the early part of the year, he progressed rapidly with his next story, *The Pursuit of the Well-Beloved*, and, at the same time, he began seriously plans for his next full-length book, *Jude the Obscure*. Compared to two years or even ten years earlier, Hardy was less tricky to live with. Emma also shared to some extent in his glory and enjoyed it. What she found more wearisome was his sense of triumph and his triumphalism. His sense of release would even have been rather frightening to her. *Tess*'s success was an enormous vindication for Hardy, the more emphatic because he had had to withstand so much rejection over the book in 1889–90. It made him more daring as a writer and, as emerged more fully only later, more daring in his personal life too.

He had recently become friends with Edward Clodd (1840–1930), a successful banker with freethinking views and literary ambitions. For Clodd, there was simply no question of the marriage vow's being binding, for instance, or divinely instituted. People must do as they felt. The sanctity of marriage was simply another superstition, which rational inquiry had exploded. Hardy consulted Clodd over financial matters in the early 1890s and, in later years, he confided in him about his private affairs. They were in frequent touch from 1890 on and Hardy made his first visit to Clodd's house in Aldeburgh, Suffolk during the summer of 1891. There, amidst a group of congenial men, Hardy discovered some of the more progressive attitudes that his contemporaries were starting to take for granted. For them, religious belief could be dispensed with quite calmly – without anguish or regret, and without putting positivism's godless Christianity in its place and – and similarly, for them religious strictures on behaviour had no force whatever. Encountering these opinions – even though he did not fully share them – was another factor that helped begin to embolden him.

Hardy's visits to Aldeburgh became regular over the years but Emma never once joined him there. It was the first social setting that Hardy kept entirely separate from her. Some of his London dining clubs forbade women and Hardy rather liked that old-fashioned rule. Clodd took the more contemporary line and welcomed women to his Aldeburgh house parties, though undoubtedly these remained male-dominated occasions. Hardy's decision to keep Emma at a distance was taken partly and ostensibly to avoid embarrassment. She would not have remotely fitted in and Hardy would have been uncomfortable. Once she knew what was said and thought, still more if she suspected what went on, Emma would have done everything in her power to stop Hardy from going back so it was fear partly that led Hardy to keep her in the dark. Nonetheless, befriending Clodd and keeping up with his slightly faster set, were self-assertive things to do. Hardy was keeping up appearances less rigidly than he had done before; he was risking comment among his more conservative friends and risking Emma's disapproval too. He was subtly changing the terms of their life together.

All these forms of withdrawal from her were the more cruel because at the same period when Hardy lost his father, Emma lost both her parents: her father died in the summer of 1890 and her mother at the end of the following year, just as *Tess* was being published as a book. We know that Hardy passed on Lady Jeune's sympathy over Emma's first bereavement but about the second, nothing is heard (not, that is, until six months later when Hardy is writing letters about his own bereavement). He was with Emma at Max Gate at the time her mother died, however, so the silence in the record may be misleading. Perhaps privately he did do his best to help her through this sad time. Nonetheless, the letters of his that do survive from late in 1891 reveal a near-total obsession with the fortunes of the book, its reception, its reviews, and its merits. The death of Emma's beloved mother is never mentioned and seems forgotten.[3]

Though their bereavements were almost simultaneous, they came at very different points in Hardy's and Emma's lives. For Hardy, the death of his father coincided with his surge in self-confidence in the wake of *Tess*; it came at a time when he was feeling liberated both professionally and emotionally whereas the death of Emma's parents could be worked through less easily. *Some Recollections* reveals how strongly she was attached to her relatives and to her family's roots in Devon. She had travelled down to her father's deathbed but whether she attended her mother's funeral is not known and although Hardy had often promised to travel into the south-west with her, he had never actually done so. Now (as in 1882 after Caddell Holder's death) it felt as if they had waited too long – as if, more specifically, Hardy had kept her waiting too long. Emma's sense of entrapment in Dorset, and in Max Gate in particular, was inevitably made worse since she no longer possessed an alternative setting – even if only an imaginary one – to counterbalance Hardy's family and his Dorset environment.

Meanwhile, the death of Hardy's father brought his relatives nearer. It's often been suggested that when Thomas Hardy, senior, died a mollifying influence was removed, leading to greater friction between Jemima and Mary, on one side, and Emma on the other. The signs of conflict are certainly more frequent after 1892 and Hardy's father was a more easy-going character than his wife was, more able to step back from a fight and see squabbles in proportion so that without him, feelings were likely to run higher. In addition, with her husband dead and her second son moving out, Jemima was almost bound to turn to Hardy more often, and as a poor widow she naturally had more of a hold over him. To make matters even worse for Emma, just when she needed Hardy's support most, his career whisked him away into the arms of fame and glamour.

One result was a shift in Emma's loyalties that corresponded to Hardy's moves away from her. During the 1890s she became an active supporter of women's rights, though never a militant one – a suffragist, as they were called, though not a suffragette – and she became distinctly more religious too. Once the powerful imaginative presence of her religiously freethinking, politically conservative father had disappeared, it was easier for her to move in these directions. In her old-fashioned religion and her newfangled politics, Emma could also be aggressive towards Hardy without having to recognize that that was what she was doing. Hardy was an agnostic and, interestingly, he was not in favour of votes for women. By coming down so clearly on the other side over both these issues, Emma was challenging his views. She was choosing to break their established rule of avoiding difficult areas and outright disagreements. It was her equivalent to his going away on holiday to Clodd's house and leaving her behind. Meanwhile, Emma could view these actions as her duty, because in what she did she was only following the demands of her faith and her conscience. Loyalty to her mother's memory played its part as well because in her orthodoxy, Emma was expressing her love for her mother, who (just like her) had been devout and had lived unhappily with an overbearing husband.

As Emma adopted something of her mother's attitude, so Hardy repeated his father's role as comforter of his mother in her old age. Consequently, as they grew more like their parents, the estranged coexistence that characterized both parents' marriages exerted a greater influence over their own life together. Furthermore, of course, these bereavements came when Hardy's new-found fame was already causing strain. Little of Emma's correspondence has survived from the early 1890s but letters to her do exist from her friend Alfred Pretor, a don at Cambridge and a minor writer. Pretor's side of the correspondence reveals indirectly the difficulty Emma had in accepting Hardy's growing stature during 1892 and afterwards. She found it harder and harder to do the wifely thing by leaving the limelight to him.

At the same time, and naturally enough, Hardy's increasingly obvious, sexually charged interest in aristocratic and/or literary women infuriated her. Nevertheless, what underlay all of her discontent, her tantrums, her fights with the family and her often quite successful spoiling campaigns was, in essence, a feeling of betrayal. After years of supporting Hardy through thick and thin, she had been cast off in favour of a succession of fawning society beauties.

*

Hardy himself was seeking out such company with emboldened self-assurance as his fame spread. His appearance changed radically too. He had grown a full beard during his twenties, either while in London or, perhaps more likely, when he came back to Dorset in 1867 and had kept it ever since, as his hair first thinned and later receded. He wore hats more often as his baldness worsened. In 1892, he shaved off his beard, while keeping the moustache, which he started to wax. The 1892 cartoon by 'Spy', the famous cartoonist, in which Hardy wears a bowler hat, spats on his shoes and carries a cane, establishes this new look as that of a man about town. A fine photographic portrait, taken by Barraud in 1891, just before the change, shows by contrast a bearded Hardy, gazing past the camera. He is far less dapper than in the cartoon and much more soulful as well. Another picture from 1892 – a tense sketch used in *Black and White* to accompany a profile of the author – presents the new image once again and, unusually for him, Hardy looks straight out at us from the picture. It is as if one motive for the change of appearance was a desire on Hardy's part to face the onlooker directly. He wished to make the most of the opportunity *Tess* had created for him so he nerved himself to this more public role and altered the way he looked in order to distance his true self from the public image.[4]

This look gradually became one he was comfortable with. In pictures from 1894 and 1895, he looks more relaxed, as if by then he had completed the shift from an old-fashioned Victorian look to something more up to date. Beards were going out in the 1890s and moustaches coming in, creating a style that paved the way for Edwardian elegance. As with so much else in Hardy's life, however, this comparatively late development established itself for posterity. The first of William Strang's portraits was painted in 1893 and for the rest of his life Hardy began to sit regularly for portrait painters. All the portraits showed the middle-aged and then elderly figure, with the long moustaches Hardy continued to wear until his death. This body of pictures tends to obscure the earlier, Victorian Hardy, with his high-minded idealism, his passionate, sometimes almost savage intensity and his beard, the mark of the Victorian sage. That figure is replaced first by the gentleman of letters, coming up to town, then by the grandiose imperial figure of Winifred Thompson's 1895 portrait, and lastly (and most influentially) by the grand old man of Max Gate, venerable and wise.

If Hardy felt he needed to be more fashionable in order to carry his career forward after *Tess*'s success, he also keenly wanted to take his place in a glamorous world. He became, in London at least, rather dressy and sleek and during the early 1890s, Emma did the same. She had been rather painfully flamboyant with her clothes when they were in Tooting in the late 1870s; from around 1900 on, she returned to that manner, sporting large hats with feathers and the lacy frills that visitors found so eccentric. The few pictures dating from the period in between show a more conventional middle-aged woman wearing a well-made, expensive silk dress or a dark, rather severe travelling coat. The flowing ringlets of her days in Cornwall, when Hardy first met her, and the loosely cut, lightly coloured dress have disappeared; in their place are a tight collar and a corseted waist; her hair is combed back and gathered in a bun. A cross hangs round her neck, instead of the locket she carried before. Evidently too, during the 1890s, Emma began to put on weight and her hair turned grey.

These various changes show the loss of beauty that Hardy observed so remorselessly (responding to it first, perhaps, in his portrait of Viviette at the end of *Two on a Tower*); they also reflect the severity of feeling and opinion that took over Emma's character as she grew older. They show too, though, Emma's adaptability – her willingness to dress the part of the famous author's wife, despite her private feelings of resentment and her largely unacknowledged envy. It is a stage in her life that, as with Hardy himself, has been obscured by the notoriety of her later appearance – the bizarreness of her clothes and behaviour as an old lady have made it easy to forget the normality of her emotions and impulses. And, quite naturally, quite normally, Hardy's actions during the 1890s turned her unease at his sudden success into outright jealousy.

Hardy's involvement with younger, more attractive and more gracious women was at first only a continuation of the relations he had developed earlier – with Lady Portsmouth's daughters and Mary Jeune's, or with women met through his circle of literary friends. Agatha Thornycroft, for instance, wife of the sculptor Hamo Thornycroft, was someone Hardy met in 1889 and flirted with, though more affectionately than predatorily. When Hamo was away, Hardy's friends Edmund Gosse and his wife Nellie helped to look after her. Hardy encouraged this, and even, as Agatha amusedly informed Hamo, urged her to enjoy herself as best she could in her husband's absence: 'he considered it right I should be gay while you were away, fearful morals with which to corrupt an inexperienced and innocent person'. Agatha was a strikingly beautiful woman – the most beautiful woman in England, Hardy said, and 'her on whom I thought' when I wrote' *Tess*. She took no special interest in her middle-aged admirer, however, giving him only the attention that was due to one of her husband's friends and a friend of the Gosses. Whatever Hardy might have hoped or yearned for when close to Agatha seems never to have crossed her mind – that innocence was part of the attraction for Hardy, of course, and one reason why he thought of her as Tess.[5]

Attractions like this were harmless enough, probably – at least Emma may have thought so – but others proved more dangerous. In 1892, Hardy was introduced to and became close friends with a devoted admirer of his work, Rebekah Owen (1858–1939), a wealthy American, and a year later, he met Florence Henniker (1855–1923) for the first time. He and Emma were invited to stay with the Lord Lieutenant of Ireland at his lodge in Dublin. The Lord Lieutenant's father was Richard Monckton Milnes, Lord Houghton, a man of letters as well as an aristocrat, whom Hardy had known since 1880 through the Rabelais Club. Monckton Milnes was staying with his son in Dublin – hence Hardy's invitation and the literary flavour of the gathering there. His daughter was hosting the occasion and she was Florence Henniker.

Despite these grand social connections, Florence was married only to an army officer, Arthur Henniker (1855–1912). Though her background was top drawer, in other words, her means and her station in life were both comparatively modest. Money did not place her utterly out of Hardy's reach and she was perfectly positioned to fit in with his lifelong dream of the Poor Man and the Lady. Furthermore, she wrote elegant novels that sold well. Physically, she was quite different from Emma – petite and birdlike, almost pinched. Her health was delicate and she had never had children, but she dressed beautifully, with flowers woven into her hair. The impact she had on Hardy was instantaneous. It was, for him at least, quite literally love at first sight.

After ten days in Ireland, Hardy, Florence and Emma travelled back to London in a group, along with others from the house party.[6] Hardy had rented a house in town for the whole of the season and he returned to it after the Dublin trip. Florence was in London too and Hardy began writing to her at once; he sent letters on 3, 7, 10, 20, 29 and 30 June, and there may have been still more that have gone missing. Although Emma stayed in the capital too, Hardy went to the theatre with Florence; he planned 'architectural lessons' with her as well – visits to London churches where Hardy would instruct her in the styles of medieval architecture and their different dates. 'I want you to be able to walk into a church and pronounce upon its date at a glance,' he announced on 7 June. On 10 June he sounds schoolmasterly: 'Will you please first impress upon your mind the elementary facts of date given at pp. 19–20' (in the handbook he had given her).[7] Hardy's earnestness over these lessons, his dramatic manner, and his sudden tyrannies are slightly comic to look back on though their effect at the time on Florence Henniker is more difficult to judge.

In any case, despite Emma's continuing presence in London, Florence and Hardy saw a great deal of each other there, before Hardy travelled back to Max Gate in early July, as the season drew to a close. Near the end of this time Hardy told Florence that he was sleeping hardly at all 'and seem not to require any'. Writing to her from Dorchester, he remarked: 'The first night of my arrival here I slept more soundly than I had done for weeks.' Still, a day or two later, he is restless once again.

> As to my beginning to write again Heaven only knows when I shall do it. – I feel much more inclined to fly off to foreign scenes or plunge into wild dissipation.[8]

This sounds very unlike him and, although it is undoubtedly to some extent an arch, self-parodic remark there is some truth in it too. Hardy's behaviour around Florence Henniker did become almost manic during this summer, especially during June and July.

In the *Life* as a coda to these hectic weeks he adds a notebook entry made at the time.

> I often think that women, even those who consider themselves experienced in sexual strategy, do not know how to manage an *honest* man.[9]

The other side of this remark emerges in one of his letters to Florence, written at the end of June. He is telling her about an encounter at 'the

Academy crush' – the opening of the summer exhibition at the Royal Academy.

> Where, of course, we met a great many vain people we knew. One amusing thing occurred to me. A well known woman in society, who is one of those despicable creatures a flirt, said to me when I was talking to her: "Don't look at me so!" I said, "Why? – because you feel I can see *too much of you*?" (she was excessively *décolletée*). "Good heavens!" said she. "I am not coming to pieces, am I?" and clutching her bodice she was quite overcome. When next I met her she said bitterly: "You have spoilt my evening: and it was too cruel of you!" However, I don't think it was, for she deserved it.[10]

Though this purports to be simply an 'amusing thing', mentioned to entertain his friend, Hardy's disapproval is venomous. Moreover, it sounds as if, really, he was attracted to her (he was staring, after all), hated that and blamed her for it, rationalizing his hostility as a proper dislike of her flirting with him. The society woman was, Hardy informs Florence, one of the very many 'vain' people who thronged the party. She displayed their customary dishonesty and selfishness. Part of the point about the incident is the assumption that Florence could not possibly be 'one of those despicable creatures a flirt'. Whatever has happened or will happen between her and Hardy will be, the letter insists, absolutely different from a society flirtation. It will be private, honest and lacking in vanity; in other words, it will be pure.

In his very first description of Florence Henniker, Hardy said that he found her to be a 'charming, *intuitive* woman apparently' (and it was Hardy who underlined the word 'intuitive'). What drew him to her was the belief that understanding between them would be effortless, and as easy as her own actions would be spontaneous and natural. He thought he had found in her the purity of Tess – purity that did not mean chastity so much as purity of heart – and found it combined with all the charming elegance of a cultivated woman. Florence Henniker seemed to possess the simplicity of heart which allowed one to know one's own instincts and to follow them. That appearance (although it turned out not to be the whole story) held the promise for Hardy of an erotic relation that was 'pure', as he understood that word. Because of their intuitive understanding, the relationship could never degenerate into heartless flirtation and in addition it would remain pure even if it were consummated – even if, that is to say, they committed adultery together.

Florence's literary ambitions meant that she shared with Hardy the common ground of writing and publishing, and several times Hardy gave Florence detailed advice about her work. During the autumn of 1893 they even began to collaborate on a short story, 'The Spectre of the Real', which was published early in 1894. Nevertheless, the collaboration itself was of importance for what it expressed more than for what it brought about. Florence's temperament was her most significant quality as far as Hardy was concerned because he found he could trust and confide in her – things he was otherwise extremely unwilling to do – and the conviction that he and Florence were naturally allied drew from him a string of chatty and unwary letters, full of the personal feelings he habitually kept back. 'If ever I were to consult any woman on a point in my own novels I should let that woman be yourself,' he wrote within weeks of their meeting; 'my belief in your insight and your sympathies being strong, and increasing.'[11]

On her side, Florence's feelings for Hardy were undoubtedly complicated. She was much more sincerely committed to him than Rosamund Tomson had ever been; on the other hand, she was more wary and more critical than Rebekah Owen, for whom essentially Hardy was a prophet and hero. Florence's feelings were volatile too, particularly when Hardy's interest in her became alarming. In a postscript to his jolly, anecdotal letter of 10 June, Hardy wrote anxiously:

> I am afraid my chronicle is mere "frivel", or a great part of it: but having made a serious business of un-serious things I must follow on for the present, to redress by any possible means the one-sidedness I spoke of, of which I am still keenly conscious.
>
> I sincerely hope to number you all my life among the most valued of my friends.

In subsequent letters, he told her, 'I *have* entered on my scheme – the plan I spoke of' and 'I adhere desperately to my plan, with poor results; but time may help it.' This plan, as he calls it, involved dining out frequently and meeting lots of people, as if by these means to cure himself of an obsessive interest in Florence herself. Though he called it *his* plan and a one-sidedness *he* was keenly conscious of, he communicated it to her anxiously and so gives the impression that, as early as this in their relationship, Florence had taken a step back – that she had attempted, so very tactfully, to hold his interest in check.

Hardy's tone suggests too that she had reason to be wary because at times he coud sound a note of near-desperation. Amidst his euphoria over Florence, his elation at finding himself in love, a kind of panic emerges. The intensity of the feelings she had unleashed in him confronts him once again with his own vulnerability. He could not stand the thought of being flirted with and disappointed a second time, and that fear made him insistent and even nagging. It is a remarkable feature of his temperament, revealed most when he was in love, that he needed so desperately to feel certain of the other person in a relationship and to be convinced that they were completely on his side.

He and Florence were apart in mid July and they met up again on 19 July at Southsea, the refined seaside resort near Portsmouth where Florence was living at the time. Hardy made a detour on his way from Dorchester up to London and continued throughout the month to write frequent letters; gradually, however, his letters became more analytical. Hardy said less about his 'plan' and more about Florence's convention-ality – her weddedness to 'the ordinances of Mother Church', and his regret that she 'should have allowed herself to be enfeebled to a belief in ritualistic ecclesiasticism'. 'My impression,' he concluded, 'is that you do not know your own views.' Four days later, and a day after their meeting in Southsea, Hardy wrote to her again, this time from London, and was a little more accommodating: 'I cannot help wishing you were free from certain retrograde superstitions,' he wrote, nearly apologizing for his aggressiveness, and adding, 'I believe you will be some day, and none the less happy for the emancipation.'[12] To help bring this about, Hardy planned to send her a copy of Swinburne's notoriously pagan, and notoriously erotic, *Poems and Ballads*.

Hardy stayed in London until 27 July at least, perhaps a little longer, though by 31 July he was definitely back in Dorchester and he wrote once more to Florence on 3 August. This letter has disappeared.[13] It must have included arrangements for a day out together in Winchester, which took place on 8 August. Hardy came up by train from Dorchester, and Florence from Southsea. They met at Eastleigh, Hampshire and shared a compartment from there to Winchester, a journey that took a quarter of an hour or so. It was a day Hardy frequently remembered and commemorated, in the almost superstitious way he had. He spoke about it in detail to Rebekah Owen soon afterwards; three years later, he told the story to his friend Edward Clodd, and Florence Hardy, who did not meet Hardy for another fifteen years, knew the exact sequence of events. In 1898, he included 'At an Inn', a poem that referred to the visit, in *Wessex Poems*, and on the day itself he made his first entry in his prayer book for twenty years.

He and Florence had lunch in Winchester at the George Inn and were assumed by the landlord to be a married couple; they attended evensong, and, according to Clodd, they clasped hands before the high altar; later, they walked out of town to the place where, in *Tess*, Angel Clare and Liza-Lu look back and see the black flag raised, signalling that Tess has died. Outwardly, it was a harmless, slightly quaint and middle-aged excursion. Inwardly, it was traumatic. Hardy went away soon afterwards with Emma to stay with friends in Shropshire; and on his return, he answered a letter Florence had sent in the interim. His reply is full of arrangements and plans, as energetic as he usually is when writing to her; repeatedly, however, he sounds surprisingly formal: 'We are here again', Hardy begins; the next paragraph opens, 'We liked the evenings at Wenlock', and the third in the same vein: 'You will have learnt that I may go to Mrs Dugdale later on.' His gallantry is more perfect than before and far more constrained. Only in the final paragraph is there some sort of explanation for this change of tone:

> You allude to the letter of Aug 3. If I shd never write to you again as in that letter you must remember that it was written *before* you expressed your views – "morbid" indeed! *petty* rather – in the railway carriage when we met at Eastleigh. But I am always your friend
>
> T.H.[14]

Whatever she had said in person her letter must have confirmed, so that Hardy's letter came in response to his additional disappointment that she had not relented or changed her mind (as he had hoped she one day would). If anything, she was more absolute. Florence admitted that her views were 'morbid' and Hardy immediately pounced on this concession, calling them 'petty' as well. Similarly, his previous letters had all ended 'Ever sincerely yours' or 'Your ever sincere friend' or something of the kind. Now he was 'always your friend' and nothing more. The phrasing, which signalled his hurt and his refusal ever to be anything less than meticulously kind, was Hardy's first and last protest at her cruelty.

We do not know what Florence Henniker said, nor how far Hardy had gone in his earlier letter. Her father, Monckton Milnes, was a close friend of Swinburne and a dedicated proponent of John Keats, whose sensuality was excessive for some Victorian tastes. Furthermore,

15. 1 Arundel Terrace, Trinity Road, Upper Tooting, where Hardy and Emma lived from 1878 to 1881.

16. Lanherne, The Avenue (now Avenue Road), Wimborne, the Hardys' home from 1881 to 1883.

17. Max Gate when newly built in 1885. Notice the exposed location and the planted pine trees beginning to grow.

18. Max Gate, c.1900, with the new turret and the extensions to the rear; the large window of Hardy's third study is very visible at the back of the house.

19. Hardy around 1894, without a beard for the first time since his youth, photographed by the London firm of Elliot & Fry.

20. Emma, photographed for *The Young Woman: A Monthly Journal and Review* in 1895–6.

21. *Left.* Agnes Grove (1863–1926), the frontispiece to her book, *The Social Fetich* (1913), which was dedicated to Hardy.

22. *Below, left.* Florence Henniker (1855–1923), the frontispiece to her volume of short stories, *Outlines* (1894).

23. *Below, right.* Rosamund Tomson (1863–1911) became Rosamund Marriott Watson after her divorce and re-marriage. This picture was reproduced in her posthumous *Poems of Rosamund Marriott Watson* (1912).

24. Hardy photographed in 1905 for the volume *Memorials of Old Dorset*.

25. Emma Hardy at the same period, as visitors to Max Gate would have seen her.

26. *Above.* Florence Dugdale (1879–1937) and Hardy on the beach at Aldeburgh during one of their visits to Edward Clodd.

27. *Left.* Florence and Hardy seated on a bench in the garden of Max Gate, around 1920.

28. Gertrude Bugler (1897–1992), photographed in 1924, the year she played the role of Tess in Dorchester.

29. Florence, drawn by the portrait painter William Strang, who painted Hardy several times.

30. Higher Bockhampton as it looks today. The path running along the back of the house leads to Rushy Pond and Rainbarrows.

as became known only after his death, Milnes collected pornography, especially the works of de Sade. From evenings at the Rabelais Club, Hardy would have known the tone of his 'enfranchised' mind and it would have encouraged him to think his daughter might secretly be in sympathy with such views.

In his poem about the Winchester episode, Hardy presents a couple, mistakenly thought to be 'more than friends', who 'had all resigned | For love's dear ends'. Presumably, as it turned out, there were things Florence could not resign – the principles of her religious faith and her conventional ideas about marital fidelity – despite (or possibly because of) her father's more advanced views. Hardy might readily have described such principles and ideas as 'petty' or 'morbid' and his literary heroes would have agreed with him. Swinburne, whom he wanted her to read, and Shelley, whose *Epipsychidion* they were reading together in July, both asserted that 'love's dear ends' overrode all other laws, conventions and scruples.[15] That was why he wanted her to read them.

Likewise 'At an Inn', though it is predominantly a rueful and fatalistic poem, ends on a grand, Romantic note:

> O severing sea and land,
> O laws of men,
> Ere death, once let us stand
> As we stood then!

They had been 'left alone | As Love's own pair', privately secure, yet into that sanctum the world's values had intruded. Something had mysteriously 'chilled the breath | Of afternoon, | And palsied unto death | The pane-fly's tune.' These haunting, bereft lines dwell on the feeling of inexplicability – that what had and had not happened came as a numbing shock. Only at the poem's close does Hardy step back and think of the possible reasons. Then it emerges that part of the explanation is the 'laws of men', violating the secret 'world within the world', which according to *Epipsychidion* love may attain.[16]

Hardy's poems about Florence Henniker are some of his best. They return to ideas of 'severing', with titles such as 'The Division' and 'In Death Divided'. (The word 'division' may hint at Florence's husband, a soldier who dealt with the 'divisions' of an army.) And what had happened felt like 'division' to Hardy because a possible union had been shattered, leaving him in a comfortless world. More important than the thwarting of his sexual desire (which he felt as a humiliation as much as anything else, a humiliation he masked by accusing her of feebly losing her nerve and bowing to convention) – more important than this was the sudden whisking away of a context where he could hope to be candid. He wrote, on 15 January 1894, when their relationship was apparently settling into one of friendly fondness:

> I have been thinking that the sort of friend one wants most is a friend with whom mutual confessions can be made of weaknesses without fear of reproach or contempt. What an indescribable luxury! Do you want such a one for yourself?[17]

The sad truth was that despite her affection for Hardy, Florence Henniker did not really want anything quite so intimate as this. She refused a sexual liaison directly; more slowly, she disappointed his hope of a friendship of real depth. They remained friends, of course, and Hardy was unfailingly loyal both to her and to his belief in her 'intuitiveness'. Nonetheless, she never responded to him quite as he wanted her to. Part of his loyalty arose from his denial of that.

Hardy has to take some of the blame for this reluctance because Florence's first impulse after 8 August was to retrieve the situation as best she could. She sent him a present of a silver inkstand, inscribed 'T. H. from F. H.', which he kept on his writing-desk for the rest of his life. Later in the autumn, she sent portrait photographs of herself, while in her letters she discussed their collaborative work and asked his advice about her stories. All this was less flirtatious than perhaps it may appear because the inkstand symbolized their shared interests, signalling that their relationship should focus on that area of their lives, and sending photographs was not at all unusual between friends. Tennyson sent a portrait photograph to Walt Whitman in 1872. ('It brings you very near me. I have it now before me,' Whitman wrote, thanking him for the gift.) Sending a picture was something a gentleman should be equipped to do and it was quite as frequent between the sexes as between men. Lady Layard, Enid Guest (1843–1913), an aristocratic married woman, sent out signed photographs of herself to all the members of her circle. There was nothing exceptional and nothing disreputable in Florence giving Hardy a photograph to remember her by.[18]

Florence's keenness to stay in touch with Hardy indicates instead the extent to which she did need him, because her letters from the latter part of 1893 show that she could easily be hurt and was frequently anxious that she might have caused hurt. Several times during the autumn, Hardy needed to reassure her of his continuing friendship: 'So far from my not forgiving you anything, & not feeling as friendly as ever,' he wrote on 6 October, 'I can say that if we are not to be the *thorough* friends in future that we hitherto have been, life will have lost a very very great attraction.' Again two months later, he reaffirmed his feelings:

> Of course I shall *never* dislike you, unless you do what you cannot do – turn out to be a totally different woman from what I know you to be. I won't have you say that there is little good in you. [. . .] If you have only *one* good quality, a good *heart*, you are good enough for me.

Behind the scenes, however, his feelings were by this time far more conflicted than this, even though he was sincere in what he said.

There was a lot of literary discussion in his letters to Florence – of *Jude the Obscure*, which Hardy was working on, and of *Life's Little Ironies*, his new collection of short stories, to be published early in 1894. Nowhere, though, does he mention that he is writing another, quite separate short story, 'An Imaginative Woman'. It is referred to in the *Life*: 'December. Found and touched up a short story called "An Imaginative Woman"', but this note and dating are probably a blind. In truth, the story was essentially new when Hardy worked on it in the winter of 1893–4 and it unmistakably drew on his relationship with Florence. The imaginative woman of the title, Ella Marchmill, is a poetess, who publishes under the name 'John Ivy'. She is married to an unliterary businessman, a gunmaker (not a very different career from being a soldier), and at the opening, the couple are on holiday in 'Solentsea', modelled on Southsea, where the Hennikers lived.

A young poet, Robert Trewe, stays in the Marchmills' holiday home during their absences. Ella does not meet but hears of him and he starts to fascinate her; she reads his poetry ardently while her husband goes yachting, and when she discovers his picture, she puts it beside her bed as she reads and hides it under the pillow when her husband returns. Later, back at their home in the Midlands, she starts a correspondence with Trewe, using her pseudonym. Soon afterwards, Trewe commits suicide and when Ella discovers this she acquires his picture and a lock of his hair. Her husband begins to suspect she is having an affair and after she too has died, in childbirth, he comes across the picture of the poet. Comparing the picture with their son, now 'a sturdy toddler', he notices an uncanny resemblance between the two and although Ella has, in fact, never been unfaithful to her husband, he believes she has and the story ends with his rejection of the child.

'An Imaginative Woman' was published in April 1894 in the *Pall Mall Magazine*, where Florence almost certainly read it soon afterwards. She could not have missed the allusions to herself. As Ella Marchmill, she is depicted as an affected person, superficial and mediocre as a writer, and foolishly impressionable as a person. Trewe, the equivalent to Hardy, is by contrast a genuine artist and an innocent victim. His truth (declared by his name) encounters her falsity – her use of a pseudonym and her choice of one that implies something parasitic and exploitative. That he is true and she is false is then made part of the story: the narrator explains that Trewe's suicide came about because he never found a devoted woman he could love. By using her pseudonym in their correspondence, Ella prevented him from finding her so that her professional disguise is made responsible for his death.

These oblique attacks on Florence were hurtful enough and they were equalled at least by the story's mean depiction of Ella's husband, as first a boor and later a bad father. Florence was evidently devoted to Arthur Henniker and would have been wounded by this caricature of him. Unsurprisingly, a long gap appears in the surviving correspondence between Florence and Hardy, which lasts from January 1894 to summer 1895. Although this gap may have occurred accidentally (and there's evidence that the couple were in touch on literary matters in the interim), nonetheless, when the letters resume, Hardy's tone has quite changed: 'Why didn't you go on being my pupil?' he asked, plaintively, in August 1895. Florence was on holiday in Nuremburg at the time. 'How I shd like to explain the quaint architecture,' he murmured. 'But that's all over, I suppose.'

It seems very likely that 'An Imaginative Woman' was one cause of their estrangement and very odd that Hardy did not foresee this happening. He may have believed that he was attacking Rosamund Tomson once again, who used a pseudonym whereas Florence did not, and who shared her initials with Robert Trewe. All the same, allusions to Florence were unmistakable in the story and they implied an author who was both extremely resentful of her and childishly self-pitying. It was very hard for Florence to remain attached to a person so likely to transform his own need for a mothering presence into hostility towards that mothering presence, and so confused about how to balance dependence and self-assertion. The story seemed, in other words, to prove Florence's worst fears well founded – that beneath the chivalrous manner and the unfailing kindness, Hardy held her in contempt. It seemed to show, in other words, that his letters were insincere and, to someone like Florence, with her anxious need for reassurance, this discovery would have been especially hard to bear. Even so, Hardy's story and his letters to Florence are not entirely in conflict. When Hardy imagines a friendship where anything can be confessed without 'fear of reproach' (as in his letter of January 1894), he is looking to Florence for absolute pity and entire understanding. The story implies the same demand by making a full confession of Hardy's petulant hostility, so that Florence's reaction would be a measure of her friendship. Eventually, obliquely, Hardy did get a kind of answer.

Florence's next book of short stories, *In Scarlet and Grey*, appeared in 1896. Hardy seems to have helped her with some of the pieces because 'Bad and Worthless' and 'A Page from a Vicar's History' both crop up in their correspondence and the volume also collected their collaborative story, 'The Spectre of the Real'. Its first story, though, 'The Heart of the Color Sergeant', had never been mentioned between them and it reads in some ways like a retelling, from Florence's point of view, of her relationship with Hardy. Florence's heroine, Kitty Malone, is about to make 'the most prosaic of marriages – to join her lot to that of an entirely respectable elder son of a rich peer', a soldier by profession; her fiancé is not attractive particularly; in fact, his 'grave, commonplace face [is] poised on an ungainly neck'. Kitty then meets a junior officer in the regiment, Sergeant Rhodes – a gentleman who has 'gone downhill' through not mixing with his own class and, specifically, through his never meeting 'ladies'. '[O]ne becomes coarser in tastes and pleasures', the Sergeant says, when deprived of civilized women's company, 'harder also, and more cynical. You have done me good, and I thank you.'[19]

The Sergeant, Kitty's husband and the rest of the regiment are about to set off to Egypt to fight. Likewise, Arthur Henniker was about to set off on the Egyptian Expedition in 1893, when Florence first met Hardy, so some sort of autobiographical link does seem to be being made. Before he leaves, the Sergeant asks Kitty to give him a nosegay of forget-me-nots as a keepsake and she agrees, performing what is seen as a generous action. Into the 'heart of a man, reckless and dissipated enough, but a gentleman still [. . .] she had brought some short glimpses of hope and retrieval'. During the campaign, Kitty's fiancé behaves heroically when he saves the Sergeant's life. The Sergeant returns home badly wounded and must be confined in the army hospital, where Kitty wishes to visit him but her husband and father-in-law dissuade her from doing so. Her final action is to send the Sergeant instead a second bunch of forget-me-nots, and clutching these he dies. He had passed, the narrator concludes, 'where time and space exist not, and memory is, perhaps, by God's mercy, no longer the twin-sister of pain'.[20]

The volume was dedicated to Florence's husband and clearly this story praises him for his military heroism and, in his conduct towards Kitty, for his delicacy and sensitivity too. At the same time, though Kitty learns a lesson in the story, her dubious actions – of consorting with the Sergeant at a party and perhaps of encouraging his feelings for her – are, nevertheless, defended because by acting as she did she has helped to redeem a fallen man. Even so, Kitty must recognize that she should and can go only so far. A married woman's kindliness to other men is vindicated (even when it makes them fall in love with her); simultaneously, its limits are defined. 'The Heart of the Color Sergeant' is in many ways a conventional story with a conventional sentiment at its close and, insofar as it has autobiographical links, it reveals some unselfconscious vanity. Kitty's mere presence and simple kindness have a redemptive effect on the Sergeant, who needs her influence to escape his life of unspecified dissipation.

The Sergeant, meanwhile, is not directly a portrait of Hardy, but there are points of contact. What he says about becoming coarser and more cynical through the absence of congenial women is something Hardy had said in the past (to Geneviève Smith in 1874) and he may easily have repeated the thought to Florence. Moreover, if the story is seen as in part a response to Hardy's feelings for Florence, it comes across as more self-defining and less complacent. Hardy had asked to be pitied and comforted; the story agrees to that and sets terms. Florence, like Kitty, will do what she can and no more, because she does sincerely wish to help him, but it would be wrong for him to ask her to do more than she should. Similarly, and perhaps in reply to 'An Imaginative Woman', the story rebukes Hardy's contempt for commonplace men – for Ella Marchmill's husband, Kitty Malone's and, behind them both, for Florence's own. Florence must keep herself properly restrained and Hardy must learn to be more roundedly kind. It is the proper way forward for them both.

Partly as a consequence of the story, perhaps, and partly through her effort to put its principles into practice, Hardy and Florence did gradually find a stable footing for their friendship. After 1896, his letters contained few of the niggling, snide rebukes that he had made before but, inevitably perhaps, they became more impersonal and wary as well. There is something mannered about their perfect gentlemanliness and something rehearsed about Hardy's allusions to the past; still, he would never be anything less than affectionate. Florence, as far as we can tell, regained her trust in his fondness for her and was anxious only about his opinion of her work; and meanwhile, Hardy grew increasingly to admire her husband, 'the most perfect type of the practical soldier that I know', as he said in 1899.[21] Much earlier than this he and Florence had reached a confirmed understanding, which lasted until her death in 1923. The two of them were to remain close and trusted friends. Though Hardy had initially wanted far more than that, by 1895 he was becoming increasingly anxious to settle for what he had.

– 21 –

No balm for all your sorrow

WHEN SHE looked back in later years, Emma identified the early 1890s as the turning point in her marriage – or as what we might call the tipping point. In 1899, Elspeth Grahame, soon after her wedding to Kenneth Grahame (the author of *The Wind in the Willows*), wrote to Emma, asking her for any advice she might have to offer about married life, especially marriage to a writer. In her reply, Emma remarked caustically that:

> at fifty, a man's feelings too often take a new course altogether. Eastern ideas of matrimony secretly pervade his thoughts, & he wearies of the most perfect, & suitable wife chosen in his earlier life. Of course he gets over it usually, somehow, or hides it, or is lucky![1]

Hardy had turned fifty during 1890, the year after his brief infatuation with Rosamund Tomson, and just before he met Rebekah Owen and Florence Henniker. That was the time, according to Emma, when he began to have 'Eastern ideas of matrimony' – polygamous ideas, that is to say, unfaithful ones.

After Emma's death in 1912, Hardy's second wife, Florence, gave the same date for the deterioration of the marriage. 'Mr Hardy', she told his niece, Lilian Gifford, 'had more than twenty years of insults'; similarly, according to Florence, family rows started at the same time: 'for the twenty years preceding Nov. 1912', she claimed, Mary and Kate Hardy 'had not been allowed inside Max Gate'.[2] Twenty years is a convenient round number and Florence did not mean to be precise. Still, she was pointing to the early 1890s and it was probably around this time that Emma began to write her embittered, savage diaries recording Hardy's ill-treatment – diaries which he read after her death.

At the time, nonetheless, letters between the two create a slightly different impression. Hardy's letters to Emma were as prosaic as ever and as unworriedly frank. 'My dearest Em,' he wrote from London in December 1890, 'Here I am – & as it wants a few minutes to breakfast I write a line to let you know.' He had planned to stay in town for the whole week but returned sooner, having heard 'that my wife's lameness is no better: so I return tomorrow morning'. A few weeks later, when he was back in London, Hardy wrote chattily again, describing trips to the theatre, mutual friends and his visit to Emma's dressmaker.

> I called at Miss Gryll's – the gown was sent off Wedny night – so I paid the bill. She hopes to do more for you, & to have more time & opportunity of getting your pattern – She seems anxious to go on with you.

This is encouraging and considerate, even if a little overdone, and a similar tone of familiarity and some intimacy continued through 1891 and beyond. To judge from the correspondence, it broke down only in 1893, soon after Hardy's first meeting with Florence Henniker. Then Emma changed from 'My dearest Em', sometimes 'My dearest Emmie', into 'My dear Em'.[3] It is a tiny change in itself but a symptom of growing chilliness. Hardy's usually elaborate concern to make sure Emma knew exactly when he would be arriving home became at the same period perfunctory and reluctant. 'I will let you know time of my arrival', he tersely asserted on 24 July 1893. This was a particularly uneasy letter and it's the only one to Emma which survives from that summer. Probably, given Hardy's infatuation with Florence Henniker during these months, letters to Emma were few enough.

By spring 1894, Hardy was again addressing his wife as 'My dearest Em', but a year later, he had reverted to the more brittle 'My dear Em' and the change again corresponded with a noticeably bad patch between them. Hardy's surviving letters to Emma were nearly always rather impersonal affairs. Where to meet, how to travel, what to bring, where to leave the key to the desk – these were the things they usually discussed. During 1895, however, hardly anything else is mentioned at all. Moreover, Hardy approached these matters with a cold nerviness. Arrangements appear to have been especially difficult to make, as if Emma were being obstructive. Instead of probing her underlying reasons for that obstructiveness, Hardy tried to find ways of resolving the immediate, superficial difficulty. The result were arrangements that became almost laughably involved and the effort required to make them clearly grew tiresome. If Emma's obstructiveness derived from a feeling of not being wanted, then of course Hardy's betraying any impatience or annoyance would confirm it. And the desire to have this feeling confirmed was one of her motives for digging her heels in. Emma wanted to flush out the indifference she believed Hardy to feel – an indifference he was at pains to disguise. It is a familiar marital pattern: tense discussion of mundane things both masks and betrays deep-seated problems. It became in the following years the currency of the Hardys' relationship and the mode they fell back into whenever their efforts at reconciliation foundered.

To judge by these letters, the marriage was certainly disturbed during 1893 by Hardy's unrequited love for Florence Henniker. And how could it not have been? Emma had been with Hardy in Dublin when he and Florence first met so she would have seen Florence's effect on him at first hand. She knew Hardly was prone to these infatuations and may even have recognized that his feelings for Florence were of a worryingly different order from what he had felt before for other women. Certainly, she could not have been unaware of Hardy's obsessive interest in this attractive, highly civilized woman because, for the rest of the summer, he was forever in London or visiting Winchester or stopping off at Southsea. It suited her perhaps to pretend not to notice and, as the letter to Elspeth Grahame shows, she gradually learnt to treat these aberrations with plucky contempt. It was a front, of course – one she could keep up so long as she felt herself still to be Hardy's wife, felt herself to be, as it were, still in possession. So long as her status remained secure she could afford to sound dismissive. And, being more dependent on her position as wife, Emma insisted upon it more. She became inflexible because threatened. Standing on her dignity added to the friction with Hardy's family, though Emma also picked a quarrel with them sometimes – targeting them perhaps because she could not make the slightest impression on Hardy himself.

She was also canny enough to cultivate Florence, behaving towards her with a kind of *faux naiveté*. This was a tactic Emma employed with all of Hardy's female friends after Rosamund Tomson. By seeming to assume that nothing untoward could possibly be going on, she risked appearing foolish, even complaisant. At the same time, however, she made much of these women, taking them up and cultivating their friendship herself. She made them welcome and thus contrived to get in the way of their relations with Hardy. Women as refined and as socially adept as Florence Henniker could not have mistaken Emma's watchfulness; similarly, women as morally upright as Florence could not remain unaffected by the plea Emma implicitly made to their better nature. Emma gave the appearance of taking for granted that her rival's relationship to Hardy was innocent and the woman's intentions pure. This was accommodating and in other circumstances it would have been merely a polite fiction, used by the betrayed wife to help keep up appearances. Given Hardy's instinct for propriety (an instinct he never lost despite his enfranchized morals, his 'Eastern ideas of matrimony' and the new, man-about-town style of his clothes), and given that the women he fell for were (after Rosamund) eminently respectable too, Emma could intervene quite successfully. Taking the women at face value was a way of keeping them up to the mark.

By early 1894, the pattern of 1889–90 seemed to have repeated itself exactly. Hardy's obsession with Florence had ended in disappointment and his feelings, at that stage, were turning bitter. Even without reading 'An Imaginative Woman' (it is not known whether she ever did, before it was published or afterwards), Emma would have been around Hardy enough to guess his state of mind. And from her point of view, they had both been 'lucky' once again. Florence's rejection was a boon to Hardy because, of course, it was better to have loved and lost than to have made both a fool of yourself and a spectacle of your wife. And during spring 1894, if there was not a definite reconciliation, there was a thawing of relations between them; the letters show Hardy being friendlier to her, at least a little more confiding and once more using shared work as a means of retrieving the relationship.

*

Emma had helped Hardy with *Tess of the d'Urbervilles* in the aftermath of his encounter with Rosamund Tomson. She helped with the laborious transcriptions that the revision demanded and probably some details in the novel derive from her suggestions – the idea of Angel's mother sending Tess her jewellery as a wedding present was, as Hardy admitted, Emma's. Over *Jude*, on the other hand, it has usually been assumed that Emma was kept in the dark. She always said so, insisting that she had had absolutely no prior knowledge of the book before it was published. Some pages of the surviving manuscript of the book, however, have been excised from it for no immediately obvious reason. The same thing occurs in several other of Hardy's manuscripts and often these missing sections can be shown to have provided evidence of Emma's contributions to the to the book. That almost certainly was the reason why Hardy cut them out and this could be what happened with *Jude* as well, in which case, despite all her denials, Emma had been assisting her husband even with this final novel, the only one of his she came actually to loathe. The most likely time for her to have done so was in 1894 because in that year Hardy was once again committed to the tedious job of writing a novel in two versions simultaneously.[4]

Jude the Obscure, like *Tess*, had a complicated history – both of composition and then of publication. Hardy stated later that the plot was 'jotted down in 1890, from notes made in 1887' and that it was then written 'in outline in 1892 and the spring of 1893'. It is hard to be sure about these claims but certainly he started work on a full-length version around August 1893. The book was contracted for serial publication with *Harper's Magazine* but Hardy realized, as he was writing it, that the story would not be suitable for a magazine at all. It was too bleak and too outspoken. In April 1894, therefore, he warned *Harper's* about the nature of the planned book and offered to withdraw from the contract. *Harper's* declined his offer, as Hardy perhaps expected they would, and Hardy set about the task instead of making his adult story acceptable to a family audience.

Perhaps he raised the issue with *Harper's* to avoid having to endure the same trauma of rejection that he had experienced with *Tess*. At any rate, it left him repeating what he had undergone with the earlier novel. He had to rewrite his draft version while also preserving it intact for future, uncensored publication. It would have been complicated enough with computer support, and Hardy had available only pen and various inks. There was, moreover, an additional complication with *Jude*, which was Hardy's changing sense of what he wanted to say.

The serial version was published in monthly instalments from December 1894 until a year later, and at that point, as usual, the book appeared in volume form. As Hardy was changing the draft in one direction to make it suitable for the magazine, he was also reworking it for volume publication – both recovering its original state and incorporating his new conceptions because by the summer of 1895, his feelings about both characters and events had significantly altered. So, there are essentially three versions of the book: the one he wrote first, in 1893–4; the one modified for *Harper's* during 1894–5, and the 'restored' version, rewritten during 1895, which became the first edition, published at the end of the year.

Jude was bound to cause the same problems as *Tess* had done – the same only more so – because it was an extraordinarily scandalous and aggressive book. The difficulty, felt even at the time by friends like Gosse, was to understand why Hardy's manner and posture had altered so much and so quickly. There had, in fact, been a few warning signs earlier. In many respects, the novel does not follow on from *Tess* at all, but from *A Group of Noble Dames* and *Life's Little Ironies*, the collection of short stories Hardy produced early in 1894 (containing 'The Son's Veto' and 'To Please His Wife', among others). Both sets of stories have the pointedness, the lack of compromise and the harshness that became so evident in *Jude*.

In other words, *Tess*'s elegiac pathos had disappeared from Hardy's work before he wrote this last novel; regret for a lost past had already been supplanted by caustic indignation at contemporary society. Few of Hardy's readers had noticed the change, however, and when they did they usually brushed it aside. *A Group of Noble Dames* and *Life's Little Ironies* were only short stories, after all; they lacked the weight and seriousness of a three-volume novel and they could be construed as authorial self-indulgences, or *jeux d'esprit*. What's more, neither book was especially successful and both received less attention from reviewers than a novel would have done.

Another reason for the change of tone was Hardy's characteristic restlessness as a writer. The stories in *Life's Little Ironies* tend to be more up to date in period than most of his fiction had been before. Hardy's more fashionable appearance in the early 1890s accompanied a desire to make his fiction more modern too and *Jude* continues in this direction: the world it describes is decisively closer to the audience it addresses and very little of the story takes place within the country communities that had been Hardy's background up until now. Their absence removes a source of comfort and a sense of value that the other novels had cherished, even though the comforts were fragile, often illusory, and the values were recognized as being outdated.

After *Far From the Madding Crowd*, Hardy had produced *The Hand of Ethelberta*, a book that his audience found bafflingly different and almost unrecognizable. *Tess* was his most successful novel since *Far From the Madding Crowd* and, once again, Hardy changed tack instantly. Success produced in him a wish to elude his readership, by disappointing their expectations, and at the same time a desire to overwhelm them – to prove himself a far more complex and considerable writer than they would imagine on the basis of a single book. Even so, these impulses do not fully account for the extreme bleakness and rage of *Jude*, for the hateful symmetries of its narrative, its depiction of class prejudice remorselessly extinguishing hope, and its tragic climax, in which two children are killed by a third who then commits suicide.

Emotionally and tonally, the germ of the book was Hardy's experience in 1893–4, when his love for Florence was rejected. Yet most of the anger in the book is directed towards things that Emma held particularly dear: Church, State, university and the institution of marriage. Florence was loyal to these things too but the novel seemed gratuitously offensive to Emma as a loyal churchwoman, committed to the sanctity of marriage and with family connections in Oxford. Certainly, she reacted to it as if it were a personal attack. The stories are apochryphal that recount her asking eminent friends to dissuade Hardy from publishing the book, but the grain of truth in them is the force of her outrage. On many topics, the novel was only expressing views that Hardy had put forward before and Emma should not have been surprised by them. *Jude*, though, made it impossible for her to suppose he was not absolutely in earnest in his views – she had often maintained to herself and to others that he was writing merely for effect. Nor could she rid herself of the belief that behind the gloomy world view and the harsh social satire, there lay dislike of her in particular.[5]

Naturally, she felt deceived. Hardy had appeared to Emma to be (and would later in life once more appear to be) an agnostic who was inclined to positivism and attached to the traditions of the Church – its music, its architecture, and its moral ideals. Such a person was a very different proposition from the embittered, anti-clerical, tragic writer of *Jude the Obscure*. Had Hardy simply been deceiving her all these years? How could he disregard her feelings so completely? And how, most of all, could he threaten his high standing as a successful novelist – something they had both worked so hard to achieve for more than twenty years?

What was really at issue between Hardy and Emma was, however, none of these external things. He did not dislike her because she was a Christian nor because she had relatives living in Oxford. *Jude* was most of all an attack on Emma's desire to make the best of things as cheerfully as one could. To Hardy, this heartiness looked coarse, whereas to Emma Hardy's gloom appeared selfish and heartless. One of Hardy's poems suggests that, late in his life at least, he identified this as the underlying problem in their marriage and recognized too that there had been fault on both sides.

'Alike and Unlike', not published until 1925, is sub-titled 'Great-Orme's Head', and this suggests some link to the situation of 1893, because on their way to Dublin, the Hardys stopped off at Llandudno and rode in a carriage around Great-Orme's Head, the famous beauty spot on the western end of the bay. It was the only time that Hardy visited the place. His poem records the grandeur of the scenery, the 'magnificent purples', which the travellers came expecting and duly saw. Nevertheless, their experiences were very different.

> But our eye-records, like in hue and line,
> Had superimposed on them, that very day,
> Gravings on your side deep, but slight on mine! –
> Tending to sever us thenceforth alway;
> Mine commonplace; yours tragic, gruesome, gray.[6]

In manuscript the poem was given a second sub-title, 'She speaks'.

This means that it is a woman who is made to confess that her experience was 'slight' and 'commonplace' by comparison with the man's perception of 'gruesome' tragedy. 'Gruesome', however, is no improvement on 'commonplace'. Neither the man nor the woman is seeing it better; they simply and unfortunately see it differently. Because neither point of view is preferred, the speaker comes across as resigned and perceptive, rather than enraged or even insulted. As in the poem set in Bournemouth, 'We Sat at the Window', published a few years earlier, whoever saw things more truly, if either of them did, the difference in outlook was the problem. It was the relentless force 'tending to sever us thenceforth alway'.

Jude was a much more hostile, aggressive work than either poem, and in many ways a remorselessly unfair one. It insists on the difference in view and on the superiority of Hardy's perspective – the greater sincerity of his apparently unreasonable sense of tragedy. The novel will not give up the conviction that what happened in 1893 was terrible for Hardy, terrible in ways Emma could not perceive or appreciate. *Jude*'s grimness expresses Hardy's utter refusal to set aside either his miserable view of the world or his feelings of personal disappointment. It is almost petulantly possessive about his suffering. As Emma became increasingly impatient with Hardy's misery, which she considered both unfounded and cowardly, *Jude* took misery to an extreme, flaunting it almost and implicitly ridiculing Emma's belief that a good dose of common sense would see you through. More specifically, the novel declared that his feelings for Florence Henniker had been serious – too serious to be dismissed or forgotten or consigned to the past.

This was one reason why, although *Jude* did have unfortunate consequences for their joint social life and for Hardy's professional one, Emma's reaction to it was so particularly extreme. She regretted that Hardy gave up writing novels soon afterwards – that is, just when he began to make money at it; it seemed a waste of all the effort involved in establishing himself. And she was made lonelier than ever in Dorset when the book's notoriety meant that she and her husband were ostracized by good society. Still, she was not simply scandalized. The attack on her went deeper than that. It made out that courage and loyalty, the qualities in her that Hardy had never failed to appreciate before, were pointless and self-deceiving. And it was attacking faith itself as well as the institutions of the Church. Emma's own writing, whatever its literary merits or lack of them, was passionately religious, mystical and visionary. By condemning the Church as the repository of worn-out superstitions and oppressive morals, Hardy was clearly goading conservative opinion. From Emma's point of view, he was denigrating her personal faith, her perceptions – even her whole way of being.

At the end of the novel, Sue becomes a self-destructive religious devotee, who insists on going back to Phillotson, even though she finds physical relations with him intolerable. Jude tries to stop her: 'affliction has brought you to this unreasonable state', he says. Sue answers with rehearsed serenity.

> Dear friend, my only friend, don't be hard with me! I can't help being as I am, and I am convinced I am right – that I see the light at last. But O, how to profit by it![7]

Emma's poem, 'The Living Word', presents 'Beseeching man' who cries out to God:

> "Who art Thou?"
> The Invisible replies,
> "I am," and none in his heart denies,
> That power which rules the earth and skies[.][8]

This was written in 1907 and reflects in its style Emma's reading of *The Dynasts*, which Hardy was writing at the time, but all through her adult life, Emma believed in the inner light of religious faith. Though she became such an insistent anti-Catholic Protestant in old age, essentially her religion was more romantic and sentimental than doctrinal or dogmatic. The idea of inner conviction, mystically given, was more important to her than orthodoxy itself, and here in *Jude* Hardy was calling such convictions 'unreasonable' – aberrant and diseased.

By the time *Jude* was published Emma was already becoming acutely sensitive to accusations that she was mad. Soon afterwards, in February 1896, she wrote an incandescent letter to Hardy's sister, Mary.

> As you are in the habit of saying of people whom you dislike that they are "mad" you should, & may well, fear, least [*sic*] the same be said of you [. . . .] I defy you ever to say such a thing of me or for you, or any one, to say that I have done anything that can be called unreasonable, or wrong, or mad, or *even unkind*! And it is a wicked, spiteful & most malicious habit of yours.

The same word, unreasonable, recurs here first in the list, as if it touched a nerve. Clearly Emma felt there was some sort of whispering campaign against her, conducted by her sister-in-law, Mary, who had, she said, 'secured [Hardy] on your side by your crafty ways'.[9] The closing chapters of *Jude*, where Sue suffers her breakdown and religious conversion, seemed terrible confirmation to Emma of Mary's success and Hardy's disloyalty.

In truth, by 1896, Hardy was already beginning to shift in his affections back towards his wife and it may be, ironically, that this was the very thing that provoked Mary's hostility. In summer and autumn 1895, when Hardy revised the manuscript and took out again the changes he had made for the serial version, he also toned down some of the original's anti-religious statements. Probably, in part, he was hoping to avoid too great a scandal (hoping entirely in vain); also, I suspect, rather late in the day, he was trying to alleviate Emma's distress. Similarly, at the same stage of the book's development, he became more severe about his heroine, Sue Bridehead, distancing the narrative from her and making it more critical.

Sue Bridehead, the novel's ambiguous heroine, had first come into focus for Hardy between autumn 1893 and spring 1894, as he developed his outline into the complete novel. He wrote to Florence Henniker in January about his progress:

> I am creeping on a little with the long story, & am beginning to get interested in my heroine as she takes shape & reality: though she is very nebulous at present.

He mentioned the book to almost no one else but persistently to Florence. In August 1895, when bogged down in the 'clerical drudgery' of 'restoring the MS', he told her that 'Curiously enough I am more interested in this Sue story than in any I have written.'[10] To Florence Henniker, he makes both himself and the book appear preoccupied almost exclusively with Sue Bridehead. The rueful disinterest of the second letter invites curiosity: why should he be so interested in this story? And why should he mention that fact to Florence of all people? It hints, certainly, at a connection between the character of Sue and Florence Henniker's personality – a connection that the novel bears out – and even, perhaps, it invites Florence to notice the similarity. If, though, Florence did begin to see links between herself and Sue when she read the book, she would not have been flattered.

By saying that Sue's religious belief was a malaise, a piece of self-destructive madness, Hardy was criticizing Florence as much as Emma because both women were, in their different ways, sincerely religious people. More seriously, perhaps, the book accused Florence of secret indifference and exploitativeness – of not knowing how to handle an honest man. Jude is completely devoted to Sue while Sue always holds something of herself in reserve. 'You have never loved me as I love you,' Jude bursts out at the end:

> never – never! Yours is not a passionate heart – your heart does not burn in a flame! You are, upon the whole, cold, – a sort of fay, or sprite – not a woman!

Jude is furious here, and with some justification. Hardy, in the poems he wrote about Florence, was fairer and kinder; still, his underlying belief remained the same. In 'A Broken Appointment' he said, 'You love not me, | And love alone can lend you loyalty; | – I know and knew it'; in 'Wessex Heights' Florence was Hardy's 'one rare fair woman', but to her too he had become just a passing thought. 'Yet my love for her in its fulness she herself even did not know'.[11]

Sue was one of Hardy's most sensitively imagined characters. Her contradictions, scruples, self-deceptions and impulsive acts of kindness, her charm and stubbornness, her unselfconscious egotism: all these appear in the book with extraordinary naturalness. Nothing in the portrait seems forced or contrived, even though the book in other respects is deliberately artificial – its structure is geometrically symmetrical, its plot has a fatalistic circularity, and its events parallel myth and tragedy, the Bible and the classics. Amidst all this, however, Sue comes across as unquenchably herself. That contrast creates some of the book's most painful and moving effects. Alongside Jude's tragedy, in other words, is Sue's: the story of her vibrant, idiosyncratic nature being gradually snuffed out by relentless external forces, the social and religious structures that surround and come to control her, outwardly and still worse internally too.

'I had a regret,' Hardy wrote to Florence Henniker in July 1893 at the height of his infatuation:

> that one who is pre-eminently the child of the Shelleyan tradition [. . .] should have allowed herself to be enfeebled to a belief in ritualistic ecclesiasticism.[12]

This was a pompous and self-righteous accusation, perhaps. Perhaps, too, it was based on a misapprehension because Florence was by temperament never as radical as Hardy thought she should be. Nonetheless, this 'regret' generated much of *Jude the Obscure* as Hardy's disappointment with Florence became Sue's narrative. He wrote a book which attacked everything Florence held dear and its heroine (so like Florence) became enfeebled in the end by ritualistic Christianity. Worse still, she proved a crueller partner for Jude than Arabella had ever been.

If Sue looked to Emma like Florence Henniker, her rival, Arabella (Sue's rival) offered her no comfort. The novel does not narrate a return back to first love, not in anything but a hurtful, parodic way. Arabella's sexual frankness and vulgarity stand, instead, at the opposite extreme from Emma's genteel manners. The book suggests that if women are not like Sue then they are like Arabella. Arabella implies that beneath a veneer of civility women are voracious and controlling. Yet, strangely, the book prefers a lack of civility. It's not unsympathetic to Arabella, though many of its readers are. Arabella's crude desire for Jude (like Alec's behaviour to Tess by comparison with Angel's) has something to be said for it. Unrefined and shamelessly self-centred, she does not torment her husband as Sue had done. Emma was encouraged to see herself as either no better than Arabella or as worse.

Emma had good reasons, therefore, to feel personally attacked by the book and intimately too – in ways that few, if any, outside the marriage could fully comprehend. Still, in the evidence of Hardy's increasing dislike for Sue as he reworked the novel during 1895, there might be some crumbs of comfort. The loss of sympathy for his heroine implied that he might eventually think himself 'lucky', in Emma's terms, to have suffered Florence's rejection. One day, he might value Emma's loyalty again – as he had done in 1887 and again, more mutedly, in 1890. And, indeed, over the following years, something of this sort did take place. In 1895, however, Emma could hardly be expected to glean much reassurance from the book or see in it signs of any happier future for her marriage. For one thing, inside Sue Bridehead, other women apart from Florence were faintly visible.

The surname included 'Head', the baptismal name of Hardy's paternal grandmother, Mary Head, who had lived at Fawley in Berkshire, where the novel opens – a location given away by Jude's surname, Fawley. Family connections tied in with Hardy's allusion to his cousin, Tryphena Sparks, in the Preface; 'some of the circumstances' were suggested, he said, 'by the death of a woman' in 1890. Hardy made Sue and Jude into first cousins, seeming to model their relationship partly on his own with Tryphena. Emma's first rival had, it now appeared, never been fully dislodged from her husband's heart and, to judge from the novel she, Emma, had never really been his true love.[13]

Moreover, for the first time, the heroine was evidently modelled on somebody else. Sue was not a generic country girl, like Tess, and not an imaginary portrait of Emma, like Elfride Swancourt, Bathsheba, Paula Power or even Lady Constantine; instead, she was evidently akin to Florence Henniker. Jude, to make matters worse, was clearly a portrait of Hardy. He referred to him in later life as 'that entirely imaginary personage', but mostly because he and everyone else had noticed the similarities. Jude's class, his trade, his academic aspirations were signs all his readers could have followed; the encoded names and Jude's hopes of entering the Church were more private signals Emma would have understood.

This novel showed Emma that she had been ousted now even from her husband's imaginative life and from his imaginary biography; everything about the novel seemed to confirm that he no longer felt anything for her and, by its closing chapters, he seemed to be saying that his wife's religion, like all religious faith, was hysterical or demented or both. Two of Emma's surviving letters reveal the consequences. In

November 1894, just as the serialization began, she wrote to Mary Haweis, a campaigner for women's suffrage. Hardy, she remarked, was indifferent to the cause.

> His interest in the Suffrage Cause is nil, in spite of "Tess" & his opinions on the woman question not in her favour. He understands only the women he *invents* – the others not at all – & he only writes for *Art*, though ethics show up.

Emma was being typically robust – dismissive about her husband but from a position of practised familiarity. She wanted to give the impression that she at least, if nobody else, knew all the hidden vanities of this recently acclaimed man. She was, she implied, perfectly able to put up with his considerable shortcomings.

Little more than a year later, Emma had become vulnerable and enraged. 'Your brother,' she wrote to Mary Hardy, 'has been outrageously unkind to me – which is *entirely your* fault.'

> If you did not know, & pander to his many weaknesses, & have secured him on your side by your crafty ways, you could not have done me the irreparable mischief you have. And doubtless you are elated that you have spoilt my life as you love power of any kind, but you have spoilt your brother's & your own punishment must inevitably follow – for God's promises are true for ever.[14]

Whether or not she had reason to be so furious – whatever, in other words, the rights and wrongs of the family arguments – Emma had by now drastically lost her composure. The stance of the unfairly neglected but still loyal spouse had become impossible. And, of course, as she lost her temper, she weakened her position. You might suspect that Mary preserved this letter (presumably there were others) precisely because it proved her point so well, confirming her judgement that Emma was at best a harridan and at worst a lunatic. The peppery, rather sophisticated woman has disappeared in this outburst behind childish paranoia and, for the first time in her extant writing, behind religious denunciation. Hardy had shown how Sue Bridehead became 'unreasonable' under the terrible afflictions she suffered – fanatical, obstinate, and self-destructive. With a nasty irony, his portrayal of his heroine seemed to have ensured that exactly the same change took place in his wife.

~ 22 ~

The day goeth away

MEANWHILE, a storm of criticism broke over them. Famously, the Bishop of Wakefield threw his copy of *Jude* into the fire; other people did the same and sent Hardy the ashes through the post. The *Athenaeum* called it a 'titanically bad book' that read 'almost like one prolonged scolding from beginning to end'. Margaret Oliphant went even further in *Blackwood's Magazine*.

> There may be books more disgusting, more impious as regards human nature, more foul in detail, in those dark corners where the amateurs [i.e. lovers] of filth find garbage to their taste; but not [. . .] from any Master's hand[.]

The success of *Tess* had gone dramatically to Hardy's head, Oliphant implied, and led to 'the tremendous downfall of the present book'. He had let himself down and simultaneously he had appeared in his true colours, proving himself to be nothing like a true 'Master'. Even Hardy's long-standing allies disapproved: the American novelist William Dean Howells, who had known Hardy since 1883 and greatly admired *The Mayor of Casterbridge*, conceded that there were 'many displeasing things' in the new novel and many 'incidents are revolting'.[1] Worst of all, Edmund Gosse, perhaps the only one of Hardy's literary acquaintances who became genuinely a friend, called it a 'grimy' story; more damagingly, he saw no motive for its hostility to life and little truth in its exaggerations: 'We think the fortunes, even of the poorest, are more variegated with pleasures, or at least with alleviations, than Mr. Hardy chooses to admit.'[2]

The book's reception traumatized Hardy, over Christmas 1895 and for the rest of the following year, though, characteristically, the *Life* struggles to present what happened with a lofty, philosophical air: 'The clamour is not worth reviving in detail at this distance of time,' Hardy wrote, even though 'he was called by the most opprobrious names, the criticisms being outrageously personal, unfair, and untrue'. As always, this was the heart of the matter as far as Hardy was concerned. When he recalls to mind the personal insults, the name-calling, and the absence of any fair-mindedness in his reviewers, resignation vanishes and his language becomes suddenly impassioned. Just as quickly, however, the *Life* suppresses this betrayal of his real feelings. 'Hardy with his quick sense of humour could not help seeing a ludicrous side to it all.' Moreover, the end-result was ultimately 'the best thing that could have happened' because Hardy felt compelled to change direction. *Jude*'s reception meant that:

> if he wished to retain any shadow of self-respect, [he had] to abandon at once a form of literary art he had long intended to abandon at some indefinite time, and resume openly that form of it which had always been more instinctive with him[.][3]

In other words, after *Jude*, he stopped writing novels and turned to poetry instead. Although this move did ultimately take place, it did not happen straight away and it was, in many ways, a hesitant and even a reluctant transition – more dangerous for Hardy and more of a wrench than the *Life* attempts to imply.

Glossing over Hardy's heartache is typical of the *Life*; so too is the tendency to downplay his ambitions as a novelist. The biography strives to give the impression that he never invested much in his prose works and that he had started to leave novels behind long before his experience with *Jude*. A diary entry from Christmas Day 1890 serves this purpose.

> While thinking of resuming 'the viewless wings of poesy' before dawn this morning, new horizons seemed to open, and worrying pettinesses to disappear.

Similarly, according to the *Life*, when Hardy was 'putting the finishing touches to *Tess*', he was already thinking of '"A Bird's Eye View of Europe at the beginning of the nineteenth century [. . .]"'. That is, he was planning *The Dynasts*, begun ten years later. And *Tess*, he claims, 'notwithstanding its exceptional popularity, was the beginning of the end of his career as a novelist'. This sentence concludes the first volume of the *Life*. The second half of the book begins with a section entitled, '"Tess", "Jude" and the End of Prose'. Hardy uses the structure of the book to help suggest that his impatience with novel writing had been building up for some time. The break he made after *Jude* looks overdue and clear-cut; it is made into a new start.[4]

In fact, of course, things were much more complicated than that. No doubt Hardy did hanker after the chance to write poetry and drama while he was writing novels. *The Dynasts* was a long-standing and precious idea and writing poetry did frequently offer him a sense of release by comparison with writing prose. Poetry took him out of the hubbub and jostling of the literary marketplace because it was the form in which he had always written when writing for himself. This is what the diary entry emphasizes and it's significant that the ideas came to him 'before dawn' on Christmas Day 1890. Early morning waking is a symptom of depression and one certainly that Hardy experienced. There are numerous references to waking early in his extant notebooks and diaries; the world always looked especially bleak to him at that time of day and life more than ever a useless struggle.

Christmas 1890 was, however, completely unlike Christmas the following year when *Tess* was being acclaimed from all sides. Though he maintained that the novel 'was the beginning of the end of his career as a novelist', its reception at the time felt like a culmination and his first impulse thereafter was by no means to withdraw into poetry. Quite the opposite: he capitalized on his success first by writing *The Pursuit of the Well-Beloved*, then by putting together another collection of short stories and thirdly by embarking on his most ambitious novel to date. In almost all respects – stylistic, thematic, tonal as well as geographical – *Jude* was a calculated bid to extend his range and Margaret Oliphant's review was so dangerous to him because it was so acute. Oliphant recognized the ambition of the novel – its hubris, if you like. She saw that, far from wishing to give up novels, Hardy was trying to dominate the form – to revolutionize it and redefine its terms.

This attempt also involved an effort to keep up. The critical condemnation *Jude* received left Hardy so bewildered and alarmed because he thought he had been moving in quite a fashionable direction. Ever since its first reviews, *Jude* has been seen as indebted to French novels, especially the Naturalist school, led by Émile Zola. Zola was born in 1840, so he was Hardy's exact contemporary and in his novels, as in *Jude*, human beings behave sordidly, social structures are repressive and immovable, and animalistic sexual desire is an overwhelming force. Hardy resisted the comparison, nevertheless: 'You mistake in supposing I admire Zola,' he told Florence Henniker.

> It is just what I don't do. I think him no artist, & too material. I
> feel that the animal side of human nature should never be dwelt on
> except as a contrast or foil to its spiritual side.

This was in 1897, when Hardy had read a dozen reviews saying that *Jude* was as unclean as Zola's *La Terre* or *Germinal.*

When much earlier in his career Hardy had been compared to George Eliot, he had obstinately insisted on his complete independence. He did so again now and there's a suspicion that he was protesting too much. He had read Zola and he owned several of the novels. It's unlikely there was no influence at all, even if some of it arose out of Hardy's wish to differentiate himself from the French novelist.[5] *Jude* does dwell on 'the animal side of human nature'; that was undeniable, and its view of the 'spiritual side' is equivocal, to say the least. Similarly, Hardy had been working for a decade or more at bringing English novels nearer to their more frank and adult French counterparts. Zola's example must have had some importance for him.

Nonetheless, Hardy did have a point because *Jude* drew much more for its inspiration on Henrik Ibsen, the Norwegian playwright whose work had scandalized and enthralled London audiences in the early 1890s. Some contemporaries did sense the similarity – William Archer, for instance, Ibsen's best known translator, chose *Jude* as his book of the year in 1896. Hostile reviews renamed the book 'Jude the Obscene' in the same way that the fashion for Ibsen was called 'Ibsceneism' by its enemies. And Hardy had evidently come across Ibsen's works. After 1890, when *Hedda Gabler* appeared, Ibsen became a European phenomenon and new plays were put on in all the major capitals almost as soon as they were written. Edmund Gosse was an early advocate and Hardy had been to see Gosse's version of *Hedda Gabler* when it was first performed in 1891. This may have added to Hardy's feelings of disappointment and failure when Gosse of all people disliked *Jude.* He saw Gosse's version of the play again in 1893, along with two more of Ibsen's plays, *Rosmersholm* and, in Florence Henniker's company, *The Master Builder.*

This was an eerie choice of play for them to watch because *The Master Builder* concerns a middle-aged architect in an unhappy marriage who has an unconsummated though passionate affair with a younger woman. When he falls in love with her and she with him, at least with a romantic image of him, the younger woman urges him to leave behind his now limited aspirations and start once more to pursue the glorious ambitions of his youth. Her encouragment leads, however, only to his death. When Florence Henniker and Hardy saw the play together in early summer 1893, Hardy's obsession with her was just taking hold. The parallels between their situation and the play's could hardly have been more striking, so much so that Hardy seems almost to have been living out the play for the rest of the year.

Clearly, the play's closeness to his own experience would have drawn him to Ibsen as he wrote the novel. Just as significantly for Hardy, Ibsen had caused a scandal while also achieving popularity. Attempts to suppress him had been defeated by the public's enthusiasm for his work, in a sequence of events that exactly paralleled Hardy's experience with *Tess*. Hardy would have seen in Ibsen a kindred spirit and found in his career additional evidence that 'candour' was acceptable in the 1890s, in a way that it had not been only a few years before. Likewise, Oscar Wilde's challenging, witty satires were doing a roaring trade in the West End and the 'New Woman' novel was the latest thing. 'New Woman' novels addressed questions of marriage and divorce, female emancipation and even female sexuality. Though Hardy persistently denied the similarity, *Jude* was evidently a 'New Woman' novel in some respects. It draws directly at points on Grant Allen's best-selling *The Woman Who Did* (1895). Hardy had also got to know 'Sarah Grand' the author of *The Heavenly Twins* (1893), another highly successful 'New Woman' novel, and he commended her method to Florence Henniker in September 1893, as he was beginning to write *Jude*.

> If you mean to make the world listen to you, you must now say what they will be thinking & saying five & twenty years hence: & if you do that you must offend your conventional friends. "Sarah Grand," who has not, to my mind, such a sympathetic & intuitive knowledge of human nature as you, has yet an immense advantage over you in this respect – in the fact of having decided to offend her friends (so she told me)[.][6]

This advice typifies the spirit in which Hardy began his own book.

Ibsen's example of candour leads to the new novel's subject-matter and plot. The reviewers especially hated Father Time's suicide near the end of the story and his murder of the other children. It is an incident that can still be very hard to take, yet it's not dissimilar from an episode Ibsen could have written. At the end of his play *The Wild Duck*, for example, the young girl Hedvig shoots herself. Like Father Time, Hedvig believes that she is unwanted by her parents, and, like *Jude*, *The Wild Duck* concerns itself with the destructive effect of moral idealism. Ibsen's influence can be detected in the style of the novel too, which is strikingly dramatic. Jude and Sue's relationship is often depicted via conversation alone, so that their unadorned dialogue reads like a theatrical text.[7]

Ibsen's example inspired Hardy's willingness to court controversy in *Jude* and, after *Tess*, he was more inclined to outspokenness anyway. In 1890 he was already arguing that different walks of life and different personalities required 'a different code of observances' and observed in his notebook that 'The morality of actresses, dancers, &c., cannot be judged by the same standard as that of people who lead slower lives.' In August 1893, in reply to a newspaper's straw poll, Hardy wrote that:

> I consider a social system based on individual spontaneity to promise better for happiness than a curbed and uniform one under which all temperaments are bound to shape themselves to a single pattern of living. To this end I would have society divided into *groups of temperaments*, with a different code of observances, for each group.

This is a much more radical and innovative version of fundamentally the same point of view. Ibsen was 'indeed a revelation', encouraging Hardy to come out so boldly here in support of social change.[8]

As 1893 turned into 1894, however, Hardy's relationship with Florence Henniker failed to live up to his expectations and Ibsen's popularity proved temporary. Respectable opinion, Florence Henniker included, turned decisively against the new realism in drama, just as it proved hostile to *Jude*. Similarly in 1895, as the novel was appearing, Oscar Wilde was put on trial for his homosexuality, found guilty and sentenced to two years' hard labour – a sentence that destroyed his career and ruined his health. A revolutionary, visionary moment in English culture seemed to have come and then just as rapidly gone again. What came in its wake was narrow-mindedness and reaction. The pillars of society did not object to being teased but they would not be threatened. Decency, normalcy, and the established gender roles: all these were reaffirmed, discreetly if possible, firmly where necessary, and *Jude* was caught up in a widespread backlash against the Naughty Nineties.

Naturally enough, not all of this came home to Hardy at once. He and Emma always tried to find some sort of distraction when one of his novels first came out. Around Christmas and New Year 1895–6, they could not go on holiday; instead, they took to cycling. In January 1896, Hardy told a friend:

> I have almost forgotten there is such a pursuit as literature in the arduous study of – bicycling! – which my wife is making me learn to keep her company, she doing it rather well.

In truth, of course, he had not forgotten literature remotely and he was not simply keeping Emma company. That was the pretext. Cycling was a fashionable hobby, probably recommended to them by the Thornycrofts, and being taken up by many of the best people. Lady Gregory of the Abbey Theatre, Dublin, and the friend of W. B. Yeats, commented in 1897 that riding a bicycle was 'simple torture, like sitting on a skate balanced on a cartwheel'.[9] Both Emma and Hardy enjoyed it more than this, Emma particularly, and it became during 1896 one means of protection from the grisly experience of Hardy's being reviewed.

As the furore surrounding *Jude* continued, however, not even cycling could entirely keep their spirits up. On a visit to London in February 1896, Hardy complained of 'fearful depression, slight headache &c'; in April he went down with a 'chill, or whatever it was' which 'left rheumatism' and meant he could only 'move about the house with difficulty'. It was unusual for him to be unwell in his fifties; evidently the book's reception was undermining his health that spring and it was making Emma poorly too. Still, they travelled up to London as normal and were received, Hardy later wrote, 'just the same as ever'.[10]

This is a doubtful assertion because, unusually, they did not stay. They left London for Brighton in May, apparently once more in search of better health. Back in London during the summer, they did do some socializing, but 'Hardy's chief pleasure' was:

> a pretty regular attendance with his wife [. . .] at the Imperial Institute [. . .] where they would sit and listen to the famous bands of Europe that were engaged year after year [. . .] but were not, to Hardy's regret, sufficiently appreciated by the London public.

Emma was especially fond of Brighton and, like Hardy, she loved music of many different kinds, especially perhaps the robust, wholesome flavour of 'the famous bands of Europe'. In this eccentric habit, they were opposing together the provincial, bad taste of 'the London public' – in music as in literature. They were cherishing too something that most people regarded as old-fashioned, a posture in relation to music particularly that Hardy struck more and more frequently in the coming years. Music – whether folk tunes or long-forgotten music-hall songs or the melodies of the metrical psalms – became a repository of the past, fleetingly retrieved, as the notes came up from musicians playing in the street outside or Hardy picked out a melody on his father's violin or when he overheard Emma singing at the piano in the front room of Max Gate.[11]

These hints of solidarity between the Hardy and Emma became if anything stronger later in the summer when attacks on *Jude* resumed. After the initial flurry of bad reviews, more thoughtful ones had appeared during the spring. Then in the summer the Bishop of Wakefield's denunciation of the book appeared along with Margaret Oliphant's essay. The pattern of *Tess* (of initial, self-righteous rejection followed by gradual acceptance) was not being repeated. Instead, the considered opinion of the serious critics confirmed the predictable, relatively harmless outrage of the book's first reviewers. Hardy began also to feel that he was being ostracized because of the book and London became intolerable. He and Emma left, first for Max Gate and then for a lengthy holiday, touring the English countryside.

Emma travelled around 'on "The Grasshopper" (her green bicycle), & I on foot' as Hardy told his new literary friend, Agnes Grove. They visited Malvern, Worcester, Warwick, Kenilworth and Stratford-on-Avon, seeing their own country 'with the eyes of a stranger, guide book in hand'. They went to the 'regular hotels' and found themselves usually 'the only two English people – the rest being all Americans'. This choice of holiday feels like a retreat, one that was unplanned perhaps. Visiting England became, rather to their surprise and delight, an escape from the English, restoring the solitude in which they had always been happiest together. It is curious and touching that their posture, with Emma riding and Hardy walking, evoked their times in Cornwall together, when she rode on horseback and he walked along beside – as her courtly lover and the squire to her lady.

After the Midlands, they travelled on first to Reading, then Dover and from there across the Channel to Belgium, the bicycle going with them all the way. The holiday seems to have gained its own momentum, its spontaneity full of nostalgia. In Brussels, they 'put up for association's sake at the same hotel they had patronized twenty years before'. Hardy visited Waterloo again, and did probably have *The Dynasts* somewhere in his mind though it is hard to see their journey simply as a research trip. Away from London and Dorset, free from the maddening intrusions of Hardy's relations, removed from the London critics' dislike, Hardy and Emma were struggling to recover their physical health, keep their emotional equilibrium and also to rebuild their marriage.[12] Things were by no means rosy between them, or comfortable. Emma felt personally wounded by *Jude*; she sympathized with a lot of the critics and, like Hardy, she had been made unwell by the stress of it all. Instinctively, though, they stuck together, closing ranks against the world.

When they came home, Hardy did begin to work again and, whatever he later claimed, the change to poetry had still not taken place. He had been working on his first Collected Edition ever since the beginning of 1895, which had become a major undertaking. He had regained possession of the copyright to all his books, and made an agreement with the publishers Osgood, McIlvaine & Co., for a complete, uniform edition, thoroughly revised and with short introductions written for each volume. By June 1896, he had got as far as the completion of volumes XIV and XV, *Life's Little Ironies* and *A Group of Noble Dames*; in August, just before leaving on holiday, he finished volume XVI, *Under the Greenwood Tree*. Now he set about the more demanding business of revising his 1892 story *The Pursuit of the Well-Beloved*, for its first appearance in book form. It would be the seventeenth and final volume in the new edition but he could expect reviews of what was, essentially, a new book.

Hardy said that this revision of a minor story was something he only 'consented' to, in order to complete the collected edition. That attitude was consistent with the picture he presented of himself as a writer fulfilling previous engagements and nothing more. He did, however, hope and believe that this 'new work' might help him make his peace with his readership, after the catastrophic reception of *Jude*. *The Well-Beloved* was, he thought, 'a book which nobody could say anything against'. It was 'a bygone, wildly romantic fancy', which 'would please Mrs Grundy & her young Person, & her respected husband, by its absolutely "harmless" quality'. When *Two on a Tower* had ruffled feathers in 1882–3, Hardy had done something similar, writing the relatively anodyne 'Romantic Adventures of a Milkmaid' and his story for boys, 'Our Exploits at West Poley'. He was hoping that *The Well-Beloved* would have the same effect, reassuring his readership and placating them.

Unfortunately, the new story was attacked almost as violently as *Jude* had been and several reviewers seemed just to be pouncing on the opportunity it offered to condemn him, as if they felt they had missed their chance the last time round. The most violent review came in the *World*. Hardy told Lady Jeune that he was 'surprised & distressed' by this 'ferocious attack'; he described it to Gosse as an 'extraordinary stab in the back'; and he told Sir George Douglas that he could not understand how his 'fanciful' tale 'should be stigmatized as sexual & disgusting'.[13] Complaining to and seeking reassurance from his trusted friends were things Hardy frequently did when badly reviewed; his reaction here is different only in its strength and in the change of mind it produced in him. Even when his initial feelings had subsided, Hardy remained convinced that he could expect from now on to be deliberately misread. He and his books were both 'innocent' but they would suffer 'cruel misrepresentation' because, in some quarters, he was now anathema. During 1896, he had been stalled for a while and picked himself up again. His holiday in the autumn had revived him – the 'eight weeks of nearly continual movement [had] been upon the whole an agreeable & instructive time', as he told Florence Henniker.[14] It had done nothing, though, to change the climate of opinion in which he had to work. It had only deceived him into underestimating the degree of entrenched opposition he now faced.

It was in this defeated state of mind, when he was 'surprised & distressed', that Hardy decided he could not write any further novels. It was an opportune moment to do so because he had a collected edition at last, a monument to his achievements over the last quarter-century. In it, he had found ways of uniting the different books – with their various origins and atmospheres – into a coherent *oeuvre*, centred on Wessex, and he could foresee the edition establishing his future reputation as well as securing him financially. If and when the public caught up with his advanced opinions, they would have this handsome set of volumes to go back to. For the present, there seemed no way of recovering, not at least in prose, the sense of intimacy with his audience that *Tess* in particular had brought him. The reviewers blocked his path and, under their influence, as the culture became more conservative, the public was abandoning him.

The decision to give up writing did, all the same, give Hardy the sense of freedom that he recalled later. Around New Year 1897, soon after the copy of *The Well-Beloved* had gone off to the printers and Hardy had at long last completed the edition, he told Florence Henniker that 'I have lately grown to feel that I should not much care if I never set eyes on London again.' A couple of months before, just after getting home from abroad, he had expressed similar feelings more self-assertively, finding in poetry a way of going forward.

> Poetry. Perhaps I can express more fully in verse ideas and emotions which run counter to the inert crystallized opinion – hard as a rock – which the vast body of men have vested interests in supporting.

During his two years' work spent on the collected edition, Hardy had spent a lot of effort altering place names and even locations sometimes in order to ensure consistency and as much topographical accuracy as possible; he added many details of local history as well and in summer 1896 he paid particular attention to *Under the Greenwood Tree*, re-entering its scenes with evident fondness – scenes from the novel of his that came closest to home.[15]

Tired of London, returning imaginatively to Wessex, and writing poetry again – these three developments go in the same direction. They are the actions of someone rejecting those who have rejected him. The treatment that *The Well-Beloved* received in the spring of 1897 had prompted this new stance and, for the next fifteen years or so, Hardy had a sense of beleaguered isolation; he viewed his public with icy, touchy anger and continued working only out of a determination not to be cowed though he felt the pointlessness of carrying on. Poetry ran counter to inert, crystallized opinion, Hardy claimed; that might be meritorious but did not mean it could begin to overcome something 'which the vast body of men have vested interests in supporting'.

*

Despite their companionship in adversity during 1896, Hardy withdrew once again from Emma when he gave up writing novels. He knew she would rather he supported more the world's inert, crystallized opinions and, as a poet, he had less need of her assistance or her support. He would not need a secretary very often or a hostess. Even so, the degree of their estrangement from this period onwards is not accounted for by his change of professional direction alone.

One sign of Hardy's change of attitude towards London and litera-ture is his decision in spring 1897 not to rent lodgings in the capital during the season. This was breaking a habit that dated back to 1883.

He and Emma did travel up, though not until mid May – the previous year they had left Dorchester as early as March – and after only two weeks in town, they retreated to Basingstoke. From there, they travelled in and out, seeing friends, exhibitions and plays. Even this compromise arrangement lasted no more than a further fortnight and by 11 June they were back in Dorchester. A week after that they were abroad, holidaying in Switzerland.[16]

It was the Queen's Diamond Jubilee in 1897 so London was unusually busy. Hardy disliked the 'racket' it all caused and Emma did not much enjoy it all either. She wrote to Rebekah Owen in February, 'We are all going frantic this year about honouring the Queen [. . . .] I suppose London will be blocked everywhere & we shall be all staring at each other.'[17] Ten years earlier 'in the brilliant Jubilee-year' Hardy had passed his time in London 'gaily enough', amused if not enthused. This time he could not bear it any more than Emma could. The best option was to go away, and for three weeks, over the Jubilee itself, they went to Switzerland, enjoying the emptiness of the resorts. Emma recorded the trip in a diary and, although her comments are briefer and less animated than they were in her holiday diaries from the 1870s and 1880s, they are not overpoweringly dark or bitter. She was disappointed by the weather, which was poor at first, though improved after Jubilee day itself (20 June), when the couple travelled from Berne on to Interlaken: 'the sweetest place of all, & we cheerful again', as Emma wrote.

Hardy's account of the holiday in the *Life* is rather over-literary and self-regarding. It dwells on the poems he wrote – which of them were inspired where – and his feelings when visiting literary pilgrimage sites: Edward Gibbon's garden in Geneva, or Byron's and Shelley's houses on the Lake. In letters at the time, he is full of literary matters too. On the other hand, he and Emma went on lengthy walks in the mountains – Hardy on foot and Emma usually on horseback, just like the previous summer when she rode her bicycle and he walked. Both of them found the scenery uplifting. The 'rosy glow from the Jungfrau' seemed 'an exhibition got up for themselves alone', Hardy wrote. It was to Emma, 'Exquisite like a bride'. There were one or two moments of tension, though remarkably few and, typically, these arose out of jealousy.

When they visited the Matterhorn, Emma remarked that 'T. H. talked of Whymper – he *knows* him.' Edward Whymper, the only Englishman to survive a famous climbing accident on the mountain in 1865, was someone Hardy had met at Aldeburgh, during one of Edward

Clodd's house parties. Emma disapproved of Clodd more than ever. She had written to him in February 1897 tenaciously disputing the anti-religious arguments of his book *Pioneers of Evolution*, and, despite Hardy's quite established pattern of visiting Clodd, she had never been invited to Aldeburgh herself. Her 'he *knows* him' sounds mocking, as if she thought Hardy was being a bore, name-dropping about his famous acquaintance. Probably he was, but Emma also overreacted. She always disliked it when Hardy tried to live a more separate life; as time went on she became increasingly impatient with men generally, particularly men in groups, largely because Hardy used single-sex clubs and dining societies as another means of avoiding her.[18] On the other hand, so long as they were together, so long as she felt in possession of him, the marriage still worked reasonably well. Hardy's literary preoccupations did not worry her. If Hardy was cheerful, he was always going to be pursuing his writing in one way or another; that was simply in his nature and Emma in fact encouraged him. Better he should be vain and slightly irritating than miserable and torpid. She bridled only when he bragged about the life she did not share.[19]

Something resembling harmony continued when they returned to England in July. They went straight back to Dorset and Hardy began working again – revising a short story, 'The Grave by the Handpost'. In August, they went on a short holiday, visiting Somerset and Salisbury. Arthur Blomfield was carrying out some repairs on the cathedral there, and this may have been what prompted Hardy to return. He was always curious about his old employer's projects (*Jude* had featured the church Blomfield had built in Oxford, St Barnabas in Jericho, renaming it 'St Silas Church' and recording many details of its High Church style). During and after his writing *Jude*, Hardy's interest in architecture generally had increased. He had done restoration work again himself in 1893, on the parish church in West Knighton, a village near Broadmayne, something that may have encouraged him to make Jude a stonemason.

During 1896, he took a marked interest in the notorious restoration of Peterborough Cathedral and in autumn 1897, he was inspecting a church in East Lulworth and an inn in Maiden Newton, on behalf of the Society for the Preservation of Ancient Buildings. Restoration was planned for both and Hardy was called in as an expert, to advise about what work was 'absolutely necessary to be done' and what would be excessive. The SPAB, founded by William Morris in 1877, was devoted to reining in Victorian restorers, to preventing them from rebuilding insensitively and in ways that ignored the meanings enshrined in ancient buildings, whatever their supposed faults of style. Hardy had been in sympathy with the Society's views from its foundation and suspicious about 'restoration' in all its forms from the late 1870s onwards. He was not dogmatic even so and at West Knighton did create more orderliness in the building than had been present before. His preferences and practice still show, more than anything else, the influence of the training Hicks gave him as an apprentice architect.

Whatever the motive for revisiting Salisbury, Hardy and Emma went to evensong together in the cathedral two days running. Four years earlier, almost to the day, he had heard evensong with Florence Henniker in Winchester. Again this time, he noted the event in his Bible and prayer book. A diary entry is reproduced in the *Life*:

> August 10. Continued – 'The day goeth away . . . the shadows of the evening are stretched out . . . I set watchmen over you, saying, Hearken to the sound of the trumpet. But they said, We will not hearken [. . . .]' Passages from the first lesson (Jer. VI.) at the Cathedral this afternoon. E. and I present. A beautiful chapter, beautifully read by the old Canon.

It was perhaps as close as they would ever get to achieving a reconciliation. The Bishop of Wakefield had died just a few days before and Hardy was moved by his death to reflect that:

> It is painful to think that people should so recklessly and bitterly attack others who have the same objects in life as themselves [. . . .] Apart from theological points I don't know that my ultimate object is far removed from that of the late bishop.

This sounds more like the positivist view of Christianity that Hardy had embraced during the 1880s and his differences with the Bishop were fundamentally little different from his disagreements with Emma. In this mood, he would think it unfortunate if superficial differences obscured a more profound shared purpose. And both he and Emma were seeking out common ground this year: Emma had been reading Ibsen in February and Hardy was going to church again in August – a habit he had long since fallen out of. The compromise they had reached ten years earlier seemed almost possible again.[20]

It did not last. The following year saw a return to their established routine – Max Gate with its gloomy surroundings remained their home;

Hardy's family continued to be a source of friction; the couple resumed in the spring their annual visit to London. They were getting too old perhaps to change their ways and many of these ways were corrosive to their happiness, as individuals and as a couple. Much worse as far as Emma was concerned was Hardy's repeated emotional infidelity – his inability to avoid entanglements with the literary women who, in Emma's eyes, had been trying to take advantage of his fame and his weakness for nearly a decade.

*

Hardy had first met Agnes Grove (1863–1926) in 1891. She was well born – the daughter of General Augustus Pitt-Rivers, her mother was one of Mary Jeune's sisters and hence the daughter of a baron; Agnes's husband succeeded to a baronetcy in 1897, making her a lady. Like Florence Henniker, Agnes was both beautiful and a rather gifted writer, especially of journalism and social commentary, though she tried her hand at fiction too. Her work at its best was polemical and political, acute and merciless about bourgeois, pseudo-genteel vulgarity; meanwhile, in her personal and social life, she was perfectly poised. After the turn of the century, as Emma grew older and suffered more from arthritis, Agnes hosted the tea parties that the Hardys gave when up in London. By then, all three enjoyed an amicable friendship. Agnes's book, *The Social Fetich*, published in 1907, was dedicated to Hardy, and Emma cultivated the acquaintance of her husband's charming lady-friend. Reaching this accommodation involved, however, a by now familiar struggle.

In Hardy's first reference to Agnes, she is one of 'a pair of beauties', and 'with her violet eyes, [she] was the more seductive'. When they met again in 1895, it was at a ball, held outdoors on a moonlit September night at her father's house, Rushmore – a romantic setting bound to impress Hardy, especially when he and 'the beautiful Mrs Grove' led off the dancing. According to a poem he wrote years later, they sat 'apart in the shade [. . .] | After the dance | The while I held her hand'. They danced again the following summer, waltzing to the 'Blue Danube' at the Imperial Institute. At this time, Agnes sought Hardy's advice about her writing and he proved more than willing to help; indeed, she became his 'pupil'. During the spring of 1896, she worked on an article, 'What Children Should be Told'; Hardy made suggestions and corrections and when the piece appeared in June, Agnes sent him a copy plus a photograph – 'a beautiful little picture', as Hardy called it. In July, Hardy reluctantly turned down an invitation to visit her.

> I shall reserve the prospect of seeing the Downs some day in your company as a pleasant thought to lighten the future with – which, with me, is in sad lack of lightening, as with a good many others.

At the end of August, when Hardy was on holiday with Emma, he again disappointed her:

> I am so sorry to be unable to come to the play. I would have given anything to see you, as you know very well, *even* in a character not your own.

They were in touch again around Christmas 1896 and briefly in the spring of 1897. A gap then followed and by the time they were corresponding again, in October 1897, Hardy's tone had changed a little. He was more formal and more disengaged, slightly suspicious and touchy, as he had been with Rosamund Tomson years earlier.

Even so, Emma can hardly have welcomed this resumption of a regular correspondence between her husband and a younger woman she had tried, indirectly, to keep out of her marriage. A year earlier she had welcomed the chance of a holiday (and had perhaps prolonged it) because their cycling trip around England and then Belgium took Hardy beyond Agnes's reach – and vice versa. It may also be that Emma was forceful and unbending in private about this latest flirtation because it was during 1896 that Hardy first began to write poems which bemoan a change of heart towards him from someone very dear. In 'The Dead Man Walking', for instance, he is the dead man who died 'one more degree', 'when my Love's heart kindled | In hate of me, | Wherefore I knew not'. The conviction became established with Hardy in the following years that Emma had mysteriously started to hate him, and the first sign of this belief occurs in 1896.

This can only be a suspicion; nonetheless, on their holiday together in 1896, there does seem to have been something punitive going on: 'my wife on her bicycle, & I walking frantically to overtake her', as Hardy put it to Edward Clodd.[21] Regimented activity, structure and discipline – Emma's leadership in short – were probably what he needed in this terrible summer; and there was some element of gratitude too in his willingness to become dependent on her. On the other hand, Emma cuts a ludicrous, sterotypically comic figure, charging along on her bicycle with a small, frail man trailing in her wake. She had been seriously unwell herself over the previous six months and her feelings over *Jude* were as raw as Hardy's. The situation cast her, however, in the role of the strident, domineering woman so many people laughed at over the next decade or so. She had not stopped loving Hardy, far from it, and if Hardy had been more self-aware he would have seen the obvious reasons she had for being angry with him. She did conclude, though, that she had had enough. Her husband was ruining himself professionally and seemed about to do the same yet again in his personal life. Hardy needed not only her support but her moral guidance too; he needed to be removed from the corrupting influence of his family and of the vain women who preyed upon his vanity.

Outwardly, it worked. Hardy's spirits did lift a little during the following year and his gallant instincts towards Emma ensured that they rubbed along quite well together so long as they were left to themselves. There were not many men who would have accepted the power relations implied by Emma's bicycle. It seemed to prove that he continued to respect her, and even to admire her as a lover should. Moreover, in a way he sincerely did: his poem 'In a Wood', celebrating Emma's 'life-loyalties', was finished in 1896. He did, at some level, accept the kindness of what she was doing. Yet bossing Hardy was always fatal. He had been so pushed by his mother when young that he instinctively baulked at it. His compliance masked withdrawal. He would not resist but neither would he actually submit. The back room, the unspoken loyalty to family, home and labouring-class values, the private literary work – these were what Hardy now cared about. Emma became a duty.

And secretly he would defy her. The letters he wrote to Agnes at regular intervals during 1898 were centred ostensibly on one of Agnes's short stories and Hardy's tone remained strictly professional. He gave Emma no immediate pretext for jealousy or rage, yet he knew she was likely to feel both. He was doing something that he knew she disliked and doing it in such a way as to discredit her dislike. There was nothing to be ashamed of in his helping a respectable married woman, a Lady, to improve her chances of literary success.[22] The dry, emotionless tone was not altogether insincere, even so. Hardy was not simply trying to antagonize Emma. He was mainly proving that she did not control him and the same was true of Agnes – the coolness towards her made another claim to independence.

At the same time as he renewed this friendship, Hardy began compiling *Wessex Poems*, his first collection of poetry. It appeared in the autumn of 1898 and, deliberately or otherwise, it offended Emma, who took particular exception to one or two of the poems, especially and unsurprisingly, 'The Ivy-Wife'. Perhaps she was wrong to bridle because what the volume reveals most is how despairing Hardy had become. He could not be positive about anything, now, not even his grievances with his wife. Some of the poems Hardy included in the volume had been written in the 1860s, several in the intervening years and the rest more recently, since Hardy began shifting his focus back to poetry from prose. The volume is weighted, however, towards his earlier work: thirty or so of the fifty-two poems are dated to various times before 1895, and it excluded several of Hardy's most powerful recent poems. As in *Wessex Tales*, published a decade earlier, Hardy chose pieces that highlighted his Dorset background and left out, for instance, the 'In Tenebris' poems written in 1895–6.

Naturally, he wanted to make this new departure attractive and to tone down the gloom that was becoming his notorious trademark. To that end, perhaps, he decided to include illustrations and during 1898 the principal energy Hardy expended on the volume was in doing the drawings for it. This was, he told Florence Henniker in August 1898, 'a mysterious occupation I have been amusing myself with lately'. At the time, he was 'up & down in spirits', he said; '*down* as a rule'.[23] The strange sketches he drew are the best record we have of this dark state of mind and give the clearest insight into it: a clearer one than the poems themselves, which either come from quite different times in his life or were carefully selected to give a more positive impression.

Some of the pictures look fairly straightforward, providing images of settings, as had been done in the complete edition just two years earlier. In others, death and decay are revealed with an almost gleeful pleasure. One picture, for example, shows an ornate coffin being brought downstairs by three or four men; these figures are drawn crudely in outline and their faces remain out of the picture. By comparison with the weighty, decorated dead, the people barely exist. In another illustration, a couple (again merely outlined), stand together in a church; the building is shown in side elevation like an architectural drawing but, unusually for building designs, the vaults beneath the church are included, along with their skeletons and rotting bones.

The poems in the volume are sometimes melancholy; beside them, the pictures appear nonetheless both more desperate and more lifeless. One of the striking characteristics of all Hardy's poetry is its rhythmic dynamism. Although his lines are not always mellifluous or fluent, they have rhythm always – a pulse that Hardy can carry forward or interrupt. In 'Thoughts of Phena At News of her Death', for example, Hardy's first stanza reads:

> Not a line of her writing have I,
>> Not a thread of her hair,
> No mark of her late time as dame in her dwelling, whereby
>> I may picture her there;
>> And in vain do I urge my unsight
>> To conceive my lost prize
> At her close, whom I knew when her dreams were upbrimming
>> with light,
>> And with laughter her eyes.

There's enormous energy in the rhythms of these irregular lines, especially at the end when Hardy recalls how Phena was as a girl. The second to last line seems filled up to the very brim; its extra length reflects all the latent power of Phena's hopes and dreams, when she was a girl and a young woman.[24] Likewise, the handwriting in the manuscript possessed Hardy's usual briskness and force. His holographs and fair copies are always very clear yet seem to be made without laborious effort; the letters are formed speedily; they lean slightly forward, to the right and the downstrokes are sharply finished, with the brightness and agility of his customary quick walk. The pictures could not be more of a contrast. For 'Thoughts of Phena', Hardy drew in profile a woman lying stretched out on a couch, a sheet covering her. Again, the object is drawn in detail and the figure sketched in outline. It seems to regard the feelings in the poem from an enormous distance, as if no longer capable of caring anything for Phena.

At the beginning of 1897, Hardy noted in his journal:

> To-day has length, breadth, thickness, colour, smell, voice. As soon as it becomes *yesterday*, it is a thin layer among many layers, without substance, colour, or articulate sound.[25]

The illustrations are very close in feeling to this. The collection is in many respects nostalgic – it tells tales of the Napoleonic Wars; it uses dialect. Drawing itself was, likewise, an old skill for Hardy, learnt when a boy and developed during his architectural training. He had studied how to paint in watercolours while a teenager, learning from H. J. Moule. It had been another of his enthusiasms, this one shared with Mary Hardy, whose painting became very skilful. Drawing implied family in other ways too: during March 1898, Hardy was in touch with James and Nathaniel Sparks, Phena's brothers, both of whom were accomplished artists, and he returned to them a 'Case of Drawings'.[26] In its nostalgia, the book considers the clash between time's destructiveness and memory's power of preservation – this is one of the issues at the heart of 'Thoughts of Phena'. But the pictures seem radically to question memory's power. What's done seems to be utterly gone. Relics are left behind – objects, tombs, pieces of furniture – but nothing of the vitality that once was: no substance, colour or articulate sound.[27] Looking back at his past seemed now only to prove that it was dead and buried. The illustrations convey more than anything else a sense that even the most intense emotions were soon outlived and soon died away. They are, like one of the poems in the volume, 'A Meeting with Despair'.

During 1898, this sense of the featureless emptiness of all things affected Hardy's attitude to Agnes, to Florence Henniker, and to all his youthful hopes and fears. Naturally, it extended to Emma, whose disapproval he risked in the volume, as if he wanted to prove he was indifferent to it – that like all other feelings his pain at her anger scarcely mattered. Consequently, when Emma took offence at some of the poems, Hardy left her to it. He had given her reason: 'The Impercipient' evoked their attendance at church services together, and spoke more frankly of their religious differences than Hardy had done before and probably than he ever did in person. It exaggerated them too. Several others are anti-religious, too, though less personal. 'At an Inn' referred unmistakably to an attempted affair. Mary Hardy, Emma's enemy, was celebrated; so, of course, was Phena. And, though there was an affectionate 'Ditty' inscribed to Emma, there was also 'The Ivy-Wife'.

The ivy speaks in the poem, boasting of her conquests. She had tried to climb several of the trees and, though the beech and plane resisted her, the ash tree could not. With her 'soft green claw', she 'cramped and bound' it, forgetting in her triumph that a weakened tree must fall.

> Soon he,
> Being bark-bound, flagged, snapped, fell outright,
> And in his fall felled me!

The competitive parasite receives her comeuppance in the end: mutual destruction. While the man (all the trees are conspicuously male) remains entirely innocent – 'he in trust received my love' – the woman sounds malicious, and possibly demented: 'Such was my love: ha-ha!' Hardy probably did not consciously intend an attack on Emma – not solely on her, at least. The poem originated also in Hardy's experience with Rosamund Tomson and even Florence Henniker. Ella Marchmill in 'An Imaginative Woman', who was so similar to Florence, used 'John Ivy' as a pseudonym; Rosamund actually used a *nom de plume* and always struck Hardy as the most exploitative and parasitic woman he had fallen for.[28] Still, whatever his intentions, the damage had been done – part of the damage being Hardy's conviction that damage had been done. When Emma abreacted to the book, he acquiesced. He saw no point in making an attempt to explain or conciliate. He flinched away from the pain involved.

Emma did make some further efforts to retrieve the situation. She gave Hardy a Bible on his birthday in 1899 – a gift he would have viewed with irony as well as pathos. There is only one marginal note in it, beside the same chapter of Jeremiah that Hardy marked two years before, and the note referred back to that occasion: 'Salisbury Cathedral, E. L. H. and T. H. Aug 1897'. Hardy visited Salisbury with his brother Henry in August 1899 and probably made the note then. Two years earlier, he had been struck by several verses in the chapter; this time he underlined only one: 'Woe unto us! for the day goeth away, for the shadows of the evening are stretched out.'[29] He was nearly sixty, and starting to contemplate the prospect of old age. He made the verse into a lament for himself and his wife, facing the diminishing future with little to remember apart from their failed attempts to love one another.

~ 23 ~

Few persons are more martial than I

IN 1902, EMMA wrote to Louise MacCarthy, whose son Desmond was an aspiring writer, friendly with Hardy. Louise asked Emma what she felt about writing as a career. Emma replied that for the mother of a writer, it was probably harmless as a choice of profession.

> To those who *marry* authors, & ask my advice, I say, "Do not help – him – so much as to extinguish your own life – but go on with former pursuits".

In August 1899, Elspeth Grahame had asked her a similar question. 'Keeping separate a good deal is a wise plan in crises,' Emma replied:

> & *expecting little* neither gratitude, nor attentions, love, nor *justice*, nor *anything* you may set your heart on. Love interest – adoration, & all that kind of thing is usually a *failure – complete* – some one comes by & upsets your pail of milk in the end.[1]

As Emma foresaw, this probably sounded 'gruesome, horrid' to a newlywed.

The two letters give essentially the same advice. Keeping separate and going on with former pursuits was evidently how Emma managed or, at least, how she saw herself as managing. Her tone is fresher and more humorous in 1899, nonetheless. By 1902, she has become rigid about the question and overemphatic so her advice sounds embittered and strident. And now, she says you have to preserve your separate sphere all the time, not only 'in crises'. Emma frequently turned misery into boldness – into an abrasive, overstated self-certainty. She had taken that line with Hardy ever since 1896, if not before. Still, she was not simply a harridan. She felt dominance was being forced on her by her husband's neglect and his lack of proper respect. From her point of view, she was being left in sole charge of the common decencies and must respond accordingly. This meant that the last ten years of her life – the period when she was most frequently observed – were years dominated by an enraged obstinacy that obscured her underlying grief and her self-pity.

After her death, there's little doubt that Hardy recognized some of this and regretted it. 'You Were the Sort that Men Forget', a poem he published in 1917, is filled with sympathy:

> You'd not the art – you never had
>   For good or bad –
> To make men see how sweet your meaning,
>   Which, visible, had charmed them glad.
>
> You would, by words inept let fall,
>   Offend them all[.]

It's a disarmingly frank judgement, excused by Hardy's loyalty to her: 'Your slighted weakness,' he says, 'Adds to the strength of my regret!' And what he says here was truly a part of the story of their life together. Emma was socially awkward; her natural shyness made her forceful and impatient. On the other hand, the poem talks down to her. Treating her as a girl and an innocent, Hardy forgives her inadequacies. What might have caused them, what they meant, how he might have made them worse – all these issues are set aside. By removing himself from the equation, Hardy makes it easier to pity her. Yet there's a shrug of the shoulders in the poem too. It blames 'Nature' for the problem and, ironically enough, it was this fatalism in Hardy, his emotional disengagement and his essential abandonment of her that made her so difficult, so 'inept'.[2]

Both of them found ways of living apart from 1898 onwards. This is clear from their holidays. In the autumn of 1903, Emma went to France with her niece Lilian Gifford, on a trip lasting three weeks or so. She did the same in 1908, staying away for more than a month. That year, she and Hardy had not taken a flat in London during the summer, although Hardy spent several weeks in the capital by himself during May and June. Similarly in 1911, Hardy was in London alone and soon after his return, Emma went away to Worthing. When she came home, Hardy went away – this time to Somerset. They avoided each other around the house as well. When Max Gate was extended in 1895, two rooms were built in the attic above Hardy's new study, designed as servants' quarters. Certainly by February 1899, perhaps a little earlier, Emma was using them as her 'little apartment where not a sound – even the dinner-bell – scarcely reaches me'. By April, she was sleeping up there too. 'My boudoir', she told Rebekah Owen, 'is my sweet refuge and solace.'[3] It lay at the top of a cramped staircase, very hard for an elderly, lame woman to climb. And the rooms themselves were poky. It was easy to bang your head on the sloping ceilings.

Hardy did not banish Emma to these rooms; she chose them herself, loving the romance of her eyrie, as well as its seclusion. It allowed her to feel superior to Hardy, the great man of letters, as he ground out his grim, blasphemous poetry day by day in the spacious, purpose-built study below. She, in her garret, was the truer, purer artist – more inspired, and less corrupted by egotism or ambition. This arrangement also meant they had to meet each other only once a day, over dinner – a ritual that was strictly kept up. Although, in these new rooms, Emma could reject the role of abandoned wife and rise above it, the set-up only encouraged her eccentricity. Physically isolated and lonely, with few friends and with many of those friendships dominated by her estranged husband, Emma deteriorated. Her causes became hobby-horses, her moral courage turned into obsessiveness, and her religious faith was overtaken by anti-Catholic paranoia. Her remarkable energy was wasted in querulous, self-dramatizing fussiness and in the outbursts of rage she directed towards her husband. Hardy lived alongside this decline for more than a decade and must have seen it taking place but he did nothing about it; instead, he ignored her more and more. His sole concession was to build a dormer window in one of her attic rooms, though even that had to wait until 1908.

There were numerous visitors to Max Gate during the latter years of the Hardys' marriage and many of them wrote down their impressions. These records are either critical of Emma or sympathetic towards her, contemptuous or pitying. What they have in common is the image of Hardy's silence when Emma attacked him, decried his writings or abused his family. Her fury consistently met with a bleak, infuriating, stubborn refusal to answer back. In public at least, the most she could hope to provoke was a hostile glance – though these were withering enough when they came, frightening in their total contempt.

Hardy's barber recalled how Hardy in old age always sat with his head 'nicely dropped'.

On the few occasions when he was waiting for attention, and always when in the haircutting chair, he would hold his head down. [. . .] It was his normal sitting position whenever he thought anyone could see him.[4]

The posture reflects Hardy's extreme shyness in public, which was a trait that Dorchester exaggerated. Maud Lugg, who worked in the town's branch of Lloyds Bank, 'used to say that Mr. Hardy always asked for her because he knew she wouldn't talk of his affairs'. Hardy perceived that he and his eccentric wife were the subject of gossip, some of it malicious. Emma was laughed at for riding around the streets on her bicycle, and Hardy, because of his novels, was not well liked.[5] Keeping his head down also became, however, his habitual response to Emma's treatment of him. Although he spoke much less about it than Emma, Hardy was actually much better than she was at 'keeping separate'. Marriage was less central to his identity as a man than it was to Emma as a woman; he had his writing career, after all. And he had been taught by his mother both to expect hostility and to practise self-reliance. He had also seen, from watching his father's lack of response to his mother's rages, that passivity was a powerful weapon.

In 1898 and 1899, Hardy's whole demeanour became rather broken-down – to a degree that was unusual even for him. He did almost no writing at all for most of 1899 – something that had not happened for more than thirty years – and this inactivity may have been brought on by the reception of *Wessex Poems*, which was not very favourable. Several reviewers criticized the poems for metrical clumsiness and strange, coarse diction. Mellifluousness was valued extremely highly in the period, and Hardy began to think he should have revised some of the poems more carefully. More significantly, the book was seen as no more than a stopgap, in a form of writing that was, in any case, not very highly regarded in the 1890s – not as highly, certainly, as it had been in mid century, when Tennyson's *In Memoriam* (1849) was revered by the Queen and Swinburne's *Poems and Ballads* (1866) caused outrage. The *Academy* review began by saying, 'It has become almost the fashion for prose-writers of all kinds to make at least one attempt in verse.' E. K. Chambers, writing in the *Athenaeum*, took the same tack: 'Much that Hardy has amused himself by collecting', he wrote, 'is quite trifling.' It was assumed that Hardy would soon revert to his real business, that of writing novels.[6] This reaction showed Hardy that he would have to make an immense effort in order to establish himself as a poet rather than a novelist. It seemed a quite impossible task and, in his generally dejected state, it struck him as barely worthwhile.

This torpor was disturbed by a war. In autumn 1899, English troops began to embark for South Africa to fight against the Boers and Hardy was instantly caught up in the excitement. He travelled to Southampton on 20 October to watch some of the troops embark – a distance of fifty miles in each direction: astonishingly he cycled both ways. Florence Henniker's husband, Arthur, was sailing and Hardy wrote to Florence, supportively though sincerely too.

> I constantly deplore the fact that 'civilized' nations have not learnt some more excellent & apostolic way of settling disputes than the old & barbarous one, after all these centuries; but when I feel that it must be, few persons are more martial than I, or like better to write of war in prose & rhyme.
>
> Such a position appears to have been now reached; & the sooner we get at it, & get it done, the better, I think.[7]

It is an unfamiliar Hardy speaking here. He was by no means a warmonger nor an imperialist. He knew Kipling but disapproved of (what he saw as) Kipling's uncritical approval of Empire. Similarly, though an admirer of Swinburne he disliked Swinburne's jingoistic poem 'The Transvaal', published as the war began, and he praised Gissing for his criticism of it. Even so, he was clearly inspired by the heroism and tragedy of war, both at this particular moment and more generally.

In 1899, the war supplied a sense of change and an impetus that went above and beyond personal desire. Things had finally come to the point where something had to be done, like it or not, so, 'the sooner we get at it, & get it done, the better, I think'. It was an external, impersonal stimulus that freed Hardy from mournful introspection and disabling self-consciousness. People were forced to act by a war and to act nobly; greatness was thrust upon them. Personal ambition – with its niggles and competitiveness – was subsumed in the demands of the moment. Similarly, in war there was no time to consider whether your actions had ultimate value or point. There were far more pressing questions to address, and Hardy, though obviously he could not fight, began at once to address them through his writing.

The first result was a number of war poems, written in autumn 1899 and published at once in prominent magazines – the *Sphere*, the *Cornhill*, the *Westminster Gazette*, and the *Daily Chronicle* as well as the *Graphic*. Some of these rank alongside Hardy's best work – 'The Souls of the Slain', 'Drummer Hodge' and 'A Wife in London' are particularly strong. Though none were enthusiastic celebrations of war, like Swinburne's or Kipling's, they differed from poems in *Wessex Poems* by addressing national and contemporary issues directly. Hardy was seeking both to catch and to mould the country's mood – he was aiming to achieve a public voice. The same endeavour is reflected in his second volume of poetry, *Poems of the Past and the Present*, published in autumn 1901. The book opened with an elegy for Queen Victoria, who had died earlier in the year, and a section of 'War Poems' came second. This was confident and timely because by 1901, after more than two years of a costly war, which had still not brought a victory, people were becoming wary of the war-fever of 1899. They were ready to listen to Hardy's elegies for the dead, laments for the bereaved and prophecies of a more peaceful future.

Altogether, in fact, this second volume was more mainstream than Hardy's first. There were translations from great classical and European poets, Catullus, Heine, Schiller and Sappho. There were 'Poems of Pilgrimage', recalling Hardy's visits to Italy and Switzerland, and invoking famous literary names: Shelley, Keats, and Edward Gibbon. The book contained none of Hardy's eerie and peculiar illustrations and conveyed through its structure and subject matter a positive, targeted attitude. It was difficult to treat it as the whimsical self-indulgence of an established novelist. Its thinking, too, was more palatable. Hardy never accepted that he was, in truth, a pessimist though the claim was repeatedly made. In *Poems of the Past and the Present*, he published several of his darkest poems – all three of the 'In Tenebris' sequence, for example – but the 'War Poems' section and the collection as a whole closed on a note of cautious hope. The last of the war poems was 'The Sick Battle-God'. There Hardy found reason to believe that the Boer War would be one of the last wars that mankind fought. The Battle-God had been powerful as recently as the Napoleonic Wars but afterwards 'modern meditation broke | His spell' and 'seeds of crescent sympathy | Were sown by those more excellent than he'. In consequence, although 'wars arise', 'zest grows cold' and 'The lurid Deity of heretofore | Succumbs to one of saner nod'.[8]

Likewise, in the book's final poem, addressed 'To the Unknown God', Hardy asserts that:

> in unwonted purlieus, far and nigh,
>   At whiles or short or long,
>   May be discerned a wrong
> Dying of self-slaughter; whereat I
>   Would raise my voice in song.

Even though the creation seemed to be created blindly (by a God 'labouring all-unknowingly') and although it seemed to operate mechanically and predictably, in 'rote-restricted ways', nonetheless, just occasionally, there was evidence that it was improving – that wrongs were naturally dying out one by one.[9] This optimism does not always ring true; instead, it sounds contrived, as if Hardy were trying to find some source of consolation for himself and for his audience in a time of unease and fear. 'The Darkling Thrush' is perhaps the single and key exception to this rule. The bird's song, heard when 'every spirit upon earth | Seemed fervourless as I', is a sign near at hand of 'Some blessed Hope, whereof he knew | And I was unaware'. It's such a moving piece because in it for a moment Hardy's tentative and abstract optimism found living proof.[10]

Even if his hopefulness was sometimes willed, willing himself in that direction was, nonetheless, an important task for Hardy because life, like his marriage, seemed to have become stuck in a rut. War gave him a prompt and the chance of finding useful employment for his talents. There was another reason too, though, for Hardy to write in this way. In 'I Have Lived with Shades', a poem near the end of the volume, he described seeing himself as a frail and uninspiring figure.

> Into the dim
> Dead throngs around
> He'll sink, nor sound
> Be left of him.

This fear of utter obscurity motivated Hardy, as it had always done, perhaps. As he grew older, though, his childlessness weighed on him more; lacking an heir he felt more fiercely than ever the need to keep his name alive. An acceptable and successful collection of poems would help to achieve this, after five or more years in which he had seemed increasingly forgotten, despite the great scandal of *Jude* and the grand achievement of a collected edition. Similar motives contributed, in 1902, to his changing his publisher – from Osgood & McIlvaine to Macmillan.

Ostensibly the move came about because Osgood & McIlvaine had been incorporated into the American firm of Harper Brothers with the result that Hardy had 'only a subsidiary branch of an American house as my English publishers'.[11] Even so, it was a bold move to approach Macmillan – one of the most prestigious London houses. Hardy had had dealings with them off and on right from the beginning and still never quite succeeded in establishing himself as a Macmillan author. It was all the more heartening, therefore, when they agreed immediately to taking him on now. They were soon republishing his novels and his poems, in a new edition that began to appear in October 1902, as soon as the rights had been transferred. At the same time, and partly for similar reasons, Hardy embarked at last on his long-imagined project, *The Dynasts*, 'an Epic-Drama of the War with Napoleon'.

It was an enormous undertaking: to put into quasi-dramatic form the history of ten years of the Napoleonic Wars, from the build-up to the Battle of Trafalgar in 1805 until the Battle of Waterloo in 1815. Hardy had done some research into the subject before – during several holidays in Belgium and Italy and when writing *The Trumpet-Major* – and the *Life* certainly wants to give the impression that this period of history had been somewhere in his mind throughout his adult life. This may be an exaggeration but it cannot be entirely false. Even so, his aims in *The Dynasts* required him to present a vast historical sweep. He wanted to bring before the reader's mind the military campaigns, political upheavals and diplomatic intrigues all across Europe over a turbulent decade – events that determined the fate of the continent for the rest of the nineteenth century. A lifelong amateur interest would have to be turned into professional expertise. He needed to acquire precise knowledge of the period's military hardware and its naval tactics, for example, as well as its convoluted politics in England and the rest of Europe.

Amazingly, the whole thing took him only six years to complete: the three volumes appeared in 1904, 1906 and 1908. A year later he had enough lyric poems finished to publish another book, *Time's Laughing-stocks*. It was a burst of creative energy comparable to what he had experienced in 1872–5 and 1889–91, and all the more extraordinary because he was approaching seventy years old. Furthermore, although its reputation now is relatively low, at the time *The Dynasts* established Hardy's seriousness as a thinker and his stature as a poet.[12] By 1908, he was no longer seen as a versifying novelist; he had gained a separate reputation as a philosophical poet. Persistence in this unexpected endeavour had brought high rewards – higher perhaps than he had ever expected. In 1904, the first volume was received sceptically and with some bemusement. In 1908, the whole work was being hailed as 'the most notable literary achievement of the last quarter-century' and 'a work of such undoubted genius'. 'For a like achievement,' Harold Child wrote in the *Times Literary Supplement,* 'we can only go back to one thing – the historical plays of Shakespeare.'[13]

Reviewers found it strange nevertheless, with its multiple perspectives and its choruses spoken by the 'Spirit of the Years', the 'Spirit of the Pities' or the 'Spirit Ironic'. Strangeness, though, was part of the point and Hardy had, according to Henry Newbolt, made 'a new departure in English poetry'.[14] He was inventing a new genre that portrayed events as the recently developed medium of film might do. As in many of his novels, the search for originality takes place amidst much that is conventional because, in many respects, *The Dynasts* does feel familiar. It's patriotic and gung-ho, full of oratory and derring-do, while its elaborate battle scenes add the excitement that action sequences give to a film. Hardy's Wessex, too, reappears: wherever the British Army is found, Dorsetshire worthies are found as well. They embody the valour, the resilience and the good sense that lead the English nation ultimately to victory.

There is no doubt that Hardy enjoyed working on the project. When it was all finished and he was correcting the proofs, he told Florence Henniker that 'It is a good thing to have nearly got rid of it, though I shall miss the work.' To Edward Clodd, he was more wryly amused on the same subject.

It is well that the business should be over, for I have been living in Wellington's campaigns so much lately that, like George IV, I am almost positive that I took part in the battle of Waterloo, & have written of it from memory.[15]

Perhaps more than anything else he wrote, *The Dynasts* took up all of his mind as he worked on it. The historical events he had got to know so fully became a world that he lived in, wandered over in his thoughts and saw before him, both in remarkable detail and as a single whole. He felt about this historical reality the same pleasure that a boy might find in an imaginary world, carefully realized and mapped out like Tolkien's Middle-earth.

Narrating history also meant, of course, that Hardy was not responsible for the events he described, which was a relief. He could depict scandalous goings-on and not be blamed for them or accused of maliciously falsifying human life. In addition, of course, these events were the heroic actions that had thrilled his boyhood. He could re-enter via them his childhood, when memories of Waterloo were fresh. When he was just starting out on the project, he wrote a poem about Mary Head, his paternal grandmother, who had lived with Hardy's family in Bockhampton until her death in 1857. She, the poem said:

> told of that far-back day when they learnt astounded
>   Of the death of the King of France:
> Of the Terror; and then of Bonaparte's unbounded
>   Ambition and arrogance.

Like Hardy as he worked on his great epic-drama, Mary grew immersed in her memories: 'Past things retold were to her as things existent, | Things present but as a tale.'[16] Hardy sought the same withdrawal from the present into a local past, hearing voices from the beginning of the century as clearly as the voices from the graveyard that filled his famous poem 'Friends Beyond'.

The Dynasts, in other words, provided a place of retreat from his miserable domestic life. As he and Emma grew ever further apart, as her animosity became more violent and unpredictable, Hardy found an artistic project that could become his real world, both in the present and, when he started it, for the foreseeable future. It secured him and gave him purpose. It took him imaginatively into what was predominantly a man's world, and the need for detailed, extensive research took him away physically as well, into the sanctuary of the British Museum Library. Hardy intended that the finished product should strike the same balance as *Poems of the Past and the Present* – that it should woo a patriotic readership without compromising Hardy's scepticism about nationalist feelings. Although, like the 'War Poems' of 1899, *The Dynasts* offered reflections on the heroism of war instead of celebrations of it, the epic-drama went further by presenting with such complexity and even-handedness the leaders of the two sides in the conflict: England's national hero and future prime minister, Wellington, and his enemy, the hated Napoleon.

Instead of vilifying Napoleon and celebrating his downfall, Hardy made the 'Spirit of the Years' say, after the Allied victory at Waterloo, that 'Europe's wormy dynasties rerobe | Themselves in their old gilt, to dazzle anew the globe!'[17] Napoleon's defeat, which was one of England's most famous triumphs, is presented as a return to the unjust status quo and as the sad end of a revolutionary hope. This turn of events may be inevitable, given the determining will of the blind God who rules the world; even so, Hardy suggests you might feel disappointed by it (whatever your reservations about Napoleon himself). Wellington is put forward, therefore, both as the consummate British military commander and as the agent of reactionary powers – powers that crushed freedom, prevented equality and restored the absolute monarchies of Europe after 1815. This approach meant that the work was challenging Hardy's audience about a historical narrative, which they took absolutely for granted. Wellington's victory over Napoleon was not simply 'a good thing', as *1066 and All That* would put it, and as Victorian and Edwardian histories consistently represented it. Probably, even so, it was a better outcome than victory for Napoleon would have been, although some of its consequences were unequivocally bad.

This aspect of *The Dynasts* enabled Hardy to reconsider his own left-wing sympathies too – the sometimes fiery socialism that had animated his youth and never entirely gone away. At the same time, the work's fatalistic viewpoint was a way of accepting disappointment. One of its unconscious purposes was to find a way of coming to terms with the defeat of Hardy's own desires for political and social change. Napoleon's Waterloo was, in some ways, Hardy's *Jude*. He was trying in *The Dynasts* to reach an accommodation with an audience that had grown more conservative during his lifetime and, as in *Poems of the Past and the Present*, Hardy achieved this via a vision of long-term, gradual improvement. In 1908 *The Dynasts* concluded with an 'After Scene', spoken by the various Spirits. Its closing words were:

> But – a stirring thrills the air
> Like to sounds of joyance there
>   That the rages
>   Of the ages
> Shall be cancelled, and deliverance offered from the darts that
>   were,
> Consciousness the Will informing, till It fashion all things fair![18]

Envisaging some ultimate deliverance for suffering humanity and a tragic world comforted Hardy's sense of historical disappointment – his feeling of having been born into an unheroic period when progressive ideas were either ignored or crushed. His marital distress probably found comfort in such a prospect as well, a future where the repetitious enmity of his and Emma's life together was no longer the whole truth of human relations. Somewhere beyond the seemingly endless, all-too familiar disagreements they experienced, a different possibility existed, in which consciousness would govern will, and reason reassert its authority.

*

The Dynasts' fond evocation of Wessex – fonder and less ambivalent than in any other of his writings – is, oddly enough, another aspect of this concern to find a reason to believe that the future might be better than the present. Hardy's Wessex figures become in the drama the repository of enduring values – of the decency, humour, affection, stoicism and compassion that human history is moving towards even as it appears to leave behind the rural culture in which those qualities are found. Hardy's affection for the past had, however, a more personal source as well, because on 3 April 1904 his mother Jemima died. She had been unwell for some months and by late March Hardy already knew the end was inevitable. She 'suffered latterly, & wished to go, so that there is really nothing for commonsense to regret', he told Clodd. 'Yet one does regret.' It is such a restrained and eloquently self-aware way of putting it. As Jemima died, so too did other great friends from Hardy's past: Henry Moule, the eldest of the Moule brothers, had passed away earlier in the spring, as had Leslie Stephen.

Hardy mourned all three, though Jemima of course most of all. Amidst his 'regret', his principal feeling seems to have been that one of the focal points of his existence had suddenly evaporated. 'After the Last Breath', the poem he wrote in her memory that year, begins: 'There's no more to be done, or feared, or hoped'.

> Blankly we gaze. We are free to go or stay;
> Our morrow's anxious plans have missed their aim;
> Whether we leave to-night or wait till day
>   Counts as the same.[19]

It is a blessed release for her, the poem says, yet also, curiously, for them – the family standing by the bedside. Jemima no longer needs their solicitude or care and, although that leaves them rather uselessly idle, it brings a kind of liberation too. After her last breath, they seem to breathe again. They can resume their lives. For better as well as worse, nothing will be asked of them any longer.

If Hardy sensed that, at long last, he might do as he pleased, he was aware too that there was very little he still desired. Nonetheless, Jemima's death did initiate a change. It was a year after the death of Hardy's father in 1892 that he fell passionately in love with Florence Henniker. Following precisely the same pattern, it was in 1905, a year after Hardy's mother died, that he fell in love again and became convinced, perhaps for the first time, that he might escape the prison of his marriage.

At first, nothing dramatic occurred. Later in the spring of 1904, Hardy and Emma went up to London for the season and stayed there off and on until late in the summer. It was their first visit since 1901. In 1902, they had stayed away to avoid the Coronation, and in 1903, Hardy had spent some weeks in the capital, mostly alone, Emma being 'rather unwell & fearful of facing London again just yet'. At least, this was what he told George Douglas. In truth, 1903 was an especially difficult year in their marriage and they kept apart as much as they could. Typically, in 1904, at what was a difficult time for Hardy, Emma lent her support. Partly she sympathized, but partly too she hoped for a change in their relationship, now that Jemima was dead.

To her companionship was added a new friendship – something more unusual for Hardy than for many people because friendship, ever since Horace Moule's death if not earlier, did not come easily to him. Edmund Gosse was a friend, though Hardy never quite trusted him, particularly after his review of *Jude*; Hardy suspected that with Gosse he had been drawn into the circle of a man of remarkable charm as well as genuine, if sometimes rather superficial, kindness. It was Emma's affection for Gosse's wife, Nellie, and Nellie's for Emma, that helped keep the two men in touch because nowhere else in his literary acquaintance was it possible for two couples to establish a foursome. In general, actually Hardy's literary friendships were rarely intimate – not even with Swinburne, for instance, despite his sense of kinship with him. When the two men got to know one another personally, Hardy's attitude remained studied and unconfiding and he was nearly always like this with other writers – too wary and competitive for close friendship to develop, his personality being too sharply divided between the professional and the personal, between required behaviour and real feeling. London's literary circles were a part of his professional life – albeit a part he rather enjoyed, for their elegance and for the opportunity they offered of seeing great men's feet of clay. To a degree he welcomed the impersonality too; certainly, he never saw them as places where sincerity was possible, still less a confession of your true feelings. One of the reasons why Hardy spent so much time with literary women was the relief they offered from the more gladiatorial encounters he had with his male literary rivals.

It also explains why he was so much more at ease with non-literary people. Hardy was not especially good at hobnobbing with ordinary country folk, though he understood their way of life so acutely. He was more comfortable with students of the countryside, those with a conscious affection for it that went beyond purely literary taste for the pastoral. T. E. Lawrence won Hardy's admiration partly for this reason when they met after the First World War. George Douglas, his old friend, was another instance and so too was H. J. Moule, who had recently died. Hermann Lea became a friend for similar reasons. Hardy had first got to know him in 1898, though not well; the friendship blossomed after 1904 when Lea began work on what became *A Handbook to the Wessex Country of Thomas Hardy's Novels and Poems*. The book appeared in 1905 and was the forerunner of Lea's *Highways and Byways in Hardy's Wessex*, published in 1913. Lea frequently consulted Hardy over these books, and over the picture postcards he was producing at the same time: cards that depicted sites from the novels.

Naturally, Hardy would welcome someone whose books encouraged an interest in Hardy's own. Despite his solid financial security since *Tess*'s success in 1891, Hardy never lost his anxiety about money. The servants all found him stingy. He kept the house far colder than was comfortable and would even take coals off the fire if he thought it had been built up too high, placing them neatly in a row across the hearth, to show the servant what he had done and so rebuke her. Builders, gardeners, messengers all complained that Hardy drove a hard bargain and gave no tips. In 1904, when Lea was researching his book, the new Macmillan edition of Hardy's novels had recently started coming out and Hardy was of course keen that it should sell well. Lea's work would help sustain an audience for the novels as they were reprinted. It would cater especially to the ever increasing touristic interest that his books appeared to create.

On neither side, though, was the relationship simply pragmatic. Lea was discreetly devoted to Hardy and Hardy was fond of him in return. Lea's presence, especially after 1907 when he moved to a cottage near Max Gate, always cheered him up. Lea moved into Higher Bockhampton when Henry and Hardy's sisters left the house for Talbothays in 1913 and he lived there until 1921, where Hardy frequently visited him. They became over the years intimate friends, sharing confidences and secrets, sharing too an interest in the details and oddities of country life. Lea was also one of the very few people – Edward Clodd was another – with whom Hardy ever discussed his personal life.

1904–5 marked the beginning of this friendship. Lea always wanted to know exactly which real places had inspired Hardy and as a result, the two of them, sometimes joined by their mutual friend Revd Thomas Perkins, Vicar of Turnworth, and sometimes by Emma and Lilian Gifford as well, made a number of excursions in and around Dorset hunting out locations. These outings took Hardy away from his grief, while also keeping him in touch with his mother's memory. In Lea, he found a kindred spirit, someone like the son he had never had. He could discuss personal matters and he could be rude too, indulging with Lea in a Rabelaisian humour that Emma would not countenance.[20]

The following summer – much of it again spent in London in a busy round of social events – a second friendship began. The first sign of it we have is a note sent by Hardy to a woman called Florence Dugdale on 5 August 1905.

> Dear Madam:
>   As you are not going to print anything about your visit I shall be happy to be at home to you some afternoon during this month, if you will send a post card a day or two before you are coming.
>
> > Yours truly
> > T. Hardy

It seems from this that he did not know her a little at the time. She, like many other journalists, had approached him for an interview and received the standard reply, a reply Florence was canny enough to have foreseen. Whether she did in fact visit Max Gate during the summer is not known but by January 1906, she seems to have done so and Hardy's tone had softened utterly.

> Dear Miss Dugdale:
>   I must thank you for the box of sweet flowers that you sent me. They are at this moment in water on the table, & look little the worse for their journey.

I do not think you stayed at all too long, & hope you will come
again some other time.

Yours sincerely

Thomas Hardy.

At this stage, their exchanges remained essentially formal and Emma
would have taken no notice. Florence was only one of many literary
people calling on her by-now famous husband. She was much more
attractive than most, of course, but Hardy had shown little interest in
other women for five or six years. Emma probably thought that all that
sort of thing was, thankfully, over and done with.

Ever since his mother's death, though, Hardy's mood had been
shifting, secretly and probably unconsciously. He wrote to Florence
Henniker on 17 September 1904, when she was about to travel back
to Ireland, the place where they had first met. 'Let me know when
you go,' Hardy told her.

Your being over there will remind me of old times – very romantic
ones – when I was younger than I am now, though you seem the
same as you were then.

This was gallant and one of the very few times that Hardy allowed
himself to address her as anything like an old flame. The following
February, he sounded flirtatious again, teasingly wounded: 'You have
become such a will of the wisp lately', he wrote, ' – or rather jill of the
wisp – that I hardly know how to address this.'[21]

The same signs of some subterranean readjustment in Hardy's
feelings can be found in the creative work. In the summer of 1904, he
wrote a poem, 'The Revisitation' (first entitled 'Time's Laughingstocks'
and later used to begin the volume of that name). The subject matter –
love's susceptibility to the ravages of time – was not unusual for him but
the approach to it was. The male speaker is completely unapologetic
about rejecting the woman he had once loved simply because she has
now grown old and ugly: 'Well I knew my native weakness, | Well I
know it still.' And he adds, even more strikingly: 'I cherished her
reproach like physic-wine.' Her anger at his unfairness pleases him, he
says, because it shows that she possessed 'A nobler soul than mine'.
There is a tone of insouciant resignation here, an amoral carelessness
and a decadent self-acceptance, even a delight in being rebuked. Hardy
was dramatizing the mindset of a self-indulgent man of the world, the

sort of person he had last thought of becoming in 1892 when he shaved off his beard. He lets slip in the poem and the letters to Florence Henniker the sense of newly rediscovered freedom that Jemima's death gradually produced in him.

Though Emma knew little about the change at the time, it became responsible for the last and possibly the most painful period of her marriage. Hardy, believing he might at last relinquish some of his self-imposed and his inherited inhibitions, became especially susceptible to Florence Dugdale – a woman who, like Rosamund Tomson in 1889, was concerned to make herself attractive to him.

— 24 —

We kissed at the barrier

FLORENCE Emily Dugdale was born in 1879 in Enfield, a small town near London, which at that time was still surrounded by countryside. Her father was headmaster of the local church school and Florence worked as a member of his staff from January 1898 until February 1908, when she resigned on the grounds of ill-health. Teaching had always been liable to make her ill and, although she had become a qualified teacher in 1906, with special credit in English Literature, Composition and the Principles of Education, she had never taken to it enthusiastically. She was much more interested in becoming a writer. Florence was a petite woman, delicate-looking, and with large, soulful, dark eyes. Her health was fragile and her tastes self-consciously refined. In several ways, she was naturally in sympathy with Hardy – their backgrounds were not dissimilar. Her father, the son of a Dorset blacksmith, had risen up the social scale via teaching, just as Hardy's sisters and cousins did. She also shared many of Hardy's 'advanced' views, though she was elaborately cautious about expressing them. She was an agnostic, for instance, and she rather disliked clergymen – her condescending employers while she was a teacher. By temperament, too, she tried like Hardy to sidestep conflict wherever possible. Emma was a more sturdy woman and could sometimes be forceful, both physically and in her relationships; Florence by contrast was frail, discreet and deferential.

She was brought up by a strict, conservative father and a mother prone to illness, sometimes to depression. Florence had grown used to looking after her and throughout her adult life she gravitated towards relationships in which she could care for people. From 1899 onwards, for four years or more, she co-wrote a children's column for the *Enfield Observer*, supplying a prose passage to accompany a piece of poetry – a piece written in each case by her close friend, Alfred Hyatt. Hyatt was ten years older than Florence and a semi-invalid, who suffered from tuberculosis and a terrible stammer. He maintained himself precariously by freelance writing, publishing and journalism. He was never in a position to marry her though there was little doubt of his feelings. Hyatt died in December 1911, aged forty. 'I lost a friend,' Florence later recalled:

who was more to me than anything else in the world – for whom I know I would *gladly* have died. [. . .] I think I lost, then, the only person who ever loved me – for I am not loveable.

Hyatt's devotion was entire; Florence's made more uncertain only by her low self-esteem. Believing herself to be unlovable, she found it hard to love in return; so she tended to love people obliquely, indirectly, thinking herself unworthy and so always holding something in reserve.

Her relationship with Hardy bears out the underlying truth of this letter though the writing is characteristically overstated. Florence was sending a letter of condolence to Rebekah Owen, whose beloved sister Catherine had recently died. 'As I write,' Florence declared, 'I feel the old dull ache spring into life again – & so I know your pain.' She wrote in the way she did out of her eagerness to establish common ground and prove fellow-feeling.[1] This fluid adaptability makes another contrast with Emma, of course, who was strident and, as Hardy put it, 'inept'. Florence went to the opposite extreme. She adapted herself completely to the person she was addressing – to what she imagined were their needs or preferences. She studied the art of blending in with more dominant personalities – it was instinctive with her and it helped to make her an excellent 'companion', especially for women older and from a higher class than she was. At other times, it made her almost dishonest – she could be craven to her social superiors, imitative and sycophantic to those she wanted to please. Constantly well-mannered, constantly accommodating, Florence could cross the fine line into insincerity. There were private, internal motives at work when she did so, alongside the social ones, because politeness established control over her own turbulent emotions as well as the distressing situations she encountered. Consequently this manner also tended to keep Florence's own emotions invisible even from herself. She habitually put herself second, embracing passivity and fatalism in order, partly, to preserve herself intact. Like this, she could remain at the side of her own life – kind and conscientious, ministering to others. It made her prone to depression, as her mother had been – perhaps it was symptomatic of a pre-existing depressive character – and at times it made her rather an unpredictable person to deal with. Hidden, surprising feelings burst out in unexpected places.

When Florence first approached Hardy, it was almost certainly in connection with Hyatt, who was planning an anthology of Hardy's writings. Hardy agreed to it in a letter to his publishers on 11 May 1906 and the book – *The Pocket Thomas Hardy* – appeared later in the year.[2] Hyatt could not have travelled to Dorset himself and so Florence went down instead, to prepare the ground and encourage Hardy to give his consent. Quite how the relationship developed over the next year or so remains unclear. Hardy was in London with Emma from mid April to mid July in 1906; a period when he and Florence could easily have met. By November, Florence was applying for a reader's ticket to the British Museum, in order 'to verify certain facts concerning the Napoleonic Era, & this for the use, & under the direction of, Mr Thomas Hardy'. The following spring she was definitely helping with his work. That brought them together, both providing a convenient pretext and actually endearing Florence to Hardy, since (unlike his previous women friends) she made herself useful to him, as Emma had done before.[3]

The library closed for renovation from the middle of April 1907. Hardy wrote almost immediately to arrange a meeting with Florence 'at the South Kensington Museum' on a Saturday afternoon. Help with his research was once more the reason he gave, but the meeting feels much more like an assignation: 'I will look for you in the architectural gallery at 4 – say by the Trajan column'.[4] During that summer Hardy also gave her an inscribed copy of *Wessex Poems* and *Poems of the Past and the Present*, recently reprinted in one volume. He recommended her to Maurice Macmillan, the publisher, and to Archibald Marshall, editor of the *Daily Mail*'s book supplement. He helped her place her short story 'The Apotheosis of the Minx' with the *Cornhill Magazine*. Hardy's assistance with Florence's writing career continued in 1908, after she had given up teaching. He recommended two more of her short stories to editors, including his friend Clement Shorter. Probably Florence wrote for the *Sphere*, edited by Shorter, during the second half of 1908.[5]

Until the end of 1907, Hardy was still finishing *The Dynasts* – he was, in other words, committed to the completion of what was becoming a burdensome task. 'It has dragged its slow length along through too many years already', he told Desmond MacCarthy, and 'This uses up all my energy.'[6] When the third and final part was finished, proofread and published in early 1908, his spirits naturally rose, the more so as the warmly appreciative reviews came in. He and Emma did not take lodgings in London together that year; instead, Hardy occupied hotel rooms and based himself at the Athenaeum for several weeks at a time. He told friends, such as Florence Henniker, that Emma could not travel up because of ill health. Whatever the truth of that, the arrangement gave him the chance of frequent meetings with Florence.

The Dynasts was not the same roaring, popular success as *Tess* had been. Hardy was also fifteen years older and nearing seventy. Yet he felt something of the same elation and vindication during 1908–9 as he had in 1893. And, as in 1893, two things happened at once: Emma was alienated by Hardy's success (and possibly his self-satisfaction) while Hardy became closely involved with another woman. It was not the same whirlwind infatuation as came over him when he travelled to Dublin in 1893. Instead, friendship and an almost paternal affection gradually changed into, from his side, sexual love.

He did not expect, at least initially, to receive love in return. The memory of Florence Henniker's rejection of him coloured this new relationship, as did Hardy's by now almost instinctual acquiescence. When his next volume of poems, *Time's Laughingstocks*, came out in autumn 1909, Hardy sent a copy to Florence Dugdale, enclosing in it fair copies of three poems: 'On the Departure Platform' and 'After the Visit', both of which evidently referred to her. He also sent her a copy of 'The Division', written years before in connection with Florence Henniker. The poem ends:

> But that thwart thing betwixt us twain,
>   Which nothing cleaves or clears,
> Is more than distance, Dear, or rain,
>   And longer than the years!

What exactly Hardy was thinking of when he first wrote about 'that thwart thing' cannot be said for certain. Florence Henniker's obstinately respectable morals, perhaps, or his ruined but immovable marriage, the 'laws of men' that helped produce both – all of these are implied. It's clearer though that when he sent the same poem to Florence Dugdale fifteen years later, Hardy was implying that some similar obstacle existed. He seemed to accept that their relationship was likely to remain unfulfilled. Or was he being more cunning? Is the poem a hint of how miserable he was so long as they remained apart from one another? He was not above emotional blackmail.

And during 1909, the two of them were becoming bolder. Hardy confided in Edward Clodd about his difficulties with Emma and his friendship with Florence. Clodd responded by offering to invite Florence with Hardy to one of his house parties at Aldeburgh. 'Your timely hint that I might bring her to Aldeburgh is really charming,' Hardy wrote. Clodd and Florence had already met, at the first night in London of an opera based on *Tess*, given in July. The libretto was in Italian and the music written by Baron Frédéric d'Erlanger (1868–1943); and the work had been put on successfully in Naples in 1906 (despite its first performance coinciding with an eruption of Vesuvius); the London production went off well too. Queen Alexandra was in the audience for the premiere and 'They have not had such a first night for many years,' Hardy told Agnes Grove. Hardy had intended to take Florence until Emma insisted on attending this star-studded occasion, then he asked Clodd to chaperone Florence instead.[7]

Because of her ill-health – something that Hardy always worried about – Florence could not get away to Aldeburgh until mid August. When she did visit, however, she stayed for an entire week. In October, she travelled with him and Henry Hardy around the north of England, visiting cathedrals. Hardy had never been around her for so long at a time before. Nor had they enjoyed the privacy of holidays away from home and away from London's scrutinizing social circles. Whether or not they began sexual relations at this time, their friendship became erotic.[8]

One symptom of this was that, from 1909 onwards, Florence began consciously to exert her influence over Hardy. She introduced him to fellow women novelists, like Nella Syrett (d. 1943); and she encouraged him to be generally more polite and amiable. His correspondence starts to be filled with polite notes to people, thanking them for their kind wishes on his birthday or wishing them a merry Christmas. Commonplace actions of this kind had become unusual for Hardy, and Florence gave him the confidence to make the right social noises. Soon after, for example, Hardy and Florence met Clement Shorter and his wife, the poet Dora Sigerson, Hardy wrote to Shorter: 'I quite agree with my young friend, who said she had been surprised & delighted to find what a sweet woman she was.' Similarly, after Florence Henniker had been widowed, Hardy wrote a poem, celebrating her late husband. He told Florence Henniker:

though I had *thought* of doing some myself, the immediate cause of
their being written was dear F.D., who assured me that you would
like them – which I had not felt certain of till then[.][9]

Florence was mediating and smoothing the way for Hardy, taking up
the wifely role already and exercising with him the skills she had
developed as a lady's companion.

In the same period, Hardy also reclaimed his freedom as a writer.
His next volume of poetry, *Time's Laughingstocks*, was consciously more
outspoken than his last. This may be because the success of *The Dynasts*
gave him extra confidence, rather as *Tess* had done; if so, Florence's
presence was influential too. She was connected in Hardy's mind with:

> the modern intelligent, mentally emancipated young woman of
> cities [. . .] by far the most interesting type of femininity the world
> provides for men's eyes at the present day.[10]

In fact, Florence was not straightforwardly all of these things. There was
a strong streak of conservatism in her nature, arising from her father's
example and from her anxious desire to conform to the moment. Even
so, more than has been recognized, Hardy did discover these qualities
in her. Here at last was the emancipated ('enfranchized') woman he had
hoped to meet for so long. With Florence by his side he could dare to –
he was obliged to – assert once more the mission of his writing:

> on one point I am determined – to exhibit what I feel ought to be
> exhibited about life to show that what we call immorality, irreligion,
> &c, are often true morality, true religion, &c, quite freely to the
> end[.][11]

This was written in June 1909. Swinburne had died in April that year
and George Meredith in May. Hardy wrote a poem at once in memory
of Meredith (and another a year later for Swinburne). Meredith was one
'of those whose wit can shake | [. . .] The counterfeits that Time will
break'. So, 'No matter,' Hardy declared, that Meredith had died.

> Further and further still
> Through the world's vaporous vitiate air
> His words wing on – as live words will.[12]

The poems show Hardy consciously taking up their mantle and carrying on their mission. He did so with greater self-belief because he enjoyed Florence's support and could ignore Emma's disapproval.

Time's Laughingstocks was a notable success both with the reviewers and the public. It was reprinted before the end of December 1909, having been published only at the beginning of the month – 'a very unusual event in the history of verse', Hardy observed with evident pleasure. When Gosse later wrote his overview of Hardy's poetry (a piece written in consultation with Hardy himself), the volume's popularity was put down to its candour. It was, Gosse wrote:

> a more daring collection than its predecessors. We find the poet here entirely emancipated from convention, and guided both in religion and morals exclusively by the light of his reflection. His energy now interacts on his clairvoyance with a completeness which he had never quite displayed before, and it is here that we find Mr. Hardy's utterance peculiarly a quintessence of himself.[13]

The volume was a vindication both of Hardy's innate originality and, in the background, of Florence's modernity. Through her, Hardy was regaining his own voice and reaching a new audience.

Being up to the minute with literary fashion was always important to Hardy, even though he often pretended to look askance at the literary world. *Jude* had responded to several of the most avant-garde trends in 1890s writing and at that time Hardy was also a friend of Arthur Symons, for example, one of the leading lights of the Decadent movement. He gave encouragement in 1907 to Desmond MacCarthy who was then writing a laudatory article about Symons, at a time when Symons was still viewed with suspicion.[14] Hardy similarly took a serious interest in the younger generation of poets writing before the First World War – poets like John Masefield, Harold Monro, and Walter de la Mare. This may have been partly the direct consequence of Florence's enthusiasm. She especially admired Masefield's work and generally knew her way around the contemporary literary world better than Hardy did. He appreciated how she kept him in touch.[15]

The most striking way, however, in which Florence sought to influence Hardy was in relation, curiously, to Emma. Over Easter 1910, Hardy went once more to Aldeburgh, again with Florence. That summer, when he would be seventy and would, as he knew in advance, be awarded the Order of Merit, he took a flat in London. Emma was reluctant to come but did so in the end, rather at Hardy's insistence. In his letters discussing possible flats with Emma, Hardy behaved with apparently infinite consideration yet he was also absolutely firm about it. He was determined she should be in attendance, and while she was in London that summer, Emma got to know Florence. They met first at the Lyceum – the women's club where both of them were members – and seem to have become friends almost at once. Later, in August, Emma invited Florence down to Max Gate for a visit. Florence had already started to type up some of Emma's manuscript stories and poems, including *The Maid on the Shore*, and she was starting to offer them to publishers. This project was, she told Emma, 'the great campaign which lies before us', for which 'you will need all your strength'.[16] The visit to Max Gate finally took place from 9 to 29 September. Just beforehand (from 2 to 6 September), Florence had been with Hardy at Aldeburgh again. That fact seems not to have caused any difficulty because the visit was a complete success and it was followed by several more during the autumn.

Florence's own circumstances had recently changed in a significant way. At various times between late 1906 and 1910, she had acted as a companion to Lady Stoker, the wife of Sir Thornley Stoker, an eminent Dublin doctor. Lady Stoker was physically and mentally unwell and, in June 1910, she had finally to be incarcerated as a lunatic. The connection between Florence and the family lapsed in consequence, although she was fondly remembered. When Sir Thornley himself died in 1912, he bequeathed Florence £2,000 – a considerable sum of money and enough, finally, to release her from the need to earn a living. In 1910, however, Lady Stoker's illness meant that Florence would no longer be needed there and so her options were narrowed. If she took no action, she would be consigned to a life of literary hack work in London as a journalist and children's writer, plus time in Enfield with her family, most of it spent nursing her sick mother. Becoming acquainted with Emma might be a step on the way towards occupying the same role at Max Gate as she had filled with the Stokers.

Florence was by this time an accomplished lady's companion. She was used to dealing with difficult elderly women and with the stresses created in families and marriages by long-term illness. Her father, a self-made and driving man, was probably unsympathetic towards his depressive wife. Sir Thornley Stoker was a more gracious and kindly person yet his social eminence made his wife's strange behaviour especially embarrassing. Hardy and Emma were comparable to both these couples and Florence believed she could help them. She would pour oil on troubled waters and provide the female companionship that Emma lacked. Hardy must have been aware of what Florence was thinking of and they may very well have decided jointly on this course, since it suited Hardy perfectly. All the same, Florence is more likely to have initiated and driven forward the idea, although, instead of suggesting it directly herself, she would have encouraged Hardy to do so. That was very much her way and it all made absolute sense. There was enough space at Max Gate for all three of them to live comfortably together and, by acting as Emma's companion, Florence could live in Hardy's house without creating a scandal.

Florence still had attachments to Enfield too – her mother's health deteriorated, in fact, late in 1910 and made additional demands on her. So, as had been the case with the Stokers, Florence probably envisaged becoming a frequent visitor rather than a permanent resident in the Hardy household. That understanding was establishing itself when she wrote to Edward Clodd on 11 November 1910. Hardy, she told him, would be unlikely to visit London until the following spring and would stay instead in Dorset, the reason being that 'I go there now so often.'[17]

Although Florence's involvement with Emma can look suspect and even deceitful, she would have been reluctant to see it like that; and the way she construed it had a bearing on how it was. Evidently, Hardy wanted her near him and cultivating Emma was a way of their bringing that about. Florence, too, was in search of a household where she could be usefully placed. She also believed, though, that by approaching Emma and supporting her (in ways that Hardy did not or could not) she would be helping the situation – alleviating the tension and suffering of their married life. She had a talent for conciliation, she felt, and was willing to perform this task if it improved Hardy's state of mind. She was as worried as Emma had always been by his 'fits of depression' and she sought, again like Emma, to find ways of keeping them at bay.[18]

For her part, Emma's evident warmth towards Florence during 1910 and thereafter was a little bit calculating too. Emma had become adept at heading off the other women whom Hardy grew interested in and she did so most often by taking them up herself. She corresponded for years with Rebekah Owen, for instance, and entertained both her and her sister, despite their tactless, intrusive habits. She had made Agnes Grove and Florence Henniker into fond acquaintants at least, if never quite friends. Florence Dugdale was more attractive to her than either Agnes or Mrs Henniker had been. She could not exert class or literary superiority over Emma as both her predecessors had been able to; she was neither an aristocrat nor an established author and these things made her considerably more congenial, because more malleable.

It is hard, even so, to decide how much of either Emma's or Florence's behaviour was artful and how much of it was sincere. Emma was clearly flattered by Florence's encouragement of her writing and charmed by Florence herself, who was attentive and deferential. On the other hand, when Florence was visiting later in November 1910, Emma did take measures to see her off. Florence reported to Edward Clodd that:

> Mrs Hardy seems to be queerer than ever. She has just asked me whether I have noticed how extremely like *Crippen* Mr TH. is, in personal appearance. She added darkly that she would not be surprised to find herself in the cellar one morning. All this in deadly seriousness. I thought it was time to depart or she would be asking me if I didn't think I resembled Miss Le Neve.[19]

Dr Crippen was executed for the murder of his wife on 23 November; Miss Le Neve was his mistress, acquitted of charges connected with Crippen's attempts to leave the country. Hardy and Florence both came to believe, after Emma's death, that Emma in her last years had gone mad and here Florence gives Clodd, who had very little time for Emma, a comic anecdote that confirmed Emma's eccentricity. She presents an absurd world and her own droll, detached response to it: 'I thought it was time to depart'. Perhaps, though, Emma rather wanted to alarm Florence (whom she would have seen as a naive, bourgeois little thing); perhaps she was trying to produce exactly the fear of being found out that Florence ironically confesses. Madness (supposing that Emma was indeed mad) is often purposeful, after all.

On the other hand, Emma genuinely warmed to Florence too. She is 'good to me, beyond words, & instead of cooling towards me she grows more & more affectionate', Florence told Clodd on 11 November. At this time, Florence's own feelings were startlingly contradictory too. She could be gossipy about Emma in one letter, even bitchy about her, but in another written within ten days, she would say, 'I am *intensely* sorry for her, sorry indeed for both.'[20] In any event, whatever Florence's or Hardy's intentions, the arrangement collapsed over Christmas 1910.

Florence had got to know Hardy's sisters earlier in the autumn – she sent Kate a postcard from Enfield in October, saying it was 'of course not nearly so sweet as Bockhampton' – and naturally enough at Christmas, Hardy wanted her to go with him to see the family. Emma by this stage never met Hardy's family and objected to Florence's doing so. There was an appalling row at the end of which Hardy went to Bockhampton by himself, Emma retired upstairs and Florence was left alone 'in the drawing-room [. . .] & vowed that no power on earth would ever induce me to spend another Christmas day at Max Gate'. Though this account dates from fifteen years later, it looks as if Florence did make just this decision at the time. From that day on, she never entered Max Gate when both Emma and Hardy were there.[21]

Instead, she spent more time with Florence Henniker. Just before Christmas, Hardy thanked his old friend for having Florence Dugdale as her guest – '*Nobody* but you does kind things like that, & I am sincerely grateful to you' – and from January 1911 onward, Hardy's 'young assistant' starting performing in Florence Henniker's household her accustomed role of secretary and companion. Meanwhile, all through the year, Florence Dugdale and Hardy continued to meet: at Aldeburgh over Easter; visiting cathedrals soon after; in the North of England during June; in the West Country in July; to Aldeburgh again on 20–23 October; in Weymouth the same month and probably on trips elsewhere in September and November. On 11 September, Hardy told Hermann Lea that he was going away 'for a few days' and on 9 November, he mentioned to Sydney Cockerell, 'I have been gadding for a few days.'[22]

Some of these trips were (as in 1909) chaperoned by Henry Hardy and now by Kate as well, giving Emma every right to feel that the Hardy family was ranged against her. In 1911, for the first time, Florence's family too were let in on the secret of her relationship with Hardy. Her younger sister, Constance, and sometimes her father accompanied them on their jaunts. Some of these trips, nevertheless, especially the ones later in the year, remained entirely private. Everywhere, then, apart from Max Gate, Hardy's relationship with Florence continued to develop during 1911. It became an established fact – gossiped about in Dorchester, and known about by Emma, though as often quite what and how much she knew is hard to be sure about.

Nonetheless, what had happened the previous Christmas left Hardy lastingly enraged. When Florence started coming to Max Gate in 1910, Hardy was hoping to engineer some sort of *menage à trois*, similar to those he found, or thought he found, among the country people of Dorset. Emma refused to cooperate and drove Florence out. That left Hardy with a choice between either leaving Emma or conducting the affair with Florence outside the home. He chose the latter, not least because his own commitment to the appearance of conventional respectability (a commitment that was quite independent of Emma's views) prevented him from making a public break. May O'Rourke, who worked as Hardy's secretary in the 1920s, recalled the 'ironclad Victorian decorum of his private life'.

> At one moment he was visited (very unusually) by two or three persons who had gone through the divorce court. Mrs Hardy [Florence] told me how he said to her: 'We should put up a notice at the gate, "Only divorced people come here!"' And again, for it evidently rankled: 'Why do *all* the divorced people come here?'[23]

Hardy's scruples were rather extreme in the interwar years and even while Emma was still alive they were becoming old-fashioned. Divorce was slowly becoming more acceptable at the end of the nineteenth century and Hardy knew several people who had separated from their partners – Edward Clodd was the most intimate of them; others were the novelists Eliza Lynn Linton and Sarah Grand. Most of Hardy's closest friends, nonetheless, thought more strictly: Florence Henniker, Agnes Grove, Lady Jeune (later Lady St Helier) all believed in the permanence of marriage and Hardy felt himself allied to them, despite differences of opinion in other areas. His own mother had stuck by her husband through thick and thin, despite her feelings of discontent. Another factor, of course, was Hardy's obsessive hatred of media attention and either divorce or separation was bound to bring that in its wake.

Hardy could tell Florence Henniker in October 1911, 'what I have thought for many years: that marriage should not thwart nature, & that when it does thwart nature it is no real marriage', yet he would not separate from his wife, still less divorce her. Because divorce was so personally exposing – because it involved citing co-respondents, for instance – it remained unthinkable to him: 'the legal contract should,' he said, 'be as speedily cancelled as possible' when the parties wanted it to be. 'Half the misery of human life would I think disappear if this were made easy.' Since, however, it was not by any means easy, the contract remained effectually binding for Hardy – binding and miserable.[24]

Christmas 1910 was perhaps the very first time that Emma had scored a decisive victory over Hardy. Never before had she had thwarted him in a matter he cared about deeply. He had felt impatience, contempt and dislike before; now these turned to positive hatred. At Easter 1911, he published a short series of poems, 'Satires of Circumstance'. He claimed of course that they were entirely impersonal: 'being *satires* they are rather brutal', he told Florence Henniker. 'I express no feeling or opinion myself at all.' Nothing could be more untrue. A few years later, and after Emma's death, Gosse made the more honest confession, semi-authorized by Hardy.

> We can with little danger assume [. . .] hard and cruel searchlights
> as they seem, that Mr. Hardy was passing through a mental crisis
> when he wrote them.[25]

The 'Satires' are bitter, punchy poems, and remorselessly cynical about marriage, which is seen as the result of male vanity combined with female greed. The sequence ended with 'Over the Coffin', in which two wives meet as their husband is being buried. The first had divorced him because of the other woman, whom he later married. Now, looking back, she thinks she should have acted differently.

> I would I had let alone you two!
> And both of us, scorning parochial ways,
> Had lived like the wives in the patriarchs' days.[26]

Emma had accused Hardy of secretly adopting 'Eastern ideas of matrimony' before and she was sensitive also to the 'parochial' mores of Dorset because she suffered so much from the social rejection that his outspoken views on marriage brought down on them. So, the poem is attacking her conventionality and interfering moralism. What it recommends as an alternative runs along the same lines as Shelley's *Epipsychidion* – the poem Hardy had commended to Florence Henniker almost twenty years before. Monogamy should not be compulsory and divorce should not be the only alternative. Wives ought instead to tolerate their husbands' other attachments. Hardy knew this was an ideal that Emma's character made quite unrealizable as events over Christmas had shown her absolute refusal to 'let alone you two'. He had no form of redress available except to vilify her – nothing left except an old man's fury.

Florence would herself have been reluctant for Hardy to divorce Emma. During the rest of the year, she helped persuade him that it would not be necessary. They found ways of being together behind

Emma's back and without her knowing too much. There are some signs, even so, that Emma's actions had had a more profound impact still. At Christmas 1911, Hardy sent Florence a card, inscribed:

> With best wishes for Christmas and the New Year.
> "Ye have been called unto liberty". – Gal. V. 13.[27]

It was a curious text to choose because, little more than a month earlier, Alfred Hyatt had died. Florence had, right to the end of his life, been asking her friends to help, in 'the hope that something *might* be done for him'[28]. His last illness and death drew her back, in other words, to her life in Enfield, to its atmosphere of rigid respectability and to the memory of Hyatt's pure love for her – a passion that remained faithful and unconsummated.

It may be that Florence had been resisting Hardy's sexual advances over the preceding few years and been giving Hyatt's love for her as the reason for her reluctance. If so, then Hardy's note suggested that, although Florence's bereavement was painful to her, it had a positive side as well: she was freer now; the situation had fortuitously (providentially) altered in favour of their love affair. If, on the other hand, an affair had already started between them, perhaps during the previous year, then Hyatt's death might easily have filled Florence with guilt and anxiety. She would have felt she had betrayed him and fallen short of his noble standards. Life in her hometown would have reminded her, too, of the dangers involved in becoming identified as somebody's mistress. If this was the situation then Hardy's note was an attempt to reassure and comfort her, and to oppose the forces that might be drawing her away from him.

Unlike previous years, no letters have been found from Florence to Hardy written during 1912 and Hardy's surviving letters to her from this year are fragmentary and mostly literary. Their chattiness, however, implies a much larger correspondence and their partial destruction suggests intimacies that have been suppressed.[29] The two of them continued, certainly, to meet: there was a trip to Aldeburgh in May and a journey to Felixstowe in July. These were fewer, though, than in 1911 perhaps because Hardy became heavily committed to preparing his novels for a further complete edition (published in 1912). The project meant writing new prefaces for some of the novels, revising nearly all, though usually in quite minor ways, and reading through volume after volume of proof. His sister, Mary, was in deteriorating health too, which deterred him from travelling so much. For her part, Florence spent much of the year at home in Enfield, writing *In Lucy's Garden*, (published that year by H. Frowde, Oxford University Press and Hodder). After Hyatt's death the previous autumn, she suffered a further loss when Sir Thornley Stoker died. Arthur Henniker died too, early in the year. Florence had become well established in the Henniker household and often went there in 1912, comforting Florence Henniker in her grief.

Despite all these external factors keeping them apart, it does look as if relations between Hardy and Florence cooled in 1912, if only a little. Something rather similar had happened in 1909–10: during 1909, the couple seemed nearly always to be together, either travelling or in London; then, in 1910, Florence tried to befriend Emma. That is to say, she sought some way of making her relationship with Hardy more socially acceptable. In 1912, she seems to have drawn back once more, as if uneasy with the situation and the role of mistress. Her troubled reaction to Emma's mention of Dr Crippen implies this sort of anxiety. It left her and Hardy in an impasse, their relationship successfully blocked firstly by Emma and secondly by their own unwillingness to court a scandal.

What would have happened had Emma lived, cannot be known, of course. There's little doubt, nonetheless, that by this time Florence was in love with Hardy; her physical withdrawal from him, if that was what was taking place, did not arise from a change of heart. It was partly circumstantial, and partly a struggle to find some way of resolving an impossible situation. The truth of this emerged when Emma died, suddenly, on 27 November 1912. Afterwards, signs of the intimacy between Florence and Hardy reappeared at once. Florence moved into Max Gate before Christmas; and from Easter 1913 onwards, she was there nearly continuously. As early as February 1913 Hardy began planning repairs and redecorations to the house that would make it more to Florence's taste, and these were under way by April. By then, he had already proposed to her and by the summer, she had accepted him.

Florence had just reached thirty-five and Hardy was approaching seventy-four yet for both of them, late on, things had suddenly, extraordinarily, come right. Hardy had never expected to outlive Emma and be given a second chance at marriage. Florence had begun to see herself as someone in love, once again, with a man she would never be able to marry. She had started to feel condemned to a secret, inward battle between respectability and fulfilment. For both of them, Emma's death was the unforeseen gift of a new beginning.

The mind goes back to the early times

WHEN EMMA died in November 1912, things had probably never been so bad between Hardy and herself. The 1880s had been patchy for them, the 1890s turbulent and the first decade of the new century increasingly rancorous, with both sides more uncompromising as irritation turned to resentment and then to hate. The events of Christmas 1910 made matters even worse. There is no doubt, nonetheless, that Hardy was stricken by Emma's death – by grief and remorse. He felt guilty about details of her last days. He had believed Emma to be generally healthy and strong, and assumed that her attack of severe indigestion (as it was first diagnosed) would soon pass off. So, he had paid little attention until it was too late. There are reports too that their very last conversation, a day or two before she died, was full of recrimination and anger. Whether or not the last conversation really happened, it typified the situation that had existed between them for the last two years; likewise, Hardy's worries over small matters betrayed more profound alarm.

Hardy felt their life together had ended with all their long-standing differences further than ever from being resolved and dislike exacerbated by recent events. Writing, family, church – the three things that mattered to both of them most – had all turned into areas of utter disagreement that grew only more extreme as the years passed. Most recently, Emma had driven Florence Dugdale away from Max Gate and ruined Hardy's hopes of keeping her close to him. He could not bear either his own disappointment or Emma's triumphant assertion of her own will. Consequently, during 1911, he spent as much time as he possibly could away from her. For most of the year, he was either in London or travelling around England. When he was not on holiday with Florence himself, she went away with Emma. In late July and early August, the two women spent a fortnight in Worthing, one of Emma's favourite resorts. In 1912, although Hardy travelled less, he immersed himself in work on the new edition of the novels. He told Florence in April that he 'read ten hours yesterday – finishing the *proofs* of the *Native*'. He kept up a similar work rate for most of the year. More absolutely and finally than ever before, he shut Emma out of his life.

There were two visits to Max Gate in the summer of that year when Hardy and Emma were observed very closely. On 2 June, Hardy's seventy-second birthday, Sir Henry Newbolt and W. B. Yeats came to present him with a gold medal, awarded by the Royal Society of Literature. In September, Edmund Gosse came down to see his old friends, accompanied by A. C. Benson, a Fellow of Magdalene College, Cambridge, a poet and a man of letters. Hardy knew Gosse well, of course, but Benson less so, although he had sent Hardy copies of his poems as early as 1892.

All of these visitors found Hardy both withdrawn and faded. He was 'an exquisitely remote figure' in Newbolt's eyes and 'far away' when Gosse met him:

> grown, it seems to me, very small, very dry, very white. [. . .] His eyes are smaller than ever, drawn with fatigue down deeper between the thin pencilled eyelids. [. . .] The thin lips tremble a little, not from age so much as an excess of introspection. One would say that under that cover of extensive leafage he had grown pallid and bloodless.

Gosse was evidently concerned for Hardy's health and well-being. The thick trees all round Max Gate, planted nearly thirty years earlier, now produced an 'extensive leafage', darkening the house and making its inhabitants etiolated and ill. This was the simple explanation Gosse used to account for the problem. Blaming unfortunate circumstances allayed his suspicion that Hardy was depressed by other, more intractable things – a hopeless marriage and the 'excess of introspection' it gave rise to. Benson (1862–1925) was less attached to Hardy and less guarded. Max Gate to him was 'like a house wrapped up and put away in a box'; it contained 'the crazy and fantastic wife' and 'the stolid niece', Lilian.

> It gave me a sense of something intolerable in the thought of his having to live day and night with the absurd, inconsequent, huffy, rambling old lady. They don't get on together at all. [. . .]
> He is not agreeable to her either, but his patience must be incredibly tried. She is so queer, and yet has to be treated as

rational, while she is full, I imagine, of suspicions and jealousies and affronts which must be half insane.

Benson – like George Gissing twenty years earlier – evidently loathed Emma the amount he met her. Life in an all-male Cambridge college encouraged dislike of women in general and Emma's manner was neither suitably anodyne for Benson's taste, nor properly submissive. Despite this misogynist bias, the cattiness and the rather lofty distaste, Benson does give a vivid, more blow-by-blow account of the couple's relentless conflict than most other visitors did. And his reaction, typically, is to dismiss Emma as irrational and 'half insane'.

For all his strength of feeling, Benson had a donnish terror of embarrassment. During their lunch, 'Mrs H. produced cigarettes' and tried, at Gosse's invitation, to smoke one. She:

> coughed cruelly at intervals, every now and then laying it down
> and saying, 'There that will be enough' but always resuming it, till
> I feared disaster. Hardy looked at her so fiercely and scornfully that
> I made haste to say that I had persuaded my mother to smoke.

This fierce and scornful look alarmed Benson enough to make him intervene on Emma's side. And it is a frightening moment, even taking into account Benson's hypersensitivity. Christine Wood Homer (1883–1975) wrote in her old age about Hardy and Emma. Her parents, who lived at Bardolf Manor near Puddletown, were friends of the Hardys and the family had been the last people Emma visited. According to Christine, Hardy 'would look at [Emma] in a rather quizzical but kindly way when she said something particularly childish'. This mild account flatters him and rather excuses her; Emma is sometimes foolish, but harmlessly so, and Hardy is admirably patient. With Gosse and Benson, the literary people Hardy was always anxious to impress, and notably too in front of men, Hardy treated his silly wife with utter contempt.[1]

When he had the opportunity, he expressed the same contempt more positively. Newbolt and Yeats came to dinner in July, as the sole guests of Emma and Hardy, though they had arrived expecting a much bigger party. The meal itself was uncomfortable, exceptionally 'unusual and anxious', as Newbolt expressed it. Emma dined with cats sitting on either side of her plate; Yeats, talking to her, looked like 'an Eastern Magician overpowered by a Northern Witch'. Altogether, Newbolt felt,

'We were no longer in the world of our waking lives.' When dinner ended, however, and the medal was to be presented, things got much worse.

> Hardy rose from his seat and looked towards his wife: she made no movement, and he walked to the door. She was still silent and unmoved: he invited her to leave us for a few minutes [. . . .] She at once remonstrated, and Yeats and I begged that she should not be asked to leave us. But Hardy insisted and she made no further appeal but gathered up her cats and her train with perfect simplicity and left the room.

Newbolt's bewildered mixture of alarm and amusement closely resembles Florence's feeling that life at Max Gate was simultaneously ridiculous and pitiable. And Florence's occasional sympathy for Emma is repeated in Newbolt's description of Emma's leaving 'with perfect simplicity'. She became a figure of sudden pathos, cruelly treated by her husband, and although Emma's dramatic instinct sought to produce that impression, Hardy's treatment was gratuitously unkind.[2] This, though, was neither an accident nor so unusual. It simply took things to an extreme. Four years before Hardy had refused a knighthood, when it was offered by Prime Minister Asquith, in part at least because he was unwilling that Emma should share in his glory by being made a 'Lady'. That, at least, was how Emma saw it although Hardy always maintained that he turned it down because he did not want to be connected with a particular government or party. The award of the Order of Merit when it came, in 1910, was less tainted by political links and it was his alone.

Emma was with him in London when the announcement was made on 9 July 1910, in the Birthday Honours list, because he had made sure she came up that year. She left for Dorchester, however, on 12 July, apparently suffering from a cold, and as a result she was not in London for the investiture, which took place on the 19th. Florence Dugdale was in town and, at Emma's request, she made sure that Hardy was 'all right' on the day.[3] It looks from this sequence of events as if Hardy had not told Emma about the award beforehand though he knew all about it himself. If that was the case, then the announcement must have come as a complete shock and not an entirely pleasant one. It meant, from Emma's point of view, the end of any lingering hope that she might one day be made a Lady. Indignant and upset, she withdrew to Max Gate, defending herself against accusations of neglecting her husband by pleading illness and by calling on Florence's help. Hardy's sending her from the room two years later when he was about to receive a further honour would have come as no surprise. Emma made her protest and then kept her dignity. It was the least she could expect of herself and it would, on this occasion, find a sympathetic audience in Newbolt and Yeats.

Matters were, of course, no better between them in November when Emma grew ill. Hardy's *Life* recorded some early signs – 'she was noticed to be weaker later on in the autumn' of 1912 – and there's external evidence to suggest she had some inkling of what was to come. She published two volumes of her poems and prose, *Alleys* and *Spaces*, in December 1911 and April 1912 respectively. Florence Dugdale's encouragement of her writing contributed to their appearance but so too perhaps did Emma's sense that time was running short. Then, as the year wore on:

> she one day suddenly sat down to the piano and played a long series of her favourite old tunes, saying at the end that she would never play any more.

On 22 November, Emma went out on 'a damp, dark afternoon' to visit the Wood Homers in Puddletown, six or seven miles away. Next day, she was unwell and did not recover.

On 25 November, Rebekah and Catherine Owen called. Emma felt obliged to welcome them but, at the end of their long visit, she went straight to bed. She felt so bad in the morning that she agreed at last to see a doctor. He diagnosed severe indigestion, accounting for her physical weakness as the result of her not absorbing any food for several days. The following day, however, Hardy was told by the maid, 'in answer to his inquiry [. . .] that she now seemed worse'.

> Hastening to her he was shocked to find her much worse, lying with her eyes closed and unconscious. The doctor came quite quickly, but before he arrived her breathing had softened and ceased.[4]

One comfort was that it had been a mercifully quick release.

The cause of death was given as heart failure and impacted gallstones and revealed that Emma must have endured considerable pain from the gallstones, probably for a long time. There was a note on her desk, requesting painkillers, which evidently she had meant one of the servants to take to the chemist's. Hardy had not noticed anything out of the ordinary before her last illness but, more tellingly, neither had any of their visitors. Emma had seemed pretty much her usual self and then suddenly died of a heart attack. There was little, in truth, for Hardy to feel guilty about surrounding her death itself. Yet he had delayed going up to see her on the day she died – for long enough to prevent his saying goodbye. Emma had fallen unconscious by the time he entered her bedroom. So, although he had been present when she died, Emma could not have known. They had not spoken. She was isolated to the very end by their pointless hatreds.

*

The funeral took place only a few days later, 30 November, and Florence was able to be there. She had travelled down to Dorset for the first time in many months because there was a production of *The Trumpet-Major* being put on by the Hardy Players, the amateur Dorchester company that performed several of Hardy's plays. Emma's death occurred the same day as the first night, though naturally Florence missed it as of course did Hardy. She remained at Max Gate for a few more days before returning home to Enfield. A week or so later, she was back at Max Gate and soon afterwards Hardy began answering the many letters of condolence sent by his friends. He had been quite unable to do so until Florence was there to help and encourage him. 'I have felt so inert that I have been able to do very little,' he told Florence Henniker later in the month.[5] His first letters were to Clodd and to Edmund Gosse's wife, Nellie (who had been very fond of Emma). A few days later he wrote to Gosse himself, to Lady Hoare (1861–1947) at Stourhead, who had been a friend of Emma first, and Clement Shorter (1857–1926), the London editor and publisher Hardy knew and trusted. By 17 December he was able to write less formally and at greater length to Florence Henniker:

> I have reproached myself for not having guessed there might be some internal mischief at work, instead of blindly supposing her robust & sound & likely to live to quite old age. In spite of the differences between us, which it would be affectation to deny, & certain painful delusions she suffered from at times, my life is intensely sad to me now without her.

Letter-writing continued up until Christmas, by which time Hardy was becoming exhausted. Some of the notes to less intimate friends were typed by Florence and just signed by Hardy. That was only the most visible sign of her general influence.

Her very presence enlivened him and she also found practical ways of helping him cope. The couple became, almost at once, touchingly devoted to each other: Hardy wrote to Florence when she returned to Enfield in January, 'If I once get you here again won't I clutch you tight.' Florence herself told Edward Clodd that she was 'absolutely happy in being' at Max Gate '& able to look after Mr Hardy, to the best of my ability'. In March, in another letter to Clodd, she declared, 'I have never before realized the depth of his affection, & his goodness & unselfishness as I have done these last three months.'[6] Florence complained only about Hardy's reawakened affection for his dead wife, repeatedly speaking of it to Clodd. Clodd himself, however, understood Hardy's feelings. 'Yes,' Hardy wrote to him early in his bereavement:

> what you say is true. One forgets all the recent years & differences,
> & the mind goes back to the early times when each was much to
> the other – in her case & mine intensely much.

The dozens of poems about Emma that Hardy wrote over the next year return again and again to their early life together, 'when | Our days were a joy, and our paths through flowers'. He went back in his mind to the days before Emma 'had changed from the one who was all to me' and was 'as at first, when our day was fair'.[7]

In the sequence 'Poems of 1912–13' (published in 1914 in *Satires of Circumstance*), these memories come to him, at first, when he is 'faltering forward' or 'but a dead man held on end | To sink down soon'. Later in the series, though, he makes stronger affirmations.

> Trust me, I mind not, though Life lours,
>> The bringing me here; nay, bring me here again!
>> I am just the same as when
> Our days were a joy, and our paths through flowers.

This is from 'After a Journey'. In 'At Castle Boterel', Hardy recalls the time he and Emma walked along the road near Boscastle during his first visit to Cornwall in 1870:

> It filled but a minute. But was there ever
>> A time of such quality, since or before,
> In that hill's story? To one mind never,

> Though it has been climbed, foot-swift, foot-sore
> By thousands more.

The poems are extraordinarily moving portrayals of grief and have been widely admired, especially over the last thirty years. It was understandable, nonetheless, that Florence found Emma's 'virtues', as extolled by Hardy, 'beginning to weigh heavilly [*sic*] on my shoulders'.[8]

Paradoxically, Hardy could not have written them without Florence; and their very existence is in some ways the greatest compliment he ever paid her. Nearly in the middle of the sequence comes the poem 'His Visitor', spoken in Emma's voice. She comes from her grave at Stinsford Church to look in at the windows of Max Gate and finds everything changed: 'The rooms new painted, and the pictures altered'. This newness drives her away:

> So I don't want to linger in this re-decked dwelling,
> I feel too uneasy at the contrasts I behold,
> And I make again for Mellstock to return here never,
> And rejoin the roomy silence, and the mute and manifold
> > Souls of old.

Redecorating was taking place in early 1913 – Hardy was 'very anxious to get the house in a little better shape before you come', Florence told Clodd in March. 'It was really in a bad state & the walls have great patches of discolouration & damp.' The 're-decked dwelling' of the poem corresponds to the actual Max Gate, as it was being taken over by Hardy's future, by Florence's tastes and requirements.[9] It is these changes that lay Emma finally and properly to rest. The agitated, triple rhythms of her speech come to a striking, absolute halt when she rejoins the 'Souls of old'.

This is a harsh outcome perhaps yet also a natural change and a necessary one. Grief involves putting an end to grief. It requires the bereaved to accept that the dead person really has gone. Hardy's poems move from inertia towards the moment when he can definitively accept that death has taken Emma away. From there, he could move forward and regain the past through writing poems that celebrated Emma and Hardy's love for her. While the sequence is psychologically acute about the grieving process, biographically it reveals Florence's importance in Hardy's coming to terms with Emma's death. Without her, he would have remained 'inert' far longer, perhaps indefinitely.

Emma had written vicious diaries about Hardy since the 1890s and Hardy discovered them when going through her papers after her death. They added immeasurably to his distress and guilt and, if he were left to himself, they threatened to break him down. It would have been almost impossible to escape the tangle of remorse and self-criticism they provoked. As it was, Hardy could imagine Emma and their past together so clearly and so happily precisely because his prospects were rosier. And this meant too that he could return later on to the lingering anguish he felt about Emma – in poems written and published after the First World War. Naturally, he could address darker areas of his feelings more successfully when he was over the worst of the shock. The extraordinary thing in some ways is that he recovered and so quickly.

Even so, for Florence, Hardy's restored affection for Emma was inevitably hurtful. Hardy had been devoted to Florence before Emma died; now he seemed more ambivalent. As his wife, Florence naturally wanted both to occupy Emma's place and to be loved for herself alone. Hardy seemed at times to be in love with his first wife still, or in love with Florence only as a reincarnation of the young Emma. Perhaps that was not surprising in the first onset of grief and Florence certainly tried to persuade herself that it would pass as time went on. Hence perhaps some of the energy she put into prompting Hardy to restore the house, including the addition of a new conservatory, backing on to the drawing room downstairs. She must keep his hands busy of course if he were not to mope; she must also keep him moving forward into their life together. She was the moving force behind other changes too, perhaps. Henry, Kate and Mary moved from Bockhampton to Talbothays during the first half of 1913. The old family home at Bockhampton was falling into disrepair, so there was reason enough to leave but their deciding to do so at this moment was certainly something Florence would not have discouraged.

Hardy's attachment to Emma's memory persisted, however, throughout his marriage to Florence and this led Florence gradually to hate her and to blacken her name. Hardy had accounted for Emma's diaries early on by saying she was deluded – mad: 'It was, of course, sheer hallucination in her, poor thing, & not wilfulness,' he told Florence. Florence's first response to this was sceptical. 'I feel', she told Clodd, 'as if I can hardly keep back my true opinion much longer.'[10] Over the following months and years, she changed her mind, tending to agree with Hardy and even encouraging the belief that Emma had been insane. This bias colours many of the stories reported by Florence about Emma, especially after Hardy's death, and during his lifetime, Florence's views led Hardy to see settled madness in Emma where earlier he had spoken only of delusions and 'hallucination'. This comforted his fear that he had played a part in her sad decline. If it was some medical condition, some weakness she had inherited through her family, then Hardy himself was not to blame. Florence, and others around him, accepted this narrative – even if it was a lie, it was to be welcomed if it helped diminish Hardy's morbid concern about his behaviour towards his dead wife.

Hardy, though, was never consistent about Emma's 'madness'. In one of his most brilliantly handled poems, 'In Front of the Landscape', published in 1914, he depicts her as one of the ghosts who surround him as he walks. Outside in the landscape, he does not see what everyone else might see – the hills, fields, milestones and so on – but faces from his past instead, from its happy days and sorrowful ones.

> Yes, I could see them, feel them, hear them, address them –
>> Halo-bedecked –
> And, alas, onwards, shaken by fierce unreason,
>> Rigid in hate,
> Smitten by years-long wryness born of misprision,
>> Dreaded, suspect.[11]

This is strikingly fair, as well as honest, though it takes time to unravel. Mentioning 'fierce unreason' goes along with the idea that Emma was mad but, by saying 'shaken by fierce unreason', Hardy makes it seem temporary, like an aberration or an illness and not her true self. He admits too that she frightened him, that she was 'Dreaded'. Most importantly, though, he offers an explanation of why all this happened: Emma's rigid hate came about because she was 'Smitten by years-long wryness born of misprision'. Her sense of being badly spoken of produced a stance of sardonic, feigned indifference. This was false to her character, and pretending to be other than she was, caused her harm. The pose of indifference, the wryness, gradually made her 'Rigid in hate' – it produced the immovable hostility that made their life together so hard.

Hardy knew before Emma died that this rigidity was mutually destructive. In a way he respected Emma's strong-mindedness. In 'Had

You Wept', for instance, he presents her reluctance to find a compromise as a principled refusal to be manipulative.

> The deep strong woman is weakest, the weak one is the strong;
> The weapon of all weapons best for winning, you have not
>   used; [. . . .]
> When I bade me not absolve you on that evening or the
>   morrow,
> Why did you not make war on me with those who weep like
>   rain?
> You felt too much, so gained no balm for all your torrid
>   sorrow,
> And hence our deep division, and our dark undying pain.[12]

This poem is less directly autobiographical than some he wrote and the situation it describes is probably imaginary. Still, it is heartfelt, especially in the bleak last line. The woman's admirable qualities, her strength and integrity, hold back her tears. Sadly, though, it is this strength that produces the 'deep division' between them in the end, and Hardy's 'dark undying pain'. The belief that Emma was simply mad was in some ways an attempt to rid himself of this pain, and something similar underlay the extreme discretion and internal contradictions of his autobiography, written a few years later. While he wanted to recall their early love affair, Hardy also wanted to pretend the marriage had been coolly impersonal for many years. At all costs, he wanted to sweep out of sight their long history of misery and conflict. He would prefer to pity her, condescend to her and even travesty the person she was, rather than properly recall their worst times. His poetry about her becomes at times so convoluted because Hardy's remarkable truthfulness comes up against this equally powerful need for comfort.

In consequence of course Emma herself has been lost. Certainly, she behaved oddly in later life. If she was suffering from painful gallstones as she grew older and was supplying herself with painkillers, these would have been opium based (like laudanum for instance) and would have had side effects. Emma's father had been an alcoholic – a matter she was always strangely candid about. In her 1876 holiday diary, Emma wrote 'T. angry about the brandy flask'. In late middle age, she put on weight rapidly – T. P. O'Connor described her at this period as 'full-blown, with an ample figure, a large rubicund face'.[13] Although O'Connor is not especially reliable, perhaps she had started to drink.

The stories of her strange behaviour are equally well accounted for by alcohol and laudanum as by actual mental illness. Emma was, moreover, more like her father than she cared to admit. She inherited both his acerbic tongue and his lawyer's skill in marshalling arguments. Her letters to the newspapers – about how to educate children, women's suffrage or cruelty to animals – are forcefully written, cogent and incisive. So too, although she is defending a creationist position, is her critique of Edward Clodd's account of evolution. Christine Wood Homer said that Emma as a young woman was 'pleasant but never brainy'.[14] She was herself too young to know this and the opposite was perhaps closer to the truth: brainy – or quite brainy at least – and never pleasant. Emma had the kind of mind it did not suit a woman to have in the late nineteenth century. She was not gifted as an imaginative writer and she was precisely not the 'intuitive' woman Hardy found in Florence Henniker. The feminine posture of gracious submissiveness, lightness and urbanity, was very hard for her and unnatural. Instead, she had force, energy and powers of organization, none of which were fully developed. Hardy did not encourage them and neither did her culture. Moreover, Emma's self-perception, partly out of loyalty to her mother and partly from dislike of her father, was excessively ladylike. She falsified and misunderstood her own strengths, romanticizing her nature and embarking on the fruitless quest to become an author.

It was her ambitions as a writer, of course, that helped to make her attractive to Hardy at the beginning. Marrying him meant that what was essentially an adolescent passion for literature became a prison for life. She found herself confronted by the reality of the romance of authorship – hard work, for years very little money, and the constant pressure of the artist's unyielding will. If Hardy felt fooled by Emma's conventionality and snobbishness, she felt equally fooled by his necessary self-centredness, since without admitting it to either of them, Hardy exerted a subtle form of tyranny over their life together. Emma took refuge in causes, visionary religion, and, I suspect, in drink as well. Her girlish whimsicality had fascinated Hardy too and in later years Emma returned to it in the hope of regaining his heart. She gave up the severe, matronly clothes she had worn in the 1890s and dressed herself once more in frills and feathers. She thought she deserved such opulence and it showed her errant husband that she at least was still the same – that she still possessed the grace, as she saw it, which had won his heart all those years ago. The theatrical eccentricities that so embarrassed her husband were to an extent a bid for attention – attention he rarely gave her. Though so good at remembering dates and so attached to annual rituals (so superstitious about them really), Hardy never did anything on Emma's birthday. Not once.

Florence Dugdale, in 1913, was faced with an easier situation than Emma had encountered when she married Hardy nearly forty years earlier. Hardy was older, mellower and more content. Florence herself was more emollient than Emma, wilier too. Even so, she grew to fear the oppressiveness of her husband's house and its unchanging routine. She wondered just before she married 'if there is not something in the air of Max Gate that makes us all a little crazy'. It was as near as she came to finding common ground with Emma – this dead, 'crazy' woman who was still her rival.[15]

~ 26 ~

The sustaining power of poetry

FLORENCE and Hardy were married on 10 February 1914, very quietly, in her home town of Enfield. They travelled back to Max Gate the same day. There was no honeymoon; instead, the couple went on a number of short holidays together over the next few months – to Devon first, and later London. Hardy downplayed the marriage when he wrote of it to friends and well-wishers. 'The step has been so soberly taken, I may even say gravely,' he told the Vicar of St Juliot, J. H. Dickinson, 'that my wife & I hope we shall not be disappointed in it.' With his close friends, he was keen to say that Emma would not be forgotten. 'I am very glad she [Florence] knew Emma well,' he wrote to Florence Henniker, who had expressed some surprise at the marriage. Because his two wives had known each other and even been friends, the second marriage would not 'obliterate an old affection'; rather affection for Emma would be continued in his marriage to Florence. This was not only a social scruple in Hardy, however; it was a personal need.

His wreath for Emma fifteen months earlier had used the same phrase: 'From her lonely husband, with the old affection'. He told A. C. Benson that Florence:

> was a friend of my first wife as she has been for a long time of my sisters, so that there is not that rupture of continuity in my life by this event which I so much dislike.

It was a sentiment that became a refrain in his letters at this time: he remarked to his old friend Frederic Harrison: 'It may seem odd to you but the sense of continuity through her [Florence] having been attached to my late wife is not the least part of my satisfaction.' He told Dickinson, 'there is no rupture of continuity in my life'.[1] Continuity and old affection. The marriage was secretly, of course, logical to Hardy because he and Florence had been involved together for several years.

There was no rupture in the continuity of his hidden life. The references in his letters to Emma and Florence's friendship with her try to suppress that guilty secret. Likewise he tries to downplay the romance and suggest that he married Florence simply because it was convenient and sensible for him to marry his secretary. All the same, he is not just being disingenuous because continuity was in itself increasingly important for Hardy. Emma's death and the sudden, total disruption it made in his private life seemed to parallel rapid, disturbing changes in the world around. In politics, Hardy was by this time a gradualist – fearful of revolution and searching instead for signs of evolutionary change. Domestically he was old and set in his ways – routine had become, in fact, a precious source of stability during his unhappy life with Emma, with its unpredictable eruptions and tirades. He was anxious that Florence might alter these patterns and, even if she did not, that her presence would feel like an alteration.

There was an equally powerful other side to this. He and Florence fully expected the marriage to be 'prosy' and 'humdrum' but it proved to be 'not without romance'. Hardy loved 'the fine morning' in a 'quiet old church' where they were married; he relished the secrecy. 'Although the church door stood wide open nobody walked in,' he told friends, 'people passed by the open door without turning their heads.' This actual wedding recalled the secret marriages he had written about so often – it felt innocent and naively brave to try to make the dream into reality. The solitude of the wedding and its intimacy invoked as well Hardy's visit to Salisbury Cathedral with Florence Henniker – especially, the moment of unspoken dedication to one another that took place when they held hands before the high altar. Also, of course, it repeated the quietness of his first wedding. He was by now a famous man and had to take steps to avoid publicity. That necessity dovetailed with what he wanted – an event that would look both forward and back; a marriage ceremony that would not cause a 'rupture in continuity' and would in consequence be 'not without romance'.[2]

For her part, Florence married Hardy, she said, so that she 'might have the right to express my devotion – & to endeavour to add to his comfort & happiness'. This, at least, was the account she gave to Sydney Cockerell, agreeing wholeheartedly with what he had 'so happily expressed' in his letter of congratulation. Subsequently, many observers of the marriage saw Florence in this light, as a wife selflessly devoted to her husband – his nurse, his secretary and his housekeeper. Ellen

Titterington, who was a parlourmaid at Max Gate from 1921 until 1928, felt that Hardy exploited Florence's kindness:

> Mrs Hardy [. . .] was devoted to her husband's comfort. She was relatively young and night after night she would dutifully read to him for two or three hours. She was like a nursemaid caring for her charge.

Florence was 'very attentive and devoted to his comfort', Ellen said elsewhere, even though the lonely, uneventful life at Max Gate depressed her.[3] Joyce Scudamore, an 'intimate friend' of Florence's, first met her near the beginning of the marriage and stayed in close touch until 1920. She was much more hostile to Hardy, who:

> seemed to resent my presence, as indeed he resented anyone who took Mrs. Hardy's attention, as she was not then immediately available to him at his beck and call. [. . .] When we were talking, Mr Hardy would sometimes put his head round the door and say to his wife, 'I'm ready when you are,' and Mrs Hardy would say to me, 'I'm afraid I must go now. My husband wants me.'

Florence was, according to Joyce Scudamore, 'always monopolised by her husband' in what was 'more a marriage of convenience than an emotional union'.[4]

With almost forty years separating them and with Hardy already so old, this account of their marriage does appear plausible, at first anyway. And all the visitors to Max Gate agree about Florence's meticulous care for her husband. Most reveal too how entirely life there revolved around his needs: his work demanded quiet so quiet was insisted on, even from small children. Florence's nephew, Tommy Soundy, visited when he was five years old.

> My memory of Max Gate in those days was of complete tranquillity, broken only by the sound of the ticking of the grandfather clocks of which Thomas Hardy was so fond. [. . .] Every Monday morning after breakfast, Thomas Hardy would wind the clocks and check the time with his watch.

Nobody else was allowed near them and even after Hardy's death they were sacrosanct. A 'man from Dorchester would come weekly on a bicycle to check and rewind them.' According to Soundy, 'No one else was allowed to touch the clocks right up to the death of Aunt Florence.'

Likewise, Hardy's rigid preferences about food were religiously observed and unwanted visitors were kept at bay by the combined efforts of Florence, the servants and, if need be, the gardener too. On these occasions, naturally, Hardy himself stayed well out of sight. Even so, despite Hardy's insistence that his needs were exactly catered for, Joyce Scudamore's account of 'a marriage of convenience' does not ring entirely true.[5]

Hardy, although he never had a car of his own, often went on rides around Dorset, chauffeured early on by Hermann Lea and in later years by Harold Voss, from Tilley's Garage in Dorchester. Voss recalled the outings years later and much of his account squares with Ellen's or Bertie Stephens's, the gardener. Hardy comes across as quiet, reserved, gentlemanly and remote. Much less friendly than his brother Henry or sister Kate, Hardy was also less generous. He tipped meanly and generally kept himself to himself. But when Voss was asked 'Did you find Hardy an interesting companion?', he answered with great warmth:

> Oh yes! He was indeed! He was a very interesting companion to have with you on a motor tour. You see, he had known me for a good many years and he was more talkative to me than to most people, and when motoring, apart from Mrs. Hardy, we were usually alone.[6]

The poet and critic Edmund Blunden, when he visited Max Gate in 1922, also found Hardy to be 'not so reserved as he seemed in some of the portraits'. Both when alone with Blunden and when Florence was with them, Hardy was 'completely candid, without the least emphasis: he did not guard his knowledge or sentiment in any way'. Ellen Titterington recalled Hardy chatting similarly to Lady Hester Pinney 'who was a very animated person'. Lady Hester, who had married a major general and moved to Racedown in Somerset, was the sister of Hardy's long-standing friend, the eminent local doctor Henry Head (who attended him on his deathbed), so she was in Hardy's confidence.

> She would sit on the hearth rug and talk and talk, and Hardy would laugh out loud and chuckle over bits she told him of the local gossip.

A servant like Ellen 'did not often hear Hardy laugh', but Lady Hester must have done so many times.

It's evident that, with friends he could trust and in private conversation, Hardy became a very different person from the withdrawn, austere character so many outsiders met. He would chat, confidingly and enthusiastically, about the things that interested or mattered to him. He could be friendly, funny and, as they consistently reported, sympathetic too. He treated the people he cared about with great kindness and an at times uncanny degree of understanding. Even Tommy Soundy, who had been led to expect a 'monster', found instead 'a very kindly white-haired old gentleman with a beaming smile [. . . .] I shall never forget that kindly welcome and the gentleness to a small bewildered boy.'[7] Blunden, Harry Voss and Lady Hester all saw this side of Hardy's personality and Florence must have seen it too. Better than anyone else, she knew what he was like when alone with a single other person – when his guard was down and his shyness disappeared. Hardy was demanding, no doubt, and imposed on Florence, yet the marriage survived because Florence also saw and knew the private man. Their long-term clandestine relationship guaranteed that: Florence had always provided Hardy with a context where he did not need to be quite so defensive or wary or self-conscious and that remained the case in their marriage. He could share jokes with her too, as he had not been able to do with Emma for years and years. Hermann Lea remembered Hardy most of all for his sense of humour and Kate, his cheery youngest sister, also knew he was far more comic than his reputation implied. May O'Rourke, when she helped out with Hardy's typing during the 1920s, noticed Hardy and Florence seeing the funny side of things. Her recollections bring out the relaxed, amused atmosphere that often characterized their life together – a side of things less visible to the servants simply because Hardy kept up more of a front with them.

In such a stable and tranquil home, Hardy's pattern of work continued unchanged day by day, month by month and year by year. He had always worked extremely hard and, in the last years of his marriage to Emma, especially so – he had gone back during 1912 to spending ten or twelve hours each day at his desk, just as he had done a quarter of a century before when writing *The Woodlanders*. He now did so in a much more supportive and companionable environment. As Ellen noticed, Florence read aloud to Hardy every evening, usually until ten o'clock when they went to bed. As well as running the house for him (much more smoothly than Emma had ever done), she continued to act as his personal assistant and handled much of his correspondence. Moreover, without fail she encouraged him in his work. Whatever she sometimes felt privately, especially when Hardy's poems celebrated Emma, she would not have dreamt of running him down as a writer, nor of attacking and criticizing his work as Emma had done. Protective of his well-being in all these respects (sometimes ferociously so), Florence made possible Hardy's extraordinary productiveness in the last fifteen years of his life.

Between 1914 and 1928 (that is, between the ages of seventy-three and eighty-seven), Hardy published five books of poetry – numbering more than 650 poems in all, nearly all of them new – plus a one-act verse drama, *The Famous Tragedy of the Queen of Cornwall* (1923); a complete de luxe edition of his works, 'The Mellstock Edition' (1920); and two volumes of selected poems (1916 and 1929 – Hardy made the selection for the second during autumn 1927, at the very end of his life). Additionally, between 1916 and 1919, he compiled and wrote the two volumes of his ghosted autobiography, published in an updated version with a few minor revisions under Florence's name in 1928 and 1930. There were further, less onerous projects as well. Hardy revised his dramatization of *Tess* and wrote an acting version of the mummers' play from *The Return of the Native*. He frequently became involved in the production of these and other plays by a group of local amateurs, helping with scripts, music and details of performance. Meanwhile, he wrote obituaries of several relatives and friends, and short recollections of literary contemporaries like Robert Louis Stevenson and George Meredith. None of this would have happened without Hardy's gift and his demonic will. Equally, though, he would not have lived so long without Florence's support and could not have written anything like so much.

As with many married couples, Hardy and Florence did take some time to settle down with one another and establish their relationship. During the first few months of the marriage, Florence's letters sounded ill at ease. She told Sydney Cockerell (1867–1962), Director of the Fitzwilliam Museum in Cambridge, that 'My one fear in marrying Mr Hardy was that the friends for whom he has the greatest affection would disapprove of the marriage.' Cockerell was one such, himself a possessive friend of Hardy who was busily placing Hardy's manuscripts in libraries around the country. Anxiety made Florence overanxious to please, especially when it came to Rebekah Owen or Lady Hoare – to the socially superior women among Hardy's circle of friends. Unsurprisingly, given her temperament and her unspectacular middle-class background, she found establishing herself a difficult and worrying business. The playful tone of her earlier letters to Clodd, with their flirtatiousness and comedy, disappeared as she solemnly adopted the forms of speech appropriate to wifeliness: 'My husband admires them [Rebekah Owen's wedding gift of spoons] so much. [. . .] My husband's brother has had a slight stroke.' And so on.[8]

. This unease was worsened by Hardy's next book of poetry, published in their first year together. It included both the elegiac 'Poems of 1912–13' and the 'Satires of Circumstance' sequence. The former Florence found personally difficult, and the second she rather disliked. The process of producing a book made Hardy as anxious as it always did, but to Florence this was a new experience. Their relationship had taken off once Hardy had completed *The Dynasts* in 1908, when, that is, he was comparatively free of work, and they had seen relatively little of each other during 1912, when he laboured over the Wessex Edition. She was probably surprised by how preoccupied and tetchy he could be when nerving himself to face the public – to stand up to be shot at, as he called it. There may also have been a question as to whether they would have or attempt to have children. Florence may have been hoping to do so, even though she expressed doubts about it – in particular, understandable qualms about whether Hardy was strong enough to deal with the strains of fatherhood during his seventies. Perhaps the hopes were vague on her part and fairly fleeting as motherhood does not seem to have been especially important to her. She spoke about it as if it were more a conventional expectation – one that she worried about fulfilling – than a positive desire, though this manner was usual with her in lots of areas and tended to disguise her true feelings. Hardy seems by all accounts to have been sexually able in old age – whether fertile or not is unknown – and he had not ruled out the possibility. You could not put it any more strongly than that, even so. The tension arose from Florence's sense of uncertainty – a desire to conceive or to resolve that they would not, a wish to settle the matter one way or the other.

These perfectly normal tensions early in a marriage were overtaken by world events. Hardy's new volume of poems was sent in manuscript to Macmillan on 10 August 1914, though Hardy did wonder whether it was still expected: another volume of his poetry, perhaps of any serious poetry, might not seem a good bet for a publisher just as war had been declared – when Dorchester, like many other towns, was 'teeming with soldiers, mostly drunk'.[9] This polite doubt addressed to his publishers masked a profound degree of shock. 'The horror of this is making a great change in him,' Florence wrote in September, 'I can see. To me he seems ten years older. The thought of it all obsesses him.' Hardy told Gosse around the same time:

> I think I have not heard from you since the war broke out. The effect of it upon me was for a long while to prevent my doing anything, & still is to a great extent.

He confided more bleakly to Sydney Cockerell that:

> the recognition that we are living in a more brutal age than that, say, of Elizabeth [. . .] does not inspire one to write hopeful poetry, or even conjectural prose, but simply make one sit still in an apathy, & watch the clock spinning backwards[.]

'I prefer to write nothing,' he told Alfred Gardiner, editor of the *Daily News*, when asked for some comment on the war. Yet soon after he did write a deliberately popular poem, 'Men Who March Away', which he intended as a song. 'The army badly wants some new marching songs,' he told Arthur Symons and the poem was quickly set to music by Edgar Lane, a Dorset composer. Soon afterwards several other settings were made. The poem won, as Hardy put it, 'an enormous popularity' after its appearance in *The Times* on 9 September.[10]

Patriotic duty roused him from torpor and he was grateful for the opportunity it offered. Early in October, for example, Hall Caine (1853–1931), the Manx novelist, wrote to Hardy, as to many others, asking him to contribute something to an anthology of artistic and literary responses to the war. Hardy replied on 18 October, much earlier than others, and supplied a poem on 21 October, 'On the Belgian Expatriation'.[11] Hardy by temperament felt the call of duty very powerfully and because he was exaggeratedly conscientious any dithering would have unsettled him. Even so, this request sounds like something he welcomed; possibly, like so many older men during 1914 as at other times of war, Hardy envied the young who could enlist and act on behalf of their country. Writing poetry was the closest he could get to military service. Perhaps too he could not endure to sit by any longer contemplating the horror of it all.

He was roused again when Harley Granville-Barker, the impresario and playwright, asked if some extracts from *The Dynasts* might be staged. 'Nothing could be more apt than The Dynasts at the present time',

Hardy agreed; the production would be 'so timely and patriotic'.[12] Though initially reluctant to take an active part, he helped in the adaptation and attended some rehearsals, and when the stage version was a success – it had a run of seventy-two performances during the first winter of the war – he was distinctly cheered. *Satires of Circumstance*, published in November, was also warmly received. Apart from the pleasure of good reviews and quick sales, Hardy was, he said, 'relieved to look upon [the poems] as past productions'. It was now possible to move on.[13] He even became 'bright & cheerful', Florence said, as the first shock of war receded and he found himself able to be of some use. During the second half of 1914, it was widely assumed in England that the war would be 'over by Christmas' and, although Hardy never shared such optimism, he did manage to resist despair.

Like many others at the time, however, Hardy found 1915 and the succeeding years a far worse ordeal. He and Florence travelled up to London in April 1915 but did not stay long. Hardy became ill at once and, even though they travelled back up in May, it was one of his last visits. The annual stay in the capital for the season was at an end. 'I dislike being there more & more,' Hardy told Florence Henniker:

> especially with the incessant evidences of this ghastly war under ones [*sic*] eyes everywhere in the streets, & no power to do anything[.]

'The war casts such a shade over everything,' he wrote to the American authoress, Edith Wharton, apologizing that his 'sojourn in London this year has not been a long one'.[14] The war now appeared a 'brutal European massacre' and, he wrote as early as March 1915, it was likely to last:

> till one of the combatants is exhausted & sues for peace without being beaten, or till one or more country is bankrupt, or starved, or till there is a revolution in Germany[.][15]

These were acutely prophetic thoughts and plainly very dismal ones. Much of the time, Hardy thought it more than likely that Germany was bound to win.

Then, later in 1915, the general horror afflicted him personally. Frank George was Hardy's second cousin once removed but much closer to him than that in feeling. He was 'a young barrister in whom I am interested', Hardy wrote in March when recommending him for a commission in the Dorsetshire regiment. Indeed, he thought of him as a probable future heir. Frank duly received a commission, visited Max Gate in April and then in July, as Hardy noted to Florence Henniker, he sailed for the Dardanelles. There he died on 22 August, 'during a brave advance'.[16] Hardy heard the news at the end of the month and was 'much distressed' even though, as he admitted, again to Florence Henniker, the 'death of a "cousin" does not seem a very harrowing matter as a rule'. Florence Henniker was the first person he told about Frank's death. She was the widow of a professional soldier so could be expected to understand and she also remained probably Hardy's most trusted and intimate friend. He would turn to her when most upset, even though the things he wrote on these occasions were usually understated and overformal. Florence Hardy was, as often, more forth-coming: '[Frank George] was, as my husband says, "*our one*".'[17] In the absence of children of their own, Frank was seen as their chosen successor and adopted child. Florence makes it sound as if he was the only one who could fill that empty place in their lives.

Hardy wrote an elegy for Frank George almost immediately – 'Before Marching and After (In Memoriam F. W. G.)' – which appeared in the *Fortnightly Review* in October. It was included among the 'Poems of War and Patriotism' published in his next collection, *Moments of Vision* (1917). Most of these war poems date from 1915 and it is a further sign of Hardy's growing despair about the 'Time of Slaughter' he was living through that from 1916 onwards he wrote much less about it. His poems shifted their focus, returning once more to personal matters – his first marriage, the absence of an heir, and thoughts about what his life amounted to overall.[18] Another reason for this change, apart from the desolating war news, was the death on 24 November 1915 of Hardy's beloved sister, Mary. She was seventy-three years old and had suffered worsening health for several years. Florence described Hardy as 'won-derfully calm and composed'.

> I think he felt that her death was a release from pain to her and hence not to be much lamented – but of course he was fond of her.[19]

This was probably designed to reassure Florence's correspondent, the rather gushing Rebekah Owen, though it does also reflect Hardy's capacity for resignation. He had said similar things when Jemima died in 1904. Now, though, all of his childhood family were dead: father, mother and sister. Henry and Kate were born too late to share in Hardy's most formative experiences, so that Mary's death left him peculiarly isolated from his past. Along with the catastrophe of the war, her death increased his feeling of having outstayed his welcome in life – of being useless and de trop.

In 'Looking Across', a poem written in December 1915, Hardy counts up, stanza by stanza, the four people now buried in Stinsford Churchyard. 'Tired, tired am I', he concludes:

> Of this earthly air,
> And my wraith asks: Why,
> Since these calm lie,
> Are not Five out there?

'The Five Students', another poem in *Moments of Vision*, extends this feeling beyond the family. In it, Hardy sees himself as the last survivor of his youthful friends – Horace Moule and his brother Henry Moule, Emma's sister Helen, possibly Tryphena Sparks too. 'I still stalk the course' of life, the speaker remarks, flatly, as if he sees little purpose in it.[20]

Other poems written during the war reflect the same state of mind. Hardy had made Emma complain in an earlier, 1913 poem, 'I thought you would join me soon.' In the 1916 poem 'Quid Hic Agis?', he wonders what value there can be in his continued existence. The title means 'What are you accomplishing here?' and is quoted from one of Hardy's favourite biblical passages, 1 Kings 19, when the prophet Elijah hears a still small voice – a voice that asks this question. Hardy had quoted the passage in his first surviving letter – a letter addressed to Mary – and would in old age occasionally make a point of attending church on the day in the calendar when the passage was read. He presents himself in the poem as another Elijah, another disheartened prophet:

> spiritless
> In the wilderness
> I shrink from sight
> And desire the night [. . .]
> And the voice catch clear,
> 'What doest thou here?'[21]

Though the melancholy is so deeply felt and 'spiritless' – so destructive of his energy – there is an almost equally strong sense of rebuke and demand. The clear sound of the voice feels like a summons, a reminder of courage and resolve, so the poem sounds suddenly as if it expects Hardy to find an answer to the question. Over the next few years, still surrounded by the war, he did succeed in finding one.

First of all, with Florence's encouragement and Sydney Cockerell's, Hardy began to work on his biography, commencing the task early in 1916. It meant going through his old notebooks, diaries and letters, putting them into chronological order and selecting from them passages that were interesting or characteristic. It meant, too, deciding how much to admit about his unhappy marriage to Emma, his humble upbringing and the controversial sides of his output. Once Hardy had chosen the passages he wanted to preserve, though, he could string them together in a third-person narrative and then destroy the originals, usually by burning them.[22]

The *Life* that resulted from all this has frequently been criticized for obscuring so much of Hardy's personal life and, secondly, for slanting his career so much away from the novels and towards *The Dynasts* – a work that was popular at the time Hardy wrote but has generally been seen as a failure by post-war critics. In 1916, though, this bias was psychologically necessary. Hardy had to prove that his present life, as a poet, was valuable; otherwise he would see no purpose in carrying on. So his biography gave the impression that poetry was what he had always wanted to do – his life in London during the 1860s was presented as that of a would-be poet, who was following architecture only out of necessity. Likewise, his career as a novelist is made to look like something that grew up almost accidentally, simply because Hardy needed to earn a crust – because poetry would not pay and novels would. Thankfully, according to the *Life*, Hardy was able during the 1890s to resume his real vocation and write poetry.

These are the broad lines of the account Hardy gives in the *Life* and they give, of course, nothing like the full picture. The story they tell, however, is the one Hardy needed to hear during the First World War, when he felt he had 'no power to do anything' and no living sources of continuity with the past. Going back into his past was, of course, a means of overcoming the severances that bereavement caused. Florence almost certainly saw this and encouraged the project for that reason. Hardy had become ill after Mary's death with another attack of diarrhoea, an affliction that coincided more and more with periods of emotional stress. This time, it had confined him to bed for nearly a month over Christmas 1915, so must have been especially severe. In this context, the *Life* can be seen more clearly as a form of therapy.

The book was therapeutic too because it gave Hardy the chance to make other biographies redundant. F. A. Hedgcock had produced the first in 1911 and aroused Hardy's violent hostility by drawing biographical conclusions from his fictional writing, from *A Pair of Blue Eyes* in particular. Ernest Brennecke published a similar study in 1925 in New York but Hardy was so indignant about its inaccuracies and intrusiveness that he stopped it from appearing in the UK. A biography he wrote himself would always have greater authority than such books, especially if primary evidence was destroyed. It would also lessen the impact of the future biographies that, as Hardy was well aware, would be difficult to prevent being written after his death. Their speculations and insinuations would be powerless so long as his 'true account' dominated posterity.

Florence and Sydney also encouraged Hardy's writing more generally and his last two volumes, *Human Shows* (1925) and *Winter Words* (1928), were compiled with Cockerell's help from Hardy's manuscripts. Hardy needed less assistance in 1916–17 but he was stimulated by their constant affirmation of the worth of what he was doing. Poetry became for the first time something Hardy began to believe in as a force for good. Hardy wrote to his young friend and disciple, the poet Siegfried Sassoon, in May 1917. Sassoon, a decorated officer who had recently been wounded on the Western Front, had sent Hardy a copy of *The Old Huntsman and Other Poems*, a book dedicated 'To Thomas Hardy, O.M.'. Hardy thanked him for it, mentioned poems he particularly liked and hoped he was recovering from his injuries.

> Improving surely, I hope, even if slowly. I don't know how I should stand the suspense of this evil time if it were not for the sustaining power of poetry. May the war be over soon.[23]

Moments of Vision was being completed at this time (the manuscript was posted off in August) and the collection reflects this idea of the 'sustaining power of poetry'. For Hardy, poetry made it possible both to confront and to bear the worst that life could inflict, just as his work on the volume, on the *Life* and on his first *Selected Poems*, had helped him to cope with a conflict that otherwise caused him to despair. Hardy's understanding of poetry's 'sustaining power' altered nonetheless during the war.

The mechanization of battle destroyed any heroism fighting might have once possessed – in, say, the Napoleonic Wars. Humanity's return to such brutal bloodletting seemed also utterly to disprove the belief in progress that had buoyed up Hardy through the Boer War and earlier. Civilization appeared to have failed and the Christian religion, for all its fine words, looked useless against humanity's evil. Hardy's meliorism – his conviction, expressed in *The Dynasts* and *Time's Laughingstocks*, that history was on a forward course – now seemed groundless. Old age condemned him to witness the disappointment of this last hope as he sat and 'watch[ed] the clock spinning backwards'. In some ways, it was simply unbearable. London was impossible for him, far worse was the thought of a visit to the front lines. The novelist John Buchan (author of *The Thirty-Nine Steps*) invited Hardy to make such a trip in summer 1917 and Hardy's friend, the playwright J. M. Barrie, did go but Hardy would not consider it. He refused, pleading the frailty of age although more compelling really was his sense of horror. The front lines were, as he put in in 1919, 'the scene of desolation'.[24]

As heroism faded, Hardy began to feel that the war must simply be got through somehow – that the end of getting it over justified the means. These views were not unusual at the time. Hardy was in agreement, for instance, with Sydney Cockerell 'that the democratic principle must be suspended in conducting a war, from the very nature of things'. Politically, Hardy had always tended to remain fairly inscrutable, espousing neutrality in public at least and saying he needed to be neutral in order to pursue his art properly. An underlying loyalty first to the Liberals and later Labour comes through consistently nevertheless – it probably was inherited from his family to some extent – and there's evidence as well that he was more radical as a young man than in middle age. During the war, his position was complicated, more complicated than critics have allowed when they criticize his war poetry for jingoism. In line with *The Dynasts*, Hardy saw the conflicting forces in the war as the ruling elites of the countries involved – the monarchies and the oligarchies that controlled them. The First World War was a 'dynastic struggle' between these militaristic oligarchies, and these 'Dynasts' had no more concern for popular needs than those of a hundred years earlier; they sacrificed the people just as ruthlessly to their own ends.[25] Your government was as bad as your enemy's and hence, on these grounds, the war had neither sense nor justification. On the other hand, Hardy did see the Germans as aggressors. Even if you were supporting a dubious regime in your own country, and sacrificing your civil liberties in the cause of war, aggression had to be defeated. Your support was demanded despite your feeling that patriotism should extend to all humanity and not just to your own country.

Nonetheless, the war was such a dreadful experience for Hardy that these views were subtly altered as time went on. He became more passive about the conflict and more quietist. His writing and his behaviour became both apolitical and withdrawn, so that in his poetry he focused on his talent for observation most of all. Hardy writes of himself in the book, famously, as 'a man who used to notice such things', valuing that ability above all. He's someone who pays attention to the apparently trivial and because he notices them and records them, he brings them back to mind; he helps them live on into the future, which they may help to change for the better. Hardy mentions an old psalm tune in *Moments of Vision*, and makes it into a source of tentative hope. He finds it 'Here in these turmoiled years of belligerent fire | Living still on – and onward, maybe'. Likewise, Shakespeare's 'discourse to-day', 'throbs on | In harmonies that cow Oblivion'; they 'Maintain a sway | Not fore-desired, in tracks unchosen and unchecked'. Accidentally, unpredictably, Shakespeare's work lives on, altering events in quite unexpected ways – and in places that only an observant, quiet man would ever notice. Hardy's noticing becomes his contribution to the war, because it offers a future.

There is a feeling of retreat, even so. When Sue Bridehead exclaimed miserably near the end of *Jude the Obscure* that 'We must conform', Jude himself refused to agree and the novel had endorsed Jude's persistent defiance of convention. Yet the First World War moved Hardy himself closer to Sue. Conformity was needed because the country needed to pull together if the war was to be won. Secondly, without order of some kind, small, obscure but infinitely precious things would fall out of view. Chaos would overwhelm poetry, destroying the hope it offered, and weakening its 'sustaining power'.

Hardy's mixture of conservative and progressive feeling is full of contradictions, making him easy to criticize as a traitor to his youthful principles or as a reactionary in his old age. His response to the Easter Rising of 1916 was, for example, notably (and surprisingly) imperialist. Florence Henniker's Ascendancy background and Florence Hardy's connections with the Anglo-Irish Stoker family may have had something to do with this, but he was alarmed too by the Russian Revolution of 1917. He asked the young poet, Robert Graves, whom he had recently got to know, whether he had 'any sympathy with the Bolshevik regime'.

Or should Hardy trust 'the Conservative newspaper that he took in its accounts of the Red Terror'?[26] Florence, although sometimes in sympathy with progressive opinion (her father, she said, 'always abused her for being a Radical'), may also have been a contributing factor in this gradual change of views. She was, certainly, during the war, anxiously patriotic. She was also very fond of the writings of Richard Jefferies, which celebrated a sort of nature-mysticism. Her friend, Alfred Hyatt, had introduced her to Jefferies and she imitated his style in her own journalism and her later books – particularly, *In Lucy's Garden* (1912).[27] Hardy's feelings about the natural world had never been so enraptured. His novels had emphasized both the harshness of rural life and its transience. He had always acknowledged (and reflected upon) the countryside's alteration over time.

In *Moments of Vision* and the volumes that followed, Hardy did move a lot closer to the feelings of Jefferies and other younger writers – closer, that is, to a belief in the natural world's healing power. That went along with his political stance and was accompanied by a delight in, what he began to call, 'the West Country'. He constantly invited friends to holiday and even to live in its healthy atmosphere. He roamed its famous and not-so-famous places by bicycle and later in Hermann Lea's car or Voss's. He responded warmly to people such as Harley Granville-Barker and Eden Philpotts when they claimed, like him, allegiance to one or other county in the region. All this increased with age, as was natural enough, but was heightened too by Hardy's withdrawal from London. Once the habit of staying in the capital had been broken, he never resumed it and he became less and less willing to uproot himself from Max Gate. He could not face 'the turmoil of the streets', he said. Hardy could cling on to some sort of hope for the future only by withdrawing from the present day.[28]

– 27 –

No mean power in the contemporary world

THE DYNASTS and *Moments of Vision* confirmed Hardy's reputation and his popularity. Strangely, perhaps, they also turned him into a guru figure for soldiers coming back from the war. Siegfried Sassoon was only one of many young writers who sought him out. T. E. Lawrence, 'Lawrence of Arabia', a greater war hero than Sassoon, took refuge in assumed identities and in the life of an ordinary soldier. One of the few people who knew the real name of 'Private T. E. Shaw' was Hardy, whom Lawrence visited very frequently, driving over on his motorcycle from his cottage at Clouds Hill, a few miles away, and sweeping dramatically up the drive of Max Gate before knocking discreetly on the kitchen door. If Hardy was busy, Lawrence would retreat without disturbing him but if not, he would grab the chance of a talk. He 'is so assured', Lawrence remarked. 'There is an unbelievable dignity and ripeness about Hardy.'[1]

A young woman, Marjorie Lilly, who visited Hardy, almost by accident, in the company of her brother and a group of his fellow-soldiers, assessed the attraction that Lawrence and others like him felt so powerfully.

> After the war, young intellectuals who had lost their way flocked to Max Gate with their problems, confident that they would find in him their leading spokesman and soul-mate[.]

Hardy did not come across as 'the professional prophet of doom' whom she had expected; instead, 'he looked alert, serene, in fact incorrigibly cheerful'. Serenity amidst widespread uncertainty was something Hardy could offer, almost without trying. And, although he had not experienced the war directly himself, for many *The Dynasts* proved his intimate understanding of a soldier's experience. According to Major General Sir Harry Marriott-Smith, one of Hardy's near neighbours in the 1920s, *The*

Dynasts showed 'an almost uncanny knowledge of how soldiers thought and how they behave'. It had 'that insight which is really a form of genius', plus 'the indomitable courage with which he always refused to blur in any way the ugly facts of the world'.[2]

The major general had been nearly forty when war broke out in 1914. Sassoon, Graves, T. E. Lawrence, Edmund Blunden and the other ordinary ex-servicemen who sought Hardy out were nearly all far younger. Lawrence had been in his mid twenties when war began; the others had been barely out of their teens. For this generation, the First World War destroyed the social order that they had been educated to serve and lead. They had not yet experienced much of it at first hand and consequently they tended to believe wholeheartedly in its purposes and ideals. It came as a catastrophic shock to them to find that their own government was amoral and quite prepared to behave with the same ruthlessness and cynicism as their enemies showed. Their moral universe and their sense of identity were being destroyed.

It felt to many of them like the end of the country that they had been taught to love. John Middleton Murry, another young literary man who visited Hardy in the post-war years, felt this more intensely once peace had been declared:

> as the news of its shameful terms gradually became known the sense
> of the hideous waste and the utter futility of the whole monstrous
> war became steadily deeper and deeper. One felt that England, the
> true England, had ceased to exist[.]

This was a common experience. A certain kind of 'England' had gone with the war, leaving behind a terrible gap. Murry's anguished, over-wrought prose suggests something like hysteria and Hardy's serenity, his fatherly acceptance of the young men who came to him, offered stability amidst confusion and deracination. Blunden felt, for instance, when he met Hardy, that he 'had joined a new commanding officer [. . .] like the best I had served under'. T. E. Lawrence wondered at Hardy's absolute lack of 'side': 'He feels interest in everyone, and veneration for no-one [. . . .] any little man finds this detachment of Hardy's a vast compliment and comfort.' If 'the true England' seemed to have disappeared, some of its gentlemanliness, its sense of fair play and its paternalism survived in Hardy; some of its grace and civility lingered still at Max Gate.[3]

In Sassoon's semi-autobiographical narrative, *The Complete Memoirs of*

George Sherston, Sherston takes *Far From the Madding Crowd* and *The Return of the Native* with him to the trenches: 'to preserve the spirit of old England in him – the spirit that so many of his generation idealized'.[4] The same thing happened in reality: Marriott-Smith bought *The Dynasts* 'in 1915 between the retreat from Mons and the landing in Gallipoli'. Charles Sorley, a poet killed during the war, who was known and admired by both Blunden and Sassoon, also praised *The Dynasts* ardently and its influence was clear in Sorley's own poetry. These among Hardy's works – *Far From the Madding Crowd*, *The Return of the Native* and *The Dynasts* – evoke with particular affection an idyllic English rural world. It is possible to find in them traces of Hardy's characteristic ambivalence about country life but doubts rarely rise to the surface. It's much less evident in these than in *Tess* or *Jude*, for example. Moreover, in *The Dynasts*, Hardy places Wessex folk at the heart of the English war effort. They epitomize all that is good about the English people and they prove that the rural world is the true, enduring England.

After the war, there was a sudden growth in novels written to celebrate English rural life – Mary Webb, Constance Holme, Sheila Kaye-Smith and John Cowper Powys all wrote 'ruralist' fiction of this kind, and were cruelly parodied by Stella Gibbons in *Cold Comfort Farm* (1932). D. H. Lawrence's *The Rainbow* (1915) and *Women in Love* (completed by 1916, published in 1921) had things in common with these novels and, like the others, Lawrence was indebted to Hardy's work. John Cowper Powys knew Hardy and visited him; his first novel, *Wood and Stone* (1917), was dedicated to Hardy, as was Mary Webb's most famous book, *Precious Bane* (1924).

Gustav Holst, the composer, was similarly an ardent admirer of Hardy. Before the war, he set several of his poems to music and afterwards wrote an orchestral evocation of Hardy's landscapes, *Egdon Heath* (1927). The piece was first performed the following year, a few months after Hardy's death, with Florence in the audience. Again, Holst focused on the rural aspect of Hardy – the heath that is the environment of *The Return of the Native* – and like others who admired Hardy, Holst admired A. E. Housman too and the Georgian poet Edward Thomas. Thomas, who had died on the front line in 1917, had been himself a leading advocate of Hardy. He published a full-length critical appreciation in 1913 and in 1915 compiled *This England: An Anthology from Her Writers*, where Hardy figured prominently. Ivor Gurney was another war poet influenced by Hardy's poetry, and he was a gifted composer as well. He set to music two sequences of A. E. Housman poems and several of Edward Thomas's. The new ruralist novels, the poetry and these songs aligned Hardy with Housman and the Georgians, with Englishness, in other words, and smoothed away from his work its characteristic oddness and discontent. Housman's first collection, *A Shropshire Lad* (1896) had encouraged Hardy to begin publishing poetry; it became enormously popular during the First World War and, after years of silence, Housman produced a second book, *Last Poems*, in 1922. He and Hardy were seen, however strange it now appears, in a similar light.

Broadly speaking Hardy accepted this view of himself, though without being confined by it. The warmth of the admiration he received was exceeded only by the range of his admirers. Sassoon organized a 'Poets' Tribute' in honour of Hardy's seventy-ninth birthday in June 1919. This consisted of poems, handwritten by forty-three poets, bound together and given to Hardy in October. There were poems by Robert Bridges (then the Poet Laureate), W. B. Yeats, D. H. Lawrence, Robert Graves, Sassoon himself and a host of others, from Sir Henry Newbolt and Sir Arthur Quiller-Couch to Walter de la Mare, Alfred Noyes and Harold Monro. It was (and is) an amazing list.

Even Ezra Pound consulted him. In November 1920, Pound sent two volumes of his poetry to Max Gate, *Quia Pauper Amavi* (1919) and *Hugh Selwyn Mauberley* (1920). He also enclosed a recent number of the *Dial*, which was an avant-garde literary periodical published in New York. This kind of magazine was not a usual outlet for Hardy, but he agreed to contribute something and his poem 'The Two Houses' appeared there the following year. A few months later, in answer to a further letter, he wrote with care and perceptiveness about Pound's work.[5] Hardy began by emphasizing the difference between his outlook and that of the 'recent poets who apparently aim at obscurity' but then, disarmingly, he proved that Pound's obscurity was by no means obscure to him. The sequence 'Hugh Selwyn Mauberley' had 'so much packed away in it, its racy satire included', Hardy said, that it was by no means 'thin' (as Pound feared); on the contrary, it would be called 'very solid indeed by those who really read it'.

Likewise, 'Homage to Sextus Propertius' – Pound's collection of pseudo-translations from the Latin poet – only needed, Hardy thought, 'a few notes for the general reader' and perhaps a change in title:

don't you think that you give the reader a wrong start at the outset
by naming it "Homage to S. P.", and not "S. P. soliloquizes", or
something of the sort?[6]

Hardy's title suggests one of Robert Browning's dramatic monologues,
which might seem fuddy-duddy but is actually very perceptive. Hardy
loved Browning and had been influenced by him profoundly. He would
not have known – except from Pound's poems – that Pound was an
admirer too. More remarkable than this insightfulness, however, is
Hardy's way of being encouraging. 'I refrain from criticizing', he wrote,
'feeling it best to leave you to the light of your own soul for guidance,
and not to be bothered by my "reactions".' He did make various
comments all the same but each one was designed to help Pound feel
confident about following the light of his own soul. The 'deprecatory
remark' Pound made about his work was, Hardy reassured him, 'unde-
served'. Hardy's uninvasive encouragement ignored literary fashion (with
all its silly rancour and cliqueyness); he tried instead to restore young
writers' sense of self-worth and independence. This was a dignified
stance, true to some of Hardy's deepest instincts and principles, and it
also suited the moment exactly.[7]

The original and important poet, Charlotte Mew, who also came
into Hardy's orbit at this time, was a slightly different case. She was
older (born in 1869), a woman and had no direct war experience. And,
like Pound, she wrote the modernist poetry that Hardy usually found
less to his taste. Mew's poems were, he initially thought, 'rather too
obscure'; over time, though, he grew to admire them. Charlotte became
one of Florence's personal friends and Florence wrote to her about
Hardy's response. She had 'read the first verse' of one of Mew's poems
aloud to her husband, 'without telling him who had written it'. Hardy
'sat up alert & interested at once. "That's *good*" he said "Who wrote it?"'
It was his typical, disinterested question.

Hardy's willingness to see worth in all sorts of poetry – Georgian
and modernist, formal and free verse – typified the old, gentlemanly
code that he was made an emblem of. And he was genuinely as kind
and helpful to Pound and Mew as he was to Blunden and Sassoon. Mew
first came to visit the Hardys in December 1918. 'What a pathetic little
creature,' Florence said of her. She was not Hardy's 'type of woman at
all' yet he 'did not dislike her & felt very sorry for her, & talked very
kindly to her'. Florence was writing to Sydney Cockerell, Mew's keenest

supporter, and some of her customary anxiety to please comes through here. Even so, 'We have been wondering could anything be done for Miss Mew', Florence wrote, mentioning that Hardy had suggested trying to get her a Civil List pension. This was brought about successfully in 1923 and Hardy signed the letter of application, his support carrying considerable weight. His intervention saved Charlotte, a genteel and delicate woman, from debilitating financial worries and it probably prolonged her life.[8]

Siegfried Sassoon, however, was the younger writer who grew closest to Hardy. He was Hamo Thornycroft's nephew and that connection may have encouraged the friendship that grew up between him and Hardy. He became, in Florence's words, 'my husband's *adored* young friend' and he visited Max Gate more than anyone, recording his impressions in extensive diaries. His feelings summed up those of his generation. In one of Sassoon's dreams, he found himself and Hardy:

> alone on a ship, in some sort of crisis. Walking along the deck, I took his hand and said, 'I do like being here with you.' Afterwards we were having breakfast together in the small smoking-room at Weirleigh. (I've never had breakfast in that room.) I had put a plate of bacon down by the fire to keep it hot for him. Then he came trotting in, very cheerful and rubbing his hands, and we ate our breakfast very happily (as we have often done at Max Gate).

Weirleigh was the house where Sassoon's mother still lived and where Sassoon had lived himself in his early twenties – 'almost continuously from December 1906 [. . .] to September 1913'. These were what Sassoon called his years of 'arrested development, when I got into a groove of minor poetry and sport'.[9] He had revisited the house in August 1923, a few months before this dream took place.

The affection in the dream is touchingly childlike – quite *un*erotic, I think, though Sassoon was homosexual. Hardy is a father figure offering reassurance during 'some sort of crisis'. During the second scene, which is intimate too, Sassoon seems to be returning the favour – he looks after Hardy by keeping the bacon warm, in the same way that Hardy had cared for him on the ship. Young children can often enjoy taking on these roles around the house, so the second part of the dream continues to cherish a happy father–son relationship with Hardy. Returning the favour also establishes comradeship, however, and the second scene recalls Sassoon's life in the trenches. It carries on the good side of the war – the enlivening impact of a call to arms. This was something Sassoon had felt very powerfully after his wasted, inert youth and he was remembering the change after his recent visit to Weirleigh. It was a change for the better that he now feared would not be lasting.

Hardy suggested it might go on. He was vigorous in old age, 'trotting in, very cheerful and rubbing his hands', and one of his roles with Sassoon and others was to comfort the traumatized – to hold their hand, psychologically if not physically. A second function was more dynamic. Against drift, purposeless and a sense of waste, Hardy's example declared the continuing value of old virtues. Sassoon had become an opponent of the war and his poems were controversially outspoken about military incompetence and patriotic cant. He was no pacifist, though. He remained firmly attached to ideas of discipline, courage and determination. Hardy's presence declared that these qualities were still worthwhile and were not the prerogative of a discredited system. Resolve and cheerfulness and energy all persisted in him; therefore they survived in England; therefore they need not fade away in the disillusioned post-war world.

Florence contributed a great deal to what Hardy came to stand for. These visitors celebrated the household at Max Gate almost as much as Hardy himself, seeing it as an epitome of hospitality and well-ordered friendliness. Florence was seen as providing both. Her scrupulous care for Hardy appeared an ideal of both womanly behaviour and motherly love – love that seemed extended to the young men like Sassoon and Blunden when they entered the house. Florence was also much closer to them in age than Hardy was. She set an example of how the young might cherish the old – of how the confusing present might keep in contact with the pre-war past, with its certainties and graciousness. Moreover, as Marjorie Lilly realized, Hardy benefited too: 'the robust outlook' of the soldiers 'provided him, in his turn, with relief from too much earnestness'. Sassoon's gift in 1919 of the 'charming volume of holograph poems' evidently moved him deeply and over the following months, he wrote individual letters of thanks to all the contributors. In the *Life*, he pinpointed this moment as:

> almost his first awakening to the consciousness that an opinion had silently grown up, as it were in the night, that he was no mean power in the contemporary world of poetry.

In the Old Testament, the prophet, Jonah, is comforted in his despair by a 'gourd' that 'came up in a night'. It cast its 'shadow over his head, to deliver him from his grief'. Hardy thought of himself, momentarily, in similar terms. The sudden proof of admiration from his peers delivered him from grief – from the general despondency produced by the war and its aftermath, from particular feelings of personal loss and from the grief he felt at second hand in the sufferings of his friends. Lady Hoare's only child, Henry Hoare, had been killed at the end of 1917; in early 1919, Sir Arthur Quiller-Couch's only son died of pneumonia while awaiting demobilization; Alfred Pope, one of Hardy's longest-standing Dorchester friends, lost his son Edward in April the same year. 'That is the insidious evil of campaigning,' Hardy wrote, 'what it leaves behind.'[10] The war lingered on in the peace, in the terrible flu epidemic of 1919 and in the minds of all the survivors.

Sassoon's was not the only mark of recognition and source of deliverance from grief. In 1919, the volume of *Georgian Poetry 1918–19* was dedicated 'To Thomas Hardy'. The following year, Hardy was awarded an honorary degree by the University of Oxford. When he went up to receive the degree, he also attended a performance of *The Dynasts* put on by OUDS, the student dramatic society. It was 'everything that could be desired', 'the whole day having been of a most romantic kind'. He had received honorary degrees before – from Aberdeen and Cambridge – and he would receive more in future years, from St Andrews and Bristol. He had already been made an Honorary Fellow of Magdalene College, Cambridge. Nonetheless, acceptance by the institution he had attacked so fiercely in *Jude* was particularly precious to Hardy. It finally put to rest his sense of exclusion – his feeling that his working-class, provincial origins had condemned him to being a perpetual outsider.

And it was not only the literary world that celebrated him. On his eightieth birthday in June 1920, it was almost inevitable that he should welcome to Max Gate a deputation from 'the Incorporated Society of Authors'. Less expected was his receiving a telegram from the King. Royal recognition continued in 1923, when during a visit to Dorchester, the then Prince of Wales (later King Edward VIII) called for tea at Max Gate. Florence lived long enough to witness the abdication crisis of 1936 and then recalled 'how difficult & obstinate he was with two of his secretaries'. At the time, she noticed his 'very weary, rather sulky young face' and commented (prophetically, given Edward VIII's later admiration for Hitler):

> But what a mercy for us that ours is a limited monarchy. Imagine that young man with the power to control the destiny of our empire!

Still, 'all passed off pleasantly' and 'there was no strain or flurry of any kind.'[11] Hardy and Florence behaved with deliberate informality. Hardy, who was not ever an enthusiastic royalist, acted as if the visit were simply a social duty – a tactic which helped him disguise how much the recognition meant to him.

Amidst these accolades, the first unmistakable signs appear that Hardy was growing old. He had by no means stopped working. A new, expensive edition of his novels was being prepared during 1919 and began to appear in 1920 as 'The Mellstock Edition'. Hardy was involved in some revision to the texts and the introductions, plus work proofreading. At the same time, Macmillan published a one-volume *Collected Poems* to accompany the one-volume edition of *The Dynasts*. Yet in October 1920 Florence was writing to Rebekah Owen to tell her that 'my husband has altered very much of late with regard to seeing people'.

> He cannot stand a long conversation – it seems to exhaust him so, and then too he behaves so oddly to visitors that I hardly know what to do. [. . .] The fact is – in plain English – that there are times when he doesn't care about seeing anyone, and these times tend to become more frequent.

Reclusiveness had always been part of Hardy's nature. Now it seemed to be growing more frequent and more determined. He was not simply withdrawing shyly from personal encounters, however, he seemed positively to dislike meeting people, particularly new people. This was partly just a consequence of old age. Partly too, though, it resulted from the ways Florence had helped him to cope with the war.

In 1916, when Hardy had been particularly depressed by news from the front and grief-stricken by the death of Frank George, Florence (advised by Sydney Cockerell) had suggested he should start work on the *Life*. This had proved a good idea. Writing and rewriting the biography protected Hardy to some extent from the remorseless tragedy of the war years. The disadvantage was that it encouraged him to dwell on the past – even to dwell in it. Another ruse Florence employed was to encourage visits to old haunts. Hardy and his brother Henry had travelled to Cornwall in 1913, not entirely with Florence's approval, but she and Hardy revisited the county in 1916, spending time at Tintagel Castle as well as St Juliot and Boscastle. Afterwards, Hardy told Florence that 'it was the last time in his life' that he would climb up to the castle itself; still, Florence reported to Cockerell, 'we had both enjoyed it, & I hope he has found the germ of an Iseult poem'.[12] He had indeed found that germ and, in 1923, he completed *The Famous Tragedy of the Queen of Cornwall*. This one-act verse-drama was set in Tintagel and retold the legend of Tristan and Isolde. Florence's comment suggests that they may have travelled into Cornwall with such a project already in mind and even that Cockerell may have suggested it, in the same way that he helped prompt Hardy to write the *Life*.

Florence and Cockerell give generally the impression of managing Hardy at this time. In 1911, at Cockerell's instigation, Hardy had entrusted him with the business of selling his manuscripts to libraries in England and abroad. Over the following years, Hardy grew to rely on him in literary areas and appointed him one of his literary executors. The other executor was Florence, who had met Cockerell first in 1913. She found him from the beginning to be a driving, sometimes rather high-handed person, respectful of Hardy but also bossy. She was in awe of him, partly because Hardy himself admired Cockerell's savoir faire. Nonetheless, although Hardy appreciated Cockerell's attention – and although in some ways he now needed encouragement from those close to him – he also resisted being managed, and he found ways of avoiding it. The past became his refuge. As had been his habit all his life, Hardy tried both to satisfy the demands of his audience (in this case, Florence and Cockerell) and, at the same time, to pursue his own agenda – to follow (as he put it to Pound) the guidance of his own heart. Emotionally and imaginatively, Hardy entered more and more the world of his early life. More and more, he left Max Gate behind, returning to the scenes where he and Emma had been happy.

So, for instance, the only one of his novels that he revised for 'The Mellstock Edition' was *A Pair of Blue Eyes* – the novel set in Cornwall and narrating his courtship of Emma. He went back to the story repeatedly, even including some passages from it in *The Famous Tragedy of the Queen of Cornwall*. And *Human Shows* his 1925 collection, recalled in its title the 'humanity show' Henry Knight shows Stephen Smith from his study window. The poems themselves reflect the same concern with old memories. Similarly, in his poems about Emma, fewer and fewer refer to Max Gate, while more and more of them returned in imagination to Cornwall. *Satires of Circumstance*'s famous 'Poems of 1912–13' had several times recalled Hardy's and Emma's married life in and around Max Gate; in *Moments of Vision*, the poems are all focused on their courtship. 'At the Word "Farewell"'' is set in St Juliot; 'The Figure in the Scene' and 'Why Did I Sketch' take place on the Cornish coast nearby – all three hark back to their first summer. 'The Wind's Prophecy' follows Hardy on one of his journeys down to Cornwall; 'Near Lanivet, 1872' remembers the visit when John Gifford was opposing the marriage, and 'During Wind and Rain' evokes Emma's life in Plymouth as a girl, using events Hardy found in her memoir, *Some Recollections*. And so on. The same is true of Hardy's next volume, *Late Lyrics and Earlier* (1922). There are fewer poems about Emma altogether but those included concentrate again on her as 'The West-of-Wessex Girl'. Their life together in Dorset is forgotten. Hardy did write several poems about the time he and Emma lived in Sturminster Newton – 'The Head Above the Fog', 'Overlooking the River Stour', and 'On Sturminster Foot-Bridge' in *Moments of Vision*, and 'A Two-Years' Idyll' from *Late Lyrics* – these exceptions prove the rule. Hardy remembered the two years they spent in Sturminster as the happiest of their married life and writing about it again in these poems, he was going back forty years in his mind – to the time before the marriage went so horribly wrong.

After 1916 (and again perhaps at Florence's suggestion) Hardy began going back to Sturminster physically as well. Travelling across by car, seeing his old house by the river and wandering around the secluded little town before driving home again became one of his favourite days out. Hardy was no longer in the habit of roaming Dorset and the West Country in Hermann Lea's car, searching out and photographing locations from the novels. Lea had moved away to the New Forest in 1921. Instead, he was chauffeured by Harry Voss, 'along byeways and side roads' to Sturminster and Voss recalled that Hardy was content with 'returning by a different route and leaving the selection to me'.[13] This was a quite new attitude; before, Hardy had always planned his trips minutely, with maps spread out on the table in Max Gate. The change suggests that his excursions to Sturminster were a new kind of travelling – times of reverie and reminiscence, that let Hardy drift away into a dream. He could leave behind his life as an eminent man of letters, married to an accomplished literary hostess and visited by all and sundry. It came as a relief from the duties of his quasi-public position. Sturminster, like Cornwall, gradually became his emotional centre.

It is not surprising, of course, that so old a man should start living in the past. And, not surprisingly too, it affected his poetry, which became retrospective and dreamlike. After the war, Hardy often wrote as if he no longer knew where precisely he was – as if the past and other places had become more vivid to him than his present world. This produced in *Late Lyrics and Earlier* a mellow collection of poetry that avoided controversy. Its poems were nearly all lyrical (as the title would lead you to expect) and there were hardly any of Hardy's characteristic, ballad-like, vivid or raunchy narrative poems or his versified philosophical debates. There was nothing polemical, in other words. Instead, an intense lyricism detached the collection from the present day, leaving behind all its troubles and anxieties. In its place, the book offered an alternative, poetical realm – one that was elegiac, filled with both pathos and comfort.

Hardy believed at this time that poetry could offer religious consolation. As he put it in his strongly worded 'Apology' that prefaced *Late Lyrics*, poetry could supply the spiritual needs of those, like Hardy himself, who found orthodox religious teaching impossible to believe. Matthew Arnold had made a similar claim for poetry years before and Hardy's thinking was still indebted to him. Yet this claim for poetry was also a response to the post-war situation.[14] Hardy found himself surrounded by younger writers who were desperate to find some source of order amidst chaos, while personally he was being drawn back into the world of his own past. He began to feel that these two things complemented each other. It seemed to him that his memories contained sources of certainty that the present moment needed so that by living in the past he was doing his best for those around him.

– 28 –

Wistlessness

THE NEW degree of recognition Hardy began to receive after the war was gratifying to Florence. She had sought it for him and saw its beneficial effects on him. It did not, however, make her husband any less self-involved or high-handed. Though he had done so much to improve Max Gate in 1913, he had soon reasserted his more usual resistance to change. Until 1920, for instance, he would not allow a bath to be installed in the house. He used a hip bath himself and the servants had to climb into the loft of an outhouse, where there was a bath of a kind. The house was not connected to the mains water supply until 1922 and even then Hardy mistrusted it; for his own bath he insisted on having well-water separately heated. He was extremely strict about money too and a hard taskmaster with the servants; occasionally, he would go right through the house in search of cobwebs, silently pointing out to the housemaids any he discovered. There are some reports too that, while they were sitting over dinner, he would tell Florence what she should and should not eat.

He was powerfully reluctant to allow Florence to go away on visits. Her absence made him ill. At least, he became ill whenever she started planning a trip away. When she decided she really must stay, of course Hardy miraculously recovered. He had, he was amused to find, '*many* characteristics in common with Mr Woodhouse', the fussily domineering, hypochondriac father in Jane Austen's *Emma*. He remained morbidly preoccupied with his dead relatives, too, as well as the prospect of his own death. These interests were ingrained in him and unavoidable; even so, he could when he wanted to make use of them in a manipulative way. If close friends came to visit, they would often be honoured with a walk to Stinsford churchyard, where Hardy's relatives were buried and where he wanted to be buried himself. Usually, according to J. M. Barrie:

he says he is to be buried exactly in between his two wives; but sometimes he is to be so many inches nearer to the first; sometimes, so many inches nearer to the second.[1]

Florence would gather from these changing measurements just how well she came up to expectations and where exactly she stood in Hardy's favour.

It comes as no surprise, therefore, to find that servants disliked him. Annie Mitchell, the cook from 1913–14, said Hardy was 'very particular over his meals'. Bertie Stephens, the gardener, said he was 'kindly' but 'fussy (he liked things done neatly)'. The builders who worked repairing or extending Max Gate were incensed by his continual interference and Ellen Titterington, whose sympathies were often with Florence, remembered her 'day after day attending to the wants of an exacting old man'. Doing so certainly imposed an enormous strain on her – a 'very nice, considerate woman', Annie Mitchell said, 'but she was not strong'. In fact, by late 1917, Florence's nerves had got very bad. During a visit to London in December, she burst into tears when old friends asked her a few 'sympathetic questions'. In 1919, her doctor diagnosed a nervous breakdown and insisted that she go away on holiday for a while. Later, in 1924, Florence needed to undergo an operation and spent some time afterwards convalescing in a London nursing-home. She was, she wrote, 'ashamed to confess that I am rather enjoying these last few days' – days being visited by Charlotte Mew and Siegfried Sassoon, among others. 'I feel better – & happier – than I have felt for years', she said.[2]

Loneliness was particularly difficult for Florence – it was something she both hated and feared, sensing how much she shared her mother's depressive personality. She needed friendly light chatter and like Emma she was isolated at Max Gate and personally unfulfilled. It was worst during the winter, when the house was freezing cold and nobody came to see them. The darkness of the surrounding trees, the damp and chill, the remorselessly static pattern of their lives – these combined to make Florence feel she was sinking into the grave. 'I did not think Mr Hardy was going to live as long as he has,' she wailed once to Ellen, the maid she trusted most.[3]

As Hardy grew more reclusive and she 'hardly knew what to do' with him, Florence had worsening anxieties about her own future. What on earth she would do if Hardy's indifference drove visitors away? If he slipped away into vague dreams of his long-ago life, she would be doubly deserted – friends would lose interest in the old fool as he lost interest in them and she would be abandoned by husband and friends alike – abandoned and trapped. Usually, all the same, Florence could manage life reasonably well. For much of the year, Max Gate was a busy place and all year round she could find consolation in the thought that she was looking after a great artist. She was performing her allotted task as well as she could and better perhaps than anyone else could have done. It was only when Hardy's past life threatened to come back into the present, in the form of a beautiful actress, that Florence found her life intolerable.

*

Hardy first encountered Gertrude Bugler when she played the part of Marty South in the local amateur production of *The Woodlanders*. She was then sixteen years old and evidently talented as well as strikingly good-looking. Hardy wrote a part specially for her in the next production by the 'Hardy Players' – selected scenes from *The Dynasts*. This took place in 1916. Via Florence, he had already tried to arrange a meeting between Gertrude and J. M. Barrie, in the hope that Barrie might help develop a career for her on the London stage. The war prevented this idea from coming to anything and interrupted the Hardy Players' performances too. In 1920, when the company resumed its activities, Gertrude played Eustacia Vye in *The Return of the Native* and in 1924, she was given the part of Tess. Hardy thought her the 'very incarnation' of his heroine and delighted in the idea that she was related to one of Tess's originals. Her mother, Augusta Way, had been a dairymaid at Kingston Maurward during the early 1890s and Hardy had visited the dairy when he was researching the book.[4] How close the connection was is impossible to say but Hardy would undoubtedly have seen in Gertrude a girl from very nearby who was remarkably beautiful and remarkably sensitive – all the things, in other words, that he saw in Tess.

His feeling for her was increased by the powerful erotic effect drama always had on him. He had been an enthusiastic theatregoer in the 1860s and had written 'To an Impersonator of Rosalind', addressed to the actress Mary Frances Scott-Siddons. When *Far From the Madding Crowd* was performed in 1882, Hardy travelled up to Liverpool to see the first night and one reason why he made the journey was his fascination with Marion Terry, the actress playing Bathsheba. Subsequently, attending *The Master Builder* with Florence Henniker had helped turn the attraction he felt for her into a near-obsessive fascination and he was always especially susceptible to portrayals of Tess. At a private performance in Max Gate, where Gwen Ffrangcon-Davies, an established London actress, took the part of Tess, Hardy was visibly moved to tears. Gertrude was less accomplished than Gwen Ffrangcon-Davies, though to Hardy she was more compelling because she did not only perform Hardy's heroines, she revived them before his very eyes. Eustacia and Tess had been objects of imaginary erotic interest when he wrote the books. When they seemed to appear before him and the past he so often dreamt of seemed to come back to life, the impact was overpowering.

Florence, because she sensed this, hated Gertrude from the beginning. All her letters to her are edgy and condescending. Judging from them, Florence did little more than obediently go through the motions when approaching J. M. Barrie on Gertrude's behalf just before war began. In 1921, when she was far better established as Hardy's wife, she still became mightily offended when Gertrude called and asked to see Hardy. 'In the first place,' she informed her social inferior:

> all invitations to Max Gate, naturally come from me, as is the custom, & again it is not usual in our station of life for any lady to call upon a gentleman. It is simply "not done". Since my marriage all calls at this house have been made on me[.]

Her letter continued in this vein for several pages. She was mollified only by Gertrude's explanation that a man – William Watkins, who directed the players – was the source of the problem. Neither woman mentioned to the other that Hardy himself had invited Gertrude to 'come over' whenever she wanted to.[5]

By this time, Gertrude had appeared as Eustacia and, according to Florence, Hardy had 'lost his heart to her entirely'. He 'is quite crazy about her', she told Louise Yearsley:

> & also much admires the photograph of the new Mrs Clement Shorter – sent us by the proud husband. I say there's safety in numbers.

Florence also comforted herself with the thought that Gertrude was soon to be married (to her cousin who lived in Beaminster). Hardy's infatuation would not 'cast me down *too* much', she said.

But the other members of the company are being a <u>little</u> upset by
<u>all</u> the applause being given to her [. . . .] So you see it <u>is</u> possible
to have <u>too</u> good a leading lady.

Florence's letters were often sharp and witty about people. Nobody else,
though, made her as bitchy as she is here – with all her fiercely
triumphant underlinings. And these feelings would not properly subside.
The following year, the Hardy Players put on a version of *Desperate
Remedies*, this time without Gertrude, who was pregnant. Florence noted
that, 'Poor Gertrude Bugler seems to have suffered agonies at being
cut out by a rival leading lady, Ethel Fare,' and, Florence went on,
'the tragic climax is that she had a still-born son on the day of the
performance'. Emma had been enraged by Hardy's disloyalties – his
emotional, if not physical, infidelities. Florence's reaction was more
underhand and malevolent though, in its way, her response was just as
reckless. Emma alienated her husband by attacking his friends and
making scenes in front of them; Florence did so by trusting them too far.
As here, in a letter written to Sydney Cockerell, with whom she later
quarrelled, Florence thoughtlessly teamed up with outsiders, gossiping
about her husband behind his back and making snide jokes about a
woman he was temporarily devoted to. This was no doubt cathartic for
her and of course understandable, given her lack of human contact in
Max Gate. Where else could she vent her feelings? Even so, it won her
no respect from Cockerell and others like him, and, more importantly,
it tended to estrange her husband.[6]

Did Florence have any reason to think that Hardy was in love with
Gertrude – conducting or hoping to conduct an affair with her? Hardy
was really a very old man – eighty-four in 1924 – and Gertrude, though
wonderfully good-looking, shows no sign of having led him on. She was
friendly towards him, admiring of him and sought his advice about
playing the roles he had written. As far as she was concerned, there was
nothing more to it than that. She had a warm, innocent fondness for the
old gentleman whose plays were providing her with such good parts.
None of this, though, made any difference to Florence because it made
no difference to Hardy. He fell in love with Gertrude because of her
resemblance to Eustacia and later Tess. Nothing Gertrude did or
intended played a significant part in his feelings for her because they
were not really feelings for her at all. He was seeing Tess. As he wrote
to his old friend A. C. Benson that year, he was living 'close to the spots

of my childish memories' and could 'revive them very often'.[7] Gertrude Bugler's performance felt like the perfect revival. He had no immoral intentions; he was not, as he saw it, being even emotionally unfaithful to Florence. If his feelings excluded her, that was simply because they were rooted in parts of his life that were remote from her experience. *Tess* was written years before they met and the dairymaids he was remembering had lived and some of them died before Florence was born.

Ellen Titterington, in a remarkable passage from her recollections of Hardy, says that she thought this revisiting of the past was something that happened all the time.

> Mr Hardy seemed to come out of his shell when talking to younger women as if a light was suddenly breaking through and he could see them in one of his books. Myself, I do not think he thought of them as women, but just shadowy figures fitting into a space like a jig-saw.

Of course, these younger women were no threat to Ellen because she was just the parlourmaid. And to Florence, often, Hardy's cheerfulness was compensation for his interest in other women. She feared Hardy's glooms (finding them infectious, among other things), so if a younger woman brought him 'out of his shell', that was all to the good.[8] Until 1924, Florence managed by and large to take this view of Gertrude; her dislike and jealousy could both be argued away and held in check. The production of *Tess* proved, however, to be a different matter.

It was first mooted in the summer of 1924 and Hardy agreed in August to allow a performance. The players were to use his thirty-year-old adaptation rather than come up with a version of their own, so the production came, from the outset, nearer to Hardy than previous ones had done, where the adaptation had been made by members of the cast. Rehearsals began during the autumn and the first performance took place on 26 November. During this period, Florence had to go away to hospital in London and have a cancerous growth removed from her neck, meaning she was absent from Max Gate for ten days at the beginning of October. Hardy evidently fretted in her absence. His deeply felt poem 'Nobody Comes' was written as he waited anxiously for her return. Perhaps to help distract himself from these worries, Hardy became energetically involved in preparations for the play and, consequently, when Florence re-entered Max Gate, after the strain of an operation and with the threat of cancer still hanging over her, she found her husband more than ever besotted with a younger woman, who was full of life and health.

She saw history repeating itself. Like her predecessor, Emma, she was now ill; she was being compelled to live with jealousy and the fear of jealousy. She saw herself as doomed to a future of humiliating neglect – a terror that Hardy confirmed by doing nothing about it. Moreover, Florence had recently been learning more of her husband's history. A year earlier, in April 1923, Hardy's old friend Florence Henniker had died and, as was customary, his letters to her were returned after her death. Florence 'opened the parcel before T. H.'

> thinking it was an autograph album from some tiresome stranger, and it was a most painful moment when I saw what I had. I think the most painful experience one can have is to receive a legacy from someone one has loved. I have put them away for the present, but later on shall carefully type them.

Florence had herself become a close friend of Florence Henniker (who had asked her to come and look after her early in 1923) so the death had brought personal grief to her as well as to Hardy. Of course, she had been told years before that her husband had felt deeply for Florence Henniker for a time during the 1890s. His old letters were unsettling nevertheless because they made the violence of his feelings clearer and showed his capacity for a near-obsessive sexual love. This discovery lingered in Florence's mind as Hardy began to show an ever-deepening interest in Gertrude Bugler.

From witnessing his earlier treatment of Emma, Florence feared most of all that Hardy would simply withdraw from her, focusing all his thoughts and energy on Gertrude and on his work. Nearly twenty years before he had done exactly the same thing, leaving Emma to her own devices while behaving with overpowering charm and consideration to Florence herself. Florence remained genuinely devoted to Hardy and her self-esteem depended almost entirely on her being Hardy's wife. This meant that his possible rejection of her was terrifying. It made her imagine herself suffering a lingering, lonely death in a house filled, as Ellen Titterington put it, with 'noiseless gloom'. Meanwhile, the thought of being ousted by a local girl made her superstitiously fearful. It felt as if the countryside, where Florence would always be a stranger, was taking its revenge on her through Gertrude, the spirit of the place.

Florence knew Hardy well enough to know that she could not confront this directly. He would only become more attached to Gertrude if she were to protest. And, as the marriage had arranged itself, she was in no position to resist. Emma had taken up her husband's other women, finding through her attention to Florence Henniker, Agnes Grove and in turn Florence herself, a way of disempowering her husband. For Florence, the same kind of involvement was something her husband now asked of her and entirely expected. With nearly all his personal and business contacts, Florence performed much of the everyday work – she managed visits so that he was not disturbed or exhausted, she handled correspondence, and smoothed over anything uncomfortable. The same applied to his dealings with Gertrude, even though this meant that Florence was expected to act in a way that helped the 'affair' along.

As the production of *Tess* continued to be a great success, there was an idea of putting on some matinée performances in the West End, with Gertrude again taking the lead role. Gertrude was enthusiastic, although her husband was less so and she did feel anxiety about leaving her young child. Hardy supported the idea too, although he evidently felt possessive about his young actress: 'We are so proud of you down here that we wish to keep you for ourselves,' he told her. 'However, you must have your own way I suppose.'[9] Florence was, to start with anyway, happy enough. 'Everything is going on well,' she informed Gertrude, '& I am sure the Haymarket production will be an accomplished fact.' This was written on 22 December, at a point when Florence felt reassured: 'Fortunately all seems quite happy now here, & the foolish trouble has blown over – for good I hope.' She may have thought that Gertrude's going to London would remove her from the scene and so might help ensure that the foolish trouble remained over. She was confident enough to express the hope that, since Hardy's feelings had calmed down, she and Gertrude might resume their friendship and even, she said, find it strengthened.[10]

By early February, such ideas seemed hopelessly naive. Rehearsals in London were looming; Hardy was still infatuated with Gertrude, if anything more than before, and gossip was starting to spread, locally at least. Florence impulsively decided she must take some sort of action. She travelled to Beaminster, saw Gertrude privately and dissuaded her from performing in London. The excitement would endanger Hardy's health, she claimed; worse still perhaps, he would be bound to reveal to the whole world his feelings for Gertrude and this would cause not only his reputation but hers as well irreparable harm. Whether or not Gertrude believed any of this, she behaved discreetly and wrote to Hardy giving her husband's disapproval and her baby's needs as her reasons for withdrawing. More privately, she wrote to Florence questioning the reality of her fears. Florence was undeterred. 'I would give all I possess to be able to believe that all I have been so worried about was the result of overstrained nerves,' she replied:

> but I put that question to Dr Head, & he told me very emphatically that I was to put that out of my head at once, & not to be persuaded that my anxieties were a delusion. He has seen so much of the kind. And then Mr Cockerell [. . .] when I asked him if it were possible that I was suffering from an hallucination, he said he was afraid it was real enough. You see I know all that has been said here – to myself & other people.

Shrill, frightened and self-defensive, Florence insisted that Hardy had become fixated on Gertrude, despite Gertrude's innocent scepticism. A list of Florence's influential, eminent friends is called to witness but evidently, she had been obsessed herself, pressurizing people into agreeing with her.

Though the visit to Beaminster was kept strictly secret, Hardy must have had an inkling of Florence's feelings. He could not have missed or mistaken the hostility his wife felt for Gertrude nor been completely unaware that she was marshalling their friends against him. His suspicions had, in fact, been building up for some time. On 12 January 1925 as preparations for the London performances continued, there was a scene, witnessed by Cockerell, who was visiting at the time. Hardy was rude to Florence, telling her to her face that she was in the way and making it abundantly clear he was fully taken up with helping Gertrude get ready for the London stage. It was entirely typical of him that when Florence betrayed signs of jealousy, Hardy punished her by giving even more of his time and attention to Gertrude. 12 January was furthermore Florence's birthday and Hardy made no reference to it, just as he had always ignored Emma's birthday while she was alive. The row and its date confirmed that Florence now occupied Emma's place and must be prepared to suffer as Emma had suffered. Going to see Gertrude a few weeks later was Florence's way of fighting back against this repetition.[11] And it did appear to work. When Gertrude withdrew, Hardy did not protest; instead, drama temporarily lost all interest for him.

Early in February 1925 he had given his friend St John Ervine permission to revise the adaptation of *Tess*, with a view to performance in London. On the 19 February, after Gertrude's decision to turn down the part, Hardy suddenly changed his mind and told Ervine that he would not contemplate any further revision. And, with that, the project lapsed. Similarly, negotiations with Sybil Thorndike, who was keen to play the role, became tricky during 1925. Eventually, Hardy's nagging obstructiveness meant they came to nothing. He made himself busy with other projects, in particular the completion (with Sydney Cockerell's assistance) of another volume of poetry, *Human Shows*, whose manuscript was delivered in early August. These obstinacies and this busyness in his professional life proved that, although Florence might have seen off Gertrude – at least for the present – she had not dislodged her rival from her husband's heart nor won back his affection. She never really did.

Hardy became frailer, naturally, as he grew older and Florence turned more and more into his nurse. She believed that the 'un-natural excitement' caused by Gertrude's presence endangered Hardy's health, so she cosseted him. She encouraged the quietness that she had found oppressive before, successfully opposing for instance the idea of any further productions by the Hardy Players. Not surprisingly, she grew overprotective in some respects, and even stifling. While Hardy accepted her tender care and often felt grateful for it, there was no longer the same trust or intimacy between them after February 1925. Hardy's self-involvement and his dwelling on the past grew more pronounced. His engagement with his wife faded away. This was not quite the same as his coldness towards Emma after 1910 – after she had done to Florence what Florence was doing now to Gertrude; nonetheless, there were things in common. Hardy's anger about Gertrude turned into another lingering resentment, less fully acknowledged and never acted upon, except negatively, but resentment all the same.

Human Shows reveals something of this. It is another retrospective book, with very many of its poems set in the distant past – they recall Hardy's childhood in Bockhampton and the girls he fell for when a boy. Others look back to his time in London. As always, some of the poems remember Emma and several reinvoke Hardy's love for Florence Henniker. There are fewer than before expressing love for Florence Hardy herself. The one that comes closest also registers unease. When I am dead, the speaker confesses:

I shall be more myself, Dear, then,
Than I am now.

No sign of querulousness
To wear you out
Shall I show there[.][12]

Is this an apology or a shrug of the shoulders – a strangely unapologetic moment of self-acceptance? It is hard to tell. There seems no possibility of change during his lifetime in any case, so he and Florence must look forward to the afterlife for their proper happiness. The tone is very different from 'I Sometimes Think' and 'A Jog-Trot Pair', poems from *Late Lyrics*, celebrating the joy within their uneventful married life, or 'Conjecture' in *Moments of Vision*, which says that without 'Emma, Florence, Mary', Hardy would have died already.

And the poems Hardy wrote after *Human Shows* was finished were similarly preoccupied with areas of his life that Florence had no part in. *Winter Words*, when it was posthumously published, shed light on his relationship with Horace Moule, his 'romance' with Agnes Grove and his love for Louisa Harding, a girl he had known ever so slightly when a teenager. There was no reference in the book to Florence or to their life together. It is a self-referential volume, concerned to set the record straight before the end and determined to insist that Hardy's views, however uncomfortable and unpopular, remained the same. A number of poems, such as 'Our Old Friend Dualism' and 'A Philosophical Fantasy', were in the polemical, anti-religious vein he had avoided in recent collections and in fact both of these had been started earlier and set aside. Some of the poems Florence actively disliked, particularly the gruesome drama 'Aristodemus the Messenian', and she was 'afraid I annoyed T. H. by saying so'.[13] Annoyed or not, Hardy carried on regardless. Saying his piece was part of his response to the nearness of death – he would go down into silence unbowed, and he would at long last do what little he could to set his mind at rest about Horace Moule.

Even so, he did these things with greater commitment because, unjustly or not, he thought Florence had imprisoned him. Like his mother first and later Emma, Florence had tried to restrict his freedom of attachment. Lady Julia Martin had been taken away from him when he was a boy; Florence Henniker and Agnes Grove in middle age; Florence's treatment of Gertrude Bugler repeated the pattern yet again. There was little fight left in Hardy now and his life was enmeshed in

Florence's care for him. His only revenge lay in his poems. Where they do not insist on familiar, unpopular opinions, they are oblique to the point of obscurity; they burrow back into the past and refuse either to compromise or be drawn. The solitariness of the voice derives from Hardy's return, at the end of his life, to a determined solitude.

That went on amidst a breathtaking amount of work. Just as he was finishing *Human Shows*, in autumn 1925, Hardy heard from Philip Ridgeway, a young theatre producer. Ridgeway suggested that *Tess* could be performed in London, at first in the out-of-town Barnes theatre and afterwards, if it was successful, somewhere in the West End. Ridgeway was a dynamic and persuasive character and Hardy decided, whimsically almost, to give him a chance. He hoped at first that Ridgeway would consider Gertrude Bugler for the leading role but much to Florence's relief, Ridgeway refused and, surprisingly perhaps, Hardy did not take umbrage; instead, he helped as much as he could with the new production. It brought him increased publicity and the novel was serialized for a second time, in *John o'London's Weekly*, beginning in September 1925 when the play started its run. This reprinting brought Hardy more than £600. The play's success also had a knock-on effect on Hardy's other works. Macmillans felt able, for instance, to reprint a second time *The Famous Tragedy of the Queen of Cornwall*. The play had been warmly received when it was first published in 1923 and a pocket edition had followed early in 1924. An opera based on the play was performed at Glastonbury that summer, with music by Rutland Boughton and it too was highly regarded. Now the play appeared again, in one volume with *Late Lyrics*. In November, Hardy's new volume *Human Shows* came out. Although he feared he might be publishing too much too quickly, the book's first impression sold almost at once and was reprinted in the New Year.

Hardy had not enjoyed such popularity since *Tess* was a bestseller in 1892. Throughout 1926, buoyed up by the play and the press attention it received, his sales boomed. His royalties for the year to June 1925 were, in all, £4,400; for the year to October 1926, they were nearly £5,400, up by nearly a quarter. In response, Macmillan proposed several further new editions – early in 1926 an illustrated limited edition of *Tess* came out (Hardy was paid £300 for signing 325 copies); in April a standard-sized version of the same book was under way and in the summer *The Dynasts* came out in a limited edition. In the autumn, there was a London production of *The Mayor of Casterbridge* and, as with *Tess* the previous year, the novel was serialized again. Meanwhile, St John Ervine suggested dramatizing *Jude*. And so it went on into 1927. *John o'London* published one of Hardy's poems every week for six months that year; the *Argosy* began reprinting his short stories. Hardy, meanwhile, prepared a new *Selected Poems* and a one-volume *Short Stories* was set in motion.

The flurry of activity, attention and success excited and also exhausted Hardy. By autumn 1927, Florence's letters were becoming full of references to his tiredness: at the end of November, she reported 'T. H. is fairly well, but he feels very tired today, for no reason apparently, which always rather worries me.' A few days later, she said that he 'very soon becomes tired, especially when he has been talking'. Then, on the morning of 11 December, her worst fears began to be realized. That day Hardy:

> sat at the writing-table in his study, and felt totally unable to work. This, he said, was the first time that such a thing had happened to him.
>
> From then his strength waned daily.

He had become 'over-tired' Florence told friends and 'this has affected his heart'.

Until Christmas, Hardy still sat downstairs for some part of the day but after that he was in bed continuously. Early in the new year, there were some signs of improvement and on 11 January, after a month of illness, he seemed considerably better. He ate well that day, appreciated receiving the gift of a bunch of flowers and dictated two sardonic epitaphs – one directed against George Moore, who had attacked Hardy and his work several times, and one mocking G. K. Chesterton, the Catholic writer who had disputed with Hardy's religious views and ridiculed the person who could put them forward.[14] Seeing off these two old enemies meant that Hardy had, at last, 'cleared everything up'. The *Life* was as finished as he could make it; his extant, unpublished poems were ready to appear, and detailed arrangements had been made with his publishers about any future editions of his novels and poems. Meanwhile, Sydney Cockerell and Florence were both on hand to carry out his posthumous wishes. He had, he told Florence, 'done all he meant to do, but he did not know whether it had been worth doing'.[15]

Hardy had an exaggerated love of order and tidiness. His daily life was regulated down to the last detail while his writing controlled the turbulence of his inner life. It was this insistence on structured pattern rather than his old age that prevented him from trusting free verse, the modern style he certainly possessed the technical skill to embrace, if he had wanted to. All his life Hardy took pride in his reliable, efficient competence, whatever it was he was doing – in punctuality and thoroughness. Now he had cleared the desk of his life.

At the end of the day, Ellen Titterington took her turn watching Hardy. The rest of the household were downstairs eating dinner: Florence, her sister Eva, who was a trained nurse and had come to help, plus Sydney Cockerell who arrived a day or two earlier at Florence's request. When Eva came back upstairs after her meal, she and Ellen 'noticed a difference in Mr. Hardy'. Then, he suddenly cried out, 'Eva! Eva! what is this?' Ellen rushed to gather eiderdowns – 'just grabbing them from beds in the different rooms'; the doctor was called and the maids were sent downstairs to wait. Just before nine o'clock, Hardy died, from 'a sharp heart-attack'. Florence was at his side.[16] Businesslike as always, Sydney Cockerell immediately phoned the BBC. He was just in time to catch the nine o'clock news.

Max Gate

THERE WERE one or two loose ends – the manuscript of *Winter Words*, for instance, ran to only one hundred poems. Hardy had intended to publish the book on his ninetieth birthday, 2 June 1930, and by then, would have expected to have another fifty poems or so. Still, what he had written would make a considerable volume already and although Florence and Sydney Cockerell had one or two qualms about some of the poems, none of these were major. As in other areas, things seemed in place and Hardy seemed to have died pretty well in control of his future – the biography was written, its publication arranged and his literary executors appointed, both of them well acquainted with his wishes. The burial arrangements were elaborately thorough too and Hardy's desire to rest with his family in the graveyard at Stinsford was widely known. Almost at once, nevertheless, things started going wrong. Florence was thrown into shock as well as grief-stricken by his death. It 'is all too terrible', she told Rebekah Owen, 'like a dreadful nightmare'. Though her husband had lived longer than anyone expected, his death had come with appalling suddenness. Florence had seen nothing very out of the ordinary in his being laid up by illness during the winter and then in a moment he was gone. Sydney Cockerell and J. M. Barrie were the people she relied on at this time; both were friends equally of Hardy and herself and, of course, neither was affected quite as badly as Florence was. As she struggled to cope, they took control. Understandably, I think, Florence in the pain of her bereavement rather wanted them to take over and relieve her of the burden of responsibility.

Both men insisted that a funeral at Westminster Abbey was the least her husband deserved. It was what the nation would expect. It would be absurd and offensive to bury 'the one [. . .] figure of fulfilled genius in English literature' in an obscure country churchyard. Everybody knew perfectly well what Hardy had wanted. To share in death the same plot of Dorsetshire ground as the rest of his family had been extremely important to him.[1] Cockerell and Barrie went ahead regardless and the funeral took place in the Abbey on 16 January. The single concession to Hardy's desires (and those of his surviving relatives) was the removal of his heart from the body and its burial in Stinsford churchyard. In London, Hardy's pall-bearers were the Prime Minister, the Leader of the Opposition, A. E. Housman, George Bernard Shaw, Rudyard Kipling, John Galsworthy, Edmund Gosse and Barrie himself, plus the Master of Magdalene College, Cambridge and the President of the Queen's College, Oxford. Other eminent people occupied reserved seats in the Abbey. Crowds lined the streets in pouring rain. It is almost impossible to conceive of a writer being given such a send-off now – not in Britain anyway. Hardy's funeral was like Beethoven's or Tennyson's. It was one of the last echoes of the Victorian culture that venerated artists as prophets and sages and as sources of national identity. At exactly the same time, in a quiet and still remote part of the English countryside, Henry Hardy was chief mourner at the burial of Hardy's heart. Kate travelled up to London with Florence but she was glad to learn afterwards that at Stinsford, 'the good sun [had] shone & the birds sang & everything was done simply, affectionately & well'.[2]

Perhaps, as people said at the time, this division of Hardy's remains was symbolically appropriate. He had straddled two worlds, by being both a national celebrity and a local writer. In speaking for Dorset, he had come to speak for England as a whole. Florence, though, lived deeply to regret what had happened. Her decision – which at the time had really been her acquiescence in Cockerell's decision – felt like a betrayal. The family had been wounded by it; local pride had been hurt and, most importantly, Hardy's wishes had been ignored. No one much liked the fact that his body had been cut up and the Dean of Westminster had some doubts about burying a notorious unbeliever within the walls of his Abbey. Furthermore, almost before the funerals were over, life was moving rapidly on and leaving Hardy behind. There were plans for a memorial but an appeal for funds produced next to nothing and nothing would be done, it turned out, unless Florence and Kate provided the cash. A statue was erected eventually and unveiled by Barrie in September 1931; even so, it was an anticlimactic moment.

Similarly, the first volume of the *Life* when it was published at the end of 1928 sold poorly and Hardy's reputation fell into sudden decline as taste changed. With the Great Crash of 1929, followed by the

Depression of the 1930s, more explicitly political writing – by the Auden generation, George Orwell and Edward Upward – became more popular. This work did, at times, owe a great deal to Hardy but the similarities were ignored. In 1932, F. R. Leavis's *New Bearings in English Poetry* made modernism fashionable and consigned Hardy to the unfashionable Victorian past; likewise T. S. Eliot's critical influence grew enormously during the 1930s and his loathing for Hardy was virulent. In his 1933 book *After Strange Gods*, he accused Hardy of being literally possessed by the devil. Florence lived until 1937 and witnessed this decline in her husband's standing. As she aged, Hardy's achievements seemed to be fading away. Metropolitan opinion-formers disparaged his work and locals started to voice their dislike for the man.

Initially, once the first phase of intense grief had passed, Florence had felt some sense of relief at Hardy's death. It released her from her duty of care; she was well provided for, and she could please herself a little more both inside Max Gate and beyond. At one stage, she believed that J. M. Barrie wanted to marry her and that a future in London beckoned, a comfortable, cultured life surrounded by the literary and theatre people Barrie mixed with. When Barrie realized what Florence was hoping for, he instantly backed off, leaving Florence marooned in Dorchester and confronted by a new task – that of preserving Hardy's memory and legacy at a time when both threatened to disappear. This duty seemed to be hers alone because Sydney Cockerell was no help. As Florence's joint literary executor he had proved a bully, contemptuous of her and self-opinionated. Pretty quickly, the two of them could not get on. Edmund Gosse, whom Hardy had also considered as a possible executor and who would have done the job far more sensitively than Cockerell did, died soon after Hardy in the summer of 1928. Others who might have assisted had died already: Hamo Thornycroft in 1926, Agnes Grove the same year, Florence Henniker, whom Florence respected and relied upon, in 1923. She was left isolated and uncertain; those friends who did survive, such as Edward Clodd, who lived until 1930, she found to be untrustworthy. They lacked the disinterested dedication to Hardy's good that was required.

Three forces came to her and Hardy's rescue. American scholars and collectors like Richard Purdy and Frederick Adams ensured, during Florence's lifetime, that Hardy's work began to be properly preserved, collated and studied. Purdy's conversations with Florence became an important, if unreliable, biographical source. At the same time, unfashionable but gifted English writers such as Siegfried Sassoon and Edmund Blunden, who had known Hardy personally, kept arguing for the permanent value of his work. Blunden's concise biography of Hardy, published in 1942, was the first sign of Hardy's slow return to critical favour.[3] Thirdly, Florence received help from Hardy's family. Henry Hardy died the same year as his brother (on 8 December), leaving Kate, the youngest child of the four, as the closest surviving blood relative. She was the last of the line – none of the siblings had had children – and, like Florence, she felt responsible for her brother's memory. The two women, who had always got along pretty well, formed an alliance.

In 1937, when Florence knew she was dying, she bequeathed Max Gate to Kate. Kate, in her turn, gave the house to the National Trust when she died three years later. She added a clause in her will insisting that all the money raised by Max Gate was to contribute to the upkeep of Hardy's birthplace in Higher Bockhampton. None of the family had lived in the house for nearly thirty years and in 1938 it had been sold to a local farmer. Kate must have believed when she died that the house would, in time, be given to the nation and, in 1948, that is what happened. Erecting a statue, maintaining Max Gate and raising funds to do the same for Higher Bockhampton, encouraging scholarship: these were the public aspects of Kate and Florence's work on Hardy's behalf. Florence also performed more personal acts of homage and reparation. In the summer of 1929, Philip Ridgeway, who had put on *Tess* four years earlier, did so again at the Duke of York's Theatre. Florence approached Gertrude offering her the leading role and successfully persuaded her to accept it. She was a great success, being billed as 'Thomas Hardy's Own Tess' during the London run; and as Gertrude enjoyed her taste of theatre life, Florence's guilty conscience was set at rest.

Florence also erected informal memorials at Max Gate. During 1928, she installed a sundial, which had been designed by Hardy himself and made by local iron-founders in either 1926 or 1927. This addition left the house complete at last, just as Hardy would have wanted it. Placing a sundial so that it tells the time accurately is not straightforward, especially when the dial is fixed to a house, rather than free-standing. You need to know the longitude of the site and the alignment of the wall where the dial is placed. Hardy's plans show that he had worked out just the right angle required and the dial is accurate to within one minute. As an architect, perhaps he would have learnt how to make these calculations and there were dials on several of the churches where he worked in the 1860s and 1870s. Yet not all architects would have known how, nor still possessed the skills fifty years afterwards. His sundial is DIY taken to a sublime extreme. It is typical of his retentiveness, his thrift with expertise and his home-grown professionalism.

Hardy was in many areas an autodidact and critics have made fun of him for that. This reveals ignorance as well as prejudice – ignorance of the learning and talent of those who taught him: the Moule family, John Hicks and, most of all perhaps, of William Barnes. Although he felt (and was) socially disadvantaged by his provincial background, Hardy's experience actually reveals the extraordinary spread of talent across Victorian culture. He benefited from a semi-official network that distributed knowledge into far-flung corners of the country and to new classes of society – to those beyond the pale of Oxbridge and the public schools. Furthermore, in William Barnes, Hardy came across a quite outstanding mind.

Barnes was serenely unconventional, unambitious in worldly terms, and devoted to the pursuit of knowledge. If received wisdom thought his interests eccentric, Barnes was undeterred. He was, in the full sense, an independent scholar.

Hardy never equalled Barnes's self-containment and his true content; nonetheless, those qualities did rub off on him, and helped him maintain his self-belief despite disappointment and rejection. Moreover, without Barnes's example, Hardy would have been less able to comfort the demobbed soldiers who came to him after the First World War. He could not have conveyed the same calm, the awareness of horrors and ability all the same to sustain himself through them. By temperament, nonetheless, Hardy was a more conflicted person than Barnes – more driven, ambitious and needy. Praise mattered to him. London mattered. His self-sufficiency was more embattled – it expressed as much defiance as unconcern. Hardy would not be made to conform but neither would he be forced to retreat. Doing things his own way and doing them himself proved he was somebody to be reckoned with.

Even so, this stance has left him something of an outsider. For all his lasting popularity, he has never quite been granted the status of a classic and his reputation in the academy remains equivocal. Meanwhile, his persistent determination to remain independent of the mainstream has

made him hard to find. When Llewelyn Powys (younger brother of John
Cowper Powys) saw Hardy's statue unveiled, he was unimpressed. The
'soul of the man' was not visible in 'the graven image', he said.

> It is away somewhere else – on Bockhampton Heath perhaps, or
> hovering over the crinkled waters of the Frome or the Stinsford
> meadows[.][4]

This is still true, despite changes in the landscape. The use of fertilizers
has made the water meadows that Hardy knew a thing of the past. The
network of sluice ditches, dug during the eighteenth century when water
meadows were first introduced, stand empty and dry all down the Frome
valley east of Dorchester. Bockhampton Heath has been planted with
pines since the Second World War, though efforts are now being made
to restore some areas to their original vegetation. Despite the trees,
walking near Rushy Pond, you still follow the narrow, chalky pathways
of *The Return of the Native* and they are still littered with flints. You'll find
there the same ants' nests Hardy described. The green lane still runs
across the Frome Valley, from Norris Hill farm to West Stafford, which
Hardy's father would have used going to and from the brickworks at
Broadmayne or to Woodsford Castle, the first building Hardy surveyed.
Hardy's routes to school can still be found as well: the various tracks
across the fields down Stinsford Hill, or down to Lower Bockhampton,
and the path across the meadows from Kingston Maurward to Grey's
Bridge.

The scenes Llewelyn Powys identifies were and are the Hardy
territory – an area marked out by the houses at Higher Bockhampton
and Max Gate and by Talbothays too, with the working men's cottages
nearby. He explored it as a boy and in the course of his lifetime helped
his family to make it their own. His soul hovers over it still – over a tiny,
private kingdom, secretly and stubbornly independent, like Hardy himself, and over Max Gate too. The public sees just what Hardy intended
them to see: the two downstairs rooms at the front looking out over a
spacious lawn. The upstairs and the back of the house remain private;
the lawn to the right, the outhouses and side entrance to the left, and
the kitchen garden behind are inaccessible too. Visitors in Hardy's day
called at the front door and were shown in, as now, to the dining room
on the left, a shrine to the great writer, filled with what an admirer
might wish to see: a collection of his published works, sketches and
watercolours of the places he described, and a glass case showing the

Roman finds discovered when the house was built. On the days when May O'Rourke worked for the Hardys, she set up her typewriter in this room. It was the front office, where Hardy presented himself to his public, and just the appropriate place for May to type up fair copies of his poems and help Florence with the correspondence.

If you were asked to tea, you would cross the hall into the living room, with its large window, eight feet by nearly nine, and reaching down almost to floor level, which looked onto the front lawn, and a second giving a glimpse of the side lawn, through the conservatory. It was an airy, sometimes chilly room, filled with objects – a multitude of chairs and side-tables, pictures on the walls, and almost every available surface occupied by china ornaments of different kinds. Everything in it had a history, everything was in a sense a conversation piece, though the room displayed more of Hardy the gentleman than Hardy the writer. It was less biographical and more social; by being invited to tea, you were being invited, after admiring his achievements, to meet the man behind the books – the middle-class professional, the local historian, the magistrate, the man who could have spent his life (as Hardy sometimes wished he had done) in quiet, respectable usefulness as a country architect.

Hardy did live in these rooms – both he and Florence came in and out when May was working downstairs and they ate their meals together at the front of the house. The divisions between public and private were not rigid, not at least during the fifteen years when he was married to Florence. Equally Hardy genuinely embraced the role of country gentleman, not merely playing it or donning its mask when forced into the open. On the other hand, he did carefully arrange retreats and escape routes. The walled garden had a small back gate at the far end of the side lawn. There was a green velvet door as well inside the house across the passage that led from the hall to the kitchen. Behind that door were the backstairs that led up to the first floor, just beside Hardy's bedroom (his first study), concealed behind the main staircase. From there the backstairs went on up into the attics, where the servants slept. If Hardy wanted to avoid visitors, for whatever reason, he could slip round to the top of the backstairs, descend them, go out of a back door, across the garden and away. He would be, quite truthfully, not at home.

Likewise, his study became increasingly remote within the house as time went on. He lived in Max Gate for a little over forty years; for more than thirty of these, he wrote in a room hidden away at the back of the house. A stranger would not find it easily, because to reach it you turned unexpectedly off the main stairs two-thirds of the way up, went through two doorways and then walked down an unlit corridor. You might easily think these were servants' rooms, too modest and poky for the master of the house. At the end of the corridor, there is simply a door and on its left a tiny, cramped staircase going up to the loft. It is all entirely unpromising and yet behind the door, Hardy's study (which hardly anyone outside the household ever saw) proves to be a grand room, elegantly furnished, spacious and, after the darkness of the corridor, surprisingly light. It was painted a coral colour in Hardy's time, not the deep red used in the reconstruction of the room in the Dorset County Museum. The window beside Hardy's desk is, similarly, large for the room and looks east and south, bringing in the morning. When you enter the study, in other words, you come out into a secluded haven. This repeats on a small scale something that is true of the house overall. In Hardy's later life, when the trees he planted had grown, you would have had to go through a dark, forbidding circle of pines before arriving at the house, with its unexpectedly confident proportions and the airy elegance of the front room.

Amidst the neat orderliness of Hardy's workspace, you would have found as well almost innumerable pieces of memorabilia. Downstairs in the hall, a barometer that had belonged to William Barnes hung on the wall; over the mantelpiece in the front room, the serial illustrations to *Jude* by William Hatherill, which Hardy greatly admired, were displayed. In the study there was more of the same kind – further relics of Barnes, Hardy's first writing desk, his childhood books too and the music books owned by his father and grandfather. Their musical instruments were kept in this room, and on the table where Hardy wrote stood other reminders of his intimate life: the inkwell Florence Henniker had sent him, for instance, and a calendar showing the date when he first met Emma. With these objects around him, he could maintain his relation to himself, protecting it there. He needed such a rigidly maintained private space because without it his responsiveness to others and to the moment, his ability to be so various, would have overwhelmed his sense of who he intrinsically was. That essentially was what he feared in London; being so aware of his vulnerability to circumstance made him determined to create a sanctum, an inviolable place for himself.

Hardy was a polymath, expert in all sorts of different areas, and he was fascinated by the world – natural objects, famously, politics too, the Irish Home Rule debate, Palmerston's funeral, classical history, the history of farming, military uniforms, drains, sundials. His mind was voracious and so was his heart: right into extreme old age, women could sweep him off his feet. Against that eagerness for life and knowledge, he placed the discipline of work – to keep him in check, to lend him direction, to avoid disappointment – and similarly he stuck to his attachments. Lots of people observed the extraordinary accuracy of Hardy's memory, again right into his old age; as much he held on to facts, though, he held on to those he had loved – Moule, Barnes, Tryphena, Jemima, Florence Henniker, and Emma too. That was, in one respect, what his study was for and that too was his purpose in writing.

Emma's maid, Dolly Gale, rushed downstairs from Emma's bedroom on the day she died, knocked on Hardy's study door and told him, breathlessly, that her mistress seemed much worse. As Dolly remembered these events eighty years later:

> Hardy seemed oblivious to the request to come. "Right now," according to Dolly, "all he could say was 'Your collar is crooked', and was not a bit concerned". Even now Dolly still has apprehension in her voice as she recounts this incident. Dolly also remembers staring at a plaque on the desk rather than looking at Hardy's cold eyes. The words on the plaque are engraved forever on her mind and read: "Write, and with mine eyes I'll drink the words".[5]

This quotation was before him whenever he wrote. It promises that he will be heard: that if he writes someone, somewhere will eagerly, devotedly read what he has written; also, someone wants to hear from him.

The words are a quotation from *Cymbeline*, one of Hardy's favourite Shakespeare plays, and are spoken by Posthumus, the hero, to Imogen his wife. They come from near the beginning of the play, when the newly married couple is forced to part, a separation that sets the plot in train. Posthumus is a 'poor but worthy gentleman' and Imogen a princess, whose father Cymbeline is enraged by their secret marriage, imprisons Imogen and banishes Posthumus. It is a situation close to some of Hardy's deepest concerns; he would have seen himself in Posthumus, a poor man separated from his lady by class and parental self-interest; he would have known too from his courtship of Emma how desperately important letters could be between lovers, how fiercely you would 'drink' their written words.

Writing became for him a precious medium between human beings who were divided from each other by the accidents of circumstance and separated at a deeper level just by the condition of being an individual. Writing resolved the conflict he felt between loneliness and the frightening self-forgetfulness that social life could bring about. Through writing and reading, you could and did sustain yourself, asserting your feelings amd opinions, amidst the din of competing voices; at the same time, with luck, you spoke to others; you reached them and you gave them something essential that they needed, a drink for their thirsty soul. In that respect, Hardy was not a political writer (despite his political commitments and interests), nor was he a philosophical one, though he was similarly preoccupied with final questions. The sustaining power of poetry lay, for Hardy, in its ability to enable both you and other people fully to be.

Perhaps the most valuable thing Hardy left behind was his belief in 'loving kindness' – the quality Giles Winterbourne exemplifies and Marty South too, the way of life led by William Barnes. Much of Hardy's own behaviour of course fell far short of that ideal: he was not compassionate to Emma nor kind to her; he was as impatient, surly, resentful and small-minded as she was in their quarrels. He was demanding too with Florence, inflexible, tyrannical and sometimes querulously manipulative. Hardy was no hypocrite, though. He sought to be gentle and kind, and he knew how hard that was. He knew how much strength was needed to overcome vindictiveness or a hunger for power. That was why he needed his privacy so badly. As Hardy saw it and felt it, you could not show loving kindness unless you were self-possessed; without that, your commitment to other people's welfare would be compelled by them, or fickle, or a kind of self-abandonment to their needs. You would be no judge; you might indulge them where you should in fact hold back. And to be self-possessed you had to have a place where you could gather your strength. 'Loving kindness' was an ordeal in Hardy's eyes. It threatened the self and did not, despite Christ's promise, bring life in all its fullness. Instead, it was both supremely valuable and somehow against nature; it went against the grain of evolutionary self-interest and yet you could not give it up because that would mean sinking back into barbarism and war.

In his study, sheltered by the house and beyond it by the trees, Hardy gathered himself to face people and to reach out to them. He had to do that, if he was to go on fully being a person and fully being himself. To turn back into the shelter of his own occupations was his only way of engaging with the world outside. That did not make it easy to do or straightforwardly pleasurable to try. Hardy had a strong sense of humanity as anomalous within nature, that consciousness and sensitivity had not been intended by the Creator and set people at odds with the rest of creation. In such conditions, oblivion seemed preferable; writing disturbed oblivion, enhancing awareness and responsiveness, so perhaps it was a foolhardy or even a damaging activity. Hardy could at times believe or fear this; more often, though, he saw in writing his particular means of carrying out a responsibility borne by everyone alike – he found in it a test of his capacity to be human and loving, gentle and kind.

Notes

Life Thomas Hardy, *The Life and Work of Thomas Hardy*, edited by Michael Millgate (London and Basingstoke: Macmillan, 1984)

LiteraryN *The Literary Notebooks of Thomas Hardy*, vol. 1, edited by Lennart A. Björk (Basingstoke and London: Macmillan, 1985)

Millgate Michael Millgate, *Thomas Hardy: A Biography Revisited* (Oxford: Oxford University Press, 2004)

Monographs *Monographs on the Life, Times and Works of Thomas Hardy: nos. 1–72*, general editor, J. Stevens Cox (Guernsey: The Toucan Press, 1963–71)

PersonalN *The Personal Notebooks of Thomas Hardy*, edited by Richard H. Taylor (London and Basingstoke: Macmillan, 1978)

PersonalW *Thomas Hardy's Personal Writings: Prefaces – Literary Opinions – Reminiscences*, edited by Harold Orel (London and Melbourne: Macmillan, 1967)

Public Voice *Thomas Hardy's Public Voice: The Essays, Speeches, and Miscellaneous Prose*, edited by Michael Millgate (Oxford: Clarendon Press, 2001)

Seymour-Smith Martin Seymour-Smith, *Hardy* (London: Bloomsbury, 1994)

Sotheby's *The Library of Frederick B. Adams, Jr. Part II: Thomas Hardy* (London: Sotheby's, 2001)

SR Emma Hardy, *Some Recollections*, edited by Evelyn Hardy and Robert Gittings (London, New York, Toronto: Oxford University Press, 1961)

'SSN' *Thomas Hardy's 'Studies, Specimens &c.' Notebook*, edited by Pamela Dalziel and Michael Millgate (Oxford: Clarendon Press, 1994)

THJ *The Thomas Hardy Journal*

WA Thomas Hardy, *The Withered Arm and Other Stories: 1874–1888*, edited by Kristin Brady (Harmondsworth: Penguin, 1999)

References to Hardy's novels use the chapter and book numbering in the recent Penguin series, general editor, Patricia Ingham.

Introduction – Higher Bockhampton

1 *CP*, 588, 590, no. 545.
2 *CP*, 870–1, no. 855.
3 *CP*, 137, no. 100.

1 – A railway bore him through

1 *Under the Greenwood Tree*, Part 1, chapter 4.
2 *Under the Greenwood Tree*, Part 1, chapter 8.

3 *Under the Greenwood Tree*, TH's preface to the 1912 edition.
4 *Under the Greenwood Tree*, Part 1, chapter 4. Moule's review was in the *Saturday Review*, 28 September 1872.
5 *Life*, 25.
6 The same is true of Worcester. At one stage during the railway boom, there was a choice between Swindon and Worcester as regional centres of the railway industry. When Swindon was selected, Worcester was 'saved' and consigned to history.
7 *The Woodlanders*, chapter 1; the phrase was used as the title for a recent selection of Hardy's short stories (London and Vermont: Everyman Paperbacks, 1996).

2 – One who lived and died where he was born

1 See *Life*, 501–2. TH's copy of *The Boy's Own Book* was in Frederick B. Adams's collection, auctioned in 2001. TH's recollections of it are preserved in a note made by J. M. Barrie. See *Sotheby's*, 15.
2 *Life*, 19–21.
3 *Life*, 12, 17; 'The Dorsetshire Labourer', *PersonalW*, 188.
4 *Life*, 19, 26. J. Vera Mardon recalls Hardy's fondness for old folk tunes and folk dances in 'Thomas Hardy as a Musician', *Monographs*, no. 15, 14ff.
5 The Mellstock Band's CDs, *The Dance at the Phoenix* (Beautiful Jo Records, 1999) and *Under the Greenwood Tree* (Saydisc, 1986, recently reissued) include performances of several west gallery tunes. I'm grateful to Dave Townsend, director of the band, for talking to me about this topic. For a more detailed account, see Nicholas Temperley, *The Music of the English Parish Church*, 2 vols (Cambridge, London, New York, Melbourne: Cambridge University Press, 1979); for Hardy's use of this music in his novels, look at Caroline Jackson-Houlsten, *Ballads, Songs and Snatches* (Aldershot and Vermont: Ashgate, 1999)
6 The west gallery group, Vital Spark, perform the Magnificat from Jackson's E flat setting on their CD *Vital Spark*; see www.internetinsight.co.uk/vitalspark.
7 *Life*, 17.
8 *Life*, 11.
9 See *Millgate*, 18. I am indebted here to John Doheny's research; see his article, 'Biography and Thomas Hardy's Maternal Ancestors: the Swetmans', *THJ*, 11:2 (May 1995), 46–60.
10 *Life*, 11.
11 *Life*, 26, 'Hermann Lea's Notes for a Biography of Thomas Hardy', in *Monographs*, no. 20, 38.
12 'SSN', 3, 88.
13 Edwin Last, 'Thomas Hardy's Neighbours', *Monographs*, no. 51, 186.

3 – *She who upheld me and I*

1 *IR*, 135, quoted from Graves's *Goodbye to All That* (1929).

2 The journey took place either in 1847 or 1848, no one knows for sure which. In either year, Jemima was recovering from illness, suffering bereavement and enduring either imminent or recent separation from Mary. 1848 seems more likely because of Martha Caroline's death, which Jemima would have wanted to respond to.

3 *Life*, 501. This anecdote was not included by Hardy himself; J. M. Barrie encouraged Florence to add it and may have composed the wording.

4 'The Roman Road', 'In Tenebris III', *CP*, 169, 265, nos. 138, 218.

5 *Life*, 23.

6 *Life*, 22–3.

7 *Life*, 24–5.

8 *CP*, 715, no. 681.

9 *CP*, 458–9, 474–5, 601, nos. 388, 414, 555. See also 'A Young Man's Epigram on Existence', *CP*, 299, no. 245.

10 *Life*, 20.

11 *Life*, 23–4.

12 *Life*, 11–12; *CP*, 3, 274–5, nos. 1 and 227.

13 *CP*, 3; *Two on a Tower*, Vol. 1, ch. 2.

4 – *'The playground of TH's childhood'*

1 *Life*, 36.

2 *Life*, 27, 29.

3 *Life*, 502.

4 TH had drawn the same view in a sketch from 1863 which, like the watercolour, shows a sunken lane, shadowed by trees on the left and with fencing on the right. In the middle of the background, as the focal point of the composition, lie the houses and spires of Dorchester. He chooses the same perspective in his novels. Fanny Robin, in *Far From the Madding Crowd* (1874), struggles towards Casterbridge from this direction and she too sees, TH says, a 'halo' over the town. Near the beginning of *The Mayor of Casterbridge*, Susan and Elizabeth-Jane see the town from the same angle, laid out before them. These passages are worth comparing with Jude's view of Christminster from the downs near Marygreen.

5 *Monographs*, no. 70, 485.

6 *Monographs*, no. 44 ('Memories of Thomas Hardy as a Schoolboy' by Charles Lacey), 102.

7 *Life*, 28, 36.

8 *Life*, 32.

9 Quoted in Giles Dugdale, *William Barnes of Dorset* (London: Cassell & Co., 1953), 168.

10 He had written one poem in dialect before, but the majority of his 1860s poetry had been highly literary.

11 *PersonalW*, 102.

5 – His kindred they, his sweetheart I

1 *Life*, 36, 468.

2 Henry Bastow to TH, 17 February 1861 (DCM).

3 'Memories of Church Restoration' (1906), *Public Voice*, 251.

4 In 1849, Ferrey built a church and a village school at Tincleton, just a few miles from where Hardy was growing up.

5 *Life*, 20.

6 *Monographs*, no. 27, 'Paupers, Criminals, and Cholera at Dorchester in 1854'.

7 TH wrote about these events in his late short story 'A Changed Man' (1900) and he portrayed Fordington – as the Mr Hyde to Dorchester's Dr Jekyll – in the Mixen Lane community of *The Mayor of Casterbridge*.

8 Handley C. G. Moule, *Memories of a Vicarage* (London: Religious Tract Society, 1913), 50. TH read this book when it appeared. See *CL*, IV, 326 and n. The revival coincided with Moule's thirtieth year in Fordington and maybe the anniversary contributed to what took place.

9 *Life*, 35.

10 Handley Moule, *Memories of a Vicarage*, 35.

11 After the cholera outbreak, Henry Moule patented an earth closet, a toilet that would convert human waste into manure, providing fertilizer while also preventing illness.

12 For the importance of Palgrave to TH's poetry, see Dennis Taylor, *Hardy's Metres and Victorian Prosody* (Oxford: Clarendon Press, 1988).

13 Horace Moule, *Christian Oratory: An Inquiry into its History During the First Five Centuries* (Cambridge: Macmillan & Co., 1859), 6.

14 *CL* I, 3.

15 *CP*, 429.

16 *Life*, 38.

17 See *Monographs*, no. 11, 'Thomas Hardy proposes to Mary Waight'.

6 – One who walks west, a city-clerk

1 *CL* I, 2. Michael Millgate identifies 'Miss A.' as Eliza Amey from Dorchester (see *Millgate*, 77).

2 Quoted in Eric de Maré, *The London Doré Saw: A Victorian Evocation* (London: Allen Lane, The Penguin Press, 1973), 32.

3 'The Woman I Met', *CP*, 592–3, no. 547.

4 *Life*, 49.
5 *Life*, 47.
6 *Life*, 38, 49.
7 Horace Moule to TH, 21 February 1864 (DCM).
8 *Life*, 49.
9 *Life*, 50.
10 *Life*, 49.
11 *Life*, 58.
12 *Life*, 50.

7 – If but some vengeful god would call to me

1 *CP*, 468.
2 *CP*, 11.
3 *Life*, 50–1.
4 The only source of this note is TH's autobiography, so it may be doctored.
5 Henry Bastow to TH, 23 December 1863 (DCM).
6 *Life*, 12.
7 'SSN', 6 and 94.
8 'SSN', 1, 9, 10; *CP*, 81, no. 52.
9 'SSN', 46–7.
10 'SSN', 48.
11 'SSN', 60, 62.
12 TH to Mary Hardy [1866], *CL* I, 7; *Life*, 52–3.

8 – Red roses and smug nuns

1 *CP*, 16, no. 17.
2 *CP*, 14, no. 13.
3 *Life*, 43.
4 Maybe it's far-fetched to think of Angel Clare's fatal conversation with Tess as carrying some memory of TH's relationship with Moule. Clare confesses to Tess that he has had an affair in the past – in London, with a prostitute – and even though she forgives him, he finds himself unable to reciprocate when she confesses her own sexual history. Insofar as Clare portrays Moule, this incident would suggest that TH saw in his friend a moral severity that resisted confidences – a severity made more severe by guilt – and that if he had wanted to talk about his sexual life to somebody in 1866, Moule would not have been the best person to choose.
5 TH quoted this letter in his *Life*, 371; see also *Life*, 42–3.
6 From 'Hymn to Proserpine', 'To Victor Hugo', 'Laus Veneris' and 'Dolores', all in Swinburne's *Poems and Ballads: First Series*.
7 'SSN', 57.

8 'Laus Veneris', ll.305–16.
9 *CP*, 323, no. 265.
10 'SSN', 70–1; Habakkuk 1:2–4.
11 'SSN', 69.
12 Here and quotations in two preceding paragraphs from *Life*, 54.

9 – Believed-in things

1 *Life*, 57–8.
2 TH in conversation with Edmund Gosse, 1921; passage quoted from Thomas Hardy, 'An Indiscretion in the Life of an Heiress', ed. Terry Coleman (London: Hutchinson, 1976), 12.
3 *Life*, 13.
4 *LiteraryN* I, 7, entry no. 20. The entry is dated sometime between 1865 and 1867.
5 'SSN', 77, 80–2; *PersonalN*, 3.
6 *Far From the Madding Crowd*, chapter 56; 'SSN', 81–2.
7 *Life*, 57.
8 'An Indiscretion', 49.
9 See Lois Deacon and Terry Coleman, *Providence & Mr Hardy* (London: Hutchinson, 1966), 20–4, 112–20, 183–96.
10 *Seymour-Smith*, 92–8; *Millgate*, 98–9.
11 Robert Gittings suggests this in *Young Thomas Hardy*, 122. See also *Providence & Mr Hardy*, 123–34.
12 *Millgate*, 98.
13 *Return of the Native*, Bk VI, chapter 3.
14 *CP*, 62–3, nos. 38 and 39.
15 Fancy plays the organ in church, as Mary did when she was teaching in Denchworth in the early 1860s. The vicar of Mellstock is young and full of plans to reform both building and services. The same was true in Stinsford and in Denchworth too: Thomas Hawkins, the incumbent during Mary's time there, was in his early thirties and energetically restoring the fabric.

10 – Rising and falling with the tide

1 TH to Alexander Macmillan, 25 July 1868, *CL* I, 7.
2 Quoted from Charles Morgan, *The House of Macmillan, 1843–1943* (London: Macmillan & Co., 1943), 87–8; Hardy paraphrased Morley's report in *Life*, 60, toning it down if anything.
3 Morgan, *House of Macmillan*, 88–91.
4 *CL*, 8.
5 *CP*, 75, no. 49; first published in *Wessex Poems*.

6 *Life*, 59.
7 Arthur Waugh, *A Hundred Years of Publishing: being the story of Chapman & Hall, Ltd.*, (London: Chapman & Hall, 1930), 146.
8 Note recorded in *Life*, 60.
9 The church hall at Windsor, designed by Hardy, was built finally during the 1980s. Blomfield's more famous Oxford commission, the church of St Barnabas in Jericho (1869), probably came just too late for Hardy to have been involved, though he certainly knew of it; he used Blomfield's building as the model for the Tractarian church that ensnares Sue at the end of *Jude the Obscure*.
10 Waugh, *A Hundred Years of Publishing*, 149.
11 *Life*, 65.
12 *Life*, 66.
13 *CP*, 224, no. 174.

11 – With magic in my eyes

1 *IR*, 33.
2 *SR*, 55.
3 *Life*, 77–8; *CP*, 351, 353, nos. 291, 292.
4 *Life*, 81; *CP*, 336, no. 276, 'Under the Waterfall'.
5 *CP*, 455, no. 384.
6 *CP*, 256, 479–80, nos. 191, 'The Minute before Meeting' and 420. See *CP*, 346, no. 285.
7 *SR*, 60; *Life*, 80, 85.
8 *CP*, 18, no: 18, ll. 37–40.
9 *Life*, 79.
10 Simon Gattrell, *Hardy the Creator: A Textual Biography* (Oxford, 1988) has done a lot to open up this aspect of Hardy's working practice.
11 The *Analysis* included more than 700 examples of doors and windows from parish churches up and down the country; *Parish Churches* chose sixty-three churches, again from all over England, and provided perspective drawings of each, plus a ground plan and short description. *Open Timber Roofs* did the same for thirty-five of the finest church roofs in the country.
12 Gosse records this in his autobiography, *Father and Son* (1907).
13 *Life*, 81, 82.
14 Alexander Macmillan to TH, 18 October 1871, *The House of Macmillan*, 99.
15 *Life*, 89.
16 *Life*, 89.

12 – That there should have come a change

1 See *CL* I, 18, 19; *Life*, 91–2.
2 *Life*, 100.

3 *PersonalN*, 5–8.

4 *Life*, 89.

5 *Life*, 92, 98–9; *CL* I, 24.

6 *IR*, 8; reprinted from William Tinsley, *Random Recollections of an Old Publisher* (London, 1900); *CL* I, 34.

7 *CL* I, 34.

8 In the *Life*, Hardy remembers George Smith, at Macmillan, suggesting he ask Tinsley to sell him back the copyright; see *Life*, 104.

9 *CL* I, 23.

10 *A Pair of Blue Eyes*, Vol. II, chapter 5. TH is describing a well-established pattern in the period, 'as (mainly male) reviewers judged the work of (mainly female) new novelists, whose work had initially been accepted by male editors' (Valerie Sanders, 'Women, fiction and the marketplace', *Women and Literature in Britain 1800–1900*, ed. Joanne Shattock (Cambridge: Cambridge University Press, 2001), 142–61 (145). Women began to enter journalism more widely during the 1870s.

11 *Far From the Madding Crowd*, chapter 20.

12 *Far From the Madding Crowd*, chapter 55.

13 *Life*, 102–3; *LettersEF*, 3.

14 West Stafford and the Smith family are evoked well in Margaret Smith's article in *THJ* 19:3 (October 2003), 57–66.

15 *CL* I, 26.

16 *CP*, 621, no. 577.

17 *Life*, 96.

18 Report of the inquest in the London *Standard*, 23 September 1873, 3.

19 *Life*, 98–9.

20 *PersonalN*, 6–7.

21 *CP*, 887, no. 874.

13 – Wasted were two souls in their prime

1 *PersonalN*, 14–17.

2 F. W. Maitland, ed., *The Life and Letters of Leslie Stephen* (London: Duckworth, 1906), 266.

3 R. L. Purdy, *Thomas Hardy: A Bibliographical Study* (London: Oxford University Press, 1954), 336–8; on this subject, see Tony Slade's persuasive article in *THJ* 1:2 (May 1985), 31–40.

4 See Hermione Lee, *Virginia Woolf* (London: Chatto & Windus, 1996), 50–78 for a vivid portrait of Stephen.

5 Leslie Stephen, 'The Broad Church', *Essays on Freethinking and Plainspeaking* (London: Longmans, Green & Co., 1873), 20, 39.

6 George Eliot's early short story, 'Janet's Repentance', in *Scenes of Clerical Life* (1857) sums up this view of Christianity.

7 *SR*, 50, 53.

8 *CL* I, 31.
9 These details have recently been discovered by Mark Davison and Colin Prendergast; see *Hook Remembered Again* (Reigate: Mark Davison, 2001), 10–18.
10 *Life*, 188, 218; Henry James to Alice James, 17 February 1878, quoted Hermione Lee, *Virginia Woolf*, 94.
11 *Life*, 110; *EHDiaries*, 56.
12 *EHDiaries*, 103.
13 *CP*, 429, no. 355. The poem was first published in *Moments of Vision* in 1917. Hardy revisited Swanage in 1916 and the visit may have prompted the poem.
14 *EHDiaries*, 54, 103. In quotations, I have reproduced as far as possible the layout of the original.
15 *EHDiaries*, 75; *Life*, 113.
16 *EHDiaries*, 40.
17 *EHDiaries*, 36.
18 *Life*, 114; *EHDiaries*, 90, 93.
19 *EHDiaries*, 88, 90, 93, 100–1; *Life*, 114; *SR*, 48.
20 *EHDiaries*, 23; To Lady Hoare, 24 April 1910, *LettersEF*, 48.
21 *SR*, 51–2.
22 Quoted in *SR*, 91.
23 *IR*, 33.

14 – Lifelong to be I thought it

1 *CL* I, 41, 43.
2 When TH quoted from Stephen's letter in the *Life*, he cut out the sentence about Sand. Sand had also been recommended before, in the 1860s.
3 The rest of his early poetry was notably literary, drawing heavily on Shakespearean models, on other Renaissance poets and on Swinburne.
4 The poem first appeared in the *Gentleman's Magazine* and *Appleton's Journal*; it was later retitled 'The Bride-Night Fire' and included in *Wessex Poems*; *CL* I, 38, 40. Hardy had not read *Lorna Doone* until this year, when he had also met Blackmore.
5 See *PersonalN*, 12 and 'The Withered Arm' *WA*, 343–4 and *SR*, 40–1.
6 *SR*, 46–7, 58–9.
7 *SR*, 59.
8 *EHDiaries*, 65. The 'k' in 'Picknic' is crossed out.
9 Kate Hardy to ELH, dated by TH 1881–3 (their time living in Wimborne) (DCM). It's more likely because of the letter's style and its references to Bournemouth that it dates from 1875 when they were at Swanage.
10 Kate Hardy to ELH, dated respectively 23 September 1881, 1882, 1881–3 and 1882 (DCM).
11 Mary Hand's letter is held in the DCM.
12 *ECStories*, 16.
13 *Life*, 118–19.

14 See Denys Kay-Robinson, *The First Mrs Thomas Hardy* (London and Basingstoke: Macmillan, 1979), 127–8.

15 *CL* VII, 5, TH to Lady Pinney, 20 January 1926.

16 The most direct instance of voyeurism in TH's work can be found in *A Laodicean* (1881), Bk II, chapter 7, where the heroine is observed doing gymnastics; an older man looking through a hole in the wall of the gym sees her in 'a pink flannel costume which showed to perfection every curve of her figure', rather as Martha Browne's bodice does.

17 *SR*, 16–17.

18 See *SR*, 57, 59: 'my sister was very important'; and FEH to Rebekah Owen, 24 October 1915; see also Kay-Robinson, *First Mrs Thomas Hardy* 78, 112, 179.

19 *SR*, 29, 50, 56.

20 At some unknown date, she crossed these out; *EHDiaries*, 55–6.

15 – Some hid dread afoot

1 *Life*, 121.

2 See Gattrell, *Hardy the Creator*.

3 See John Sutherland, *Victorian Novelists and Publishers* (London: Athlone Press, 1976).

4 *CL* I, 52, 54–5, 59.

5 'A Two-Years' Idyll', *CP*, 629, no. 587.

6 *CL* I, 65.

7 Helen Allingham, née Paterson, had drawn the illustrations for *Far From the Madding Crowd*. See above, chapter 12.

8 *CL* I, 79–81.

9 *Life*, 142–3.

10 See *LiteraryN*, 134, 370; entries 1203–12 and n. Hillebrand's article appeared in the June 1880 number of the *Nineteenth Century*.

11 *CL* I, 70.

12 *ECStories*, 152; see *Millgate*, 201; *Seymour-Smith*, 264–5.

13 *Life*, 96, 145.

14 *CL* I, 71.

15 *WA*, 111.

16 *CP*, 466, 733; nos. 400, 701.

16 – No such bower will be known

1 *CL* I, 82–6.

2 *Life*, 151, 153.

3 *LiteraryN*, 136, no. 1217.

4 See Brenda Flint, *Thomas Hardy in Wimborne 1881–1883* (Ferndown: Power Publications, 1995).

5   *PersonalN*, 21–4; *Life*, 158.

6   *CL* I, 92, 101–2; *Life*, 154, 155.

7   *CL* VII, 93–4; *Life*, 156.

8   *CL* I, 99–103, 104, 108.

9   *CL* I, 109; *Life*, 160; *CL* I, 114.

10 *Seymour-Smith*, 295–7.

11 *CL* VII, 94.

12 *CL* I, 89.

13 *IR*, 108, quoted from Ann Thwaite, *Portraits from Life* (London, 1991).

14 *CP*, 256–7, no. 192.

15 See *Public Voice*, 62–3; *IR*, 20–3; the article, entitled 'Celebrities at Home', appeared in the *World*, February 1886; it gives further details about the Roman remains discovered at Max Gate, using the same wording as TH's paper to the Dorset Field Club (not yet published in 1886), so it was very likely TH's work, at least in part; the whole article is reprinted in *THJ* 2: 2 (May 1986), 42–7.

16 *Life*, 167.

17 It may be he adopted this design from their house in Surbiton.

17 – Taking the universe seriously

1   *CL* VII, 94.

2   *CL* I, 114; *CritHeritage*, 100–2.

3   To Gosse, 10 December 1882; *CL* I, 110.

4   The illustrations to 'The Romantic Adventures of a Milkmaid' are reprinted in Philip Allingham's article in *THJ* 16: 3 (October 2000), 45–62.

5   The *Graphic*'s weekly parts could not be bound together into book form as the monthly parts of other magazines were, so using this outlet may have made it easier for TH to keep separate in his mind the magazine version of his novels and their book version.

6   *CL* I, 65, 116.

7   *CL* I, 111 (TH to Alfred Austin, 16 December 1882) and 113 (TH to A. P. Watt (?), 15 January 1883).

8   *CL* I, 107. It's a sign of TH's prestige that he was asked to contribute to a new project; a similar request was made in March 1883 by Wilfred Meynell, for his new magazine *Merry England*; see *CL* II, 15–16; in 1880 *A Laodicean* had been commissioned for serial publication in the new European edition of *Harper's New Monthly Magazine*.

9   *CL* I, 119.

10 See *PersonalN*, pp. 150–2, no. 1296; and Simon Trezise, ' "Here's Zixpence Towards That Please God": Thomas Hardy, Joseph Arch and Hodge', *THJ* 6: 2 (June 1990), 48–62.

11 'The Dorsetshire Labourer', *Public Voice*, 52.

12 *Public Voice*, 44, 53–4.

13 *Public Voice*, 38–9.

14 In the second passage Hardy combines two senses of watch – to observe and to stay awake. There are numerous examples of Elizabeth-Jane's watching; see particularly chapters 15, 22 and 24. It's a similar idea to that in Doris Lessing's *Mara and Dann: An Adventure* (London: Flamingo, 1999) where education is conducted solely through a process of question and answer at the end of the day, the question being, again and again, 'What have you seen today?'

15 *CL* I, 121, 123.

16 'Our Exploits at West Poley' began to be serialized in the *Household* in November 1892.

17 The notebook is held in DCM and has recently been published: *Thomas Hardy: The 'Facts' Notebook*, edited by William Greenslade (Aldershot and Burlington, VT: Ashgate, 2004).

18 Greenslade (ed.), *Facts Notebook*, 7, 121, 124–5.

19 Thomas Hardy, 'The Late Mr. T. W. H. Tolbort, B.C.S.', DCC, 16 August 1883, *Public Voice*, 59.

20 *Life*, 168.

21 See *Millgate*, 20.

22 *WA*, 251.

23 Jemima had been pregnant with TH when she married; in the *Life*, TH stated that the germ of 'Interlopers at the Knap' was a story he heard in December 1882 concerning a girl 'who had been betrayed and deserted by her lover' and who then refused to marry, 'not caring to be "made respectable"'. (*Life*, 162–3.)

24 *Mayor of Casterbridge*, chapter 12; *Jude the Obscure*, Part VI, chapter 11.

18 – Life-loyalties

1 See his poem, 'Great Things', *CP*, 474–5, no. 414.

2 It was not unusual to do so. The temperance movement was a powerful influence around this time, especially in Liberal circles, and TH would often stay at the West Central Temperance Hotel, in Bloomsbury, when visiting London for short periods. See *Life*, 163; *THJ* 9: 2 (May 1993), 19–22 – in Fran Chalfont's third article on TH's residences.

3 *Life*, 173, 179.

4 *Life* 177, 209.

5 *Life*, 186, *CL* I, 144, 148–9.

6 *Life*, 187.

7 *CL* I, 146, 149, 154, 157; Gissing's letter is quoted in *Life*, 189.

8 Emma was, Hardy said, 'almost the last person – if not the very last – outside his family, whom he was able to converse with' (*CL* I, 153.)

9 *Life*, 167.

10 *Life*, 191, 192.

11 *Life*, 192.
12 *EHDiaries*, 125, 173, 186.
13 *Life*, 196; *EHDiaries*, 113, 138, 144, 146.
14 *Life*, 183.
15 *CP*, 64, no. 40; *Woodlanders* chapter 3.
16 *CL* I, 136.
17 *CL* I, 167.
18 *CL* I, 171.
19 *CL* I, 174, 182, 187, 188, 189.
20 *CL* I, 172.

19 – If the true artist ever weeps

1 R. H. Hutton, *Spectator*, 26 March 1887, *CritHeritage*, 142.
2 *CL* I, 250.
3 *Life*, 232; *CL* I, 200, 201.
4 *CL* I, 149; *Life*, 189.
5 His prefaces to the collected editions in 1895–6 and 1912, plus his 'Apology' in *Late Lyrics* of 1922, make up the rest of his published critical writing.
6 'Candour in English Fiction', *New Review*, January 1890, *PersonalW*, 126, 129, 130.
7 *PersonalW*, 112.
8 *CritHeritage* 147, 176.
9 *CL* I, 192. Millgate dates the visit to September 1889, Gittings to 1885. Mabel says (in the letter from 1937 which is the sole source of information) that Max Gate was 'then raw-new' and that TH read aloud from a novel he was 'engaged on', either *The Woodlanders* in 1885 or *Tess* in 1889.
10 Graham R. Tomson, *The Bird-Bride: A Volume of Ballads and Sonnets* (London: Longmans, Green & Co., 1889); for inscription, see Maggs Sale Catalogue, 1938, No. 664, item 197; *CL* I, 199, 206, 207.
11 TH to Rosamund Tomson, 6 October 1889, *CL* I, 200.
12 *CL* II, 24.
13 *Tess of the d'Urbervilles*, chapter 11.
14 *CL* I, 238, 239.
15 *Life*, 229, 230. Thomas Campion (1567–1620) describes a beautiful woman's lips as 'rose-buds filled with snow' in his poem 'There is a Garden in her Face'.
16 *Life*, 247.
17 *CP*, 480, no. 421. See *Life*, 233 for the date of composition (and the names of the bevy).
18 *CL* I, 249; *Tess of the d'Urbervilles*, chapters 23, 24.
19 'Thoughts of Phena', ll. 7–8, *CP*, 62, no. 38.

20 – That we had all resigned for love's dear ends

1 See TH to ELH, 5 December 1890: 'Probably I shall just save the Copyright of Tess in America – owing to delay. If all goes well how fortunate.' (*CL* I, 222.)

2 *Life*, 252, 268.

3 Hardy referred to the death in the *Life* but this passage was cut by FEH when preparing the manuscript. See Denys Kay-Robinson, *The First Mrs Hardy*, 143.

4 See *THJ* 5: 1 (January 1989); Hardy also looks straight out of William Strang's remarkable and little-known 1896 portrait, which is reproduced in *THJ* 9: 1 (February 1993) and discussed there by Dennis Taylor.

5 See Helen Upton, 'Hamo Thornycroft and Thomas Hardy', *THJ* 13: 2 (May 1997), 60–5.

6 Among them, Lena Milman, another society novelist, and her father, Keeper of the Tower of London.

7 *CL* II, 11, 13.

8 *CL* II, 20, 22, 23; letters of 2 July, 13 July, 16 July.

9 *Life*, 273.

10 To FH, 29 June 1893, *CL* II, 18.

11 *CL* II, 18.

12 *CL* II, 23, 26; letters of 16 July, 20 July.

13 *Life*, 273, 274.

14 *CL* II, 27–8.

15 See *CL* II, 23; letter of 16 July.

16 *CP*, 68–9, no. 45; FH and TH were both reading *Epipsychidion* in summer 1893, see *CL* II, 23. The poem closes in a long invitation from the speaker to his beloved, Emily, to join him on an idyllic Greek island and live there alone, 'Possessing and possest by all that is | Within that calm circumference of bliss, | And by each other, till to love and live | Be one' (ll. 549–52).

17 *CL* II, 48.

18 Hallam Tennyson, *Alfred Lord Tennyson: A Memoir*, 2 vols (London: Macmillan & Co., 1897), II, 115; A. M. Terhune, *The Life of Edward Fitzgerald* (London: Oxford University Press, 1947), 62, records Fitzgerald's embarrassment when he cannot provide a photograph of himself for Charles Eliot Norton. Hardy asked FH for a photograph of her husband when he went off to fight in South Africa in 1899.

19 'The Heart of the Color Sergeant' in Florence Henniker, *In Scarlet and Grey: Stories of Soldiers and Others and 'The Spectre of the Real'* by Thomas Hardy and Florence Henniker (Boston and London: Roberts Bros. and John Lane, 1896), 12, 13. See *CL* II, 44 (to FH, 18 December 1893), 71–2 (to Clement Shorter, 7 and 14 March 1895). Roger Ebbatson writes interestingly about their collaboration in *An Imaginary England: Nation, Landscape and Literature, 1840–1920* (Aldershot and Burlington, VT: Ashgate, 2005), 83–97.

20 *In Scarlet and Grey*, 15, 29
21 *CL* II, 233.

21 – No balm for all your sorrow

1 *LettersEF*, 15; ELH to Elspeth Grahame, 20 August 1899.
2 *LettersEF*, 76, 86, 88.
3 To ELH, 9 December 1890, 24 January 1891 and to Edmund Gosse, 10 December 1890, *CL* I, 223, 224, 227. For 'dear Em' and 'dearest Em', see among others his letters to ELH, 10 December 1890 and 24 July 1893, *CL* I, 223, II, 27. His previous extant letter to ELH, dated 16 March 1893, a few months before the meeting with FH, begins 'My dearest Em' (*CL* II, 5).
4 Simon Gatrell suggests this in *Hardy the Creator*, 42–3.
5 'A Tragedy of Two Ambitions' (1888), collected in *Life's Little Ironies* (1894) foreshadows *Jude* more directly through its plot.
6 *CP*, 789, no. 762.
7 *Jude the Obscure*, Part VI, chapter 3.
8 Emma Lavinia Hardy, *Poems and Religious Effusions*, *Monographs* no. 29, 8, from her volume *Alleys* (1911).
9 ELH to Mary Hardy, 22 February 1896, *LettersEF*, 8.
10 To FH, 15 January 1894 and 12 August 1895, *CL* II, 47, 84.
11 *Jude*, Part VI, chapter 3; *CP*, 136, 320, nos. 99, 261.
12 To FH, 16 July 1893, *CL* II, 23.
13 'Bridehead' also echoes 'Bird-Bride', the title of Rosamund Tomson's book of poetry; some of Sue's clothing resembles Rebekah Owen's. In this novel, apparently, all of Hardy's recent romantic interests were being resurrected – the last and most serious of them with the greatest intensity.
14 ELH to Mary Haweis, 13 November 1894, and to Mary Hardy, 22 February 1896, *LettersEF*, 6–8.

22 – The day goeth away

1 *CritHeritage*, 249–50, 255, 257.
2 *St James Gazette*, 8 November 1895, 4.
3 *Life*, 287, 288, 309.
4 *Life*, 241, 245.
5 See *LiteraryN*, 385, entry 1321n.
6 *CL* II, 33; 'Sarah Grand' was the pseudonym of Mrs Frances Elizabeth MacFall (1862–1943).
7 Arguably, *Jude* is also the novel that has transferred to film with least distortion, in the version with Christopher Eccleston and Kate Winslet.
8 *Life*, 237, 274. TH had always been interested in 'temperament' as a way of differentiating between people. In 1863, he had drawn diagrams showing the

various types of temperament that people fall into, based on the French philosopher, Charles Fourier's *Passions of the Human Soul*. *The Mayor of Casterbridge* was subtitled '*The Story of a Man of Character*' and when he published a revised version of *The Pursuit of the Well-Beloved* he called it *The Well-Beloved: A Sketch of a Temperament*. See *LiteraryN*, 3–4.

9   *Lady Gregory's Diaries, 1892–1902*, edited James Pethica (Gerrards Cross: Colin Smythe, 1996), 126.

10 *Life*, 292, 293; TH to Grant Allen, 7 January 1896, to ELH, 3 February 1896, to Lady Jeune, 20 April 1896, *CL* II, 106, 109, 116.

11 It is not known where the piano was kept, but there was nowhere suitable apart from the front living room.

12 *Life*, 298; TH to Agnes Grove, 25 August 1896, *CL* II, 128; *Life*, 299, 301.

13 TH to Sir George Douglas, 25 March 1897, to Lady Jeune, 29 March 1897, to Edmund Gosse, 31 March 1897, *CL* II, 154, 156, 157.

14 TH to FH, 12 October 1896, *CL* II, 134.

15 *Life*, 302. Simon Gattrell has studied these revisions closely; see his *Thomas Hardy's Vision of Wessex* (Palgrave: Basingstoke and New York, 2002) and the related website: <http://www.english.uga.edu/Wessex>.

16 TH to FH, 30 December 1896, *CL* II, 141. See *Life*, 310 and *CL* II, 162–6.

17 *Life*, 211; ELH to Rebekah Owen, 19 February 1897, *LettersEF*, 9.

18 *EHDiaries*, 201, 207; Edward Clodd, *Pioneers of Evolution. From Thales to Huxley* (London, 1896); see *LettersEF*, 11–12.

19 See *Life*, 310–13; TH to FH, 3 July 1897, *CL* II, 168–9; *EHDiaries*, 201.

20 *Life*, 317; see ELH to Rebekah Owen, 19 February 1897: 'I have been reading John Gabriel Borkman. Ibsen has excelled himself in it – pathetic, powerful & true to the characters in their positions.' (*LettersEF*, 9). The letter's buoyant tone suggests better relations in the marriage at this point – better than two years before or two years later.

21 Photo for the *Young Woman* magazine, 1895–6; TH to Clodd, 30 October 1896, *CL* II, 136.

22 There are seven extant letters from TH to Lady Grove between 21 October 1897 and 20 July 1898, see *CL* II, 180–196; *Life*, 286, 298; 'Concerning Agnes', ll. 9–11, *CP*, 878, no. 862.

23 TH to FH, 30 August 1898 and 22 September 1898, *CL* II, 199, 202.

24 'Thoughts of Phena', ll. 1–8, *CP*, 62, no. 38.

25 See *Wessex Poems*, 1898, new edition (London: Macmillan & Co., 1903), 165; *Life*, 302.

26 See *CL* II, 188.

27 Hardy uses 'relic' in 'Thoughts of Phena': 'Thus I do but the phantom retain [. . .] | As my relic; yet haply the best of her' (ll. 17–19).

28 'The Ivy-Wife', 16–18, 22–4; *CP*, 57, no. 33; see also 'The Impercipient', *CP*, 67–8, no. 44.

29 See Kenneth Phelps, 'Annotations by Thomas Hardy in his Bibles and Prayer-Book', *Monographs*, no. 32, 12.

23 – Few persons are more martial than I

1 *LettersEF*, 15, 26.

2 *CP*, 434–5, no. 364.

3 ELH to Rebekah Owen, 14 February 1899, *LettersEF*, 14; ELH to Rebekah Owen, 24 April 1899, quoted *Millgate*, 362.

4 *Monographs*, no. 5, 7.

5 See *THJ* 4: 3 (May 1988), 26–7, letter from Ben Toobe.

6 *CritHeritage*, 322, 325.

7 TH to FH, 11 October 1899, *CL* II, 232.

8 'The Sick Battle-God', *CP*, 98–9, no. 64.

9 '[Greek title: to the unknown God]', *CP*, 187, no. 151.

10 *CP*, 115, 150, nos. 78, 119.

11 *CP*, 184, no. 149; TH to Clarence McIlvaine, 4 March 1902, *CL* III, 7. McIlvaine was evidently not best pleased; he called the transfer an 'abrupt termination' – language which Hardy disputed (see *CL* III, 10).

12 Glen Wickens's recent study of *The Dynasts – Thomas Hardy, Monism, and the Carnival Tradition* (Toronto, Buffalo, London: University of Toronto Press, 2002) – is one sign of the work's recently improved standing.

13 *CritHeritage*, 371, 372, 385.

14 *CritHeritage*, 394.

15 *CL* III, 287.

16 *CP*, 274–5, no. 227, dated '20 May 1902'. It was first published in *Time's Laughingstocks* (1909).

17 *The Dynasts*, Part 3, Act VII, scene viii; *CPW*, Vol. 5, 247.

18 *The Dynasts*, Part 3, 'After Scene', *CPW*, Vol. 5, 255.

19 TH to Edward Clodd, 12 April 1904, *CL* III, 120; *CP*, 270, no. 223. The poem was dated '1904' and first published in *Time's Laughingstocks* (1909).

20 TH to Sir George Douglas, 27 May 1903, *CL* III, 62. See *Monographs*, no. 20, 23–7; TH to Hermann Lea, 6 October 1904, *CL* III, 137–8.

21 TH to FH, 25 September 1904 and 26 February 1905, *CL* III, 134, 159.

24 – We kissed at the barrier

1 FEH to Rebekah Owen, 1 December 1914, *LettersEF*, 101–2. Other information here about FEH is taken from Robert Gittings and Jo Manton, *The Second Mrs Hardy*, revised edition (Oxford, New York, Toronto, Melbourne: Oxford University Press, 1981).

2 TH to George Macmillan, *CL* III, 205; *The Pocket Thomas Hardy: Being Selections from the Wessex Novels and Poems*, compiled by Alfred H. Hyatt (London: Chatto & Windus, 1906).

3 FED to British Museum, 20 November 1906, *LettersEF*, 59.

4 TH to FED, 29 April 1907, *CL* III, 253.

5 *Sotheby's*, 106; *CL* III, 261–2; *ECStories*, 334.

6 TH to Desmond MacCarthy, 30 September 1907, *CL* III, 276.

7 *CL* IV, 36; see *CL* III, 204 and *Life*, 374.

8 The opera version of *Tess* would have been a strong romantic impetus too – watching Ibsen with Florence Henniker had been intoxicating to him; similarly, much later, Gertrude Bugler's performance as Tess made Hardy fall in love with her.

9 TH to Clement Shorter, 4 May 1911 and TH to FH, 22 May 1912, *CL* IV, 151, 215–16.

10 TH to FH, 26 May 1911, *CL* IV, 154.

11 TH to Maurice Hewlett, 11 June 1909, *CL* IV, 28.

12 'George Meredith', *CP*, 298, no. 243; see 'A Singer Asleep', *CP*, 323–5, no. 265.

13 TH to FH, 24 December 1909, *CL* IV, 66; *CritHeritage*, 450.

14 Desmond MacCarthy (1877–1952), knighted in 1951; his piece on Symons appeared in 1907.

15 Hardy told Frank Hedgcock in July 1910 that 'a revival [in poetry] was overdue, and there were signs of it in the writings of some of the younger men – Walter de la Mare, Laurence Binyon, Wilfrid Gibson, Edward Thomas.' Masefield was also praised in the interview. See *IR*, 97.

16 FED to ELH, ?15 July 1910 and 18 August 1910, *LettersEF*, 61.

17 *LettersEF*, 66.

18 FED to Edward Clodd, 11 December 1911, *LettersEF*, 73.

19 FED to Edward Clodd, 19 November 1910, *LettersEF*, 68.

20 FED to Edward Clodd, 11 November 1910, *LettersEF*, 66.

21 FED to Kate Hardy, [20 October 1910] and FEH to Sydney Cockerell, 25 December 1925, *LettersEF*, 64, 234.

22 *CL* IV, 132, 173, 189.

23 May O'Rourke, 'Thomas Hardy: His Secretary Remembers', *Monographs*, no. 8, 29. Was TH still remembering Rosamund Tomson, the divorcee who had tried to ensnare him?

24 TH to FH, 3 October 1911, *CL* IV, 177.

25 TH to FH, 3 May 1911, *CL* IV, 151; *CritHeritage*, 451.

26 'Over the Coffin', *CP*, 423, no. 350. When 'Satires of Circumstance' were collected in *Satires of Circumstance* (1914), Hardy added 'In the Moonlight' at the end of the sequence. Typically, after Emma's death, the new poem depicts a man in mourning for the woman he 'did not love', whom 'during her life I thought nothing of'. (*CP*, 423, no. 351).

27 *CL* IV, 195.

28 FED to Edward Clodd, 11 December 1911, *LettersEF*, 73–4.

29 See TH to FED, [22 April 1913] and [Late October 1912], *CL* IV, 212, 232.

25 – The mind goes back to the early times

1   *IR*, 99, 106, 108, extracts from A. C. Benson's diary and Ann Thwaite, *Portraits from Life* (London, 1991); Christine Wood Homer, 'Thomas Hardy and His Two Wives', *Monographs*, no. 18, 12.

2   *IR*, 99–100, extract taken from *The Later Life and Letters of Sir Henry Newbolt* (London, 1942).

3   TH to ELH, [18 July 1910], *CL* IV, 106. See also FED to ELH, [15 July 1910], *LettersEF*, 61 and *Millgate*, 432.

4   *Life*, 386–7. *Alleys* and *Spaces* were reprinted in 'Poems and Religious Effusions by Emma L. Hardy', *Monographs*, no. 29.

5   *CL* IV, 243.

6   FED to Edward Clodd, 16 January 1913, [30 January 1913], 7 March 1913, *LettersEF*, 75, 77, 78. Hardy's words are from a letter quoted by Florence to Clodd.

7   TH to Edward Clodd, 13 December 1913, *CL* IV, 239; 'After a Journey', 'The Voice', *CP*, 346, 349, nos. 285, 289.

8   'The Voice', 'The Going', 'After a Journey', 'At Castle Boterel', *CP*, 338, 346, 349, 352, nos. 277, 285, 289, 292; FED to Edward Clodd, [30 January 1913], *LettersEF*, 77.

9   'His Visitor', *CP*, 347, no. 286. There are nine poems in the sequence before this one and eleven after. FED to Edward Clodd, 7 March 1913, *LettersEF*, 78.

10 FED to Edward Clodd, [30 January 1913], 77; TH to FH, 17 December 1912, *CL* IV, 243.

11 *CP*, 303, no. 246.

12 *CP*, 318, 380, nos. 259, 313.

13 *EHDiaries*, 80; T. P. O'Connor, 'Personal Traits of Thomas Hardy', *Monographs*, no. 54, 238.

14 'Thomas Hardy and His Two Wives', *Monographs*, no. 18, 12. See *LettersEF*, 11–12, 16–17, 24–6, 39–40.

15 FEH to Edward Clodd, 3 December 1913, *LettersEF*, 86.

26 – The sustaining power of poetry

1   *CL* V, 15–16, 16–17, 18, 19.

2   TH to FH and Lucy Clifford, 11 and 12 February 1914, *CL* V, 10–11.

3   Ellen Titterington, 'The Domestic Life of Thomas Hardy (1921–28)', *Monographs*, no. 4, 8, 16.

4   Joyce Scudamore, 'Florence and Thomas Hardy: A Retrospect', *Monographs*, no. 19, 10.

5   Soundy's recollections in *THJ* 4: 3 (October 1988), 77–8, reprinted from *Thomas Hardy Society Review*, 1977. TH recalled Barnes's interest in accurate

timekeeping in his obituary; his own was again a piece of discipleship and a keeping up of standards – a sign that he was professional, enlightened and modern, even though he lived in the backwoods and was thought to be a mere rustic.

6 Harold Lionel Voss, 'Motoring with Thomas Hardy', *Monographs*, no. 7, 12.

7 Edmund Blunden, 'Guest of Thomas Hardy', *Monographs*, no. 10, 9, 11; Ellen Titterington, 'Domestic Life', *Monographs*, no. 4, 18 and 'Afterthoughts of Max Gate', *Monographs*, no. 59, 342–3.

8 FH to Sydney and Kate Cockerell and to Rebekah Owen, 13 February and 20 March 1914, *LettersEF*, 93, 94

9 TH to George Macmillan and Edward Clodd, 9 and 18 August 1914, *CL* V, 41, 42.

10 FH to Rebekah Owen, 5 September 1914, *LettersEF*, 100; *CL* V, 43, 45, 46, 48. See *THJ* 15: 3 (October 1999), 85–7, the article by James Whitehead.

11 See Sarah Wootton's article in *THJ* 17: 2 (May 2001), 70–5, which publishes TH's letters to Caine for the first time.

12 TH to Harley Granville-Barker, 27 September 1914, *CL* V, 51.

13 TH to A. C. Benson, 30 December 1914, *CL* V, 72.

14 *LettersEF*, 105; *CL* V, 99, 118

15 TH to FH, 23 March 1915, *CL* V, 86.

16 TH to Sir Evelyn Wood, 19 March 1915, *CL* V, 85; *Life*, 401.

17 TH to FH, 2 September 1915, *CL* V, 121; FEH to Lady Hoare, 30 August 1915, *LettersEF*, 109.

18 *CP*, 544–5, no. 502. 'In Time of Slaughter' was the original title of 'Quid Hic Agits?', a poem first published in the *Spectator* in 1916 and collected in *Moments of Vision* (see *CP*, 440–2, no. 371 and n.).

19 FH to Rebekah Owen, 3 December 1915, *LettersEF*, 110.

20 *CP*, 493, 499, nos. 439, 446.

21 'Something Tapped', dated 'August 1913' and 'Quid Hic Agis?', *CP*, 442, 464, nos. 371, 396.

22 See *Life* xi–xvi on how the book was composed.

23 TH to Siegfried Sassoon, 18 May 1917, *CL* V, 213. Sassoon had asked permission to dedicate the volume in February.

24 See TH to Buchan and to Barrie, 20 and 23 June 1917, and TH to Thomas Humphry Ward, 15 March 1919, *CL* V, 220–, 299. Ward's wife, the novelist Mary Ward, had just 'got back from her third visit to the scene of desolation'.

25 TH to Clodd [18 August 1914?], *CL* V, 42. See also TH to FH, 23 March 1915, *CL* V, 86–7, where Hardy refers to 'the group of oligarchs and munition-makers whose interest is war'.

26 Robert Graves, *Goodbye to All That* (1929), reprinted *IR*, 134.

27 FEH to Louise Yearsley, 10 November 1918, *LettersEF*, 150.

28 TH to C. E. S. Chambers, 27 June 1924, *CL* VI, 261.

27 – No mean power in the contemporary world

1 T. E. Lawrence to Robert Graves, 8 September 1923, *IR*, 182–3. Lawrence was introduced to Hardy through Graves.

2 Marjorie Lilly, 'The Hardy I Knew' (1978), Major General Smith, speaking on BBC radio in 1955, *IR*, 144–5, 181–2.

3 Hardy was not the only writer to be approached in this way. Edward Carpenter, the Socialist and 'simple lifer', was another. Almost the same age as Hardy, Carpenter too was living in the country (on a smallholding near Sheffield) and could claim a similar kind of independence from corrupt city life, from the government and Establishment that had produced the war. Carpenter was openly gay and in other respects more positively alternative than Hardy. His example helped Forster (and to a lesser extent Sassoon) to accept and come to terms with their own homosexual orientation. Like Hardy, though, Carpenter radiated the maturity, wisdom and calm that attracted and comforted these young men. Hardy was sought out more than anyone else, because his work epitomized the England that seemed lost.

4 See Michael Thorpe, *Siegfried Sassoon: A Critical Study* (London: Universitaire Press, 1966), 97. See also Max Egremont, *Siegfried Sassoon: A Biography* (London: Picador, 2005), 221–2, 266, 289.

5 'The Two Houses', *CP*, 595–6, no. 549.

6 TH to Ezra Pound, 18 March 1921, *CL* VI, 77, see also 47, 49.

7 *CL* VI, 77.

8 FEH to Sydney Cockerell, 22 June, 6 and 22 December 1918, *LettersEF*, 143, 151–2, 153; see also 201n.

9 *Siegfried Sassoon's Diaries: 1923–25*, edited by Rupert Hart-Davis (London and Boston: Faber & Faber, 1985), 53, 80.

10 *IR*, 145, *Life*, 422; Jonah 4: 6, 11; see FEH to Lady Hoare, *LettersEF*, 142; TH to Alfred Pope, *CL* V, 302.

11 *LettersEF*, 201, 341; *Life*, 455.

12 *LettersEF*, 120, 168–9.

13 Voss, 'Motoring with Thomas Hardy', *Monographs*, no. 7, 8.

14 See the 'Apology', prefacing *Late Lyrics and Earlier*, *CP*, 556–62.

28 – Wistlessness

1 FEH to Sydney Cockerell, 8 August 1920, *LettersEF*, 167; Lady Cynthia Asquith, 'Thomas Hardy at Max Gate', *Monographs*, no. 63, 384.

2 *Monographs*, no. 4, 19; no. 6, 17; no. 65, 398, 399, *LettersEF*, 135, 163n., 211, 212.

3 *Monographs*, no. 59, 341.

4 See F. B. Pinion's article in *THJ* 8: 3 (October 1992), 29–35.

5 *LettersEF*, 182–3 and n., see also 127–8 and 183–5.

6 *LettersEF*, 171, 172, 193

7 TH to A. C. Benson, 27 September 1924, *CL* VI, 276.

8 *Monographs*, no. 59, 342.

9 TH to Gertrude Bugler, 16 December 1924, *CL* VI, 297.

10 *LettersEF*, 217–18.

11 These events are recorded in Sydney Cockerell's diary; see W. S. Blunt, *Cockerell*, 214–15 and *Millgate*, 515.

12 'When Dead. To ——', *CP*, 721, no. 689.

13 *CP*, 848–53, 892–7, nos. 832, 881, 884; *LettersEF*, 277.

14 *CP*, 954, nos. 946, 947.

15 *Life*, 478–9.

16 *Monographs*, no. 4, 16 and no. 59, 344.

Conclusion – Max Gate

1 FEH to Rebekah Owen, 26 January 1928, *LettersEF*, 264; review of *A Changed Man* (1913), quoted in Edmund Blunden, *Thomas Hardy* (London: Macmillan, 1942), 140.

2 Kate Hardy's diary, 16 January 1928, quoted *Millgate*, 536.

3 W. H. Rutland, *Thomas Hardy: A Study of his Writings and their Background* (1938) and Carl J. Weber, *Hardy of Wessex* (1940), both published in America, were part of the same trend.

4 'Two Essays by Llewelyn Powys', *Monographs*, 70 (1971).

5 Beryl Baigent's interview with Dolly in her article from *THJ* 8: 3 (October 1992), 73.

Further Reading

PUBLISHED SOURCES

Extremely valuable editorial work, beginning in the 1960s and accelerating since, has succeeded in bringing almost all of Hardy's miscellaneous writing into print.

Beatty, C. J. P., ed., *The Architectural Notebook of Thomas Hardy*, Dorchester: Dorset Natural History and Archaeological Society, 1966

Orel, Harold, ed., *Thomas Hardy's Personal Writings: Prefaces – Literary Opinions – Reminiscences*, London: Macmillan, 1967

Taylor, Richard H., ed., *The Personal Notebooks of Thomas Hardy*, London: Macmillan, 1978

Purdy, Richard Little, and Michael Millgate, eds., *The Collected Letters of Thomas Hardy*, 7 vols. Oxford: Clarendon Press, 1978–88

Björk, Lennart A., ed., *The Literary Notebooks of Thomas Hardy*, 2 vols., London: Macmillan, 1985

Dalziel, Pamela and Michael Millgate, eds., *Thomas Hardy's 'Studies, Specimens &c.' Notebook*, Oxford: Clarendon Press, 1994

Millgate, Michael, ed., *Thomas Hardy's Public Voice: The Essays, Speeches, and Miscellaneous Prose*, Oxford: Clarendon Press, 2001

Greenslade, William, ed., *Thomas Hardy: The 'Facts' Notebook*, Aldershot and Burlington, Vermont: Ashgate, 2004

MANUSCRIPT SOURCES

The Dorset County Museum, Dorchester holds an extensive collection of Hardy manuscripts, letters, sketches, watercolours, and books from his library. The Beinecke Library at Yale University possesses two particularly interesting sets of manuscripts, Richard Purdy's conversations with Florence Hardy and Sydney Cockerell's notes from his meetings with Hardy.

Biographies and Biographical Records
(in Chronological Order)

The full-length studies by Robert Gittings, Michael Millgate and Martin Seymour-Smith are the most substantial recent biographies, drawing on and contesting the image of Hardy created over the previous half-century, not least by Hardy himself.

Hedgcock, F. A., *Thomas Hardy: Penseur et Artiste*, Paris: Librarie Hachette, 1911

Brennecke, Ernest, *The Life of Thomas Hardy*, New York: Greenpoint Press, 1925

Hardy, F. E., *The Early Life of Thomas Hardy, 1840–1891* and *The Later Years of Thomas Hardy, 1892–1928*, London: Macmillan, 1928 and 1930 (This ghosted autobiography was edited by Michael Millgate as *The Life and Work of Thomas Hardy, by Thomas Hardy*, London: Macmillan, 1984)

Weber, Carl, *Hardy of Wessex: His Life and Literary Career*, New York: Columbia University Press, 1940

Hardy, Evelyn, *Thomas Hardy: A Critical Biography*, London: Hogarth Press, 1954

Deacon, Lois and Terry Coleman, *Providence and Mr Hardy*, London: Hutchinson & Co., 1966

Stewart, J. I. M., *Thomas Hardy: A Critical Biography*, Harlow: Longman, 1971

Gittings, Robert, *Young Thomas Hardy*, London: Heinemann, 1975

O'Sullivan, Timothy, *Thomas Hardy: An Illustrated Biography*, London: Macmillan, 1975

Gittings, Robert, *The Older Thomas Hardy*, London: Heinemann, 1978

Millgate, Michael, *Thomas Hardy: A Biography*, Oxford and New York: Oxford University Press, 1982 (revised edition, *Thomas Hardy: A Biography Revisited*, Oxford, Oxford University Press, 2004)

Pinion, F. B., *Thomas Hardy: His Life and Friends*, Basingstoke and London: Macmillan, 1992

Seymour-Smith, Martin, *Hardy*, London: Bloomsbury, 1994

Gibson, James, *Thomas Hardy: A Literary Life*, Macmillan Literary Lives, London: Macmillan, 1996

Turner, Paul, *The Life of Thomas Hardy*, Blackwell Critical Biographies, Oxford: Blackwell, 1998

In addition to the following documents and studies relating to Hardy, his life and context, back numbers of *The Thomas Hardy Journal* supply a wealth of detail, both anecdotal and scholarly.

Cox, J. Stevens, general editor, *Monographs on the Life, Times and Works of Thomas Hardy: nos. 1–72*, Guernsey: The Toucan Press, 1963–71 (These useful, though unreliable materials were repeated by the same publisher in two volumes as *Thomas Hardy: Materials for a Study of His Life, Times and Works* and *Thomas Hardy: More Materials for a Study of His Life, Times and Works*)

Hardy, Emma, *Some Recollections*, ed. Evelyn Hardy and Robert Gittings, London: Oxford University Press, 1961

Pinion, F. B., *A Hardy Companion: a Guide to the Works of Thomas Hardy and their Background*, London: Macmillan, 1968

Kay-Robinson, Denys, *The First Mrs Thomas Hardy*, London: Macmillan, 1979

Gittings, Robert and Jo Manton, *The Second Mrs Hardy*, Oxford: Oxford University Press, 1981

Fowles, John, ed., *Thomas Hardy's England*, text by Jo Draper, London: Jonathan Cape, 1984

Taylor, Richard H., *Emma Hardy Diaries*, Ashington, Northumberland and Manchester: MidNAG and Carcanet, 1985

Hands, Timothy, *A Hardy Chronology*, London: Macmillan, 1992

Millgate, Michael, ed., *Letters of Emma and Florence Hardy*, Oxford: Clarendon Press, 1996

Gibson, James, ed., *Thomas Hardy: Interviews and Recollections*, London: Macmillan, 1999

TEXTS

Over the last few years, Hardy's novels have been reprinted by Penguin Classics, under the general editorship of Patricia Ingham. These editions use the first volume versions of the novels as the basis for the text, instead of Hardy's later, revised editions. Annotated editions of the major novels aimed particularly at students are numerous; the Broadview Press has recently produced excellent editions of *Tess of the d'Urbervilles* (1996, ed. Sarah E. Maier), *The Mayor of Casterbridge* (1997, ed. Norman Page) and *Jude the Obscure* (1999, ed. Cedric Watts). The World's Classics editions, published by Oxford University Press, offer extensive notes and detailed textual analysis.

Hardy's poems are available complete in either *The Complete Poetical Works of Thomas Hardy*, ed. Samuel Hynes, 5 vols., Oxford: Clarendon Press, 1982–95 or in *The Complete Poems*, ed. James Gibson, London: Macmillan, 1976. Volumes IV and V of Hynes's edition contain *The Dynasts* and Hardy's other dramatic works. Tim Armstrong's edition of Thomas Hardy, *Selected Poems*, Longman Annotated Texts, Harlow: Longman, 1993 is very helpful.

Editions of the short stories are available in both Penguin Classics and World's Classics. Pamela Dalziel edited *Thomas Hardy: The Excluded and Collaborative Stories*, Oxford: Clarendon Press, 1992, which is of particular interest in relation to Florence Henniker and Florence Hardy.

CRITICISM

An enormous amount has been written about Hardy's works. Good introductions are provided by:

Kramer, Dale, ed. *The Cambridge Companion to Thomas Hardy*, Cambridge: Cambridge University Press, 1999

Page, Norman, ed., *The Oxford Reader's Companion to Hardy*, Oxford: Oxford University Press, 2000

Ingham, Patricia, *Thomas Hardy*, Authors in Context, Oxford: Oxford University Press, 2003

Mallett, Philip, ed., *Palgrave Advances in Thomas Hardy Studies*, Basingstoke and New York, 2004

Each of these provides a helpful bibliography of Hardy criticism. The most stimulating and thought-provoking critical works that I have come across are:

Armstrong, Tim, *Haunted Hardy: Poetry, History, Memory*, Basingstoke and New York: Palgrave, 2000

Beer, Gillian, 'Can the Native Return?', *Open Fields: Science in Cultural Encounter*, Oxford: Clarendon Press, 1996

Boumelha, Penny, *Thomas Hardy and Women: Sexual Ideology and Narrative Form*, Brighton: Harvester, 1982

Brodsky, Joseph, 'Wooing the Inanimate (Four Poems by Thomas Hardy)', *On Grief and Reason: Essays*, New York: Farrar, Straus & Giroux, 1995

Bullen, J. B., *The Expressive Eye: Fiction and Perception in the Works of Thomas Hardy*, Oxford: Clarendon Press, 1986

Butler, Lance St John, ed., *Thomas Hardy after Fifty Years*, London and Basingstoke: Macmillan, 1977

——, *Alternative Hardy*, Basingstoke: Macmillan, 1989

Devereux, Joanna, *Patriarchy and its Discontents: Sexual Politics in Selected Novels and Stories of Thomas Hardy*, London: Routledge, 2002

Ebbatson, Roger, *Hardy: The Margin of the Unexpressed*, Sheffield: Sheffield Academic Press, 1993

Elliott, Ralph W. V., *Thomas Hardy's English*, Oxford: Basil Blackwell, 1984

Fisher Joe, *The Hidden Hardy*, Basingstoke and London: Macmillan, 1992

Garson, Marjorie, *Hardy's Fables of Integrity: Woman, Body, Text*, Oxford: Clarendon Press, 1991

Gatrell, Simon, *Hardy the Creator: A Textual Biography*, Oxford: Clarendon Press, 1988

Goode, John, *Thomas Hardy: The Offensive Truth*, Oxford: Basil Blackwell, 1988

Gregor, Ian, 'Hardy's World', *ELH*, 38 (1971), 274–93

Hardy, Barbara, *Thomas Hardy: Imagining Imagination: Hardy's Poetry and Fiction*, London: Athlone Press, 2000

Higonnet, M. R., ed., *The Sense of Sex: Feminist Perspectives on Hardy*, Urbana: University of Illinois Press, 1993

Ingham, Patricia, 'Dialect in the Novels of Hardy and George Eliot', *Literary English Since Shakespeare*, ed. George Watson, London: Oxford University Press, 1970

Irwin, Michael, *Reading Hardy's Landscapes*, Basingstoke and New York: Palgrave, 2000

Jacobus, Mary, 'Tess's Purity', *Essays in Criticism*, 26 (1976), 318–38

Kramer, Dale, *Thomas Hardy: The Forms of Tragedy*, Detroit: Wayne State University Press, 1975

Lock, Charles, 'Hardy Promises: *The Dynasts* and the Epic of Imperialism', *Reading Thomas Hardy*, ed. Charles P. C. Pettit, Basingstoke and New York: Macmillan, 1998

Moore, Kevin Z., *The Descent of the Imagination: Postromantic Culture in the Later Novels of Thomas Hardy*, New York: New York University Press, 1990

Morgan, Rosemarie, *Cancelled Words: Rediscovering Thomas Hardy*, London: Routledge, 1992

Neill, Edward, *The Secret Life of Thomas Hardy*, Aldershot: Ashgate, 2004

Ray, Martin, *Thomas Hardy: A Textual Study of the Short Stories*, Aldershot: Ashgate, 1997

Springer, Marlene, *Hardy's Art of Allusion*, London: Macmillan, 1983

Taylor, Dennis, *Hardy's Metres and Victorian Prosody*, Oxford: Clarendon Press, 1988

Thomas, Jane, *Thomas Hardy, Femininity and Dissent: Reassessing the 'Minor' Novels*, London: Macmillan, 1999

Widdowson, Peter, *Hardy in History: A Study in Literary Sociology*, London and New York; Routledge, 1989

Widdowson, Peter, ed., *Thomas Hardy: Tess of the d'Urbervilles*, New Casebooks Series, Basingstoke and London: Macmillan, 1993

Index

Illustration Acknowledgements

All photographs courtesy of the Dorset County Museum, except:
8 – Lambeth Palace Library, ICBS 04850;
15, 16 – the author;
20 – by permission of the British Library;
21, 22, 23, 24 – by permission of the Syndics of Cambridge University Library;
30 – photographs by Colin Graham, by permission of Dorset Publishing Company.

Visit **www.panmacmillan.com** to read more about all our books and to buy them. You will also find features, author interviews and news of any author events, and you can sign up for e-newsletters so that you're always first to hear about our new releases.